Designing the User Interface

Strategies for Effective
Human-Computer Interaction
Third Edition

Ben Shneiderman
The University of Maryland

An imprint of Addison Wesley Longman, Inc.

Reading, Massachusetts • Harlow, England • Menlo Park, California
Berkeley, California • Don Mills, Ontario • Sydney • Bonn • Amsterdam
Tokyo • Mexico City

Many of the designations used by manufacturers and sellers to distinguish their products are claimed as trademarks. Where those designations appear in this book, and Addison-Wesley was aware of a trademark claim, the designations have been printed in initial caps or all caps.

Library of Congress Cataloging-in-Publication Data

Shneiderman, Ben.
    Designing the user interface : strategies for effective human
    -computer-interaction / Ben Shneiderman. -- 3rd ed.
        p.   cm.
    Includes bibliographical references and index.
    ISBN 0-201-69497-2
    1. Human-computer interaction.   2. User interfaces (Computer
systems)   I. Title.
QA76.9.H85S54   1998
004'.01'9--dc21   96-37974
                                                              CIP

Access the latest information about Addison-Wesley titles from our World Wide Web site: http://www.awl.com/cseng

Chapter opener illustrations from art provided by Mark Kostabi. Reproduced with permission.

Cover art © Boris Lyubner/SIS

Reprinted with corrections, March 1998.

14 - MA - 05 04 03

Preface to the Third Edition

Designing the User Interface is intended primarily for designers, managers, and evaluators of interactive systems. It presents a broad survey of designing, implementing, managing, maintaining, training, and refining the user interface of interactive systems. The book's second audience is researchers in human–computer interaction, specifically those who are interested in human performance with interactive systems. These researchers may have backgrounds in computer science, psychology, information systems, library science, business, education, human factors, ergonomics, or industrial engineering; all share a desire to understand the complex interaction of people with machines. Students in these fields also will benefit from the contents of this book. It is my hope that this book will stimulate the introduction of courses on user-interface design in all these and other disciplines. Finally, serious users of interactive systems will find that the book gives them a more thorough understanding of the design questions for user interfaces. My goals are to encourage greater attention to the user interface and to help develop a rigorous science of user-interface design.

Since publication of the first two editions of this book in 1986 and 1992, researchers in the field of human–computer interaction and practitioners of user-interface design have grown more numerous and influential. The quality of interfaces has improved greatly, and the community of users has grown dramatically. Researchers and designers could claim success, but user expectations are higher and the applications are more demanding. Today's interfaces are good, but novice and expert users still experience anxiety and frustration all too often. To achieve the goal of universal access, designers will have to continue to work harder. This book is meant to help them keep up the momentum, and thus to encourage further progress.

Keeping up with the innovations in human–computer interaction is a demanding task. Requests for an update to my second edition began shortly after its publication, but I had to wait until a sabbatical year allowed me to set aside enough time to complete this third edition. I've gone to the library, the World Wide Web, conferences, and colleagues to harvest information, and then returned to my keyboard to write. My first drafts were only a starting point to generate feedback from colleagues, practitioners, and students. The work was intense and satisfying.

New in the Third Edition

Comments from instructors who used the second edition were influential in my revisions of the structure. Since many courses include design, evaluation, and construction projects, the chapters on development methodologies, evaluation techniques, and software tools were moved toward the beginning. Since direct manipulation is the dominant user-interface style, it is presented first, followed by menus, form fillin, and command languages. The material on computer-supported cooperative work has changed dramatically as research ideas and prototypes have become commercial tools. Information visualization is still in its early phases, but vigorous research and emerging commercial activity are widespread. The closing chapter on the rapidly growing World Wide Web is totally new.

Instructors wanted more guidelines and summary tables; these elements are now shown in boxes throughout the book. The Practitioner Summaries and Researcher Agendas remain popular; they have been updated. The references have been expanded and freshened with many new sources, with classic papers still included. Because some of the previously cited works were difficult to find, a much larger percentage of the references now are widely available sources. Figures—especially those showing screen designs—age quickly. In this edition, numerous new user interfaces are shown, many in full color.

Readers will see the dynamism of human–computer interaction reflected in the substantial changes to this third edition. Controversy continues about the future of speech input and output, natural-language interaction, anthropomorphic design, and agents. I emphasize empirical reports, try to present both sides fairly, and offer my opinions.

The presence of the World Wide Web has a profound effect on researchers, designers, educators, and students. I want to encourage intense use of the web by all these groups and to ease integration of the web into common practice. However, the volatility of the web is not in harmony with the permanence of printed books. Publishing website URLs in the book would have been risky, because changes are made daily. For these and other reasons, with the cooperation of my publisher and Prof. Blaise Liffick (Millersville University), we have established an ambitious web site (http://www.aw.com/DTUI) to accompany this book. It contains pointers to web sites related to each chapter's topics, updates on fast-changing topics, interesting reviews, and instructional support. Exercises, homework assignments, projects, and examination questions are just a few of the elements of this evolving site. Contributions from professionals, faculty, and students are making this resource increasingly valuable, and the community using it is lively and growing. I hope that every reader will visit the site, will participate in discussion groups, and will contribute to it. Send us your ideas and contributions.

Ways to Use This Book

I hope that practitioners and researchers who read this book will want to keep it on their shelves to consult when they are working on a new topic or seeking pointers to the literature.

Instructors may choose to assign the full text in the order that I present it, or to make selections from it. The opening chapter is a good starting point for most students, but instructors may take different paths depending on their disciplines. For example, instructors might emphasize the following chapters, listed by area:

- Computer science: 2, 5, 6, 13, 14, 15
- Psychology: 2, 4, 9, 10, 14
- Library and information science: 2, 4, 12, 15, 16
- Business and information systems: 3, 4, 14, 15
- Education technology: 2, 4, 11, 12, 14, 16
- Communication arts and media studies: 4, 11, 12, 16
- Technical writing and graphic design: 3, 4, 11, 12, 15, 16

The book's web site provides syllabi from many instructors, and offers supplemental teaching materials.

Acknowledgments

Writing is a lonely process; revising is a social one. I am grateful to the many colleagues and students who contributed their suggestions. My close daily partners at the University of Maryland have the greatest influence and my deepest appreciation: Gary Marchionini, Kent Norman, Catherine Plaisant, and Anne Rose. I give special thanks to Charles Kreitzberg and Jenny Preece for their personal and professional support. Other major contributors of useful comments include Richard Bellaver, Tom Bruns, Stephan Greene, Jesse Heines, Eser Kandogan, Chris North, Arkady Pogostkin, Richard Potter, Marilyn Saltzman, Michael Spring, Egemen Tanin, and Craig Wills. The many people and organizations that provided figures are acknowledged in the relevant captions.

I also appreciate the students around the world who sent me comments and suggestions. Their provocative questions about our growing discipline and profession encourage me daily.

Ben Shneiderman (ben@cs.umd.edu)

Contents

Designing the User Interface

Strategies for Effective Human-Computer Interaction

Third Edition

Mark Kostabi, *Technological Obsession (Moon and Mystery)*, 1996

Human Factors of Interactive Software

Designing an object to be simple and clear takes at least twice as long as the usual way. It requires concentration at the outset on how a clear and simple system would work, followed by the steps required to make it come out that way—steps which are often much harder and more complex than the ordinary ones. It also requires relentless pursuit of that simplicity even when obstacles appear which would seem to stand in the way of that simplicity.

T. H. Nelson, *The Home Computer Revolution*, **1977**

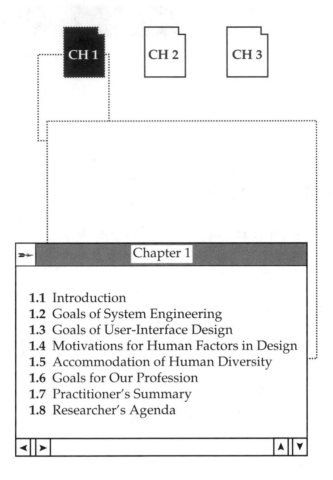

1.1 Introduction

New technologies provide extraordinary—almost supernatural—powers to those people who master them. Computer systems and accessible interfaces are still new technologies that are being rapidly disseminated. Great excitement spreads as designers provide remarkable functions in carefully crafted interactive and networked systems. The opportunities for youthful system builders and mature entrepreneurs are substantial, and the impacts on individuals and organizations are profound.

Like early photography equipment or automobiles, computers have been available only to people who were willing to devote effort to mastering the technology. Harnessing the computer's power is a task for designers who understand the technology and are sensitive to human capacities and needs.

Human performance in the use of computer and information systems will remain a rapidly expanding research and development topic in the coming decades. This interdisciplinary journey of discovery combines the data-gathering methods and intellectual framework of experimental psychology with the powerful and widely used tools developed from computer science. Contributions also accrue from educational and industrial psychologists, instructional and graphic designers, technical writers, experts in human factors or ergonomics, and adventuresome anthropologists or sociologists.

Applications developers who apply human-factors principles and processes are producing exciting interactive systems. Provocative ideas emerge in the pages of the numerous thick computer magazines, the shelves of the proliferating computer stores, and the menus of the expanding computer networks. User interfaces produce corporate success stories and Wall Street sensations such as Netscape, America Online, or Lycos. They also produce intense competition (with Microsoft as a favorite enemy), copyright-infringement suits (such as Apple's suit against Microsoft covering the Windows interface), mega-mergers (such as Bell Atlantic and NYNEX), takeovers (such as IBM grabbing Lotus), and international liaisons (such as British Telecom's link to MCI).

At an individual level, user interfaces change many people's lives: doctors can make more accurate diagnoses, children can learn more effectively, graphic artists can explore more creative possibilities, and pilots can fly airplanes more safely. Some changes, however, are disruptive; too often, users must cope with frustration, fear, and failure when they encounter excessive complexity, incomprehensible terminology, or chaotic layouts.

The steadily growing interest in user-interface design spans remarkably diverse systems (Figs. 1.1 to 1.7 and Color Plates A1 to A6). Word processors and desktop-publishing tools are used routinely, and many businesses employ photo scanning and image-manipulation software. Electronic mail, computer conferencing, and the World Wide Web have provided new communication media. Digital image libraries are expanding in applications from medicine to space exploration. Scientific visualization and simulator workstations allow safe experimentation and inexpensive training. Electronic spreadsheets and decision-support systems serve as tools for analysts from many disciplines. Educational and public access to information from museum kiosks or government sources is expanding. Commercial systems include inventory, personnel, reservations, air traffic, and electric-utility control. Computer-assisted software-engineering tools and programming environments allow rapid prototyping, as do computer-assisted design, manufacturing, and engineering workstations. Most of us use various consumer electronics, such as VCRs, telephones, cameras, and appliances. Art, music, sports, and entertainment all are assisted or enhanced by computer systems.

Practitioners and researchers in many fields are making vital contributions. Academic and industrial theorists in computer science, psychology, and human factors are developing perceptual, cognitive, and motor theories

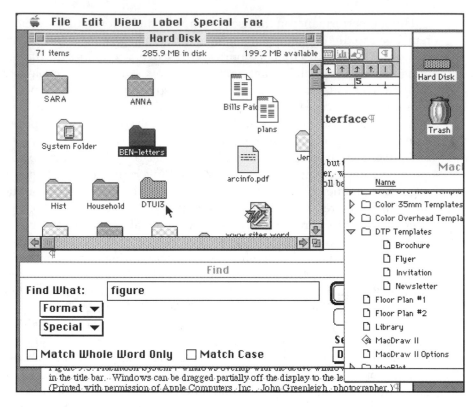

Figure 1.1

Macintosh System 7.5. The active window, which shows stripes in the title bar, is on top. Windows can be dragged partially off the display to the left, right, and bottom. File and folder icons can be dragged to new folders or to the trashcan for deletion. (Used with permission of Apple Computer, Inc., Cupertino, CA.)

and models of human performance, while experimenters are collecting empirical data.

Software designers are exploring how best to organize information graphically. They are developing query languages and visually attractive facilities for input, search, and output. They are using sound (such as music and voice), three-dimensional representations, animation, and video to improve the appeal and information content of interfaces. Techniques such as direct manipulation, telepresence, and virtual realities may change the ways that we interact with and think about computers.

Hardware developers and system builders are offering novel keyboard designs and pointing devices, as well as large, high-resolution color displays. They are designing systems that both provide rapid response times for increasingly complex tasks and have fast display rates and smooth transitions

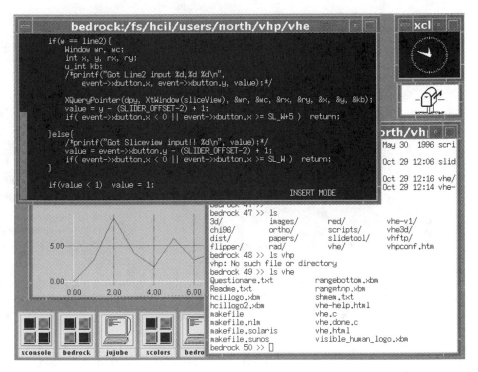

Figure 1.2

Unix Motif environment. A programmer is shown at work.

for increasingly complex 3-dimensional manipulations. Technologies that allow speech input and output, gestural input, and tactile or force-feedback output increase ease of use, as do input devices such as the touchscreen and stylus.

Developers with an orientation toward educational psychology, instructional design, and technical writing are creating engaging online tutorials, training, reference manuals, demonstrations and sales materials, and are exploring novel approaches to group lectures, distance learning, personalized experiential training, and video presentations. Graphic designers are actively engaged in visual layout, color selection, and animation. Sociologists, anthropologists, philosophers, policy makers, and managers are dealing with organizational impact, computer anxiety, job redesign, retraining, distributed teamwork, computer-supported cooperation strategies, work-at-home schemes, and long-term societal changes.

We are living in an exciting time for developers of user interfaces. The hardware and software foundations for the bridges and tunnels have been built. Now the roadway can be laid and the stripes painted to make way for the heavy traffic of eager users.

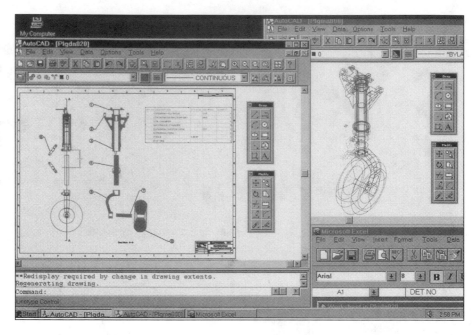

Figure 1.3

AutoCAD R13 for Windows. This design environment has multiple windows and palettes for an aircraft landing-gear assembly. (Used with permission of AutoDesk, San Rafael, CA.)

The rapid growth of interest in user-interface design is international in scope. In the United States, the Association for Computing Machinery (ACM) Special Interest Group in Computer Human Interaction (SIGCHI) had more than 6000 members in 1997. The annual CHI conferences draw almost 2500 people. The Usability Professionals Association focuses on commercial approaches, and the Human Factors & Ergonomics Society, the American Society for Information Science, and other professional groups attend to research on human–computer interaction. Regular conferences in Europe, Japan, and elsewhere draw substantial audiences of researchers and practitioners. In Europe, the ESPRIT project devotes approximately 150 person-years of effort per year to the topic. In Japan, the Ministry of International Trade and Industry promotes commercially-oriented projects and consortia among many companies.

This chapter gives a broad overview of human–computer interaction from practitioner and research perspectives. Specific references cited in the chapter appear on page 33, and a set of general references begins on page 35.

Figure 1.4

Realistic textures add to this outdoor setting that leads the player to one of the islands making up the world of *Riven: The Sequel to MYST* (Copyright Cyan, Inc.) MYST (1994) and Riven (1997), created by Rand and Robyn Miller, are entrancing environments that bridge literary styles with video games. (Used with permission of Broderbund, Inc.)

1.2   Goals of System Engineering

The high-level goal of making the user's quality of life better (see Afterword) is important to keep in mind, but designers have more specific goals. Every designer wants to build a high-quality interactive system that is admired by colleagues, celebrated by users, circulated widely, and imitated frequently. Appreciation comes not from flamboyant promises or stylish advertising, but rather from inherent quality features that are achieved through thoughtful planning, sensitivity to user needs, and diligent testing.

Managers can promote attention to user-interface issues by selection of personnel, preparation of schedules and milestones, construction and application of guidelines documents, and commitment to testing. Designers then propose multiple design alternatives for consideration, and the leading contenders are subjected to further development and testing (see Chapters 3 and

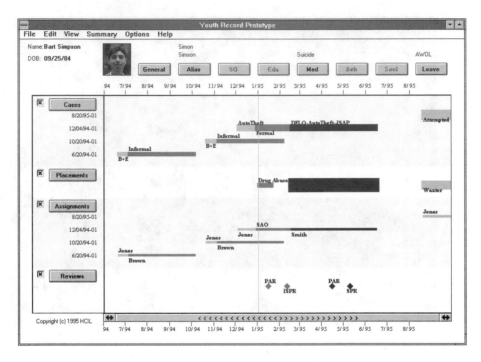

Figure 1.5

Youth Record prototype using the Lifelines display to show a case history for the Maryland Department of Juvenile Justice. (Used with permission of the University of Maryland Human–Computer Interaction Laboratory, College Park, MD.)

4). User-interface building tools (see Chapter 5) enable rapid implementation and easy revision. Evaluation of designs refines the understanding of appropriateness for each choice.

Successful designers go beyond the vague notion of "user friendliness," probing deeper than simply making a checklist of subjective guidelines. They have a thorough understanding of the diverse community of users and the tasks that must be accomplished. Moreover, they are deeply committed to serving the users, which strengthens their resolve when they face the pressures of short deadlines, tight budgets, and weak-willed compromisers.

Effective systems generate positive feelings of success, competence, mastery, and clarity in the user community. The users are not encumbered by the computer and can predict what will happen in response to each of their actions. When an interactive system is well designed, the interface almost disappears, enabling users to concentrate on their work, exploration, or pleasure. Creating an environment in which tasks are carried out almost effortlessly and users are "in the flow" requires a great deal of hard work from the designer.

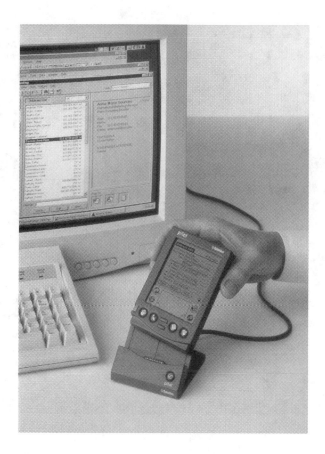

Figure 1.6

U.S. Robotics Pilot portable computer. The convenient docking station allows easy synchronization of files with a desktop computer. (Used with permission of U.S. Robotics.)

Setting explicit goals helps designers to achieve those goals. In getting beyond the vague quest for user-friendly systems, managers and designers can focus on specific goals that include well-defined system-engineering and measurable human-factors objectives. The U.S. Military Standard for Human Engineering Design Criteria (1989) states these purposes:

- Achieve required performance by operator, control, and maintenance personnel
- Minimize skill and personnel requirements and training time
- Achieve required reliability of personnel–equipment combinations
- Foster design standardization within and among systems

1.2.1 Proper functionality

The first step is to ascertain the necessary functionality—what tasks and subtasks must be carried out. The frequent tasks are easy to determine, but the occasional tasks, the exceptional tasks for emergency conditions, and the

Figure 1.7

Children's educational game computer (Talking Teacher from Radio Shack, Tandy Corp., Ft. Worth, TX 76102), which has voice instructions and feedback with a one-line visual display. Games have three levels of difficulty and include word, number, and musical exercises.

repair tasks to cope with errors in use of the system are more difficult to discover. Task analysis is central, because systems with inadequate functionality frustrate the user and are often rejected or underutilized. If the functionality is inadequate, it does not matter how well the human interface is designed. Excessive functionality is also a danger, and providing it is probably the more common mistake of designers, because the clutter and complexity make implementation, maintenance, learning, and usage more difficult.

1.2.2   Reliability, availability, security, and data integrity

A vital second step is ensuring proper system reliability: commands must function as specified, displayed data must reflect the database contents, and updates must be applied correctly. Users' trust of systems is fragile; one experience with misleading data or unexpected results will undermine for a long time a person's willingness to use a system. The software architecture, hardware components, and network support must ensure high availability. If the system is not available or introduces errors, then it does not matter how well the human interface is designed. Designers also must pay attention to ensuring privacy, security, and data integrity. Protection must be provided from unauthorized access, inadvertent destruction of data, or malicious tampering.

1.2.3   Standardization, integration, consistency, and portability

As the number of users and software packages increases, the pressures for and benefits of standardization grow. Slight differences among systems not only increase learning times, but also can lead to annoying and dangerous errors. Gross differences among systems require substantial retraining and burden users in many ways. Incompatible storage formats, hardware, and software versions cause frustration, inefficiency, and delay. Designers must decide whether the improvements they offer are useful enough to offset the disruption to the users.

Standardization refers to common user-interface features across multiple applications. Apple Computers (1987) successfully developed an early standard that was widely applied by thousands of developers, enabling users to learn multiple applications quickly. IBM's Common User Access (1989, 1991, 1993) specifications came later; and when the Microsoft Windows (1995) interface became standardized, it became a powerful force.

Integration across application packages and software tools was one of the key design principles in Unix. (Portability across hardware platforms was another.) The command language was standard from the beginning (with some divergences), but there are now competing graphical user interfaces (GUIs), many built around the X and Motif standards.

Consistency primarily refers to common action sequences, terms, units, layouts, color, typography, and so on within an application program. Consistency is a strong determinant of success of systems. It is naturally extended to include compatibility across application programs and compatibility with paper or non–computer-based systems. Compatibility across versions is a troubling demand, since the desire to accommodate novel functionality or improved designs competes with the benefits of consistency.

Portability refers to the potential to convert data and to share user interfaces across multiple software and hardware environments. Arranging for portability is a challenge for designers who must contend with different display sizes and resolutions, color capabilities, pointing devices, data formats, and so on. Some user-interface building tools help by generating code for Macintosh, Windows, OS/2, Unix, and other environments so that the interfaces are similar in each environment or resemble the style in those environments. Standard text files (in ASCII) can be moved easily across environments, but graphic images, spreadsheets, video images, and so on are more difficult to convert.

1.2.4   Schedules and budgets

Careful planning and courageous management are needed if a project is to be completed on schedule and within budget. Delayed delivery or cost over-runs can threaten a system because of the confrontational political atmos-phere in a company, or because the competitive market environment contains potentially overwhelming forces. If an in-house system is delivered late, then other projects are affected, and the disruption may cause managers to choose to install an alternative system. If a commercial system is too costly, customer resistance may emerge to prevent widespread acceptance, allow-ing competitors to capture the market.

Proper attention to human-factors principles and rigorous testing often leads to reduced cost and rapid development. A carefully tested design generates fewer changes during implementation and avoids costly updates after release. The business case for human factors in computer and information systems is strong (Klemmer, 1989; Chapanis, 1991; Landauer, 1995), as demonstrated by many successful products whose advantage lay in their superior user interfaces.

1.3   Goals of User-Interface Design

If adequate functionality has been chosen, reliability is ensured, standardiza-tion addressed and schedule plus budgetary planning is complete, then developers can focus their attention on the design and testing process. The multiple design alternatives must be evaluated for specific user communities and for specific benchmark tasks. A clever design for one community of users may be inappropriate for another community. An efficient design for one class of tasks may be inefficient for another class.

The relativity of design played a central role in the evolution of informa-tion services at the Library of Congress (Marchionini et al., 1993). Two of the major uses of computer systems were cataloging new books and searching the online book catalog. Separate systems for these tasks were created that optimized the design for one task and made the complementary task diffi-cult. It would be impossible to say which was better because both were fine systems, but they were serving different needs. Posing such a question would be like asking whether the New York Philharmonic Orchestra was better than the New York Yankees baseball team.

The situation became even more complex when Congressional staffers and then the public were invited to use the search systems. Three- to six-hour training courses were appropriate for Congressional staffers, but the first-time public users were overwhelmed by the command language and complex cataloging rules. Eventually a touchscreen interface with reduced functionality and better information presentation was developed and became a big success in the public reading rooms. The next step in evolution was the development of a World Wide Web version of the catalog to allow users anywhere in the world to access the catalog and other databases. These changing user communities and requirements each led to interface changes, even though the database and services remained similar.

Careful determination of the user community and of the benchmark set of tasks is the basis for establishing human-factors goals. For each user and each task, precise measurable objectives guide the designer, evaluator, purchaser, or manager. These five measurable human factors are central to evaluation:

1. *Time to learn*   How long does it take for typical members of the user community to learn how to use the commands relevant to a set of tasks?

2. *Speed of performance*   How long does it take to carry out the benchmark tasks?

3. *Rate of errors by users*   How many and what kinds of errors do people make in carrying out the benchmark tasks? Although time to make and correct errors might be incorporated into the speed of performance, error handling is such a critical component of system usage that it deserves extensive study.

4. *Retention over time*   How well do users maintain their knowledge after an hour, a day, or a week? Retention may be linked closely to time to learn, and frequency of use plays an important role.

5. *Subjective satisfaction*   How much did users like using various aspects of the system? The answer can be ascertained by interview or by written surveys that include satisfaction scales and space for free-form comments.

Every designer would like to succeed in every category, but there are often forced tradeoffs. If lengthy learning is permitted, then task-performance times may be reduced by use of complex abbreviations, macros, and shortcuts. If the rate of errors is to be kept extremely low, then speed of performance may have to be sacrificed. In some applications, subjective satisfaction may be the key determinant of success; in others, short learning times or rapid performance may be paramount. Project managers and designers must be aware of the tradeoffs and must make their choices explicit and public. Requirements documents and marketing brochures should make clear which goals are primary.

After multiple design alternatives are raised, the leading possibilities should be reviewed by designers and users. Low-fidelity paper mockups are useful, but high-fidelity online prototypes create a more realistic environment for review. Design teams negotiate the guidelines document to make explicit the permissible formats, sequences, terminology, and so on. Then, the interface design is created with suitable prototyping tools, and testing can begin to ensure that the user-interface design goals are met. The user manual and the technical reference manual can be written before the implementation to provide another review and perspective on the design. Next, the implementation can be carried out with proper software tools; this task should be a modest one if the design is complete and precise. Finally, the acceptance test certifies that the delivered system meets the goals of the designers and customers. The development and evaluation process is described in greater detail in Chapters 3 and 4.

1.4   Motivations for Human Factors in Design

The enormous interest in human factors of interactive systems arises from the complementary recognition of how poorly designed many current systems are and of how genuinely developers desire to create elegant systems that serve the users effectively. This increased concern emanates from four primary sources: life-critical systems; industrial and commercial uses; office, home, and entertainment applications; and exploratory, creative, and collaborative systems.

1.4.1   Life-critical systems

Life-critical systems include those that control air traffic, nuclear reactors, power utilities, staffed spacecraft, police or fire dispatch, military operations, and medical instruments. In these applications high costs are expected, but they should yield high reliability and effectiveness. Lengthy training periods are acceptable to obtain rapid, error-free performance, even when the users are under stress. Subjective satisfaction is less of an issue because the users are well motivated. Retention is obtained by frequent use of common functions and practice sessions for emergency actions.

1.4.2   Industrial and commercial uses

Typical industrial and commercial uses include banking, insurance, order entry, inventory management, airline and hotel reservations, car rentals, utility billing, credit-card management, and point-of-sales terminals. In these cases, costs shape many judgments; lower cost may be preferred even if there is some sacrifice in reliability. Operator training time is expensive, so ease of learning is important. The tradeoffs for speed of performance and error rates are governed by the total cost over the system's lifetime. Subjective satisfaction is of modest importance; retention is obtained by frequent use. Speed of performance becomes central for most of these applications because of the high volume of transactions, but operator fatigue or burnout is a legitimate concern. Trimming 10 percent off the mean transaction time means 10-percent fewer operators, 10-percent fewer terminal workstations, and possibly a 10-percent reduction in hardware costs. A study by developers of a system to manage telephone directory assistance indicated that a 0.8-second reduction in the 15-second mean time per call would save $40 million per year (Springer, 1987).

1.4.3   Office, home, and entertainment applications

The rapid expansion of office, home, and entertainment applications is the third source of interest in human factors. Personal-computing applications include word processing, automated transaction machines, video games, educational packages, information retrieval, electronic mail, computer conferencing, and small-business management. For these systems, ease of learning, low error rates, and subjective satisfaction are paramount because use is frequently discretionary and competition is fierce. If the users cannot succeed quickly, they will abandon the use of a computer or try a competing package. In cases where use is intermittent, retention is likely to be faulty, so online assistance becomes important.

Choosing the right functionality is difficult. Novices are best served by a constrained simple set of actions; but as users' experience increases, so does their desire for more extensive functionality and rapid performance. A layered or level-structured design is one approach to graceful evolution from novice to expert usage. Low cost is important because of lively competition, but extensive design and testing can be amortized over the large number of users.

1.4.4   Exploratory, creative, and cooperative systems

An increasing fraction of computer use is dedicated to supporting human intellectual and creative enterprises. Electronic encyclopedias, World Wide Web browsing, collaborative writing, statistical hypothesis formation, business decision making, and graphical presentation of scientific simulation results are examples of exploratory environments. Creative environments include writer's toolkits or workbenches, architecture or automobile design systems, artist or programmer workstations, and music-composition systems. Decision-support tools aid knowledgeable users in medical diagnosis, finance, industrial-process management, satellite-orbit determination, and military command and control. Cooperative systems enable two or more people to work together, even if the users are separated by time and space, through use of electronic text, voice, and video mail; through electronic meeting systems that facilitate face-to-face meetings; or through groupware that enables remote collaborators to work concurrently on a document, spreadsheet, or image.

In these systems, the users may be knowledgeable in the task domain but novices in the underlying computer concepts. Their motivation is often high, but so are their expectations. Benchmark tasks are more difficult to describe because of the exploratory nature of these applications. Usage can range from occasional to frequent. In short, it is difficult to design and evaluate these systems. At best, designers can pursue the goal of having the computer vanish as users become completely absorbed in their task domain. This goal seems to be met most effectively when the computer provides a direct-manipulation representation of the world of action. Then, tasks are carried out by rapid familiar selections or gestures, with immediate feedback and a new set of choices.

1.5   Accommodation of Human Diversity

The remarkable diversity of human abilities, backgrounds, motivations, personalities, and workstyles challenges interactive-system designers. A right-handed female designer with computer training and a desire for rapid interaction using densely packed screens may have a hard time developing a successful workstation for left-handed male artists with a more leisurely and freeform workstyle. Understanding the physical, intellectual, and personality differences among users is vital.

1.5.1   Physical abilities and physical workplaces

Accommodating the diverse human perceptual, cognitive, and motor abilities is a challenge to every designer. Fortunately, there is much literature reporting research and experience from design projects with automobiles, aircraft, typewriters, home appliances, and so on that can be applied to the design of interactive computer systems. In a sense, the presence of a computer is only incidental to the design; human needs and abilities are the guiding forces.

Basic data about human dimensions comes from research in *anthropometry* (Dreyfus, 1967; Roebuck et al., 1975). Thousands of measures of hundreds of features of people—male and female, young and adult, European and Asian, underweight and overweight, and tall and short—provide data to construct means and 5- to 95-percentile groupings. Head, mouth, nose, neck, shoulder, chest, arm, hand, finger, leg, and foot sizes have been carefully cataloged for a variety of populations. The great diversity in these static measures reminds us that there can be no image of an "average" user, and that compromises must be made or multiple versions of a system must be constructed.

The choice of keyboard design parameters (see Section 9.2) evolved to meet the physical abilities of users in terms of distance between keys, size of keys, and required pressure. People with especially large or small hands may have difficulty in using standard keyboards, but a substantial fraction of the population is well served by one design. On the other hand, since screen-brightness preferences vary substantially, designers must provide a knob to enable user control. Controls for chair seat and back heights, or for display-screen angles, also allow individual adjustment. When a single design cannot accommodate a large fraction of the population, then multiple versions or adjustment controls are helpful.

Physical measures of static human dimensions are not enough. Measures of dynamic actions—such as reach distance while seated, speed of finger presses, or strength of lifting—are also necessary (Bailey, 1996).

Since so much of work is related to perception, designers need to be aware of the ranges of human perceptual abilities (Schiff, 1980). Vision is especially important and has been thoroughly studied (Wickens, 1992). For example, researchers consider human response time to varying visual stimuli, or time to adapt to low or bright light. They examine human capacity to identify an object in context, or to determine the velocity or direction of a moving point. The visual system responds differently to various colors, and some people are color blind. People's spectral range and sensitivity vary. Peripheral vision is quite different from perception of images in the fovea. Flicker, contrast, and motion sensitivity must be considered, as must the impact of glare and of visual fatigue. Depth perception, which allows three-dimensional viewing, is based on several cues. Some viewing angles and distances make the screen easier to read. Finally, designers must consider the needs of people who have eye disorders, damage, or disease, or who wear corrective lenses.

Other senses are also important: touch for keyboard or touchscreen entry, and hearing for audible cues, tones, and speech input or output (see Chapter 9). Pain, temperature sensitivity, taste, and smell are rarely used for input or output in interactive systems, but there is room for imaginative applications.

These physical abilities influence elements of the interactive-system design. They also play a prominent role in the design of the workplace or workstation (or playstation). The American National Standard for Human Factors Engineering of Visual Display Terminal Workstations (1988) lists these concerns:

- Work-surface and display support height
- Clearance under work surface for legs
- Work-surface width and depth
- Adjustability of heights and angles for chairs and work surfaces
- Posture—seating depth and angle; back-rest height and lumbar support

- Availability of armrests, footrests, and palmrests
- Use of chair casters

Workplace design is important in ensuring high job satisfaction, high performance, and low error rates. Incorrect table heights, uncomfortable chairs, or inadequate space to place documents can substantially impede work. The Standard document also addresses such issues as illumination levels (200 to 500 lux); glare reduction (antiglare coatings, baffles, mesh, positioning); luminance balance and flicker; equipment reflectivity; acoustic noise and vibration; air temperature, movement, and humidity; and equipment temperature.

The most elegant screen design can be compromised by a noisy environment, poor lighting, or a stuffy room, and that compromise will eventually lower performance, raises error rates, and discourage even motivated users.

Another physical-environment consideration involves room layout and the sociology of human interaction. With multiple workstations for a classroom or office, alternate layouts can encourage or limit social interaction, cooperative work, and assistance with problems. Because users can often quickly help one another with minor problems, there may be an advantage to layouts that group several terminals close together or that enable supervisors or teachers to view all screens at once from behind. On the other hand, programmers, reservations clerks, or artists may appreciate the quiet and privacy of their own workspace.

The physical design of workplaces is often discussed under the term *ergonomics*. Anthropometry, sociology, industrial psychology, organizational behavior, and anthropology may offer useful insights in this area.

1.5.2   Cognitive and perceptual abilities

A vital foundation for interactive-systems designers is an understanding of the cognitive and perceptual abilities of the users (Kantowitz and Sorkin, 1983; Wickens, 1992). The human ability to interpret sensory input rapidly and to initiate complex actions makes modern computer systems possible. In milliseconds, users recognize slight changes on their displays and begin to issue a stream of commands. The journal *Ergonomics Abstracts* offers this classification of human *cognitive processes*:

- Short-term memory
- Long-term memory and learning
- Problem solving
- Decision making
- Attention and set (scope of concern)
- Search and scanning
- Time perception

They also suggest this set of *factors affecting perceptual and motor performance*:

- Arousal and vigilance
- Fatigue
- Perceptual (mental) load
- Knowledge of results
- Monotony and boredom
- Sensory deprivation
- Sleep deprivation
- Anxiety and fear
- Isolation
- Aging
- Drugs and alcohol
- Circadian rhythms

These vital issues are not discussed in depth in this book, but they have a profound influence on the quality of the design of most interactive systems. The term *intelligence* is not included in this list, because its nature is controversial and measuring pure intelligence is difficult.

In any application, background experience and knowledge in the task domain and the interface domain (see Section 2.2) play key roles in learning and performance. Task- or computer-skill inventories can be helpful in predicting performance.

1.5.3   Personality differences

Some people dislike computers or are made anxious by them; others are attracted to or are eager to use computers. Often, members of these divergent groups disapprove or are suspicious of members of the other community. Even people who enjoy using computers may have very different preferences for interaction styles, pace of interaction, graphics versus tabular presentations, dense versus sparse data presentation, step-by-step work versus all-at-once work, and so on. These differences are important. A clear understanding of personality and cognitive styles can be helpful in designing systems for a specific community of users.

A fundamental difference is one between men and women, but no clear pattern of preferences has been documented. It is often pointed out that the preponderance of video-arcade game players and designers are young males. There are women players of any game, but popular choices among women for early videogames were Pacman and its variants, plus a few other games such as Donkey Kong or Tetris. We have only speculations regarding why women prefer these games. One female commentator labeled Pacman "oral aggressive" and could appreciate the female style of play. Other women have identified the compulsive cleaning up of every dot as an attraction. These games are distinguished by their less violent action and sound track. Also, the board is fully visible, characters have personality, softer color patterns are used, and there is a sense of closure and completeness. Can these informal conjectures be converted to measurable criteria and then validated? Can designers become aware of the needs and desires of women, and create video games that will be more attractive to women than to men?

Turning from games to office automation, the largely male designers may not realize the effect on women users when the command names require the users to KILL a file or ABORT a program. These and other potential unfortunate mismatches between the user interface and the user might be avoided by more thoughtful attention to individual differences among users. Huff (1987) found a bias when he asked teachers to design educational games for boys or girls. The designers created gamelike challenges when they expected boys as users and used more conversational dialogs when they expected girls as users. When told to design for students, the designers produced boy-style games.

Unfortunately, there is no simple taxonomy of user personality types. A popular technique is to use the Myers–Briggs Type Indicator (MBTI) (Shneiderman, 1980), which is based on Carl Jung's theories of personality types. Jung conjectured that there were four dichotomies:

- *Extroversion versus introversion*   Extroverts focus on external stimuli and like variety and action, whereas introverts prefer familiar patterns, rely on their inner ideas, and work alone contentedly.

- *Sensing versus intuition*   Sensing types are attracted to established routines, are good at precise work and enjoy applying known skills, whereas intuitive types like solving new problems and discovering new relations but dislike taking time for precision.

- *Perceptive versus judging*   Perceptive types like to learn about new situations, but may have trouble making decisions, whereas judging types like to make a careful plan and will seek to carry through the plan even if new facts change the goal.

- *Feeling versus thinking*   Feeling types are aware of other people's feelings, seek to please others and relate well to most people, whereas thinking types are unemotional, may treat people impersonally and like to put things in logical order.

The theory behind the MBTI provides portraits of the relationships between professions and personality types and between people of different personality types. It has been applied to testing of user communities and has provided guidance for designers.

Many hundreds of psychological scales have been developed, including risk taking versus risk avoidance; internal versus external locus of control; reflective versus impulsive behavior; convergent versus divergent thinking; high versus low anxiety; tolerance for stress; tolerance for ambiguity, motivation, or compulsiveness; field dependence versus independence; assertive versus passive personality; and left- versus right-brain orientation. As designers explore computer applications for home, education, art, music, and entertainment, they will benefit from paying greater attention to personality types.

1.5.4   Cultural and international diversity

Another perspective on individual differences has to do with cultural, ethnic, racial, or linguistic background (Fernandes, 1995). It seems obvious that users who were raised learning to read Japanese or Chinese will scan a screen differently from users who were raised learning to read English or French. Users from cultures that have a more reflective style or respect for ancestral traditions may prefer interfaces different from those chosen by users from cultures that are more action oriented or novelty based.

Little is known about computer users from different cultures, but designers are regularly called on to make designs for other languages and cultures. The growth of a worldwide computer market (many U.S. companies have more than one-half of their sales in overseas markets) means that designers must prepare for internationalization. Software architectures that facilitate customization of local versions of user interfaces should be emphasized. For example, all text (instructions, help, error messages, labels) might be stored in files, so that versions in other languages could be generated with no or little additional programming. Hardware concerns include character sets, keyboards, and special input devices. User-interface design concerns for internationalization include the following:

- Characters, numerals, special characters, and diacriticals
- Left-to-right versus right-to-left versus vertical input and reading
- Date and time formats
- Numeric and currency formats
- Weights and measures
- Telephone numbers and addresses
- Names and titles (Mr., Ms., Mme., M., Dr.)
- Social-security, national identification, and passport numbers
- Capitalization and punctuation

- Sorting sequences
- Icons, buttons, colors
- Pluralization, grammar, spelling
- Etiquette, policies, tone, formality, metaphors

The list is long and yet incomplete. Whereas early designers were often excused from cultural and linguistic slips, the current highly competitive atmosphere means that more effective localization will often produce a strong advantage. To promote effective designs, companies should run usability studies with users from each country, culture, and language community (Nielsen, 1990).

1.5.5   Users with disabilities

The flexibility of computer software makes it possible for designers to provide special services to users who have disabilities (Edwards, 1995; McWilliams, 1984; Glinert and York, 1992). The U.S. General Services Administration's (GSA) guide, *Managing End User Computing for Users with Disabilities* (1991), describes effective accommodations for users who have low vision or are blind, users who have hearing impairments, and users who have mobility impairments. Enlarging portions of a display (Kline and Glinert, 1995) or converting displays to braille or voice output (Durre and Glander, 1991) can be done with hardware and software supplied by many vendors. Text-to-speech conversion can help blind users to receive electronic mail or to read text files, and speech-recognition devices permit voice-controlled operation of some software. Graphical user interfaces were a setback for vision-impaired users, but technology innovations facilitate conversion of spatial information into nonvisual modes (Poll and Waterham, 1995; Thatcher, 1994; Mynatt and Weber, 1994).

Users with hearing impairments often can use computers with only simple change (conversion of tones to visual signals is often easy to accomplish), and can benefit from office environments that make heavy use of electronic mail and facsimile transmission (FAX). Telecommunications devices for the deaf (TDD) enable telephone access to information (such as train or airplane schedules) and services (federal agencies and many companies offer TDD access). Special input devices for users with physical disabilities will depend on the user's specific impairment; numerous assisting devices are available. Speech recognition, eye-gaze control, head-mounted optical mouse, and many other innovative devices (even the telephone) were pioneered for the needs of disabled users (see Chapter 9).

Designers can benefit by planning early to accommodate users who have disabilities, since substantial improvements can be made at low or no cost. The term *computer curbcuts* brings up the image of sidewalk cutouts to permit wheelchair access that are cheaper to build than standard curbs if they are planned rather than added later. Similarly, moving the on–off switch to the front of a computer adds a minimal change to the cost of manufacturing and helps mobility-impaired users, as well as other users. The motivation to accommodate users who have disabilities has increased since the enactment of U.S. Public Laws 99–506 and 100–542, which require U.S. government agencies to establish accessible information environments that accommodate employees and citizens who have disabilities. Any company wishing to sell products to the U.S. government should adhere to the GSA recommendations (1991). Further information about accommodation in workplaces, schools, and the home is available from many sources:

- Private foundations (e.g., the American Foundation for the Blind)
- Associations (e.g., the Alexander Graham Bell Association for the Deaf, the National Association for the Deaf, and the Blinded Veterans Association)
- Government agencies (e.g., the National Library Service for the Blind and Physically Handicapped of the Library of Congress and the Center for Technology in Human Disabilities at the Maryland Rehabilitation Center)
- University groups (e.g., the Trace Research and Development Center on Communications and the Control and Computer Access for Handicapped Individuals at the University of Wisconsin)
- Manufacturers (e.g., Apple, AT&T, DEC, and IBM)

Learning-disabled children account for two percent of the school-age population in the United States. Their education can be positively influenced by design of special courseware with limits on lengthy textual instructions, confusing graphics, extensive typing, and difficult presentation formats (Neuman, 1991). Based on observations of 62 students using 26 packages over 5.5 months, Neuman's advice to designers of courseware for learning-disabled students is applicable to all users:

- Present procedures, directions, and verbal content at levels and in formats that make them accessible even to poor readers.
- Ensure that response requirements do not allow students to complete programs without engaging with target concepts.
- Design feedback sequences that explain the reasons for students' errors and that lead students through the processes necessary for responding correctly.

- Incorporate reinforcement techniques that capitalize on students' sophistication with out-of-school electronic materials.

Our studies with minimally learning-disabled fourth, fifth, and sixth graders learning to use word processors reinforce the need for direct manipulation (see Chapter 6) of visible objects of interest (MacArthur and Shneiderman, 1986). The potential for great benefit to people with disabilities is one of the unfolding gifts of computing. The Association for Computing Machinery (ACM) Special Interest Group on Computers and the Physically Handicapped (SIGCAPH) publishes a quarterly newsletter of interest to workers in this area and runs the annual conference on Assistive Technology (ASSETS).

1.5.6   Elderly users

Most people grow old. There can be many pleasures and satisfactions to seniority, but there are also negative physical, cognitive, and social consequences of aging. Understanding the human factors of aging can lead us to computer designs that will facilitate access by the elderly. The benefits to the elderly include meeting practical needs for writing, accounting, and the full range of computer tools, plus the satisfactions of education, entertainment, social interaction, communication, and challenge (Furlong and Kearsley, 1990). Other benefits include increased access of the society to the elderly for their experience, increased participation of the elderly in society through communication networks, and improved chances for productive employment of the elderly.

The National Research Council's report on Human Factors Research Needs for an Aging Population describes aging as

> A nonuniform set of progressive changes in physiological and psychological functioning.... Average visual and auditory acuity decline considerably with age, as do average strength and speed of response.... [People experience] loss of at least some kinds of memory function, declines in perceptual flexibility, slowing of "stimulus encoding," and increased difficulty in the acquisition of complex mental skills,... visual functions such as static visual acuity, dark adaptation, accommodation, contrast sensitivity, and peripheral vision decline, on average, with age. (Czaja, 1987)

This list has its discouraging side, but many people experience only modest effects and continue participating in many activities, even through their nineties.

The further good news is that computer-systems designers can do much to accommodate elderly users, and thus to give the elderly access to the beneficial aspects of computing and network communication. How many young people's lives might be enriched by electronic-mail access to grandparents or great-grandparents? How many businesses might benefit from electronic consultations with experienced senior citizens? How many government agencies, universities, medical centers, or law firms could advance their goals by easily available contact with knowledgeable elderly citizens? As a society, how might we all benefit from the continued creative work of senior citizens in literature, art, music, science, or philosophy?

As the U.S. population grows older, designers in many fields are adapting their work to serve the elderly. Larger street signs, brighter traffic lights, and better nighttime lighting can make driving safer for drivers and pedestrians. Similarly, larger fonts, higher display contrast, easier-to-use pointing devices, louder audio tones, and simpler command languages are just a few of the steps that user-interface designers can take to improve access for the elderly (Tobias, 1987; Christiansen et al., 1989). Many of these adjustments can be made through software-based control panels that enable users to tailor the system to their changing personal needs. System developers have yet to venture actively into the potentially profitable world of golden-age software, in parallel to the growing market in kidware. Let's do it *before* Bill Gates turns 65!

Electronic-networking projects, such as the San Francisco–based Senior-Net, are exploring the needs of elderly users (anyone over 55 years of age may join) for computing services, networking, and training. Computer games are also attractive for the elderly because they stimulate social interaction, provide practice in sensorimotor skills such as eye–hand coordination, enhance dexterity, and improve reaction time. In addition, meeting a challenge and gaining a sense of accomplishment and mastery are helpful in improving self-image for anyone (Whitcomb, 1990).

In our research group's brief experiences in bringing computing to two residences for elderly people, we also found that the users' widespread fear of computers and belief that they were incapable of using computers gave way quickly with a few positive experiences. These elderly users, who explored video games, word processors, and educational games, felt quite satisfied with themselves, were eager to learn more, and transferred their new-found enthusiasm to trying automated bank machines or super-market touchscreen computers. Suggestions for redesign to meet the needs of elderly users (and possibly other users) emerged, such as the appeal of high-precision touchscreens compared with the mouse (see Chapter 9).

In summary, computing for elderly users provides an opportunity for the elderly, for system developers, and for all society. The Human Factors & Ergonomics Society has a Technical Group on Aging that publishes a newsletter at least twice a year and organizes sessions at conferences.

1.6   Goals for Our Profession

Clear goals are useful not only for system development but also for educational and professional enterprises. Three broad goals seem attainable: (1) influencing academic and industrial researchers; (2) providing tools, techniques, and knowledge for commercial systems implementors; and (3) raising the computer consciousness of the general public.

1.6.1   Influencing academic and industrial researchers

Early research in human–computer interaction was done largely by introspection and intuition, but this approach suffered from lack of validity, generality, and precision. The techniques of controlled psychologically-oriented experimentation can lead to a deeper understanding of the fundamental principles of human interaction with computers.

The reductionist scientific method has this basic outline:

- Understanding of a practical problem and related theory
- Lucid statement of a testable hypothesis
- Manipulation of a small number of independent variables
- Measurement of specific dependent variables
- Careful selection and assignment of subjects
- Control for bias in subjects, procedures, and materials
- Application of statistical tests
- Interpretation of results, refinement of theory, and guidance for experimenters

Materials and methods must be tested by pilot experiments, and results must be validated by replication in variant situations.

Of course, the highly developed and structured method of controlled experimentation has its weaknesses. It may be difficult or expensive to find adequate subjects, and laboratory conditions may distort the situation so much that the conclusions have no application. When we arrive at results for large groups of subjects by statistical aggregation, extremely good or poor performance by individuals may be overlooked. Furthermore, anecdotal evidence or individual insights may be given too little emphasis because of the authoritative influence of statistics.

In spite of these concerns, controlled experimentation provides a productive basis that can be modified to suit the situation. Anecdotal experiences and subjective reactions should be recorded, thinking aloud or protocol approaches should be employed, field or case studies with extensive performance data collection should be carried out, and the individual insights of researchers, designers, and experimental participants should be captured.

Within computer science, there is a growing awareness of the need for greater attention to human-factors issues. Researchers who propose new programming languages or data-structure constructs are more aware of the need to match human cognitive skills. Developers of advanced graphics systems, agile manufacturing equipment, or computer-assisted design systems increasingly recognize that the success of their proposals depends on the construction of a suitable human interface. Researchers in these and other areas are making efforts to understand and measure human performance.

There is a grand opportunity to apply the knowledge and techniques of traditional psychology (and of recent subfields such as cognitive psychology) to the study of human–computer interaction. Psychologists are investigating human problem solving with computers to gain an understanding of cognitive processes and memory structures. The benefit to psychology is great, but psychologists also have the golden opportunity to influence dramatically an important and widely used technology.

Researchers in information science, business and management, education, sociology, anthropology, and other disciplines are benefitting and contributing by their study of human–computer interaction (National Research Council, 1983; Marchionini and Sibert, 1991). There are so many fruitful directions for research that any list can be only a provocative starting point. Here are a few.

- *Reduced anxiety and fear of computer usage*   Although computers are widely used, they still serve only a fraction of the population. Many otherwise competent people resist use of computers. Some elderly users avoid helpful computer-based devices, such as bank terminals or word processors, because they are anxious about—or even fearful of—breaking the computer or making an embarrassing mistake. Interviews with nonusers of computers would help us to determine the sources of this anxiety and to formulate design guidelines for alleviating the fear. Tests could be run to determine the effectiveness of the redesigned systems and of improved training procedures.

- *Graceful evolution*   Although novices may begin their interactions with a computer by using menu selection, they may wish to evolve to faster or more powerful facilities. Methods are needed to smooth the transition from novice to knowledgeable user to expert. The differing requirements of novice and experts in prompting, error messages, online assistance, display complexity, locus of control, pacing, and informative feedback all need investigation. The design of control panels to support adaptation and evolution is also an open topic.

- *Specification and implementation of interaction*   User interface building tools (Chapter 5) reduce implementation times by an order of magnitude when they match the task. There are still many situations in which extensive coding in procedural languages must be added. Specification languages have been proposed, but these are still a long way from being complete and useful. Advanced research on tools to aid interactive-systems designers and implementers might have substantial pay-off in reducing costs and improving quality. Tools for World Wide Web designers to enable automatic conversion for different computers, screen sizes, or modem speeds could be substantially improved, thereby facilitating universal access.

- *Direct manipulation*   Visual interfaces in which users operate on a representation of the objects of interest are extremely attractive (Chapter 6). Empirical studies would refine our understanding of what is an appropriate analogical or metaphorical representation, and of what is the role of rapid, incremental, reversible operations. Newer forms of direct manipulation—such as visual languages, spatial visualization, remote control, telepresence, and virtual reality—are further topics for research.

- *Input devices*   The plethora of input devices presents opportunities and challenges to system designers (Chapter 6). There are heated discussions about the relative merits of the high-precision touchscreen; stylus, pen, voice, eye-gaze, and gestural input; the mouse; the dataglove; and the force-feedback joystick. Such conflicts could be resolved through extensive experimentation with multiple tasks and user communities. Underlying issues include speed, accuracy, fatigue, error correction, and subjective satisfaction.

- *Online assistance*   Although many systems offer some help or tutorial information online, we have only limited understanding of what constitutes effective design for novices, knowledgeable users, and experts (Chapter 12). The role of these aids and of online user consultants could be studied to assess effects on user success and satisfaction. The goal of *just-in-time* (JIT) training is elusive, but appealing.

- *Information exploration*   As navigation, browsing, and searching of multimedia digital libraries and the World Wide Web become more common, the pressure for more effective strategies and tools will increase (Chapter 15). Users will want to filter, select, and restructure their information rapidly and with minimum effort, without fear of disorientation or of getting lost. Large databases of text, images, graphics, sound, and scientific data will become easier to explore with emerging information-visualization tools.

1.6.2   Providing tools, techniques, and knowledge for systems implementers

User-interface design and development are current hot topics, and international competition is lively. There is a great thirst for knowledge, software tools, design guidelines, and testing techniques. New user interface building tools (see Chapter 5) provide support for rapid prototyping and system development while aiding design consistency and simplifying evolutionary refinement.

Guidelines documents are being written for general audiences and for specific applications. Many projects are taking the productive route of writing their own guidelines, which are specifically tied to the problems of their application environment. These guidelines are constructed from experimental results, experience with existing non–computer-based systems, review of related computer-based systems, and knowledgeable guesswork.

Iterative usability studies and acceptance testing are appropriate during system development. Once the initial system is available, refinements can be made on the basis of online or printed surveys, individual or group interviews, or more controlled empirical tests of novel strategies (see Chapter 4).

Feedback from users during the development process and for evolutionary refinement can provide useful insights and guidance. Online electronic-mail facilities may allow users to send comments directly to the designers. Online user consultants and telephone hot-line workers can provide not only prompt assistance, but also much information about the activities and problems of the user community.

1.6.3   Raising the computer consciousness of the general public

The media are so filled with stories about computers that raising public consciousness of these tools may seem unnecessary. In fact, however, many people are still uncomfortable with computers. When they do finally use a bank machine or word processor, they may be fearful of making mistakes, anxious about damaging the equipment, worried about feeling incompetent, or threatened by the computer "being smarter than I am." These fears are generated, in part, by poor designs that have complex commands, hostile and vague error messages, tortuous and unfamiliar sequences of actions, or a deceptive anthropomorphic style.

One of my goals is to encourage users to translate their internal fears into outraged action. Instead of feeling guilty when they get a message such as SYNTAX ERROR, they should express their anger at the system designer who was so inconsiderate and thoughtless. Instead of feeling inadequate or foolish because they cannot remember a complex sequence of commands, they should complain to the designer who did not provide a more convenient mechanism or should seek another product that does.

As examples of successful and satisfying systems become more visible, the crude designs will appear increasingly archaic and will become commercial failures. As designers improve interactive systems, some of these fears will recede and the positive experiences of competence, mastery, and satisfaction will flow in. Then, the images of computer scientists and of data-processing professionals will change in the public's view. The machine-oriented and technical image will give way to one of personal warmth, sensitivity, and concern for the user.

1.7   Practitioner's Summary

If you are designing an interactive system, a thorough task analysis can provide the information for a proper functional design. You should pay attention to reliability, availability, security, integrity, standardization, portability, integration, and the administrative issues of schedules and budgets. As design alternatives are proposed, they can be evaluated for their role in providing short learning times, rapid task performance, low error rates, ease of retention, and high user satisfaction. As the design is refined and implemented, you can test for accomplishment of these goals with pilot studies, expert reviews, usability tests, and acceptance tests. The rapidly growing literature and sets of design guidelines may be of assistance in developing your project standards and practices, and in accommodating the increasingly diverse and growing community of users.

1.8   Researcher's Agenda

The opportunities for researchers are unlimited. There are so many interesting, important, and doable projects that it may be hard to choose a direction. Each experiment has two parents: (1) the practical problems facing designers, and (2) the fundamental theories based on psychological principles of human behavior. Begin by proposing a lucid, testable hypothesis. Then consider the appropriate research methodology, conduct the experiment, collect the data, and analyze the results. Each experiment also has three children: (1) specific recommendations for the practical problem, (2) refinements of your theory of human performance, and (3) guidance to future experimenters. Each chapter of this book ends with specific research proposals.

World Wide Web Resources WWW

This book is accompanied by an extensive website, prepared by Blaise Liffick (http://www.aw.com/DTUI), that includes pointers to additional resources tied to the contents of each chapter. In addition, this website contains information for instructors, students, practitioners, and researchers. The links for Chapter 1 include general resources on human-computer interaction, such as professional societies, government agencies, companies, bibliographies, and guidelines documents.

People seeking references to scientific journals and conferences now have an online bibliography for human–computer interaction. Built under the heroic leadership of Gary Perlman at Ohio State (perlman@turing.acm.org), it makes available almost 8000 journal, conference, and book abstracts. Some parts are searchable online, but most users FTP the files for personal use.

Three wonderful sets of pointers to World Wide Web resources are maintained by

1. Keith Instone (http://usableweb.com/hciel)

2. Hans de Graaf (http://is.twi.tudelft.nl/hci/)

3. Mikael Ericsson (http://www.ida.liu.se/labs/aslab/groups/um/hci/)

An excellent electronic mailing list (chi-announcements@acm.org) is maintained by SIGCHI. To subscribe, send electronic mail to `listserv@acm.org` with this line:

`subscribe chi-announcements <your full name>.`

Andrew Cohill (cohill@bev.net) maintains several listservs for the Human Factors & Ergonomics Society, including the lively CSTG-L. To subscribe, send electronic mail to listserv@listserv.vt.edu with this line:

`subscribe cstg-L <your full name>.`

http://www.aw.com/DTUI

References

Specialized references for this chapter appear here; general information resources are given in the section that follows immediately.

Chapanis, Alphonse, The business case for human factors in informatics. In Shackel, Brian and Richardson, Simon (Editors), *Human Factors for Informatics Usability*, Cambridge University Press, Cambridge, U.K. (1991), 39–71.

Christiansen, M., Chaudhary, S., Gottshall, R., Hartman, J., and Yatcilla, D., EASE: A user interface for the elderly. In Salvendy, G. and Smith, M. J. (Editors), *Designing and Using Human–Computer Interfaces and Knowledge Based Systems*, Elsevier Science Publishers B.V., Amsterdam, The Netherlands (1989), 428–435.

Czaja, Sara J. (Editor), *Human Factors Research Needs for an Aging Population*, National Academy Press, Washington, D.C. (1990).

Durre, Karl P. and Glander, Karl W., Design considerations for microcomputer based applications for the blind. In Nurminen, M. I., Jarvinen, P., and Weir, G. (Editors), *Human Jobs and Computer Interfaces*, North-Holland, Amsterdam, The Netherlands (1991).

Edwards, Alistair D.N., *Extra-Ordinary Human–Computer Interaction: Interfaces for Users with Disabilities*, Cambridge University Press, Cambridge, U.K. (1995).

Furlong, Mary and Kearsley, Greg, *Computers for Kids Over 60*, SeniorNet, San Francisco, CA (1990).

General Services Administration, Information Resources Management Services (GSI, IRMS), *Managing End User Computing for Users with Disabilities*, GSI, IRMS, Washington, D.C. (1991).

Glinert, Ephraim, P. and York, Bryant W., Computers and people with disabilities, *Communications of the ACM*, 35, 5 (May 1992), 32–35.

Huff, C. W. and Cooper, J., Sex bias in educational software: The effect of designers' stereotypes on the software they design, *Journal of Applied Social Psychology*, 17, 6 (June 1987), 519–532.

Kline, Richard L. and Glinert, Ephraim P., Improving GUI accessibility for people with low vision, *Proc. CHI' 95 Human Factors in Computer Systems*, ACM, New York (1995), 114–121.

MacArthur, Charles and Shneiderman, Ben, Learning disabled students' difficulties in learning to use a word processor: Implications for instruction and software evaluation, *Journal of Learning Disabilities*, 19, 4 (April 1986), 248–253.

Marchionini, Gary, Ashley, Maryle, and Korzendorfer, Lois, ACCESS at the Library of Congress, In Shneiderman, Ben (Editor), *Sparks of Innovation in Human–Computer Interaction*, Ablex Publishers, Norwood, NJ (1993), 251–258.

Marchionini, Gary and Sibert, John (Editors), An agenda for human–computer interaction: Science and engineering serving human needs, *ACM SIGCHI Bulletin* (October 1991), 17–32.

Mynatt, Elizabeth D. and Weber, Gerhard, Nonvisual presentation of graphical user interfaces: Contrasting two approaches, *CHI' 94 Human Factors in Computer Systems*, ACM, New York (1994), 166–172

National Research Council Committee on Human Factors, *Research Needs in Human Factors*, National Academy Press, Washington, D.C. (1983).

Neuman, Delia, Learning disabled students' interactions with commercial courseware: A naturalistic study, *Educational Technology Research and Development*, 39, 1 (1991), 31–49.

Poll, Leonard H. D. and Waterham, Ronald P., Graphical user interfaces and visually disabled users, *IEEE Transactions on Rehabilitation Engineering*, 3, 1 (March 1995), 65–69.

Springer, Carla J., Retrieval of information from complex alphanumeric displays: Screen formatting variables' effect on target identification time. In Salvendy, Gavriel (Editor), *Cognitive Engineering in the Design of Human–Computer Interaction and Expert Systems*, Elsevier, Amsterdam, The Netherlands (1987), 375–382.

Thatcher, James W., Screen Reader/2: Access to OS/2 and the graphical user interface, *Proc. ACM SIGCAPH—Computers and the Physically Handicapped, ASSETS '94* (1994), 39–47.

Tobias, Cynthia L., Computers and the elderly: A review of the literature and directions for future research, *Proc. Human Factors Society Thirty-First Annual Meeting*, Santa Monica, CA (1987), 866–870.

Whitcomb, G. Robert, Computer games for the elderly, *Proc. Conference on Computers and the Quality of Life '90*, ACM SIGCAS, New York (1990), 112–115.

General information resources

Primary journals include the following:

ACM Transactions on Computer–Human Interaction. Quarterly, ACM, 1515 Broadway, New York, NY 10036.

ACM Interactions: A Magazine for User Interface Designers. Quarterly, ACM, 1515 Broadway, New York, NY 10036.

Behaviour & Information Technology (BIT). Six times per year, Taylor & Francis Ltd, 4 John Street, London WCIN 2ET, U.K.

Human–Computer Interaction. Quarterly, Lawrence Erlbaum Associates, Inc., 365 Broadway, Hillsdale, NJ 07642.

Interacting with Computers. Quarterly, Butterworth Heinemann Ltd, Linacre House, Jordan Hill, Oxford OX2 8DP U.K.

International Journal of Human–Computer Studies, formerly *International Journal of Man–Machine Studies (IJMMS).* Monthly, Academic Press, 24–28 Oval Road, London NW1 7DX, U.K.

International Journal of Human–Computer Interaction. Quarterly, Ablex Publishing Corporation, 355 Chestnut Street, Norwood, NJ 07648.

Other journals that regularly carry articles of interest are these:

ACM Computing Surveys

Communications of the ACM (CACM)

ACM Transactions on Graphics

ACM Transactions on Information Systems

Cognitive Science

Computer Supported Cooperative Work

Computers and Human Behavior

Ergonomics

Human Factors (HF)

Hypermedia

IEEE Computer
IEEE Computer Graphics and Applications
IEEE Software
IEEE Transactions on Systems, Man, and Cybernetics (IEEE SMC)
Journal of Visual Languages and Computing

The Association for Computing Machinery (ACM) has a Special Interest Group on Computer & Human Interaction (SIGCHI) that publishes a quarterly newsletter and holds regularly scheduled conferences. Other ACM Special Interest Groups such as Graphics (SIGGRAPH), Computers and the Physically Handicapped (SIGCAPH), and hypertext plus multimedia (SIGLINK) also cover this topic in their conferences and newsletters. The American Society for Information Science (ASIS) has a Special Interest Group on Human–Computer Interaction (SIGHCI) that publishes a quarterly newsletter and participates by organizing sessions at the annual ASIS convention. The International Federation for Information Processing has Technical Committee and Working Groups on human–computer interaction. The Human Factors & Ergonomics Society also has a Computer Systems Technical Group with a quarterly newsletter.

Conferences—such as the ones held by the ACM (the SIGCHI and SIGGRAPH especially), IEEE (the Visual Languages Symposium especially), ASIS, Human Factors & Ergonomics Society, and IFIP—often have relevant papers presented and published in the proceedings. The INTERACT, the Human–Computer Interaction International, and the Work with Display Units series of conferences (held approximately every other year) are also important resources with broad coverage of user-interface issues. Several more specialized ACM conferences may be of interest: User Interfaces Software and Technology, Hypertext, and Computer-Supported Cooperative Work.

The list of guidelines documents and books is a starting point to the large and growing literature in this area. Gerald Weinberg's 1971 book, *The Psychology of Computer Programming*, is a continuing inspiration to thinking about how people interact with computers. James Martin provided a thoughtful and useful survey of interactive systems in his 1973 book, *Design of Man–Computer Dialogues*. My 1980 book, *Software Psychology: Human Factors in Computer and Information Systems*, promoted the use of controlled experimental techniques and the reductionist scientific method. Rubinstein and Hersh, *The Human Factor: Designing Computer Systems for People* (1984), offered an appealing introduction and many useful guidelines. The first edition of this book, published in 1987, reviewed critical issues, offered guidelines for designers, and suggested research directions.

Don Norman's 1988 book, *The Psychology of Everyday Things*, is a refreshing look at the psychological issues in the design of the everyday technology that surrounds us. As a reader I was provoked equally by the sections dealing with doors or showers and computers or calculators. This book has a wonderful blend of levity and great depth of thinking, practical wisdom, and thoughtful theory. A lively collection of essays was assembled in 1990 by Brenda Laurel in close collaboration with Apple, under the title *The Art of Human–Computer Interface Design*.

Recent recommended books are Hix and Hartson's 1993 *Developing User Interfaces*, Jakob Nielsen's 1993 *Usability Engineering*, Preece et al.'s 1994 *Human–Computer Interaction*, and Landauer's 1995 *The Trouble with Computers*. Two ambitious collections of papers appeared in 1995: Baecker et al.'s thoughtful and thorough commentaries enrich their 950 pages of reprints, and Perlman et al.'s careful selection of 79 papers on human–computer interaction from the Human Factors & Ergonomic Society conferences covers most topics.

An important development for the field was the creation (in late 1991) of a professional group, Usability Professionals Association (UPAdallas@aol.com), for usability testers, and a newsletter called *Common Ground*. The beginning of 1994 marked the appearance of ACM's professional magazine entitled *interactions*, and ACM's academic journal *Transactions on Computer–Human Interaction*.

Guidelines documents

General guidelines

American National Standard for Human Factors Engineering of Visual Display Terminal Workstations, ANSI/HFS Standard No. 100–1988, Human Factors Society, Santa Monica, CA (February 1988).

—Carefully considered standards for the design, installation, and use of visual display terminals. Emphasizes ergonomics and anthropometrics.

Engel, Stephen E. and Granda, Richard E., *Guidelines for Man/Display Interfaces*, Technical Report TR 00.2720, IBM, Poughkeepsie, NY (December 1975).

—An early and influential document that is the basis for several of the other guidelines documents.

Human Engineering Design Criteria for Military Systems, Equipment and Facilities, Military Standard MIL-STD–1472D, U.S. Government Printing Office, Washington, D.C. (March 14, 1989, and later changes).
ftp://archive.cis.ohiostate.edu/pub/hci/1472/

—Almost 300 pages (plus a 100-page index) covering traditional ergonometric or anthropometric issues. Later editions pay increasing attention to user–computer interfaces. Interesting and thought provoking, but sometimes outdated and difficult to read due to a six-level organization.

International Standards Organization, ISO 9241. Ergonomic Requirements for Office Work with Visual Display Terminals (VDT)s, Available from American National Standards Institute, 11 West 42nd Street, New York, NY.

—General introduction, dialogue principles, guidance on usability, presentation of information, user guidance, menu dialogues, command dialogues, direct manipulation dialogues, form filling dialogues.

NASA User-Interface Guidelines, Goddard Space Flight Center-Code 520, Greenbelt, MD (January 1996). http://groucho.gsfc.nasa.gov/Code_520/Code_522/Documents/HCI_Guidelines/

—The purpose of this document is to present user-interface guidelines that specifically address graphic and object-oriented interfaces operating in either distributed or independent systems environments. Principles and general guidelines are given, with many graphic-interface examples for a variety of platforms.

National Institute of Standards and Technology (NIST), *The User Interface Component of the Applications Portability Profile (FIPS PUB 158–1)*. Available from National Technical Information Service, U.S. Department of Commerce, Springfield, VA 22161.

—This standard is intended for use by computing professionals involved in system and application software development and implementation for network-based bitmapped graphic systems. This standard is part of a series of specifications needed for application portability. It covers the Data Stream Encoding, Data Stream Interface, and Subroutine Foundation layers of the reference model.

Smith, Sid L. and Mosier, Jane N., *Guidelines for Designing User Interface Software*, Report ESD-TR–86–278, Electronic Systems Division, MITRE Corporation, Bedford, MA (August 1986). Available from National Technical Information Service, Springfield, VA.

—This thorough document, which has undergone several revisions, begins with a good discussion of human-factors issues in design. It then covers data entry, data display, and sequence control. Guidelines are offered with comments, examples, exceptions, and references. This report is *the* place to start if you are creating your own guidelines.

Specific guidelines

Apple Human Interface Guidelines: The Apple Desktop Interface, Addison-Wesley, Reading, MA (1987), 144 pages.

—The Human Interface Group and the Technical Publications Group teamed up to produce this readable, example-filled book that starts with a thoughtful philosophy and then delves into precise details. It is required reading for anyone developing Macintosh software, and is an inspiration to people who are designing their own guidelines document; it also stimulates interesting reflections for researchers.

Apple Computer, Inc., *Macintosh Human Interface Guidelines*, Addison-Wesley, Reading, MA (1992), 384 pages.

—A major expansion of the previous citation, and a beautifully produced color book. A well-designed CD-ROM, *Making it Macintosh*, exemplifies these Mac guidelines, Addison-Wesley, Reading, MA (1993).

Bellcore, *Design Guide for Multiplatform Graphical User Interfaces LP-R13*, Bellare, Piscataway, NJ (December 1995).

—This document makes a diligent effort to provide guidance for designers of interfaces for implementation on several platforms, including Windows and Motif.

IBM, *Object-Oriented Interface Design: IBM Common User Access Guidelines*, Que Corp., Carmel, IN (December 1992), 708 pages.

—This book is the commercially published version of IBM's *CUA Guidelines*.

IBM Systems Application Architecture: Common User Access Guide to User Interface Design, IBM Document SC34–4289–00, (October 1991), 163 pages.

—This readable introduction to user-interface design is a textbook for software and user-interface designers that covers principles, components, and techniques.

IBM Systems Application Architecture: Common User Access Advanced Interface Design Reference, IBM Document SC34–4290–00, (October 1991), 401 pages.

—This volume is the latest version of IBM's *Guide* for application programmers who wish to adhere to the CUA design. It identifies what the interface components are and when to use them.

IBM System Application Architecture: Common User Access, Advanced Interface Design Guide, IBM Document SC26–4582–0, Boca Raton, FL (June 1989), 195 pages.

—This now-outdated version of the IBM standards shows progress over the 1987 document. It places heavy emphasis on graphic interaction, use of pointing devices, and windows. International standards for multiple languages are also given attention.

IBM System Application Architecture: Common User Access, Panel Design and User Interaction, IBM Document SC26–4351–0, Boca Raton, FL (December 1987), 328 pages.

—This older version of IBM's standards took years to prepare. It has been highly influential in the development of all IBM products, and therefore also of many corporate standards.

Microsoft, *The Windows Interface Guidelines for Software Design*, Microsoft Press, Redmond, WA (1995), 556 pages.

—This thoughtful analysis of usability principles (user in control, directness, consistency, forgiveness, aesthetics, and simplicity) gives detailed guidance for Windows software developers regarding how to make it happen.

Open Software Foundation, *OSF/Motif Style Guide* and *OSF/Motif User's Guide*, Prentice-Hall, Englewood Cliffs, NJ (1990).

—This book provides readable explanations for designers and for users to create or use applications under the OSF/Motif environment. Covers menus, windows, dialog boxes, and help facilities.

Books

Classic books

Bolt, Richard A., *The Human Interface: Where People and Computers Meet*, Lifelong Learning Publications, Belmont, CA (1984), 113 pages.

Cakir, A., Hart, D. J., and Stewart, T. F. M., *Visual Display Terminals: A Manual Covering Ergonomics, Workplace Design, Health and Safety, Task Organization*, John Wiley and Sons, New York (1980).

Card, Stuart K., Moran, Thomas P., and Newell, Allen, *The Psychology of Human–Computer Interaction*, Lawrence Erlbaum Associates, Hillsdale, NJ (1983), 469 pages.

Coats, R. B. and Vlaeminke, I., *Man–Computer Interfaces: An Introduction to Software Design and Implementation,* Blackwell Scientific Publications, Oxford, U.K. (1987), 381 pages.

Crawford, Chris, *The Art of Computer Game Design: Reflections of a Master Game Designer,* Osborne/McGraw-Hill, Berkeley, CA (1984), 113 pages.

Dreyfus, W., *The Measure of Man: Human Factors in Design* (Second Edition), Whitney Library of Design, New York (1967).

Dumas, Joseph S., *Designing User Interfaces for Software,* Prentice-Hall, Englewood Cliffs, NJ (1988), 174 pages.

Ehrich, R. W. and Williges, R. C., *Human–Computer Dialogue Design,* Elsevier Science Publishers B.V., Amsterdam, The Netherlands (1986).

Galitz, Wilbert O., *Human Factors in Office Automation,* Life Office Management Association, Atlanta, GA (1980), 237 pages.

Galitz, Wilbert O., *Handbook of Screen Format Design* (Third Edition), Q. E. D. Information Sciences, Wellesley, MA (1989), 307 pages.

Gilmore, Walter E., Gertman, David I., and Blackman, Harold S., *User–Computer Interface in Process Control: A Human Factors Engineering Handbook,* Academic Press, San Diego, CA (1989) 436 pages.

Hiltz, Starr Roxanne, *Online Communities: A Case Study of the Office of the Future,* Ablex, Norwood, NJ (1984), 261 pages.

Hiltz, Starr Roxanne and Turoff, Murray, *The Network Nation: Human Communication via Computer,* Addison-Wesley, Reading, MA (1978).

Kantowitz, Barry H. and Sorkin, Robert D., *Human Factors: Understanding People-System Relationships,* John Wiley and Sons, New York (1983), 699 pages.

Kearsley, Greg, *Online Help Systems: Design and Implementation,* Ablex, Norwood, NJ (1988), 115 pages.

Martin, James, *Design of Man–Computer Dialogues,* Prentice-Hall, Englewood Cliffs, NJ (1973), 509 pages.

Mehlmann, Marilyn, *When People Use Computers: An Approach to Developing an Interface,* Prentice-Hall, Englewood Cliffs, NJ (1981).

Mumford, Enid, *Designing Human Systems for New Technology,* Manchester Business School, Manchester, U.K. (1983), 108 pages.

National Research Council, Committee on Human Factors, *Research Needs for Human Factors,* National Academy Press, Washington, D.C. (1983), 160 pages.

Nickerson, Raymond S., *Using Computers: Human Factors in Information Systems,* MIT Press, Cambridge, MA (1986), 434 pages.

Norman, Donald A., *The Psychology of Everyday Things,* Basic Books, New York (1988), 257 pages.

Oborne, David J., *Computers at Work: A Behavioural Approach,* John Wiley and Sons, Chichester, U.K. (1985), 420 pages.

Roebuck, J. A., Kroemer, K. H. E., and Thomson, W. G., *Engineering Anthropometry Methods,* Wiley, New York (1975).

Rubinstein, Richard and Hersh, Harry, *The Human Factor: Designing Computer Systems for People,* Digital Press, Maynard, MA (1984), 249 pages.

Schiff, W., *Perception: An Applied Approach*, Houghton Mifflin, New York (1980).

Sheridan, T. B. and Ferrel, W. R., *Man–Machine Systems: Information, Control, and Decision Models of Human Performance*, MIT Press, Cambridge, MA (1974).

Shneiderman, Ben, *Software Psychology: Human Factors in Computer and Information Systems*, Little, Brown, Boston (1980), 320 pages.

Tichauer, E. R., *The Mechanical Basis of Ergonomics*, John Wiley and Sons, New York (1978).

Turkle, Sherry, *The Second Self: Computers and the Human Spirit*, Simon and Schuster, New York (1984).

Weinberg, Gerald M., *The Psychology of Computer Programming*, Van Nostrand Reinhold, New York (1971), 288 pages.

Weizenbaum, Joseph, *Computer Power and Human Reason: From Judgment to Calculation*, W. H. Freeman, San Francisco (1976), 300 pages.

Winograd, Terry and Flores, Fernando, *Understanding Computers and Cognition*, Ablex, Norwood, NJ (1986), 207 pages.

Zuboff, Shoshanna, *In the Age of the Smart Machine: The Future of Work and Power*, Basic Books, New York (1988), 468 pages.

Recent books

Bailey, Robert W., *Human Performance Engineering: Using Human Factors/Ergonomics to Achieve Computer Usability* (Third Edition), Prentice-Hall, Englewood Cliffs, NJ (1996), 636 pages.

Barfield, Lon, *The User Interface: Concepts & Design*, Addison-Wesley, Reading, MA (1993), 353 pages.

Bass, Len and Coutaz, Joelle, *Developing Software for the User Interface*, Addison-Wesley, Reading, MA (1991), 256 pages.

Brown, C. Marlin "Lin," *Human–Computer Interface Design Guidelines*, Ablex, Norwood, NJ (1988), 236 pages.

Brown, Judith R. and Cunningham, Steve, *Programming the User Interface: Principles and Examples*, John Wiley and Sons, New York (1989), 371 pages.

Carroll, John M., *The Nurnberg Funnel: Designing Minimalist Instruction for Practical Computer Skill*, MIT Press, Cambridge, MA (1990), 340 pages.

Carroll, John, M., *Scenario-Based Design: Envisioning Work and Technology in System Development*, John Wiley and Sons, New York (1995), 406 pages.

Cooper, Alan, *About Face: The Essentials of User Interface Design*, IDG Books Worldwide, Foster City, CA (1995), 580 pages.

Dix, Alan, Finlay, Janet, Abowd, Gregory, and Beale, Russell, *Human–Computer Interaction*, Prentice Hall, New York (1993), 570 pages.

Druin, Allison and Solomon, Cynthia, *Designing Multimedia Environments for Children: Computers Creativity and Kids*, John Wiley and Sons, New York (1996), 263 pages.

Duffy, Thomas M., Palmer, James E., and Mehlenbacher, Brad, *Online Help: Design and Evaluation*, Ablex, Norwood, NJ (1993), 260 pages.

Dumas, Joseph S. and Redish, Janice C., *A Practical Guide to Usability Testing*, Ablex, Norwood, NJ (1993), 304 pages.

Eberts, Ray E., *User Interface Design*, Prentice Hall, Englewood Cliffs, NJ (1993), 649 pages.

Fernandes, Tony, *Global Interface Design: A Guide to Designing International User Interfaces*, Academic Press Professional, Boston, MA (1995), 191 pages.

Foley, James D., van Dam, Andries, Feiner, Steven K., and Hughes, John F., *Computer Graphics: Principles and Practice* (Second Edition), Addison-Wesley, Reading, MA (1990), 1174 pages.

Galitz, Wilbert O., *It's Time to Clean Your Windows: Designing GUIs that Work*, John Wiley and Sons, New York (1994), 477 pages.

Heckel, Paul, *The Elements of Friendly Software Design (The New Edition)*, SYBEX, San Francisco (1991), 319 pages.

Hix, Deborah, and Hartson, H. Rex, *Developing User Interfaces: Ensuring Usability Through Product and Process*, John Wiley and Sons, New York (1993), 381 pages.

Kantowitz, Barry H. *Experimental Psychology: Understanding Psychological Research* (Fifth Edition), West, Minneapolis/St. Paul, MN (1994).

Kobara, Shiz, *Visual Design with OSF/Motif*, Addison-Wesley, Reading, MA (1991), 260 pages.

Krueger, Myron, *Artificial Reality II*, Addison-Wesley, Reading, MA (1991), 304 pages.

Landauer, Thomas K., *The Trouble with Computers: Usefulness, Usability, and Productivity*, MIT Press, Cambridge, MA (1995), 425 pages.

Laurel, Brenda, *Computers as Theater*, Addison-Wesley, Reading, MA (1991), 211 pages.

Marchionini, Gary, *Information Seeking in Electronic Environments*, Cambridge University Press, Cambridge, U.K. (1995), 224 pages.

Marcus, Aaron, *Graphic Design for Electronic Documents and User Interfaces*, ACM Press, New York (1992), 266 pages.

Mayhew, Deborah J., *Principles and Guidelines in Software User Interface Design*, Prentice Hall, Englewood Cliffs, NJ (1992), 619 pages.

Mullet, Kevin and Sano, Darrell, *Designing Visual Interfaces: Communication Oriented Techniques*, Sunsoft Press, Englewood Cliffs, NJ (1995), 277 pages.

Myers, Brad, *Creating User Interfaces by Demonstration*, Academic Press, New York (1988), 320 pages.

Newman, William M. and Lamming, Michael G., *Interactive Systems Design*, Addison-Wesley, Reading, MA (1995), 468 pages.

Nielsen, Jakob, *Designing User Interfaces for International Use*, Elsevier Science Publishers, Amsterdam, The Netherlands (1990).

Nielsen, Jakob, *Multimedia and Hypertext: The Internet and Beyond*, Academic Press, Cambridge, MA (1995), 480 pages.

Nielsen, Jakob, *Usability Engineering*, Academic Press, Boston, MA (1993), 358 pages.

Norman, Kent, *The Psychology of Menu Selection: Designing Cognitive Control at the Human/Computer Interface*, Ablex, Norwood, NJ (1991), 350 pages.

Olsen, Jr., Dan R., *User Interface Management Systems: Models and Algorithms*, Morgan Kaufmann, San Mateo, CA (1991), 256 pages.

Preece, Jenny, *A Guide to Usability: Human Factors in Computing*, Addison-Wesley, Reading, MA (1993), 144 pages.

Preece, Jenny, Rogers, Yvonne, Sharp, Helen, Benyon, David, Holland, Simon, and Carey, Tom, *Human–Computer Interaction*, Addison-Wesley, Reading, MA (1994), 773 pages.

Ravden, Susannah and Johnson, Graham, *Evaluating Usability of Human–Computer Interfaces*, Halsted Press Division of John Wiley and Sons, New York (1989), 126 pages.

Sanders, M. S. and McCormick, Ernest J., *Human Factors in Engineering and Design* (Seventh Edition), McGraw-Hill, New York (1993).

Schuler, Douglas, *New Community Networks: Wired for Change*, ACM Press, New York, and Addison-Wesley, Reading, MA (1996), 528 pages.

Shneiderman, Ben and Kearsley, Greg, *Hypertext Hands-On! An Introduction to a New Way of Organizing and Accessing Information*, Addison-Wesley, Reading, MA (1989), 165 pages and two disks.

Thimbleby, Harold, *User Interface Design*, ACM Press, New York (1990), 470 pages.

Thorell, L. G. and Smith, W. J., *Using Computer Color Effectively*, Prentice-Hall, Englewood Cliffs, NJ (1990), 258 pages.

Tognazzini, Bruce, *Tog on Interface*, Addison-Wesley, Reading, MA (1992), 331 pages.

Travis, David, *Effective Color Displays: Theory and Practice*, Academic Press, Harcourt Brace Jovanovich, London, U.K. (1991), 301 pages.

Turkle, Sherry, *Life on the Screen: Identity in the Age of the Internet*, Simon and Schuster, New York (1995).

Vaske, Jerry and Grantham, Charles, *Socializing the Human–Computer Environment*, Ablex, Norwood, NJ (1990), 290 pages.

Wickens, Christopher D., *Engineering Psychology and Human Performance: Second Edition*, HarperCollins, New York (1992), 560 pages.

Documentation

Brockmann, R. John, *Writing Better Computer User Documentation: From Paper to Hypertext: Version 2.0*, John Wiley and Sons, New York (1990), 365 pages.

Haramundanis, Katherine, *The Art of Technical Documentation*, Digital Press, Maynard, MA (1992), 267 pages.

Horton, William K., *Designing and Writing Online Documentation: Help Files to Hypertext*, John Wiley and Sons, New York (1990), 372 pages.

Price, Jonathan, *How to Write a Computer Manual*, Benjamin/Cummings, Menlo Park, CA (1984), 295 pages.

Weiss, Edmond H., *How to Write a Usable User Manual*, ISI Press, Philadelphia, PA (1985), 197 pages.

Reference resource

ACM, *Resources in Human–Computer Interaction*, ACM Press, New York (1990), 1197
pages.

Collections

Proceedings Human Factors in Computer Systems, Washington, D.C., ACM (March
15–17, 1982), 399 pages.

The following volumes are available from ACM Order Dept., P. O. Box 64145,
Baltimore, MD 21264, or from Addison-Wesley Publishing Co., One Jacob
Way, Reading, MA 01867.

Proceedings ACM CHI '83 Conference: Human Factors in Computing Systems, Ann Janda
(Editor), Boston, MA (December 12–15, 1983).

Proceedings ACM CHI '85 Conference: Human Factors in Computing Systems, Lorraine
Borman and Bill Curtis (Editors), San Francisco (April 14–18, 1985).

Proceedings ACM CHI '86 Conference: Human Factors in Computing Systems, Marilyn
Mantei and Peter Orbeton (Editors), Boston, MA (April 13–17, 1986).

Proceedings ACM CHI + GI '87 Conference: Human Factors in Computing Systems, John
M. Carroll and Peter P. Tanner (Editors), Toronto, Canada (April 5–9, 1987).

Proceedings ACM CHI '88 Conference: Human Factors in Computing Systems, Elliot
Soloway, Douglas Frye, and Sylvia B. Sheppard (Editors), Washington, D.C. (May
15–19, 1988).

Proceedings ACM CHI '89 Conference: Human Factors in Computing Systems, Ken Bice
and Clayton Lewis (Editors), Austin, TX (April 30–May 4, 1989).

Proceedings ACM CHI '90 Conference: Human Factors in Computing Systems, Jane Carrasco
Chew and John Whiteside (Editors), Seattle, WA (April 1–5, 1990).

Proceedings ACM CHI '91 Conference: Human Factors in Computing Systems, Scott P.
Robertson, Gary M. Olson, and Judith S. Olson (Editors), New Orleans, LA (April
27–May 2, 1991).

Proceedings ACM CHI '92 Conference: Human Factors in Computing Systems, Penny
Bauersfeld, John Bennett, and Gene Lynch (Editors), Monterey, CA (May 3–7,
1992)

Proceedings ACM INTERCHI '93 Conference: Human Factors in Computing Systems,
Stacey Ashlund, Kevin Mullet, Austin Henderson, Erik Hollnagel, and Ted White
(Editors), Amsterdam, The Netherlands (April 24–29, 1993).

Proceedings ACM CHI '94 Conference: Human Factors in Computing Systems, Beth Adel-
son, Susan Dumais, and Judith Olson (Editors), Boston, MA (April 24–28, 1994).

Proceedings ACM CHI '95 Conference: Human Factors in Computing Systems, Irvin R.
Katz, Robert Mack, and Linn Marks (Editors), Denver, CO (May 7–11, 1995).

Proceedings ACM CHI '96 Conference: Human Factors in Computing Systems, Michael J.
Tauber, Victoria Bellotti, Robin Jeffries, Jock D. Mackinlay, and Jakob Nielsen
(Editors), Vancouver, Canada (April 13–18, 1996).

Proceedings ACM CHI '97 Conference: Human Factors in Computing Systems, Steven Pemberton, Jennifer J. Preece, and Mary Beth Rosson (Editors), Atlanta, GA (March 22–27, 1997).

INTERACT '84: IFIP International Conference on Human–Computer Interaction, North-Holland, Amsterdam, The Netherlands (1984).

INTERACT '87: IFIP International Conference on Human–Computer Interaction, North-Holland, Amsterdam, The Netherlands (1987).

INTERACT '90: IFIP International Conference on Human–Computer Interaction, North-Holland, Amsterdam, The Netherlands (1990).

INTERACT '93: IFIP International Conference on Human–Computer Interaction, North-Holland, Amsterdam, The Netherlands (1993).

INTERACT '96: IFIP International Conference on Human–Computer Interaction, North-Holland, Amsterdam, The Netherlands (1996).

INTERACT '97: IFIP International Conference on Human–Computer Interaction, North-Holland, Amsterdam, The Netherlands (1996).

Classic collections

Badre, Albert and Shneiderman, Ben (Editors), *Directions in Human–Computer Interaction,* Ablex, Norwood, NJ (1980), 225 pages.

Blaser, A. and Zoeppritz, M. (Editors), *Enduser Systems and Their Human Factors,* Springer-Verlag, Berlin (1983), 138 pages.

Carey, Jane (Editor), *Human Factors in Management Information Systems,* Ablex, Norwood, NJ (1988), 289 pages.

Coombs, M. J. and Alty, J. L. (Editors), *Computing Skills and the User Interface,* Academic Press, New York (1981).

Carroll, John M. (Editor), *Interfacing Thought: Cognitive Aspects of Human–Computer Interaction,* MIT Press, Cambridge, MA (1987), 324 pages.

Curtis, Bill (Editor), *Tutorial: Human Factors in Software Development,* IEEE Computer Society, Los Angeles (1981), 641 pages.

Durrett, H. John (Editor), *Color and the Computer,* Academic Press (1987), 299 pages.

Guedj, R. A., Hagen, P. J. W., Hopgood, F. R. A., Tucker, H. A., and Duce, D. A. (Editors), *Methodology of Interaction,* North-Holland, Amsterdam, The Netherlands (1980), 408 pages.

Hartson, H. Rex (Editor), *Advances in Human–Computer Interaction,* Volume 1, Ablex, Norwood, NJ (1985), 290 pages.

Hartson, H. Rex and Hix, Deborah (Editors), *Advances in Human–Computer Interaction,* Volume 2, Ablex, Norwood, NJ (1988), 380 pages.

Helander, Martin (Editor), *Handbook of Human–Computer Interaction,* North-Holland, Amsterdam (1988), 1167 pages.

Hendler, James A. (Editor), *Expert Systems: The User Interface,* Ablex, Norwood, NJ (1987), 336 pages.

Klemmer, Edmund T. (Editor), *Ergonomics: Harness the Power of Human Factors in Your Business,* Ablex, Norwood, NJ (1989), 218 pages.

Larson, James A. (Editor), *Tutorial: End User Facilities in the 1980's*, IEEE Computer Society Press (EHO 198–2), New York (1982).

Monk, Andrew (Editor), *Fundamentals of Human–Computer Interaction*, Academic Press, London, U.K. (1984), 293 pages.

Muckler, Frederick A. (Editor), *Human Factors Review: 1984*, Human Factors Society, Santa Monica, CA (1984), 345 pages.

Nielsen, Jakob (Editor), *Coordinating User Interfaces for Consistency*, Academic Press, San Diego, CA (1989), 142 pages.

Norman, Donald A. and Draper, Stephen W. (Editors), *User Centered System Design: New Perspectives on Human–Computer Interaction*, Lawrence Erlbaum Associates, Hillsdale, NJ (1986).

Salvendy, Gavriel (Editor), *Human–Computer Interaction, Proceedings of the First USA–Japan Conference on Human–Computer Interaction*, Elsevier Science Publishers, Amsterdam, The Netherlands (1984), 470 pages.

Salvendy, Gavriel (Editor), *Handbook of Human Factors*, John Wiley and Sons, New York (1987), 1874 pages.

Salvendy, Gavriel (Editor), *Cognitive Engineering in the Design of Human–Computer Interaction and Expert Systems*, Elsevier, Amsterdam, The Netherlands (1987), 592 pages.

Salvendy, Gavriel, Sauter, Steven L., and Hurrell, Jr., Joseph J. (Editors), *Social, Ergonomic and Stress Aspects of Work with Computers*, Elsevier, Amsterdam, The Netherlands (1987), 373 pages.

Salvendy, Gavriel, Smith, Michael J. (Editors), *Designing and Using Human–Computer Interfaces and Knowledge Based Systems*, Elsevier, Amsterdam, The Netherlands (1989), 990 pages.

Shackel, Brian (Editor), *Man–Computer Interaction: Human Factors Aspects of Computers and People*. Sijthoff and Noordhoof Publishers, Amsterdam, The Netherlands (1981), 560 pages.

Sime, M. and Coombs, M. (Editors), *Designing for Human–Computer Communication*, Academic Press, New York (1983), 332 pages.

Smith, H. T. and Green, T. R. G. (Editors), *Human Interaction with Computers*, Academic Press, New York (1980).

Smith, Michael J. and Salvendy, Gavriel (Editors), *Work with Computers: Organizational, Management, Stress and Health Aspects*, Elsevier Science Publishers B.V., Amsterdam, The Netherlands (1989), 698 pages.

Thomas, John C. and Schneider, Michael L. (Editors), *Human Factors in Computer Systems*, Ablex, Norwood, NJ (1984), 276 pages.

Van Cott, H. P. and Kinkade, R. G. (Editors), *Human Engineering Guide to Equipment Design*, U.S. Superintendent of Documents, Washington, D.C. (1972), 752 pages.

Vassiliou, Yannis (Editor), *Human Factors and Interactive Computer Systems*, Ablex, Norwood, NJ (1984), 287 pages.

Sherr, Sol (Editor), *Input Devices*, Academic Press, San Diego, CA (1988), 301 pages.

Wiener, Earl L., and Nagel, David C. (Editors), *Human Factors in Aviation*, Academic Press, New York (1988), 684 pages.

Recent collections

Adler, Paul S. and Winograd, Terry (Editors), *Usability: Turning Technologies into Tools*, Oxford University Press, New York (1992), 208 pages.

Baecker, R., Grudin, J., Buxton, W., and Greenberg, S. (Editors), *Readings in Human–Computer Interaction: Towards the Year 2000*, Morgan Kaufmann, Los Altos, CA (1995), 950 pages.

Bias, Randolph, and Mayhew, Deborah (Editors), *Cost-Justifying Usability*, Academic Press, New York (1994).

Bullinger, H.-J. (Editor), *Human Aspects of Computing: Design and Use of Interactive Systems and Information Management*, Elsevier Science Publishers B.V., Amsterdam, The Netherlands (1991), 1367 pages.

Carey, Jane (Editor), *Human Factors in Information Systems: An Organizational Perspective*, Ablex, Norwood, NJ (1991), 376 pages.

Carey, Jane (Editor), *Human Factors in Information Systems: Emerging Theoretical Bases*, Ablex, Norwood, NJ (1995), 381 pages.

Carroll, John M. (Editor), *Designing Interaction: Psychology at the Human–Computer Interface*, Cambridge University Press, Cambridge, U.K. (1991), 333 pages.

Cockton, G., Draper, S. W., and Weir, G. R. S. (Editors), *People and Computers IX*, Cambridge University Press, Cambridge, U.K. (1994), 428 pages.

Greenberg, Saul (Editor), *Computer-Supported Cooperative Work and Groupware*, Academic Press, London, U.K. (1991), 423 pages.

Greenberg, Saul, Hayne, Stephen, and Rada, Roy (Editors), *Groupware for Real Time Drawing: A Designer's Guide*, McGraw-Hill, New York (1995).

Hartson, H. Rex and Hix, Deborah (Editors), *Advances in Human–Computer Interaction*, Volume 3, Ablex, Norwood, NJ (1992), 288 pages.

Hartson, H. Rex and Hix, Deborah (Editors), *Advances in Human–Computer Interaction*, Volume 4, Ablex, Norwood, NJ (1993), 292 pages.

Laurel, Brenda (Editor), *The Art of Human–Computer Interface Design*, Addison Wesley, Reading, MA (1990), 523 pages.

MacDonald, Lindsay and Vince, John (Editors), *Interacting with Virtual Environments*, John Wiley and Sons, New York (1994), 291 pages.

Myers, Brad A. (Editor), *Languages for User Interfaces*, Jones and Bartlett Publishers, Boston, MA (1992).

Nielsen, Jakob (Editor), *Advances in Human–Computer Interaction*, Volume 5, Ablex, Norwood, NJ (1993), 258 pages.

Perlman, Gary, Green, Georgia K., and Wogalter, Michael S., *Human Factors Perspectives on Human–Computer Interaction: Selections from Proceedings of Human Factors and Ergonomics Society Annual Meetings 1983–1994*, Santa Monica, CA (1995), 381 pages.

Rudisill, Marianne, Lewis, Clayton, Polson, Peter B., and McKay, Timothy D., *Human–Computer Interface Design: Success Stories, Emerging Methods and Real-World Context*, Morgan Kaufmann, San Francisco (1995), 408 pages.

Shackel, Brian and Richardson, Simon (Editors), *Human Factors for Informatics Usability*, Cambridge University Press, Cambridge, U.K. (1991), 438 pages.

Winograd, Terry (Editor), *Bringing Design to Software,* ACM Press, New York, and
Addison-Wesley, Reading, MA (1996), 321 pages.

Videotapes

Video is an effective medium for presenting the dynamic, graphical, interactive nature of modern user interfaces. The Technical Video Program of the
ACM SIGCHI conferences makes it possible to see excellent demonstrations
of often-cited but seldom-seen systems.
    All CHI videos can be ordered directly through ACM:
    ACM Member Service Department, 1515 Broadway, New York, NY
10036. Email: acmhelp@acm.org Tel: (800) 342–6626 or (212) 626–0613.
VHS NTSC and PAL versions are available (http://www.acm.org/sigchi/
video):

Year	(Location)
CHI'97	(Atlanta, GA)
CHI'96	(Vancouver, CA)
CHI'95	(Denver, CO)

Older Issues (1994 and before) were published with ACM SIGGRAPH Video
Review:

SVR

Issue Number	Year	(Location)
97	CHI'94	(Boston)
88/89	CHI'93	(Amsterdam, Netherlands)
76/77	CHI'92	(Monterey, CA)
78/79	CHI'92	Special Videos and Future Scenarios
63/64/65	CHI'91	(New Orleans, LA)
55/56	CHI'90	(Seattle, WA)
57	CHI'90	All the Widgets (Special Instructional Issue)
45/46	CHI'89	(Austin, TX)
47/48	CHI'89	(Austin, TX)
58/59	CHI'88	(Washington, D.C.)
33/34	CHI+GI'87	(Toronto, Canada)
26/27	CHI'86	(Boston, MA)
18/19	CHI'85	(San Francisco, CA)
12/13	CHI'83	(Boston, MA)

User-Interface Strategies   The University of Maryland Instructional Television produces a live satellite television program and sells the tapes. Telephone (301) 405–4905.

Email: itv@eng.umd.edu.http://www.glue.umd.edu/itv

The programs are coordinated by the author of this book who does at least a one-hour opening presentation followed by hour-long guest lectures and a discussion hour:

1996   Charles Kreitzberg and Edward Yourdon
1995   Frank Stein, Kent Norman, H. Rex Hartson, and Deborah Hix
1994   Jakob Nielsen, Judith Olson, and Myron Krueger
1993   Marilyn Mantei, Tom Furness, and James Martin
1992   Tom Landauer, Brad Myers, and Brenda Laurel
1991   Andries Van Dam, Elliot Soloway, and Bill Curtis
1990   Aaron Marcus, John Carroll, and Joy Mountford
1988   Tom Malone, Don Norman, and James Foley

Consulting and design companies

Aaron Marcus and Associates, Emeryville, CA
American Institutes for Research, Washington, D.C.
Cognetics Corp., Princeton Junction, NJ; Washington, D.C.
Dray & Associates, Minneapolis, MN
Ergo Research Group, Inc., Norwalk, CT
Human Factors International, Inc., Fairfield, IA
Preface User Interface Design, Burbank, CA
Usability Engineering Services, Inc., Kirkland, WA
Usernomics, Foster City, CA
UserWorks, Rockville, MD

Mark Kostabi, *The Art of Military Strategy*, 1997

2

Theories, Principles, and Guidelines

We want principles, not only developed—the work of the closet—but applied, which is the work of life.

Horace Mann, *Thoughts*, 1867

There never comes a point where a theory can be said to be true. The most that anyone can claim for any theory is that it has shared the successes of all its rivals and that it has passed at least one test which they have failed.

A.J. Ayer, *Philosophy in the Twentieth Century*, 1982

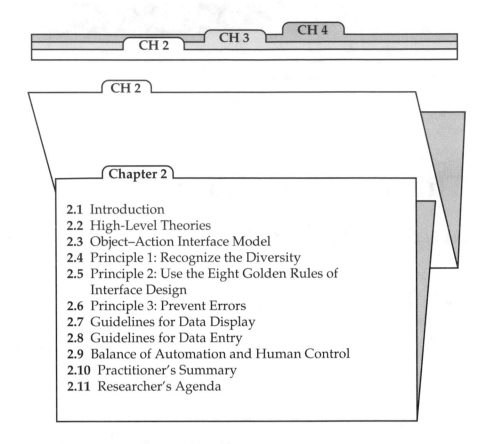

2.1 Introduction

Successful designers of interactive systems know that they can and must go beyond intuitive judgments made hastily when a design problem emerges. Fortunately, guidance for designers is beginning to emerge in the form of (1) high-level theories and models, (2) middle-level principles, and (3) specific and practical guidelines. The theories and models offer a framework or language to discuss issues that are application independent, whereas the middle-level principles are useful in creating and comparing design alternatives. The practical guidelines provide helpful reminders of rules uncovered by designers.

In many contemporary systems, there is a grand opportunity to improve the user interface. The cluttered displays, complex and tedious procedures, inadequate functionality, inconsistent sequences of actions, and insufficient informative feedback can generate debilitating stress and anxiety that lead to poor performance, frequent minor and occasional serious errors, and job dissatisfaction.

This chapter begins with a review of several theories, concentrating on the object–action interface model. Section 2.4 then deals with frequency of use, task profiles, and interaction styles. Eight golden rules of interface design are offered in Section 2.5. Strategies for preventing errors are described in Section 2.6. Specific guidelines for data entry and display appear in Sections 2.7 and 2.8. Sections 2.9 addresses the difficult question of balancing automation and human control.

2.2 High-Level Theories

Many theories are needed to describe the multiple aspects of interactive systems. Some theories are *explanatory*: They are helpful in observing behavior, describing activity, conceiving of designs, comparing high-level concepts of two designs, and training. Other theories are *predictive*: They enable designers to compare proposed designs for execution time or error rates. Some theories may focus on perceptual or cognitive subtasks (time to find an item on a display or time to plan the conversion of a boldfaced character to an italic one), whereas others concentrate on motor-task performance times. Motor-task predictions are the best established and are accurate for predicting keystroking or pointing times (see Fitts' Law, Section 9.3.5). Perceptual theories have been successful in predicting reading times for free text, lists, and formatted displays. Predicting performance on complex cognitive tasks (combinations of subtasks) is especially difficult because of the many strategies that might be employed and the many opportunities for going astray. The ratio for times to perform a complex task between novices and experts or between first-time and frequent users can be as high as 100 to 1. Actually, the contrast is even more dramatic because novices and first-time users often are unable to complete the tasks.

A *taxonomy* is a part of an explanatory theory. A taxonomy is the result of someone trying to put order on a complex set of phenomena; for example, a taxonomy might be created for input devices (direct versus indirect, linear versus rotary) (Card et al., 1990), for tasks (structured versus unstructured, controllable versus immutable) (Norman, 1991), for personality styles (convergent versus divergent, field dependent versus independent), for technical aptitudes (spatial visualization, reasoning) (Egan, 1988), for user experience levels (novice, knowledgeable, expert), or for user-interfaces styles (menus, form fillin, commands). Taxonomies facilitate useful comparisons, organize a topic for newcomers, guide designers, and often indicate opportunities for novel products.

Any theory that could help designers to predict performance for even a limited range of users, tasks, or designs would be a contribution (Card, 1989). For the moment, the field is filled with hundreds of theories competing for attention while being refined by their promoters, extended by critics, and applied by eager and hopeful—but skeptical—designers. This development is healthy for the emerging discipline of human–computer interaction, but it means that practitioners must keep up with the rapid developments, not only in software tools, but also in theories.

Another direction for theoreticians would be to try to predict subjective satisfaction or emotional reactions. Researchers in media and advertising have recognized the difficulty in predicting emotional reactions, so they complement theoretical predictions with their intuitive judgments and extensive market testing. Broader theories of small-group behavior, organizational dynamics, sociology of knowledge, and technology adoption may prove to be useful. Similarly, the methods of anthropology or social psychology may be helpful in understanding and overcoming barriers to new technology and resistance to change.

There may be "nothing so practical as a good theory," but coming up with an effective theory is often difficult. By definition, a theory, taxonomy, or model is an abstraction of reality and therefore must be incomplete. However, a good theory should at least be understandable, produce similar conclusions for all who use it, and help to solve specific practical problems.

2.2.1   Conceptual, semantic, syntactic, and lexical model

An appealing and easily comprehensible model is the four-level approach that Foley and van Dam developed in the late 1970s (Foley et al., 1990):

1. The *conceptual level* is the user's mental model of the interactive system. Two conceptual models for text editing are line editors and screen editors.
2. The *semantic level* describes the meanings conveyed by the user's command input and by the computer's output display.
3. The *syntactic level* defines how the units (words) that convey semantics are assembled into a complete sentence that instructs the computer to perform a certain task.
4. The *lexical level* deals with device dependencies and with the precise mechanisms by which a user specifies the syntax.

This approach is convenient for designers because its top-down nature is easy to explain, matches the software architecture, and allows for useful modularity during design. Designers are expected to move from conceptual to lexical, and to record carefully the mappings between levels.

2.2.2   GOMS and the keystroke-level model

Card, Moran, and Newell (1980, 1983) proposed the *goals, operators, methods, and selection rules* (GOMS) model and the *keystroke-level model*. They postulated that users formulate goals (edit document) and subgoals (insert word), each of which they achieve by using methods or procedures (move cursor to desired location by following a sequence of arrow keys). The operators are "elementary perceptual, motor, or cognitive acts, whose execution is necessary to change any aspect of the user's mental state or to affect the task environment" (Card, et al. 1983, p. 144) (press up-arrow key, move hand to mouse, recall file name, verify that cursor is at end of file). The selection rules are the control structures for choosing among the several methods available for accomplishing a goal (delete by repeated backspace versus delete by placing markers at beginning and end of region and pressing delete button).

The keystroke-level model attempts to predict performance times for error-free expert performance of tasks by summing up the time for keystroking, pointing, homing, drawing, thinking, and waiting for the system to respond. These models concentrate on expert users and error-free performance, and place less emphasis on learning, problem solving, error handling, subjective satisfaction, and retention.

Kieras and Polson (1985) built on the GOMS approach and used production rules to describe the conditions and actions in an interactive text editor. The number and complexity of production rules gave accurate predictions of learning and performance times for five text-editing operations: insert, delete, copy, move, and transpose. Other strategies for modeling interactive-system usage involve *transition diagrams* (Fig. 2.1). These diagrams are helpful during design; for instruction; and as a predictor of learning time, performance time, and errors.

Kieras (1988), however, complains that the Card, Moran, and Newell presentation "does not explain in any detail how the notation works, and it seems somewhat clumsy to use. Furthermore, the notation has only a weak connection to the underlying cognitive theory." Kieras offers a refinement with his *Natural GOMS Language* (NGOMSL) and an analysis method for writing down GOMS models. He tries to clarify the situations in which the GOMS task analyst must make a *judgment call*, must make assumptions about how users view the system, must bypass a complex hard-to-analyze task (choosing wording of a sentence, finding a bug in a program), or must check for consistency. Applying NGOMSL to guide the process of creating online help, Elkerton and Palmiter (1991) developed *method descriptions* for their

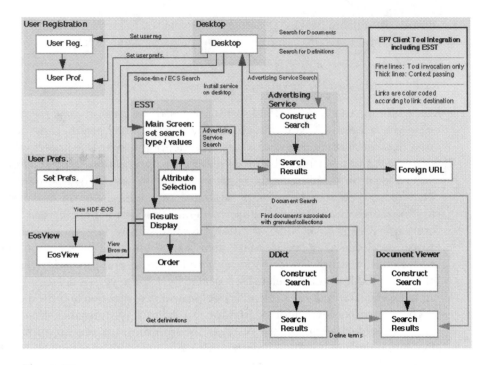

Figure 2.1

Transition diagram from the NASA search system.

interface, in which the actions necessary to accomplish a goal are broken down into steps. They also developed *selection rules,* by which a user can choose among alternative methods. For example, there may be two alternative methods to delete fields and one selection rule:

- Method 1 to accomplish the goal of deleting the field:

  Step 1:   Decide: If necessary, then accomplish the goal of selecting the field.

  Step 2:   Accomplish the goal of using a specific field-delete method.

  Step 3:   Report goal accomplished.

- Method 2 to accomplish the goal of deleting the field:

  Step 1:   Decide: If necessary, then use the Browse tool to go to the card with the field.

  Step 2:   Choose the Field tool in the Tools menu.

  Step 3:   Note that the fields on the card background are displayed.

  Step 4:   Click on the field to be selected.

Step 5:   Report goal accomplished.

- Selection rule set for goal of using a specific field-delete method:
  - If you want to paste the field somewhere else, then choose "Cut Field" from the Edit menu.
  - If you want to delete the field permanently, then choose "Clear Field" from the Edit menu.
  - Report goal accomplished.

The empirical evaluation with 28 subjects demonstrated that the NGOMSL version of help halved the time users took to complete information searches in the first of four trial blocks.

A production-rule–based cognitive architecture called Soar provides a computer-based approach to implementing GOMS models. This software tool enables complex predictions of expert performance times based on perceptual and cognitive parameters. Soar was used to model learning in the highly interactive task of videogame playing (Bauer and John, 1995). John and Kieras (1996a, 1996b) compare four GOMS-related techniques and provide ten case studies of practical applications.

2.2.3 Stages of action models

Another approach to forming theories is to describe the stages of action that users go through in trying to use a system. Norman (1988) offers *seven stages of action* as a model of human–computer interaction:

1. Forming the goal
2. Forming the intention
3. Specifying the action
4. Executing the action
5. Perceiving the system state
6. Interpreting the system state
7. Evaluating the outcome

Some of Norman's stages correspond roughly to Foley and van Dam's separation of concerns; that is, the user forms a conceptual intention, reformulates it into the semantics of several commands, constructs the required syntax, and eventually produces the lexical token by the action of moving the mouse to select a point on the screen. Norman makes a contribution by placing his stages in the context of *cycles of action* and *evaluation*. This dynamic process of action distinguishes Norman's approach from the other models, which deal mainly with the knowledge that must be in the user's mind. Furthermore, the seven-stages model leads naturally to identification of the *gulf of execution* (the mismatch between the user's intentions and the allowable actions) and the *gulf of evaluation* (the mismatch between the system's representation and the user's expectations).

This model leads Norman to suggest four principles of good design. First, the state and the action alternatives should be visible. Second, there should be a good conceptual model with a consistent system image. Third, the interface should include good mappings that reveal the relationships between stages. Fourth, the user should receive continuous feedback. Norman places a heavy emphasis on studying errors. He describes how errors often occur in moving from goals to intentions to actions and to executions.

A stages-of-action model helps us to describe user exploration of an interface (Polson and Lewis, 1990). As users try to accomplish their goals, there are four critical points where user failures can occur: (1) users can form an inadequate goal, (2) users might not find the correct interface object because of an incomprehensible label or icon, (3) users many not know how to specify or execute a desired action, and (4) users may receive inappropriate or misleading feedback. The latter three failures may be prevented by improved design or overcome by time-consuming experience with the interface (Franzke, 1995).

2.2.4   Consistency through grammars

An important goal for designers is a *consistent* user interface. However, the definition of consistency is elusive and has multiple levels that are sometimes in conflict; it is also sometimes advantageous to be inconsistent. The argument for consistency is that a command language or set of actions should be orderly, predictable, describable by a few rules, and therefore easy to learn and retain. These overlapping concepts are conveyed by an example that shows two kinds of inconsistency (A illustrates lack of any attempt at consistency, and B shows consistency except for a single violation):

Consistent	Inconsistent A	Inconsistent B
delete/insert character	delete/insert character	delete/insert character
delete/insert word	remove/bring word	remove/insert word
delete/insert line	destroy/create line	delete/insert line
delete/insert paragraph	kill/birth paragraph	delete/insert paragraph

Each of the actions in the consistent version is the same, whereas the actions vary for the inconsistent version A. The inconsistent action verbs are all acceptable, but their variety suggests that they will take longer to learn, will cause more errors, will slow down users, and will be harder for users to remember. Inconsistent version B is somehow more malicious because there is a single unpredictable inconsistency that stands out so dramatically that this language is likely to be remembered for its peculiar inconsistency.

To capture these notions, Reisner (1981) proposed an *action grammar* to describe two versions of a graphics-system interface. She demonstrated that the version that had a simpler grammar was easier to learn. Payne and Green (1986) expanded her work by addressing the multiple levels of consistency (lexical, syntactic, and semantic) through a notational structure they call *task–action grammars* (TAGs). They also address some aspects of completeness of a language by trying to characterize a complete set of tasks; for example, *up*, *down*, and *left* constitute an incomplete set of arrow-cursor movement tasks, because *right* is missing. Once the full set of task–action mappings is written down, the grammar of the command language can be tested against it to demonstrate completeness. Of course, a designer might leave out something from the task–action mapping and then the grammar could not be checked accurately, but it does seem useful to have an approach to checking for completeness and consistency. For example, a TAG definition of cursor control would have a dictionary of tasks:

move-cursor-one-character-forward	[Direction = forward, Unit = char]
move-cursor-one-character-backward	[Direction = backward, Unit = char]
move-cursor-one-word-forward	[Direction = forward, Unit = word]
move-cursor-one-word-backward	[Direction = backward, Unit = word]

Then the high-level rule schemas that describe the syntax of the commands are as follows:

1. task [Direction, Unit] → symbol [Direction] + letter [Unit]
2. symbol [Direction = forward] → "CTRL"
3. symbol [Direction = backward] → "ESC"
4. letter [Unit = word] → "W"
5. letter [Unit = char] → "C"

These schemas will generate a consistent grammar:

move cursor one character forward	CTRL-C
move cursor one character backward	ESC-C
move cursor one word forward	CTRL-W
move cursor one word backward	ESC-W

Payne and Green are careful to state that their notation and approach are flexible and extensible, and they provide appealing examples in which their approach sharpened the thinking of designers.

Reisner (1990) extends this work by defining consistency more formally, but Grudin (1989) points out flaws in some arguments for consistency. Certainly consistency is subtle and has multiple levels; there are conflicting forms of consistency, and sometimes inconsistency is a virtue (for example, to draw attention to a dangerous operation). Nonetheless, understanding consistency is an important goal for designers and researchers.

2.2.5   Widget-level theories

Hierarchical decomposition is often a useful tool for dealing with complexity, but many of the theories and predictive models follow an extreme reductionist approach, which may not always be valid. In some situations, it is hard to accept the low level of detail, the precise numbers that are sometimes attached to subtasks, and the validity of simple summations of time periods. Furthermore, models requiring numerous subjective judgments raise the question of whether several analysts would come up with the same results.

An alternative approach is to follow the simplifications made in the higher-level, user-interface building tools (see Chapter 5). Instead of dealing with atomic level features, why not create a model based on the widgets (interface components) supported in the tool? Once a scrolling-list widget was tested to determine user performance as a function of the number of items and the size of the window, then future widget users would have automatic generation of performance prediction. The prediction would have to be derived from some declaration of the task frequencies, but the description of the interface would emerge from the process of designing the interface.

A measure of layout appropriateness (frequently used pairs of widgets should be adjacent, and the left-to-right sequence should be in harmony with the task-sequence description) would also be produced to guide the designer in a possible redesign. Estimates of the perceptual and cognitive complexity plus the motor load would be generated automatically (Sears, 1992). As widgets become more sophisticated and more widely used, the investment in determining the complexity of each widget will be amortized over the many designers and projects.

Gradually, higher-level patterns of usage are appearing, in much that way that Alexander describes has occurred in architecture (1977). Familiar patterns of building fireplaces, stairways, or roofs become modular components that acquire names and are combined to form still larger patterns.

2.3   Object–Action Interface Model

Distinctions between syntax and semantics have long been made by compiler writers who sought to separate out the parsing of input text from the operations that were invoked by the text. A *syntactic–semantic model* of human behavior was originated to describe programming (Shneiderman, 1980) and was applied to database-manipulation facilities (Shneiderman, 1981), as well as to direct manipulation (Shneiderman, 1983). The early syntactic-semantic model made a major distinction between meaningfully acquired semantic concepts and rote-memorized syntactic details. Semantic concepts of the users's tasks were well-organized and stable in memory, whereas syntactic details of command languages were arbitrary and had to be rehearsed frequently to be maintained.

The maturing model described in this book's first edition stressed the separation between task-domain concepts (for example, stock-market portfolios) and the computer-domain concepts that represent them (for example, folders, spreadsheets, or databases). Then, this book's second edition amplified the important distinction between objects and actions. By now, the objects and actions have become the dominant features. In this third edition, the underlying theory of design will be called the *object–action interface* (OAI—let's pronounce it Oo-Ah!) *model.*

As GUIs have replaced command languages, intricate syntax has given way to relatively simple direct manipulations applied to visual representations of objects and actions. The emphasis is now on the visual display of user task objects and actions. For example, a collection of stock-market portfolios might be represented by leather folders with icons of engraved share certificates. Then, the actions are represented—by trashcans for deletion, or shelf icons to represent destinations for portfolio copying. Of course, there are syntactic aspects of direct manipulation, such as knowing whether to drag the file to the trashcan or to drag the trashcan to the folder, but the amount of syntax is small and can be thought of as being at the lowest level of the interface actions. Even syntactic forms such as double-clicking, mouse-down-and-wait, or gestures seem simple compared to the pages of grammars for early command languages.

Doing object–action design starts with understanding the task. That task includes the universe of real-world objects with which users work to accomplish their intentions and the actions that they apply to those objects. The

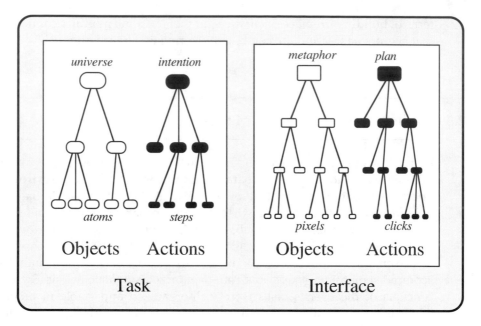

Figure 2.2

Task and interface concepts, separated into hierarchies of objects and actions.

high-level task objects might be stock-market statistics, a photo library, or a scientific journal (Fig. 2.2). These objects can be decomposed into information on a single stock and finally into atomic units such as a share price. Task actions start from high-level intentions that are decomposed into intermediate goals and individual steps.

Once there is agreement on the task objects and actions and their decomposition, the designer can create the metaphoric representations of the interface objects and actions. Interface objects do not have weight or thickness; they are pixels that can be moved or copied in ways that represent real-world task objects with feedback to guide users. Finally, the designer must make the interface actions visible to users, so that users can decompose their plan into a series of intermediate actions, such as opening a dialog box, all the way down to a series of detailed keystrokes and clicks.

In outline, the OAI model is an explanatory model that focuses on task objects and actions, and on interface objects and actions. Because the syntactic details are minimal, users who know the task domain objects and actions can learn the interface relatively easily (see Chapter 12). The OAI model also reflects the higher level of design with which most designers deal when they use the widgets in user-interface–building tools. The standard widgets have familiar and simple syntax (click, double-click, drag, or drop) and simple forms of feedback (highlighting, scrolling, or movement), leaving the designer more focused on how to use these widgets to create a business-oriented solution. The OAI model is in harmony with the software-engineering trends toward object-oriented design and programming methods that have become popular in the past decade.

2.3.1 Task hierarchies of objects and actions

The primary way to deal with large and complex problems is to decompose them into several smaller problems in a hierarchical manner until each subproblem is manageable. For example, a human body is discussed in terms of neural, muscular, skeletal, reproductive, digestive, circulatory, and other subsystems, which in turn might be described by organs, tissues, and cells. Most real-world objects have similar decompositions: buildings, cities, computer programs, and plays, for example. Some objects are more neatly decomposed than are others; some objects are easier to understand than are others.

Similarly, intentions can be decomposed into smaller action steps. A building-construction plan can be reduced to a series of steps such as surveying the property, laying the foundation, building the frame, raising the roof, and completing the interior. A symphony performance has movements, measures, and notes; a baseball game has innings, outs, and pitches.

People learn the task objects and actions independently of their implementation on a computer. People learn about buildings or books through developmental experiences in their youth, but many tasks require specialized training, such as in how to manage stock-market portfolios, to design buildings, or to diagnose medical problems. It may take years to learn the terminology, to acquire the decision-making skills, and to become proficient.

Designers who develop computer systems to support professionals may have to take training courses, to read workbooks, and to interview users. Then, the designers can sit down and generate a hierarchy of objects and actions to model the users' tasks. This model forms a basis for designing the interface objects and actions plus their representation in pixels on a screen, in physical devices, or by a voice or other audio cue.

Users who must learn to use computers to accomplish real-world tasks must first become proficient in the task domain. An expert computer user who has not studied architecture will not be able to use a building-design package any more than a computer-savvy amateur can make reliable medical diagnoses.

In summary, tasks include hierarchies of objects and actions at high and low levels. Hierarchies are not perfect, but they are comprehensible and useful. Most users accept a separation of their tasks into high- and low-level objects and actions.

2.3.2   Interface hierarchies of objects and actions

The *interface* includes hierarchies of objects and actions at high and low levels. For example, a central set of *interface-object* concepts deals with storage. Users come to understand the high-level concept that computers store information. The stored information can be refined into objects, such as the directory and the files of information. In turn, the directory object is refined into a set of directory entries, each of which has a name, length, date of creation, owner, access control, and so on. Each file is an object that has a lower-level structure consisting of lines, fields, characters, fonts, pointers, binary numbers, and so on.

The *interface actions* also are decomposable into lower-level actions. The high-level plans, such as creating a text data file, may require load, insertion, and save actions. The midlevel action of saving a file is refined into the actions of storing a file and backup file on one of many disks, of applying access-control rights, of overwriting previous versions, of assigning a name to the file, and so on. Then, there are many low-level details about permissible file types or sizes, error conditions such as shortage of storage space, or responses to hardware or software errors. Finally, the low-level action of issuing a specific command is carried out by clicking on a pull-down menu item.

Designers craft interface objects and actions based on familiar examples, then tune those objects and actions to fit the task. For example, in developing a system to manage stock-market portfolios, the designer might consider spreadsheets, databases, word processors, or a specialized graphical design that allowed users to drag stock symbols to indicate buying or selling.

Users can learn interface objects and actions by seeing a demonstration, hearing an explanation of features, or conducting trial-and-error sessions. The metaphoric representation—abstract, concrete, or analogical—conveys the interface objects and actions. For example, to explain saving a file, an instructor might draw a picture of a disk drive and a directory to show where the file goes and how the directory references the file. Alternatively, the instructor might describe how the card catalog acts as a directory for books saved in the library.

When interface objects and actions have a logical structure that can be anchored to familiar task objects and actions, we expect that structure to be relatively stable in memory. If users remember the high-level concept of saving a file, they will be able to conclude that the file must have a name, a size, and a storage location. The linkage to other objects and the visual presentation support the memorability of this knowledge.

These interface objects and actions were once novel, known by only a small number of scientists, engineers, and data-processing professionals. Now, these concepts are taught at the elementary-school level, argued over during coffee breaks in the office, and exchanged in the aisles of corporate jets. When educators talk of computer literacy, part of their plans cover these interface concepts.

The OAI model helps us to understand the multiple complex processes that must occur for users to be successful in using an interface to accomplish a task. For example, in writing a business letter using computer software, users have to integrate smoothly their knowledge of the task objects and actions and of the interface objects and actions. They must have the high-level concept of writing (task action) a letter (task object), recognize that the letter will be stored as a document (interface object), and know the details of the save command (interface action). Users must be fluent with the middle-level concept of composing a sentence, and must recognize the mechanisms for beginning, writing, and ending a sentence. Finally, users must know the proper low-level details of spelling each word (low-level task object), and must know where the keys are for each letter (low-level interface object). The goal of minimizing interface concepts (such as the syntax of a command language) while presenting a visual representation of the task objects and actions is the heart of the direct-manipulation approach to design (see Chapter 6).

Integrating the multiple levels of task and interface concepts is a substantial challenge that requires great motivation and concentration. Educational materials that facilitate the acquisition of this knowledge are difficult to design, especially because of the diversity of background knowledge and motivation levels of typical learners. The OAI model of user knowledge can provide a guide to educational designers by highlighting the different kinds of knowledge that users need to acquire (see Chapter 12) and a guide to web site designers (see Chapter 16).

Designers of interactive systems can apply the OAI model to systematize their work. Where possible, the task objects should be made explicit, and the user's task actions should be laid out clearly. Then, the interface objects and actions can be identified, and appropriate representations can be created. These designs are likely to increase comprehensibility to users and independence of specific hardware.

2.3.3 The disappearance of syntax

In the early days of computers, users had to maintain a profusion of device-dependent details in their human memories. These low-level syntactic details include the knowledge of which action erases a character (delete, backspace, CTRL-H, CTRL-G, CTRL-D, rightmost mouse button, or ESCAPE), which action inserts a new line after the third line of a text file (CTRL-I, INSERT key, I3, I 3, or 3I), which abbreviations are permissible, and which of the numbered function keys produces the previous screen.

The learning, use, and retention of this knowledge are hampered by two problems. First, these details vary across systems in an unpredictable manner. Second, acquiring syntactic knowledge is often a struggle because the arbitrariness of these minor design features greatly reduces the effectiveness of paired-associate learning. Rote memorization requires repeated rehearsals to reach competence, and retention over time is poor unless the knowledge is applied frequently. Syntactic knowledge is usually conveyed by example and repeated usage. Formal notations, such as Backus–Naur form, are useful for knowledgeable computer scientists, but are confusing to most users.

A further problem with syntactic knowledge, in some cases, lies in the difficulty of providing a hierarchical structure or even a modular structure to cope with the complexity. For example, how is a user to remember these details of using an electronic-mail system: press RETURN to terminate a paragraph, CTRL-D to terminate a letter, Q to quit the electronic-mail subsystem, and logout to terminate the session. The knowledgeable computer user understands these four forms of termination as commands in the context of the full system, but the novice may be confused by four seemingly similar situations that have radically different syntactic forms.

A final difficulty is that syntactic knowledge is system dependent. A user who switches from one machine to another may face different keyboard layouts, commands, function-key usage, and sequences of actions. Certainly there may be some overlap. For example, arithmetic expressions might be the same in two languages; unfortunately, however, the small differences can be the most annoying. One system uses K to keep a file and another uses K to kill the file, or S to save versus S to send.

Expert frequent users can overcome these difficulties, and they are less troubled by syntactic knowledge problems. Novices and knowledgeable users, however, are especially troubled by syntactic irregularities. Their burden can be lightened by use of menus (see Chapter 7), a reduction in the arbitrariness of the keypresses, use of consistent patterns of commands, meaningful command names and labels on keys, and fewer details that must be memorized (see Chapter 8).

Minimizing these burdens is the goal of most interface designers. Modern direct-manipulation styles (see Chapter 6) support the process of presenting users with screens filled with familiar objects and actions representing their task objects and actions. Modern user interface building tools (see Chapter 5) facilitate the design process by making standard widgets easily available.

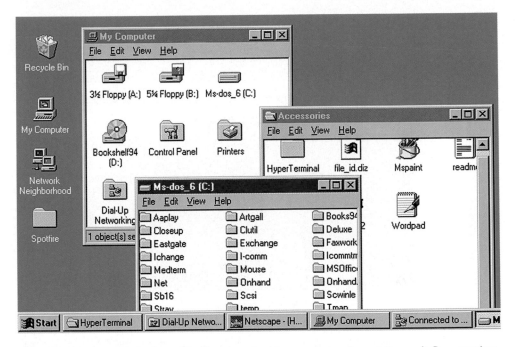

Plate A1: Microsoft Windows 95. (Reprinted with permission from Microsoft Corporation, Redmond, WA.)

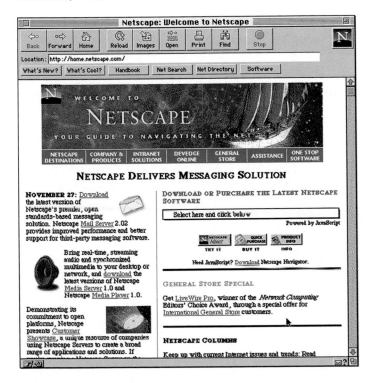

Plate A2: Netscape home page (http://home.netscape.com). (© 1996 Netscape Communication Corporation. Used with permission.)

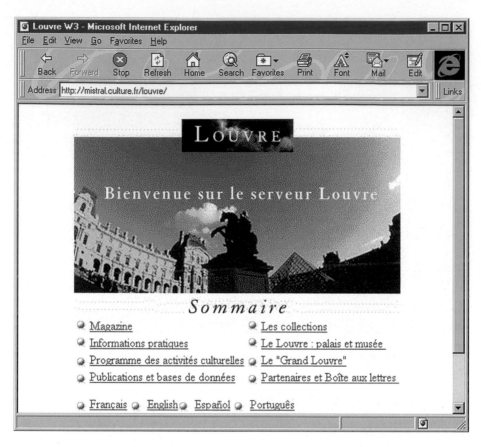

Plate A3: Microsoft Internet Explorer, showing the Louvre Museum web site (http://mistral.culture.fr/louvre).

Plate A4: White House home page (http://www.whitehouse.gov).

Plate A5: Library of Congress home page (http://www.loc.gov).

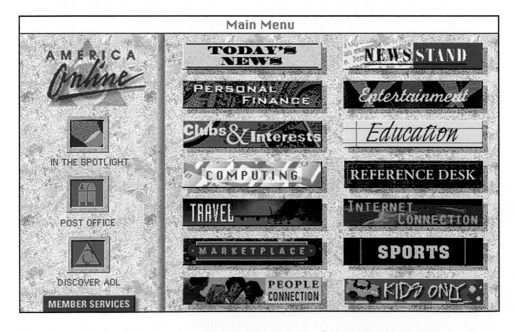

Plate A6: America Online main menu. (© 1997 America Online. Used by permission.)

Innovative designers may recognize opportunities for novel widgets that provide a closer match between the screen representation and the user's workplace.

2.4   Principle 1: Recognize the Diversity

When human diversity (see Section 1.5) is multiplied by the wide range of situations, tasks, and frequencies of use, the set of design possibilities becomes enormous. The designer can respond by choosing from a spectrum of interaction styles.

A preschooler playing a graphic computer game is a long way from a reference librarian doing bibliographic searches for anxious and hurried patrons. Similarly, a professional programmer using a new operating system is a long way from a highly trained and experienced air-traffic controller. Finally, a student surfing the net for love poems is a long way from a hotel-reservations clerk serving customers for many hours per day.

These sketches highlight the differences in users' background knowledge, training in the use of the system, frequency of use, and goals, as well as in the impact of a user error. No single design could satisfy all these users and situations, so before beginning a design, we must make the characterization of the users and the situation as precise and complete as possible.

2.4.1   Usage profiles

"Know thy user" was the first principle in Hansen's (1971) classic list of user-engineering principles. It is a simple idea, but a difficult and, unfortunately, often-undervalued goal. No one would argue against this principle, but many designers assume that they understand the users and users' tasks. Successful designers are aware that other people learn, think, and solve problems in different ways. Some users really do prefer to deal with tables rather than with graphs, with words instead of numbers, or with a rigid structure rather than an open-ended form.

It is difficult for most designers to know whether Boolean expressions are too difficult a concept for library patrons at a junior college, fourth graders learning programming, or professional controllers of electric-power utilities.

All design should begin with an understanding of the intended users, including population profiles that reflect age, gender, physical abilities, education, cultural or ethnic background, training, motivation, goals, and personality. There are often several communities of users for a system, so the design effort is multiplied. Typical user communities—such as high school teachers, nurses, doctors, computer programmers, museum patrons, or librarians—can be expected to have various combinations of knowledge and usage patterns. Users from different countries may each deserve special attention, and even regional differences exist within countries. Other variables that characterize users include location (for example, urban vs. rural), economic profile, disabilities, and attitudes toward using technology.

In addition to these profiles, users might be tested for such skills as comprehension of Boolean expressions, knowledge of set theory, fluency in a foreign language, or skills in human relationships. Other tests might cover such task-specific abilities as knowledge of airport city codes, stockbrokerage terminology, insurance-claims concepts, or map icons.

The process of getting to know the users is never ending because there is so much to know and because the users keep changing. Every step in understanding the users and in recognizing them as individuals whose outlook is different from the designer's own is likely to be a step closer to a successful design.

For example, a generic separation into novice or first-time, knowledgeable intermittent, and expert frequent users might lead to these differing design goals:

- *Novice or first-time users*   True novice users are assumed to know little of the task or interface concepts. By contrast, first-time users are professionals who know the task concepts, but have shallow knowledge of the interface concepts. Both groups of users may arrive with anxiety about using computers that inhibits learning. Overcoming these limitations is a serious challenge to the designer of the interface, including instructions, dialog boxes, and online help. Restricting vocabulary to a small number of familiar, consistently used concept terms is essential to begin developing the user's knowledge. The number of actions should also be small, so that novice and first-time users can carry out simple tasks successfully and thus reduce anxiety, build confidence, and gain positive reinforcement. Informative feedback about the accomplishment of each task is helpful, and constructive, specific error messages should be provided when users make mistakes. Carefully designed paper manuals and step-by-step online tutorials may be effective.

- *Knowledgeable intermittent users*   Many people are knowledgeable but intermittent users of a variety of systems. They have stable task concepts and broad knowledge of interface concepts, but they will have difficulty retaining the structure of menus or the location of features. The burden on their memories will be lightened by orderly structure in the menus, consistent terminology, and high interface apparency, which emphasizes recognition rather than recall. Consistent sequences of actions, meaningful messages, and guides to frequent patterns of usage will help knowledgeable intermittent users to rediscover how to perform their tasks properly. Protection from danger is necessary to support relaxed exploration of features or attempts to invoke a partially forgotten action sequence. These users will benefit from online help screens to fill in missing pieces of task or interface knowledge. Well-organized reference manuals also will be useful.

- *Expert frequent users*   Expert "power" users are thoroughly familiar with the task and interface concepts and seek to get their work done quickly. They demand rapid response times, brief and nondistracting feedback, and the capacity to carry out actions with just a few keystrokes or selections. When a sequence of three or four commands is performed regularly, the frequent user is eager to create a *macro* or other abbreviated form to reduce the number of steps. Strings of commands, shortcuts through menus, abbreviations, and other accelerators are requirements.

These characteristics of these three classes of usage must be refined for each environment. Designing for one class is easy; designing for several is much more difficult.

When multiple usage classes must be accommodated in one system, the basic strategy is to permit a *level-structured* (some times called *layered* or *spiral approach*) to learning. Novices can be taught a minimal subset of objects and actions with which to get started. They are most likely to make correct choices when they have only a few options and are protected from making mistakes—when they are given a *training-wheels* interface. After gaining confidence from hands-on experience, these users can progress to ever-greater levels of task concepts and the accompanying interface concepts. The learning plan should be governed by the users' progress through the task concepts, with new interface concepts being introduced only when they are needed to support a more complex task. For users with strong knowledge of the task and interface concepts, rapid progress is possible.

For example, novice users of a bibliographic-search system might be taught author or title searches first, followed by subject searches that require Boolean combinations of queries. Their progress is governed by the task domain, rather than by an alphabetical list of commands that are difficult to relate to the tasks. The level-structured approach must be carried out in the design of not only the software, but also the user manuals, help screens, error messages, and tutorials.

Another approach to accommodating different usage classes is to permit user control of the density of informative feedback that the system provides. Novices want more informative feedback to confirm their actions, whereas frequent users want less distracting feedback. Similarly, it seems that frequent users like displays to be more densely packed than do novices. Finally, the pace of interaction may be varied from slow for novices to fast for frequent users.

2.4.2   Task profiles

After carefully drawing the user profile, the developers must identify the tasks. Task analysis has a long, but mixed, history (Bailey, 1996). Every designer would agree that the set of tasks must be determined before design can proceed, but too often the task analysis is done informally or implicitly. If implementers find that another command can be added, the designer is often tempted to include that command in the hope that some users will find it helpful. Design or implementation convenience should not dictate system functionality or command features.

High-level task actions can be decomposed into multiple middle-level task actions that can be further refined into atomic actions that the user executes with a single command, menu selection, and so on. Choosing the most appropriate set of atomic actions is a difficult task. If the atomic actions are too small, the users will become frustrated by the large number of actions necessary to accomplish a higher-level task. If the atomic actions are too large and elaborate, the users will need many such actions with special options, or they will not be able to get exactly what they want from the system.

The relative task frequencies will be important in shaping, for example, a set of commands or a menu tree. Frequently performed tasks should be simple and quick to carry out, even at the expense of lengthening some infrequent tasks. Relative frequency of use is one of the bases for making architectural design decisions. For example, in a text editor,

- Frequent actions might be performed by special keys, such as the four cursor arrows, INSERT, and DELETE.
- Intermediately frequent actions might be performed by a single letter plus CTRL, or by a selection from a pull-down menu—examples include underscore, center, indent, subscript, or superscript.
- Infrequent actions or complex actions might require going through a sequence of menu selections or form fillins—for example, to change the printing format or to revise network-protocol parameters.

A matrix of users and tasks can help us to sort out these issues (Fig. 2.3). In each box, the designer can put a check mark to indicate that this user carries

FREQUENCY OF TASK BY JOB TITLE

Job title	Query by Patient	Update Data	Query across Patients	Add Relations	Evaluate System
Nurse	0.14	0.11			
Physician	0.06	0.04			
Supervisor	0.01	0.01	0.04		
Appointment personnel	0.26				
Medical-record maintainer	0.07	0.04	0.04	0.01	
Clinical researcher			0.08		
Database programmer			0.02	0.02	0.05

Figure 2.3

Hypothetical frequency-of-use data for a medical clinic information system. Answering queries from appointments personnel about individual patients is the highest-frequency task.

out this task. A more precise analysis would include frequencies instead of just simple check marks.

2.4.3   Interaction styles

When the task analysis is complete and the task objects and actions have been identified, the designer can choose from these primary interaction styles: menu selection, form fillin, command language, natural language, and direct manipulation (Box 2.1). Chapters 6 through 8 explore these styles in detail; here, we give a comparative overview to set the stage.

Direct manipulation When a clever designer can create a visual representation of the world of action, the users' tasks can be greatly simplified because direct manipulation of familiar objects is possible. Examples of such systems include the popular desktop metaphor, computer-assisted–design tools, air-traffic–control systems, and video games. By pointing at visual representations of objects and actions, users can carry out tasks rapidly and can observe the results immediately. Keyboard entry of commands or menu choices is

Box 2.1

Advantages and disadvantages of the five primary interaction styles.

Advantages	*Disadvantages*
Direct manipulation	
visually presents task concepts	may be hard to program
allows easy learning	may require graphics display and pointing devices
allows easy retention	
allows errors to be avoided	
encourages exploration	
affords high subjective satisfaction	
Menu selection	
shortens learning	presents danger of many menus
reduces keystrokes	may slow frequent users
structures decision making	consumes screen space
permits use of dialog-management tools	requires rapid display rate
allows easy support of error handling	
Form fillin	
simplifies data entry	consumes screen space
requires modest training	
gives convenient assistance	
permits use of form-management tools	
Command language	
is flexible	has poor error handling
appeals to "power" users	requires substantial training and memorization
supports user initiative	
allows convenient creation of user-defined macros	
Natural language	
relieves burden of learning syntax	requires clarification dialog
	may require more keystrokes
	may not show context
	is unpredictable

replaced by use of cursor-motion devices to select from a visible set of objects and actions. Direct manipulation is appealing to novices, is easy to remember for intermittent users, and, with careful design, it can be rapid for frequent users. Chapter 6 describes direct manipulation and its application.

Menu selection In menu-selection systems, users read a list of items, select the one most appropriate to their task, and observe the effect. If the terminology and meaning of the items are understandable and distinct, then users can accomplish their tasks with little learning or memorization and just a few actions. The greatest benefit may be that there is a clear structure to decision making, since all possible choices are presented at one time. This interaction style is appropriate for novice and intermittent users and can be appealing to frequent users if the display and selection mechanisms are rapid.

For designers, menu-selection systems require careful task analysis to ensure that all functions are supported conveniently and that terminology is chosen carefully and used consistently. Advanced user interface building tools to support menu selection are an enormous benefit in ensuring consistent screen design, validating completeness, and supporting maintenance.

Form fillin When data entry is required, menu selection usually becomes cumbersome, and form fillin (also called *fill in the blanks*) is appropriate. Users see a display of related fields, move a cursor among the fields, and enter data where desired. With the form-fillin interaction style, users must understand the field labels, know the permissible values and the data-entry method, and be capable of responding to error messages. Since knowledge of the keyboard, labels, and permissible fields is required, some training may be necessary. This interaction style is most appropriate for knowledgeable intermittent users or frequent users. Chapter 7 provides a thorough treatment of menus and form fillin.

Command language For frequent users, command languages provide a strong feeling of locus of control and initiative. Users learn the syntax and can often express complex possibilities rapidly, without having to read distracting prompts. However, error rates are typically high, training is necessary, and retention may be poor. Error messages and online assistance are hard to provide because of the diversity of possibilities plus the complexity of mapping from tasks to interface concepts and syntax. Command languages and lengthier query or programming languages are the domain of expert frequent users, who often derive great satisfaction from mastering a complex set of semantics and syntax.

Natural language The hope that computers will respond properly to arbitrary natural-language sentences or phrases engages many researchers and system developers, in spite of limited success thus far. Natural-language interaction usually provides little context for issuing the next command, frequently requires *clarification dialog,* and may be slower and more cumbersome than the alternatives. Still, where users are knowledgeable about a task domain whose scope is limited and where intermittent use inhibits command-language training, there exist opportunities for natural-language interfaces (discussed at the end of Chapter 8).

Blending several interaction styles may be appropriate when the required tasks and users are diverse. Commands can lead the user to a form fillin where data entry is required, or menus can be used to control a direct-manipulation environment when a suitable visualization of actions cannot be found.

2.5   Principle 2: Use the Eight Golden Rules of Interface Design

Later chapters cover constructive guidance for design of direct manipulation, menu selection, command languages, and so on. This section presents underlying principles of design that are applicable in most interactive systems. These underlying principles of interface design, derived heuristically from experience, should be validated and refined.

1. *Strive for consistency.* This rule is the most frequently violated one, but following it can be tricky because there are many forms of consistency. Consistent sequences of actions should be required in similar situations; identical terminology should be used in prompts, menus, and help screens; and consistent color, layout, capitalization, fonts, and so on should be employed throughout. Exceptions, such as no echoing of passwords or confirmation of the delete command, should be comprehensible and limited in number.

2. *Enable frequent users to use shortcuts.* As the frequency of use increases, so do the user's desires to reduce the number of interactions and to increase the pace of interaction. Abbreviations, special keys, hidden commands, and macro facilities are appreciated by frequent knowledgeable users. Short response times and fast display rates are other attractions for frequent users.

3. *Offer informative feedback.* For every user action, there should be system feedback. For frequent and minor actions, the response can be modest, whereas for infrequent and major actions, the response should be more substantial. Visual presentation of the objects of interest provides a con-

venient environment for showing changes explicitly (see discussion of direct manipulation in Chapter 6).

4. *Design dialogs to yield closure.* Sequences of actions should be organized into groups with a beginning, middle, and end. The informative feedback at the completion of a group of actions gives operators the satisfaction of accomplishment, a sense of relief, the signal to drop contingency plans and options from their minds, and an indication that the way is clear to prepare for the next group of actions.

5. *Offer error prevention and simple error handling.* As much as possible, design the system such that users cannot make a serious error; for example, prefer menu selection to form fillin and do not allow alphabetic characters in numeric entry fields. If users make an error, the system should detect the error and offer simple, constructive, and specific instructions for recovery. For example, users should not have to retype an entire command, but rather should need to repair only the faulty part. Erroneous actions should leave the system state unchanged, or the system should give instructions about restoring the state.

6. *Permit easy reversal of actions.* As much as possible, actions should be reversible. This feature relieves anxiety, since the user knows that errors can be undone, thus encouraging exploration of unfamiliar options. The units of reversibility may be a single action, a data-entry task, or a complete group of actions such as entry of a name and address block.

7. *Support internal locus of control.* Experienced operators strongly desire the sense that they are in charge of the system and that the system responds to their actions. Surprising system actions, tedious sequences of data entries, inability or difficulty in obtaining necessary information, and inability to produce the action desired all build anxiety and dissatisfaction. Gaines (1981) captured part of this principle with his rule *avoid acausality* and his encouragement to make users the *initiators* of actions rather than the *responders* to actions.

8. *Reduce short-term memory load.* The limitation of human information processing in short-term memory (the rule of thumb is that humans can remember "seven-plus or minus-two chunks" of information) requires that displays be kept simple, multiple page displays be consolidated, window-motion frequency be reduced, and sufficient training time be allotted for codes, mnemonics, and sequences of actions. Where appropriate, online access to command-syntax forms, abbreviations, codes, and other information should be provided.

These underlying principles must be interpreted, refined, and extended for each environment. The principles presented in the ensuing sections focus on increasing the productivity of users by providing simplified data-entry procedures, comprehensible displays, and rapid informative feedback that increase feelings of competence, mastery, and control over the system.

2.6   Principle 3: Prevent Errors

There is no medicine against death, and against error no rule has been found.

Sigmund Freud (Inscription he wrote on his portrait)

Users of word processors, spreadsheets, database-query facilities, air-traffic–control systems, and other interactive systems make mistakes far more frequently than might be expected. Card et al. (1980) reported that experienced professional users of text editors and operating systems made mistakes or used inefficient strategies in 31 percent of the tasks assigned to them. Brown and Gould (1987) found that even experienced authors made errors in almost half their spreadsheets. Other studies reveal the magnitude of the problem of—and the loss of productivity due to—user errors.

One way to reduce the loss in productivity due to errors is to improve the error messages provided by the computer system. Shneiderman (1982) reported on five experiments in which changes to error messages led to improved success at repairing the errors, lower error rates, and increased subjective satisfaction. Superior error messages were more specific, positive in tone, and constructive (telling the user what to do, rather than merely reporting the problem). Rather than using vague and hostile messages, such as SYNTAX ERROR or ILLEGAL DATA, designers were encouraged to use informative messages, such as UNMATCHED LEFT PARENTHESIS or MENU CHOICES ARE IN THE RANGE OF 1 TO 6.

Improved error messages, however, are only helpful medicine. A more effective approach is to prevent the errors from occurring. This goal is more attainable than it may seem in many systems.

The first step is to understand the nature of errors. One perspective is that people make mistakes or "slips" (Norman, 1983) that designers help them to avoid by organizing screens and menus functionally, designing commands or menu choices to be distinctive, and making it difficult for users to take irreversible actions. Norman offers other guidelines, such as do not have modes, do offer feedback about the state of the system, and do design for consistency of commands. Norman's analysis provides practical examples and a useful theory.

Three techniques can reduce errors by ensuring complete and correct actions: correct matching pairs, complete sequences, and correct commands.

2.6.1   Correct matching pairs

A common problem is the lack of correct matching pairs. It has many manifestations and several simple prevention strategies. An example is the failure to provide the right parenthesis to close an open left parenthesis. If a bibliographic-search system allowed Boolean expressions such as `COMPUTERS AND (PSYCHOLOGY OR SOCIOLOGY)` and the user failed to provide the right parenthesis at the end, the system would produce a `SYNTAX ERROR` message or, more helpfully, a more meaningful message, such as `UNMATCHED LEFT PARENTHESES`.

Similarly, other marker pairs are required to delimit boldface, italic, or underscored text in word processors or web programming. If the text file contains `<B>This is boldface</B>`, then the three words between the markers appear in boldface. If the rightmost `</B>` is missing, additional text may be inadvertently made bold.

In each of these cases, a matching pair of markers is necessary for operation to be complete and correct. The omission of the closing marker can be prevented by use of an editor, preferably screen oriented, that puts both the beginning and ending components of the pair on the screen in one action. For example, typing a left parenthesis generates a left and right parenthesis and puts the cursor in between to allow creation of the contents. An attempt to delete one of the parentheses will cause the matching parenthesis (and possibly the contents as well) to be deleted. Thus, the text can never be in a syntactically incorrect form. Some people find this rigid approach to be too restrictive. For them a milder form of protection may be appropriate. For example, when the user types a left parenthesis, the screen displays in the lower-left corner a message indicating the need for a right parenthesis until that character is typed.

2.6.2   Complete sequences

Sometimes, an action requires several steps or commands to reach completion. Since people may forget to complete every step of an action, designers attempt to offer a sequence of steps as a single action. In an automobile, the driver does not have to set two switches to signal a left turn. A single switch causes both (front and rear) turn-signal lights on the left side of the car to flash. When a pilot throws a switch to lower the landing gear, hundreds of steps and checks are invoked automatically.

This same concept can be applied to interactive uses of computers. For example, the sequence of dialing up, setting communication parameters, logging on, and loading files is frequently executed by many users. Fortunately, most com-munications-software packages enable users to specify these processes once and then to execute them by simply selecting the appropriate name.

Users of a word processor should be able to indicate that section titles are to be centered, set in uppercase letters, and underlined, without having to issue a series of commands each time they enter a section title. Then, if the user wants to change the title style—for example, to eliminate underlin-ing—a single command will guarantee that all section titles are revised con-sistently.

As a final example, air-traffic controllers may formulate plans to change the altitude of a plane from 14,000 feet to 18,000 feet in two incre-ments; after raising the plane to 16,000 feet, however, the controller may get distracted and may thus fail to complete the action. The controller should be able to record the plan and then have the computer prompt for completion.

The notion of complete sequences of actions may be difficult to imple-ment because users may need to issue atomic actions as well as complete sequences. In this case, users should be allowed to define sequences of their own; the macro or subroutine concept should be available at every level of usage.

Designers can gather information about potential complete sequences by studying sequences of commands that people actually issue, and the pat-terns of errors that people actually make.

2.6.3 Correct commands

Industrial designers recognize that successful products must be safe and must prevent the user from making dangerously incorrect use of the prod-uct. Airplane engines cannot be put into reverse until the landing gear has touched down, and cars cannot be put into reverse while traveling forward at faster than five miles per hour. Many simpler cameras prevent double exposures (even though the photographer may want to expose a frame twice), and appliances have interlocks to prevent tampering while the power is on (even though expert users occasionally need to perform diagnoses).

The same principles can be applied to interactive systems. Consider these typical errors made by the users of command languages: They invoke commands that are not available, request files that do not exist, or enter data values that are not acceptable. These errors are often caused by annoying typographic errors, such as using an incorrect command abbre-viation; pressing a pair of keys, rather than a desired single key; mis-spelling a file name; or making a minor error such as omitting, inserting, or transposing characters. Error messages range from the annoyingly brief ?

or WHAT?, to the vague UNRECOGNIZED COMMAND or SYNTAX ERROR, to the condemning BAD FILE NAME or ILLEGAL COMMAND. The brief ? is suitable for expert users who have made a trivial error and can recognize it when they see the command line on the screen. But if an expert has ventured to use a new command and has misunderstood its operation, then the brief message is not helpful. They must interrupt their planning to deal with correcting the problem—and with their frustration in not getting what they wanted.

Some systems offer automatic command completion that allows users to type just a few letters of a meaningful command. They may request the computer to complete the command by pressing the space bar, or the computer may complete it as soon as the input is sufficient to distinguish the command from others. Automatic command completion can save keystrokes and is appreciated by many users, but it can also be disruptive because the user must consider how many characters to type for each command, and must verify that the computer has made the completion that was intended.

A more effective preventative for errors is to apply direct-manipulation strategies that emphasize selection over command-language typing. The computer presents permissible commands, menu choices, or file names on the screen, and users select their choice with a pointing device. This approach is effective if the screen has ample space, the display rate is rapid, and the pointing device is fast and accurate.

2.7 Guidelines for Data Display

The separation between basic principles and more informal guidelines is not a sharp line. However, thoughtful designers can distinguish between psychological principles (Wickens, 1993; Bridger, 1995) and practical guidelines that are gained from experience with a specific application. Guidelines for display of data are being developed by many organizations. A guidelines document can help by promoting consistency among multiple designers, recording practical experience, incorporating the results of empirical studies, and offering useful rules of thumb (see Chapters 3 and 11). The creation of a guidelines document engages the design community in a lively discussion of input or output formats, command sequences, terminology, and hardware devices (Brown, 1988; Galitz, 1993). Inspirations for design guidelines can also be taken from graphics designers (Tufte, 1983, 1990, 1997; Mullet and Sano, 1995).

2.7.1   Organizing the display

Smith and Mosier (1986) offer five high-level objectives for data display that remain vital:

1. *Consistency of data display*   During the design process, the terminology, abbreviations, formats, colors, capitalization, and so on should all be standardized and controlled by use of a written (or computer-managed) dictionary of these items.

2. *Efficient information assimilation by the user*   The format should be famil-iar to the operator and should be related to the tasks required to be per-formed with these data. This objective is served by rules for neat columns of data, left justification for alphanumeric data, right justifica-tion of integers, lining up of decimal points, proper spacing, use of com-prehensible labels, and appropriate measurement units and numbers of decimal digits.

3. *Minimal memory load on user*   Users should not be required to remember information from one screen for use on another screen. Tasks should be arranged such that completion occurs with few actions, minimizing the chance of forgetting to perform a step. Labels and common formats should be provided for novice or intermittent users.

4. *Compatibility of data display with data entry*   The format of displayed infor-mation should be linked clearly to the format of the data entry. Where pos-sible and appropriate, the output fields should also act as editable input fields.

5. *Flexibility for user control of data display*   Users should be able to get the information from the display in the form most convenient for the task on which they are working. For example, the order of columns and sorting of rows should be easily changeable by users.

This compact set of high-level objectives is a useful starting point, but each project needs to expand these into application-specific and hardware-dependent standards and practices. For example, these generic guidelines emerge from a report on design of control rooms for electric-power utilities (Lockheed, 1981):

- Be consistent in labeling and graphic conventions.
- Standardize abbreviations.
- Use consistent format in all displays (headers, footers, paging, menus, and so on).
- Present a page number on each display page, and allow actions to call up a page via entry of a page number.
- Present data only if they assist the operator.

- Present information graphically where appropriate by using widths of lines, positions of markers on scales, and other techniques that relieve the need to read and interpret alphanumeric data.
- Present digital values only when knowledge of numerical value is necessary and useful.
- Use high-resolution monitors and maintain them to provide maximum display quality.
- Design a display in monochromatic form using spacing and arrangement for organization and then judiciously add color where it will aid the operator.
- Involve users in the development of new displays and procedures.

Chapter 11 further discusses data-display issues.

2.7.2   Getting the user's attention

Since substantial information may be presented to users for the normal performance of their work, exceptional conditions or time-dependent information must be presented so as to attract attention (Wickens, 1992). Multiple techniques exist for getting attention:

- *Intensity*   Use two levels only, with limited use of high intensity to draw attention.
- *Marking*   Underline, enclose in a box, point to with an arrow, or use an indicator such as an asterisk, bullet, dash, plus, or X.
- *Size*   Use up to four sizes, with larger sizes attracting more attention.
- *Choice of fonts*   Use up to three fonts.
- *Inverse video*   Use inverse coloring.
- *Blinking*   Use blinking displays (2 to 4 hertz) with great care and in limited areas.
- *Color*   Use up to four standard colors, with additional colors reserved for occasional use.
- *Color blinking*   Use changes in color (blinking from one color to another) with great care and in limited areas.
- *Audio*   Use soft tones for regular positive feedback and harsh sounds for rare emergency conditions.

A few words of caution are necessary. There is a danger in creating cluttered displays by overusing these techniques. Novices need simple, logically organized, and well-labeled displays that guide their actions. Expert users do not need extensive labels on fields; subtle highlighting or positional presentation is sufficient. Display formats must be tested with users for comprehensibility.

Similarly highlighted items will be perceived as being related. Color coding is especially powerful in linking related items, but this use makes it more difficult to cluster items across color codes. User control over highlighting—for example, allowing the operator in an air-traffic–control environment to assign orange to images of aircraft above 18,000 feet—may provide a useful resolution to concerns about personal preferences. Highlighting can be accomplished by increased intensity, blinking, or other methods.

Audio tones can provide informative feedback about progress, such as the clicks in keyboards or ringing sounds in telephones. Alarms for emergency conditions do alert users rapidly, but a mechanism to suppress alarms must be provided. If several types of alarms are used, testing is necessary to ensure that users can distinguish among alarm levels. Prerecorded or synthesized voice messages are an intriguing alternative, but since they may interfere with communications among operators, they should be used cautiously.

2.8   Guidelines for Data Entry

Data-entry tasks can occupy a substantial fraction of the operator's time and are the source of frustrating and potentially dangerous errors. Smith and Mosier (1986) offer five high-level objectives for data entry:

1. *Consistency of data-entry transactions*   Similar sequences of actions should be used under all conditions; similar delimiters, abbreviations, and so on should be used.

2. *Minimal input actions by user*   Fewer input actions mean greater operator productivity and—usually—fewer chances for error. Making a choice by a single keystroke, mouse selection, or finger press, rather than by typing in a lengthy string of characters, is potentially advantageous. Selecting from a list of choices eliminates the need for memorization, structures the decision-making task, and eliminates the possibility of typographic errors. However, if users must move their hands from a keyboard to a separate input device, the advantage is defeated because home-row position is lost. Experienced users often prefer to type six to eight characters instead of moving to a lightpen, joystick, or other selection device.

   A second aspect of this guideline is that redundant data entry should be avoided. It is annoying for users to enter the same information in two locations, since the double entry is perceived as a waste of effort and an opportunity for error. When the same information is required in two places, the system should copy the information for the user, who still has the option of overriding by retyping.

3. *Minimal memory load on users*   When doing data entry, users should not be required to remember lengthy lists of codes and complex syntactic command strings.

4. *Compatibility of data entry with data display*   The format of data-entry information should be linked closely to the format of displayed information.

5. *Flexibility for user control of data entry*   Experienced data-entry operators may prefer to enter information in a sequence that they can control. For example, on some occasions in an air-traffic control environment, the arrival time is the prime field in the controller's mind; on other occasions, the altitude is the prime field. Flexibility should be used cautiously, since it goes against the consistency principle.

2.9   Balance of Automation and Human Control

The principles described in the previous sections are in harmony with the goal of simplifying the user's task—eliminating human actions when no judgment is required. Users can then avoid the annoyance of handling routine, tedious, and error-prone tasks, and can concentrate on critical decisions, planning, and coping with unexpected situations (Sanders and McCormick, 1993). Computers should be used to keep track of and retrieve large volumes of data, to follow preset patterns, and to carry out complex mathematical or logical operations (Box 2.2 provides a detailed comparison of human and machine capabilities).

The degree of automation will increase over the years as procedures become more standardized, hardware reliability increases, and software verification and validation improves. With routine tasks, automation is preferred, since the potential for error may be reduced. However, I believe that there will always be a critical human role, because the real world is an *open system* (there is a nondenumerable number of unpredictable events and system failures). By contrast, computers constitute a *closed system* (there is only a denumerable number of normal and failure situations that can be accommodated in hardware and software). Human judgment is necessary for the unpredictable events in which some action must be taken to preserve safety, to avoid expensive failures, or to increase product quality (Hancock and Scallen, 1996).

Box 2.2

Relative capabilities of humans and machines. *Sources:* Compiled from Brown, 1988; Sanders and McCormick, 1993.

Humans Generally Better	Machines Generally Better
Sense low level stimuli	Sense stimuli outside human's range
Detect stimuli in noisy background	Count or measure physical quantities
Recognize constant patterns in varying situations	Store quantities of coded information accurately
Sense unusual and unexpected events	Monitor prespecified events, especially infrequent ones
Remember principles and strategies	Make rapid and consistent responses to input signals
Retrieve pertinent details without a priori connection	Recall quantities of detailed information accurately
Draw on experience and adapt decisions to situation	Process quantitative data in prespecified ways
Select alternatives if original approach fails	Reason deductively: infer from a general principle
Reason inductively: generalize from observations	Perform repetitive preprogrammed actions reliably
Act in unanticipated emergencies and novel situations	Exert great, highly-controlled physical force
Apply principles to solve varied problems	Perform several activities simultaneously
Make subjective evaluations	Maintain operations under heavy information load
Develop new solutions	Maintain performance over extended periods of time
Concentrate on important tasks when overload occurs	
Adapt physical response to changes in situation	

For example, in air-traffic control, common actions include changes to altitude, heading, or speed. These actions are well understood and can potentially be automatable by a scheduling and route-allocation algorithm, but the controllers must be present to deal with the highly variable and unpredictable emergency situations. An automated system might deal successfully with high volumes of traffic, but what would happen if the airport manager closed two runways because of turbulent weather? The controllers would have to reroute planes quickly. Now suppose that there is only one active runway and one pilot calls in to request special clearance to land because of a failed engine, while another pilot in a second plane reports a passenger with a potential heart attack. Human judgment is necessary to decide which plane should land first, and how much costly and risky diversion of normal traffic is appropriate. Air-traffic controllers cannot just jump into the emergency; they must be intensely involved in the situation as it develops if they are to make an informed and rapid decision. In short, real-world situations are so complex that it is impossible to anticipate and program for every contingency; human judgment and values are necessary in the decision-making process.

Another example of the complexity of real-world situations in air-traffic control emerges from an incident on a Boeing 727 that had a fire on board near an airport. The controller cleared other traffic from the flight path and began to guide the plane in for a landing. The smoke was so thick that the pilot had trouble reading his instruments. Then the onboard transponder burned out, so the air-traffic controller could no longer read the plane's altitude from the situation display. In spite of these multiple failures, the controller and the pilot managed to bring down the plane quickly enough to save the lives of many—but not all—of the passengers. A computer could not have been programmed to deal with this particular unexpected series of events.

A tragic outcome of excess automation occurred during a 1995 flight to Cali, Colombia. The pilots relied on the automatic pilot and failed to realize that the plane was making a wide turn to return to a location that they had already passed. When the ground-collision alarm sounded, the pilots were too disoriented to pull up in time; they crashed 200 feet below the mountain peak.

The goal of system design in many applications is to give operators sufficient information about current status and activities, so that, when intervention is necessary, they have the knowledge and the capacity to perform correctly, even under partial failures. Increasingly, the human role is to respond to unanticipated situations, equipment failure, improper human performance, and incomplete or erroneous data (Eason, 1980; Sheridan, 1988; Billings, 1997).

The entire system must be designed and tested, not only for normal situations, but also for as wide a range of anomalous situations as can be anticipated. An extensive set of test conditions might be included as part of the requirements document. Operators need to have enough information that they can take responsibility for their actions.

Beyond performance of productive decision-making tasks and handling of failures, the role of the human operator will be to improve the design of the system. In complex systems, an opportunity always exists for improvement, so systems that lend themselves to refinement will evolve via continual incremental redesign by the operators.

The balance of automation and human control also emerges as an issue in systems for home and office automation. Some designers promote the notion of autonomous, adaptive, or anthropomorphic agents that carry out the users' intents and anticipate needs (Maes, 1994, 1995; Hayes-Roth, 1995; Hendler, 1996). Their scenarios often show a responsive, butler-like human being to represent the agent (such as the bow-tied, helpful young man in Apple Computer's 1987 video on the *Knowledge Navigator*), or refer to the agent on a first-name basis (such as Sue or Bill in Hewlett-Packard's 1990 video on future computing). Microsoft's unsuccessful BOB program used cartoon characters to create onscreen partners. Other people have described *knowbots* or *softbots*—agents that traverse the World Wide Web in search of information of interest, such as where to find a low price for a Hawaiian tour.

Many people are attracted to the idea of a powerful functionary carrying out their tasks and watching out for their needs. The wish to create an autonomous agent that knows people's likes and dislikes, makes proper inferences, responds to novel situations, and performs competently with little guidance is strong for some designers. They believe that human–human interaction is a good model for human–computer interaction, and they seek to create computer-based partners, assistants, or agents. They promote their designs as intelligent and adaptive, and often they pursue anthropomorphic representations of the computer (see Section 11.3 for a review) to the point of having artificial faces talking to users. Anthropomorphic representations of computers have been unsuccessful in bank terminals, computer-assisted instruction, talking cars, and postal-service stations; however, these designers believe that they can find a way to attract users.

A variant of the agent scenario, which does not include an anthropomorphic realization, is that the computer employs a *user model* to guide an adaptive system. The system keeps track of user performance and adapts its behavior to suit the users' needs. For example, several proposals suggest that, as users make menu selections more rapidly, indicating proficiency, advanced menu items or a command-line interface appears. Automatic adaptations have been proposed for response time, length of messages, density of feedback, content of menus, order of menu items (see Section 7.3 for evidence against the helpfulness of this strategy), type of feedback (graphic or tabular), and content of help screens. Advocates point to video games that increase the speed or number of dangers as users progress though stages of the game. However, games are notably different from most work situations, where users have external goals and motivations to accomplish their tasks. There is much discussion of user models, but little empirical evidence of their efficacy.

There are some opportunities for adaptive user models to tailor system responses, but even occasional unexpected behavior has serious negative side effects that discourages use. If adaptive systems make surprising changes, users must pause to see what has happened. Then users may become anxious because they may not be able to predict the next change, interpret what has happened, or restore the system to the previous state. Suggestions that users could be consulted before a change is made are helpful, but such intrusions may still disrupt problem-solving processes and annoy users.

The agent metaphor is based on the design philosophy that assumes users would be attracted to "autonomous, adaptive, intelligent" systems. Designers believe that they are creating a system that is lifelike and smart; however, users may feel anxious about and unable to control these systems. Success stories for advocates of adaptive systems include a few training and help systems that have been studied extensively and refined carefully to give users appropriate feedback for the errors that they make. Generalizing from these systems has proved to be more difficult than advocates had hoped.

These difficulties have led many agent proponents to shift to distributed World Wide Web searching and collaborative filtering (see Section 15.5). There is no visible agent or adaptation in the interface, but the applications aggregate information from multiple sources in some, often proprietary, way. Such blackbox approaches have great entertainment and even practical value in cases such as selecting movies, books, or music. However, in searching for antidotes in a toxicology database, physicians may want more predictable behavior and more control over what happens as they narrow their search.

The philosophical alternative to agents is *user-control, responsibility, and accomplishment.* Designers who emphasize a direct-manipulation style believe that users have a strong desire to be in control and to gain mastery over the system. Then, users can accept responsibility for their actions and derive feelings of accomplishment (Lanier, 1995; Shneiderman, 1995). Historical evidence suggests that users seek comprehensible and predictable systems and shy away from those that are complex or unpredictable; pilots may disengage automatic piloting devices if they perceive these systems are not performing as they expect.

Comprehensible and predictable user interfaces should mask the underlying computational complexity, in the same way that turning on an automobile ignition is comprehensible to users but invokes complex algorithms in the engine-control computer. These algorithms may adapt to varying engine temperatures or air pressures, but the action at the user-interface level remains predictable.

A critical issue for designers is the clear placement of responsibility for failures. Agent advocates usually avoid discussing responsibility, even for basic issues as violation of someone's copyright or for more serious flaws such as bugs that cause data destruction. Their designs rarely allow for monitoring the agent's performance, and feedback to users about the current user model is often given little attention. However, most human operators recognize and accept their responsibility for the operation of the computer, and therefore designers of financial, medical, or military applications ensure that detailed feedback is provided.

An alternative to agents and user models may be to expand the control-panel metaphor. Users use current control panels to set physical parameters, such as the speed of cursor blinking, rate of mouse tracking, or loudness of a speaker, and to establish personal preferences such as time and date formats, placement and format of menus, or color schemes (Figs. 2.4 and 2.5). Some software packages allow users to set parameters such as the speed of play in games or the usage level as in HyperCard (from browsing to editing buttons,

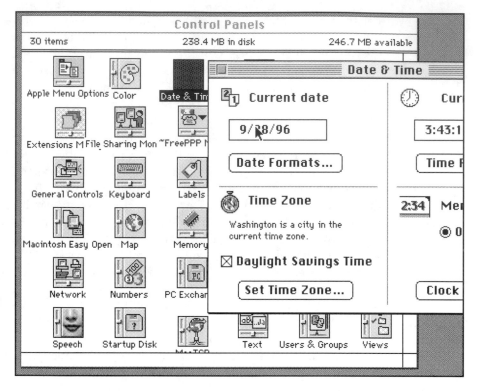

Figure 2.4

Macintosh MacOS 7.5 control panels, with Date & Time selected. Current control panels are used to set physical parameters (such as the speed of cursor blinking, rate of mouse tracking, or loudness of a speaker), and to establish personal preferences (such as time and date formats, placement and format of menus, or color schemes). (Used with permission of Apple Computer, Inc., Cupertino, CA.)

to writing scripts and creating graphics). Users start at level 1 and can then choose when to progress to higher levels. Often users are content remaining experts at level 1 of a complex system rather than dealing with the uncertainties of higher levels. More elaborate control panels exist in style sheets of word processors, specification boxes of query facilities, and information-visualization tools. Similarly, scheduling software may have elaborate controls to allow users to execute planned procedures at regular intervals or when triggered by other processes.

Computer control panels, like cruise-control mechanisms in automobiles and remote controllers for televisions, are designed to convey the sense of control that users seem to expect. Increasingly, complex processes are specified by direct-manipulation programming (see Chapter 6) or by graphical specifications of scheduled procedures, style sheets, and templates.

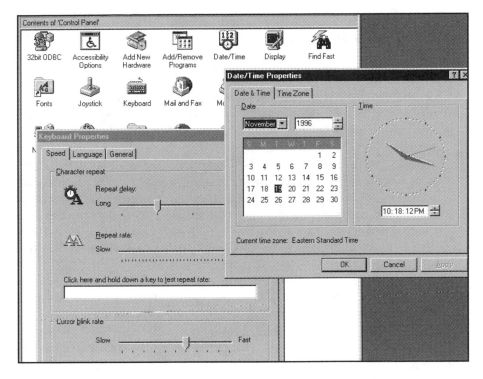

Figure 2.5

Microsoft Windows 95 control panel. (Used with permission of Microsoft Corp., Redmond, WA.)

2.10 Practitioner's Summary

Designing user interfaces is a complex and highly creative process that blends intuition, experience, and careful consideration of numerous technical issues. Designers are urged to begin with a thorough task analysis and a careful specification of the user communities. Explicit recording of task objects and actions can lead to construction of useful metaphors for interface objects and actions that benefit novice and expert users. Extensive testing and iterative refinement are necessary parts of every development project.

Design principles and guidelines are emerging from practical experience and empirical studies. Organizations can benefit by reviewing available guidelines documents and then constructing a local version. A guidelines document records organizational policies, supports consistency, aids the application of tools for user-interface building, facilitates training of new designers, records results of practice and experimental testing, and stimulates discussion of user-interface issues.

2.11   Researcher's Agenda

The central problem for psychologists, human-factors professionals, and computer scientists is to develop adequate theories and models of the behavior of humans who use interactive systems. Traditional psychological theories must be extended and refined to accommodate the complex human learning, memory, and problem-solving required in these applications. Useful goals include descriptive taxonomies, explanatory theories, and predictive models.

A first step might be to investigate thoroughly a limited task for a single community, and to develop a formal notation for describing task actions and objects. Then the mapping to interface actions and objects can be made precisely. This process would lead to predictions of learning times, performance speeds, error rates, subjective satisfaction, or human retention over time, for competing designs.

Next, the range of tasks and user communities could be expanded to domains of interest, such as word processing, information retrieval, or data entry. More limited and applied research problems are connected with each of the hundreds of design principles or guidelines that have been proposed. Each validation of these principles and clarification of the breadth of applicability would be a small but useful contribution to the emerging mosaic of human performance with interactive systems.

World Wide Web Resources   WWW

Websites include theories and information on user models. A major topic with many websites is agents, including skeptical views. Debates over hot topics can be found in news groups which are searchable from many standard services such as Lycos or Infoseek.

http://www.aw.com/DTUI

References

Alexander, Christopher, Ishikawa, Sara, and Silverstein, Murray, *A Pattern Language: Towns, Buildings, Construction*, Oxford University Press, New York (1977).

Bailey, Robert W., *Human Performance Engineering: Using Human Factors/Ergonomics to Achieve Computer Usability* (Third Edition), Prentice-Hall, Englewood Cliffs, NJ (1996).

Bauer, Malcolm I., and John, Bonnie E., Modeling time-constrained learning in a highly interactive task, *Proc. CHI '95 Conference: Human Factors in Computing Systems*, ACM, New York (1996), 19–26

Billings, Charles E., *Animation Automation: The Search for a Human-Centered Approach*, Lawrence Erlbaum Assoc., Publishers, Mahwah, NJ (1997).

Bridger, R. S., *Introduction to Ergonomics*, McGraw-Hill, New York (1995).

Brown, C. Marlin, *Human–Computer Interface Design Guidelines*, Ablex, Norwood, NJ (1988).

Brown, P., and Gould, J., How people create spreadsheets, *ACM Transactions on Office Information Systems*, 5 (1987), 258–272.

Card, Stuart K., Theory-driven design research, in McMillan, Grant R., Beevis, David, Salas, Eduardo, Strub, Michael H., Sutton, Robert, and Van Breda, Leo (Editors), *Applications of Human Performance Models to System Design*, Plenum Press, New York (1989), 501–509.

Card, Stuart K., Mackinlay, Jock D., and Robertson, George G., The design space of input devices, *Proc. CHI '90 Conference: Human Factors in Computing Systems*, ACM, New York (1990), 117–124.

Card, Stuart, Moran, Thomas P., and Newell, Allen, The keystroke-level model for user performance with interactive systems, *Communications of the ACM*, 23 (1980), 396–410.

Card, Stuart, Moran, Thomas P., and Newell, Allen, *The Psychology of Human–Computer Interaction*, Lawrence Erlbaum Associates, Hillsdale, NJ (1983).

Eason, K. D., Dialogue design implications of task allocation between man and computer, *Ergonomics*, 23, 9 (1980), 881–891.

Eberts, Ray E., *User Interface Design*, Prentice Hall, Englewood Cliffs, NJ (1993).

Egan, Dennis E., Individual differences in human–computer interaction. In Helander, Martin (Editor), *Handbook of Human–Computer Interaction*, Elsevier Science Publishers, Amsterdam, The Netherlands (1988), 543–568.

Elkerton, Jay and Palmiter, Susan L., Designing help using a GOMS model: An information retrieval evaluation, *Human Factors*, 33, 2 (1991), 185–204.

Foley, James D., van Dam, Andries, Feiner, Steven K., and Hughes, John F., *Computer Graphics: Principles and Practice* (Second Edition), Addison-Wesley, Reading, MA (1990).

Franzke, Marita, Turning research into practice: Characteristics of display-based interaction, *Proc. CHI '95 Conference: Human Factors in Computing Systems*, ACM, New York (1995), 421–428.

Gaines, Brian R., The technology of interaction: Dialogue programming rules, *International Journal of Man–Machine Studies*, 14, (1981), 133–150.

Galitz, Wilbert O., *It's Time to Clean Your Windows: Designing GUIs that Work*, John Wiley and Sons, New York (1994).

Gilbert, Steven W., Information technology, intellectual property, and education, *EDUCOM Review*, 25, (1990), 14–20.

Grudin, Jonathan, The case against user interface consistency, *Communications of the ACM*, 32, 10 (1989), 1164–1173.

Hancock, P. A. and Scallen, S. F., The future of function allocation, *Ergonomics in Design*, 4, 4 (October 1996), 24–29.

Hansen, Wilfred J., User engineering principles for interactive systems, *Proc. Fall Joint Computer Conference*, 39, AFIPS Press, Montvale, NJ (1971), 523–532.

Hayes-Roth, Barbara, An architecture for adaptive intelligent systems, *Artificial Intelligence: Special Issue on Agents and Interactivity*, 72, (1995), 329–365.

Hendler, James A. (Editor), Intelligent agents: Where AI meets information technology, Special Issue, *IEEE Expert: Intelligent Systems & Their Applications 11*, 6 (December 1996), 20–63.

John, Bonnie and Kieras, David E., Using GOMS for user interface design and evaluation: Which technique? *ACM Transactions on Computer–Human Interaction 3*, 4 (December 1996a), 287–319.

John, Bonnie and Kieras, David E., The GOMS family of user interface analysis techniques: Comparison and contrast, *ACM Transactions on Computer–Human Interaction 3*, 4 (December 1996b), 320–351.

Kieras, David, Towards a practical GOMS model methodology for user interface design. In Helander, Martin (Editor), *Handbook of Human–Computer Interaction*, Elsevier Science Publishers, Amsterdam, The Netherlands (1988), 135–157.

Kieras, David, and Polson, Peter G., An approach to the formal analysis of user complexity, *International Journal of Man–Machine Studies*, 22, (1985), 365–394.

Lanier, Jaron, Agents of alienation, *ACM interactions*, 2, 3 (1995), 66–72

Lockheed Missiles and Space Company, *Human Factors Review of Electric Power Dispatch Control Centers. Volume 2: Detailed Survey Results*, (Prepared for) Electric Power Research Institute, Palo Alto, CA (1981).

Maes, Pattie, Agents that reduce work and information overload, *Communications of the ACM*, 37, 7 (July 1994), 31–40.

Maes, Pattie, Artificial life meets entertainment: Lifelike autonomous agents, *Communications of the ACM*, 38, 11 (November 1995), 108–114.

Mullet, Kevin and Sano, Darrell, *Designing Visual Interfaces: Communication Oriented Techniques*, Sunsoft Press, Englewood Cliffs, NJ (1995).

National Research Council, *Intellectual Property Issues in Software*, National Academy Press, Washington, D.C. (1991).

Norman, Donald A., Design rules based on analyses of human error, *Communications of the ACM*, 26, 4 (1983), 254–258.

Norman, Donald A., *The Psychology of Everyday Things*, Basic Books, New York (1988).

Norman, Kent L., Models of the mind and machine: Information flow and control between humans and computers, *Advances in Computers*, 32, (1991), 119–172.

Panko, Raymond R. and Halverson, Jr., Richard P., Spreadsheets on trial: A survey of research on spreadsheet risks, *Proc. Twenty-Ninth Hawaii International Conference on System Sciences* (1996).

Payne, S. J., and Green, T. R. G., Task-action grammars: A model of the mental representation of task languages, *Human–Computer Interaction*, 2, (1986), 93–133.

Payne, S. J., and Green, T. R. G., The structure of command languages: An experiment on task-action grammar, *International Journal of Man–Machine Studies*, 30, (1989), 213–234.

Polson, Peter, and Lewis, Clayton, Theory-based design for easily learned interfaces, *Human–Computer Interaction*, 5, (1990), 191–220.

Reisner, Phyllis, Formal grammar and design of an interactive system, *IEEE Transactions on Software Engineering*, SE–5, (1981), 229–240.

Reisner, Phyllis, What is consistency? In Diaper et al. (Editors), *INTERACT '90: Human–Computer Interaction*, North-Holland, Amsterdam, The Netherlands (1990), 175–181.

Sanders, M. S. and McCormick, Ernest J., *Human Factors in Engineering and Design* (Seventh Edition), McGraw-Hill, New York (1993).

Sears, Andrew, *Widget-Level Models of Human–Computer Interaction: Applying Simple Task Descriptions to Design and Evaluation*, PhD. Dissertation, Department of Computer Science, University of Maryland, College Park, MD (1992).

Sheridan, Thomas B., Task allocation and supervisory control. In Helander, M. (Editor), *Handbook of Human–Computer Interaction*, Elsevier Science Publishers, Amsterdam, The Netherlands (1988), 159–173.

Shneiderman, Ben, *Software Psychology: Human Factors in Computer and Information Systems*, Little, Brown, Boston, MA (1980).

Shneiderman, Ben, A note on the human factors issues of natural language interaction with database systems, *Information Systems*, 6, 2 (1981), 125–129.

Shneiderman, Ben, System message design: Guidelines and experimental results. In Badre, A. and Shneiderman, B. (Editors) *Directions in Human–Computer Interaction*, Ablex, Norwood, NJ (1982), 55–78.

Shneiderman, Ben, Direct manipulation: A step beyond programming languages, *IEEE Computer*, 16, 8 (1983), 57–69.

Shneiderman, Ben, Looking for the bright side of agents, *ACM Interactions*, 2, 1 (January 1995), 13–15.

Smith, Sid L. and Mosier, Jane N., *Guidelines for Designing User Interface Software*, Report ESD-TR–86–278, Electronic Systems Division, MITRE Corporation, Bedford, MA (1986). Available from National Technical Information Service, Springfield, VA.

Tufte, Edward, *The Visual Display of Quantitative Information*, Graphics Press, Cheshire, CT (1983).

Tufte, Edward, *Envisioning Information*, Graphics Press, Cheshire, CT (1990).

Tufte, Edward, *Visual Explanations*, Graphics Press, Cheshire, CT (1997).

Wickens, Christopher D., *Engineering Psychology and Human Performance* (Second Edition), HarperCollins Publishers, New York (1992).

Mark Kostabi, *Computer Klatsch*, 1996

3

Managing Design Processes

Just as we can assert that no product has ever been created in a single moment of inspiration ... nobody has ever produced a set of requirements for any product in a similarly miraculous manner. These requirements may well begin with an inspirational moment but, almost certainly, the emergent bright idea will be developed by iterative processes of evaluation until it is thought to be worth starting to put pencil to paper. Especially when the product is entirely new, the development of a set of requirements may well depend upon testing initial ideas in some depth.

W. H. Mayall, *Principles in Design*, 1979

The Plan is the generator. Without a plan, you have lack of order and willfulness. The Plan holds in itself the essence of sensation.

Le Corbusier, *Towards a New Architecture*, 1931

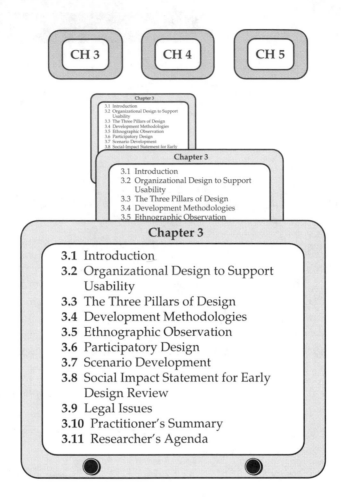

3.1   Introduction

In the first decades of computer-software development, technically oriented programmers designed text editors, programming languages, and applications for themselves and their peers. The substantial experience and motivation of these users meant that complex interfaces were accepted and even appreciated. Now, the user population for office automation, home and personal computing, and digital libraries is so vastly different from the original that programmers' intuitions may be inappropriate. Current users are not dedicated to the technology, their background is more tied to workflow, and their use of computers may be discretionary. Designs should be based on careful observation of current users, refined by thoughtful analysis of task frequencies and sequences, and validated through early, careful, and thorough prototype, usability, and acceptance tests.

In the best designs, the techno-centric style of the past is yielding to a genuine desire to accommodate to the users' skills, goals, and preferences. Designers are seeking direct interaction with users during the design phase, during the development process, and throughout the system lifecycle. Iterative design methods that allow early testing of prototypes, revisions based on feedback from users, and incremental refinements suggested by usability-test administrators are catalysts for high-quality systems. Around the world, *usability engineering* is becoming a recognized discipline with established practices and some standards. The Usability Professionals Association, formed in 1991, has become a respected community with active participation from large corporations and numerous small design, test, and build firms.

The variety of design situations precludes a comprehensive strategy. Managers will have to adapt the strategies offered in this chapter to suit their organization, projects, schedules, and budgets. These strategies begin with the organizational design that gives appropriate emphasis to support usability. Next, are the three pillars of successful user-interface development: guidelines document and process, user-interface software tools, and expert review and usability testing. The Logical User-Centered Interaction Design (LUCID) methodology is a framework for scheduling, on which strategies such as ethnographic observation, participatory design, scenario development, and possibly a Social Impact Statement review can be hung. Finally, legal concerns should be addressed during the design process.

3.2   Organizational Design to Support Usability

Corporate-marketing and customer-assistance departments are becoming more aware of the importance of usability and are a source of constructive encouragement. When competitive products provide similar functionality, usability engineering is vital for product acceptance. Many organizations have created usability laboratories to provide expert reviews and to conduct usability tests of products during development. Outside experts can provide fresh insights, while usability-test subjects perform benchmark tasks in carefully supervised conditions (Whiteside et al., 1988; Klemmer, 1989; Nielsen, 1993; Dumas and Redish, 1993). These and other evaluation strategies are covered in Chapter 4.

Companies may not yet have a chief usability officer (CUO) or a vice president for usability, but they often have user-interface architects and usability engineering managers. High-level commitment helps to promote attention at every level. Organizational awareness can be stimulated by "Usability Day" presentations, internal seminars, newsletters, and awards. Of course, resistance to new techniques and a changing role for software engineers can cause problems in organizations. Organizational change is difficult, but creative leaders blend inspiration and provocation. The high road is to appeal to the desire for quality that most professionals share. When they are shown data on shortened learning times, faster performance, or lower error rates on well-designed interfaces, they are likely to be more sympathetic to applying usability-engineering methods. The low road is to point out the frustration, confusion, and high error rates due to the current complex designs, while citing the successes of competitors who apply usability-engineering methods.

Most large and many small organizations maintain a centralized human-factors group or a usability laboratory as a source of expertise in design and testing techniques (Gould et al., 1991; Nielsen, 1994). However, each project should have its own user-interface architect who develops the necessary skills, manages the work of other people, prepares budgets and schedules, and coordinates with internal and external human-factors professionals when further expertise, references to the literature, or usability tests are required. This dual strategy balances the needs for centralized expertise and decentralized application. It enables professional growth in the user-interface area and in the application domain (for example, in geographic information or imaging systems).

The field has now matured to the point that many projects have grown large in complexity, size, and importance. Role specialization is emerging, as it has in architecture, aerospace, and book design. Eventually, individuals will become highly skilled in specific problems, such as user–interface building tools, graphic-display strategies, voice and audio tone design, and message, or online tutorial writing. Consultation with graphic artists, book designers, advertising copy writers, instructional-textbook authors, or film-animation creators is expected. Perceptive system developers recognize the need to employ psychologists for conducting experimental tests, sociologists for evaluating organizational impact, educational psychologists for refining training procedures, and social workers for guiding user consultants or customer-service personnel.

As design moves to implementation, the choice of user interface building tools is vital to success. These rapidly emerging tools enable designers to build novel systems quickly and support the iterative design–test–refine cycle.

Guidelines documents were originally seen as the answer to usability questions, but they are now appreciated as a broader social process in which the initial compilation is only the first step. The management strategies for the three Es—enforcement, exemption, enhancement—are only beginning to emerge and to become institutionalized.

The business case for focusing on usability has been made powerfully and repeatedly in the past decade (Mantei and Teorey, 1988; Karat, 1990; Chapanis, 1991). It apparently needs frequent repetition because traditional managers and engineers are often resistant to changes that would bring increased attention to the users' needs. Karat's (1990, 1994) businesslike reports within IBM became influential documents when they were published externally. She reported up to $100 payoffs for each dollar spent on usability, with identifiable benefits in reduced program-development costs, reduced program-maintenance costs, increased revenue due to higher customer satisfaction, and improved user efficiency and productivity. Other economic analyses showed fundamental changes in organizational productivity (as much as 720 percent improvements) when people kept usability in mind from the beginning of development projects (Landauer, 1995). Even minimal application of usability testing followed by correction of 20 of the easiest-to-repair faults improved user efficiency from 19 percent to as much as 80 percent.

Usability engineers and *user-interface architects* are gaining experience in managing organizational change. As attention shifts from software-engineering or management-information systems, battles for control and power manifest themselves in budget and personnel allocations. Well-prepared managers who have a concrete organizational plan, defensible cost–benefit analyses, and practical development methodologies are most likely to be winners.

Design is inherently creative and unpredictable. Interactive system designers must blend a thorough knowledge of technical feasibility with a mystical esthetic sense of what attracts users. Carroll and Rosson (1985) characterize design in this way:

- Design is a *process;* it is not a state and it cannot be adequately represented statically.
- The design process is *nonhierarchical;* it is neither strictly bottom-up nor strictly top-down.
- The process is *radically transformational;* it involves the development of partial and interim solutions that may ultimately play no role in the final design.
- Design intrinsically involves the *discovery of new goals.*

These characterizations of design convey the dynamic nature of the process. But in every creative domain, there can also be discipline, refined techniques, wrong and right methods, and measures of success. Once the early data collection and preliminary requirements are established, more detailed design and early development can begin. This chapter covers strategies for managing early stages of projects and offers design methodologies. Chapter 4 focuses on evaluation methods.

3.3   The Three Pillars of Design

If standardization can be humanized and made flexible in design and the economics brought to the home owner, the greatest service will be rendered to our modern way of life. It may be really born—this democracy, I mean.

Frank Lloyd Wright, The Natural House, 1954

The three pillars described in this section can help user-interface architects to turn good ideas into a successful system (Fig. 3.1). They are not guaranteed to work, but experience has shown that each pillar can produce an order-of-magnitude speedup in the process and can facilitate the creation of excellent systems.

3.3.1   Guidelines documents and processes

Early in the design process, the user-interface architect should generate, or require other people to generate, a set of working guidelines. Two people might work for one week to produce a 10-page document, or a dozen people might work for two years to produce a 300-page document. One component of Apple's success with the Macintosh was that machine's early and readable guidelines document that provided a clear set of principles for the many applications developers to follow and thus ensured a harmony in design across products. Microsoft's Windows guidelines have also been refined over the years, and they provide a good starting point and an educational experience for many programmers. These and other guidelines documents are referenced and are described briefly in the general reference section at the end of Chapter 1.

Each project has different needs, but guidelines should be considered for

- Words and icons
  - Terminology (objects and actions), abbreviations, and capitalization
  - Character set, fonts, font sizes, and styles (bold, italic, underline)
  - Icons, graphics, and line thickness
  - Use of color, backgrounds, highlighting, and blinking

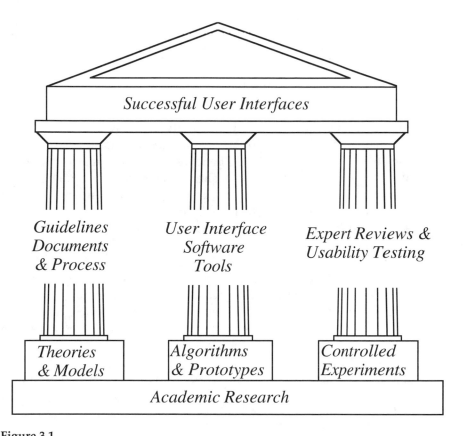

Figure 3.1

The three pillars of successful user-interface development.

- Screen-layout issues
    - Menu selection, form fillin, and dialog-box formats
    - Wording of prompts, feedback, and error messages
    - Justification, whitespace, and margins
    - Data entry and display formats for items and lists
    - Use and contents of headers and footers
- Input and output devices
    - Keyboard, display, cursor control, and pointing devices
    - Audible sounds, voice feedback, touch input, and other special input modes or devices
    - Response times for a variety of tasks
- Action sequences
    - Direct-manipulation clicking, dragging, dropping, and gestures
    - Command syntax, semantics, and sequences

- • Programmed function keys
- • Error handling and recovery procedures
- • Training
  - • Online help and tutorials
  - • Training and reference materials

Guidelines creation should be a social process within an organization to gain visibility and build support. Controversial guidelines (for example, on when to use voice alerts) should be reviewed by colleagues or tested empirically. Procedures should be established to distribute the guidelines, to ensure enforcement, to allow exemptions, and to permit enhancements. Guidelines documents must be a living text that is adapted to changing needs and refined through experience. Acceptance may be increased by a three-level approach of rigid standards, accepted practices, and flexible guidelines. This approach clarifies which items are firmer and which items are susceptible to change.

The creation of a guidelines document (Box 3.1) at the beginning of an implementation project focuses attention on the interface design and provides an opportunity for discussion of controversial issues. When the guideline is adopted by the development team, the implementation proceeds quickly and with few design changes. For large organizations, there may be two or more levels of guidelines to provide organizational identity while allowing projects to have distinctive style and local control of terminology.

3.3.2   User-interface software tools

One difficulty in designing interactive systems is that customers and users may not have a clear idea of what the system will look like when it is done. Since interactive systems are novel in many situations, users may not realize the implications of design decisions. Unfortunately, it is difficult, costly, and time consuming to make major changes to systems once those systems have been implemented.

Even though this problem has no complete solution, some of the more serious difficulties can be avoided if, at an early stage, the customers and users can be given a realistic impression of what the final system will look like (Gould and Lewis, 1985). A printed version of the proposed displays is helpful for pilot tests, but an onscreen display with an active keyboard and mouse is more realistic. The prototype of a menu system may have only one or two paths active, instead of the thousands of paths envisioned for the final system. For a form-fillin system, the prototype may simply show the fields, but may not process them. Prototypes have been developed with simple drawing or word-processing tools, but graphical design environments such as HyperCard and MacroMind Director are widely used. Development envi-

Box 3.1

Recommendations for guidelines documents.

Provides a social process for developers

Records decisions for all parties to see

Promotes consistency and completeness

Facilitates automation of design

Allows multiple levels

   Rigid standards
   Accepted practices
   Flexible guidelines

Announces policies for

   Enforcement: who reviews?
   Exemption: who decides?
   Enhancement: how often?

ronments such as Microsoft's Visual Basic/C++ and Borland's Delphi are easy to learn yet powerful. More sophisticated tools such as Visix's Galaxy and Sun's Java provide cross-platform development and a rich variety of services. These tools are covered in Chapter 5.

3.3.3   Expert reviews and usability testing

Theatrical producers know that previews to critics and extensive rehearsals are necessary to ensure a successful opening night. Early rehearsals may require only one or two performers wearing street clothes; but, as opening night approaches, dress rehearsals with the full cast, props, and lighting are expected. Aircraft designers carry out wind-tunnel tests, build plywood mockups of the cabin layout, construct complete simulations of the cockpit, and thoroughly flight test the first prototype. Similarly, interactive-system designers are now recognizing that they must carry out many small and some large pilot tests of system components before release to customers (Dumas and Redish, 1993). In addition to a variety of expert review methods, tests with the intended users, surveys, and automated analysis tools are proving to be valuable. Procedures vary greatly depending on the goals of the usability study, the number of expected users, the dangers of errors, and the level of investment. Chapter 4 covers expert reviews, usability testing, and other evaluation methods in depth.

3.4   Development Methodologies

Many software development projects fail to achieve their goals. Some estimates suggest that the failure rate is as high as 60 percent, with about 25 percent of projects never being completed and perhaps another 35 percent only achieving partial success. Much of this problem can be traced to lack of attention to design issues during the initial stages of development. Careful attention to user-centered design issues at the early stages of software development has been shown to reduce both development time and cost dramatically. Well-designed systems are less expensive to develop and have lower maintenance costs over their lifetime. They are easier to learn, produce faster performance, reduce user errors substantially, and provide users with a sense of mastery and the confidence to explore features that go beyond the minimum required to get by.

The relationship between software developers and users has not always been a smooth one. Software-engineering development methodologies have helped developers meet budgets and schedules (Boehm, 1988; Sutcliffe and McDermott, 1991; Preece and Rombaugh, 1994; Humphrey, 1995), but have not always provided guidance in developing a usable interface (Chapanis and Budurka, 1990). A number of academics with consulting experience produced a first generation of design methodologies focused on user interface (Hix and Hartson, 1993; Nielsen, 1993). Commercial firms that specialize in user-centered design have built on this foundation and created a second generation of design methodologies.

These business-oriented approaches specify detailed deliverables for the various stages of design and incorporate cost/benefit and return on investment (ROI) analyses to facilitate decision making. In addition to the interface design elements that were basic to the academic systems, the commercial methodologies highlight management strategies used to keep to schedule and budget. Any user-centered design methodology must also mesh with the software-engineering methodology used.

The *Logical User-Centered Interactive Design Methodology* (LUCID, formerly Quality Usability Engineering (QUE)) (Kreitzberg, 1996) identifies six stages (see Table 3.1):

Stage 1: Develop product concept

Stage 2: Perform research and needs analysis

Stage 3: Design concepts and key-screen prototype

Stage 4: Do iterative design and refinement

Stage 5: Implement software

Stage 6: Provide rollout support

In the first stage, a product concept is developed. Surprisingly, many software development efforts are launched without a clear concept of the prod-

Table 3.1

Logical User-Centered Interaction Design Methodology from Cognetics Corporation, Princeton Junction, NJ (Kreitzberg, 1996).

Stage 1: Develop product concept

> Create a high concept.
> Establish business objectives.
> Set up the usability design team.
> Identify the user population.
> Identify technical and environmental issues.
> Produce a staffing plan, schedule, and budget.

Stage 2: Perform research and needs analysis

> Partition the user population into homogeneous segments.
> Break job activities into task units.
> Conduct needs analysis through construction of scenarios and participatory design.
> Sketch the process flow for sequences of tasks.
> Identify major objects and structures which will be used in the software interface.
> Research and resolve technical issues and other constraints.

Stage 3: Design concepts and key-screen prototype

> Create specific usability objectives based on user needs.
> Initiate the guidelines and style guide.
> Select a navigational model and a design metaphor.
> Identify the set of key screens: login, home, major processes.
> Develop a prototype of the key screens using a rapid prototyping tool.
> Conduct initial reviews and usability tests.

Stage 4: Do iterative design and refinement

> Expand key-screen prototype into full system.
> Conduct heuristic and expert reviews.
> Conduct full-scale usability tests.
> Deliver prototype and specification.

Stage 5: Implement software

> Develop standard practices.
> Manage late stage change.
> Develop online help, documentation and tutorials.

Stage 6: Provide rollout support

> Provide training and assistance.
> Perform logging, evaluation, and maintenance.

uct. At the center of the LUCID methodology is creation of a "high concept" for the product—a brief statement that defines the goals, functionality and benefits of the product. For example,

> The new home banking system will provide customers with unified access to their accounts. It will support balance inquiry, management of credit accounts and loans, transfer of funds among accounts, electronic bill payment and investment in the bank's family of mutual funds. The system will provide the customer with year-end accounting for tax purposes.

As part of the product concept stage, project leaders define business objectives, establish the design team, identify environmental, technical or legal constraints, specify the user population, and prepare a project plan and budget. During the first stage, the product concept is illustrated by simple screen sketches (which may be created on paper or on-screen). The goal of these sketches is to convey the system concept to nontechnical users.

With the project plan in place, the design team meets with users to understand their needs and competencies, the business process to be supported and the functional requirements of the system. LUCID uses participatory design sessions to solicit user input, construct workflow scenarios and define the objects that are central to the design.

A distinctive aspect of LUCID is its focus on a key-screen prototype that incorporates the major navigational paths of the system. The key-screen prototype is used to show users the design of the proposed system and allow them to evaluate and refine it. The key-screen prototype is also used for usability testing and heuristic review. Key screens usually evoke strong reactions, generate early participation, and create momentum for the project.

Like most user-centered design methodologies, LUCID employs rapid prototyping and iterative usability testing (Chapter 4). Because rapid prototyping is key to meeting schedule and budget, LUCID relies on user interface building tools (Chapter 5). The prototypes are usually developed by a programmer who is part of the software engineering team. One of this programmer's responsibilities is to identify interface issues that have implications for the technical architecture of the product. When completed and approved by users, the prototype serves as part of the programming specification for the software engineers.

Finally, LUCID describes a phased rollout approach built on theories of organizational change. Project leaders identify barriers to and construct incentives for adoption of the software. The goal is to ensure a positive reception by customers, users, and managers.

As a management strategy, LUCID makes the commitment to user-centered design explicit and highlights the role of usability engineering in software development by focusing on activities, deliverables, and reviews. At each of the LUCID stages, 12 areas of activity are evaluated; each is tied to specified deliverables and timely feedback through reviews:

1. *Product definition*: high concept for managers and marketers
2. *Business case*: pricing, expected revenues, return on investment, competition
3. *Resources*: duration, effort levels, team members, back-up plans
4. *Physical environment*: ergonomic design, physical installation, communication lines
5. *Technical environment*: hardware and software for development and integration
6. *Users*: multiple communities for interviews, user testing, marketing
7. *Functionality*: services provided to users
8. *Prototype*: early paper prototypes, key screens, running prototypes
9. *Usability*: set measurable goals, conduct tests, refine interface and goals
10. *Design guidelines*: modification of existing guidelines, implementation of review process
11. *Content materials*: identification and acquisition of copyrighted text, audio, and video
12. *Documentation, training and help*: specification, development, and testing paper, video, and online versions

The thoroughness of LUCID comes from its validation and refinement in multiple projects. However, each project has special needs, so any design methodology is only a starting point for project management. LUCID is designed to promote an orderly process, with iterations within a stage and predictable progress among stages. The reality is sometimes more complex, especially for novel projects that may require a return to earlier stages for some parts of the design.

3.5   Ethnographic Observation

The early stages of most methodologies include observation of users. Since interface users form a unique culture, ethnographic methods for observing them in the workplace are likely to become increasingly important. An "ethnographer participates, overtly or covertly, in people's daily lives for an extended period of time, watching what happens, listening to what is said, asking questions" (Hammersley and Atkinson, 1983). As ethnographers, user-interface designers gain insight into individual behavior and the organizational context. User-interface designers differ from traditional ethnographers; in addition to understanding their subjects, user-interface designers observe interfaces in use for the purpose of changing and improving those interfaces. Whereas traditional ethnographers immerse themselves in cultures for weeks or months, user-interface designers need to limit this process to a period of days or even hours, and still to obtain the relevant data needed to influence a redesign (Hughes et al., 1995). Ethnographic methods have been applied to office work (Suchman, 1983), air-traffic control (Bentley et al., 1992), and other domains (Vaske and Grantham, 1989).

The goal of an observation is to obtain the necessary data to influence interface redesign. Unfortunately, it is easy to misinterpret observations, to disrupt normal practice, and to overlook important information. Following a validated ethnographic process reduces the likelihood of these problems. Guidelines for preparing for the evaluation, performing the field study, analyzing the data, and reporting the findings might include the following (Rose et al., 1995):

Preparation
- Understand organization policies and work culture.
- Familiarize yourself with the system and its history.
- Set initial goals and prepare questions.
- Gain access and permission to observe or interview.

Field Study
- Establish rapport with managers and users.
- Observe or interview users in their workplace, and collect subjective and objective quantitative and qualitative data.
- Follow any leads that emerge from the visits.
- Record your visits.

Analysis
- Compile the collected data in numerical, textual, and multimedia databases.
- Quantify data and compile statistics.
- Reduce and interpret the data.
- Refine the goals and the process used.

Reporting
- Consider multiple audiences and goals.
- Prepare a report and present the findings.

These notions seem obvious when stated but they require interpretation and attention in each situation. For example, understanding the differing perceptions that managers and users have about the efficacy of the current interface will alert you to the varying frustrations that each group will have. For example, managers may complain about the unwillingness of staff to update information promptly, but staff may be resistant to using the interface because the login process takes 6 to 8 minutes. In preparing for one observation, we appreciated that the manager called to warn us that graduate students should not wear jeans because the users were prohibited from doing so. Learning the technical language of the users is also vital for establishing rapport. It is useful to prepare a long list of questions that you can then filter down by focusing on the proposed goals. Awareness of the differences among user communities, such as those mentioned in Section 1.5, will help to make the observation and interview process more effective.

Data collection can include a wide range of subjective impressions that are qualitative or of subjective reactions that are quantitative, such as rating scales or rankings. Objective data can consist of qualitative anecdotes or critical incidents that capture user experiences, or can be quantitative reports about, for example, the number of errors that occur during a one-hour observation of six users. Deciding in advance what to capture is highly beneficial, but remaining alert to unexpected happenings is also valuable. Written report summaries have proved to be valuable, far beyond expectations; in most cases, raw transcripts of every conversation are too voluminous to be useful.

Making the process explicit and planning carefully may seem awkward to many people whose training stems from computing and information technology. However, a thoughtful applied ethnographic process has proved to have many benefits. It can increase trustworthiness and credibility, since designers learn about the complexities of an organization firsthand by visits to the workplace. Personal presence allows designers to develop working relationships with several end users to discuss ideas; most important, the users may consent to be active participants in the design of their new interface.

3.6 Participatory Design

Many authors have urged participatory design strategies (Olson and Ives, 1981; Mumford, 1983; Ives and Olson, 1984; Gould and Lewis, 1985; Gould et al., 1991; Damodaran, 1996), but the concept is controversial. The arguments in favor suggest that more user involvement brings more accurate information about tasks, an opportunity for users to influence design decisions, the sense of participation that builds users' ego investment in successful implementation, and the potential for increased user acceptance of the final system (Baroudi et al., 1986; Greenbaum and Kyng, 1991; Monk et al., 1993).

On the other hand, extensive user involvement may be costly and may lengthen the implementation period, build antagonism with people who are not involved or whose suggestions are rejected, force designers to compromise their design to satisfy incompetent participants, and simply build opposition to implementation (Ives and Olson, 1984).

Participatory-design experiences are usually positive, and advocates can point to many important contributions that would have been missed without it. People who are resistant might appreciate the somewhat formalized multiple-case-studies *plastic interface for collaborative technology initiatives through video exploration (PICTIVE)* approach (Muller, 1992). Users sketch interfaces, then use slips of paper, pieces of plastic, and tape to create low-fidelity early prototypes. A scenario walkthrough is then recorded on videotape for presentation to managers, users, or other designers. With the right leadership, PICTIVE can effectively elicit new ideas and be fun for all involved (Muller et al., 1993).

Careful selection of users helps to build a successful participatory design experience. A competitive selection increases participants' sense of importance and emphasizes the seriousness of the project. Participants may be asked to commit to repeated meetings and should be told what to expect about their roles and their influence. They may have to learn about the technology and business plans of the organization, and to act as a communication channel to the larger group of users that they represent.

The social and political environment surrounding the implementation of complex interfaces is not amenable to study by rigidly defined methods or controlled experimentation. Social and industrial psychologists are interested in these issues, but dependable research and implementation strategies may never emerge. The sensitive project leader must judge each case on its merits and must decide what is the right level of user involvement. The personalities of the design-team members and of the users are such critical determinants that experts in group dynamics and social psychology may be useful as consultants.

The experienced user-interface architect knows that organizational politics and the preferences of individuals may be more important than the technical issues in governing the success of an interactive system. The warehouse managers who see their positions threatened by an interactive system that provides senior managers with up-to-date information through desktop displays will ensure that the system fails by delaying data entry or by being less than diligent in guaranteeing data accuracy. The interface designer should take into account the effect on users, and should solicit their participation to ensure that all concerns are made explicit early enough to avoid counterproductive efforts and resistance to change. Novelty is threatening to many people, so clear statements about what to expect when can be helpful in reducing anxiety.

3.7   Scenario Development

When a current interface is being redesigned or a well-polished manual system is being automated, there often are available reliable data about the range and distribution of task frequencies and sequences. If current data do not exist, then logging usage can quickly provide insight. When substantial changes are anticipated, such as in business-process re-engineering, or when a novel application is planned, identifying the tasks and estimating their frequencies is more difficult.

A table with user communities listed across the top and tasks listed down the side is helpful. Each box can then be filled in with the relative frequency with which each user performs each task. Another representation tool is a table of task sequences, indicating which tasks follow other tasks. Often, a flowchart or transition diagram helps designers to record and convey the sequences of possible actions. The thickness of the connecting lines indicates the frequency of the transitions.

In less well-defined projects, many designers have found day-in-the-life scenarios helpful to characterize what happens when users perform typical tasks. During the early design stages, data about current performance should be collected to provide a baseline. Information about similar systems can be gathered, and interviews can be conducted with interested parties, such as users and managers (Carroll, 1995).

An early and easy way to describe a novel system is to write scenarios of usage and then, if possible, to act them out as a form of theater. This technique can be especially effective when multiple users must cooperate (for example, in control rooms, cockpits, or financial trading rooms) or multiple physical devices are used (for example, at customer-service desks, medical laboratories, or hotel check-in areas). Scenarios can represent common or emergency situations, with both novice and expert users.

In developing the National Digital Library, the design team began by writing 81 scenarios that portrayed typical needs of potential users. Here is an example:

> *K–16 Users*: A seventh-grade social-studies teacher is teaching a unit on the Industrial Revolution. He wants to make use of primary source material that would illustrate the factors that facilitated industrialization, the manner in which it occurred, and the impact that it had on society and on the built environment. Given his teaching load, he only has about four hours total to locate and package the supplementary material for classroom use.

Other scenarios might describe how users explore a system, such as this optimistic vision, written for the U.S. Holocaust Museum and Education Center:

A grandmother and her 10- and 12-year old grandsons have visited the museum before. They have returned this time to the Learning Center to explore what life was like in her shtetl in Poland in the 1930s. One grandson eagerly touches the buttons on the welcome screen, and they watch the 45-second video introduction by the museum director. They then select the button on "History before the Holocaust" and choose to view a list of towns. Her small town is not on the list, but she identifies the larger nearby city, and they get a brief textual description, a map of the region, and a photograph of the marketplace. They read about the history of the town and view 15-second videos of the market-place activity and a Yiddish theater production. They bypass descriptions of key buildings and institutions, choosing instead to read biographies of a famous community leader and a poet. Finally, they select "GuestBook" and add their names to the list of people who have indicated an affiliation with this town. Further up on the list, the grandmother notices the name of a childhood friend from whom she has not heard in 60 years—fortunately, the earlier visitor has left an address.

This scenario was written to give nontechnical museum planners and the Board of Directors an idea of what could be built if funding were provided. Such scenarios are easy for most people to grasp, and they convey design issues such as physical installation (room and seats for three or more patrons with sound isolation) and development requirements (video production for the director's introduction and conversion of archival films to video).

Some scenario writers take a further step and produce a videotape to convey their intentions. There are famous future scenarios, such as Apple's Knowledge Navigator, made in 1988, which produced numerous controversies. It portrayed a professor using voice commands to talk with a bow-tied preppie character on the screen and touch commands to develop ecological simulations. Many viewers enjoyed the tape, but thought that it stepped over the bounds of reality by having the preppie agent recognize the professor's facial expressions, verbal hesitations, and emotional reactions. In 1994, Bruce Tognazzini's Starfire scenario for Sun Microsystems gave his elaborate but realistic impression of a large-screen work environment that supported rich collaborations with remote users. Bill Gates took video scenarios one step further at the November 1994 Comdex show, screening an hour-long police drama set in 2005 to illustrate digital wallets, interactive home TV, educational databases, and medical communications.

3.8   Social Impact Statement for Early Design Review

Interactive systems often have a dramatic impact on large numbers of users. To minimize risks, a thoughtful statement of anticipated impacts circulated among stakeholders can be a useful process for eliciting productive suggestions early in the development, when changes are easiest.

Information systems are increasingly required to provide services by governments, utilities, and publicly regulated industries. However, some critics have strong negative attitudes about modern technologies: "technological evolution is leading to something new: a worldwide interlocked monolithic, technical-political web of unprecedented negative implications. And it is surely creating terrible and possibly catastrophic impacts on the earth" (Mander, 1991).

This negative view does not help us to shape more effective technology or to prevent damage from technology failures. Constructive criticism and guidelines for design could be helpful in reversing the long history of disruptions in telephone, banking, or charge-card systems; dissatisfaction with privacy protection or incorrect credit histories; dislocation through deskilling or layoffs; and deaths from flawed medical instruments. While guarantees of perfection are not possible, policies and processes can be developed that will more often than not lead to satisfying outcomes.

A *social impact statement,* similar to an environmental-impact statement (Battle et al., 1994) might help to promote high-quality systems in government-related applications. Reviews for private-sector corporate projects would be optional and self-administered. Early and widespread discussion can uncover concerns and enable stakeholders to state their positions openly (Ralls, 1994). Of course, there is the danger that these discussions will elevate fears or force designers to make unreasonable compromises, but these risks seem reasonable in a well-managed project. The practicality of writing social impact statements was addressed by Huff (1996), who used them as a teaching tool. An outline for a social impact statement might include these sections (Shneiderman and Rose, 1996):

Describe the new system and its benefits
- Convey the high-level goals of the new system.
- Identify the stakeholders.
- Identify specific benefits.

Address concerns and potential barriers
- Anticipate changes in job functions and potential layoffs.

- Address security and privacy issues.
- Discuss accountability and responsibility for system misuse and failure.
- Avoid potential biases.
- Weigh individual rights versus societal benefits.
- Assess tradeoffs between centralization and decentralization.
- Preserve democratic principles.
- Ensure diverse access.
- Promote simplicity and preserve what works.

Outline the development process
- Present an estimated project schedule.
- Propose process for making decisions.
- Discuss expectations of how stakeholders will be involved.
- Recognize needs for more staff, training, and hardware.
- Propose plan for backups of data and equipment.
- Outline plan for migrating to the new system.
- Describe plan for measuring the success of the new system.

A social impact statement should be produced early enough in the development process to influence the project schedule, system requirements, and budget. It could be developed by the system design team, which might include end users, managers, internal or external software developers, and possibly clients. Even for large systems, the social impact statement should be of a size and complexity that make it accessible to users with relevant background.

After the social impact statement is written, it is evaluated by the appropriate review panel plus managers, other designers, end users, and anyone else who will be affected by the proposed system. Potential review panels include federal government units (for example, General Accounting Organization, Office Personnel Management), state legislatures, regulatory agencies (for example, Securities and Exchange Commission or Federal Aviation Administration), professional societies, and labor unions. The review panel receives the written report, holds public hearings, and requests modifications. Citizen groups also are given the opportunity to present their concerns and to suggest alternatives.

Once the social impact statement is adopted, it must be enforced. A social impact statement documents the intentions for the new system, and the stakeholders need to see that those intentions are backed up by actions. Typically, the review panel is the proper authority for enforcement.

The effort, cost, and time should be appropriate to the project, while facilitating a thoughtful review. The process can offer large improvements by preventing problems that could be expensive to repair, improving privacy protection, minimizing legal challenges, and creating more satisfying work environments. Information-system designers take no Hippocratic Oath, but pledging themselves to strive for the noble goal of excellence in design can win respect and inspire others.

3.9 Legal Issues

As user interfaces have become prominent, serious legal issues have emerged. Every development process should include a review of legal issues that may affect design, implementation, or marketing.

Privacy is always a concern whenever computers are used to store data or to monitor activity. Medical, legal, financial, military, or certain other data often have to be protected to prevent unapproved access, illegal tampering, inadvertent loss, or malicious mischief. Physical security to prohibit access is fundamental; in addition, privacy protection can involve user-interface mechanisms for controlling password access, file-access control, identity checking, and data verification. Users at a public workstation or kiosks want assurance that their password cannot be seen by other people. Effective protection should provide a high degree of privacy with a minimum of confusion and intrusion into work. Encryption and decryption processes may involve complex dialog boxes to specify keys.

A second concern encompasses safety and reliability. User interfaces for aircraft, automobiles, medical equipment, military systems, or nuclear-reactor control rooms can affect life-or-death decisions. If an air-traffic controller is temporarily confused by the contents of the display, that could lead to disaster. If the user interface for such a system is demonstrated to be difficult to understand, it could leave the designer, developer, and operator open to a law suit alleging improper design. Designers should strive to make high-quality and well-tested interfaces that adhere to state-of-the-art design guidelines. Documentation of testing and usage should be maintained to provide accurate data on actual performance. Unlike architecture or engineering, user-interface design is not yet an established profession with clear standards.

A third issue is copyright protection for software and information (Gilbert, 1990; Computer Science and Telecommunications Board, 1991; Samuelson, 1995; 1996). Software developers who have spent time and money to develop a package are frustrated in their attempts to recover their costs and to make a profit if potential users pirate (i.e., make illegal copies of) the package, rather than buy it. Various technical schemes have been tried to prevent copying, but clever hackers can usually circumvent the barriers. It is unusual for a company to sue an individual for copying a program, but cases have been brought against corporations and universities. Site-license agreements are one solution because they allow copying within a site once the fees have been paid. More complicated situations arise in the context of access to online information. If a customer of an online information service pays for time to access to the database, does the customer have the right to extract and store the retrieved information electronically for later use? Can the customer send an electronic copy to a colleague, or sell a bibliography carefully culled from a large commercial database? Do individuals, their employers, or network operators own the information contained in electronic-mail messages? The emergence of the World Wide Web and efforts to build vast digital libraries have raised the temperature and pace of copyright discussions. Publishers are seeking to protect their intellectual assets, and librarians are torn between their desire to serve patrons and their obligations to publishers. If copyrighted works are disseminated freely, then what incentives will there be for publishers and authors? If it is illegal to transmit any copyrighted work without permission or payment, then science, literature, and other fields will suffer. The fair-use doctrine of limited copying for personal and educational purposes helped cope with the questions raised by photocopying technologies, but the perfect rapid copying and dissemination permitted by the network demands a thoughtful update.

A fourth issue is freedom of speech in electronic environments. Do users have a right to make controversial or potentially offensive statements through electronic mail or newsgroups? Are such statements protected by the First Amendment? Are networks like street corners, where freedom of speech is guaranteed, or are networks like television broadcasting, where community standards must be protected? Should network operators be responsible for or prohibited from eliminating offensive or obscene jokes, stories, or images? Controversy has raged over whether network operators have a right to prohibit electronic-mail messages that are used to organize a rebellion against themselves. Another controversy emerged over whether a network operator has a duty to suppress racist electronic-mail remarks or postings to a bulletin board. If libelous statements are transmitted, can a person sue the network as well as the source?

Other legal concerns include adherence to laws requiring equal access for disabled users and attention to changing laws in countries around the world.

The most controversial issue for user-interface designers is that of copyright and patent protection for user interfaces. When user interfaces comprised coded commands in all-capital letters transmitted via Teletype, there was little that could be protected. But the emergence of artistically designed GUIs with animations and extensive online help has led developers to file for copyright protection. This activity has led to many controversies:

- *What material is eligible for copyright?* Since fonts, lines, boxes, shading, and colors cannot usually be accorded copyrights, some people claim that most interfaces are not protectable. Advocates of strong protection claim that the ensemble of components is a creative work, just like a song that is composed of uncopyrightable notes or a poem of uncopyrightable words. Although standard arrangements, such as the rotated-L format of spreadsheets, are not copyrightable, collections of words, such as the

Lotus 1–2–3 menu tree, have been accepted as copyrightable, but such decisions have later been overturned by higher courts. Apple lost its copyright-infringement suit against Microsoft for the Windows interface, in part because the judge insisted on decomposing the interface into elements rather than looking at the overall look and feel. Maybe the most confusing concept is the separation between ideas (not protectable) and expressions (protectable). Generations of judges and lawyers have wrestled with this issue; they agree only that there is "no bright shining line" between idea and expression, and that the distinction must be decided in each case. Most informed commentators would agree that the idea of working on multiple documents at once by showing multiple windows simultaneously is not protectable, but that specific expressions of windows (border decorations, animations for movement, and so on) is protectable. A key point is that there should be a variety of ways to express a given idea. When there is only one way to express an idea—for example, a circle for the idea of a wedding band—the expression is not protectable.

- *Are copyrights or patents more appropriate for user interfaces?* Traditionally, copyright is used for artistic, literary, and musical expressions, whereas patent is used for functional devices. There are interesting crossovers, such as copyrights for maps, engineering drawings, and decorations on teacups, and patents for software algorithms. In the United States, copyrights are easy to obtain (just put a copyright notice on the user interface and file a copyright application), are rapid, and are not verified. Patents are complex, slow, and costly to obtain, because they must be verified by the U.S. Patent and Trademark Office. Copyrights last 75 years for companies and life plus 50 years for individuals. Patents last for only 17 years but are considered more enforceable. The strength of patent protection has raised concerns over patents that were granted for what appear to be fundamental algorithms for data compression and display management. Copyrights for printed user manuals and online help can also be obtained.

- *What constitutes copyright infringement?* If another developer copies your validly copyrighted user interface exactly, that is clearly a case of infringement. More subtle issues arise when a competitor makes a user interface that has elements strikingly similar, by your judgment, to your own. To win a copyright-infringement case, you must convince a jury of "ordinary observers" that the competitor actually saw your interface and that the other interface is "substantially similar" to yours.

- *Should user interfaces be copyrighted?* There are many respected commentators who believe that user interfaces should not be copyrighted. They contend that user interfaces should be shared and that it would impede progress if developers had to pay for permission for every user-interface feature that they saw and wanted to include in their interface. They claim also that copyrights interfere with beneficial standardization and that unnecessary artistic variations would create confusion and inconsistency. Advocates of copyrights for user interfaces wish to recognize creative accomplishments and, by allowing protection, to encourage innovation while ensuring that designers are rewarded for their works. Although ideas are not protectable, specific expressions would have to be licensed from the creator, presumably for a fee, in the same way that each photograph in an art book must be licensed and acknowledged, or each use of a song, play, or quote must be granted permission. Concern over the complexity and cost of this process and the unwillingness of copyright owners to share is legitimate, but the alternative of providing no protection might slow innovation.

In the current legal climate, interface designers must respect existing expressions and would be wise to seek licenses or cooperative agreements to share user interfaces. Placing a copyright notice on the title screen of a system and in user manuals seems appropriate. Of course, proper legal counsel should be obtained.

3.10   Practitioner's Summary

Usability engineering is maturing rapidly, and once-novel ideas have become standard practices. Usability has increasingly taken center stage in organizational and product planning. Development methodologies, such as Cognetics' LUCID, help designers by offering a validated process with predictable schedules and meaningful deliverables. Ethnographic observation can provide information to guide task analysis and to complement carefully supervised participatory design processes. Logs of usage provide valuable data about the task sequences and frequencies. Scenario writing helps to bring common understanding of design goals and is useful for managerial and customer presentations. For interfaces developed by governments, public utilities, and regulated industries, an early social-impact statement can elicit public discussion that is likely to identify problems and produce interfaces that have high overall societal benefits. Designers and managers should obtain legal advice to ensure adherence to laws and protection of intellectual property.

3.11   Researcher's Agenda

Human-interface guidelines are often based on best-guess judgments rather than on experimental data. More experimentation could lead to refined standards that are more complete and dependable, and to more precise knowledge of how much improvement can be expected from a design change. Because of changing technology, we will never have a stable and complete set of guidelines, but the benefits of scientific studies will be enormous in terms of the reliability and quality of decision making about user interfaces. The design processes, ethnographic methods, participatory design activities, scenario writing, and social impact statements are rapidly evolving. Thoughtful case studies of successes and failures would lead to refinement and more widespread application. Creative processes are notoriously difficult to study, but well-documented examples of success stories might inform and inspire.

World Wide Web Resources   WWW

Design methods promoted by companies and standards organizations are covered, with information on how to develop style guidelines. References to guidelines documents are included in Chapter 1.

http://www.aw.com/DTUI

References

Baroudi, Jack J., Olson, Margrethe H., and Ives, Blake, An empirical study of the impact of user involvement on system usage and information satisfaction, *Communications of the ACM*, 29, 3 (March 1986), 232–238.

Battle, Jackson, Fischman, Robert, and Squillace, Mark, (1994), *Environmental Law. Volume 1: Environmental Decision making NEPA and the Endangered Species Act*, Anderson Publishing, (1994). World Wide Web version prepared in April 1994 by Robert Fischman, Indiana University, School of Law, Bloomington, IN, http://www.law.indiana.edu/envdec

Bentley, R., Hughes, J., Randall, D., Rodden, T., Sawyer, P., Shapiro, D., and Sommerville, I., Ethnographically-informed systems design for air traffic control, *Proc. CSCW '92—Sharing Perspectives* (1992), 123–129.

Boehm, Barry, A spiral model of software development and enhancement, *IEEE Computer*, 21, 5 (May 1988), 61–72.

Carroll, John, M., *Scenario-Based Design: Envisioning Work and Technology in System Development*, John Wiley and Sons, New York (1995).

Carroll, John M. and Rosson, Mary Beth, Usability specifications as a tool in iterative development. In Hartson, H. Rex (Editor), *Advances in Human–Computer Interaction 1*, Ablex, Norwood, NJ (1985), 1–28.

Chapanis, Alphonse, The business case for human factors in informatics. In Shackel, Brian and Richardson, Simon (Editors), *Human Factors in Informatics Usability*, Cambridge University Press, Cambridge, U.K. (1991), 39–71.

Chapanis, Alphonse and Budurka, William J., Specifying human–computer interface requirements, *Behaviour and Information Technology*, 9, 6 (1990), 479–492.

Computer Science and Telecommunications Board, National Research Council, *Intellectual Property Issues in Software*, National Academy Press, Washington, D.C. (1991).

Damodaran, Leela, User involvement in the systems design process—a practical guide for users, *Behaviour & Information Technology*, 15, 6 (1996), 363–377.

Dumas, Joseph and Redish, Janice, *A Practical Guide to Usability Testing*, Ablex, Norwood, NJ (1993).

Gilbert, Steven W., Information technology, intellectual property, and education, *EDUCOM Review*, 25, (1990), 14–20.

Gould, John, How to design usable systems. In Helander, Martin (Editor), *Handbook of Human–Computer Interaction*, North-Holland, Amsterdam, The Netherlands (1988), 757–789.

Gould, John D., and Lewis, Clayton, Designing for usability: Key principles and what designers think, *Communications of the ACM*, 28, 3 (March 1985), 300–311.

Gould, John D., Boies, Stephen J., and Lewis, Clayton, Making usable, useful productivity-enhancing computer applications, *Communications of the ACM*, 34, 1 (January 1991), 75–85.

Greenbaum, Joan and Kyng, Morten (Editors), *Design at Work: Cooperative Design of Computer Systems*, LEA Publishers, Hillsdale, NJ (1991).

Hammersley, M., and Atkinson, P., *Ethnography Principles and Practice*, Routledge, London (1983).

Hix, Deborah and Hartson, H. Rex, *Developing User Interfaces: Ensuring Usability Through Product and Process*, John Wiley and Sons, New York (1993).

Huff, Chuck, Practical guidance for teaching the Social Impact Statement, *Proc. CQL '96, ACM SIGCAS Symposium on Computers and the Quality of Life* (Feb. 1996), 86–89.

Hughes, J., King, V., Rodden, T., and Anderson, H., The role of ethnography in interactive systems design, *Interactions*, 2, 2 (1995), 56–65.

Humphrey, Watts, *A Discipline for Software Engineering*, Addison-Wesley, Reading, MA (1995).

Ives, Blake, and Olson, Margrethe H., User involvement and MIS success: A review of research, *Management Science*, 30, 5 (May 1984), 586–603.

Karat, Claire-Marie, Cost-benefit analysis of usability engineering techniques, *Proc. Human Factors Society Annual Meeting* (1990), 839–843.

Karat, Claire-Marie, A business case approach to usability. In Bias, Randolph, and Mayhew, Deborah (Editors), *Cost-Justifying Usability*, Academic Press, New York (1994), 45–70.

Klemmer, Edmund T. (Editor), *Ergonomics: Harness the Power of Human Factors in Your Business*, Ablex, Norwood, NJ (1989).

Kreitzberg, Charles, Managing for usability. In Alber, Antone F. (Editor), *Multimedia: A Management Perspective*, Wadsworth, Belmont, CA (1996), 65–88.

Landauer, Thomas K., *The Trouble with Computers: Usefulness, Usability, and Productivity*, MIT Press, Cambridge, MA (1995).

Mander, Jerry, *In the Absence of the Sacred: The Failure of Technology and the Survival of the Indian Nations*, Sierra Club Books, San Francisco, CA (1991).

Mantei, Marilyn and Teorey, Toby, Cost-benefit analysis for incorporating human factors in the software life cycle, *Communications of the ACM,* 31, 4 (1988), 428–439.

Monk, A., Wright, P., Haber, J., and Davenport, L., *Improving Your Human–Computer Interface: A Practical Technique,* Prentice-Hall, Englewood Cliffs, NJ (1993).

Muller, Michael J., Retrospective on a year of participatory design using the PICTIVE technique, *Proc. CHI '92—Human Factors in Computing Systems,* ACM, New York (1992), 455–462.

Muller, M., Wildman, D., and White, E., Taxonomy of PD practices: A brief practitioner's guide, *Communications of the ACM,* 36, 4 (1993), 26–27.

Mumford, Enid, *Designing Participatively,* Manchester Business School, Manchester, U.K. (1983).

Nielsen, Jakob (Editor), Special Issue on Usability Laboratories, *Behaviour & Information Technology,* 13, 1 & 2 (January–April 1994).

Nielsen, Jakob, *Usability Engineering,* Academic Press, New York (1993).

Olson, Margrethe H. and Ives, Blake, User involvement in system design: An empirical test of alternative approaches, *Information and Management,* 4, (1981), 183–195.

Preece, Jenny and Rombach, Dieter, A taxonomy for combining Software Engineering (SE) and Human–Computer Interaction (HCI) measurement approaches: Towards a common framework, *International Journal of Human–Computer Studies,* 41, 4 (1994), 553–583.

Ralls, Scott, *Integrating Technology with Workers in the New American Workplace,* U.S. Department of Labor, Office of the American Workplace, Washington, D.C. (1994).

Rose, Anne, Plaisant, Catherine, and Shneiderman, Ben, Using ethnographic methods in user interface re-engineering, *Proc. DIS '95: Symposium on Designing Interactive Systems,* ACM Press, New York (August 1995), 115–122.

Samuelson, Pamela, Copyright and digital libraries, *Communications of the ACM,* 38, 3 (1995), 15–21, 110.

Samuelson, Pamela, Legal protection for database contents, *Communications of the ACM,* 39, 12 (1996), 17–23.

Shneiderman, Ben and Rose, Anne, Social impact statements: Engaging public participation in information technology design, *Proc. CQL '96, ACM SIGCAS Symposium on Computers and the Quality of Life* (Feb. 1996), 90–96.

Sutcliffe, A. G. and McDermott, M., Integrating methods of human–computer interface design with structured systems development, *International Journal of Man–Machine Studies,* 34, 5 (1991), 631–656.

Thomas, John C., Organizing for human factors. In Vassiliou, Y. (Editor), *Human Factors in Interactive Computer Systems,* Ablex, Norwood, NJ (1984), 29–46.

Suchman, L., Office procedure as practical action: Models of work and system design, *ACM Transactions on Office Information Systems,* 1, 4 (1983), 320–328.

Vaske, Jerry and Grantham, Charles, *Socializing the Human–Computer Environment,* Ablex, Norwood, NJ (1989).

Whiteside, John, Bennett, John, and Holtzblatt, Karen, Usability engineering: Our experience and evolution. In Helander, Martin (Editor), *Handbook of Human–Computer Interaction,* North-Holland, Amsterdam, The Netherlands (1988), 791–817.

Mark Kostabi, *Gumball Market*, 1996

4

Expert Reviews, Usability Testing, Surveys, and Continuing Assessments

The test of what is real is that it is hard and rough.
. . . What is pleasant belongs in dreams.

Simone Weil, *Gravity and Grace*, 1947

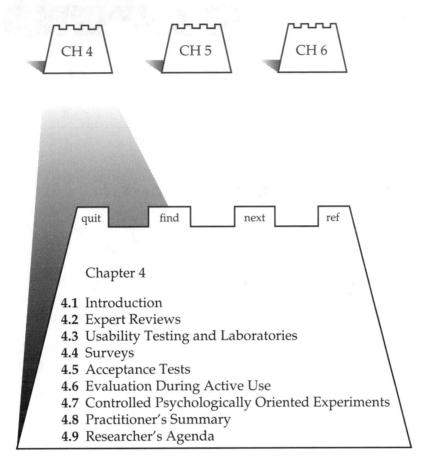

CH 4   CH 5   CH 6

quit   find   next   ref

Chapter 4

4.1 Introduction
4.2 Expert Reviews
4.3 Usability Testing and Laboratories
4.4 Surveys
4.5 Acceptance Tests
4.6 Evaluation During Active Use
4.7 Controlled Psychologically Oriented Experiments
4.8 Practitioner's Summary
4.9 Researcher's Agenda

4.1 Introduction

Designers can become so entranced with their creations that they may fail to evaluate those objects adequately. Experienced designers have attained the wisdom and humility to know that extensive testing is a necessity. If feedback is the "breakfast of champions," then testing is the "dinner of the gods." However, careful choices must be made from the large menu of evaluation possibilities to create a balanced meal.

The determinants of the evaluation plan include (Nielsen, 1993; Hix and Hartson, 1993; Preece et al., 1994; Newman and Lamming, 1995)

- Stage of design (early, middle, late)
- Novelty of project (well defined versus exploratory)
- Number of expected users

- Criticality of the interface (for example, life-critical medical system versus museum-exhibit support)
- Costs of product and finances allocated for testing
- Time available
- Experience of the design and evaluation team

The range of evaluation plans might be from an ambitious two-year test with multiple phases for a new national air-traffic–control system to a three-day test with six users for a small internal accounting system. The range of costs might be from 10 percent of a project down to 1 percent.

A few years ago, it was just a good idea to get ahead of the competition by focusing on usability and doing testing, but now the rapid growth of interest in usability means that failure to test is risky indeed. The dangers are not only that the competition has strengthened, but also that customary engineering practice now requires adequate testing. Failure to perform and document testing could lead to failed contract proposals or malpractice lawsuits from users when errors arise. At this point, it is irresponsible to bypass some form of usability testing.

One troubling aspect of testing is the uncertainty that remains even after exhaustive testing by multiple methods. Perfection is not possible in complex human endeavors, so planning must include continuing methods to assess and repair problems during the lifecycle of an interface. Second, even though problems may continue to be found, at some point a decision has to be made about completing prototype testing and delivering the product. Third, most testing methods will account appropriately for normal usage, but performance with high levels of input such as in nuclear-reactor–control or air-traffic–control emergencies is extremely difficult to test. Development of testing methods to deal with stressful situations and even with partial equipment failures will have to be undertaken as user interfaces are developed for an increasing number of life-critical applications.

The Usability Professionals Association was founded in 1991 to exchange information among workers in this arena. The annual conference focuses attention on forms of usability evaluations and provides a forum for exchanges of ideas among the more than 4000 members.

4.2   Expert Reviews

While informal demos to colleagues or customers can provide some useful feedback, more formal expert reviews have proved to be effective (Nielsen and Mack, 1994). These methods depend on having experts available on staff or as consultants, whose expertise may be in the application or user-interface domains. Expert reviews can be conducted on short notice and rapidly.

Expert reviews can occur early or late in the design phase, and the outcomes can be a formal report with problems identified or recommendations for changes. Alternatively, the expert review could result in a discussion with or presentation to designers or managers. Expert reviewers should be sensitive to the design team's ego involvement and professional skill, so suggestions should be made cautiously: It is difficult for someone just freshly inspecting a system to understand all the design rationale and development history. The reviewer notes possible problems for discussion with the designers, but solutions generally should be left for the designers to produce. Expert reviews usually entail half day to one week, although a lengthy training period may be required to explain the task domain or operational procedures. It may be useful to have the same as well as fresh expert reviewers as the project progresses. There are a variety of expert-review methods from which to choose:

- *Heuristic evaluation*   The expert reviewers critique an interface to determine conformance with a short list of design heuristics such as the eight golden rules (Chapter 2). It makes an enormous difference if the experts are familiar with the rules and are able to interpret and apply them.

- *Guidelines review*   The interface is checked for conformance with the organizational or other guidelines document. Because guidelines documents may contain a thousand items, it may take the expert reviewers some time to master the guidelines, and days or weeks to review a large system.

- *Consistency inspection*   The experts verify consistency across a family of interfaces, checking for consistency of terminology, color, layout, input and output formats, and so on within the interface as well as in the training materials and online help.

- *Cognitive walkthrough*   The experts simulate users walking through the interface to carry out typical tasks. High-frequency tasks are a starting point, but rare critical tasks, such as error recovery, also should be walked through. Some form of simulating the day in the life of the user should be part of expert-review process. Cognitive walkthroughs were developed for interfaces that can be learned by exploratory browsing (Wharton et al., 1994), but they are useful even for interfaces that require substantial training. An expert might try the walkthrough privately and explore, but then there also would be a group meeting with designers, users, or managers to conduct the walkthrough and to provoke a discussion. This public walkthrough is based on the successful code walkthroughs promoted in software engineering (Yourdon, 1989).

- *Formal usability inspection*   The experts hold courtroom-style meeting, with a moderator or judge, to present the interface and to discuss its merits and weaknesses. Design-team members may rebut the evidence about problems in an adversarial format. Formal usability inspections can be educational experiences for novice designers and managers, but they may take longer to prepare and more personnel to carry out than do other types of review.

Expert reviews can be scheduled at several points in the development process when experts are available and when the design team is ready for feedback. The number of expert reviews will depend on the magnitude of the project and on the amount of resources allocated.

Comparative evaluation of expert-review methods and usability-testing methods is difficult because of the many uncontrollable variables; however, the studies that have been conducted provide evidence for the benefits of expert reviews (Jeffries et al., 1991; Karat et al. 1992). Different experts tend to find different problems in an interface, so three to five expert reviewers can be highly productive, as can complementary usability testing.

Expert reviewers should be placed in the situation most similar to the one that intended users will experience. The expert reviewers should take training courses, read manuals, take tutorials, and try the system in as close as possible to a realistic work environment, complete with noise and distractions. In addition, expert reviewers may also retreat to a quieter environment for detailed review of each screen.

Getting a *bird's-eye view* of an interface by studying a full set of printed screens laid out on the floor or pinned to walls has proved to be enormously fruitful in detecting inconsistencies and spotting unusual patterns.

The dangers with expert reviews are that the experts may not have an adequate understanding of the task domain or user communities. Experts come in many flavors, and conflicting advice can further confuse the situation (cynics say, "For every PhD, there is an equal and opposite PhD"). To strengthen the possibility of successful expert review, it helps to chose knowledgeable experts who are familiar with the project situation and who have a long-term relationship with the organization. These people can be called back to see the results of their intervention, and they can be held accountable. Moreover, even experienced expert reviewers have great difficulty knowing how typical users, especially first-time users, will behave.

4.3   Usability Testing and Laboratories

The emergence of usability testing and laboratories since the early 1980s is an indicator of the profound shift in attention to user needs. Traditional managers and developers resisted at first, saying that usability testing seemed like a nice idea, but that time pressures or limited resources prevented them from trying it. As experience grew and successful projects gave credit to the testing process, demand swelled and design teams began to compete for the scarce resource of the usability-laboratory staff. Managers came to realize that having a usability test on the schedule was a powerful incentive to complete a design phase. The usability-test report provided supportive confirmation of progress and specific recommendations for changes. Designers sought the bright light of evaluative feedback to guide their work, and managers saw fewer disasters as projects approached delivery dates. The remarkable surprise was that usability testing not only sped up many projects, but also produced dramatic cost savings (Gould, 1988; Gould et al., 1991; Karat, 1994).

Usability-laboratory advocates split from their academic roots as these practitioners developed innovative approaches that were influenced by advertising and market research. While academics were developing controlled experiments to test hypotheses and support theories, practitioners developed usability-testing methods to refine user interfaces rapidly. Controlled experiments have at least two treatments and seek to show statistically significant differences; usability tests are designed to find flaws in user interfaces. Both strategies use a carefully prepared set of tasks, but usability tests have fewer subjects (maybe as few as three), and the outcome is a report with recommended changes, as opposed to validation or rejection of hypotheses. Of course, there is a useful spectrum of possibilities between rigid controls and informal testing, and sometimes a combination of approaches is appropriate.

The movement toward usability testing stimulated the construction of usability laboratories (Dumas and Redish, 1993; Nielsen, 1993). Many organizations spent modest sums to build a single usability laboratory, while IBM built an elaborate facility in Boca Raton, Florida, with 16 laboratories in a circular arrangement with a centralized database for logging usage and recording performance. Having a physical laboratory makes an organization's commitment to usability clear to employees, customers, and users (Nielsen, 1994) (Fig. 4.1). A typical modest usability laboratory would have two 10- by 10-foot areas, one for the participants to do their work and another, divided by a half-silvered mirror, for the testers and observers (designers, managers, and customers) (Fig. 4.2). IBM was an early leader in developing usability laboratories, Microsoft started later, but embraced the idea forcefully, and hundreds of software-development companies have followed suit. A consulting community that will do usability testing for hire also has emerged.

The usability laboratory is typically staffed by one or more people with expertise in testing and user-interface design, who may serve 10 to 15 projects per year throughout the organization. The laboratory staff meet with the user-interface architect or manager at the start of the project to make a test plan with scheduled dates and budget allocations. Usability-laboratory staff participate in early task analysis or design reviews, provide information on software tools or literature references, and help to develop the set of tasks for the usability test. Two to six weeks before the usability test, the detailed test plan is developed, comprising the list of tasks, plus subjective satisfac-

Figure 4.1

Usability lab test, with subject and observer seated at a workstation. Video recorders capture the user's actions and the contents of the screens, while microphones capture thinking-aloud comments. (Used with permission of Sun Microsystems, Mountain View, CA.)

tion and debriefing questions. The number, types, and source of participants are identified—sources, for example, might be customer sites, temporary personnel agencies, or advertisements placed in newspapers. A pilot test of the procedures, tasks, and questionnaires, with one to three subjects is conducted one week ahead of time, while there is still time for changes. This stereotypic preparation process can be modified in many ways to suit each project's unique needs.

After changes are approved, participants are chosen to represent the intended user communities, with attention to background in computing, experience with the task, motivation, education, and ability with the natural language used in the interface. Usability-laboratory staff also must control for physical concerns (such as eyesight, left- versus right-handedness, age, and gender), and for other experimental conditions (such as time of day, day of week, physical surroundings, noise, room temperature, and level of distractions).

Participants should always be treated with respect and should be informed that it is not *they* who are being tested; rather, it is the software and user interface that are under study. They should be told about what they will be doing (for example, typing text into a computer, creating a drawing using a mouse, or getting information from a touchscreen kiosk) and how long they will be expected to stay. Participation should always be voluntary, and

Figure 4.2

Usability lab control room, with test controllers and observers watching the subject through a half-silvered window. Video controls allow zooming and panning to focus on user actions. (Used with permission of Sun Microsystems, Mountain View, CA.)

informed consent should be obtained. Professional practice is to ask all subjects to read and sign a statement like this one:

- I have freely volunteered to participate in this experiment.
- I have been informed in advance what my task(s) will be and what procedures will be followed.
- I have been given the opportunity to ask questions and have had my questions answered to my satisfaction.
- I am aware that I have the right to withdraw consent and to discontinue participation at any time, without prejudice to my future treatment.
- My signature below may be taken as affirmation of all the above statements; it was given prior to my participation in this study.

An effective technique during usability testing is to invite users to think *aloud* about what they are doing. The designer or tester should be supportive of the participants, not taking over or giving instructions, but prompting and listening for clues about how they are dealing with the interface. After a suitable time period for accomplishing the task list—usually one to three hours—the participants can be invited to make general comments or suggestions, or to respond to specific questions. The informal atmosphere of a thinking-aloud session is pleasant, and often leads to many spontaneous suggestions for improvements. In their efforts to encourage thinking aloud, some usability laboratories found that having two participants working together produces more talking, as one participant explains procedures and decisions to the other.

Videotaping participants performing tasks is often valuable for later review and for showing designers or managers the problems that users encounter (Lund, 1985). Reviewing videotapes is a tedious job, so careful logging and annotation during the test is vital to reduce the time spent finding critical incidents (Harrison, 1991). Participants may be anxious about the video cameras at the start of the test, but within minutes they usually focus on the tasks and ignore the videotaping. The reactions of designers to seeing videotapes of users failing with their system is sometimes powerful and may be highly motivating. When designers see subjects repeatedly picking the wrong menu item, they realize that the label or placement needs to be changed. Most usability laboratories have acquired or developed software to facilitate logging of user activities (typing, mousing, reading screens, reading manuals, and so on) by observers with automatic time stamping.

At each design stage, the interface can be refined iteratively, and the improved version can be tested. It is important to fix quickly even small flaws, such as of spelling errors or inconsistent layout, since they influence user expectations.

Many variant forms of usability testing have been tried. Nielsen's (1993) *discount usability engineering*, which advocates quick and dirty approaches to task analysis, prototype development, and testing, has been widely influential because it lowered the barriers to newcomers.

Field tests attempt to put new interfaces to work in realistic environments for a fixed trial period. Field tests can be made more fruitful if logging software is used to capture error, command, and help frequencies, plus productivity measures. Portable usability laboratories with videotaping and logging facilities have been developed to support more thorough field testing. A different kind of field testing supplies users with test versions of new software. The largest field test of all time was probably the beta-testing of Microsoft's Windows 95, in which reportedly 400,000 users internationally received early versions and were asked to comment.

Early usability studies can be conducted using paper mockups of screen displays to assess user reactions to wording, layout, and sequencing. A test administrator plays the role of the computer by flipping the pages while asking a participant user to carry out typical tasks. This informal testing is inexpensive and rapid, and usually is productive.

Game designers pioneered the *can-you-break-this* approach to usability testing by providing energetic teenagers with the challenge of trying to beat new games. This destructive testing approach, in which the users try to find fatal flaws in the system or otherwise to destroy it, has been used in other projects and should be considered seriously. Software purchasers have little patience with flawed products and the cost of sending out tens of thousands of replacement disks is one that few companies can bear.

Competitive usability testing can be used to compare a new interface to previous versions or to similar products from competitors. This approach is close to a controlled experimental study, and staff must be careful to construct parallel sets of tasks and to counterbalance the order of presentation of the interfaces. Within subjects designs seem more powerful because participants can make comparisons between the competing interfaces, so fewer participants are needed, although they will each be needed for a longer time period.

For all its success, usability testing does have at least two serious limitations: It emphasizes first-time usage and has limited coverage of the interface features. Since usability tests are usually two to four hours, it is difficult to ascertain how performance will be after a week or a month of regular usage. Within the typical two to four hours of a usability test, the participants may get to use only a small fraction of the features, menus, dialog boxes, or help screens. These and other concerns have led design teams to supplement usability testing with the varied forms of expert reviews.

4.4 Surveys

Written user surveys are a familiar, inexpensive, and generally acceptable companion for usability tests and expert reviews. Managers and users grasp the notion of surveys, and the typically large numbers of respondents (hundreds to thousands of users) offer a sense of authority compared to the potentially biased and highly variable results from small numbers of usability-test participants or expert reviewers. The keys to successful surveys are clear goals in advance and then development of focused items that help to attain those goals. Experienced surveyors know that care is also needed during administration and data analysis (Oppenheim, 1992).

A survey form should be prepared, reviewed among colleagues, and tested with a small sample of users before a large-scale survey is conducted. Similarly, statistical analyses (beyond means and standard deviations) and presentations (histograms, scatterplots, and so on) should also be developed before the final survey is distributed. In short, directed activities are more successful than unplanned statistical-gathering expeditions (no wild goose chases, please). My experience is that directed activities also seem to provide the most fertile frameworks for unanticipated discoveries.

Survey goals can be tied to the components of the OAI model of interface design (see Section 2.3). Users could be asked for their subjective impressions about specific aspects of the interface, such as the representation of

- Task domain objects and actions
- Interface domain metaphors and action handles
- Syntax of inputs and design of displays

Other goals would be to ascertain the user's

- Background (age, gender, origins, education, income)
- Experience with computers (specific applications or software packages, length of time, depth of knowledge)
- Job responsibilities (decision-making influence, managerial roles, motivation)
- Personality style (introvert versus extravert, risk taking versus risk averse, early versus late adopter, systematic versus opportunistic)
- Reasons for not using an interface (inadequate services, too complex, too slow)
- Familiarity with features (printing, macros, shortcuts, tutorials)
- Feelings after using an interface (confused versus clear, frustrated versus in control, bored versus excited)

Online surveys avoid the cost and effort of printing, distributing, and collecting paper forms. Many people prefer to answer a brief survey displayed on a screen, instead of filling in and returning a printed form, although there is a potential bias in the self-selected sample. One survey of World Wide Web utilization generated more than 13,000 respondents. So that costs are kept low, surveys might be administered to only a fraction of the user community.

In one survey, users were asked to respond to eight statements according to the following commonly used scale:

1. Strongly agree
2. Agree
3. Neutral
4. Disagree
5. Strongly disagree

The items in the survey were these:

1. I find the system commands easy to use.
2. I feel competent with and knowledgeable about the system commands.
3. When writing a set of system commands for a new application, I am confident that they will be correct on the first run.

4. When I get an error message, I find that it is helpful in identifying the problem.

5. I think that there are too many options and special cases.

6. I believe that the commands could be substantially simplified.

7. I have trouble remembering the commands and options, and must consult the manual frequently.

8. When a problem arises, I ask for assistance from someone who really knows the system.

This list of questions can help designers to identify problems users are having, and to demonstrate improvement to the interface as changes are made in training, online assistance, command structures, and so on; progress is demonstrated by improved scores on subsequent surveys.

In a study of error messages in text-editor usage, users had to rate the messages on 1-to-7 scales:

Hostile	1 2 3 4 5 6 7	Friendly
Vague	1 2 3 4 5 6 7	Specific
Misleading	1 2 3 4 5 6 7	Beneficial
Discouraging	1 2 3 4 5 6 7	Encouraging

If precise—as opposed to general—questions are used in surveys, then there is a greater chance that the results will provide useful guidance for taking action.

Coleman and Williges (1985) developed a set of bipolar semantically anchored items (pleasing versus irritating, simple versus complicated, concise versus redundant) that asked users to describe their reactions to using a word processor. Another approach is to ask users to evaluate aspects of the interface design, such as the readability of characters, the meaningfulness of command names, or the helpfulness of error messages. If users rate as poor one aspect of the interactive system, the designers have a clear indication of what needs to be redone.

The *Questionnaire for User Interaction Satisfaction* (QUIS) was developed by Shneiderman and was refined by Norman and Chin (Chin et al., 1988) (http://www.lap.umd.edu/QUISFolder/quisHome.html). It was based on the early versions of the OAI model and therefore covered interface details, such as readability of characters and layout of displays; interface objects, such as meaningfulness of icons; interface actions, such as shortcuts for frequent users; and task issues, such as appropriate terminology or screen sequencing. It has proved useful in demonstrating the benefits of improvements to a videodisc-retrieval program, in comparing two Pascal programming environments, in assessing word processors, and in setting requirements for redesign of an online public-access library catalog. We have since applied QUIS in many projects with thousands of users and have created new versions that include items relating to website design and video-conferencing. The University of Maryland Office of Technology Liaison (College Park, Maryland 20742; (301) 405-4209) licenses QUIS in electronic and paper forms to over a hundred organizations internationally, in addition to granting free licenses to student researchers. The licensees have applied QUIS in varied ways, sometimes using only parts of QUIS or adding domain-specific items.

Table 4.1 contains the long form that was designed to have two levels of questions: general and detailed. If participants are willing to respond to every item, then the long-form questionnaire can be used. If participants are not likely to be patient, then only the general questions in the short form need to be asked.

Other scales include the Post-Study System Usability Questionnaire, developed by IBM, which has 48 items that focus on system usefulness, information quality, and interface quality (Lewis, 1995). The Software Usability Measurement Inventory contains 50 items designed to measure users' perceptions of their effect, efficiency, and control (Kirakowski and Corbett, 1993).

4.5   Acceptance Tests

For large implementation projects, the customer or manager usually sets objective and measurable goals for hardware and software performance. Many authors of requirements documents are even so bold as to specify mean time between failures, as well as the mean time to repair for hardware and, in some cases, for software. More typically, a set of test cases is specified for the software, with possible response-time requirements for the hardware-software combination. If the completed product fails to meet these acceptance criteria, the system must be reworked until success is demonstrated.

These notions can be neatly extended to the human interface. Explicit acceptance criteria should be established when the requirements document is written or when a contract is offered.

Rather than the vague and misleading criterion of "user friendly," measurable criteria for the user interface can be established for the following:

- Time for users to learn specific functions
- Speed of task performance
- Rate of errors by users
- User retention of commands over time
- Subjective user satisfaction

Table 4.1

Questionaire for User Interaction Satisfaction (© University of Maryland, 1997)

Identification number: _____ System: _____ Age: _____ Gender: __ male __ female

PART 1: System Experience

1.1 How long have you worked on this system?

___ less than 1 hour

___ 1 hour to less than 1 day

___ 1 day to less than 1 week

___ 1 week to less than 1 month

___ 1 month to less than 6 months

___ 6 months to less than 1 year

___ 1 year to less than 2 years

___ 2 years to less than 3 years

___ 3 years or more

1.2 On the average, how much time do you spend per week on this system?

___ less than one hour

___ one to less than 4 hours

___ 4 to less than 10 hours

___ over 10 hours

PART 2: Past Experience

2.1 How many operating systems have you worked with?

___ none

___ 1

___ 2

___ 3–4

___ 5–6

___ more than 6

2.2 Of the following devices, software, and systems, check those that you have personally used and are familiar with:

___ computer terminal	___ personal computer	___ lap top computer
___ color monitor	___ touch screen	___ floppy drive
___ CD-ROM drive	___ keyboard	___ mouse
___ track ball	___ joy stick	___ pen based computing
___ graphics tablet	___ head mounted display	___ modems
___ scanners	___ word processor	___ graphics software
___ spreadsheet software	___ database software	___ computer games
___ voice recognition	___ video editing systems	___ internet
___ CAD computer aided design	___ rapid prototyping systems	___ e-mail

PART 3: Overall User Reactions

Please circle the numbers which most appropriately reflect your impressions about using this computer system. Not Applicable = NA.

3.1 Overall reactions to the system:

terrible   wonderful

1 2 3 4 5 6 7 8 9   NA

3.2

frustrating   satisfying

1 2 3 4 5 6 7 8 9   NA

3.3

dull   stimulating

1 2 3 4 5 6 7 8 9   NA

3.4

difficult   easy

1 2 3 4 5 6 7 8 9   NA

3.5

inadequate power   adequate power

1 2 3 4 5 6 7 8 9   NA

3.6

rigid   flexible

1 2 3 4 5 6 7 8 9   NA

Table 4.1   (continued)

PART 4: Screen

4.1 Characters on the computer screen	hard to read easy to read	
	1 2 3 4 5 6 7 8 9	NA
4.1.1 Image of characters	fuzzy sharp	
	1 2 3 4 5 6 7 8 9	NA
4.1.2 Character shapes (fonts)	barely legible very legible	
	1 2 3 4 5 6 7 8 9	NA
4.2 Highlighting on the screen	unhelpful helpful	
	1 2 3 4 5 6 7 8 9	NA
4.2.1 Use of reverse video	unhelpful helpful	
	1 2 3 4 5 6 7 8 9	NA
4.2.2 Use of blinking	unhelpful helpful	
	1 2 3 4 5 6 7 8 9	NA
4.2.3 Use of bolding	unhelpful helpful	
	1 2 3 4 5 6 7 8 9	NA
4.3 Screen layouts were helpful	never always	
	1 2 3 4 5 6 7 8 9	NA
4.3.1 Amount of information that can be displayed on screen	inadequate adequate	
	1 2 3 4 5 6 7 8 9	NA
4.3.2 Arrangement of information can be displayed on screen	illogical logical	
	1 2 3 4 5 6 7 8 9	NA
4.4 Sequence of screens	confusing clear	
	1 2 3 4 5 6 7 8 9	NA
4.4.1 Next screen in a sequence	unpredictable predictable	
	1 2 3 4 5 6 7 8 9	NA
4.4.2 Going back to the previous screen	impossible easy	
	1 2 3 4 5 6 7 8 9	NA
4.4.3 Progression of work related tasks	confusing clearly marked	
	1 2 3 4 5 6 7 8 9	NA

Please write your comments about the screens here:

PART 5: Terminology and System Information

5.1 Use of terminology throughout system	inconsistent consistent	
	1 2 3 4 5 6 7 8 9	NA
5.1.2 Work related terminology	inconsistent consistent	
	1 2 3 4 5 6 7 8 9	NA
5.2.3 Computer terminology	inconsistent consistent	
	1 2 3 4 5 6 7 8 9	NA

Table 4.1   (continued)

5.2 Terminology relates well to the work you are doing?	never always 1 2 3 4 5 6 7 8 9	NA
5.2.1 Computer terminology is used	too frequently appropriately 1 2 3 4 5 6 7 8 9	NA
5.2.2 Terminology on the screen	ambiguous precise 1 2 3 4 5 6 7 8 9	NA
5.3 Messages which appear on screen	inconsistent consistent 1 2 3 4 5 6 7 8 9	NA
5.3.1 Position of instructions on the screen	inconsistent consistent 1 2 3 4 5 6 7 8 9	NA
5.4 Messages which appear on screen	confusing clear 1 2 3 4 5 6 7 8 9	NA
5.4.1 Instructions for commands or functions	confusing clear 1 2 3 4 5 6 7 8 9	NA
5.4.2 Instructions for correcting errors	confusing clear 1 2 3 4 5 6 7 8 9	NA
5.5 Computer keeps you informed about what it is doing	never always 1 2 3 4 5 6 7 8 9	NA
5.5.1 Animated cursors keep you informed	never always 1 2 3 4 5 6 7 8 9	NA
5.5.2 Performing an operation leads to a predictable result	never always 1 2 3 4 5 6 7 8 9	NA
5.5.3 Controlling amount of feedback	impossible easy 1 2 3 4 5 6 7 8 9	NA
5.5.4 Length of delay between operations	unacceptable acceptable 1 2 3 4 5 6 7 8 9	NA
5.6 Error messages	unhelpful helpful 1 2 3 4 5 6 7 8 9	NA
5.6.1 Error messages clarify the problem	never always 1 2 3 4 5 6 7 8 9	NA
5.6.2 Phrasing of error messages	unpleasant pleasant 1 2 3 4 5 6 7 8 9	NA

Please write your comments about terminology and system information here:

_____

PART 6: Learning

6.1 Learning to operate the system	difficult easy 1 2 3 4 5 6 7 8 9	NA
6.1.1 Getting started	difficult easy 1 2 3 4 5 6 7 8 9	NA

Table 4.1   (continued)

6.1.2 Learning advanced features	difficult	easy	
		1 2 3 4 5 6 7 8 9	NA
6.1.3 Time to learn to use the system	difficult	easy	
		1 2 3 4 5 6 7 8 9	NA
6.2 Exploration of features by trial and error	discouraging	encouraging	
		1 2 3 4 5 6 7 8 9	NA
6.2.1 Exploration of features	risky	safe	
		1 2 3 4 5 6 7 8 9	NA
6.2.2 Discovering new features	difficult	easy	
		1 2 3 4 5 6 7 8 9	NA
6.3 Remembering names and use of commands	difficult	easy	
		1 2 3 4 5 6 7 8 9	NA
6.3.1 Remembering specific rules about entering commands	difficult	easy	
		1 2 3 4 5 6 7 8 9	NA
6.4 Tasks can be performed in a straight-forward manner	never	always	
		1 2 3 4 5 6 7 8 9	NA
6.4.1 Number of steps per task	too many	just right	
		1 2 3 4 5 6 7 8 9	NA
6.4.2 Steps to complete a task follow a logical sequence	never	always	
		1 2 3 4 5 6 7 8 9	NA
6.4.3 Feedback on the completion of sequence of steps	unclear	clear	
		1 2 3 4 5 6 7 8 9	NA

Please write your comments about learning here:

PART 7: System Capabilities

7.1 System speed	too slow	fast enough	
		1 2 3 4 5 6 7 8 9	NA
7.1.1 Response time for most operations	too slow	fast enough	
		1 2 3 4 5 6 7 8 9	NA
7.1.2 Rate information is displayed	too slow	fast enough	
		1 2 3 4 5 6 7 8 9	NA
7.2 The system is reliable	never	always	
		1 2 3 4 5 6 7 8 9	NA
7.2.1 Operations	undependable	dependable	
		1 2 3 4 5 6 7 8 9	NA
7.2.2 System failures occur	frequently	seldom	
		1 2 3 4 5 6 7 8 9	NA
7.2.3 System warns you about potential problems	never	always	
		1 2 3 4 5 6 7 8 9	NA

Table 4.1   (continued)

7.3 System tends to be	noisy quiet 1 2 3 4 5 6 7 8 9	NA
7.3.1 Mechanical devices such as fans, disks, and printers	noisy quiet 1 2 3 4 5 6 7 8 9	NA
7.3.2 Computer generated sounds	annoying pleasant 1 2 3 4 5 6 7 8 9	NA
7.4 Correcting your mistakes	difficult easy 1 2 3 4 5 6 7 8 9	NA
7.4.1 Correcting typos	complex simple 1 2 3 4 5 6 7 8 9	NA
7.4.2 Ability to undo operations	inadequate adequate 1 2 3 4 5 6 7 8 9	NA
7.5 Ease of operation depends on your level of experience	never always 1 2 3 4 5 6 7 8 9	NA
7.5.1 You can accomplish tasks knowing only a few commands	with difficulty easily 1 2 3 4 5 6 7 8 9	NA
7.5.2 You can use features/shortcuts	with difficulty easily 1 2 3 4 5 6 7 8 9	NA

Please write your comments about system capabilities here:

PART 8: Technical Manuals and On-line help

8.1 Technical manuals are	confusing clear 1 2 3 4 5 6 7 8 9	NA
8.1.1 The terminology used in the manual	confusing clear 1 2 3 4 5 6 7 8 9	NA
8.2 Information from the manual is easily understood	never always 1 2 3 4 5 6 7 8 9	NA
8.2.1 Finding a solution to a problem using the manual	impossible easy 1 2 3 4 5 6 7 8 9	NA
8.3 Amount of help given	inadequate adequate 1 2 3 4 5 6 7 8 9	NA
8.3.1 Placement of help messages on the screen	confusing clear 1 2 3 4 5 6 7 8 9	NA
8.3.2 Accessing help messages	difficult easy 1 2 3 4 5 6 7 8 9	NA
8.3.3 Content of on-line help messages	confusing clear 1 2 3 4 5 6 7 8 9	NA
8.3.4 Amount of help given	inadequate adequate 1 2 3 4 5 6 7 8 9	NA

Table 4.1   (continued)

8.3.5 Help defines specific aspects of the system	inadequately adequately 1 2 3 4 5 6 7 8 9	NA
8.3.6 Finding specific information using the on-line help	difficult easy 1 2 3 4 5 6 7 8 9	NA
8.3.7 On-line help	useless helpful 1 2 3 4 5 6 7 8 9	NA

Please write your comments about technical manuals and on-line help here:

PART 9: On-line Tutorials

9.1 Tutorial was	useless helpful 1 2 3 4 5 6 7 8 9	NA
9.1.1 Accessing on-line tutorial	difficult easy 1 2 3 4 5 6 7 8 9	NA
9.2 Maneuvering through the tutorial was	difficult easy 1 2 3 4 5 6 7 8 9	NA
9.2.1 Tutorial is meaningfully structured	never always 1 2 3 4 5 6 7 8 9	NA
9.2.2 The speed of presentation was	unacceptable acceptable 1 2 3 4 5 6 7 8 9	NA
9.3 Tutorial content was	useless helpful 1 2 3 4 5 6 7 8 9	NA
9.3.1 Information for specific aspects of the system were complete and informative	never always 1 2 3 4 5 6 7 8 9	NA
9.3.2 Information was concise and to the point	never always 1 2 3 4 5 6 7 8 9	NA
9.4 Tasks can be completed	with difficulty easily 1 2 3 4 5 6 7 8 9	NA
9.4.1 Instructions given for completing tasks	confusing clear 1 2 3 4 5 6 7 8 9	NA
9.4.2 Time given to perform tasks	inadequate adequate 1 2 3 4 5 6 7 8 9	NA
9.5 Learning to operate the system using the tutorial was	difficult easy 1 2 3 4 5 6 7 8 9	NA
9.5.1 Completing system tasks after using only the tutorial	difficult easy 1 2 3 4 5 6 7 8 9	NA

Please write your comments about on-line tutorials here:

Table 4.1   (continued)

PART 10: Multimedia

10.1 Quality of still pictures/photographs	bad good 1 2 3 4 5 6 7 8 9	NA
10.1.1 Pictures/Photos	fuzzy clear 1 2 3 4 5 6 7 8 9	NA
10.1.2 Picture/Photo brightness	dim bright 1 2 3 4 5 6 7 8 9	NA
10.2 Quality of movies	bad good 1 2 3 4 5 6 7 8 9	NA
10.2.1 Focus of movie images	fuzzy clear 1 2 3 4 5 6 7 8 9	NA
10.2.2 Brightness of movie images	dim bright 1 2 3 4 5 6 7 8 9	NA
10.2.3 Movie window size is adequate	never always 1 2 3 4 5 6 7 8 9	NA
10.3 Sound output	inaudible audible 1 2 3 4 5 6 7 8 9	NA
10.3.1 Sound output	choppy smooth 1 2 3 4 5 6 7 8 9	NA
10.3.2 Sound output	garbled clear 1 2 3 4 5 6 7 8 9	NA
10.4 Colors used are	unnatural natural 1 2 3 4 5 6 7 8 9	NA
10.4.1 Amount of colors available	inadequate adequate 1 2 3 4 5 6 7 8 9	NA

Please write your comments about multimedia here:

PART 11: Teleconferencing

11.1 Setting up for conference	difficult easy 1 2 3 4 5 6 7 8 9	NA
11.1.1 Time for establishing the connections to others	too long just right 1 2 3 4 5 6 7 8 9	NA
11.1.2 Number of connections possible	too few enough 1 2 3 4 5 6 7 8 9	NA
11.2 Arrangement of windows showing connecting groups	confusing clear 1 2 3 4 5 6 7 8 9	NA
11.2.1 Window with view of your own group is of appropriate size	never always 1 2 3 4 5 6 7 8 9	NA

Table 4.1   (continued)

11.2.2 Window(s) with view of connecting group(s) is of appropriate size	never always 1 2 3 4 5 6 7 8 9		NA
11.3 Determining the focus of attention during conference was	confusing clear 1 2 3 4 5 6 7 8 9		NA
11.3.1 Telling who is speaking	difficult easy 1 2 3 4 5 6 7 8 9		NA
11.4 Video image flow	choppy smooth 1 2 3 4 5 6 7 8 9		NA
11.4.1 Focus of video image	fuzzy clear 1 2 3 4 5 6 7 8 9		NA
11.5 Audio output	inaudible audible 1 2 3 4 5 6 7 8 9		NA
11.5.1 Audio is in sync with video images	never always 1 2 3 4 5 6 7 8 9		NA
11.6 Exchanging data	difficult easy 1 2 3 4 5 6 7 8 9		NA
11.6.1 Transmitting files	difficult easy 1 2 3 4 5 6 7 8 9		NA
11.6.2 Retrieving files	difficult easy 1 2 3 4 5 6 7 8 9		NA
11.6.3 Using on-line chat	difficult easy 1 2 3 4 5 6 7 8 9		NA
11.6.4 Using shared workspace	difficult easy 1 2 3 4 5 6 7 8 9		NA

Please write your comments about teleconferencing here:

_____

PART 12: Software Installation

12.1 Speed of installation	slow fast 1 2 3 4 5 6 7 8 9		NA
12.2 Customization	difficult easy 1 2 3 4 5 6 7 8 9		NA
12.2.1 Installing only the software you want	confusing clear 1 2 3 4 5 6 7 8 9		NA
12.3 Informs you of its progress	never always 1 2 3 4 5 6 7 8 9		NA
12.4 Gives a meaningful explanation when failures occur	never always 1 2 3 4 5 6 7 8 9		NA

Please write your comments about software installation here:

_____

An acceptance test might specify the following:

The subjects will be 35 secretaries hired from an employment agency. They have no word-processing experience, but have typing skills in the range of 35 to 50 words per minute. They will be given 45 minutes of training on the basic features. At least 30 of the 35 secretaries should be able to complete, within 30 minutes, 80 percent of the typing and editing tasks in the enclosed benchmark test correctly.

Another testable requirement for the same system might be this:

After four half-days of regular use of the system, 25 of these 35 secretaries should be able to carry out, within 20 minutes, the advanced editing tasks in the second benchmark test, and should make fewer than six errors.

This second acceptance test captures performance after regular use. The choice of the benchmark tests is critical and is highly system dependent. The test materials and procedures must also be refined by pilot testing before use.
    A third item in the acceptance test plan might focus on retention:

After two weeks, at least 15 of the test subjects should be recalled and should perform the third benchmark test. In 40 minutes, at least 10 of the subjects should be able to complete 75 percent of the tasks correctly.

In a large system, there may be eight or 10 such tests to carry out on different components of the interface and with different user communities. Other criteria such as subjective satisfaction, output comprehensibility, system response time, installation procedures, printed documentation, or graphics appeal may also be considered in acceptance tests of complete commercial products.
    If they establish precise acceptance criteria, both the customer and the interface developer can benefit. Arguments about the user friendliness are avoided, and contractual fulfillment can be demonstrated objectively. Acceptance tests differ from usability tests in that the atmosphere may be adversarial, so outside testing organizations are often appropriate to ensure neutrality. The central goal of acceptance testing is not to detect flaws, but rather to verify adherence to requirements.
    Once acceptance testing has been successful, there may be a period of field testing before national or international distribution. In addition to further refining the user interface, field tests can improve training methods, tutorial materials, telephone-help procedures, marketing methods, and publicity strategies.
    The goal of early expert reviews, usability testing, surveys, acceptance testing, and field testing is to force as much as possible of the evolutionary

development into the prerelease phase, when change is relatively easy and inexpensive to accomplish.

4.6   Evaluation During Active Use

A carefully designed and thoroughly tested system is a wonderful asset, but successful active use requires constant attention from dedicated managers, user-services personnel, and maintenance staff. Everyone involved in supporting the user community can contribute to system refinements that provide ever higher levels of service. You cannot please all of the users all of the time, but earnest effort will be rewarded by the appreciation of a grateful user community. Perfection is not attainable, but percentage improvements are possible and are worth pursuing.

Gradual system dissemination is useful so that problems can be repaired with minimal disruption. As more and more people use the system, major changes should be limited to an annual or semiannual system revision that is announced adequately. If system users can anticipate the change, then resistance will be reduced, especially if they have positive expectations of improvement. More frequent changes are expected in the rapidly developing World Wide Web environment, but a balance between stable access to key resources even as novel services are added may be the winning policy.

4.6.1   Interviews and focus-group discussions

Interviews with individual users can be productive because the interviewer can pursue specific issues of concern. After a series of individual discussions, *focus-group discussions* are valuable to ascertain the universality of comments. Interviewing can be costly and time consuming, so usually only a small fraction of the user community is involved. On the other hand, direct contact with users often leads to specific, constructive suggestions.

A large corporation conducted 45-minute interviews with 66 of the 4300 users of an internal message system. The interviews revealed that the users were happy with some aspects of the functionality, such as the capacity to pick up messages at any site, the legibility of printed messages, and the convenience of after-hours access. However, the interviews also revealed that 23.6 percent of the users had concerns about reliability, 20.2 percent thought that using the system was confusing, and 18.2 percent said convenience and accessibility could be improved, whereas only 16.0 percent expressed no concerns. Later questions in the interview explored specific features. As a result of this interview project, a set of 42 enhancements to the system was proposed and implemented. The designers of the system had earlier proposed an alternate set of enhancements, but the results of the interviews led to a changed set of priorities that more closely reflected the users' needs.

4.6.2   Continuous user-performance data logging

The software architecture should make it easy for system managers to collect data about the patterns of system usage, speed of user performance, rate of errors, or frequency of requests for online assistance. Logging data provide guidance in the acquisition of new hardware, changes in operating procedures, improvements to training, plans for system expansion, and so on.

For example, if the frequency of each error message is recorded, then the highest-frequency error is a candidate for attention. The message could be rewritten, training materials could be revised, the software could be changed to provide more specific information, or the command syntax could be simplified. Without specific logging data, the system-maintenance staff has no way of knowing which of the many hundreds of error-message situations is the biggest problem for users. Similarly, staff should examine messages that never appear, to see whether there is an error in the code or whether users are avoiding use of some facility.

If logging data are available for each command, each help screen, and each database record, then changes to the human–computer interface can be made to simplify access to frequently used features. Managers also should examine unused or rarely used facilities to understand why users are avoiding those features. Logging of the Thomas system for access to U.S. Congress legislation revealed high-frequency terms, such as *abortion, gun control,* and *balanced budget* that could be used in a browse list of hot topics (Croft et al, 1995). Logging in an educational database identified frequently used as well and rarely used paths and features (Marchionini and Crane, 1994).

A major benefit of usage-frequency data is the guidance that they provide to system maintainers in optimizing performance and in reducing costs for all participants. This latter argument may yield the clearest advantage to cost-conscious managers, whereas the increased quality of the interface is an attraction to service-oriented managers.

Logging may be well intentioned, but users' rights to privacy deserve to be protected. Links to specific user names should not be collected, unless necessary. When logging aggregate performance crosses over to monitoring individual activity, managers must inform users of what is being monitored and how the information will be used. Although organizations may have a right to ascertain worker performance, workers should be able to view the results and to discuss the implications. If monitoring is surreptitious and is later discovered, resulting worker mistrust of management could be more damaging than the benefits of the collected data. Manager and worker cooperation to improve productivity, and worker participation in the process and benefits, are advised.

4.6.3   Online or telephone consultants

Online or *telephone consultants* can provide extremely effective and personal assistance to users who are experiencing difficulties. Many users feel reassured if they know that there is a human being to whom they can turn when problems arise. These consultants are an excellent source of information about problems users are having and can suggest improvements and potential extensions.

Many organizations offer a toll-free number via which the users can reach a knowledgeable consultant; others charge for consultation by the minute. On some network systems, the consultants can monitor the user's computer and see the same displays that the user sees while maintaining telephone voice contact. This service can be extremely reassuring: Users know that someone can walk them through the correct sequence of screens to complete their tasks.

America Online provides live (real-time) chat rooms for discussion of user problems. Users can type their questions and get responses promptly. Many groups maintain a standard electronic-mail address of staff@<organization> that allows users to get help from whomever is on duty. My several successful experiences of getting quick help late at night from our departmental staff have remained firmly in my memory. On one occasion, they helped me to unpack a file in an unfamiliar format; on another, they recovered an inadvertently deleted file.

4.6.4   Online suggestion box or trouble reporting

Electronic mail can be employed to allow users to send messages to the maintainers or designers. Such an *online suggestion box* encourages some users to make productive comments, since writing a letter may be seen as requiring too much effort.

A Library of Congress website that invites comments gets 10 to 20 per day, including thoughtful ones such as this:

> I find as I get searching through the various Web pages . . . that I am left with an unsatisfied feeling. I have been sitting in front of the PC for close to an hour . . . and have been stopped and/or slowed due to items that can be directly related to web server design.
>
> First off, the entry pages are too big and disorganized. Those links that do exist do not have adequate enough descriptions to direct a user to the information they desire. In addition, the use of a search engine would greatly facilitate sifting through the abundance of information that is thrown at the user with any one of these links. Links should be short, sweet, and specific. Large amounts of material should not be included in one document on a busy server. . . .

> Breaking up these larger documents into smaller, well organized documents may seem to create an additional burden on programming. However, if intelligence is used in the creation of such systems, it would not take much . . .

In fact, the search engine that this user wanted was available, but he could not find it, and larger documents were broken into smaller segments. A reply helped to get this user what he was seeking, and his message also led to design changes that made the interface features more visible.

An internet directory service for personal names, Knowbot Information Service, offers a `gripe` command with the invitation "Place a compliment or complaint in the KIS log file." Another service simply has a button labeled "Tell us what you think."

A large corporation installed a full-screen, fill-in-the-blanks form for user problem reports, and received 90 comments on a new internal system within three months. The user's identification number and name were entered automatically, and the user moved a cursor to indicate which subsystem was causing a problem and what the problem's seriousness was (showstopper, annoyance, improvement, other). Each problem report received a dated and signed response that was stored on a file for public reading.

4.6.5   Online bulletin board or newsgroup

Some users may have a question about the suitability of a software package for their application, or may be seeking someone who has had experience using an interface feature. They do not have any individual in mind, so electronic mail does not serve their needs. Many interface designers offer users an *electronic bulletin board* or *newsgroup* (see Section 14.3) to permit posting of open messages and questions. These newsgroups cover programming languages, software tools, or task domains. There are also mailing lists for interface designers, such as the one established on the internet by the Human Factors and Ergonomics Society's Computer Systems Technical Group (send electronic mail to list-serv@listserv.vt.edu with this line: `subscribe cstg-L <your full name>`)

Some professional societies offer bulletin boards by way of networks such as America Online, Prodigy, and CompuServe. These bulletin boards may offer information services or permit downloading of software.

Bulletin-board software systems usually offer a list of item headlines, allowing users the opportunity to select items for display. New items can be added by anyone, but usually someone monitors the bulletin board to ensure that offensive, useless, or repetitious items are removed.

4.6.6   User newsletters and conferences

When there is a substantial number of users who are geographically dispersed, managers may have to work harder to create a sense of community. *Newsletters* that provide information about novel interface facilities, suggestions for improved productivity, requests for assistance, case studies of successful applications, or stories about individual users can promote user satisfaction and knowledge. Printed newsletters are more traditional and have the advantage that they can be carried away from the workstation. A printed newsletter has an appealing air of respectability. Online newsletters are less expensive and more rapidly disseminated. World Wide Web or CD-ROM newsletters are appealing if collections of images are included or large datasets are anticipated.

Personal relationships established by face-to-face meetings also increase the sense of community among users. *Conferences* allow workers to exchange experiences with colleagues, promote novel approaches, stimulate greater dedication, encourage higher productivity, and develop a deeper relationship of trust. Ultimately, it is the people who matter in an organization, and human needs for social interaction should be satisfied. Every technical system is also a social system that needs to be encouraged and nurtured.

By soliciting user feedback in any of these ways, managers can gauge user attitudes and elicit useful suggestions. Furthermore, users may have more positive attitudes toward the interface if they see that the managers genuinely desire comments and suggestions.

4.7   Controlled Psychologically Oriented Experiments

Scientific and engineering progress is often stimulated by improved techniques for precise measurement. Rapid progress in the designs of interfaces will be stimulated as researchers and practitioners evolve suitable human-performance measures and techniques. We have come to expect that automobiles will have miles-per-gallon reports pasted to the window, appliances will have energy-efficiency ratings, and textbooks will be given grade-level designations; soon, we will expect software packages to show learning-time estimates and user-satisfaction indices from appropriate evaluation sources.

Academic and industrial researchers are discovering that the power of the traditional scientific method can be fruitfully employed in the study of interfaces (Barnard, 1991). They are conducting numerous experiments that are uncovering basic design principles. The outline of the scientific method as applied to human–computer interaction might include these tasks:

- Deal with a practical problem and consider the theoretical framework.
- State a lucid and testable hypothesis.
- Identify a small number of independent variables that are to be manipulated.
- Carefully choose the dependent variables that will be measured.

- Judiciously select subjects, and carefully or randomly assign subjects to groups.
- Control for biasing factors (nonrepresentative sample of subjects or selection of tasks, inconsistent testing procedures).
- Apply statistical methods to data analysis.

- Resolve the practical problem, refine the theory, and give advice to future researchers.

The classic experimental methods of psychology are being enhanced to deal with the complex cognitive tasks of human performance with information and computer systems. The transformation from Aristotelian introspection to Galilean experimentation that took two millennia in physics is being accomplished in two decades in the study of human–computer interaction.

The reductionist approach required for controlled experimentation yields narrow but reliable results. Through multiple replications with similar tasks, subjects, and experimental conditions, reliability and validity can be enhanced. Each small experimental result acts like a tile in the mosaic of human performance with computer-based information systems.

Managers of actively used systems are also coming to recognize the power of controlled experiments in fine tuning the human–computer interface. As proposals are made for new menu structures, novel cursor-control devices, and reorganized display formats, a carefully controlled experiment can provide data to support a management decision. Fractions of the user population could be given proposed improvements for a limited time, and then performance could be compared with the control group. Dependent measures could include performance times, user-subjective satisfaction, error rates, and user retention over time.

Experimental design and statistical analysis are complex topics (Hays, 1988; Cozby, 1996; Runyon and Haber, 1996; Winer et al., 1991.) Novice experimenters would be well advised to collaborate with experienced social scientists and statisticians.

4.8   Practitioner's Summary

Interface developers evaluate their designs by conducting expert reviews, usability tests, surveys, and rigorous acceptance tests. Once systems are released, developers perform continuous performance evaluations by interviews or surveys, and by logging user performance in a way that respects the privacy of users. If you are not measuring, you are not doing human factors!

Successful system managers understand that they must work hard to establish a relationship of trust with the user community. In addition to providing a properly functioning system, computer service managers and information-systems directors recognize the need to create social mechanisms for feedback, such as online surveys, interviews, discussions, consultants, suggestion boxes, bulletin boards, newsletters, and conferences.

4.9   Researcher's Agenda

Researchers can contribute their experience with experimentation to developing techniques for system evaluation. Guidance in conducting pilot studies, acceptance tests, surveys, interviews, and discussions would benefit commercial development groups. Experts in constructing psychological tests would be extremely helpful in preparing a validated and reliable test instrument for subjective evaluation of interactive systems. Such a standardized test would allow independent groups to compare the acceptability of their systems. In addition, assessment methods for user skill levels with software would be helpful in job-placement and training programs.

Clinical psychologists, psychotherapists, and social workers could contribute to training online or as telephone consultants—after all, helping troubled users is a human-relationship issue. Finally, more input from experimental, cognitive, and clinical psychologists would help computer specialists to recognize the importance of the human aspects of computer use. What techniques can reduce novice user anxiety? How can life-critical applications for experienced professionals be tested reliably?

World Wide Web Resources | WWW |

Prototyping and usability testing methods are covered with some information on evaluation methods, such as surveys. The full text of our QUIS is available online.

http://www.aw.com/DTUI

References

Barnard, Phil, The contributions of applied cognitive psychology to the study of human–computer interaction. In Shackel, B. and Richardson, S. (Editors), *Human Factors for Informatics Usability*, Cambridge University Press, Cambridge, U.K. (1991), 151–182.

Chin, John P., Diehl, Virginia A., and Norman, Kent L., Development of an instrument measuring user satisfaction of the human–computer interface, *Proc. CHI '88—Human Factors in Computing Systems*, ACM, New York (1988), 213–218.

Coleman, William D. and Williges, Robert C., Collecting detailed user evaluations of software interfaces, *Proc. Human Factors Society—Twenty-Ninth Annual Meeting*, Santa Monica, CA (1985), 204–244.

Cozby, Paul C., *Methods in Behavioral Research* (Sixth Edition), Mayfield, Mountain View, CA (1996).

Croft, W. Bruce, Cook, Robert, and Wilder, Dean, Providing government information on the internet: Experiences with THOMAS, *Proc. Digital Libraries '95 Conference*, ACM, New York (1995). Also available at http://www.csdl.tamu.edu/DL95/papers/croft/croft.html

Curtis, Bill, Defining a place for interface engineering, *IEEE Software*, 9, 2 (March 1992), 84–86.

Dumas, Joseph and Redish, Janice, *A Practical Guide to Usability Testing*, Ablex, Norwood, NJ (1993).

Gould, John, How to design usable systems. In Helander, Martin (Editor), *Handbook of Human–Computer Interaction*, North-Holland, Amsterdam, The Netherlands (1988), 757–789.

Gould, John D., Boies, Stephen J., and Lewis, Clayton, Making usable, useful productivity-enhancing computer applications, *Communications of the ACM*, 34, 1 (January 1991), 75–85.

Harrison, Beverly L., Video annotation and multimedia interfaces: From theory to practice, *Proc. Human Factors Society Thirty-Fifth Annual Meeting* (1991), 319–322.

Hays, William L., *Statistics* (Fourth Edition), Holt, Rinehart and Winston, New York (1988).

Hix, Deborah and Hartson, H. Rex, *Developing User Interfaces: Ensuring Usability Through Product and Process*, John Wiley and Sons, New York (1993).

Jeffries, R., Miller, J. R., Wharton, C., and Uyeda, K. M., User interface evaluation in the real world: A comparison of four techniques, *Proc. ACM CHI91 Conf.* (1991), 119–124.

Karat, Claire-Marie, A business case approach to usability. In Bias, Randolph, and Mayhew, Deborah (Editors), *Cost-Justifying Usability*, Academic Press, New York (1994), 45–70.

Karat, Claire-Marie, Campbell, Robert, and Fiegel, T., Comparison of empirical testing and walkthrough methods in user interface evaluation, *Proc. CHI '92—Human Factors in Computing Systems*, ACM, New York (1992), 397–404.

Kirakowski, J. and Corbett, M. SUMI: The Software Usability Measurement Inventory, *British Journal of Educational Technology*, 24, 3 (1993), 210–212.

Landauer, Thomas K., *The Trouble with Computers: Usefulness, Usability, and Productivity*, MIT Press, Cambridge, MA (1995).

Lewis, James R., IBM computer usability satisfaction questionnaires: Psychometric evaluation and instructions for use, *International Journal of Human–Computer Interaction*, 7, 1 (1995), 57–78.

Lund, Michelle A., Evaluating the user interfaces: The candid camera approach, *Proc. CHI '85—Human Factors in Computing Systems*, ACM, New York (1985), 93–97.

Marchionini, Gary and Crane, Gregory, Evaluating hypermedia and learning: Methods and results from the Perseus Project, *ACM Transactions on Information Systems*, 12, 1 (1994), 5–34.

Newman, William M. and Lamming, Michael G., *Interactive System Design*, Addison-Wesley, Reading, MA (1995).

Nielsen, Jakob (Editor), Special Issue on Usability Laboratories, *Behaviour & Information Technology*, 13, 1 & 2 (January–April 1994).

Nielsen, Jakob, *Usability Engineering*, Academic Press, New York (1993).

Nielsen, Jakob and Mack, Robert (Editors), *Usability Inspection Methods*, John Wiley and Sons, New York (1994).

Oppenheim, Abraham N., *Questionnaire Design, Interviewing, and Attitude Measurement*, Pinter Publishers, New York (1992).

Preece, Jenny, Rogers, Yvonne, Sharp, Helen, Benyon, David, Holland, Simon, and Carey, Tom, *Human–Computer Interaction*, Addison-Wesley, Reading, MA (1994).

Runyon, Richard P. and Haber, Audrey, *Fundamentals of Behavioral Statistics* (Eighth Edition), McGraw-Hill, New York (1996).

Wharton, Cathleen, Rieman, John, Lewis, Clayton, and Polson, Peter, The cognitive walkthrough method: A practitioner's guide. In Nielsen, Jakob and Mack, Robert (Editors), *Usability Inspection Methods*, John Wiley and Sons, New York (1994).

Winer, B. J., Brown, Donald R., and Michels, Kenneth M., *Statistical Principles in Experimental Design*, McGraw-Hill, New York (1991).

Yourdon, Edward, *Structured Walkthroughs* (Fourth Edition), Yourdon Press, Englewood Cliffs, NJ (1989).

Mark Kostabi, *Automatic Painting*, 1991

5

Software Tools

There is great satisfaction in building good tools for other people to use.

Freeman Dyson, *Disturbing the Universe,* **1979**

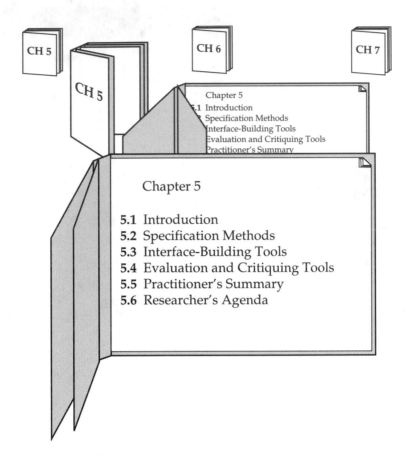

CH 5

CH 6

CH 7

CH 5

Chapter 5

5.1 Introduction

Log cabins were often built by settlers for personal housing on the American frontier, just as early user interfaces were built by programmers for their own use. As housing needs changed, windows and rooms were added in a process of iterative refinement, and dirt floors gave way to finished wood. Log cabins are still being built according to personal taste by rugged individualists, but modern private homes, apartment buildings, schools, hospitals, and offices require specialist training, careful planning, and special equipment.

The emergence of user-interface architects, design and specification methods, standard components, and automated tools for construction are indicators of the maturation of our field. There will always be room for the innovator and the eccentric, but the demands of modern life require user-interface architects to build reliable, standard, safe, inexpensive, effective, and widely acceptable user interfaces on a predictable schedule (Carey, 1988).

Building and user-interface architects must have simple and quick methods of sketching to give their clients a way to identify needs and preferences. Then, they need precise methods for working out the details with the clients (detailed floorplans become transition diagrams, screen layouts, and menu trees), for coordinating with specialized colleagues (plumbers and electricians become graphic designers and technical writers), and for telling the builders (or software engineers) what to do.

Like building architects, successful user-interface architects know that it makes good sense to complete the design before they start building, even though they know that, in the process of construction, some changes will have to be made. With large projects, multiple designers (structural engineers for the steel framework, interior designers for space planning, and decorators for the esthetics) will be necessary. The size and importance of each project will determine the level of design effort and the number of participants. Just as there are specialists for airports, hospitals, and schools, there are user-interfaces specialists for air-traffic–control, medical, and educational applications.

This chapter begins with user-interface specification methods, moves to software tools to support design and software engineering, and then closes with evaluation and critiquing tools. These tools are increasingly graphical in their user interfaces, enabling designers and programmers to build interfaces rapidly by dragging components and linking functions together. User-interface building tools have matured rapidly in the past few years, and have radically changed the nature of software development. Productivity gains of 50 to 500 percent above previous methods have been documented for many standard GUIs. But, even as the power tools for established styles improve and gain acceptance, programmers will always have to handcraft novel interface styles.

5.2 Specification Methods

The first asset in making designs is a good notation to record and discuss alternate possibilities. The default language for specifications in any field is the designer's natural language, such as English, and a sketchpad or blackboard. But *natural-language specifications* tend to be lengthy, vague, and ambiguous, and therefore often are difficult to prove correct, consistent, or complete. *Formal* and *semiformal languages* have proved their value in many areas, including mathematics, physics, circuit design, music, and even knitting. Formal languages have a specified grammar, and effective procedures exist to determine whether a string adheres to the language's grammar.

Grammars for command languages are effective, but for GUIs the amount of syntax is small. In GUIs, a grammar might be used to describe sequences of actions, but these grammars tend to be short, making transition diagrams and graphical specifications more appealing.

Menu-tree structures are popular, and therefore specifying menu trees by simply drawing the tree and showing the menu layouts deserves attention. The more general method of *transition diagrams* has wide applicability in user-interface design. Improvements such as *statecharts* have features that are attuned to the needs of interactive systems and for widget specification. New approaches such as the *user action notation* (UAN) (Hartson et al., 1990; Chase et al., 1994) are helpful in characterizing user behavior and some aspects of system responses.

5.2.1   Grammars

In computer programming, *Backus–Naur form* (BNF) also called (*Backus normal form*) is often used to describe programming languages. High-level components are described by nonterminals, and specific strings are terminals. Let us use the example of a telephone-book entry. The nonterminals describe a person's name (composed of a last name followed by a comma and a first name) and a telephone number (composed of an area code, exchange, and local number). Names consist of strings of characters. The telephone number has three components: a three-digit area code, a three-digit exchange, and a four-digit local number.

```
<Telephone book entry> ::= <Name> <Telephone number>
<Name> ::= <Last name>, <First name>
<Last name> ::= <string>
<First name> ::= <string>
<string> ::= <character>|<character><string>
<character> ::=
    A|B|C|D|E|F|G|H|I|J|K|L|M|N|O|P|Q|R|S|T|U|V|W|X|Y|Z
<Telephone number> ::= (<area code>) <exchange>-<local number>
<area code> ::= <digit><digit><digit>
<exchange> ::= <digit><digit><digit>
<local number> ::= <digit><digit><digit><digit>
<digit> ::= 0|1|2|3|4|5|6|7|8|9
```

The left-hand side of each specification line is a nonterminal (within angle brackets) that is defined by the right-hand side. Vertical bars indicate alternatives for nonterminals and terminals. Acceptable-telephone-book entries include the following:

```
WASHINGTON, GEORGE (301) 555-1234
BEEF, STU (726) 768-7878
A, Z (999) 111-1111
```

BNF notation is used widely, even though it is incomplete and must be supplemented by ad hoc techniques for specifying the semantics, such as permissible names or area codes. The benefits are that some aspects can be written down precisely, and that software tools can be employed to verify some aspects of completeness and correctness of the grammar and of strings in the language. On the other hand, grammars are difficult to follow as they grow and are confusing for many users.

Command languages are nicely specified by BNF-like grammars, such as the task–action grammar (Section 2.2.4). Reisner (1981) expanded the idea of BNF to sequences of actions, such as pushing a button, selecting a color, or drawing a shape.

Variant forms of BNF have been created to accommodate specific situations. For example, the Unix command for copying files or directories is summarized by this extract from the online manual:

```
cp [ -ip ] filename1 filename2
cp -rR [ -ip ] directory1 directory2
cp [ -iprR ] filename ... directory
```

where the square brackets indicate that zero or more options can be included, and the −rR indicates that one of these options for recursive copying is required for copying directories.

To accommodate the richness of interactive software, *multiparty grammars* (Shneiderman, 1982) have nonterminals that are labeled by the party that produces the string (typically the user, U, or the computer, C). Nonterminals acquire values during parsing for use by other parties, and therefore error-handling rules can be included easily. This grammar describes the opening steps in a login process:

```
<Session> ::= <U: Opening> <C: Responding>
<U: Opening> ::= LOGIN <U: Name>
<U: Name> ::= <U: string>
<C: Responding> ::= HELLO [<U: Name>]
```

Here, square brackets indicate that the value of the user's name should be produced by the computer in responding to the login command.

Multiparty grammars are effective for text-oriented command sequences that have repeated exchanges, such as a bank terminal. Unfortunately, two-dimensional styles, such as form fillin or direct manipulation and graphical layouts, are more difficult to describe with multiparty grammars. Menu selection can be described by multiparty grammars, but the central aspect of tree structure and traversal is not shown conveniently in a grammar-based approach.

5.2.2   Menu-selection and dialog-box trees

For many applications a *menu-selection tree* is an excellent selection style because of the simple structure that guides designers and users alike. Guidelines for the contents of the menu trees are covered in Chapter 7. Specification methods include online tools to help in the construction of menu trees and simple drawing tools that enable designers and users to see the entire tree at one time.

Menu trees are powerful as a specification tool since they show users, managers, implementers, and other interested parties the complete and detailed coverage of the system. Like any map, a menu tree shows high-level relationships and low-level details. With large systems, the menu tree may have to be laid out on a large wall or floor, but it is important to be able to see the entire structure at once to check for consistency, completeness, and lack of ambiguity or redundancy.

Similar comments apply for dialog boxes. Printing out the dialog boxes and showing their relationships by mounting them on a wall is enormously helpful in gaining an overview of the entire system to check for consistency and completeness.

5.2.3   Transition diagrams

Menu trees are incomplete because they do not show the entire structure of possible user actions, such as returns to the previous menu, jumps to the starting menu, or detours to error handling or to help screens. However, adding all these transitions would clutter the clean structure of a menu tree. For some aspects of the design process, more precise specification of every possible transition is required. Also, for many nonmenu interaction styles, there is a set of possible states and permissible transitions among the states that may not form a tree structure. For these and other circumstances, a more general design notation known as *transition diagrams* has been used widely.

Typically, a transition diagram has a set of *nodes* that represents system states and a set of *links* between the nodes that represents possible transitions. Each link is labeled with the user action that selects that link and possible computer responses. The simple transition diagram in Fig. 5.1 (Wasserman and Shewmake, 1985) represents a numbered menu-selection system for restaurant reviews that shows what happens when the user selects numbered choices: 1 (add a restaurant to the list), 2 (provide a review of a restaurant), 3 (read a review), 4 (get help, also accessed by a ?), 5 (quit), or any other character (error message). Figure 5.2 shows its text form. Figure 5.3 shows another form of transition diagram that displays frequencies along the links.

Many forms of transition diagrams have been created with special notations to fit needs of application areas, such as air-traffic control or word pro-

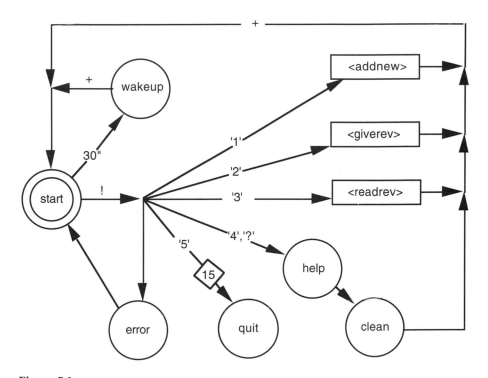

Figure 5.1

Transition diagram for a simple menu system. (Wasserman and Shewmake, 1985.)

cessing. Tools for creating and maintaining transition diagrams, dataflow diagrams, and other graphical displays are part of most *computer-assisted software engineering (CASE)* environments, such as the Software Through Pictures (Interactive Development Environments, Inc., http://www.ide.com). In most systems, the diagram is created by direct-manipulation actions, but designers can get a textual output of the transition diagram as well.

Unfortunately, transition diagrams get unwieldy as system complexity grows, and too many transitions can lead to complex spaghetti-like displays. Improvements are to replace a state transition node with a screen print to give readers a better sense of movement through the displays and dialog boxes. Such overviews are helpful in design and in training.

Designs for interfaces with hundreds of dialog boxes, or for websites with hundreds of screens, are easier to study when hung on the wall. In a memorable encounter, 350 screens of a satellite-control system were pasted on three walls of a conference room, quickly revealing the disparate styles of the design teams of the six modules. Compressed overview diagrams may be squeezed onto a single sheet of paper for user manuals, or printed as a poster to hang on users' walls.

```
node start
        cs, r2, rv, c_' Interactive Restaurant Guide', sv,
        r6, c5,  'Please make a choice:  ',
        r+2, c10,  '1:  Add new restaurant to database',
        r+2, c10,  '2:  Give review of a restaurant  ',
        r+2, c10,  '3:  Read reviews for a given restaurant',
        r+2, c10,  '4:  Help', r+2, c10,  '5:  Quit',  r+3,c5,  'Your choice:  ',   mark_A

node help
        cs, r5, c0,  'This program stores and retrieves information on',
        r+1,  c0, 'restaurants,  with emphasis on San Francisco.',
        r+1,  c0,  'You can add or update information about restaurants',
        r+1,  c0,  'already in the database,  or obtain information about',
        r+1,  c0,  'restaurants,  including the reviews of others.',
        r+2,  c0,  'To continue, type RETURN.'

node error
        r$-1, rv, 'Illegal command.',  sv,  'Please type a number from 1 to 5.',
        r$,  'Press RETURN to continue.'
node clean
        r$-1, cl,r$,cl
node wakeup
        r$,cl,rv,'Please make a choice',sv,   tomark_A
node quit
        cs,  'Thank you very much.  Please try this program again',
        nl,'and continue to add information on restaurants.'
arc start single_key
        on  '1'   to   <addnew>
        on  '2'   to   <giverev>
        on  '3'   to   <readrev>
        on  '4',   '?'  to  help
        on  '5'   to  quit
        alarm 30 to wakeup
        else to error
arc error
        else to start
arc help
        skip to clean
arc clean
        else to start
arc <addnew>
        skip to start
arc <readrev>
        skip to start
arc <giverev>
        skip to start
```

Figure 5.2

Text form of Fig. 5.1. Additional information is provided by the comment lines.

5.2.4   Statecharts

Although transition diagrams are effective for following flow or action and for keeping track of the current state plus current options, they can rapidly become large and confusing. Modularity is possible if nodes are included with subgraphs, but this strategy works well with only orderly, one-in, one-out graphs. Transition diagrams also become confusing when each node must show links to a help state, jumps back to the previous or start state, and a quit

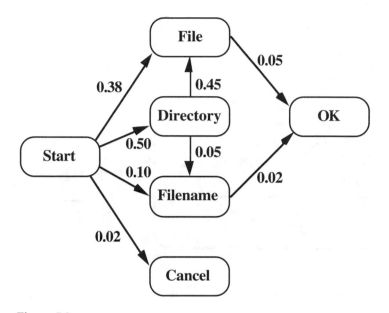

Figure 5.3

Sample transition diagram for file-manipulation actions. Link labels indicate how frequently each transition is made.

state. Concurrency and synchronization are poorly represented by transition diagrams, although some variations such as petri-nets can help. An appealing alternative is *statecharts* (Harel, 1988), which have several virtues in specifying interfaces. Because a grouping feature is offered through nested round-tangles (Fig. 5.4), repeated transitions can be factored out to the surrounding roundtangle. Extensions to statecharts—such as concurrency, external interrupt events, and user actions—are represented in Statemaster, which is a user-interface tool based on statecharts (Wellner, 1989).

Statecharts can also be extended with dataflow and constraint specification, plus embedded screen prints to show the visual states of graphical widgets (Carr, 1994). For example, in the simple case of a secure toggle switch, there are five states, so showing the visual feedback on the statechart with user-action notation (see Section 5.2.5) on the arcs helps readers to understand what is happening (Fig. 5.5).

5.2.5   User-action notation (UAN)

The grammar or diagram approaches to specification are suited for menus, commands, or form fillin, but they are clumsy with direct-manipulation interfaces, because they cannot cope conveniently with the variety of permissible

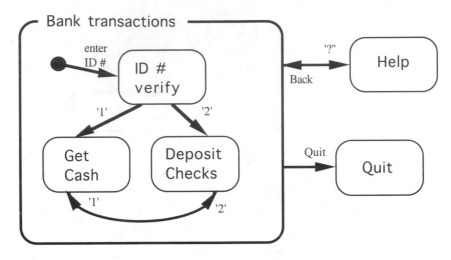

Figure 5.4

Statechart of a simplified bank transaction system showing grouping of states.

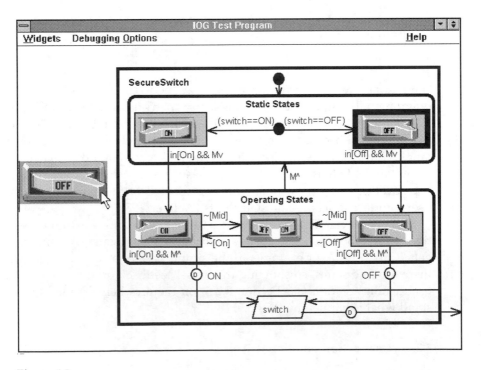

Figure 5.5

Interaction-object graphs extend statecharts with dataflow features and the user-action notation. This example shows a secure switch with bitmaps of the states at each node. (Carr, 1994)

actions and visual feedback that the system provides. In addition, direct-manipulation interfaces depend heavily on context to determine the meaning of an input. For example, a mouse-button click can mean select a file, open a window, or start an application, depending on where the cursor is when the click is applied. Similarly, it is difficult to characterize the results of dragging an icon, since they will depend on where the icon is dropped.

To cope with the rich world of direct-manipulation interfaces, high-level notations that focus on the users' tasks, that deal with pointing, dragging, and clicking, and that describe the interface feedback are more likely to be helpful. For example, to select an icon, the user must move the cursor to the icon location and click and release on the mouse button. The movement to an icon is represented by a ~[icon] and the mouse-button motion is represented by Mv (mouse-button depress) followed by M^ (mouse-button release). The system response, which is to highlight the icon, is represented by icon! The sequencing is shown by a complete *user-action notation (UAN)* description (Hartson et al., 1990; Hix and Hartson, 1993):

TASK: Select an icon

User Actions	Interface Feedback
~[icon] Mv	icon!
M^	

A more complex task might be to delete a file; that task requires user actions of dragging a file icon around the display to a trash icon while holding down the mouse button. The interface feedback is to highlight the file that is selected and to dehighlight (file-! indicates dehighlight the file) other files, then to drag an outline of the file icon to the trash icon (outline(file) > ~ means that the outline is dragged by the cursor). Then, the user drops the file-icon outline on the trash icon, the file icon is erased, and the trash icon blinks. The selected file is shown in the interface-state column:

TASK: Select an icon

User Actions	Interface Feedback	Interface State
~[file] Mv	file!, forall(file!): file-!	selected = file
~[x,y]*	outline(file) > ~	
~[trash]	outline(file) > ~, trash!	
M^	erase(file), trash!!	selected = null

The UAN has interface-specific symbols for actions (such as moving the cursor, pressing a button, entering a string, or setting a value), and for concurrency, interrupts, and feedback (such as highlighting, blinking, dragging, rubberbanding, and erasing). The symbols were chosen to mimic the actions—such as v for button depress, ^ for button release, and ~ for cursor movement—but it still takes time to get used to this novel notation. Also, UAN does not conveniently specify rich graphics, such as drawing programs or animations, relationships across tasks, and interrupt behavior. Nonetheless, UAN is a compact, powerful, and high-level approach to specifying system behavior and describing user actions (Chase et al., 1994).

5.3   Interface-Building Tools

Specification methods are important for the design of components of a system such as command languages, data-entry sequences, and widgets. Screen-transition diagrams drawn or printed on paper are an excellent means to provide an overview of the system. They allow user-interface architects, designers, managers, users, and software engineers to sit around a table, discuss the design, and prepare for the big job that lies ahead. Paper-based designs are a great way to start, but the detailed specification of complete user interfaces requires software tools.

The good news is that there has been a rapid and remarkable proliferation of software tools to accommodate most designers and software engineers in accomplishing many design goals. These tools come in colorful shrink-wrapped boxes that emphasize convenient and rapid building of onscreen prototypes. They generally allow visual editing, so designers can immediately assess the "look" of the system and can easily change color, fonts, and layout. These direct-manipulation design tools have enabled large numbers of task-domain experts who have only modest technical training to become user-interface designers.

Other tools are powerful programming languages that include extensive toolkits that enable experienced software engineers to build a richer variety of features, but that often require twice or 20 times as much code and work. Of course, there will always be special designs that require programming in languages, such as C or C++, or even in assembly language to deal with precise timing or special hardware features.

The terminology for products varies depending on the vendor. Popular terms include Rapid Prototyper, User Interface Builder, User Interface Management System, User Interface Development Environment, Rapid Application Developer. A key distinction is how extensively the system uses convenient visual programming, a relatively simple scripting language (event or object oriented), or a more powerful general-purpose programming language.

Use of these software tools brings great benefits (Box 5.1), and is spreading widely, even as the tools are rapidly improved in successive versions.

Box 5.1

Features of user-interface–building tools.

User-interface independence

- Separate interface design from internals
- Enable multiple user-interface strategies
- Enable multiple-platform support
- Establish role of user-interface architect
- Enforce standards

Methodology and notation

- Develop design procedures
- Find ways to talk about design
- Create project management

Rapid prototyping

- Try out ideas very early
- Test, revise, test, revise, . . .
- Engage end users, managers, and customers

Software support

- Increase productivity
- Offer constraint and consistency checks
- Facilitate team approaches
- Ease maintenance

The central advantage stems from the notion of *user-interface independence*— decoupling of the user-interface design from the complexities of programming. This decoupling allows the designers to lay out sequences of displays in just a few hours, to make revisions in minutes, and to support the expert-review and usability-testing processes. The programming needed to complete the underlying system can be applied once the user-interface design has been stabilized. The user-interface prototypes can serve as specifications from which writers create user manuals, and from which software engineers build the system using other tools. The latter are required to produce a system that works just like the prototype. In fact, prototypes can be the specification in government or commercial contracts for novel software.

Some early tools were limited to doing prototyping only, but most modern tools allow for quick prototyping and then system development. The design tools enable construction of complete systems but they may run slowly, limit the database size, or restrict users in many ways. The software-engineering tools allow construction of more robust systems, but the complexity, cost, and development time are usually greater.

An important consideration in choosing tools is whether they support cross-platform development, a strategy in which the interface can run on multiple environments such as Windows or Unix. There is a great benefit if only one program needs to be written and maintained, but the product is available on multiple platforms.

Another important consideration is whether the application allows the user interface to run under a web browser such as Netscape Navigator or Microsoft Internet Explorer. Since these browsers are written for multiple platforms, the cross-platform goal is automatically met. The World Wide Web is such a powerful force that web-oriented tools are likely to have the brightest future.

5.3.1   Design tools

User-interface architects recognize that creating quick sketches is important during the early stages of design to explore multiple alternatives, to allow communication within the design team, and to convey to clients what the product will look like. User-interface mockups can be created with paper and pencil, word processors, or slide-show presentation software (Adobe Persuasion or Microsoft PowerPoint). Resourceful designers have also built user-interface prototypes with computer-assisted–instruction software, such as Authorware, IconAuthor, or Quest, and with multimedia construction tools, such as Apple Hypercard, MacroMind Director, or Asymetrix Toolbook.

In the simplest case, designers create a slide show of still images, which are switched at a user-controlled pace. Most tools support more complete prototyping that allows users to select from menus, click on buttons, use scrolling lists, and even drag icons. Users can navigate through screens and go back to previous screens. The prototype may not have a full database, help, or other facilities, but it offers a carefully chosen path that gives a realistic presentation of what the interface will do.

Visual editing tools usually permit designers to lay out displays with cursor movements or mouse clicks, and to mark regions for selection, highlighting, or data entry. Then, designers can specify which button selection is linked to a related display or dialog box. Prototypes are excellent aids to design discussions and are effective in winning contracts, because clients can be given a rough idea of what the finished system will be like.

The early success Apple's HyperCard stimulated many competitors. These systems combine visual editing—by allowing designers to include buttons and other fields—with simple interface actions provided automatically (for example, clicking on a back-arrow would take the user to the previous card). For more complex actions, the innovative HyperTalk scripting language enables many users to create useful interfaces with only moderate training. Designers can write programs with easy-to-understand terms:

```
on mouseUp
    play "boing"
    wait for 3 seconds
    visual effect wipe left very fast to black
    click at 150,100
    type "goodbye"
end mouseUp
```

Of course, programming in such languages can become complex as the number of short code segments grows and their interrelationships become difficult to fathom.

Visual programming tools with direct manipulation, such as Prograph (Pictorius Systems), are an intriguing alternative. Prograph allows users to edit, execute, debug, and make changes during execution, with flowchart-like visual-programming tools that emphasize dataflow and have a deeply nested modular structure (Fig. 5.6). Visual programming for laboratory instruments was the motivating influence for LabVIEW (National Instruments) (Fig. 5.7), which has a flat structure of function boxes (arithmetic, Boolean, and more) linked with wires (Green and Petre, 1996).

Contemporary visual development tools such as Microsoft Visual Basic (Fig. 5.8), Borland Delphi (Fig. 5.9), and Symantec Cafe (Fig. 5.10) have easy-to-use design tools for dragging buttons, labels, data-entry fields, combo boxes, and more onto a workspace to assemble the visual interface. Then, users write code in a scripting language that is an extension of Basic, object-oriented Pascal, or Java to implement the actions. The visual editors in these products reduce design time for user interfaces dramatically, if designers are content to use the supplied widgets, such as labels, data-entry boxes, scroll bars, scrolling lists, or text-entry areas. Adding new widgets takes programming skill, but there are large libraries of widgets for sale. Delphi's compiled Pascal code runs faster than the interpreted Basic, and Delphi also provides good support for database access, but newer versions of each product are likely to challenge each other.

5.3.2 Software-engineering tools

Experienced programmers often build user interfaces with general-purpose programming languages such as C or C++, but this approach is giving way to using facilities that are especially tuned to user-interface development and web access (Olsen, 1991; Myers, 1995).

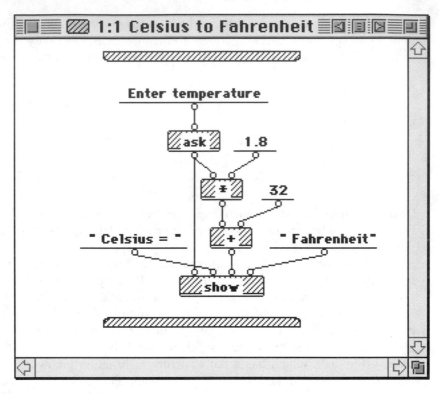

Figure 5.6

Prograph CPX, a visual language that uses object-oriented programming techniques, including inheritance, encapsulation, and polymorphism. This simple example shows a common programming problem. (Used with permission of Pictorius Inc., Halifax, Nova Scotia, Canada.)

Some products provide user-interface program libraries, often called *toolkits*, that offer common widgets, such as windows, scroll bars, pull-down or pop-up menus, data-entry fields, buttons, and dialog boxes. Programming languages with accompanying libraries are familiar to experienced programmers and afford great flexibility. However, toolkits can become complex, and the programming environments for those, such as Microsoft Windows Developer's Toolkit, Apple Macintosh MacApp, and Unix X-Windows toolkit (Xtk), require months of learning for programmers to gain proficiency. Even then, the burden in creating applications is great, and maintenance is difficult. The advantage is that the programmer has extensive control and great flexibility in creating the interface. Toolkits have become popular with programmers, but they provide only partial support for consis-

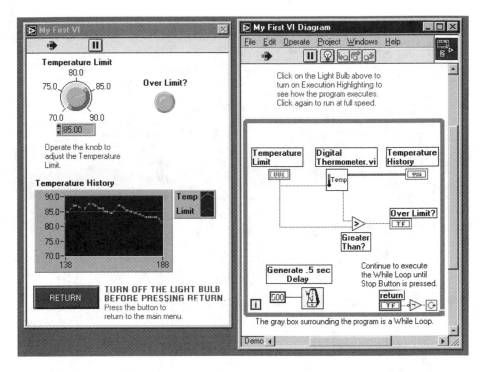

Figure 5.7

LabVIEW enables users to develop virtual instruments in a visual-programming environment. In this simple demo program, the virtual instrument on the left is controlled by the program on the right, which can show an animation of its execution. (Reprinted with permission of copyright owner, National Instruments Corporation (Austin,TX). LabVIEW is a registered trademark of National Instruments.)

tency, and designers and managers must still depend heavily on experienced programmers. The Motif example in Fig. 5.11 conveys the challenge of programming user interfaces in X.

To lighten the burden of programming, Ousterhout developed a simpler scripting language called Tcl and an accompanying toolkit called Tk (Ousterhout, 1994). Their great success was due to the relative ease of use of Tcl and the useful widgets in Tk, such as the text and canvas. Tcl is interpreted, so development is rapid, and its cross-platform capabilities are further attractions. The absence of a visual editor discourages some users, but Tcl's convenience in gluing together components has overcome the objections of most critics. This sample menu-construction program illustrates Tcl scripting (Martland, 1994, http://http2.brunel.ac.uk:8080/~csstddm/TCL2/TCL2.html):

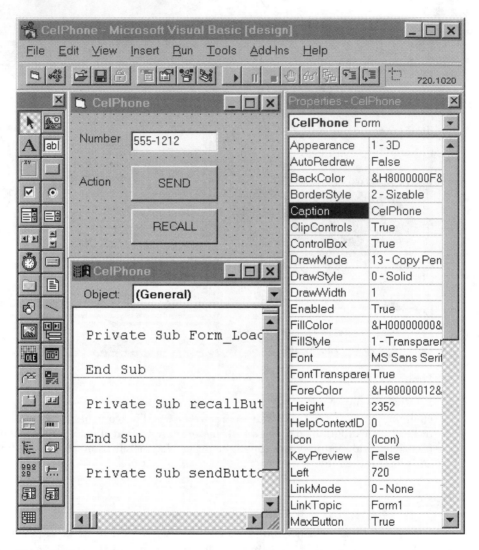

Figure 5.8

This Microsoft Visual Basic design shows a mock-up of a CelPhone interface with a text box for the phone number and two action buttons. The palette of tools on the left includes a Label, TextBox, Frame, CommandButton, CheckBox, RadioButton, ComboBox, ListBox, and scroll bars. The code window is in the bottom center and the properties window at the right allows users to set object properties. (Figures 5.8, 5.9 and 5.10 prepared by Stephan Greene, University of Maryland.) (Used with permission of Microsoft Corp., Redmond, WA.)

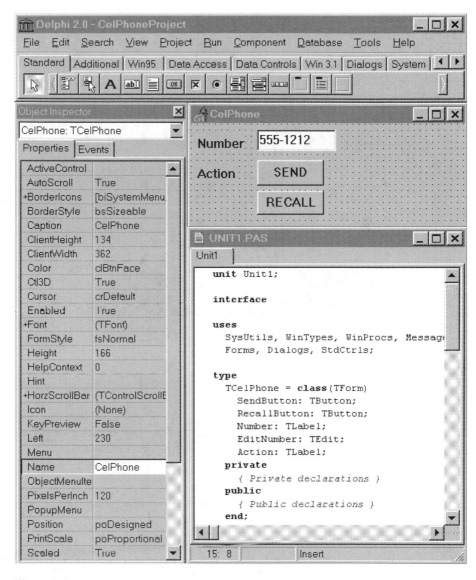

Figure 5.9

This Borland Delphi design shows the same mock-up of a CelPhone as in Fig. 5.8. The palette of tools, which is across the top, includes MainMenu, PopupMenu, Label, Edit, Memo Button, CheckBox, RadioButton, ListBox, ComboBox, ScrollBar, GroupBox, RadioGroup, and Panel. The Object Inspector window, which allows setting of properties, is at the left, and the code window is at the lower right. (Used with permission of Borland International, Inc., Scotts Valley, CA)

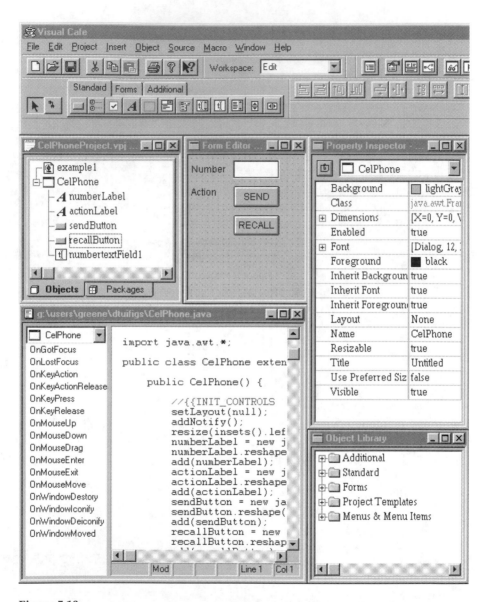

Figure 5.10

This Symantec Visual Cafe design shows the same mock-up of a CelPhone as in Fig. 5.8. The palette of tools, which is across the top, includes Button, RadioButton, CheckBox, Label, Panel, Choice, MenuBar, TextArea, TextField, List, Vertical Scrollbar, and Horizontal Scrollbar. The object hierarchy in the form is at the upper left, the code in the lower left, the properties window on the upper right, and the object library on the lower right. (Used with permission of Symantec Corp., Cupertino, CA.)

```
X/* Written by Dan Heller. Copyright 1991, O'Reilly & Associates.
X * This program is freely distributable without licensing fees and
X * is provided without guarantee or warrantee expressed or implied.
X * This program is -not- in the public domain.
X======================================================================
X      /* main window contains a MenuBar and a Label displaying a pixmap
*/
X      main_w = XtVaCreateManagedWidget("main_window",
X           xMainWindowWidgetClass,     toplevel,
X           XmNscrollBarDisplayPolicy, XmAS_NEEDED,
X           XmNscrollingPolicy,        XmAUTOMATIC,
X           NULL);
X
X      /* Create a simple MenuBar that contains three menus */
X      file = XmStringCreateSimple("File");
X      edit = XmStringCreateSimple("Edit");
X      help = XmStringCreateSimple("Help");
X      menubar = XmVaCreateSimpleMenuBar(main_w, "menubar",
X           XmVaCASCADEBUTTON, file, 'F',
X           XmVaCASCADEBUTTON, edit, 'E'
X           XmVaCASCADEBUTTON, help, 'H',
X           NULL);
X   XmStringFree(file);
X   XmStringFree(edit);
X      /* don't free "help" compound string yet — reuse it for later */
X
X      /* Tell the menubar which button is the help menu */
X      if (widget - XtNameToWidget(menubar, "button_2"))
X           XtVaSetValues(menubar, XmNmenuHelpWidget, widget, NULL);
```

Figure 5.11

Programming of user interfaces in Motif.

```
#First make a menu button
menubutton .menu1 -text "Unix commands" -menu .menu1.m
-underline 0

#Now make the menu, and add the lines one at a time
menu .menu1.m
.menu1.m add command -label "List Files" -command {ls}
.menu1.m add command -label "Get date" -command {date}
.menu1.m add command -label "Start calendar" -command {xcalendar}

pack .menu1
```

A well-developed commercial alternative is Galaxy (Visix, Reston, VA), which offers cross-platform capability by emulating GUIs on Macintosh, Windows, Motif, and other platforms. The visual editor has rich functionality that allows users to specify layouts with springs and struts to preserve the designer's intent even when screen sizes or widget sizes are changed (Hudson and Mohamed, 1990). Galaxy has rich object-oriented libraries that can be invoked from C or C++ programs, plus tools for managing network services and file directories. It requires software-engineering skills to use, but the visual editor enables prompt construction of prototypes.

Sun Microsystems has created the largest tremors on the web with its offerings of Java and Javascript. Java is a complete system-programming language that is specially designed for the World Wide Web. It is compiled on the server and is sent to clients as bytecodes that are interpreted by the browser on whatever platform the browser resides, thereby obtaining cross-platform capability. Java can be used to create complete applications that are distributed like any program, but one of its charms is its capacity to create "applets." These small program fragments can be downloaded from a web page and executed on the user's machine. This aspect enables programmers easily to make web pages dynamic and provide animations or error checking on data-entry forms. This extreme form of modularity allows software packages to be updated by way of the World Wide Web, and permits users to acquire only the components that they use.

Java is object oriented but eliminates some of the complexity of C++, such as operator overloading, multiple inheritance, pointers, and extensive automatic coercions. Automatic garbage collection and the absence of pointers eliminate common sources of bugs. Security and robustness goals were achieved by techniques such as strong typing, which requires explicit data declarations, and static binding, which means that references must be made during compilation. Software engineers have celebrated Java, because of its features and its familiar programming-language style, as indicated in this brief example from the online manual:

```
class Test {
    public static void main(String[] args) {
        for (int i = 0; i < args.length; i++)
            System.out.print(i == 0 ? args[i] : " " + args[i]);
            System.out.println();
    }
}
```

Javascript is a much simpler scripting language that is embedded in the Hypertext Markup Language (HTML) code that generates web pages. It achieves the goals of network distribution and cross-platform capability, since it is distributed within the HTML for a web page and is interpreted by the client's browser on the local machine—Macintosh, Windows, or Unix. It is relatively easy to learn, especially for someone who has learned HTML, and it supplies common features. This example shows a script to square the value of a user-entered number:

```
<HEAD>
<SCRIPT LANGUAGE="JavaScript">
<!-- to hide script contents from old browsers
   function square(i) {
     document.write("The call passed ", i ," to
       the function.",<BR>)
     return i * i
   }

   document.write("The function returned ",square(5),".")
   // end hiding contents from old browsers   -->
</SCRIPT>
</HEAD>
<BODY>
<BR>
All done.
</BODY>
```

On loading the web page, it produces this output:

```
The call passed 5 to the function.
The function returned 25.
All done.
```

Although the original Java and Javascript did not contain visual editors, other developers will supply those tools. Security problems have arisen, but Java seems likely to provide adequate security to encourage development of commercial processes, such as funds transfer, credit-card charges, or personal data sharing. Execution speed of Java is a concern, because the bytecodes must be interpreted, but compilation techniques are promised to support rapid performance, and even hardware changes have been suggested.

The rapid pace of change on the Internet is stimulated by the easy sharing of code and the capacity to build quickly on top of the work of other programmers. The frenzy is sometimes alarming, but is usually irresistible. The importance of the World Wide Web has led developers of many tools—including Tcl/Tk, Galaxy, MacroMind Director, and Visual Basic—to enable their programs to run on the web.

5.4   Evaluation and Critiquing Tools

Software tools are natural environments in which to add procedures to evaluate or critique user interfaces. Simple metrics that report numbers of displays, widgets, or links between displays capture the size of a user-interface project. But the inclusion of more sophisticated evaluation procedures can allow us to assess whether a menu tree is too deep or contains redundancies, whether widget labels have been used consistently, whether all buttons have proper transitions associated with them, and so on (Olsen and Halversen, 1988). Even straightforward tools such as spell checkers or concordances of terms would be a benefit.

A second set of tools is *run-time logging software*, which captures the users' patterns of activity. Simple reports—such as on the frequency of each error message, menu-item selection, dialog-box appearance, help invocation, form-field usage, or web-page access—are of great benefit to maintenance personnel and to revisers of the initial design. Experimental researchers can also capture performance data for alternative designs to guide their decision making. Software to analyze and summarize the performance data will be welcome.

An early example is Tullis' Display Analysis Program, which takes alphanumeric screen designs (no color, highlighting, separator lines, or graphics) and produces Tullis's display-complexity metrics plus some advice, such as this (Tullis, 1988):

```
Upper-case letters: 77% The percentage of upper-case letters
is high.
     Consider using more lower-case letters, since text printed
     in normal upper- and lower-case letters is read about 13%
     faster than text in all upper case. Reserve all upper-case
     for items that need to attract attention.

Maximum local density = 89.9% at row 9, column 8.
Average local density = 67.0%
     The area with the highest local density is identified
     ...you can reduce local density by distributing the
     characters as evenly as feasible over the entire
     screen.

Total layout complexity = 8.02 bits
Layout complexity is high.
     This means that the display items (labels and data) are
     not well aligned with each other...Horizontal complexity
     can be reduced by starting items in fewer different
     columns on the screen (that is, by aligning them verti-
     cally).
```

The movement toward GUIs with richer fonts and layout possibilities has reduced interest in Tullis's metrics, but better analyses of layouts seem possible (see Section 11.4). Evaluations based on formal user-task descriptions using NGOMSL (Byrne et al., 1994) or simpler task sequences and frequencies (Sears, 1993; 1995) are possible. Task-dependent metrics are likely to be more accurate, but the effort and uncertainty in collecting sequences and frequencies of tasks may discourage potential users.

Task-independent measurement and evaluation tools can be easily applied at low cost, early in the development process (Mahajan and Shneiderman, 1996). Simple measures such as the number of widgets per dialog box, widget density, nonwidget areas, aspect ratio, and balance of top to bottom or left to right are useful to gain some idea of the designer's style, but they have limited value in detecting anomalies. Reports on the top, bottom, left and right margins, and the list of distinct colors and typefaces often produced unreasonable variations in four systems developed using Visual Basic. Separate tools to perform spell checking and to produce interface concordances were helpful in revealing errors and inconsistencies. Software tools to check button size, position, color, and wording also revealed inconsistencies that were produced because multiple members of design teams failed to coordinate on a common style. An empirical study with 60 users demonstrated that increased variations in terminology—for example, switching from *search* to *browse* to *query*—slowed performance times by 10 to 25 percent.

Web-page and web-site analyzers also offer designers some guidance. Doctor HTML (http://imagiware.com/RxHTML/)provides link and spell checking; examines forms, tables, and images; and gives code evaluation with comments such as this:

```
Did not find the required open and close HEAD tag. You should
open and close the HEAD tag in order to get consistent per-
formance on all browsers. Found extra close STRONG tags in
this document. Please remove them.
```

5.5 Practitioner's Summary

There will always be a need to write some user interfaces with traditional programming tools, but the advantages of specialized user-interface software tools for designers and software engineers are large. They include an order-of-magnitude increase in productivity, shorter development schedules, support for expert reviews and usability testing, ease in making changes and ensuring consistency, better management control, and reduced training necessary for designers.

The profusion of current tools and the promises of improved tools requires that managers, designers, and programmers stay informed, and that they make fresh choices for each project. This educational process can be enlightening, since the benefits of improved and appropriate tools are enormous if the right tools are selected (Hix and Schulman, 1991) (Box 5.2).

From the tool maker's viewpoint, there are still great opportunities to create effective tools that handle more user-interface situations, that produce output for multiple software and hardware platforms, that are easier to learn, that are

Box 5.2

Factors in choosing among user-interface–building tools.

Widgets supported

- Windows and dialog boxes
- Pull-down or pop-up menus
- Buttons (rectangles, roundtangles, etc.)
- Radio buttons and switches
- Scroll bars (horizontal and vertical)
- Data-entry fields
- Field labels
- Boxes and separator lines
- Sliders, gauges, meters

Interface features

- Color, graphics, images, animation, video
- Varying display size (low to high resolution)
- Sounds, music, voice input–output
- Mouse, arrow keys, touchscreen, stylus

Software architecture

- Prototype only, prototype plus application-programming support, user-interface development environment
- Interface style (command language, menu, form fillin, or direct manipulation)
- Levels and strength of user-interface independence
- Programming language (specialized, standard (C, Pascal, etc.), visual)
- Evaluation and documentation tools
- Easy interface with database, graphics, networking, spreadsheets, etc.
- Logging during testing and use

Management issues

- Number of satisfied users of the tool
- Supplier reliability and stability
- Cost
- Documentation, training, and technical support
- Project-management support
- Integration with existing tools and processes

more powerful, and that provide more useful and accurate evaluation. Existing CASE tools could be expanded to include user-interface features.

5.6   Researcher's Agenda

The narrow focus of formal models of user interfaces and specification languages means that these models are beneficial for only small components. Scalable formal methods and automatic checking of user-interface features would be a major contribution. Innovative methods of specification involving graphical constraints or visual programming seem to be a natural match for creating GUIs. Improved software architectures are needed to ease the burden during revision and maintenance of user interfaces. Cooperative computing tools may provide powerful authoring tools that enable multiple designers to work together effectively on large projects. Other opportunities exist to create tools for designers of interfaces in novel environments using sound, animation, video, and virtual reality, and manipulating physical devices as in flexible manufacturing systems or home automation. Other challenges are to specify dynamic processes (gestural input), to handle continuous input (datastreams from a sensor), and to synchronize activities (to pop up a reminder box for 10 seconds, if a file has not been saved after 30 minutes of editing). As new interface styles emerge, there will always be a need to develop new tools to facilitate their construction. Metrics and evaluation tools are still open topics for user-interface and website developers. Specification by demonstration is an appealing notion (Myers, 1992), but practical application remains elusive.

World Wide Web Resources   WWW

User interface tools are widely promoted on the web by companies and others. The World Wide Web is a great resource here because the technology changes so rapidly that books are immediately out of date. Online white papers, manuals, and tutorials are often effective and enable contact with developers. An imaginative idea is to have websites that will critique your website. Such online services are likely to expand in the coming years.

http://www.aw.com/DTUI

References

Carey, Tom, The gift of good design tools. In Hartson, H. R. and Hix, D. (Editors), *Advances in Human–Computer Interaction*, Volume II, Ablex, Norwood, NJ (1988), 175–213.

Byrne, Michael D., Wood, Scott D., Sukaviriya, Piyawadee "Noi," Foley, James D., and Kieras, David E., Automating interface evaluation, *Proc. CHI '94 Conference— Human Factors in Computing Systems*, ACM, New York (1994), 232–237.

Carr, David, Specification of interface interaction objects, *Proc. CHI '94 Conference— Human Factors in Computing Systems*, ACM, New York (1994), 372–378.

Chase, J. D., Schulman, Robert S., Hartson, H. Rex, and Hix, Deborah, Development and evaluation of a taxonomical model of behavioral representation techniques, *Proc. CHI '94 Conference—Human Factors in Computing Systems*, ACM, New York (1994), 159–165.

Green, Thomas R. G. and Petre, Marian, Usability analysis of visual programming environments: A "cognitive dimensions" framework, *Journal of Visual Languages and Computing*, 7, (1996), 131–174.

Harel, David, On visual formalisms, *Communications of the ACM*, 31, 5 (May 1988), 514–530.

Hartson, H. Rex, Siochi, Antonio C., and Hix, Deborah, The UAN: User-oriented representation for direct manipulation interface designs, *ACM Transactions on Information Systems*, 8, 3 (July 1990), 181–203.

Hix, Deborah and Hartson, H. Rex, *Developing User Interfaces: Ensuring Usability Through Product and Process*, John Wiley and Sons, New York (1993).

Hix, Deborah and Schulman, Robert S., Human–computer interface development tools: A methodology for their evaluation, *Communications of the ACM*, 34, 3 (March 1991), 74–87.

Hudson, Scott E. and Mohamed, Shamim P., Interactive specification of flexible user interface displays, *ACM Transactions on Information Systems*, 8, 3 (July 1990), 269–288.

Jacob, Robert J. K., An executable specification technique for describing human–computer interaction. In Hartson, H. Rex (Editor), *Advances in Human–Computer Interaction*, Volume I, Ablex, Norwood, NJ (1985), 211–242.

Mahajan, Rohit and Shneiderman, Ben, Visual and textual consistency checking tools for graphical user interfaces, Dept. of Computer Science Tech Report CS-TR-3639, University of Maryland, College Park, MD (1996).

Myers, Brad A., Demonstrational interfaces: A step beyond direct manipulation, *IEEE Computer*, 25, 8 (August 1992), 61–73.

Myers, Brad A., User interface software tools, *ACM Transactions on Computer–Human Interaction*, 2, 1 (March 1995), 64–103.

Olsen, Jr., Dan R., *User Interface Management Systems: Models and Algorithms*, Morgan Kaufmann Publishers, San Mateo, CA (1991).

Olsen, Jr., Dan R. and Halversen, Bradley W., Interface usage measurement in a User Interface Management System, *Proc. ACM SIGGRAPH Symposium on User Interface Software and Technology*, ACM Press, New York (1988), 102–108.

Ousterhout, John, *Tcl and the Tk Toolkit*, Addison-Wesley, Reading, MA (1994).

Reisner, Phyllis, Formal grammar and design of an interactive system, *IEEE Transactions on Software Engineering*, SE-5, (1981), 229–240.

Shneiderman, Ben, Multi-party grammars and related features for defining interactive systems, *IEEE Systems, Man, and Cybernetics*, SMC-12, 2 (March–April 1982), 148–154.

Sears, Andrew, Layout appropriateness: Guiding user interface design with simple task descriptions, *IEEE Transactions on Software Engineering*, 19, 7 (1993), 707–719.

Sears, Andrew, AIDE: A step towards metrics-based interface development tools, *Proc. UIST '95 User Interface Software and Technology*, ACM, New York (1995), 101–110.

Tullis, Thomas, A system for evaluating screen formats: research and application. In Hartson, H. Rex and Hix, D. (Editors), *Advances in Human–Computer Interaction*, Volume II, Ablex, Norwood, NJ (1988), 214–286.

Wasserman, Anthony I., and Shewmake, David T., The role of prototypes in the User Software Engineering (USE) methodology. In Hartson, Rex (Editor), *Advances in Human–Computer Interaction*, Volume I, Ablex, Norwood, NJ (1985), 191–210.

Wellner, Pierre D., Statemaster: A UIMS based on statecharts for prototyping and target implementation, *Proc. CHI '89 Conference—Human Factors in Computing Systems*, ACM, New York (1989), 177–182.

Mark Kostabi, *Computer Cafe (Uploading the Future)*, 1996

Direct Manipulation and Virtual Environments

Leibniz sought to make the form of a symbol reflect its content. "In signs," he wrote, "one sees an advantage for discovery that is greatest when they express the exact nature of a thing briefly and, as it were, picture it; then, indeed, the labor of thought is wonderfully diminished."

Frederick Kreiling, "Leibniz,"
Scientific American, **May 1968**

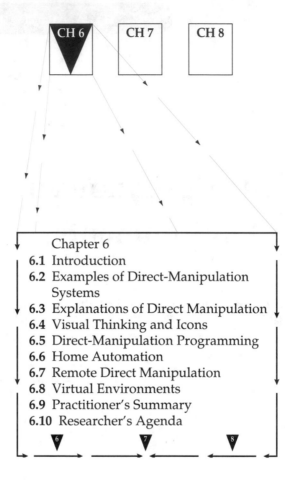

CH 6   CH 7   CH 8

Chapter 6
6.1 Introduction
6.2 Examples of Direct-Manipulation Systems
6.3 Explanations of Direct Manipulation
6.4 Visual Thinking and Icons
6.5 Direct-Manipulation Programming
6.6 Home Automation
6.7 Remote Direct Manipulation
6.8 Virtual Environments
6.9 Practitioner's Summary
6.10 Researcher's Agenda

6.1 Introduction

Certain interactive systems generate a glowing enthusiasm among users that is in marked contrast with the more common reaction of grudging acceptance or outright hostility. The enthusiastic users report the following positive feelings:

- Mastery of the interface
- Competence in performing tasks
- Ease in learning the system originally and in assimilating advanced features
- Confidence in the capacity to retain mastery over time

- Enjoyment in using the system
- Eagerness to show off the system to novices
- Desire to explore more powerful aspects of the system

These feelings convey an image of the truly pleased user. The central ideas in the systems that inspire such delight are visibility of the objects and actions of interest; rapid, reversible, incremental actions; and replacement of complex command-language syntax by direct manipulation of the object of interest (Shneiderman, 1983). The objects–actions interface (OAI) model provides a sound foundation for understanding direct manipulation since it steers designers to represent the task domain objects and actions while minimizing the interface concepts and the syntax-memorization load. Direct-manipulation thinking has spawned the new strategies of information visualization (see Chapter 15) that present thousands of objects on the screen with dynamic user controls.

6.2   Examples of Direct-Manipulation Systems

No single system has every admirable attribute or design feature—such a system might not be possible. Each of the following examples, however, has sufficient numbers of them to win the enthusiastic support of many users.

My favorite example of using direct manipulation is driving an automobile. The scene is directly visible through the front window, and performance of actions such as braking or steering has become common knowledge in our culture. To turn left, the driver simply rotates the steering wheel to the left. The response is immediate and the scene changes, providing feedback to refine the turn. Imagine trying to turn by issuing a command LEFT 30 DEGREES and then another command to see the new scene; but that is the level of operation of many office-automation tools of today! Another well-established example is air-traffic control, in which users see a representation of the airspace with brief data blocks attached to each plane. Controllers move a trackball to point at specific planes and to perform actions.

6.2.1   Command-line versus display editors versus word processors

It may be hard for new users of word processors to believe, but in the early 1980s, text editing was done with line-oriented command languages. Users might see only one line at a time and typed commands were needed to move the view window or to make any changes. The users of novel *full-page display editors* were great advocates of their systems. A typical comment was, "Once you've used a display editor, you will never want to go back to a line editor—

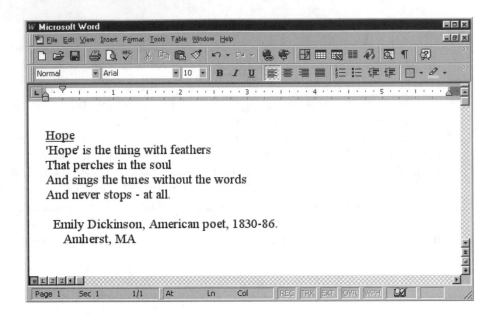

Figure 6.1

An example of a WYSIWYG (What You See Is What You Get) editor: Microsoft Word for Office 97. (Used with permission of Microsoft Corp., Redmond, WA.)

you'll be spoiled." Similar comments came from users of early personal-computer word processors, such as WORDSTAR, or display editors such as emacs or vi (for visual editor) on the Unix system. A beaming advocate called emacs "the one true editor." In these systems users viewed up to a full screen of text and could edit by using backspace or insert directly by typing.

Researchers found that performance was improved and training times were reduced with display editors so there was evidence to support the enthusiasm of display-editor devotees. Furthermore, office-automation evaluations consistently favored full-page display editors for secretarial and executive use. There are some advantages to command-language approaches, such as that history keeping is easier, more flexible markup languages are available (for example, SGML), macros tend to be more powerful, and some tasks are simpler to express (for example, change all italics to bold). Strategies for accommodating these needs are finding their way into modern direct-manipulation word processors.

By the early 1990s, *what you see is what you get (WYSIWYG)* word processors had become standard. Microsoft Word has become dominant on the Macintosh and IBM PC compatibles, with Lotus Word Pro and Corel's WordPerfect taking second place (Fig. 6.1). The advantages of WYSIWYG word processors include the following:

- *Display a full page of text*   Showing 20 to 60 lines of text simultaneously gives the reader a clearer sense of context for each sentence, while permitting simpler reading and scanning of the document. By contrast, working with the one-line-at-a-time view offered by line editors is like seeing the world through a narrow cardboard tube. Some large displays can support two full pages of text, set side by side.

- *Display the document in the form that it will appear when the final printing is done*   Eliminating the clutter of formatting commands also simplifies reading and scanning of the document. Tables, lists, page breaks, skipped lines, section headings, centered text, and figures can be viewed in their final form. The annoyance and delay of debugging the format commands are almost eliminated because the errors are usually apparent immediately.

- *Show cursor action to the user*   Seeing an arrow, underscore, or blinking box on the screen gives the operator a clear sense of where to focus attention and to apply action.

- *Control cursor motion through physically obvious and intuitively natural means*   Arrow keys or cursor-motion devices—such as a mouse, joystick, or graphic tablet—provide natural physical mechanisms for moving the cursor. This setup is in marked contrast to commands, such as UP 6, that require an operator to convert the physical action into a correct syntactic form that may be difficult to learn and hard to recall, and thus may be a source of frustrating errors.

- *Use labeled icons for actions*   Most word processors have labeled icons in a toolbar for frequent actions. These buttons act as a permanent menu-selection display to remind users of the features and to provide rapid selection.

- *Display the results of an action immediately*   When the user presses a button to move the cursor or center text, the results are shown immediately on the screen. Deletions are apparent immediately: the character, word, or line is erased, and the remaining text is rearranged. Similarly, insertions or text movements are shown after each keystroke or function-key press. In contrast, with line editors, users must issue print or display commands to see the results of changes.

- *Provide rapid response and display*   Most display editors operate at high speed; a full page of text appears in a fraction of a second. This high display rate coupled with short response time produces a satisfying sense of power and speed. Cursors can be moved quickly, large amounts of text can be scanned rapidly, and the results of actions can be shown almost instantaneously. Rapid response also reduces the need for additional commands and thereby simplifies design and learning. Line editors with slow display rates and long response times bog down the user. Speeding up line editors would add to their attractiveness, but they would still lack such features as direct overtyping, deletion, and insertion.

- *Offer easily reversible actions*   When users enter text, they repair an incorrect keystroke by merely backspacing and overstriking. They can make simple changes by moving the cursor to the problem area and overstriking, inserting, or deleting characters, words, or lines. A useful design strategy is to include natural inverse operations for each operation (for example, to increase or decrease type sizes). An alternative offered by many display editors is a simple UNDO command to return the text to the state that it was in before the previous action or action sequence. The easy reversibility reduces user anxiety about making a mistake or destroying the file.

So many of these issues have been studied empirically that someone joked that the word processor is the white rat for researchers in human–computer interaction. Switching metaphors, for commercial developers, we might say the word processor is the root for many technological sprouts:

- *Integration* of graphics, spreadsheets, animations, photographs, and so on is done in the body of a document. Advanced designs, such as the OpenDoc, even permit "hot links" so that, if the graphic or spreadsheet is changed, the copy in the document also will be changed.

- *Desktop-publishing software* produces sophisticated printed formats with multiple columns and allows output to high-resolution printers. Multiple fonts, grayscales, and color permit preparation of high-quality documents, newsletters, reports, newspapers, or books. Examples include Adobe PageMaker and QuarkXPress.

- *Slide-presentation software* produces color text and graphic layouts for use as overhead transparencies, 35-millimeter slides, or directly from the computer with a large-screen projector to allow animations.

- *Hypermedia environments* with selectable buttons or embedded menu items allow users to jump from one article to another. Links among documents, bookmarks, annotations, and tours can be added by readers.

- *Improved macro facilities* enable users to construct, save, and edit sequences of frequently used actions. A related feature is a style sheet that allows users to specify and save a set of options for spacing, fonts, margins, and so on. Another feature is the saving of templates that allows users to take the formatting work of colleagues as a starting point for their own documents. Most word processors come with dozens of standard templates for business letters, newsletters, or brochures.

- *Spell checkers and thesauri* are standard on most full-featured word processors. Spell checking can also be set to function while the user is typing, or to make automatic changes for common mistakes, such as changing "teh" to "the."

- *Grammar checkers* offer users comments about potential problems in writing style, such as use of passive voice, excessive use of certain words, or lack of parallel construction. Some writers—both novices and professionals—appreciate the comments and know that they can decide whether to apply the suggestions. Critics point out, however, that the advice is often inappropriate and therefore wastes time.

- *Document assemblers* allow users to compose complex documents, such as contracts or wills, from standard paragraphs using appropriate language for males or females; citizens or foreigners; high, medium, or low income earners; renters or home owners, and so on.

6.2.2   The VisiCalc spreadsheet and its descendants

The first electronic spreadsheet, VisiCalc, was the product of a Harvard Business School student, Dan Bricklin, who became frustrated when trying to carry out repetitious calculations for a graduate course in business. He and a friend, Bob Frankston, built an "instantly calculating electronic worksheet" (as the user manual described it) that permitted computation and immediate display of results across 254 rows and 63 columns.

The *spreadsheet* can be programmed so that column 4 displays the sum of columns 1 through 3; then, every time a value in the first three columns changes, the fourth column changes as well. Complex dependencies among manufacturing costs, distribution costs, sales revenue, commissions, and profits can be stored for several sales districts and for various months, so that the effects of changes on profits can be seen immediately.

This simulation of an accountant's spreadsheet makes it easy for novices to comprehend the objects and permissible actions. Spreadsheet users can try out alternate plans and see the effects on sales or profit. The distributor of VisiCalc explained the system's appeal as "it jumps," referring to the user's delight in watching the propagation of changes across the screen.

Competitors to VisiCalc emerged quickly; they made attractive improvements to the user interface and expanded the tasks that were supported. LOTUS 1-2-3 dominated the market in the 1980s (Fig. 6.2), but the current leader is Microsoft's Excel (Fig. 6.3), which has a large number of features and specialized additions. Excel and other modern spreadsheets offer integration with graphics, three-dimensional representations, multiple windows, and database features. The features are invoked easily with command menus or toolbars, and can be used within powerful macro facilities.

Figure 6.2

Early version of Lotus 1-2-3, the spreadsheet program that was dominant through the 1980s. (Printed with permission of Lotus Development Corporation, Cambridge, MA.)

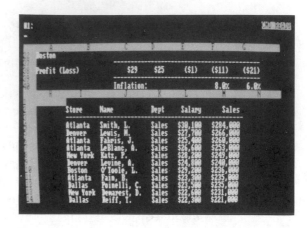

6.2.3   Spatial data management

In geographic applications, it seems natural to give a spatial representation in the form of a map that provides a familiar model of reality. The developers of the prototype Spatial Data Management System (Herot, 1980; 1984) attribute the basic idea to Nicholas Negroponte of MIT. In one early scenario, the user was seated before a color-graphics display of the world and could

	Site / Operating Exp	GL #	7/98	8/98	9/98 Q1	Q2	Q3	
2	Site	Operating Exp	GL #	7/98	8/98	9/98 Q1	Q2	Q3
3	Albany, NY			$28,675	$28,675	$28,175 $85,525	$85,525	$85,525
4		Salaries	1-1002	10000	10000	10000 30000	30000	30000
5		Supplies	1-2310	3000	2500	3000 8500	8500	8500
6		Equipment	1-2543	457	4575	4575 9607	9607	9607
7		Lease Pmts	1-7862	9600	960	9600 20160	20160	20160
8		Advertising	1-8752	1500	1500	1500 4500	4500	4500
9								
10	Memphis, TN			$28,200	$28,200	$28,200 $84,600	$84,600	$84,600
11		Salaries	2-1002	7500	7500	7500 22500	22500	22500
12		Supplies	2-2310	2000	2000	2000 6000	6000	6000
13		Equipment	2-2543	8000	8000	8000 24000	24000	24000
14		Lease Pmts	2-7862	8200	8200	8200 24600	24600	24600
15		Advertising	2-8752	2500	2500	2500 7500	7500	7500

Figure 6.3

Microsoft Excel spreadsheet for Office 97. (Used with permission of Microsoft Corp., Redmond, WA.)

zoom in on the Pacific Ocean to see markers for convoys of military ships (Fig. 6.4). By moving a joystick, the user caused the screen to be filled with silhouettes of individual ships; zooming displayed detailed data, such as, ultimately, a full-color picture of the captain.

In another scenario, icons representing such different aspects of a corporation as personnel, an organizational chart, travel information, production data, and schedules were shown on a screen. By moving the joystick and zooming in on objects of interest, the user could travel through complex *information spaces (I-spaces)* to locate the item of interest. A building floorplan showing departments might be displayed; when a department was chosen, individual offices became visible. As the cursor was moved into a room, details of the occupant appeared on the screen. If users chose the wrong room, they merely backed out and tried another. The lost effort was minimal, and there was no stigma attached to error. The recent Xerox PARC Information Visualizer is an ensemble of tools that permit three-dimensional animated explorations of buildings, cone-shaped file directories, organization charts, a perspective wall that puts featured items up front and centered, and several two- and three-dimensional information layouts (Robertson et al., 1993).

ArcView (ESRI, Inc.) is a widely used geographic-information system that offers rich, layered databases of map-related information (Fig. 6.5). Users can zoom in on areas of interest, select the kinds of information they wish to view (roads, population density, topography, rainfall, political boundaries, and much more), and do limited searches. Much simpler but widely popular highway maps are available for the entire United States on a single CD-ROM. Map servers on the World Wide Web are increasingly popular for taking tours of cities, checking weather reports, or buying a home.

The success of a spatial data-management system depends on the skill of the designers in choosing icons, graphical representations, and data layouts that are natural and comprehensible to the user. The joy of zooming in and out, or of gliding over data with a joystick, entices even anxious users, who quickly demand additional power and data.

6.2.4 Video games

For many people, the most exciting, well-engineered, and commercially successful application of the concepts that we have been discussing lies in the world of video games (Provenzo, 1991). The early but simple and popular game PONG required the user to rotate a knob that moved a white rectangle on the screen. A white spot acted as a ping-pong ball that ricocheted off the wall and had to be hit back by the movable white rectangle. Users developed speed and accuracy in placing the "paddle" to keep the increasingly speedy ball from getting past, while the computer speaker emitted a ponging sound

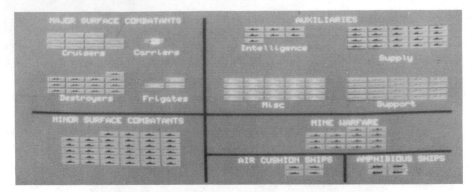

Figure 6.4

The Spatial Data Management System. Three displays to show multiple levels of detail or related information. The user moves a joystick to traverse information spaces or to zoom in on a map to see more details about ship convoys. (Courtesy of the Computer Corporation of America, Cambridge, MA.)

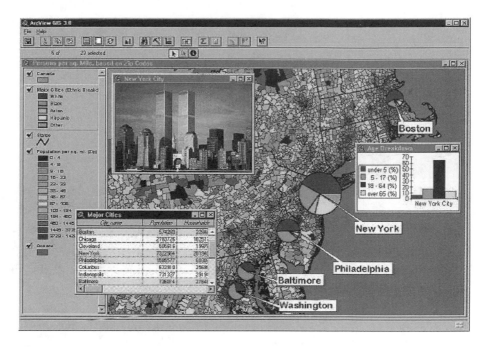

Figure 6.5

ArcView® geographic information system (GIS), which provides comprehensive mapping functions and management of related data. This map of the northeast United States shows color coding by population density for each zip code, ethnic makeup of large cities, and a photo of New York City. (Graphic image supplied courtesy of Environmental Systems Research Institute, Inc., Redlands, CA. Copyright 1996.)

when the ball bounced. Watching someone else play for 30 seconds is all the training that a person needs to become a competent novice, but many hours of practice are required to become a skilled expert.

Later games, such as Missile Command, Donkey Kong, Pac Man, Tempest, TRON, Centipede, or Space Invaders, were much more sophisticated in their rules, color graphics, and sound effects. Recent games include multi-person competitions in tennis or karate, three-dimensional graphics, still higher resolution, and stereo sound. The designers of these games provide stimulating entertainment, a challenge for novices and experts, and many intriguing lessons in the human factors of interface design—somehow, they have found a way to get people to put quarters in the sides of computers. Forty-million Nintendo game players reside across 70 percent of those American households that include 8 to 12 year olds. Brisk sales of the Mario series testify to the games' strong attraction, in marked contrast to the anxiety about and resistance to office-automation equipment that many users have

Figure 6.6

Home videogames are a huge success and employ advanced graphics hardware for rapid movement in rich three-dimensional worlds. The Nintendo 64 player can be used with a variety of games including the popular Super Mario® series (© 1997 Nintendo. Images courtesy of Nintendo of America Inc.)

shown (Fig. 6.6). The SEGA game player, Nintendo 64, and Sony Playstation have brought powerful three-dimensional graphics hardware to the home and have created a remarkable international market. Small hand-held game devices, such as the Game Boy®, provide portable fun for kids on the street or executives in their 30,000-foot-high offices.

These games provide a field of action that is visual and compelling. The commands are physical actions—such as button presses, joystick motions, or knob rotations—whose results are shown immediately on the screen. There is no syntax to remember, and therefore there are no syntax-error messages. If users move their spaceships too far left, then they merely use the natural inverse operation of moving back to the right. Error messages are unnecessary, because the results of actions are obvious and can be reversed easily. These principles can be applied to office automation, personal computing, or other interactive environments.

Most games continuously display a numeric score so that users can measure their progress and compete with their previous performance, with friends, or with the highest scorers. Typically, the 10 highest scorers get to store their initials in the game for public display. This strategy provides one form of positive reinforcement that encourages mastery. Malone's (1981), Provenzo's (1991), and our studies with elementary-school children have shown that continuous display of scores is extremely valuable. Machine-generated feedback—such as "Very good" or "You're doing great!"—is not as effective, since the same score carries different meanings for different people. Most users prefer to make their own subjective judgments and perceive the machine-generated messages as an annoyance and a deception.

Many educational games use direct manipulation effectively. Elementary- or high-school students can learn about urban planning by using Sim-City and its variants, which show urban environments visually and let students build roads, airports, housing, and so on by direct-manipulation actions.

The esthetically appealing MYST and its successor Riven (Broderbund) have drawn widespread approval even in some literary circles, while the more violent but wildly successful DOOM series has provoked controversy over its psychological effects on teens. Studying game design is fun, but there are limits to the applicability of the lessons. Game players seek entertainment and focus on the challenge of mastery, whereas applications users focus on their task and may resent too many playful distractions. The random events that occur in most games are meant to challenge the user; in nongame designs, however, predictable system behavior is preferred. Game players are engaged in competition with the system or with other players, whereas applications-systems users prefer a strong internal locus of control, which gives them the sense of being in charge.

6.2.5   Computer-aided design

Many *computer-aided design (CAD)* systems for automobiles, electronic circuitry, architecture, aircraft (see Fig. 1.3), or slide layout (Fig. 6.7) use principles of direct manipulation. The operator may see a circuit schematic on the screen and, with mouse clicks, be able to move resistors or capacitors into or out of the proposed circuit. When the design is complete, the computer can provide information about current, voltage drops, and fabrication costs, and warnings about inconsistencies or manufacturing problems. Similarly, newspaper-layout artists or automobile-body designers can easily try multiple designs in minutes, and can record promising approaches until they find even better ones.

The pleasures in using these systems stem from the capacity to manipulate the object of interest directly and to generate multiple alternatives rapidly. Some systems have complex command languages; most have moved to using cursor action and graphics-oriented commands.

Related applications are *computer-aided manufacturing (CAM)* and process control. Honeywell's process-control system provides the manager of an oil refinery, paper mill, or power-utility plant with a colored schematic view of

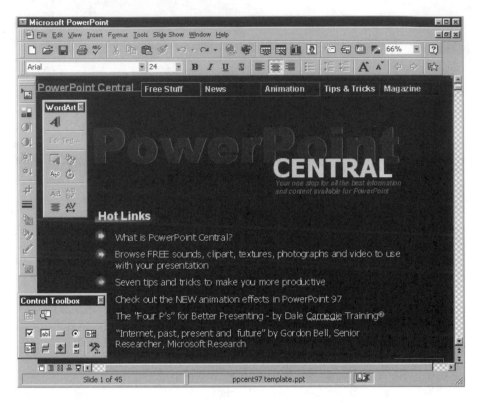

Figure 6.7

Presentation graphics or slide programs, such as Microsoft's PowerPoint for Office 97, have multiple toolbars and palettes that support a direct-manipulation style of selecting objects, moving them, and resizing them. (Used with permission of Microsoft Corp., Redmond, WA.)

the plant. The schematic may be displayed on eight displays or on a large wall-sized map, with red lines indicating a sensor value that is out of normal range. With a single click, the operator can get a more detailed view of the troubling component; with a second click, the operator can examine individual sensors or can reset valves and circuits.

A basic strategy for this design is to eliminate the need for complex commands that the operator would need to recall during a once-a-year emergency. The visual overview provided by the schematic facilitates problem solving by analogy, since the linkage between the screen representations and the plant's temperatures or pressures is so close.

6.2.6   Office automation

Designers of advanced *office-automation systems* used direct-manipulation principles. The pioneering Xerox Star (Smith et al., 1982) offered sophisticated text-formatting options, graphics, multiple fonts, and a high-resolution, cursor-based user interface (Fig. 6.8). Users could move (but not drag) a document icon to a printer icon to generate a hardcopy printout. The Apple Lisa system elegantly applied many of the principles of direct manipulation; although it was not a commercial success, it laid the groundwork for the successful Macintosh. The Macintosh designers drew from the Star and Lisa experiences, but made many simplifying decisions while preserving adequate power for users (Fig. 6.9). The hardware and software designs supported rapid and continuous graphical interaction for pull-down menus, window manipulation, editing of graphics and text, and dragging of icons. Variations on the Macintosh appeared soon afterward for other popular personal computers, and by now Windows 95 dominates the office-automation market (Color Plate 1). The Windows 95 design is still a close relative of the Macintosh design, and both are candidates for substantial improvements in window management (Chapter 13), with simplifications for novices and increased power for sophisticated users.

Studies of users of direct-manipulation interfaces have confirmed the advantages for at least some users and tasks. In a study of 30 novices, MS-DOS commands for creating, copying, renaming, and erasing files were contrasted with Macintosh direct-manipulation actions. After user training and practice, average task times were 5.8 minutes versus 4.8 minutes, and average errors were 2.0 versus 0.8 (Margono and Shneiderman, 1987). Subjective preference also favored the direct-manipulation interface. In a study of a command-line versus a direct-manipulation database interface, 55 "computer naive but keyboard literate" users made more than twice as many errors with the command-line format. No significant differences in time were found (Morgan et al., 1991). These users preferred the direct-manipulation interface overall, and rated it as more stimulating, easier, and more adequately powerful. Both reports caution about generalizing their results to more experienced users. A study with novices and experienced users was cosponsored by Microsoft and Zenith Data Systems (Temple, Barker, and Sloane, Inc., 1990). Although details about subjects, interfaces, and tasks were not reported, the results showed improved productivity and reduced fatigue for experienced users with a GUI, as compared with a character-based user interface. The benefits of direct manipulation were confirmed in other studies (Benbasat and Todd, 1993); one such study also demonstrated that the advantage was greater for experienced than for novice users (Ulich et al., 1991).

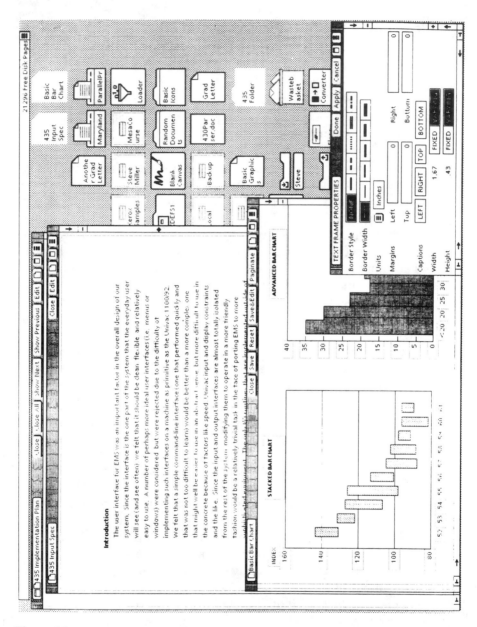

Figure 6.8

The Xerox Star 8010 with the ViewPoint system enables users to create documents with multiple fonts and graphics. This session shows the Text Frame Properties sheet over sample bar charts, with a document in the background and many desktop icons available for selection. (Prepared by Steve Miller, University of Maryland.)

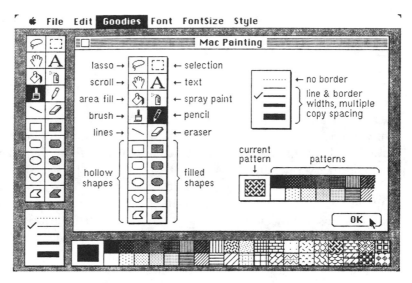

Figure 6.9

The original Apple Macintosh MacPaint. This program offers a command menu on the top, a menu of action icons on the left, a choice of line thicknesses on the lower left, and a palette of texture on the bottom. All actions can be accomplished with only the mouse. (Photo courtesy of Apple Computer, Inc., Cupertino, CA)

6.2.7 Further examples of direct manipulation

The trick in creating a direct-manipulation system is to come up with an appropriate representation or model of reality. Some designers may find it difficult to think about information problems in a visual form; with practice, however, they may find it more natural. With many applications, the jump to visual language may be difficult; later, however, users and designers can hardly imagine why anyone would want to use a complex syntactic notation to describe an essentially visual process. In fact, it is hard to think of new command languages developed after 1990. It is hard to conceive of learning the commands for the vast number of features in modern word processors, drawing programs, or spreadsheets, but the visual cues, icons, menus, and dialog boxes make it possible for even intermittent users to succeed.

Several designers applied direct manipulation using the metaphor of a stack of cards to portray a set of addresses, telephone numbers, events, and so on. Clicking on a card brings it to the front, and the stack of cards moves to preserve alphabetic ordering. This simple card-deck metaphor, combined with other notions (Heckel, 1991) led to Bill Atkinson's innovative development of HyperCard stacks in 1987 (see Section 15.4). Billed as a way to "create your own applications for gathering, organizing, presenting, searching, and customizing information," HyperCard quickly spawned variants, such as SuperCard and ToolBook. Each has a scripting language to enable users to create appealing graphics applications.

Direct-manipulation checkbook-maintenance and checkbook-searching interfaces, such as Quicken (Intuit, Inc.) display a checkbook register with labeled columns for check number, date, payee, and amount. Changes can be made in place, new entries can be made at the first blank line, and a check-mark can be made to indicate verification against a monthly report or bank statement. Users can search for a particular payee by filling in a blank payee field and then typing a ?.

Why not have web-based airline-reservations systems show the user a map and prompt for cursor motion to the departing and arriving cities? Then the user can select the date from a calendar and a time from a clock. Showing the seating plan of the plane on the screen, with a diagonal line to indicate an already-reserved seat, would enable seat selection.

"Direct manipulation" is an accurate description of the programming of certain industrial robot tools. The operator holds the robot "hand" and guides it through a spray painting or welding task while the controlling computer records every action. The control computer can then operate the robot automatically, repeating the precise action as many times as is necessary.

Why not teach students about polynomial equations by letting them move sliders to set values for the coefficients and watch how the graph changes, where the y-axis intercept occurs, or how the derivative equation reacts. Similarly, direct manipulation of sliders for red, green, and blue is a satisfying way to explore color space. Slider-based dynamic queries are a powerful tool for information exploration (see Section 15.4).

Direct manipulation has the power to attract users because it is comprehensible, rapid, and even enjoyable. If actions are simple, reversibility is ensured, and retention is easy, then anxiety recedes, users feel in control, and satisfaction flows in.

6.3 Explanations of Direct Manipulation

Several authors have attempted to describe the component principles of direct manipulation. An imaginative and early interactive system designer, Ted Nelson (1980), perceived user excitement when the interface was constructed by what he calls the *principle of virtuality*—a representation of reality that can be manipulated. Rutkowski (1982) conveyed a similar concept in his *principle of transparency*: "The user is able to apply intellect directly to the task; the tool itself seems to disappear." Heckel (1991) laments that "Our instincts and training as engineers encourage us to think logically instead of visually, and this is counterproductive to friendly design." His description is in harmony with the popular notions of logical symbolic sequential left-brain and the visual artistic all-at-once right-brain problem-solving styles.

Hutchins et al. (1986) review the concepts of direct manipulation and offer a thoughtful decomposition of concerns. They describe the "feeling of involvement directly with a world of objects rather than of communicating with an intermediary," and clarify how direct manipulation breaches the *gulf of execution* and the *gulf of evaluation*.

These writers and others (Ziegler and Fahnrich, 1988; Thimbleby, 1990; Phillips and Apperley, 1991; Frohlich, 1993) support the recognition that a new form of interactive system had emerged. Much credit also goes to the individual designers who created systems that exemplify aspects of direct manipulation.

Another perspective on direct manipulation comes from the psychology literature on *problem-solving* and *learning research*. Suitable representations of problems have been clearly shown to be critical to solution finding and to learning. Polya (1957) suggests drawing a picture to represent mathematical problems. This approach is in harmony with Maria Montessori's teaching methods for children (Montessori, 1964). She proposed use of physical objects, such as beads or wooden sticks, to convey such mathematical principles as addition, multiplication, or size comparison. The durable abacus is appealing because it gives a direct-manipulation representation of numbers.

Bruner (1966) extended the physical-representation idea to cover polynomial factoring and other mathematical principles. Carroll, Thomas, and Malhotra (1980) found that subjects given spatial representation were faster and more successful in problem solving than were subjects given an isomorphic problem with a temporal representation. Similarly, Te'eni (1990) found that the feedback in direct-manipulation designs was effective in reducing users' logical errors in a task requiring statistical analysis of student grades. The advantage appears to stem from having the data entry and display combined in a single location on the display.

Physical, spatial, or visual representations also appear to be easier to retain and manipulate than are textual or numeric representations (Arnheim, 1972; McKim, 1980). Wertheimer (1959) found that subjects who memorized the formula for the area of a parallelogram, $A = h \times b$, rapidly succeeded in doing such calculations. On the other hand, subjects who were given the structural understanding of cutting off a triangle from one end and placing it on the other end could more effectively retain the knowledge and generalize it to solve related problems. In plane-geometry theorem proving, spatial representation facilitates discovery of proof procedures over a strictly axiomatic representation of Euclidean geometry. The diagram provides heuristics that are difficult to extract from the axioms. Similarly, students are often encouraged to solve algebraic word problems by drawing pictures to represent those problems.

Papert's (1980) LOGO language created a mathematical microworld in which the principles of geometry are visible. Based on the Swiss psychologist Jean Piaget's theory of child development, LOGO offers students the opportunity to create line drawings easily with an electronic turtle displayed on a screen. In this environment, users derive rapid feedback about their programs, can determine what has happened easily, can spot and repair errors quickly, and can gain satisfaction from creative production of drawings. These features are all characteristic of a direct-manipulation environment.

6.3.1   Problems with direct manipulation

Spatial or visual representations are not necessarily an improvement over text, because they may be too spread out, causing off-page connectors on paper or tedious scrolling on displays. In professional programming, use of high-level flowcharts and database-schema diagrams can be helpful for some tasks, but there is a danger that they will be confusing. Similarly, direct-manipulation designs may consume valuable screen space and thus force valuable information offscreen, requiring scrolling or multiple actions. Studies of graphical plots versus tabular business data and of flowcharts versus program text demonstrate advantages for graphical approaches when pattern-recognition tasks are relevant, but disadvantages when the graphic gets too large and the tasks require detailed information. For experienced users, a tabular textual display of 50 document names may be more appropriate than only 10 graphic document icons with the names abbreviated to fit the icon size.

A second problem is that users must learn the meaning of components of the visual representation. A graphic icon may be meaningful to the designer, but may require as much or more learning time than a word. Some airports that serve multilingual communities use graphic icons extensively, but the meanings of these icons may not be obvious. Similarly, some computer terminals designed for international use have icons in place of names, but the meaning is not always clear. Icons with titles that appear when the cursor is over them offer only a partial solution.

A third problem is that the visual representation may be misleading. Users may grasp the analogical representation rapidly, but then may draw incorrect conclusions about permissible actions. Users may overestimate or underestimate the functions of the computer-based analogy. Ample testing must be carried out to refine the displayed objects and actions and to minimize negative side effects.

A fourth problem is that, for experienced typists, taking your hand off the keyboard to move a mouse or point with a finger may be slower than typing the relevant command. This problem is especially likely to occur if the user is familiar with a compact notation, such as arithmetic expressions, that is easy to enter from a keyboard, but that may be more difficult to select with a mouse. The keyboard remains the most effective direct-manipulation device for certain tasks.

Choosing the right objects and actions is not necessarily an easy task. Simple metaphors, analogies, or models with a minimal set of concepts are a good starting point. Mixing metaphors from two sources may add complexity that contributes to confusion. The emotional tone of the metaphor should be inviting rather than distasteful or inappropriate (Carroll and Thomas, 1982)—sewage-disposal systems are an inappropriate metaphor for electronic-message systems. Since the users may not share the metaphor, analogy, or conceptual model with the designer, ample testing is required. For help in training, an explicit statement of the model, of the assumptions, and of the limitations is necessary.

6.3.2 The OAI model explanation of direct manipulation

The attraction of direct manipulation is apparent in the enthusiasm of the users. The designers of the examples in Section 6.2 had an innovative inspiration and an intuitive grasp of what users would want. Each example has features that we could criticize, but it will be more productive for us to construct an integrated portrait of direct manipulation with three principles:

1. Continuous representation of the objects and actions of interest with meaningful visual metaphors
2. Physical actions or presses of labeled buttons, instead of complex syntax
3. Rapid incremental reversible operations whose effect on the object of interest is visible immediately

Using these three principles, it is possible to design systems that have these beneficial attributes:

- Novices can learn basic functionality quickly, usually through a demonstration by a more experienced user.
- Experts can work rapidly to carry out a wide range of tasks, even defining new functions and features.
- Knowledgeable intermittent users can retain operational concepts.
- Error messages are rarely needed.
- Users can immediately see whether their actions are furthering their goals, and, if the actions are counterproductive, they can simply change the direction of their activity.
- Users experience less anxiety because the system is comprehensible and because actions can be reversed easily.

- Users gain confidence and mastery because they are the initiators of action, they feel in control, and they can predict the system responses.

The success of direct manipulation is understandable in the context of the OAI model. The object of interest is displayed so that interface actions are close to the high-level task domain. There is little need for the mental decomposition of tasks into multiple interface commands with a complex syntactic form. On the contrary, each action produces a comprehensible result in the task domain that is visible in the interface immediately. The closeness of the task domain to the interface domain reduces operator problem-solving load and stress. This basic principle is related to stimulus-response compatibility, as discussed in the human-factors literature. The task objects and actions dominate the users' concerns, and the distraction of dealing with a tedious interface is reduced (Fig. 6.10).

In contrast to textual descriptors, dealing with visual representations of objects may be more "natural" and closer to innate human capabilities: Action and visual skills emerged well before language in human evolution. Psychologists have long known that people grasp spatial relation-

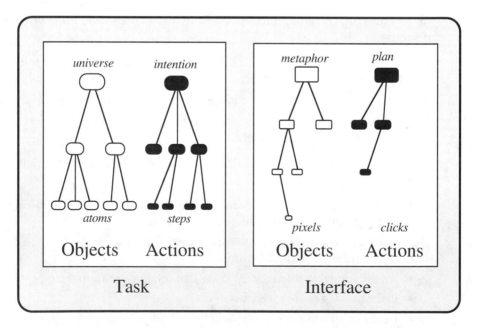

Figure 6.10

Direct-manipulation systems may require users to learn substantial task knowledge. However, users must acquire only a modest amount of interface knowledge and syntactic details.

ships and actions more quickly when those people are given visual rather than linguistic representations. Furthermore, intuition and discovery are often promoted by suitable visual representations of formal mathematical systems.

The Swiss psychologist Jean Piaget described *four stages of development: sensorimotor* (from birth to approximately 2 years), *preoperational* (2 to 7 years), *concrete operational* (7 to 11 years), and *formal operations* (begins at approximately 11 years) (Copeland, 1979). According to this theory, physical actions on an object are comprehensible during the concrete operational stage, and children acquire the concept of *conservation* or *invariance*. At about age 11, children enter the formal-operations stage, in which they use *symbol manipulation* to represent actions on objects. Since mathematics and programming require abstract thinking, they are difficult for children, and designers must link symbolic representations to actual objects. Direct manipulation brings activity to the concrete-operational stage, thus making certain tasks easier for children and adults.

6.4   Visual Thinking and Icons

The concepts of a *visual language* and of *visual thinking* were promoted by Arnheim (1972), and were embraced by commercial graphic designers (Verplank, 1988; Mullet and Sano, 1995), semiotically oriented academics (*semiotics* is the study of signs and symbols), and data-visualization gurus. The computer provides a remarkable visual environment for revealing structure, showing relationships, and enabling interactivity that attracts users who have artistic, right-brained, holistic, intuitive personalities. The increasingly visual nature of computer interfaces can sometimes challenge or even threaten the logical, linear, text-oriented, left-brained, compulsive, rational programmers who were the heart of the first generation of hackers. Although these stereotypes—or caricatures—will not stand up to scientific analysis, they do convey the dual paths that computing is following. The new visual directions are sometimes scorned by the traditionalists as *WIMP* (windows, icons, mouse, and pull-down menu) interfaces, whereas the command-line devotees are seen as inflexible, or even stubborn.

There is evidence that different people have different cognitive styles, and it is quite understandable that individual preferences may vary. Just as there are multiple ice-cream flavors or car models, so too there will be multiple interface styles. It may be that preferences will vary by user and by tasks. So respect is due to each community, and the designer's goal is to provide the best of each style and the means to cross over when desired.

The conflict between text and graphics becomes most heated when the issue of *icons* is raised. Maybe it is not surprising that the dictionary definitions of *icon* usually refer to religious images, but the central notion in computing is that an icon is an image, picture, or symbol representing a concept (Rogers, 1989; Marcus, 1992). In the computer world, icons are usually small (less than 1-inch-square or 64- by 64-pixel) representations of an object or action. Smaller icons are often used to save space or to be integrated within other objects, such as a window border or toolbar. It is not surprising that icons are often used in painting programs to represent the tools or actions (lasso or scissors to cut out an image, brush for painting, pencil for drawing, eraser to wipe clean), whereas word processors usually have textual menus for their actions. This difference appears to reflect the differing cognitive styles of visually and textually oriented users, or at least differences in the tasks. Maybe, while you are working on visually oriented tasks, it is helpful to "stay visual" by using icons, whereas, while you are working on a text document, it is helpful to "stay textual" by using textual menus.

For situations where both a visual icon or a textual item are possible—for example, in a directory listing—designers face two interwoven issues: how to decide between icons and text, and how to design icons. The well-established highway signs are a useful source of experience. Icons are unbeatable for showing ideas such as a road curve, but sometimes a phrase such as ONE WAY!—DO NOT ENTER is more comprehensible than an icon. Of course, the smorgasbord approach is to have a little of each (as with, for example, the octagonal STOP sign), and there is evidence that icons plus words are effective in computing situations (Norman, 1991). So the answer to the first question (deciding between icons and text) depends not only on the users and the tasks, but also on the quality of the icons or the words that are proposed. Textual menu choices are covered in Chapter 7; many of the principles carry over. In addition, these icon-specific guidelines should be considered:

- Represent the object or action in a familiar and recognizable manner.
- Limit the number of different icons.
- Make the icon stand out from its background.
- Consider three-dimensional icons; they are eye catching, but also can be distracting.
- Ensure that a single selected icon is clearly visible when surrounded by unselected icons.
- Make each icon distinctive from every other icon.
- Ensure the harmoniousness of each icon as a member of a family of icons.

- Design the movement animation: when dragging an icon, the user might move the whole icon, just a frame, possibly a grayed-out or transparent version, or a black box.
- Add detailed information, such as shading to show size of a file (larger shadow indicates larger file), thickness to show breadth of a directory folder (thicker means more files inside), color to show the age of a document (older might be yellower or grayer), or animation to show how much of a document has been printed (a document folder is absorbed progressively into the printer icon).
- Explore the use of combinations of icons to create new objects or actions—for example, dragging a document icon to a folder, trashcan, outbox, or printer icon has great utility. Can a document be appended or prepended to another document by pasting of adjacent icons? Can a user set security levels by dragging a document or folder to a guard dog, police car, or vault icon? Can two database icons be intersected by overlapping of the icons?

Marcus (1992) applies semiotics as a guide to four levels of icon design:

1. *Lexical qualities*   Machine-generated marks—pixel shape, color, brightness, blinking
2. *Syntactics*   Appearance and movement—lines, patterns, modular parts, size, shape
3. *Semantics*   Objects represented—concrete versus abstract, part versus whole
4. *Pragmatics*   Overall legible, utility, identifiable, memorable, pleasing

He recommends starting by creating quick sketches, pushing for consistent style, designing a layout grid, simplifying appearance, and evaluating the designs by testing with users. We might consider a fifth level of icon design:

5. *Dynamics* Receptivity to clicks—highlighting, dragging, combining

The dynamics of icons might also include a rich set of gestures with a mouse, touchscreen, or pen. The gestures might indicate copy (up and down), delete (a cross), edit (a circle), and so on. Icons might also have associated sounds. For example, if each document icon had associated with it a tone (the lower the tone, the bigger the document), then, when a directory was opened, each tone might be played simultaneously or sequentially. Users might get used to the symphony played by each directory and could detect certain features or anomalies, just as we often know telephone numbers by tune and can detect misdialings as discordant tones.

Icon design becomes more interesting as computer hardware improves and as designers become more creative. Animated icons that demonstrate their function improve online help capabilities (see Section 12.4.2). Beyond simple icons, we are now seeing increasing numbers of visual programming languages (see Section 5.3.1) and specialized languages for mechanical engineering, circuit design, and database query.

6.5   Direct-Manipulation Programming

Performing tasks by direct manipulation is not the only goal. It should be possible to do programming by direct manipulation as well, at least for certain problems. People sometimes program robots by moving the robot arm through a sequence of steps that are later replayed, possibly at higher speed. This example seems to be a good candidate for generalization. How about moving a drill press or a surgical tool through a complex series of motions that are then repeated exactly? In fact, these direct-manipulation–programming ideas are implemented in modest ways with automobile radios that users preset by tuning to their desired station and then pressing and holding a button. Later, when the button is pressed, the radio tunes to the preset frequency. Some professional television-camera supports allow the operator to program a sequence of pans or zooms and then to replay it smoothly when required.

Programming of physical devices by direct manipulation seems quite natural, and an adequate visual representation of information may make direct-manipulation programming possible in other domains. Several word processors allow users to create macros by simply performing a sequence of commands and storing it for later use. WordPerfect enables the creation of macros that are sequences of text, special function keys such as TAB, and other WordPerfect commands. emacs allows its rich set of functions, including regular expression searching, to be recorded into macros. Macros can invoke one another, leading to complex programming possibilities. These and other systems allow users to create programs with nonvarying action sequences using direct manipulation, but strategies for including loops and conditionals vary. emacs allows macros to be encased in a loop with simple repeat factors. emacs and WordPerfect also allow users to attach more general control structures by resorting to textual programming languages.

Spreadsheet packages, such as LOTUS 1-2-3 and Excel, have rich programming languages and allow users to create portions of programs by carrying out standard spreadsheet operations. The result of the operations is stored in another part of the spreadsheet and can be edited, printed, and stored in a textual form.

Macro facilities in GUIs are more challenging to design than are macro facilities in traditional command interfaces. The MACRO command of Direct

Manipulation Disk Operating System (DMDOS) (Iseki and Shneiderman, 1986) was an early attempt to support a limited form of programming for file movement, copying, and directory commands.

Smith (1977) inspired work in this area with his Pygmalion system that allowed arithmetic programs to be specified visually with icons. A number of early research projects have attempted to create direct-manipulation programming systems (Rubin et al., 1985). Maulsby and Witten (1989) developed a system that could induce or infer a program from examples, questioning the users to resolve ambiguities. In constrained domains, inferences become predictable and useful, but if the inference is occasionally wrong, users will quickly distrust it.

Myers (1992) coined the phrase *demonstrational programming* to characterize the technique of letting users create macros by simply doing their tasks and having the system construct the proper generalization automatically. Cypher (1991) built and ran a usability test with seven subjects for his EAGER system that monitored user actions within HyperCard. When EAGER recognized two similar sequences, a small smiling cat appeared on the screen to offer the users help in carrying out further iterations. Cypher's success with two specific tasks is encouraging, but it has proved to be difficult to generalize this approach.

It would be helpful if the computer could recognize repeated patterns reliably and create useful macros automatically, while the user was engaged in performing a repetitive interface task. Then, with the user's confirmation, the computer could take over and could carry out the remainder of the task automatically. This hope for automatic programming is appealing, but a more effective approach may be to give users the visual tools to specify and record their intentions. Rule-based programming with graphical conditions and actions offers a fresh alternative that may be appealing to children and adults (Fig. 6.11) (Smith et al., 1994). The screen is portrayed as a set of tiles, and users specify graphical rewrite rules by showing before-and-after tile examples. Another innovative environment conceived of initially for children is ToonTalk (Kahn, 1996), which offers animated cartoon characters who carry out actions in buildings using a variety of fanciful tools.

To create a reliable tool that works in many situations without unpredictable automatic programming, designers must meet the *five challenges of programming in the user interface (PITUI)* (Potter, 1993):

1. Sufficient computational generality (conditionals, iteration)

2. Access to the appropriate data structures (file structures for directories, structural representations of graphical objects) and operators (selectors, booleans, specialized operators of applications)

3. Ease in programming (by specification, by example, or by demonstration, with modularity, argument passing, and so on) and in editing programs

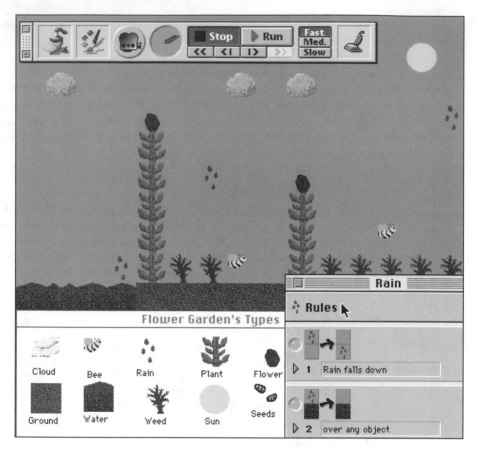

Figure 6.11

Cocoa display showing the Flower Garden world, with the control panel, the garden data types, and the graphical rules for the rain falling down and getting absorbed by any object. (Used with permission of Apple Computers, Inc., Cupertino, CA.)

4. Simplicity in invocation and assignment of arguments (direct manipulation, simple library strategies with meaningful names or icons, in-context execution, and availability of results)

5. Low risk (high probability of bug-free programs, halt and resume facilities to permit partial executions, undo operations to enable repair of unanticipated damage)

The goal of PITUI is to allow users easily and reliably to repeat automatically the actions that they can perform manually in the user interface. Rather than depending on unpredictable inferencing, users will be able to indicate their intentions explicitly by manipulating objects and actions. The design of direct-manipulation systems will undoubtedly be influenced by the need to support PITUI. This influence will be a positive step that will also facilitate history keeping, undo, and online help.

The *cognitive-dimensions framework* may help us to analyze design issues of visual-programming environments, such as those needed for PITUI (Green and Petre, 1996). The framework provides a vocabulary to facilitate discussion of high-level design issues; for example, *viscosity* is used to describe the difficulty of making changes in a program, and *progressive evaluation* describes the capacity for execution of partial programs. Other dimensions are consistency, diffuseness, hidden dependencies, premature commitment, and visibility.

Direct-manipulation programming offers an alternative to the agent scenarios (see Section 2.9). Agent promoters believe that the computer can ascertain the users' intentions automatically, or can take action based on a vague statements of goals. I doubt that user intentions are so easily determined or that vague statements are usually effective. However, if users can specify what they want with comprehensible actions selected from a visual display, then they can often and rapidly accomplish their goals while preserving their sense of control and accomplishment.

6.6 Home Automation

Internationally, many companies predict a large market in extensive controls in homes, but only if the user interfaces can be made simple. Remote control of devices (either from one part of the home to another, from outside, or by programmed delays) is being extended to channel audio and video throughout the house, to schedule lawn watering as a function of ground moisture, to offer video surveillance and burglar alarms, and to provide multiple-zone environmental controls plus detailed maintenance records.

Some designers promote voice controls, but commercially successful systems use traditional pushbuttons, remote controllers, telephone keypads, and touchscreens, with the latter proving to be the most popular. Installations with two to 10 touchscreens spread around the house should satisfy most homeowners. Providing direct-manipulation controls with rich feedback is vital in these applications. Users are willing to take training, but operation must be rapid and easy to remember even if the option is used only once or twice per year (such as spring and fall adjustments for daylight-savings time).

Studies of four touchscreen designs, all based on direct manipulation, explored scheduling operations for VCR recording and light controls (Plaisant et al., 1990; Plaisant and Shneiderman, 1991). The four designs were

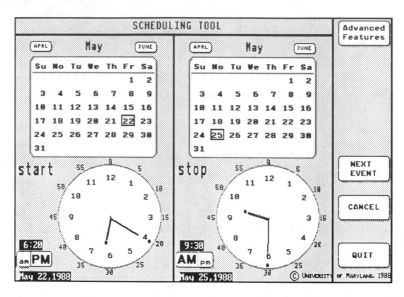

Figure 6.12

This scheduler shows two calendars for start and stop dates, plus two 12-hour circular clocks with hands that the user can drag to set start and stop times. (Used with permission of University of Maryland, College Park, MD.)

1. A digital clock that users set by pressing step keys (similar to onscreen programming in current videocassette players)
2. A 24-hour circular clock whose hands users can drag with fingers
3. A 12-hour circular clock (plus A.M.–P.M. toggle) whose hands users can drag with fingers (Fig. 6.12)
4. A 24-hour time line in which ON–OFF flags can be placed to indicate start-stop times (Fig. 6.13)

The results indicated that the 24-hour time line was easiest to understand and use. Direct-manipulation principles were central to this design; users selected dates by touching a monthly calendar, and times by moving the ON or OFF flags on to the 24-hour time line. The flags were an effective way of representing the ON or OFF actions and of specifying times without use of a keyboard. The capacity to adjust the flag locations incrementally, and the ease of removing them, were additional benefits. We are extending the design to accommodate more complex tasks, such as scheduling and synchronization of multiple devices, searching through schedules to find dates with specific events, scheduling repeated events (close curtains every night at dusk, turn lights on every Friday night at 7 P.M., record status monthly),

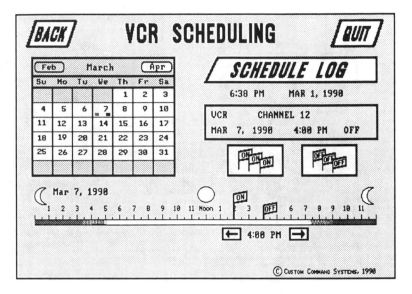

Figure 6.13

This 24-hour time-line scheduler was most successful in our usability studies. The users select a date by pointing on the calendar and then dragging ON and OFF flags to the 24-hour time lines. The feedback is a red line on the calendar and the time lines. (Used with permission of University of Maryland, College Park, MD.)

and long-duration events. A generalization of the flags-on-a-line idea was applied to heating control, where users specified upper and lower bounds by dragging flags on a thermometer.

Since so much of home control involves the room layouts and floorplans, many direct-manipulation actions take place on a display of the floorplan (Fig. 6.14), with selectable icons for each status indicator (such as burglar alarm, heat sensor, or smoke detector), and for each activator (such as curtain or shade closing and opening motors, airconditioning- or heating-vent controllers, or audio and video speaker or screen). People could route sound from a CD player located in the living room to the bedroom and kitchen by merely dragging the CD icon into those rooms. Sound-volume control would be accomplished by having the user move a marker on a linear scale.

The simple act of turning a device ON or OFF proved to be an interesting problem. Wall-mounted light switches typically show their status by up for ON and down for OFF. Most people have learned this standard and can get what they want on the first try, if they know which switch to throw to turn on a specific light. Laying out the switches to reflect the floorplan does solve

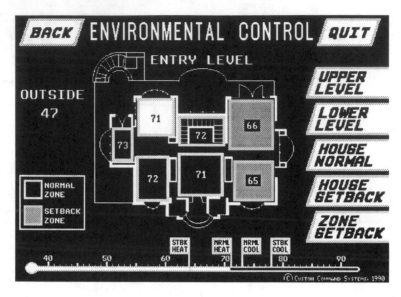

Figure 6.14

Floorplan of a private home, used to set temperatures. Direct-manipulation designs emphasize task-domain graphics. (Courtesy of Custom Command Systems, College Park, MD.)

the problem nicely (Norman, 1988). Visitors may have problems because, in some countries, ON and OFF are reversed or the up-down switches have been replaced by push buttons. To explore possibilities, we constructed six kinds of touchscreen ON-OFF buttons with three-dimensional animation and sound (Fig. 6.15). There were significant differences in user preferences, with high marks going to the simple button, the rocker, and multiple-level pushbuttons. The multiple pushbuttons have a readily comprehensible

Figure 6.15

Varying designs for toggle buttons using three-dimensional graphic characteristics. Designed by Catherine Plaisant.

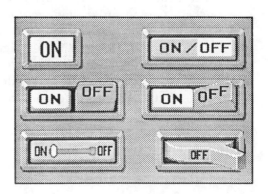

visual presentation, and they generalize nicely to multiple state devices (OFF, LOW, MEDIUM, HIGH).

Controlling complex home equipment from a touchscreen by direct manipulation reshapes how we think of homes and their residents. New questions arise, such as whether residents will feel safer, be happier, save more money, or experience more relaxation with these devices. Are there new notations, such as petri-net variants or role-task diagrams, for describing home automation and the social relations among residents? The benefits to users who have disabilities or are elderly were often on our minds as we designed these systems, since these people may be substantial beneficiaries of this technology, even though initial implementations are designed for the healthy and wealthy.

6.7 Remote Direct Manipulation

There are great opportunities for the teleoperation or remote control of devices if acceptable user interfaces can be constructed. If designers can provide adequate feedback in sufficient time to permit effective decision making, then attractive applications in office automation, computer-supported collaborative work, education, and information services may become viable. Remote-controlled environments in medicine could enable specialists to provide consultations more rapidly, or allow surgeons to conduct more complex procedures during operations. Home-automation applications could extend remote operation of telephone-answering machines to security and access systems, energy control, and operation of appliances. Scientific applications in space, underwater, or in hostile environments can enable new research projects to be conducted economically and safely (Uttal, 1989; Sheridan, 1992).

In traditional direct-manipulation systems, the objects and actions of interest are shown continuously; users generally point, click, or drag, rather than type; and feedback, indicating change, is immediate. However, when the devices being operated are remote, these goals may not be realizable, and designers must expend additional effort to help users to cope with slower response, incomplete feedback, increased likelihood of breakdowns, and more complex error recovery. The problems are strongly connected to the hardware, physical environment, network design, and the task domain.

A typical remote application is *telemedicine*: medical care delivered over communication links (Satava and Jones, 1996). In one scenario, the physician specialist being consulted and the patient's primary physician or a technician are in different locations. Then, for example, an effective telepathology

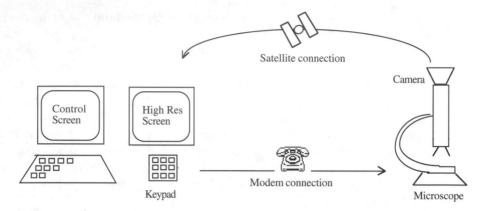

Figure 6.16

A simplified diagram of a telepathology system showing control actions sent by tele-phone and images sent by satellite.

system (Weinstein et al., 1989) allows a pathologist to examine tissue sam-ples or body fluids under a remotely located microscope (Figs. 6.16 and 6.17). The transmitting workstation has a high-resolution camera mounted on a motorized light microscope. The image is transmitted via broadband satel-lite, microwave, or cable. The consulting pathologist at the receiving work-station can manipulate the microscope using a keypad, and can see a high-resolution image of the magnified sample. The two care givers talk by telephone to coordinate control and to request slides that are placed manu-ally under the microscope. Controls include

- Magnification (three or six objectives)
- Focus (coarse and fine bidirectional control)
- Illumination (bidirectional adjustment continuous or by step)
- Position (two-dimensional placement of the slide under the microscope objective)

The architecture of remote environments introduces several complicating factors:

- *Time delays*   The network hardware and software cause delays in send-ing user actions and receiving feedback: a *transmission delay*, or the time it takes for the command to reach the microscope (in our example,

Figure 6.17

Telepathology components include a microscope with a camera attached to a workstation. This setup enables a pathologist to use remote control to examine the slides. (Used with permission of William J. Chimiak and Robert O. Rainer, The Bowman Gray School of Medicine of Wake Forest University, Winston Salem, NC.)

transmitting the command through the modem), and *operation delay,* or the time until the microscope responds (Van de Vegte et al., 1990). These delays in the system prevent the operator from knowing the current status of the system. For example, if a positioning command has been issued, it may take several seconds for the slide to start moving. As the feedback appears showing the motion, the users may recognize that they are going to overshoot their destination, but a few seconds will pass before the stopping command takes effect.

- *Incomplete feedback* Devices originally designed for direct control may not have adequate sensors or status indicators. For instance, the microscope can transmit its current position, but it operates so slowly that it cannot be used continuously. Thus, it is not possible to indicate on the control screen the exact current position relative to the start and desired positions.

- *Feedback from multiple sources* Incomplete feedback is different from no feedback. The image received on the high-resolution screen is the main feedback to evaluate the result of an action. In addition, the microscope can occasionally report its exact position, allowing recalibration of the status display. It is also possible to indicate the estimated stage position during the execution of a movement. This estimated feedback can be used as a progress indicator whose accuracy depends on the variability of the time delays. To comply with the physical incompatibility between the high-resolution feedback (analog image) and the rest of the system (digital), we spread the multiple feedbacks over several screens. Thus, the pathologists are forced to switch back and forth between multiple sources of feedback, increasing their cognitive load.

- *Unanticipated interferences*   Since the devices operated are remote, and may be also operated by other persons in this or another remote location, unanticipated interferences are more likely to occur than in traditional direct-manipulation environments. For instance, if the slide under the microscope were moved (accidentally) by a local operator, the positions indicated might not be correct. A breakdown might also occur during the execution of a remote operation, without a good indication of this event being sent to the remote site. Such breakdowns require increased status information for remote users and additional actions that allow for correction.

One solution to these problems is to make explicit the network delays and breakdowns as part of the system. The user sees a model of the starting state of the system, the action that has been initiated, and the current state of the system as it carries out the action. It may be preferable to provide spatially parameterized positioning actions (for example, move by a distance $+x$, $+y$, or move to a fixed point (x, y) in a two-dimensional space), rather than providing temporal commands (for example, start moving right at a 36° angle from the horizontal). In other words, the users specify a destination (rather than a motion), and wait until the action is completed before readjusting the destination if necessary.

Remote direct manipulation is rooted in two domains that, so far, have been independent. The first root grows from direct manipulation in personal computers and is often identified with the desktop metaphor and office automation. The second root is in process control, where human operators control physical processes in complex environments. Typical tasks are operating power or chemical plants, controlling manufacturing, flying airplanes, or steering vehicles. If the physical processes take place in a remote location, we talk about *teleoperation* or *remote control.* To perform the control task, the human operator may interact with a computer, which may carry out some of the control tasks without any interference by the human operator. This idea is captured by the notion of *supervisory control* (Sheridan, 1992). Although supervisory control and direct manipulation stem from different problem domains and are usually applied to different system architectures, they carry a strong resemblance.

6.8   Virtual Environments

Flight-simulator designers use many tricks to create the most realistic experience for fighter or airline pilots. The cockpit displays and controls are taken from the same production line that create the real ones. Then, the windows are replaced by high-resolution computer displays, and sounds are choreographed to give the impression of engine start or reverse thrust. Finally, the vibration and tilting during climbing or turning are created by hydraulic jacks and intricate suspension systems. This elaborate technology may cost almost $100 million, but even then it is a lot cheaper, safer, and more useful for training than the $400-million jet that it simulates. Of course, home videogame players have purchased millions of $30 flight simulators that run on their personal computers. Flying a plane is a complicated and specialized skill, but simulators are available for more common—and for some surprising—tasks under the alluring name of *virtual reality* or the more descriptive *virtual environments*.

High above the office desktop, much beyond multimedia, and farther out than the hype of hypermedia, the gurus and purveyors of virtuality are promoting immersive experiences (Fig. 6.18). Whether soaring over Seattle, bending around bronchial tubes to find lung cancers, or grasping complex molecules, the cyberspace explorers are moving past their initial fantasies to create useful technologies. The imagery and personalities involved in virtual reality are often colorful (Rheingold, 1991), but many researchers have tried to present a balanced view by conveying enthusiasm while reporting on problems (MacDonald and Vince, 1994; Bryson, 1996).

Architects have been using computers to draw three-dimensional representations of buildings for two decades. Most of their design systems show the building on a standard or slightly larger display, but adding a large-screen projector to create a wall-sized image gives prospective clients a more realistic impression. Now add animation that allows clients to see what happens if they move left or right, or approach the image. Then enable clients to control the animation by walking on a treadmill (faster walking brings the building closer more quickly), and allow them to walk through the doors or up the stairs. Finally, replace the large-screen projector with a head-mounted display, and monitor head movement with Polhemus trackers. Each change

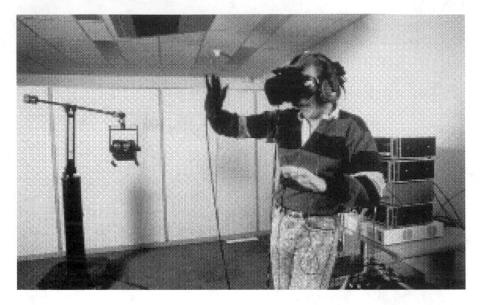

Figure 6.18

In the goggles-and-gloves approach to virtual reality, the system tracks the user's hand
and head motions, plus finger gestures, to
control the scene's movement and manipulation. To enter this virtual environment you
need special gear. Any of several types of
stereoscopic devices transform otherwise
two-dimensional image data into three-
dimensional images. Some three-dimensional viewers, called head-mounted
displays, resemble helmets with movie
screens where the visor would be. (NCSA/
University of Illinois.)

takes users a bit farther along the range from "looking at" to "being in."
Bumping into walls, falling (gently) down stairs, meeting other people, or
having to wait for an elevator could be the next variations.

The architectural application is a persuasive argument for "being in,"
because we are used to "being in" buildings and moving around them. On
the other hand, for many applications, "looking at" is often more effective,
which is why air-traffic–control workstations place the viewer above the situation display. Similarly, seeing movies on the large wraparound screens
that put viewers "in" race cars or airplanes are special events compared to
the more common "looking at" television experience. The Living Theater of
the 1960s created an involving theatrical experience and "be-ins" were popu-

lar, but most theater goers prefer to take their "suspension of disbelief" experiences from the "looking at" perspective (Laurel, 1991).

It remains to be seen whether doctors, accustomed to "looking at" a patient, really want to crawl through the patient's lungs or "be in" the patient's brains. Modern surgical procedures and technology can benefit by "looking at" video images from inside a patient's heart taken through fiber-optic cameras and from use of remote direct-manipulation devices that minimize the invasive surgery. Surgery planning can also be done with three-dimensional "looking at" visualizations shown on a traditional desktop display and guided by hand-held props (Hinckley et al., 1994). There are more mundane applications for such video and fiberoptic magic; imagine the benefits to household plumbers of being able to see lost wedding rings around the bends of a sink drain or to see and grasp the child's toy that has fallen down the pipes of a now-clogged toilet.

Other concepts that were sources for the current excitement include *artificial reality*, pioneered by Myron Krueger (1991). His VideoPlace and VideoDesk installations with large-screen projectors and video sensors combined full-body movement with projected images of light creatures that walked along a performer's arm or of multicolored patterns and sounds generated by the performer's movement. Similarly, Vincent Vincent's demonstrations of the Mandala system carried performance art to a new level of sophistication and fantasy. The CAVE, a room with several walls of high-resolution rear-projected displays with three-dimensional audio, can offer satisfying experiences for several people at a time (Cruz-Neira et al., 1993) (Fig. 6.19).

The telepresence aspect of virtual reality breaks the physical limitations of space and allows users to act as though they are somewhere else. Practical thinkers immediately grasp the connection to remote direct manipulation, remote control, and remote vision, but the fantasists see the potential to escape current reality and to visit science-fiction worlds, cartoonlands, previous times in history, galaxies with different laws of physics, or unexplored emotional territories. Virtual worlds can be used to treat patients with fear of height by giving them an immersive experience with control over their viewpoint, while preserving their sense of physical safety (Fig. 6.20) (Hodges et al., 1995).

The direct-manipulation principles and the OAI model may be helpful to people who are designing and refining virtual environments. Users should be able to select actions rapidly by pointing or gesturing, with incremental and reversible control, and display feedback should occur immediately to convey the sense of causality. Interface objects and actions should be simple, so that users view and manipulate task-domain objects. The surgeon's instruments should be readily available or easily called up by spoken command or gesture. Similarly, an interior designer walking through a house with a client should be able to pick up a window-stretching tool or pull on a handle to try out a larger window, or to use a room-painting tool to change

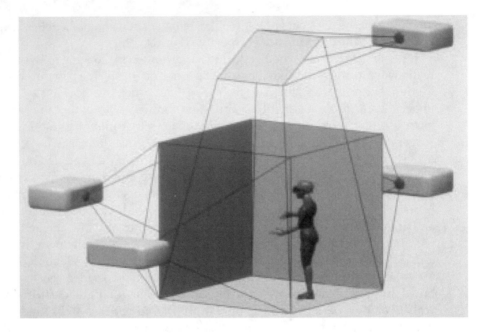

Figure 6.19

The CAVE™, a multiperson, room-sized, high-resolution, 3D video and audio environment at the University of Illinois at Chicago. The CAVE is a 10- × 10- × 9-foot theater, made up of three rear-projection screens for walls and a down-projection screen for the floor. Projectors throw full-color workstation fields (1024 × 768 stereo) onto the screens at 96 Hz. (© 1992. Image courtesy of Lewis Siegel and Kathy O'Keefe, Electronic Visualization Laboratory, University of Illinois at Chicago.)

the wall colors while leaving the windows and furniture untouched. Navigation in large virtual spaces presents further challenges, but overview maps have been demonstrated to provide useful orientation information (Darken and Sibert, 1996).

Alternatives to the immersive environment, often called *desktop* or *fishtank* virtual environments (both references are to "looking at" standard displays), are becoming more common and more accepted. The long-standing active work on three-dimensional graphics has led to user interfaces that support user-controlled exploration of real places, scientific visualizations, or fantasy worlds. Many applications run on high-performance workstations capable of rapid rendering, but some are appealing even over the web using the popular Virtual Reality Modeling Language (VRML) (Goralski, 1996).

Graphics researchers have been perfecting image display to simulate lighting effects, textured surfaces, reflections, and shadows. Data structures and algorithms for zooming in or panning across an object or room rapidly and smoothly are becoming practical on common computers. In an innova-

Figure 6.20

Virtual-reality therapy for users who have acrophobia. These users can accommodate to heights by going up in this virtual elevator with a guard rail located at waist level. The controls for the elevator are located on the guard rail: a green up arrow, a green down arrow, and a red stop square. (Hodges et al., 1995.) (Used with permission of Larry F. Hodges, Rob Kooper, and Tom Meyer, Georgia Tech, Atlanta, GA.)

tion called "augmented reality," users see the real world with an overlay of additional information; for example, while users are looking at the walls of a building, their semitransparent eyeglasses show where the electrical wires or plumbing are located. Augmented reality could show users where and how to repair electrical equipment or automobile engines (Feiner et al., 1993).

Another variant, called *situational awareness*, uses a palmtop computer with a location sensor to control the display. As the user moves the palmtop around a map, museum, or a piece of machinery, the display shows information about the city neighborhoods, the paintings, or the history of repairs (Fitzmaurice, 1993). Shopping carts with displays that advertise products as you walk down the supermarket aisle have already been installed.

Successful virtual environments will depend on smooth integration of multiple technologies:

- *Visual display*   The normal-size (12 to 15 inches diagonally) computer display at a normal viewing distance (70 centimeters) subtends an angle of about 5 degrees; large-screen (15- to 22-inch) displays can cover a 20- to 30-degree field, and the head-mounted displays cover 100 degrees horizontally and 60 degrees vertically. The head-mounted displays block other images, so the effect is more dramatic, and head motion produces new images, so the users can get the impression of 360 degree coverage. Flight simulators also block extraneous images, but they do so without forcing the users to wear sometimes-cumbersome head-mounted displays. Another approach is a boom-mounted display that senses the users' positions without requiring that they wear heavy goggles (Fig. 6.21).

  As hardware technology improves, it will be possible to provide more rapid and higher-resolution images. Most researchers agree that the displays must approach real time (probably under 100 millisecond delay) in presenting the images to the users. Low-resolution displays are acceptable while users or the objects are moving, but when users stop to stare, higher resolution is necessary to preserve the sense of "being in." Improved hardware and algorithms are needed to display rough shapes rapidly and then to fill in the details when the motion stops. A further requirement is that motion be smooth; both incremen-

Figure 6.21

A full-color head-coupled stereoscopic display. The Fakespace BOOM3C (Binocular Omni-Orientation Monitor) provides high-quality visual displays and tracking integrated with a counterbalanced articulated arm for full six-degree of freedom motion (x, y, z, roll, pitch, yaw). Pictured here is a computer model of the Basilica of St. Francis of Assisi, complete with fourteenth century frescoes by Giotto. (Composite photo of BOOM3C® courtesy of Fakespace, Inc. (241 Polaris Avenue, Mountain View, CA 94043) and Infobyte.)

tal changes and continuous display of the objects of interest are required (Hendrix and Barfield, 1996).

- *Head-position sensing* Head-mounted displays can provide differing views depending on head position. Look to the right, and you see a forest; look to the left, and the forest gives way to a city. The Polhemus tracker requires mounting on the user's head, but other devices embedded in a hat or eyeglasses are possible. Video recognition of head position is possible. Sensor precision should be high (within 1 degree) and rapid (within 100 milliseconds). Eye tracking to recognize the focus of attention might be useful, but it is difficult to accomplish while the user is moving and is wearing a head-mounted display.

- *Hand-position sensing* The DataGlove is a highly innovative invention; it surely will be refined and improved beyond its current low resolution. Bryson (1996) complains that "the problems with glove devices include inaccuracies in measurement and lack of standard gestural vocabulary." It may turn out that accurate measurement of finger position is required only for one or two fingers or for only one or two joints. Hand orientation is provided by a Polhemus tracker mounted on the glove or wrist. Sensors for other body parts such as knees, arms, or legs may yet find uses. The potential for sensors and tactile feedback on more erotic body parts has been referred to by more than one journalist.

- *Force feedback* Hand-operated remote-control devices for performing experiments in chemistry laboratories or for handling nuclear materials provide force feedback that gives users a good sense of when they grasp an object or bump into one. Force feedback to car drivers and pilots is carefully configured to provide realistic and useful tactile information. Simulated feedback from software was successful in speeding docking tasks with complex molecules (Brooks, 1988). It might be helpful for surgeons to receive force feedback as they practice difficult operations. A palmtop display mounted on a boom was shown to produce faster and more accurate performance on a remote manipulation task when haptic (touch and force feedback) feedback was added (Noma et al., 1996). Remote handshaking as part of a video conference has been suggested, but it is not clear that the experience could be as satisfying as the real thing.

- *Sound input and output* Sound output adds realism to bouncing balls, beating hearts, or dropping vases, as videogame designers found out long ago. Making convincing sounds at the correct moment with full three-dimensional effect is possible, but it too is hard work. The digital sound hardware is adequate, but the software tools are still inadequate. Music output from virtual instruments is promising; early work simulates existing instruments such as a violin, but novel instruments have emerged. Speech recognition may complement hand gestures in some applications.

- *Other sensations*   The tilting and vibration of flight simulators might provide an inspiration for some designers. Could a tilting and vibrating virtual roller coaster become popular if users could travel at 60, 600, or 6000 miles per hour and crash through mountains or go into orbit? Other effects such as a throbbing disco sound and strobe lights could also amplify some virtual experiences. Why not include real gusts of air, made hot or cold to convey the virtual weather? Finally, the power of smells to evoke strong reactions has been understood by writers from Proust to Gibson. Olfactory computing has been discussed, but appropriate and practical applications have yet to be found.

- *Cooperative and competitive virtual reality*   Computer-supported cooperative work (see Chapter 14) is a lively research area, as are cooperative virtual environments, or as one developer called it, "virtuality built for two." Two people at remote sites work together, seeing each other's actions and sharing the experience. Competitive games such as virtual racquetball have been built for two players. Software for training Army tank crews took on a much more compelling atmosphere when the designs shifted from playing against the computer to shooting at other tank crews and worrying about their attacks. The realistic sounds created such a sense of engagement that crews experienced elevated heart rates, more rapid breathing, and increased perspiration. Presumably, virtual environments could also bring relaxation and pleasant encounters with other people.

6.9   Practitioner's Summary

Among interactive systems that provide equivalent functionality and reliability, some systems emerge to dominate the competition. Often, the most appealing systems have an enjoyable user interface that offers a natural representation of the task objects and actions—hence the term *direct manipulation* (Box 6.1). These systems are easy to learn, to use, and to retain over time. Novices can acquire a simple subset of the commands, and then progress to more elaborate operations. Actions are rapid, incremental, and reversible, and can be performed with physical actions instead of complex syntactic forms. The results of operations are visible immediately, and error messages are needed less often.

Just because direct-manipulation principles have been used in a system does not ensure that system's success. A poor design, slow implementation, or inadequate functionality can undermine acceptance. For some applications, menu selection, form fillin, or command languages may be more appropriate. However, the potential for direct-manipulation programming, remote direct manipulation, and virtual reality and its variants is great. Many new products will certainly emerge. Iterative design (see Chapter 3) is espe-

Box 6.1
_____

Definition, benefits, and drawbacks of direct manipulation

Definition

- Visual representation (metaphor) of the "world of action"
  - Objects and Actions are shown
  - Analogical reasoning is tapped
- Rapid, incremental, and reversible actions
- Replacement of typing with pointing and selecting
- Immediate visibility of results of actions

Benefits over commands

- Control–display compatibility
- Less syntax reduces error rates
- Errors are more preventable
- Faster learning and higher retention
- Encourages exploration

Concerns

- Increased system resources, possibly
- Some actions may be cumbersome
- Macro techniques are often weak
- History and other tracing may be difficult
- Visually impaired users may have more difficulty

cially important in testing direct-manipulation systems, because the novelty of this approach may lead to unexpected problems for designers and users.

6.10   Researcher's Agenda

We need research to refine our understanding of the contribution of each feature of direct manipulation: analogical representation, incremental operation, reversibility, physical action instead of syntax, immediate visibility of results, and graphic form. Reversibility is easily accomplished by a generic UNDO command, but designing natural inverses for each action may be more attractive. Complex actions are well-represented with direct manipulation, but level-structured design strategies for graceful evolution from novice to expert usage would be a major contribution. For expert users, direct-manipulation programming is still an opportunity, but good methods of history keeping and editing of action sequences are needed. Software tools to create direct-manipulation environments are sorely needed to encourage exploratory development.

Beyond the desktops, and laptops, there is the allure of telepresence, virtual environments, augmented realities, and situationally aware devices. The playful aspects will certainly be pursued, but the challenge is to find the practical designs for being in and looking at three-dimensional worlds. Novel devices for walking through museums or supermarkets and teleoperation for repair seem good candidates for entrepreneurs.

World Wide Web Resources   WWW

Some creative direct manipulation services and tools are linked to, but the majority of links cover direct manipulation programming, teleoperation, and virtual environments. The web-based Virtual Reality Modeling Language enables creation of three-dimensional environments on web pages and there are numerous visually appealing websites.

http://www.aw.com/DTUI

References

Arnheim, Rudolf, *Visual Thinking*, University of California Press, Berkeley, CA (1972).

Benbasat, Izak and Todd, P., An experimental investigation of interface design alternatives: Icon versus text and direct manipulation versus menus, *International Journal of Man–Machine Studies*, 38, 3 (1993), 369–402.

Brooks, Frederick, Grasping reality through illusion: Interactive graphics serving science, *Proc. CHI '88 Conference—Human Factors in Computing Systems*, ACM, New York (1988), 1–11.

Bruner, James, *Toward a Theory of Instruction*, Harvard University Press, Cambridge, MA (1966).

Bryson, Steve, Virtual reality in scientific visualization, *Communications of the ACM*, 39, 5 (May 1996), 62–71.

Carroll, John M. and Thomas, John C., Metaphor and the cognitive representation of computing systems, *IEEE Transactions on Systems, Man, and Cybernetics*, SMC-12, 2 (March–April 1982), 107–116.

Carroll, J. M., Thomas, J. C., and Malhotra, A., Presentation and representation in design problem-solving, *British Journal of Psychology*, 71, (1980), 143–153.

Copeland, Richard W., *How Children Learn Mathematics* (Third Edition), MacMillan, New York (1979).

Cruz-Neira, C., Sandin, D. J., and DeFanti, T., Surround-screen projection-based virtual reality: The design and implementation of the CAVE, *Proc. SIGGRAPH '93 Conference*, ACM, New York (1993), 135–142.

Cypher, Allen, EAGER: Programming repetitive tasks by example, *Proc. CHI '91 Conference—Human Factors in Computing Systems*, ACM, New York (1991), 33–39.

Darken, Rudolph, P. and Sibert, John L., Navigating large virtual spaces, *International Journal of Human–Computer Interaction*, 8, 1 (1996), 49–71.

Feiner, Steven, MacIntyre, Blair, and Seligmann, Doree, Knowledge-based augmented reality, *Communications of the ACM*, 36, 7 (1993), 52–62.

Fitzmaurice, George, Situated information spaces and spatially aware palmtop computers, *Communications of the ACM*, 36, 7 (1993), 39–49.

Frohlich, David M., The history and future of direct manipulation, *Behaviour and Information Technology*, 12, 6 (1993), 315–329.

Goralski, Walter, *VRML: Exploring Virtual Worlds on the Internet*, Prentice Hall, Englewood Cliffs, NJ (1996).

Green, T. R. G. and Petre, M., Usability analysis of visual programming environments: A "cognitive dimensions" framework, *Journal of Visual Languages and Computing*, 7, (1996), 131–174.

Heckel, Paul, *The Elements of Friendly Software Design: The New Edition*, SYBEX, San Francisco (1991).

Hendrix, C., and Barfield, W., Presence within virtual environments as a function of visual display parameters, *Presence: Teleoperators and Virtual Environments*, 5, 3 (1996), 274–289.

Herot, Christopher F., Spatial management of data, *ACM Transactions on Database Systems*, 5, 4, (December 1980), 493–513.

Herot, Christopher, Graphical user interfaces. In Vassiliou, Yannis (Editor), *Human Factors and Interactive Computer Systems*, Ablex, Norwood, NJ (1984), 83–104.

Hinckley, Ken, Pausch, Randy, Goble, John C., and Kassell, Neal F., Passive real-world props for neurosurgical visualization, *Proc. CHI '94 Conference—Human Factors in Computing Systems*, ACM, New York (1994), 452–458.

Hodges, L.F., Rothbaum, B.O., Kooper, R., Opdyke, D., Meyer, T., North, M., de Graff, J.J., and Williford, J., Virtual environments for treating the fear of heights, *IEEE Computer*, 28, 7 (1995), 27–34.

Hutchins, Edwin L., Hollan, James D., and Norman, Don A., Direct manipulation interfaces. In Norman, Don A. and Draper, Stephen W. (Editors), *User Centered System Design: New Perspectives on Human–Computer Interaction*, Lawrence Erlbaum Associates, Hillsdale, NJ (1986), 87–124.

Iseki, Osamu and Shneiderman, Ben, Applying direct manipulation concepts: Direct Manipulation Disk Operating System (DMDOS), *Software Engineering Notes*, 11, 2, (March 1986), 22–26.

Krueger, Myron, *Artificial Reality II*, Addison-Wesley, Reading, MA (1991).

Laurel, Brenda, *Computers as Theatre*, Addison-Wesley, Reading, MA (1991).

MacDonald, Lindsay and Vince, John (Editors), *Interacting with Virtual Environments*, John Wiley and Sons, New York (1994).

McKim, Robert H., *Experiences in Visual Thinking* (Second Edition), Brooks/Cole, Monterey, CA (1980).

Malone, Thomas W., What makes computer games fun? *BYTE*, 6, 12 (December 1981), 258–277.

Marcus, Aaron, *Graphic Design for Electronic Documents and User Interfaces*, ACM Press, New York (1992).

Margono, Sepeedeh and Shneiderman, Ben, A study of file manipulation by novices using commands versus direct manipulation, *Twenty-sixth Annual Technical Symposium*, ACM, Washington, D.C. (June 1987), 154–159.

Maulsby, David L. and Witten, Ian H., Inducing programs in a direct-manipulation environment, *Proc. CHI '89 Conference—Human Factors in Computing Systems*, ACM, New York (1989), 57–62.

Montessori, Maria, *The Montessori Method*, Schocken, New York (1964).

Morgan, K., Morris, R. L., and Gibbs, S., When does a mouse become a rat? or . . . Comparing performance and preferences in direct manipulation and command line environment, *The Computer Journal*, 34, 3 (1991), 265–271.

Mullet, Kevin and Sano, Darrell, *Designing Visual Interfaces: Communication Oriented Techniques*, Sunsoft Press, Englewood Cliffs, NJ (1995).

Myers, Brad A., Demonstrational interfaces: A step beyond direct manipulation, *IEEE Computer*, 25, 8 (August 1992), 61–73.

Nelson, Ted, Interactive systems and the design of virtuality, *Creative Computing*, 6, 11, (November 1980), 56 ff., and G, 12 (December 1980), 94 ff.

Noma, Haruo, Miyasato, Tsutomu, and Kishino, Fumio, A palmtop display for dexterous manipulation with haptic sensation, *Proc. CHI '96 Conference—Human Factors in Computing Systems*, ACM, New York (1996), 126–133.

Norman, Donald A., *The Psychology of Everyday Things*, Basic Books, New York (1988).

Norman, Kent, *The Psychology of Menu Selection: Designing Cognitive Control at the Human/Computer Interface*, Ablex, Norwood, NJ (1991).

Papert, Seymour, *Mindstorms: Children, Computers, and Powerful Ideas*, Basic Books, New York (1980).

Phillips, C. H. E. and Apperley, M. D., Direct manipulation interaction tasks: A Macintosh-based analysis, *Interacting with Computers*, 3, 1 (1991), 9–26.

Plaisant, Catherine and Shneiderman, Ben, Scheduling ON–OFF home control devices: Design issues and usability evaluation of four touchscreen interfaces, *International Journal for Man–Machine Studies*, 36, (1992), 375–393.

Plaisant, C., Shneiderman, B., and Battaglia, J., Scheduling home-control devices: A case study of the transition from the research project to a product, *Human-Factors in Practice*, Computer Systems Technical Group, Human-Factors Society, Santa Monica, CA (December 1990), 7–12.

Polya, G., *How to Solve It*, Doubleday, New York, (1957).

Potter, Richard, Just in Time programming. In Cypher, Allen (Editor), *Watch What I Do: Programming by Demonstration*, MIT Press, Cambridge, MA (1993), 513–526.

Provenzo, Jr., Eugene R., *Video Kids: Making Sense of Nintendo*, Harvard University Press, Cambridge, MA (1991).

Rheingold, Howard, *Virtual Reality,* Simon and Schuster, New York (1991).

Robertson, George G., Card, Stuart K., and Mackinlay, Jock D., Information visual-ization using 3-D interactive animation, *Communications of the ACM,* 36, 4 (April 1993), 56–71.

Rogers, Yvonne, Icons at the interface: Their usefulness, *Interacting with Computers,* 1, 1 (1989), 105–117.

Rubin, Robert V., Golin, Eric J., and Reiss, Steven P., Thinkpad: A graphics system for programming by demonstrations, *IEEE Software,* 2, 2 (March 1985), 73–79.

Rutkowski, Chris, An introduction to the Human Applications Standard Computer Interface, Part 1: Theory and principles, *BYTE,* 7, 11 (October 1982), 291–310.

Satava, R. M. and Jones, S. B., Virtual reality and telemedicine: Exploring advanced concepts, *Telemedicine Journal,* 2, 3 (1996), 195–200.

Sheridan, T. B., *Telerobotics, Automation, and Human Supervisory Control,* The MIT Press, Cambridge, MA (1992).

Shneiderman, Ben, Direct manipulation: A step beyond programming languages, *IEEE Computer,* 16, 8, (August 1983), 57–69.

Smith, David Canfield, *Pygmalion: A Computer Program to Model and Stimulate Cre-ative Thought,* Birkhauser Verlag, Basel, Switzerland (1977).

Smith, D. Canfield, Irby, Charles, Kimball, Ralph, Verplank, Bill, and Harslem, Eric, Designing the Star user interface, *BYTE,* 7, 4 (April 1982), 242–282.

Stuart, Rory, *The Design of Virtual Environments,* McGraw-Hill, New York (1996).

Temple, Barker, and Sloane, Inc., The benefits of the graphical user interface, *Multi-media Review* (Winter 1990), 10–17.

Thimbleby, Harold, *User Interface Design,* ACM Press, New York (1990).

Ulich, E., Rauterberg, M., Moll, T., Greutmann, T., and Strohm, O., Task orientation and user-orientated dialogue design, *International Journal of Human–Computer Interaction,* 3, 2 (1991), 117–144.

Uttal, W. R., Teleoperators, *Scientific American,* 261, 6 (December 1989), 124–129.

Vince, John, *Virtual Reality Systems,* Addison-Wesley, Reading, MA (1995).

Van de Vegte, J. M. E., Milgram, P., Kwong, R. H., Teleoperator control models: Effects of time delay and imperfect system knowledge, *IEEE Transactions on Sys-tems, Man, and Cybernetics,* 20, 6 (November–December 1990), 1258–1272.

Verplank, William L., Graphic challenges in designing object-oriented user inter-faces. In Helander, M. (Editor), *Handbook of Human–Computer Interaction,* Elsevier Science Publishers, Amsterdam, The Netherlands (1988), 365–376.

Weinstein, R., Bloom, K., Rozek, S., Telepathology: Long distance diagnosis, *Ameri-can Journal of Clinical Pathology,* 91 (Suppl 1) (1989), S39–S42.

Wertheimer, M., *Productive Thinking,* Harper and Row, New York (1959).

Ziegler, J. E. and Fähnrich, K.-P., Direct manipulation. In Helander, M. (Editor), *Handbook of Human–Computer Interaction,* Elsevier Science Publishers, Amster-dam, The Netherlands (1988), 123–133.

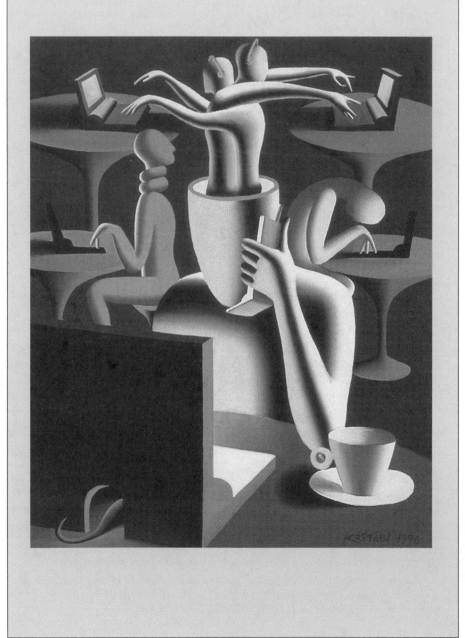

Mark Kostabi, *Message Center (Gold Rush)*, 1996

Menu Selection, Form Fillin, and Dialog Boxes

A man is responsible for his choice and must accept the consequences, whatever they may be.

W. H. Auden, *A Certain World*

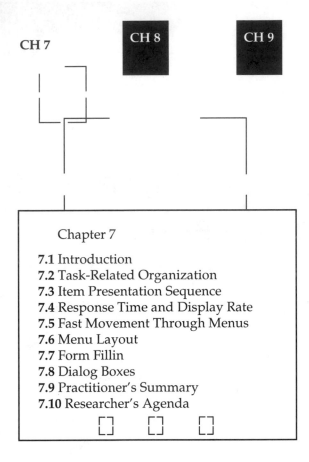

CH 7

CH 8

CH 9

Chapter 7

7.1 Introduction
7.2 Task-Related Organization
7.3 Item Presentation Sequence
7.4 Response Time and Display Rate
7.5 Fast Movement Through Menus
7.6 Menu Layout
7.7 Form Fillin
7.8 Dialog Boxes
7.9 Practitioner's Summary
7.10 Researcher's Agenda

7.1 Introduction

When designers cannot create appropriate direct-manipulation strategies, menu selection and form fillin are attractive alternatives. Whereas early systems used full-screen menus with numbered items, modern menus are usually pulldowns, check boxes or radio buttons in dialog boxes, or embedded links on World Wide Web pages, all selectable by mouse clicks. When the menu items are written with familiar terminology and are organized in a convenient structure and sequence, users can select an item easily.

Menus are effective because they offer the cues to elicit user recognition, rather than forcing the user to recall the syntax of a command from memory. Users indicate their choices with a pointing device or keystroke and get feedback indicating what they have done. Simple menu selection is especially effective when users have little training, use the system intermittently, are unfamiliar with the terminology, or need help in structuring their decision-making process. With careful design of complex menus and high-speed interaction, menu selection can become appealing even to expert frequent users.

However, just because a designer uses menu selection, form fillin, and dialog boxes, there is no guarantee that the interface will be appealing and easy to use. Effective interfaces emerge only after careful consideration of and testing for numerous design issues, such as task-related organization, phrasing of items, sequence of items, graphic layout and design, response time, shortcuts for knowledgeable frequent users, on line help, error correction, and selection mechanisms (keyboard, pointing devices, touchscreen, voice, and so on) (Norman, 1991).

This chapter starts with menus, then moves on to cover form fillin and this method's integration into dialog boxes. The examples are drawn from pull-down menus, full-screen displays, embedded links of the World Wide Web, and graphical dialog boxes. Menu items can be textual, graphic, or auditory.

7.2 Task-Related Organization

The primary goal for menu, form-fillin, and dialog-box designers is to create a sensible, comprehensible, memorable, and convenient organization relevant to the user's tasks. We can learn a few lessons by following the decomposition of a book into chapters, a program into modules, or the animal kingdom into species. Hierarchical decompositions—natural and comprehensible to most people—are appealing because every item belongs to a single category. Unfortunately, in some applications, an item may be difficult to classify as belonging to only one category, and designers are tempted to create duplicate pointers, thus forming a network.

Restaurant menus separate appetizers, soups, salads, main dishes, desserts, and beverages to help customers organize their selections. Menu items should fit logically into categories and have readily understood meanings. Restaurateurs who list dishes with idiosyncratic names such as "veal Monique," generic terms such as "house dressing," or unfamiliar labels such as "wor shu op" should expect that waiters will spend ample time explaining the alternatives, or should anticipate that customers will become anxious because of the unpredictability of their meals.

Similarly, for computer menus, the categories should be comprehensible and distinctive so that users are confident in making their selections. Users should have a clear idea of what will happen when they make a selection. Computer menus are more difficult to design than are restaurant menus, because computer displays typically have less space than do printed menus. In addition, the number of choices and the complexity is greater in many computer applications, and computer users may not have helpful waiters to turn to for an explanation (Norman and Chin, 1989).

The importance of meaningful organization of menu items was demonstrated in an early study with 48 novice users (Liebelt et al., 1982). Simple menu trees with three levels and 16 target items were constructed in both meaningfully organized and disorganized forms. Error rates were nearly halved and user think time (time from menu presentation to user's selection of an item) was reduced for the meaningfully organized form. In a later study, meaningful categories—such as food, animals, minerals, and cities— led to shorter response times than did random or alphabetic organizations (McDonald et al., 1983). This experiment tested 109 novice users who worked through 10 blocks of 26 trials. The authors concluded that "these results demonstrate the superiority of a categorical menu organization over a pure alphabetical organization, particularly when there is some uncertainty about the terms." With larger menu structures, the effect is even more dramatic.

These results and the OAI model suggest that the key to menu-structure design is first to consider the task-related objects and actions. For a music-concert ticketing system, the menus might separate out types of music (classical, folk, rock, jazz, and so on), concert locations, or dates, and might offer actions such as browsing lists, searching by performer name, or locating inexpensive performances. The interface objects might be dialog boxes with check boxes for types of music and scrolling menus of concert locations. Performer names might be in a scrolling list or typed in via form fillin.

Menu-selection applications range from trivial choices between two items to complex information systems that offer thousands of displays. The simplest applications consist of a single menu, but even within this limited format, there are many variations (Fig. 7.1). The second group of applications includes a linear sequence of menu selections; the progression of menus is independent of the user's choice. Strict tree structures make up the third and most common group. Acyclic (menus that are reachable by more than one path) and cyclic (structures with meaningful paths that allow users to repeat menus) networks constitute the fourth group. In addition, special traversal commands may enable users to jump around the branches of a tree, to go back to the previous menu, or to go to the beginning of a linear sequence.

7.2.1   Single menus

In some situations, a single menu is sufficient to accomplish a task. Single menus may have two or more items, or may allow multiple selections. Single menus may pop up on the current work area or may be permanently available (on a frame, in a separate window, or on a data tablet) while the main display is changed.

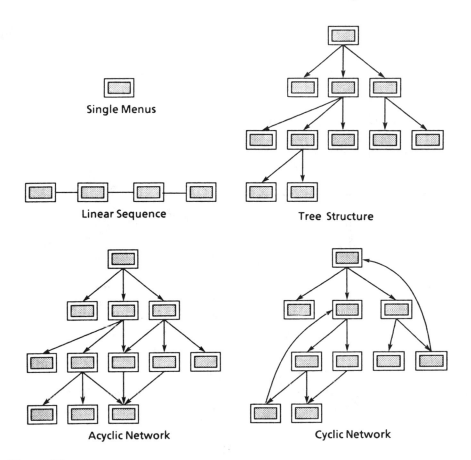

Figure 7.1

Menu systems can use a simple single menu or a linear sequences of menus. Tree-structured menus are the most common. Traversing deep trees or more elaborate acyclic or cyclic menu structures can be difficult for some users.

Binary menus The simplest case is a *binary menu* with, for example, yes-no, true-false, or male–female choices. In keyboard-oriented systems, menu items can be identified by single-letter mnemonics, as they are in this photo-library retrieval system:

```
Photos are indexed by film type
   B Black and white
   C Color
Type the letter of your choice
and press RETURN:
```

Users often prefer *mnemonic letters,* such as those in this menu, to numbered choices (see Section 7.5). The mnemonic-letter approach requires additional caution in avoiding collisions and increases the effort of translation to foreign languages, but its clarity and memorability are an advantage in many applications.

In GUIs, dialog boxes offer users selection buttons, often called *radio buttons.* Selection is made with a mouse or other cursor-control device. This box has two radio buttons.

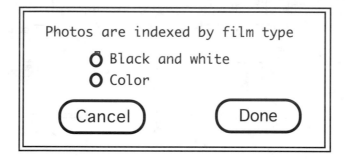

While earlier systems used text only, modern systems can show items graphically. For example, users can choose the orientation for output by selecting one of a pair of icons. The selected item is the darker (inverse highlighted) one.

Orientation

In the following example, users can choose between Cancel and OK by a mouse click, but the thickened border on OK indicates that this selection is the default, and that pressing RETURN will select it.

These simple examples demonstrate alternative ways to identify menu items and to convey instructions to the user. No optimal format for menus has emerged, but consistency across menus in a system is extremely important.

Multiple-item menus Single menus may have more than two items. One example is an online quiz displayed on a touchscreen:

```
Who invented the telephone?
   Thomas Edison
   Alexander Graham Bell
   Lee De Forest
   George Westinghouse
Touch your answer.
```

Another example is a list of options in a document-processing system:

```
EXAMINE, PRINT, DROP, OR HOLD?
```

The quiz example has distinct, comprehensible items, but the document-processing example shows an implied menu selection that could be confusing to novice users. There are no explicit instructions, and it is not apparent that single-letter abbreviations are acceptable. Knowledgeable and expert users may prefer this short form of a menu selection, usually called a *prompt*, because of its speed and simplicity.

In GUIs, radio buttons support single item selection from a multiple-item menu. This choice of paper size for printing shows US Letter as the selected item:

Paper: ⦿ **US Letter**   ○ **A4 Letter**
 ▸   ○ **US Legal**   ○ **B5 Letter**
            ○ **No. 10 Envelope**

Multiple-selection menus or check boxes A further variation on single menus is the capacity to make multiple selections from the choices offered. For example, a political-interest survey might allow multiple choice on one display (Fig. 7.2). A multiple-selection menu with mouse clicks as the selection method is a convenient strategy for handling multiple binary choices, since the user is able to scan the full list of items while deciding. In the following Macintosh example, Bold and Underline have been selected;

Figure 7.2

A multiple-selection touchscreen menu. Users can select up to three political issues.

Superscript and UPPERCASE (grayed out) become available on a pop-up menu after the check box is selected:

Pull-down and pop-up menus *Pull-down menus* are constantly available to the user via selections along a top menu bar. The Xerox Star, Apple Lisa, and Apple Macintosh (Fig. 7.3) made these possibilities widely available, and their versions have become standardized (Windows, IBM OS/2, OSF/Motif). Common items in the menu bar are File, Edit, Font, Format, View, Window, and Help. The users make a selection by moving the pointing device over the

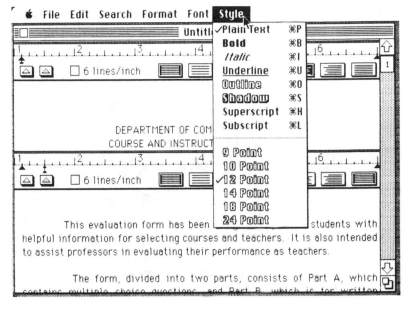

Figure 7.3

The pull-down menu on an early Apple Macintosh MacWrite program. Users can select font variations and size. (Photo courtesy of Apple Computer, Inc.)

menu items, which respond by highlighting (reverse video, a box surrounding the item, and color all have been used). Since positional constancy is such a strong principle, when an item is not available for selection it is preferable to gray it out rather than to remove it from the list. This Macintosh menu bar shows the available pull-down menus:

🍎 **File   Edit   Font   Size   Style   Format   Spelling   View**

In Windows, pull-down menu items are also selectable with a keystroke sequence.

Pop-up menus appear on the display in response to a click with a pointing device such as a mouse. The contents of the pop-up menu may depend on where the cursor is when the pointing device is clicked. Since the pop-up menu covers a portion of the display, there is strong motivation to keep the menu text small. Hierarchical sequences of pop-up menus are also used.

Pop-up menus can also be organized in a circle to form *pie menus* (Callahan et al., 1988):

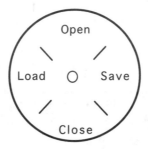

Pie menus are convenient because selection is more rapid and, with practice, can be done without visual attention. Improvements to appearance and behavior were made in a pie menus variant called marking menus in Alias StudioPaint V3 (Tapia and Kurtenbach, 1995).

Scrolling and two-dimensional menus (fast and vast)   Sometimes the list of menu items may be longer than the 20 to 60 lines that can reasonably fit on a display. One solution is to create a tree-structured menu, but sometimes the desire to limit the system to one conceptual menu is strong. A typical application is selecting a state from the 50 states in the United States. The first portion of the menu is displayed with an additional menu item that leads to the next display in the menu sequence. The scrolling (or paging) menu might continue with dozens or thousands of items using the list-box capabilities found in most GUIs. Alternatively, a multiple-column menu might be used, with the 50 states arranged in five columns of 10 items each (Fig. 7.4). These "fast and vast" *two-dimensional menus* give users an excellent overview of the choices, reduce the number of actions, and allow rapid selection. Multiple-column menus are especially useful in World Wide Web page design to minimize the scrolling needed to see a long list and to give users a single-screen overview of the full set of choices.

Alphasliders   When the menu items become too numerous to show on the screen at once without obscuring other items, more compact strategies are needed. One approach is the *alphaslider*, which uses multiple levels of granularity in moving the slider thumb (scroll box) and therefore can support tens or hundreds of thousands of items (Ahlberg and Shneiderman, 1994). The following alphaslider covers the 10,000 actors in a film database (Color Plate B4). The dark upper part of the thumb jumps over 40 actors for each move of

Select multiple states for travel information:

Alabama	Hawaii	Massachusetts	New Mexico	South Dakota
Alaska	Idaho	Michigan	New York	Tennessee
Arizona	Illinois	Minnesota	North Carolina	Texas
Arkansas	Indiana	Mississippi	North Dakota	Utah
California	Iowa	Missouri	Ohio	Vermont
Colorado	Kansas	Montana	Oklahoma	Virginia
Connecticut	Kentucky	Nebraska	Oregon	Washington
Delaware	Louisiana	Nevada	Pennsylvania	West Virginia
Florida	Maine	New Hampshire	Rhode Island	Wisconsin
Georgia	Maryland	New Jersey	South Carolina	Wyoming

(Ok)   (Cancel)

Figure 7.4

A "fast and vast" two-dimensional menu that allows rapid multiple selection from the list of 50 states. This version shows a menu with five columns of 10 states each, arranged in alphabetical order down the columns.

the mouse, and the lighter smaller lower part allows movement through each actor's name:

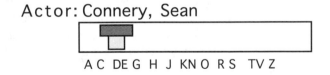

Actor: Connery, Sean

A C DE G H J KN O R S TV Z

The index at the bottom of the alphaslider gives users an idea of where to jump to start a new search.

Embedded links All the menus discussed thus far might be characterized as *explicit menus* in that there is an orderly enumeration of the menu items with little extraneous information. In many situations, however, the menu items might be *embedded* in text or graphics and still be selectable. This is the basis for hypertext designs (see Chapter 16).

In a textual database with articles about people, events, and places for a museum application, it is natural to allow users to retrieve detailed information by selecting a name in context (Koved and Shneiderman, 1986). Selectable names are highlighted, and users click with a mouse (Fig. 7.5). The names, places, or phrases are menu items embedded in meaningful text that

```
WASHINGTON, DC: THE NATION'S CAPITAL              PAGE 2 OF 3
```

   Located between **Maryland** and **Virginia,** Washington, DC
embraces the **White House** and the **Capitol,** a host of
government offices as well as the **Smithsonian museums.**
Designed by **Pierre L'Enfant,** Washington, DC is a graceful
city of broad boulevards, **national monuments,** the rustic
Rock Creek Park, and the **National Zoo.**
   First-time visitors should begin at the **mall** by walking
from the **Capitol** towards the **Smithsonian museums** and on

BACK PAGE   NEXT PAGE   RETURN TO "NEW YORK CITY"   EXTRA

Figure 7.5

Embedded links in an early version of Hyperties. The links improve comprehensibility over numbered menu lists and lowered anxiety for novice users. A reverse-video
selector box initially covers the NEXT PAGE action. Users move the selector box
over highlighted links or actions, then select by pressing RETURN. A mouse allows
them to make a selection by merely clicking on the highlighted link or action. (Created in 1983 by Human–Computer Interaction Laboratory, University of Maryland,
College Park, MD; distributed and refined by Cognetics Corporation, Princeton
Junction, NJ.)

informs users and helps to clarify the meaning of the items. Embedded links
were popularized in the Hyperties system (Color Plate C1) (Cognetics Corp.,
Princeton Junction, NJ), which was used for two early commercial hypertext
projects (Shneiderman, 1988; Shneiderman and Kearsley, 1989), and became
the preferred method for traversing links on the World Wide Web (see Color
Plates A2 to A5 and Figs. 16.5 to 16.10).

   Embedded links have emerged in other applications. Air-traffic–control
systems allow users to select airplanes in the spatial layout of flight paths to
obtain more detailed information. Many geographic-information systems
similarly allow users to select cities or other features to obtain more information. Selection of regions in a two-dimensional layout, usually called *image
maps,* was built into Hyperties in 1988 and has become popular on websites.
Embedded links permit items to be viewed in context and eliminate the need
for a distracting and screen-wasting enumeration of items. Contextual display
helps to keep the users focused on their tasks and on the objects of interest.

Iconic menus, toolbars, or palettes Menus can offer many actions that a
user can select with a click and apply to a displayed object. These menus,
often called *toolbars* or *palettes,* are widely used in paint and draw programs
(see Fig. 6.7), in computer-assisted design packages, and in other graphics

systems. Users may be able to customize the toolbar with their choices of items, and to control the placement to be at the top or side. Users who wish to conserve screen space for their documents can eliminate the toolbar.

7.2.2 Linear sequences and multiple menus

Often, a series of interdependent menus can be used to guide users through a series of choices in which they see a sequence of menus. For example, a document-printing package might have a linear sequence of menus to choose print parameters, such as device, line spacing, and page numbering. Another familiar example is an online examination that has a sequence of multiple-choice test items, each made up as a menu. Guidance for users in making complex decisions can often be provided by a sequence of cue cards or Wizards (a Microsoft term).

Linear sequences guide the user through a complex decision-making process by presenting one decision at a time. We could improve the document-printing example by offering the user several menus on the screen at once. Putting several menus on a single dialog box simplifies the user interface, allows users to enter choices in any order, and speeds usage (Fig. 7.6).

7.2.3 Tree-structured menus

When a collection of items grows and becomes difficult to maintain under intellectual control, designers can form categories of similar items, creating a *tree structure* (Clauer, 1972; Norman, 1991). Some collections can be partitioned easily into mutually exclusive groups with distinctive identifiers. Familiar examples include these groupings:

- Male, female
- Animal, vegetable, mineral
- Spring, summer, autumn, winter
- Sunday, Monday, Tuesday, Wednesday, Thursday, Friday, Saturday
- Less than 10, between 10 and 25, greater than 25
- Percussion, string, woodwind, brass
- Fonts, size, style, spacing

Even these groupings may occasionally lead to confusion or disagreement. Classification and indexing are complex tasks, and, in many situations, there is no single solution that is acceptable to everyone, for example, colors or flowers. The initial design can be improved as a function of feedback from users. Over time, as the structure is improved—and as users gain familiarity with it, success rates will improve.

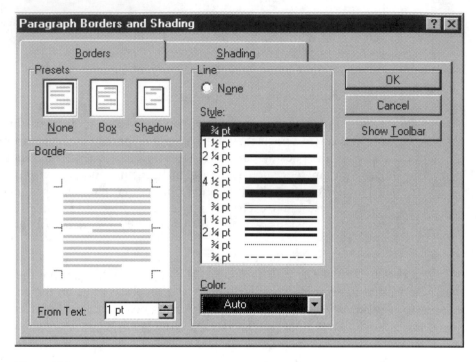

Figure 7.6

Multiple menus in a single dialog box. Users can enter choices in any order and are given a clear overview of the possibilities. (Used with permission of Microsoft Corp., Redmond, WA.)

In spite of the associated problems, tree-structured menu systems have the power to make large collections of data available to novice or intermittent users. If each menu has 30 items, then a menu tree with four levels has the capacity to lead an untrained user through a collection of 810,000 destinations. That number would be excessively large for a set of commands in a word processor, but would be realistic in a World Wide Web application such as a directory (see Fig. 16.5), a digital library (see Color Plate A5), or an online service such as America Online (see Color Plate A6).

If the groupings at each level are natural and comprehensible to users, and if users know the target, then menu traversal can be accomplished in a few seconds—it is faster than flipping through a book. On the other hand, if the groupings are unfamiliar and users have only a vague notion of the item that they seek, they may get lost for hours in the tree menus (Robertson et al., 1981; Norman and Chin, 1988).

Terminology from the user's task domain can orient the user. Instead of using a title, such as MAIN MENU OPTIONS, that is vague and emphasizes the computer domain, use terms such as FRIENDLIBANK SERVICES or simply GAMES.

Depth versus breadth The *depth*, or number of levels, of a menu tree depends, in part, on the *breadth*, or number of items per level. If more items are put into the main menu, then the tree spreads out and has fewer levels. This shape may be advantageous, but only if clarity is not compromised substantially and if a slow display rate does not consume the user's patience. Several authors urge using four to eight items per menu, but, at the same time, they urge using no more than three to four levels. With large menu applications, one or both of these guidelines must be compromised.

Several empirical studies have dealt with the depth–breadth tradeoff, and the evidence is strong that breadth should be preferred over depth. In fact, there is reason to encourage designers to limit menu trees to three levels: when the depth goes to four or five, there is a good chance of users becoming lost or disoriented.

Kiger (1984) grouped 64 items in these menu-tree forms:

8×2	Eight items on each of two levels
4×3	Four items on each of three levels
2×6	Two items on each of six levels
$4 \times 1 + 16 \times 1$	A four-item menu followed by a 16-item menu
$16 \times 1 + 4 \times 1$	A 16-item menu followed by a four-item menu

The deep narrow tree, 2×6, produced the slowest, least accurate, and least preferred version; the 8×2 was among those rated highest for speed, accuracy, and preference. The 22 subjects performed 16 searches on each of the five versions.

Landauer and Nachbar (1985) confirmed the advantage of breadth over depth and developed predictive equations for traversal times. They varied the number of items per level from 2, 4, 8, to 16 to reach 4096 target items of numbers or words. The times for the task with words ranged from 23.4 seconds down to 12.5 seconds as the breadth increased and the number of levels decreased. Over the range studied, the authors suggest that a simple function of the number of items on the screen will predict the time, T, for a selection:

$$T = k + c^*\log b,$$

where k and c are empirically determined constants for scanning the screen to make a choice, and b is the breadth at each level. Then, the total time to traverse the menu tree depends on only the depth, D, which is

$$D = \log b N,$$

where N is the total number of items in the tree. With $N = 4096$ target items and a branching factor of $b = 16$, the depth $D = 3$, and the total time is $3*(k + c*\log16)$.

Norman and Chin (1988) fixed the number of levels at four, with 256 target items, and varied the shape of the tree structure. They recommend greater breadth at the root and at the leaves, and add a further encouragement to minimize the total number of menu frames needed so as to increase familiarity. In an interesting variation, Wallace et al. (1987) confirmed that broader, shallower trees (4×3 versus 2×6) produced superior performance, and showed that, when users were stressed, they made 96 percent more errors and took 16 percent longer. The stressor was simply an instruction to work quickly ("It is imperative that you finish the task just as quickly as possible"); the control group received gentler verbal instruction to avoid rushing ("Take your time; there is no rush").

Even though the semantic structure of the items cannot be ignored, these studies suggest that the fewer the levels, the greater the ease of decision making. Of course, display rates, response time, and screen clutter must be considered, in addition to the semantic organization.

Task-related grouping in tree structures   Grouping menu items in a tree such that they are comprehensible to users and match the task structure is sometimes difficult. The problems are akin to putting kitchen utensils in order; steak knives go together and serving spoons go together, but where do you put butter knives or carving sets? Computer-menu problems include overlapping categories, extraneous items, conflicting classifications in the same menu, unfamiliar jargon, and generic terms. Based on this set of problems, here are several suggested rules for forming menu trees:

- *Create groups of logically similar items* For example, a comprehensible menu would list countries at level 1, states or provinces at level 2, and cities at level 3.
- *Form groups that cover all possibilities* For example, a menu with age ranges 0-9, 10-19, 20-29, and > 30 makes it easy for the user to select an item.
- *Make sure that items are nonoverlapping* Lower-level items should be naturally associated with a single higher-level item. Overlapping categories such as Entertainment and Events are a poor choice compared to Concerts and Sports.
- *Use familiar terminology, but ensure that items are distinct from one another* Generic terms such as Day and Night may be too vague, when compared to Before 6 P.M. and After 6 P.M.

Menu maps   As the depth of a menu tree grows, users find it increasingly difficult to maintain a sense of position in the tree; their sense of disorienta-

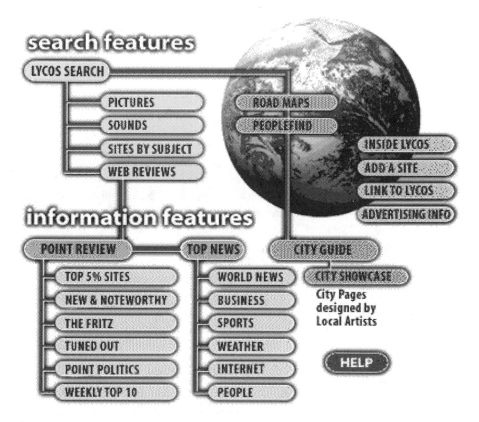

Figure 7.7

A menu map of a World Wide Web site. This example from the Lycos search service is called a sitemap.

tion, or of "getting lost," grows. Viewing one menu at a time is like seeing the world through a cardboard tube; it is hard to grasp the overall pattern and to see relationships among categories. Evidence from several early studies demonstrated the advantage of offering a spatial map to help users stay oriented. Sometimes *menu maps* are shown on web pages (Fig. 7.7); sometimes they are printed as large posters to give users a visual overview of hundreds of items at several levels. Another approach is to have the overview in the user manual as a fold-out or spread over several pages as a tree diagram or indented-text display to show levels.

Summary There is no perfect menu structure that matches every person's knowledge of the application domain. Designers must use good judgment for the initial implementation, but then must be receptive to suggested improvements and empirical data. Users will gradually gain familiarity, even with extremely complex tree structures, and will be increasingly successful in locating required items.

7.2.4   Acyclic and cyclic menu networks

Although tree structures are appealing, sometimes network structures are more appropriate. For example, in a commercial online service, it might make sense to provide access to banking information from both the financial and consumer parts of a tree structure. A second motivation for using *menu networks* is that it may be desirable to permit paths between disparate sections of a tree, rather than requiring users to begin a new search from the main menu. Network structures in the form of *acyclic* or *cyclic graphs* arise naturally in social relationships, transportation routing, scientific-journal citations, and many other applications. As users move from trees to acyclic networks to cyclic networks, the potential for getting lost increases. Confusion and disorientation are often reported among World Wide Web users who have difficulty navigating that large cyclic network.

With a tree structure, the user can form a mental model of the structure and of the relationships among the menus. Developing this mental model may be more difficult with a network. With a tree structure, there is a single parent menu, so backward traversals toward the main menu are straightforward. In networks, a stack of visited menus must be kept to allow backward traversals. It may be helpful to preserve a notion of "level," or of distance from the main menu. Users may feel more comfortable if they have a sense of how far they are from the main menu.

7.3   Item Presentation Sequence

Once the items in a menu have been chosen, the designer is still confronted with the choice of *presentation sequence*. If the items have a natural sequence—such as days of the week, chapters in a book, or sizes of eggs—then the decision is trivial. Typical bases for sequencing items include these:

- *Time*   Chronological ordering
- *Numeric ordering*   Ascending or descending ordering
- *Physical properties*   Increasing or decreasing length, area, volume, temperature, weight, velocity, and so on

Many cases have no task-related ordering, and the designer must choose from such possibilities as these:

- *Alphabetic sequence of terms*
- *Grouping of related items* (with blank lines or other demarcation between groups)
- *Most frequently used items first*
- *Most important items first* (importance may be difficult to determine and may vary among users)

Card (1982) experimented with a single 18-item vertical permanent menu of text-editing commands such as INSERT, ITALIC, and CENTER. He presented subjects with a command, and they had to locate the command in the list, to move a mouse-controlled cursor, and to select the command by pressing a button on the mouse. The menu items were sequenced in one of three ways: alphabetically, in functional groups, and randomly. Each of four subjects made 86 trials with each sequencing strategy. The mean times were as follows

Strategy	Time per trial (seconds)
alphabetic	0.81
functional	1.28
random	3.23

Since subjects were given the target item, they did best when merely scanning to match the menu items in an alphabetic sequence. The performance with the functional groupings was remarkably good, indicating that subjects began to remember the groupings and could go directly to a group. In menu applications where the users must make a decision about the most suitable menu item, the functional arrangement might be more appealing. Users' memory for the functionally grouped items is likely to surpass their memory for the alphabetic or random sequences. The poor performance that Card observed with the random sequence confirms the importance of considering alternative presentation sequences for the items.

With a 64-item menu, the time for locating a target word was found to increase from just over 2 seconds for an alphabetic menu to more than 6 seconds for a random menu (McDonald et al., 1983). When the target word was replaced with a single-line definition, the 109 subjects could no longer scan for a simple match and had to consider each menu item carefully. The advantage of alphabetic ordering nearly vanished. User reaction time went up to about 7 seconds for the alphabetic and about 8 seconds for the random organization. Somberg and Picardi (1983) studied user reaction times in a five-item menu. Their three experiments revealed a significant and nearly linear relationship between the user's reaction time and the serial position in the menu. Furthermore, there was a significant increase in reaction time if the target word was unfamiliar, rather than familiar.

If frequency of use is a potential guide to sequencing menu items, then it might make sense to vary the sequence adaptively to reflect the current pattern of use. Unfortunately, adaptations can be disruptive, increasing confusion and undermining the users' learning of menu structures. In addition, users might become anxious that other changes might occur at any moment. Evidence against the utility of such changes was found in a study in which a pull-down list of food items was resequenced to ensure that the most frequently selected items migrated toward the top (Mitchell and Shneiderman, 1988). Users were clearly unsettled by the changing menus, and their performance was better with static menus. In contrast, evidence in favor of adaptation was found in a study of a telephone-book menu tree that had been restructured to make frequently used telephone numbers more easily accessible (Greenberg, 1985). However, this study did not deal with the issue of potentially disorienting changes to the menu during usage. So that you avoid disruption and unpredictable behavior, it is probably a wise policy to allow users to specify when they want the menu restructured.

When some menu items are much more frequently selected than are others, there is a temptation to organize the menu in descending frequency. This organization does speed up selection of the topmost items, but the loss of a meaningful ordering for low-frequency items is disruptive. A sensible compromise is to extract three or four of the most frequently selected items and to put them on the top, while preserving the order for the remaining items. In controlled experiments and field studies with a lengthy font menu, the three popular fonts (Courier, Helvetica, and Times) were put on top, and the remaining list was left in alphabetical order. This split-menu strategy proved appealing and statistically significantly improved performance (Sears and Shneiderman, 1993). An improved theory of menu-selection performance emerged that showed that familiar items were selected in logarithmic time, whereas unfamiliar items were found in linear time with respect to their position in the menu. The software collected usage frequency, but the split-menu ordering remained stable until the system administrator decided to make a change.

7.4   Response Time and Display Rate

A critical variable that may determine the attractiveness of menu selection is the speed at which users can move through the menus. The two components of speed are system *response time*, the time it takes for the system to begin displaying information in response to a user selection, and *display rate*, the speed at which the menus are displayed (see Chapter 10). For most modern computers, response time is so rapid that this issue is less of a concern, but delays on the World Wide Web have revived this topic.

Deep menu trees or complex traversals become annoying to the user if system response time is slow, resulting in long and multiple delays. With slow display rates, lengthy menus become annoying because of the volume of text or graphics that must be displayed. In positive terms, if the response time is long, then designers should place more items on each menu to reduce the number of menus necessary. If the display rate is slow, then designers should place fewer items on each menu to reduce the display time. If the response time is long and the display rate is low, menu selection is unappealing and command-language strategies, in spite of the greater memory demands that they place on users, become more attractive.

With short response times and rapid display rates, menu selection becomes a lively medium that can be attractive even for frequent and knowledgeable users. In almost every case studied, user performance and preference improved with broader and shallower menus. For most situations, designers are well advised to increase the size of menus, if they can reduce the number of menus.

7.5   Fast Movement Through Menus

Even with short response times and high display rates, frequent menu users may become annoyed if they must make several menu selections to complete a simple task. There is an advantage to reducing the number of menus by increasing the number of items per menu, but this strategy may not be sufficient. As response times lengthen and display rates decrease, the need for shortcuts through the menus increases.

Instead of creating a command language to accomplish the task with positional or keyword parameters, we can refine the menu approach to accommodate expert and frequent users. Three approaches have been used: allow typeahead for known menu choices, assign names to menus to allow direct access, and create menu macros that allows users to assign names to frequently used menu sequences.

7.5.1   Menus with typeahead: The BLT approach

A natural way to permit frequent menu users to speed through the menus is to allow *typeahead*. The user does not have to wait to see the menus before choosing the items, but can type a string of letters or numbers when presented with the main menu. Typeahead becomes important when the menus are familiar and response time or display rates are slow, as they are in many voice-mail systems. Most telephone-inquiry systems, electronic-mail systems, and Windows 95 applications allow the experienced user to enter a string of keypresses to select from a series of menus.

If the menu items are identified with single letters, then the concatenation of menu selections in the typeahead scheme generates a command name that acquires mnemonic value. To users of a photo-library search system that offered menus with typeahead, a color slide portrait quickly became known as a CSP, and a black-and-white print of a landscape became known as a BPL. Each mnemonic comes to be remembered and chunked as a single concept. This strategy quickly became known as the *BLT approach*, after the abbreviation for a bacon, lettuce, and tomato sandwich.

The attraction of the BLT approach is that users can move gracefully from being novice menu users to being knowledgeable command users. There are no new commands to learn; as soon as users become familiar with one branch of the tree, they can apply that knowledge to speed up their work. Learning can be incremental; users can apply one-, two-, or three-letter typeahead, and then explore the less familiar menus. If users forget part of the tree, they simply revert to menu usage.

The BLT approach requires a more elaborate parser for user input, and handling of nonexistent menu choices is a bit more problematic. It is also necessary to ensure distinct first letters for items within each menu, but ambiguity across menus presents no problem. The typeahead or BLT approach is attractive because it is powerful, is simple, and allows graceful evolution from novice to expert.

7.5.2   Menu names or bookmarks for direct access

A second approach to support frequent users is to use numbered menu items and to assign *menu names* to each menu frame. Users can follow the menus or, if they know the name of their destination, they can type it in and go there directly. The early CompuServe Information Service had a three-letter identifier for major topics, followed by a dash and a page number. Rather than working their way through three levels of menus at 30 characters per second, users knew that they could go directly to TWP-1, the start of the subtree containing today's edition of *The Washington Post*. America Online has bookmarks (Favorite Places) and keyword access.

This strategy is useful if there is only a small number of destinations that each user needs to remember. If users need to access many different portions of the menu tree, they will have difficulty keeping track of the destination names. A list of the current destination names is necessary to ensure that designers create unique names for new entries.

An empirical comparison of the learnability of the typeahead and direct-access strategies demonstrated an advantage for the latter (Laverson et al., 1987). Thirty-two undergraduates had to learn either path names (typeahead) or destination names (direct access) for a four-level menu tree. The direct-access names proved to be significantly faster to learn and were preferred. Different tree structures or menu contents may influence the outcome of similar studies.

In World Wide Web browsers, *bookmarks* provide a way for users to take shortcuts to destinations that they have visited previously. For many users, this menu of destinations can grow quickly and require hierarchical management strategies.

7.5.3 Menu macros, custom toolbars, and style sheets

A third approach to serving frequent menu users is to allow regularly used paths to be recorded by users as *menu macros* or to be placed in the *toolbar* as a user-selected icon. A user can invoke the macro or customization facility, traverse the menu structure, and then assign a name or icon. When the name or icon is invoked, the traversal is executed automatically. This mechanism allows tailoring of the system and can provide a simplified access mechanism for users who have special needs. Many word processors provide a style-sheet facility to allow users to make multiple menu selections and to record those choices as a personal style. For example, the style for chapter titles might be set to boldface, 24-point, italic, Times font, and centered text. Then, this chapter-title style can be saved and later invoked when needed as a form of macro. Users may also be allowed to rearrange the menu items to accommodate their patterns of work.

7.6 Menu Layout

Little experimental research has been done on menu layout. This section contains many subjective judgments, which are in need of empirical validation (Box 7.1).

7.6.1 Titles

Choosing the title for a book is a delicate matter for an author, editor, or publisher. A particularly descriptive or memorable title can make a big difference in reader responses. Similarly, choosing titles for menus is a complex matter that deserves serious thought.

Box 7.1

Menu Selection Guidelines

- Use task semantics to organize menus
  (single, linear sequence, tree structure, acyclic and cyclic networks)
- Prefer broad–shallow to narrow–deep
- Show position by graphics, numbers, or titles
- Use items as titles for sub trees
- Group items meaningfully
- Sequence items meaningfully
- Use brief items, begin with the keyword
- Use consistent grammar, layout, terminology
- Allow type ahead, jump ahead, or other short cuts
- Enable jumps to previous and main menu
- Consider online help; novel selection mechanisms; and optimal response time, display rate, screen size

For single menus, a simple descriptive title that identifies the situation is all that is necessary. With a linear sequence of menus, the titles should accurately represent the stages in the linear sequence. Consistent grammatical style can reduce confusion and brief but unambiguous noun phrases are often sufficient.

For tree-structured menus, choosing titles is more difficult. Titles such as Main menu or topic descriptions such as Bank transactions for the root of the tree clearly indicate that the user is at the beginning of a session. One potentially helpful rule is to use exactly the same words in the high-level menu items and in the titles for the next lower-level menu. It is reassuring to users to see an item such as Business and financial services and, after they selected it, a screen that is titled Business and financial services. It might be unsettling to get a screen titled Managing your money, even though the intent is similar. Imagine looking in the table of contents of a book and seeing a chapter title such as "The American Revolution," but, when you turn to the indicated page, finding "Our early history"—you might worry about whether you had made a mistake, and your confidence might be undermined. Similarly, when you design World Wide Web pages, you should ensure that the embedded menu item matches the title on the destination page. Using menu items as titles may encourage the menu author to choose items more carefully so that they are descriptive in the context of the other menu items and as the title of the next menu.

A further concern is consistency in placement of titles and other features in a menu screen. Teitelbaum and Granda (1983) demonstrated that user think time nearly doubled when the position of information, such as titles or prompts, was varied on menu screens.

7.6.2   Phrasing of menu items

Just because a system has menu choices written with English words, phrases, or sentences, that is no guarantee that it is comprehensible. Individual words may not be familiar to some users (for example, "repaginate"), and often two menu items may appear to satisfy the user's needs, whereas only one does (for example, "put away" or "eject"). This enduring problem has no perfect solution. Designers can gather feedback from colleagues, users, pilot studies, acceptance tests, and user-performance monitoring. The following guidelines may seem obvious, but we state them because they are so often violated:

- *Use familiar and consistent terminology*   Carefully select terminology that is familiar to the designated user community and keep a list of these terms to facilitate consistent use.
- *Ensure that items are distinct from one another*   Each item should be distinguished clearly from other items. For example, `Slow tours of the countryside`, `Journeys with visits to parks`, and `Leisurely voyages` are less distinctive than are `Bike tours`, `Train tours to national parks`, and `Cruise-ship tours`.
- *Use consistent and concise phrasing*   Review the collection of items to ensure consistency and conciseness. Users are likely to feel more comfortable and to be more successful with `Animal`, `Vegetable`, and `Mineral` than with `Information about animals`, `Vegetable choices you can make`, and `Viewing mineral categories`.
- *Bring the keyword to the left*   Try to write menu items such that the first word aids the user in recognizing and discriminating among items—use `Size of type` instead of `Set the type size`. Users scan menu items from left to right; if the first word indicates that this item is not relevant, they can begin scanning the next item.

7.6.3   Graphic layout and design

The constraints of screen width and length, display rate, character set, and highlighting techniques strongly influence the graphic layout of menus. Presenting 50 states as menu items was natural on a large screen with rapid display rate. On the other hand, systems with small text-only displays or slow modems must add levels of subcategories to present the same information.

Menu designers should establish guidelines for consistency of at least these menu components:

- *Titles* Some people prefer centered titles, but left justification is an acceptable approach, especially with slow display rates.

- *Item placement* Typically, items are left justified, with the item number or letter preceding the item description. Blank lines may be used to separate meaningful groups of items. If multiple columns are used, a consistent pattern of numbering or lettering should be used (for example, down the columns is easier to scan than across the rows).

- *Instructions* The instructions should be identical in each menu, and should be placed in the same position. This rule includes instructions about traversals, help, or function-key usage.

- *Error messages* If the users make an unacceptable choice, the error message should appear in a consistent position and should use consistent terminology and syntax.

- *Status reports* Some systems indicate which portion of the menu structure is currently being searched, which page of the structure is currently being viewed, or which choices must be made to complete a task. This information should appear in a consistent position and should have a consistent structure.

Consistent formats help users to locate necessary information, focus users' attention on relevant material, and reduce users' anxiety by offering predictability.

In addition, since disorientation is a potential problem, techniques to indicate position in the menu structure can be useful. In books, different fonts and typefaces may indicate chapter, section, and subsection organization. Similarly, in menu trees, as the user goes down the tree structure, the titles can be designed to indicate the level or distance from the main menu. If graphics, fonts, typefaces, or highlighting techniques are available, they can be used beneficially. But even simple techniques with only fixed-size upper-case characters and indentation can be effective:

```
                          * * * * * * * * * * * * * * * * * * * * * * * * *
MAIN MENU                        *  MAIN MENU  *
                          * * * * * * * * * * * * * * * * * * * * * * * * *

HOME SERVICES             *  *  *  HOME SERVICES  *  *  *
NEWSPAPERS                -  -  NEWSPAPERS  -  -
The New York Times        THE  NEW  YORK  TIMES
```

This display gives a clear indication of progress down the tree. When users wait to do traversal back up the tree or to an adjoining menu at the same level, they feel confident about what action to take.

With linear sequences of menus, the users can be given a simple visual presentation of position in the sequence: *position marker*. In a computer-assisted instruction sequence with 12 menu frames, a position marker (+) just below the menu items might show progress. In the first frame, the position marker is

```
+---------
```

in the second frame, it is

```
-+--------
```

and in the final frame, it is

```
---------+
```

The users can gauge their progress and can see how much remains to be done.

With GUIs, many possibilities exist for showing progress through successive levels of a tree-structured menu or through linear sequences. A common approach is to show a cascade of successive menu boxes set slightly lower than and slightly to the right of the previous items. For pull-down menus, *cascading or walking menus* (in which users walk through several levels at a time) are perceptually meaningful, but can present a motor challenge a user who must to move the cursor in the appropriate direction. Microsoft Windows 95 provides a convenient Start button on the lower left, but traversing the walking menu down several layers is a challenge for some users.

Another graphic innovation is to use transparent or see-through menus or tool palettes called *magic lenses* that can be dragged near to the object of interest while only partially obscuring it (Bier et al., 1994). Harrison and Vicente (1996) showed that user performance remains unchanged as the menu becomes up to 50 percent transparent, but the users make significantly more errors and their performance slows as the transparency reaches 75 percent.

With rapid high-resolution displays, more elegant visual representations are possible. Given sufficient screen space, it is possible to show a large portion of the menu map and to allow users to point at a menu item anywhere in the tree. Graphic designers or layout artists are useful partners in such design projects.

7.7   Form Fillin

Menu selection is effective for choosing an item from a list, but some tasks are cumbersome with menus. If data entry of personal names or numeric values is required, then keyboard typing becomes more attractive. When many fields of data are necessary, the appropriate interaction style is *form fillin*. For example, the user might be presented with a name and address form (Fig. 7.8). Form fillin was an important strategy in the days of 80×24 textual displays, and it has flourished in the world of graphical dialog boxes as well as on the World Wide Web.

The form-fillin approach is attractive because the full complement of information is visible, giving users a feeling of being in control of the dialog. Few instructions are necessary, since the display resembles familiar paper forms. On the other hand, users must be familiar with keyboards, use of the TAB key or mouse to move the cursor, error correction by backspacing, field-label meanings, permissible field contents, and use of the ENTER key.

7.7.1   Form-fillin design guidelines

There is a paucity of empirical work on form fillin, but several design guidelines have emerged from practitioners (Galitz, 1993; Brown, 1988). An experimental comparison of database update by form fillin and by a command-language strategy demonstrated a significant speed advantage for the former (Ogden and Boyle, 1982): 11 of the 12 subjects expressed a preference for the form-fill-in approach. Software tools simplify design, help to ensure consistency, ease maintenance, and speed implementation. But even with excellent tools, the designer must still make many complex decisions (Box 7.2).

The elements of form-fillin design include the following:

- *Meaningful title*   Identify the topic and avoid computer terminology.
- *Comprehensible instructions*   Describe the user's tasks in familiar terminology. Be brief; if more information is needed, make a set of help screens available to the novice user. In support of brevity, just describe the necessary action (Type the address or simply Address:) and avoid pronouns (You should type the address) or references to "the user" (The user of the form should type the address). Another useful rule is to use the word type for entering information

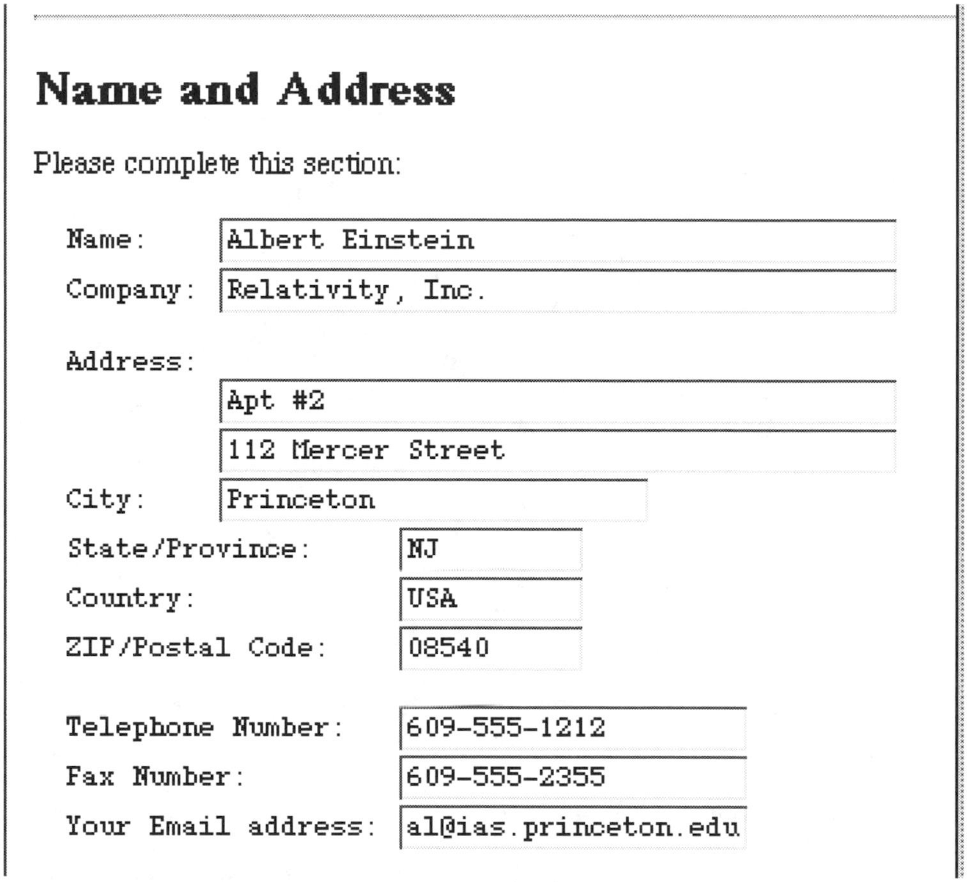

Name and Address

Please complete this section:

Name: `Albert Einstein`

Company: `Relativity, Inc.`

Address:

`Apt #2`

`112 Mercer Street`

City: `Princeton`

State/Province: `NJ`

Country: `USA`

ZIP/Postal Code: `08540`

Telephone Number: `609-555-1212`

Fax Number: `609-555-2355`

Your Email address: `al@ias.princeton.edu`

Figure 7.8

A form-fillin design for name and address entry on a web page.

and `press` for special keys such as the TAB, ENTER, cursor movement, or programmed function (PFK, PF, or F) keys. Since "ENTER" often refers to the special key, avoid using it in the instructions (for example, do not use `Enter the address`; instead, stick to `Type the address`.) Once a grammatical style for instructions is developed, be careful to apply that style consistently.

- *Logical grouping and sequencing of fields* Related fields should be adjacent, and should be aligned with blank space for separation between groups. The sequencing should reflect common patterns—for example, city followed by state followed by zip code.

Box 7.2

Form Fillin Design Guidelines

- Meaningful title
- Comprehensible instructions
- Logical grouping and sequencing of fields
- Visually appealing layout of the form
- Familiar field labels
- Consistent terminology and abbreviations
- Visible space and boundaries for data-entry fields
- Convenient cursor movement
- Error correction for individual characters and entire fields
- Error prevention where possible
- Error messages for unacceptable values
- Marking of optional fields
- Explanatory messages for fields
- Completion signal to support user control

- *Visually appealing layout of the form*   Using a uniform distribution of fields is preferable to crowding one part of the screen and leaving other parts blank. Alignment creates a feeling of order and comprehensibility. For example, the field labels Name, Address, and City can be right justified so that the data-entry fields are vertically aligned. This layout allows the frequent user to concentrate on the entry fields and to ignore the labels. If users are working from hardcopy, the screen should match the paper form.
- *Familiar field labels*   Common terms should be used. If Home Address were replaced by Domicile, many users would be uncertain or anxious about what to do.
- *Consistent terminology and abbreviations*   Prepare a list of terms and acceptable abbreviations and use the list diligently, making additions only after careful consideration. Instead of varying such terms as Address, Employee Address, ADDR., and Addr., stick to one term, such as Address.
- *Visible space and boundaries for data-entry fields*   Users should be able to see the size of the field and to anticipate whether abbreviations or other trimming strategies will be needed. Underscores can indicate the num-

ber of characters available on text-only displays, and an appropriate-sized box can show field length in GUIs.

- *Convenient cursor movement*   Use a simple and visible mechanism for moving the cursor, such as a TAB key or cursor-movement arrows.
- *Error correction for individual characters and entire fields* Allow use of a backspace key and overtyping to enable the user to make easy repairs or changes to entire fields.
- *Error prevention*   Where possible, prevent users from entering incorrect values. For example, in a field requiring a positive integer, do not allow the user to enter letters, minus signs, or decimal points.
- *Error messages for unacceptable values*   If users enter an unacceptable value, the error message should appear on completion of the field. The message should indicate permissible values of the field; for example, if the zip code is entered as 28K21 or 2380, the message might be Zip codes should have 5 digits.
- *Optional fields clearly marked* Wherever appropriate, the word Optional or other indicators should be visible. Optional fields should follow required fields, whenever possible.
- *Explanatory messages for fields*   If possible, explanatory information about a field or the permissible values should appear in a standard position, such as in a window on the bottom, whenever the cursor is in the field.
- *Completion signal*   It should be clear to the users what they must do when they are finished filling in the fields. Generally, designers should avoid automatic completion when the final field is filled because users may wish to review or alter previous field entries.

These considerations may seem obvious, but often forms designers omit the title or an obvious way to signal completion, or include unnecessary computer file names, strange codes, unintelligible instructions, unintuitive groupings of fields, cluttered layouts, obscure field labels, inconsistent abbreviations or field formats, awkward cursor movement, confusing error-correction procedures, or hostile error messages.

Detailed design rules should reflect local terminology and abbreviations. They should specify field sequences familiar to the users; the width and height of the display device; highlighting features such as reverse video, underscoring, intensity levels, color, and fonts; the cursor-movement keys; and coding of fields.

7.7.2   List and combo boxes

In graphical environments and on the World Wide Web, designers can use scrolling list boxes to reduce the users' data-entry burdens and the resultant

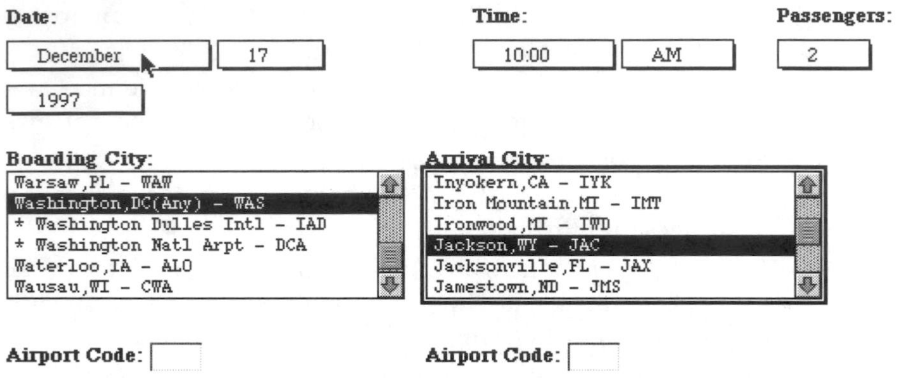

Date:

| December ▲ | | 17 |

| 1997 |

Time:

| 10:00 | | AM |

Passengers:

| 2 |

Boarding City:

```
Warsaw,PL - WAW                      ▲
Washington,DC(Any) - WAS
* Washington Dulles Intl - IAD
* Washington Natl Arpt - DCA
Waterloo,IA - ALO
Wausau,WI - CWA                      ⬇
```

Arrival City:

```
Inyokern,CA - IYK                    ▲
Iron Mountain,MI - IMT
Ironwood,MI - IWD
Jackson,WY - JAC
Jacksonville,FL - JAX
Jamestown,ND - JMS                   ⬇
```

Airport Code: [   ]   **Airport Code:** [   ]

Figure 7.9

A web page that allows users to choose a flight-booking date, time, and number of passengers from pop-up lists. The user then selects boarding and arrival cities by scrollling lists or filling in airport codes.

errors (Color Plate C2). Scrolling lists can be thousands of items long, as they are in many CD-ROM encyclopedias. Rapid selection from a long list can be facilitated by a *combo box*, in which users can type in leading characters and force scrolling through the list. Typical lists are alphabetically ordered to support user typing of leading characters, but categorical lists may be useful. The principles of menu-list sequencing apply (Section 7.3). A combination of pop-up menus, scrolling, and form fillin can support rapid selection, even for a multistep task such as airline scheduling (Fig. 7.9).

7.7.3   Coded fields

Columns of information require special treatment for data entry and for display. Alphabetic fields are customarily left justified on entry and on display. Numeric fields may be left justified on entry, but then become right justified on display. When possible, avoid entry and display of leftmost zeros in numeric fields. Numeric fields with decimal points should line up on the decimal points.

Pay special attention to such common fields as these:

- *Telephone numbers*   Offer a form to indicate the subfields:

        Telephone: (_ _ _) _ _ _-_ _ _ _

    Be alert to special cases, such as addition of extensions or the need for nonstandard formats for international numbers.

- *Social-security numbers* The pattern for U.S. social-security numbers should appear on the screen as

```
Social-security number: _ _ _ - _ _ - _ _ _ _
```

When the user has typed the first three digits, the cursor should jump to the leftmost position of the two-digit field.

- *Times* Even though the 24-hour clock is convenient, many people find it confusing and prefer A.M. or P.M. designations. The form might appear as

```
_ _:_ _ _ _ (9:45 AM or PM)
```

Seconds may or may not be included, adding to the variety of necessary formats.

- *Dates* How to specify dates is one of the nastiest problems; no good solution exists. Different formats for dates are appropriate for different tasks, and European rules differ from American rules. An acceptable standard may never emerge.

    When the display presents coded fields, the instructions might show an example of correct entry; for example,

```
Date: _ _/_ _/_ _ (04/22/98 indicates April 22, 1998)
```

For many people, examples are more comprehensible than is an abstract description, such as

```
MM/DD/YY
```

- *Dollar amounts (or other currency)* The dollar sign should appear on the screen, so users then type only the amount. If a large number of whole-dollar amounts is to be entered, users might be presented with a field such as

```
Deposit amount: $_ _ _ _ _.00
```

with the cursor to the left of the decimal point. As the user types numbers, they shift left, calculator style. To enter an occasional cents amount, the user must type the decimal point to reach the 00 field for overtyping.

Other considerations in form-fillin design include multiscreen forms, mixed menus and forms, use of graphics, relationship to paper forms, use of pointing devices, use of color, handling of special cases, and integration of a word processor to allow remarks.

7.8 Dialog Boxes

In modern GUIs, users can make some choices from pull-down or pop-up menus, but many tasks require multiple selections as well as data entry of numeric values or alphanumeric strings. The most common solution to complex tasks is to provide a dialog box for users. Familiar examples include the Open, Save, Find, Replace, and Spell Check dialog boxes (Fig. 7.10). Dialog boxes can also contain task-specific functions, such as entering customer name and address for a car rental; specifying clothing color, size, and fabric for an order-entry system; or selecting colors and textures for a geographic-information system.

Dialog-box design combines menu-selection and form-fillin issues with additional concerns about consistency across hundreds of dialog boxes and relationship with other items on the screen (Galitz, 1994). A guidelines document for dialog boxes can help to ensure appropriate consistency (Box 7.3). Dialog boxes should have meaningful titles to identify them, and should have consistent visual properties—for example, centered, mixed uppercase and lowercase, 12-point, black, Helvetica font. Dialog boxes are often shaped and sized to fit each situation, but distinctive sizes or aspect ratios may be used to signal errors, confirmations, or components of the application. Within a dia-

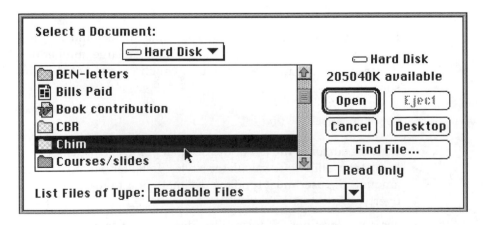

Figure 7.10

Open dialog box from Microsoft Word for the Macintosh.

Box 7.3

Dialog Box Guidelines

Internal layout: like that of menus and forms

- Meaningful title, consistent style
- Top-left to bottom-right sequencing
- Clustering and emphasis
- Consistent layouts (margins, grid, whitespace, lines, boxes)
- Consistent terminology, fonts, capitalization, justification
- Standard buttons (OK, Cancel)
- Error prevention by direct manipulation

External relationship

- Smooth appearance and disappearance
- Distinguishable but small boundary
- Size small enough to reduce overlap problems
- Display close to appropriate items
- No overlap of required items
- Easy to make disappear
- Clear how to complete/cancel

---

log box, there should be standard margins and visual organization, typically from top-left to bottom-right for languages that read left to right. A grid structure helps to organize the contents, and symmetry can be used to provide order when appropriate. Clustering of related items within a box or separation by horizontal and vertical rules gives users help in understanding the contents. Emphasis can be added by color, font size, or style of type.

The elements of a dialog box will depend on the toolkit or design tool (see Chapter 5), but they usually include buttons, check boxes, fill in fields, list boxes, combo boxes, and sliders. Standard buttons—with consistent labels, colors, and fonts—help users to navigate correctly and quickly. Where possible, users should be able to undo each step, and should be prevented from making errors.

Dialog-box design also involves the relationship with the current contents of the screen. Since dialog boxes usually pop up on top of some portion of the screen, there is a danger that they will obscure relevant information. Therefore, dialog boxes should be as small as is reasonable to minimize the overlap and visual disruption. Dialog boxes should appear near, but not on top of, the related screen items. When a user clicks on a city on a map, the dialog box about the city should appear just next to the click point. The most common annoyance is to have the Find or Spell Check box obscure a relevant part of the text.

Dialog boxes should be distinct enough that users can easily distinguish them from the background, but should not be so harsh as to be visually disruptive. Finally, dialog boxes should disappear easily with as little visual disruption as possible (see Section 13.4 and 13.5).

When tasks are complex, multiple dialog boxes may be needed, leading some designers to chose a tabbed dialog box, in which two to 20 protruding tabs indicate the presence of multiple dialog boxes. This technique can be effective, but carries with it the potential problem of too much fragmentation; users may have a hard time finding what they want underneath the tabs. A smaller number of larger dialog boxes may be advantageous, since users usually prefer doing visual search to having to remember where to find a desired control.

7.9   Practitioner's Summary

Concentrate on organizing the structure and sequence of menus to match the users' tasks, ensure that each menu is a meaningful task-related unit, and create items that are distinctive and comprehensible. If some users make frequent use of the system, then typeahead, shortcut, or macro strategies should be allowed. Permit simple traversals to the previously displayed menu and to the main menu. Be sure to conduct human-factors tests and to involve human-factors specialists in the design process. When the system is implemented, collect usage data, error statistics, and subjective reactions to guide refinement.

Whenever possible, use software tools to produce and display a menu, form fillin, or dialog box. Commercial systems reduce implementation time, ensure consistent layout and instructions, and simplify maintenance.

7.10   Researcher's Agenda

Experimental research could help to refine the design guidelines concerning organization and sequencing in single and linear sequences of menus. How can differing communities of users be satisfied with a common organization when their information needs are markedly different? Should users be allowed to tailor the structure of the menus, or is there greater advantage in compelling everyone to use the same structure and terminology? Should a tree structure be preserved even if some redundancy is introduced?

Research opportunities abound. Depth-versus-breadth tradeoffs under differing conditions need to be studied to provide guidance for designers. Layout strategies, wording of instructions, phrasing of menu items, graphic design, and response time are all excellent candidates for experimentation. Exciting possibilities are becoming available with larger screens and novel selection devices.

Implementers would benefit from advanced software tools to automate creation, management, usage-statistics gathering, and evolutionary refinement. Portability could be enhanced to facilitate transfer across systems, and internationalization could be facilitated by tools to support redesign for multiple national languages.

World Wide Web Resources   WWW

Information on menu, form fillin and dialog box design including empirical studies and examples of systems. The most interesting experience is scanning the World Wide Web to see how designers have laid out menu trees or aligned form-fillin boxes.

http://www.aw.com/DTUI

References

Ahlberg, C. and Shneiderman, B., AlphaSlider: A compact and rapid selector, *Proc. CHI '94 Human Factors in Computer Systems*, ACM, New York (April 1994), 365–371.

Bier, Eric, Stone, Maureen, Fishkin, Ken, Buxton, William, and Baudel, T., A taxonomy of see-through tools, *Proc. CHI '94 Human Factors in Computing Systems*, ACM, New York (1994), 358–364.

Brown, C. Marlin, *Human–Computer Interface Design Guidelines*, Ablex, Norwood, NJ (1988).

Callahan, Jack, Hopkins, Don, Weiser, Mark, and Shneiderman, Ben, An empirical comparison of pie versus linear menus, *Proc. CHI '88 Human Factors in Computer Systems*, ACM, New York (1988), 95–100.

Card, Stuart K., User perceptual mechanisms in the search of computer command menus, *Proc. Human Factors in Computer Systems*, Washington, D.C., Chapter of ACM (March 1982), 190–196.

Clauer, Calvin Kingsley, An experimental evaluation of hierarchical decision-making for information retrieval, IBM Research Report RJ 1093, San Jose, CA (September 15, 1972).

Galitz, Wilbert O., *It's Time to Clean Your Windows: Designing GUIs that Work*, John Wiley and Sons, New York (1994).

Greenberg, Saul and Witten, Ian H., Adaptive personalized interfaces: A question of viability, *Behaviour and Information Technology*, 4, 1 (1985), 31–45.

Harrison, Beverly L. and Vicente, Kim J., An experimental evaluation of transparent menu usage, *Proc. CHI '96, Human Factors in Computing Systems*, ACM, New York (1996), 391–398.

Kiger, John I., The depth/breadth trade-off in the design of menu-driven user interfaces, *International Journal of Man–Machine Studies*, 20, (1984), 201–213.

Koved, Lawrence, and Shneiderman, Ben, Embedded menus: Menu selection in context, *Communications of the ACM*, 29, (1986), 312–318.

Landauer, T. K., and Nachbar, D. W., Selection from alphabetic and numeric menu trees using a touch screen: Breadth, depth, and width, *Proc. CHI '85, Human Factors in Computing Systems*, ACM, New York (April 1985), 73–78.

Laverson, Alan, Norman, Kent, and Shneiderman, Ben, An evaluation of jump-ahead techniques for frequent menu users, *Behaviour and Information Technology*, 6, (1987), 97–108.

Liebelt, Linda S., McDonald, James E., Stone, Jim D., and Karat, John, The effect of organization on learning menu access, *Proc. Human Factors Society, Twenty-Sixth Annual Meeting*, Santa Monica, CA (1982), 546–550.

McDonald, James E., Stone, Jim D., and Liebelt, Linda S., Searching for items in menus: The effects of organization and type of target, *Proc. Human Factors Society, Twenty-Seventh Annual Meeting*, Santa Monica, CA (1983), 834–837.

Mitchell, Jeffrey and Shneiderman, Ben, Dynamic versus static menus: An experimental comparison, *ACM SIGCHI Bulletin*, 20, 4 (1989), 33–36.

Norman, Kent, *The Psychology of Menu Selection: Designing Cognitive Control at the Human/Computer Interface*, Ablex, Norwood, NJ (1991).

Norman, Kent L. and Chin, John P., The effect of tree structure on search in a hierarchical menu selection system, *Behaviour and Information Technology*, 7, (1988), 51–65.

Norman, Kent L. and Chin, John P., The menu metaphor: Food for thought, *Behaviour and Information Technology*, 8, 2 (1989), 125–134.

Ogden, William C. and Boyle, James M., Evaluating human–computer dialog styles: Command versus form/fill-in for report modification, *Proc. Human Factors Society, Twenty-Sixth Annual Meeting*, Santa Monica, CA (1982), 542–545.

Robertson, G., McCracken, D., and Newell, A., The ZOG approach to man–machine communication, *International Journal of Man–Machine Studies*, 14, (1981), 461–488.

Sears, Andrew and Shneiderman, Ben, Split menus: Effectively using selection frequency to organize menus, *ACM Transactions on Computer-Human Interaction*, 1, 1 (1994), 27–51.

Shneiderman, Ben (Editor), *Hypertext on Hypertext*, Hyperties disk with 1 Mbyte data and graphics incorporating July 1988 CACM, ACM Press, New York (July 1988).

Shneiderman, Ben and Kearsley, Greg, *Hypertext Hands-On! An Introduction to a New Way of Organizing and Accessing Information*, Addison-Wesley, Reading, MA; book and hypertext disk using Hyperties (May 1989).

Somberg, Benjamin, and Picardi, Maria C., Locus of information familiarity effect in the search of computer menus, *Proc. Human Factors Society, Twenty-Seventh Annual Meeting*, Santa Monica, CA (1983), 826–830.

Tapia, Mark A., and Kurtenbach, Gordon, Some design refinements and principles on the appearance and behavior of marking menus, *Proc. User Interface Software and Technology '95*, ACM, New York (1995), 189–195.

Teitelbaum, Richard C., and Granda, Richard, The effects of positional constancy on searching menus for information, *Proc. CHI '83, Human Factors in Computing Systems*, ACM, New York (1983), 150–153.

Wallace, Daniel F., Anderson, Nancy S., and Shneiderman, Ben, Time stress effects on two menu selection systems, *Proc. Human Factors Society, Thirty-First Annual Meeting*, Santa Monica, CA (1987), 727–731.

Mark Kostabi, *Oasis (Yellow Meditation)*, 1996

Command and Natural Languages

I soon felt that the forms of ordinary language were far too diffuse.... I was not long in deciding that the most favorable path to pursue was to have recourse to the language of signs. It then became necessary to contrive a notation which ought, if possible, to be at once simple and expressive, easily understood at the commencement, and capable of being readily retained in the memory.

Charles Babbage, "On a method of expressing by signs the action of machinery," 1826

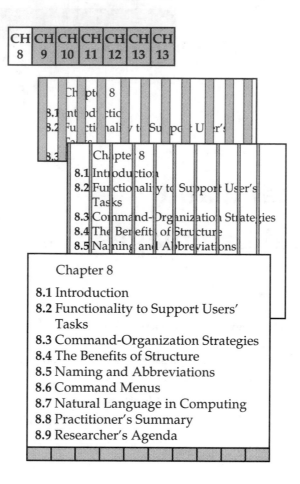

8.1 Introduction

The history of written language is rich and varied. Early tally marks and pictographs on cave walls existed for millennia before precise notations for numbers or other concepts appeared. The Egyptian hieroglyphs of 5000 years ago were a tremendous advance because standard notations facilitated communication across space and time. Eventually languages with a small alphabet and rules of word and sentence formation dominated because of the relative ease of learning, writing, and reading. In addition to these natural languages, special languages for mathematics, music, and chemistry emerged because they facilitated communication and problem solving. In the twentieth century, novel notations were created for such diverse domains as dance, knitting, higher forms of mathematics, logic, and DNA molecules.

The basic goals of language design are

- Precision
- Compactness
- Ease in writing and reading
- Completeness
- Speed in learning
- Simplicity to reduce errors
- Ease of retention over time

Higher-level goals include

- Close correspondence between reality and the notation
- Convenience in carrying out manipulations relevant to users' tasks
- Compatibility with existing notations
- Flexibility to accommodate novice and expert users
- Expressiveness to encourage creativity
- Visual appeal

Constraints on a language include

- The capacity for human beings to record the notation
- The match between the recording and the display media (for example, clay tablets, paper, printing presses)
- The convenience in speaking (vocalizing)

Successful languages evolve to serve the goals within the constraints.

The printing press was a remarkable stimulus to language development because it made widespread dissemination of written work possible. The computer is another remarkable stimulus to language development, not only because widespread dissemination through networks is possible, but also because computers are a tool to manipulate languages and because languages are a tool for manipulating computers.

The computer has had only a modest influence on spoken natural languages, compared to its enormous impact as a stimulus to the development of numerous new formal written languages. Early computers were built to perform mathematical computations, so the first programming languages had a strong mathematical flavor. But computers were quickly found to be effective manipulators of logical expressions, business data, graphics, sound, and text. Increasingly, computers are used to operate on the real world: directing robots, issuing dollar bills at bank machines, controlling manufacturing, and guiding spacecraft. These newer applications encourage language designers to find convenient notations to direct the computer while preserving the needs of people to use the language for communication and problem solving.

Therefore, effective computer languages must not only represent the users' tasks and satisfy the human needs for communication, but also be in harmony with mechanisms for recording, manipulating, and displaying these languages in a computer.

Computer programming languages such as FORTRAN, COBOL, ALGOL, PL/I, and Pascal, that were developed in the 1960s and early 1970s were designed for use in a noninteractive computer environment. Programmers would compose hundreds or thousands of lines of code, carefully check that code, and then *compile* or interpret it by computer to produce a desired result. Incremental programming was one of the design considerations in BASIC and in advanced languages such as LISP, APL, and PROLOG. Programmers in these languages were expected to build small pieces online and to test the pieces interactively. Still, the common goal was to create a large program that was preserved, studied, extended, and modified. The attraction of rapid compilation and execution led to the widespread success of the compact, but sometimes obscure, notation used in C. The pressures for team programming, organizational standards for sharing, and the increased demands for reusability promoted encapsulation and the development of object-oriented programming concepts in languages such as ADA and C++. The demands of network environments and the pursuit of cross-platform tools led to the emergence of Java.

Scripting languages emphasizing screen presentation and mouse control became popular in the late 1980s, with the appearance of HyperCard, Super-Card, ToolBook, and so on. These languages included novel operators, such as ON MOUSEDOWN, BLINK, or IF FIRST CHARACTER OF THE MESSAGE BOX IS 'A'. Java expanded the possibilities for web-oriented screen management, secure network operations, and portability.

World Wide Web addresses can be seen as a form of command language. Users come to memorize the structure and to memorize favorite sites, even though the typical usage is to click to select from a web page or a bookmark list. Web addresses begin with a protocol name (http, ftp, gopher, and so on), followed by a colon and two forward slashes. Then, the server address (which also can include country codes or domain names, such as gov, edu, mil, org), directory path, and file name; for example,

```
http://www.whitehouse.gov/WH/glimpse/top.html
```

Database-query languages for relational databases were developed in the middle to late 1970s and led to the widely used SQL. It emphasized short segments of code (three to 20 lines) that could be written at a terminal and executed immediately. The goal of the user was to create a result, rather than a program. A key part of database-query languages and information-retrieval languages was the specification of Boolean operations: AND, OR, and NOT.

Command languages, which originated with operating-systems commands, are distinguished by their immediacy and by their impact on devices or information. Users issue a command and watch what happens. If the result is correct, the next command is issued; if not, some other strategy is adopted. The commands are brief and their existence is transitory. Command histories are sometimes kept and macros are created in some command languages, but the essence of command languages is that they have an ephemeral nature and that they produce an immediate result on some object of interest.

Command languages are distinguished from menu-selection systems in that their users must recall notation and initiate action. Menu-selection users view or hear the limited set of items; they respond more than initiate. Command-language users are often called on to accomplish remarkable feats of memorization and typing. For example, this Unix command, used to delete blank lines from a file, is not obvious:

```
grep -v ^$ filea > fileb
```

Similarly, to get printout on unlined paper on a high-volume laser printer, a user at one installation was instructed to type

```
CP TAG DEV E VTSO LOCAL 2 OPTCD=J F=3871 X=GB12
```

The puzzled user was greeted with a shrug of the shoulders and the equally cryptic comment that "Sometimes, logic doesn't come into play; it's just getting the job done." This style of work may have been acceptable in the past, but user communities and their expectations are changing. While there are still millions of users of command languages, the development of new command languages has slowed dramatically due to the emergence of direct-manipulation and menu-selection interfaces.

Command languages may consist of single commands or may have complex syntax (Section 8.2). The language may have only a few operations or may have thousands. Commands may have a hierarchical structure or may permit concatenation to form variations (Section 8.3). A typical form is a verb followed by a noun object with qualifiers or arguments for the verb or noun, for example, PRINT MYFILE 3 COPIES. Abbreviations may be permitted (Section 8.5). Feedback may be generated for acceptable commands, and error messages (Section 11.2) may result from unacceptable forms or typos. Command-language systems may offer the user brief prompts or may be close to menu-selection systems (Section 8.6). Finally, natural-language interaction can be considered as a complex form of command language (Section 8.7).

8.2 Functionality to Support Users' Tasks

People use computers and command-language systems to accomplish a wide range of work, such as text editing, operating-system control, bibliographic retrieval, database manipulation, electronic mail, financial management, airline or hotel reservations, inventory, manufacturing process control, and adventure games.

People will use a computer system if it gives them powers not otherwise available. If the power is attractive enough, people will use a system despite a poor user interface. Therefore, the first step for the designer is to determine the functionality of the system by studying the users' task domain. The outcome is a list of task actions and objects, which is then abstracted into a set of interface actions and objects. These items, in turn, are represented with the low-level interface syntax.

A common design error is to provide an excessive numbers of objects and actions, which can overwhelm the user. Excessive objects and actions take more code to maintain; potentially cause more bugs; possibly incur slower execution; and require more help screens, error messages, and user manuals (see Chapters 11 and 12). For the user, excess functionality slows learning, increases the chance of error, and adds the confusion of longer manuals, more help screens, and less-specific error messages. On the other hand, insufficient objects or actions leaves the user frustrated because a desired function is not supported. For instance, users might have to copy a list with a pen and paper because there is no simple print command or to reorder a list by hand because there is no sort command.

Careful task analysis might result in a table of user communities and tasks, with each entry indicating expected frequency of use. The high-volume tasks should be made easy to carry out. The designer must decide which communities of users are the prime audience for the system. Users may differ in their position in an organization, their knowledge of computers, or their frequency of system use.

At an early stage, the destructive actions—such as deleting objects or changing formats—should be evaluated carefully to ensure that they are reversible, or at least are protected from accidental invocation. Designers should also identify error conditions and prepare error messages. A transition diagram showing how each command takes the user to another state is a highly benefi-

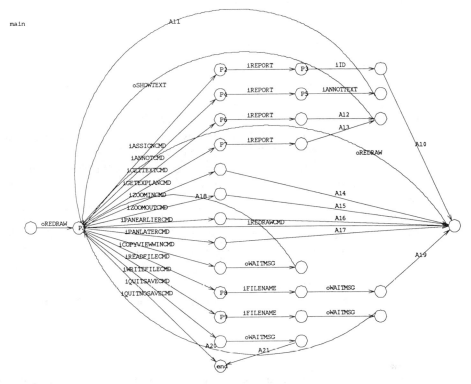

Figure 8.1

Transition diagram indicating user inputs with an "i" and computer outputs with an
"o." This relatively simple diagram shows only a portion of the system. Complete
transition diagrams may comprise many pages. (Courtesy of Robert J. K. Jacob,
Naval Research Laboratory, Washington, D.C.)

cial aid to design, as well as for eventual training of users (Fig. 8.1). A diagram
that grows too complicated may signal the need for system redesign.

Major considerations for expert users are the possibilities of tailoring the
language to suit personal work styles and of creating named macros to permit several operations to be carried out with a single command. Macro facilities allow extensions that the designers could not foresee or that are
beneficial to only a small fragment of the user community. A macro facility
can be a full programming language that might include specification of arguments, conditionals, iteration, integers, strings, and screen-manipulation
primitives, plus library and editing tools. Well-developed macro facilities are
one of the strong attractions of command languages.

8.3   Command-Organization Strategies

Several strategies for command organization have emerged. A unifying interface concept or metaphor aids learning, problem solving, and retention. Electronic-mail enthusiasts conduct lively discussions about the metaphoric merits of such task-related objects as file drawers, folders, documents, memos, notes, letters, or messages. They debate the appropriate interface actions (CREATE, EDIT, COPY, MOVE, DELETE) and the choice of action pairs: LOAD/SAVE (too much in the computer domain), READ/WRITE (acceptable for letters, but awkward for file drawers), or OPEN/CLOSE (acceptable for folders, but awkward for notes).

Designers often err by choosing a metaphor closer to the computer domain than to the user's task domain. Of course, metaphors can mislead the user, but careful design can reap the benefits while reducing the detriments. Having adopted an interface concept or metaphor for actions and objects, the designer must then choose a strategy for the command syntax. Mixed strategies are possible, but learning, problem solving, and retention may be aided by limitation of complexity.

8.3.1   Simple command set

In a *simple command set*, each command is chosen to carry out a single task, and the number of commands matches the number of tasks. When there is only a small number of tasks, this approach can produce a system that is simple to learn and use. Some MUD commands are simple, such as look, go, who, rooms, and quit. When there is a large number of commands, however, there is danger of confusion. The vi editor on Unix systems offers many commands while attempting to keep the number of keystrokes low. The result is complex strategies that employ single letters, shifted single letters, and the CTRL key plus single letters (Fig. 8.2). Furthermore, some commands stand alone, whereas others must be combined, often in irregular patterns.

8.3.2   Command plus arguments

The second option is to follow each command (COPY, DELETE, PRINT) by one or more *arguments* (FILEA, FILEB, FILEC) that indicate objects to be manipulated:

```
COPY FILEA,FILEB
DELETE FILEA
PRINT FILEA,FILEB,FILEC
```

The commands may be separated from the arguments by a blank or other delimiter, and the arguments may have blanks or delimiters between them

VI COMMANDS TO MOVE THE CURSOR

Moving within a window

H	go to home position (upper left)
L	go to last line
M	go to middle line
(CR)	next line (carriage return)
+	next line
-	previous line
CTRL-P	previous line in same column
CTRL-N	next line in same column
(LF)	next line in same column (line feed)

Moving within a line

0	go to start of line
$	go to end of line
(space)	go right one space
CRTL-H	go left one space
h	go left one space
w	forward one word
b	backward one word
e	end (rightmost) character of a word
)	forward one sentence
(	backward one sentence
}	forward one paragraph
{	backward one paragraph
W	blank out a delimited word
B	backwards blank out a delimited word
E	go to the end of a delimited word

Finding a character

fx	find the character x going forward
Fx	find the character x going backward
tx	go up to x going forward
Tx	go up to x going backward

Scrolling the window

CTRL-F	go forward one screen
CTRL-B	go backward one screen
CTRL-D	go forward one half screen
CTRL-U	go backward one half screen
G	go to line
/pat	go to line with pattern forward
pat	go to line with pattern backward

Figure 8.2

The profusion of cursor-movement commands in vi enable expert users to get tasks done with just a few actions, but they can overwhelm novice and intermittent users.

(Schneider et al., 1984). Keyword labels for arguments may be helpful to some users; for example,

```
COPY FROM=FILEA TO=FILEB
```

The labels require extra typing and thus increase chances of a typo, but readability is improved and order dependence is eliminated.

8.3.3   Command plus options and arguments

Commands may have *options* (3, HQ, and so on) to indicate special cases. For example,

```
PRINT/3,HQ FILEA
PRINT (3,HQ) FILEA
PRINT FILEA -3,HQ
```

may produce three copies of FILEA at the printer in the headquarters building. As the number of options grows, the complexity can become overwhelming and the error messages must be less specific. The arguments also may have options, such as version numbers, privacy keys, or disk addresses.

The number of arguments, of options, and of permissible syntactic forms can grow rapidly. One airline-reservations system uses the following command to check the seat availability on a flight on August 21, from Washington's National Airport (DCA) to New York's LaGuardia Airport (LGA) at about 3:00 P.M.:

```
A0821DCALGA0300P
```

Even with substantial training, error rates can be high with this approach, but frequent users seem to manage and even to appreciate the compact form of this type of command.

The Unix command-language system is widely used, in spite of the complexity of its command formats, which have been criticized severely (Norman, 1981). Here again, users will master complexity to benefit from the rich functionality in a system. Observed error rates with actual use of Unix commands have ranged from 3 to 53 percent (Hanson et al., 1984). Even common commands have generated high syntactic error rates: mv (18 percent) or cp (30 percent). Still, the complexity has a certain attraction for a portion of the potential user community. Users gain satisfaction in overcoming the difficulties and becoming one of the inner circle (gurus or wizards) who are knowledgeable about system features—command-language macho.

8.3.4 Hierarchical command structure

In a *hierarchical command structure*, the full set of commands is organized into a tree structure, like a menu tree. The first level might be the command action, the second might be an object argument, and the third might be a destination argument:

Action	Object	Destination
CREATE	File	File
DISPLAY	Process	Local printer
REMOVE	Directory	Screen
COPY		Remote printer
MOVE		

If a hierarchical structure can be found for a set of tasks, it offers a meaningful structure to a large number of commands. In this case, $5 \times 3 \times 4 = 60$ tasks can be carried out with only five command names and one rule of formation. Another advantage is that a command-menu approach can be developed to aid the novice or intermittent user, as was done in VisiCalc and later in Lotus 1–2–3 and Excel.

8.4 The Benefits of Structure

Human learning, problem solving, and memory are greatly facilitated by meaningful structure. If command languages are well designed, users can recognize the structure and can easily encode it in their semantic-knowledge storage. For example, if users can uniformly edit such objects as characters, words, sentences, paragraphs, chapters, and documents, this meaningful pattern is easy for them to learn, apply, and recall. On the other hand, if they must overtype a character, change a word, revise a sentence, replace a paragraph, substitute a chapter, and alter a document, then the challenge and potential for error grow substantially, no matter how elegant the syntax (Scapin, 1982).

Meaningful structure is beneficial for task concepts, computer concepts, and syntactic details of command languages. Yet many systems fail to provide a meaningful structure. Users of one operating system display information with the LIST, QUERY, HELP, and TYPE commands, and move objects with the PRINT, TYPE, SPOOL, SEND, COPY, or MOVE commands. Defaults are inconsistent, four different abbreviations for PRINT and LINECOUNT are required, binary choices vary between YES/NO and ON/OFF, and function-key usage is inconsistent. These flaws emerge from multiple uncoordinated design groups and reflect insufficient attention by the managers, especially as features are added over time.

An explicit list of design conventions in a *guidelines document* can be an aid to designers and managers. Exceptions may be permitted, but only after thoughtful discussions. Users can learn systems that contain inconsistencies, but they do so slowly and with a high chance of making mistakes.

8.4.1   Consistent argument ordering

Several studies have shown that there are benefits associated with using a *consistent order for arguments* (Barnard et al., 1981).

Inconsistent order of arguments	Consistent order of arguments
`SEARCH file no,message id`	`SEARCH message id,file no`
`TRIM message id,segment size`	`TRIM message id,segment size`
`REPLACE message id,code no`	`REPLACE message id,code no`
`INVERT group size,message id`	`INVERT message id,group size`

Time to perform tasks for the 48 subjects was significantly shorter with the consistent argument ordering.

8.4.2   Symbols versus keywords

Evidence that command structure affects performance comes from a comparison of 15 commands in a commercially used symbol-oriented text editor, and revised commands that had a more keyword-oriented style (Ledgard et al., 1980). Here are three sample commands:

Symbol editor	Keyword editor
`FIND:/TOOTH/;-1`	`BACKWARD TO "TOOTH"`
`LIST;10`	`LIST 10 LINES`
`RS:/KO/,/OK/;*`	`CHANGE ALL "KO" TO "OK"`

The revised commands performed the same functions. Single-letter abbreviations (`L;10` or `L 10 L`) were permitted in both editors, so the number of keystrokes was approximately the same. The difference in the revised commands was that keywords were used in an intuitively meaningful way, but there were no standard rules of formation. Eight subjects at three levels of text-editor experience used both versions in this counterbalanced-order within-subjects design. The results (Table 8.1) clearly favored the keyword editor, indicating that command-formation rules do make a difference.

Table 8.1

Effects of revised text-editor commands on three levels of users. (Ledgard et al., 1980.)

	Percentage of Task Completed		Percentage of Erroneous Commands	
	Symbol	*Keyword*	*Symbol*	*Keyword*
Inexperienced users	28	42	19.0	11.0
Familiar users	43	62	18.0	6.4
Experienced users	74	84	9.9	5.6

8.4.3 Hierarchical structure and congruence

Carroll (1982) altered two design variables to produce four versions of a 16-command language for controlling a robot (Table 8.2). Commands could be hierarchical (verb-object–qualifier) or nonhierarchical (verb only) and congruent (for example, ADVANCE/RETREAT or RIGHT/LEFT) or noncongruent (GO/BACK or TURN/LEFT). Carroll uses *congruent* to refer to meaningful pairs of opposites (*symmetry* might be a better term). Hierarchical structure and congruence have been shown to be advantageous in psycholinguistic experiments. Thirty-two undergraduate subjects studied one of the four command sets in a written manual, gave subjective ratings, and then carried out paper-and-pencil tasks.

Subjective ratings prior to performance of tasks showed that subjects disapproved of the nonhierarchical noncongruent form and gave the highest rating for the nonhierarchical congruent form. Memory and problem-solving tasks showed that congruent forms were clearly superior and that the hierarchical forms were superior for several dependent measures. Error rates were dramatically lower for the congruent hierarchical forms.

This study assessed performance of new users of a small command language. Congruence helped subjects to remember the natural pairs of concepts and terms. The hierarchical structure enabled subjects to master 16 commands with only one rule of formation and 12 keywords. With a larger command set—say, 60 or 160 commands—the advantage of hierarchical structure should increase, assuming that a hierarchical structure could be found to accommodate the full set of commands. Another conjecture is that retention should be facilitated by the hierarchical structure and congruence.

Carroll's study was conducted during a half-day period; with one week of regular use, differences probably would be reduced substantially. However, with intermittent users or with users under stress, the hierarchical congruent form might again prove superior. An online experiment might have

Table 8.2

Command sets and partial results. (Carroll 1982.)

CONGRUENT		NONCONGRUENT	
Hierarchical	*Non-hierarchical*	*Hierarchical*	*Non-hierarchical*
MOVE ROBOT FORWARD	ADVANCE	MOVE ROBOT FORWARD	GO
MOVE ROBOT BACKWARD	RETREAT	CHANGE ROBOT BACKWARD	BACK
MOVE ROBOT RIGHT	RIGHT	CHANGE ROBOT RIGHT	TURN
MOVE ROBOT LEFT	LEFT	MOVE ROBOT LEFT	LEFT
MOVE ROBOT UP	STRAIGHTEN	CHANGE ROBOT UP	UP
MOVE ROBOT DOWN	BEND	MOVE ROBOT DOWN	BEND
MOVE ARM FORWARD	PUSH	CHANGE ARM FORWARD	POKE
MOVE ARM BACKWARD	PULL	MOVE ARM BACKWARD	PULL
MOVE ARM RIGHT	SWING OUT	CHANGE ARM RIGHT	PIVOT
MOVE ARM LEFT	SWING IN	MOVE ARM LEFT	SWEEP
MOVE ARM UP	RAISE	MOVE ARM UP	REACH
MOVE ARM DOWN	LOWER	CHANGE ARM DOWN	DOWN
CHANGE ARM OPEN	RELEASE	CHANGE ARM OPEN	UNHOOK
CHANGE ARM CLOSE	TAKE	MOVE ARM CLOSE	GRAB
CHANGE ARM RIGHT	SCREW	MOVE ARM RIGHT	SCREW
CHANGE ARM LEFT	UNSCREW	CHANGE ARM LEFT	TWIST

Subjective Ratings (1 = Best, 5 = Worst)

	1.86	1.63	1.81	2.73
Test Scores	14.88	14.63	7.25	11.00
Errors	0.50	2.13	4.25	1.63
Omissions	2.00	2.50	4.75	4.15

been more realistic and would have brought out differences in command
length that would have been a disadvantage to the hierarchical forms
because of the greater number of keystrokes required. However, the hierarchical forms could all be replaced with three-letter abbreviations (for example, MAL for MOVE ARM LEFT), thereby providing an advantage even in
keystroke counts.

In summary, sources of structure that have proved advantageous
include these:

- Positional consistency
- Grammatical consistency
- Congruent pairing
- Hierarchical form

In addition, as discussed in Section 8.5, a mixture of meaningfulness, mnemonicity, and distinctiveness is helpful.

8.5 Naming and Abbreviations

In discussing command-language names, Schneider (1984) takes a delightful quote from Shakespeare's *Romeo and Juliet*: "A rose by any other name would smell as sweet." As Schneider points out, the lively debates in design circles suggest that this concept does not apply to command-language names. Indeed, the command names are the most visible part of a system and are likely to provoke complaints from disgruntled users.

Critics (Norman, 1981, for example) focus on the strange names in Unix, such as `mkdir` (make directory), `cd` (change directory), `ls` (list directory), `rm` (remove file), and `pwd` (print working directory); or in IBM's CMS, such as SO (temporarily suspend recording of trace information), LKED (link edit), NUCXMAP (identify nucleus extensions), and GENDIRT (generate directory). Part of the concern is the inconsistent abbreviation strategies that may take the first few letters, first few consonants, first and final letter, or first letter of each word in a phrase. Worse still are abbreviations with no perceivable pattern.

8.5.1 Specificity versus generality

Names are important for learning, problem solving, and retention over time. When it contains only a few names, a command set is relatively easy to master; but when it contains hundreds of names, the choice of meaningful, organized sets of names becomes more important. Similar results were found for programming tasks, where variable name choices were less important in small modules with from 10 to 20 names than in longer modules with dozens or hundreds of names.

With larger command sets, the names do make a difference, especially if they support congruence or some other meaningful structure. One naming-rule debate revolves around the question of *specificity versus generality* (Rosenberg, 1982). Specific terms can be more descriptive than general ones are, and if they are more distinctive, they may be more memorable. General terms may be more familiar and therefore easier to accept. Two weeks after a training session with 12 commands, subjects were more likely to recall and recognize the meaning of specific commands than those of general commands (Barnard et al., 1981).

In a paper-and-pencil test, 84 subjects studied one of seven sets of eight commands (Black and Moran, 1982). Two of the eight commands—the commands for inserting and deleting text—are shown here in all seven versions:

Infrequent, discriminating words	insert	delete
Frequent, discriminating words	add	remove
Infrequent, nondiscriminating words	amble	perceive
Frequent, nondiscriminating words	walk	view
General words (frequent, nondiscriminating)	alter	correct
Nondiscriminating nonwords (nonsense)	GAC	MIK
Discriminating nonwords (icons)	abc-adbc	abc-ac

The "infrequent, discriminating" command set resulted in faster learning and superior recall than did other command sets. The general words were correlated with the lowest performance on all three measures. The nonsense words did surprisingly well, supporting the possibility that, with small command sets, distinctive names are helpful even if they are not meaningful.

8.5.2   Abbreviation strategies

Even though command names should be meaningful for human learning, problem solving, and retention, they must satisfy another important criterion: They must be in harmony with the mechanism for expressing the commands to the computer. The traditional and widely used command-entry mechanism is the keyboard, which indicates that commands should use brief and kinesthetically easy codes. Commands requiring shifted keys or CTRL keys, special characters, or difficult-to-type sequences are likely to cause higher error rates. For text editing, when many commands are applied and speed is appreciated, single-letter approaches are attractive. Overall, brevity is a worthy goal, since it can speed entry and reduce error rates. Early word-processor designers pursued this approach, even when mnemonicity was sacrificed, thereby making use more difficult for novice and intermittent users.

In less demanding applications, designers have used longer command abbreviations, hoping that the gains in recognizability would be appreciated over the reduction in key strokes. Novice users may actually prefer typing the full name of a command because they have a greater confidence in its success (Landauer et al., 1983). Novices who were required to use full command names before being taught two-letter abbreviations made fewer errors with the abbreviations than did those who were taught the abbreviations from the start and than did those who could create their own abbreviations (Grudin and Barnard, 1985).

The phenomenon of preferring the full name at first appeared in our study of bibliographic retrieval with the Library of Congress's SCORPIO system. Novices preferred typing the full name, such as BROWSE or SELECT, rather than the traditional four-letter abbreviations BRWS or SLCT, or the single-letter abbreviations B or S. After five to seven uses of the command, their confidence increased and they attempted the single-letter abbreviations. A designer of a text adventure game recognized this principle and instructed novice users to type EAST, WEST, NORTH, or SOUTH; after five full-length commands, the system tells the user about the single-letter abbreviations.

With experience and frequent use, abbreviations become attractive for, and even necessary to satisfy, the "power" user. Efforts have been made to find optimal abbreviation strategies. Several studies support the notion that abbreviation should be accomplished by a consistent strategy (Ehrenreich and Porcu, 1982; Benbasat and Wand, 1984; Schneider, 1984). Here are six potential strategies:

1. *Simple truncation*   Use the first, second, third, and so on letters of each command. This strategy requires that each command be distinguishable by the leading string of characters. Abbreviations can be all of the same length or of different lengths.

2. *Vowel drop with simple truncation*   Eliminate vowels and use some of what remains. If the first letter is a vowel, it may or may not be retained. H, Y, and W may or may not be considered as vowels for this purpose.

3. *First and final letter*   Since the first and final letters are highly visible, use them; for example, use ST for SORT.

4. *First letter of each word in a phrase*   Use the popular acronym technique, for example, with a hierarchical design plan.

5. *Standard abbreviations from other contexts*   Use familiar abbreviations such as QTY for QUANTITY, XTALK for CROSSTALK (a software package), PRT for PRINT, or BAK for BACKUP.

6. *Phonics*   Focus attention on the sound; for example, use XQT for execute.

Truncation appears to be the most effective mechanism overall, but it has its problems. Conflicting abbreviations appear often, and decoding an unfamiliar abbreviation may not be easy as when vowel dropping is used (Schneider, 1984).

8.5.3   Guidelines for using abbreviations

Ehrenreich and Porcu (1982) offer this compromise set of guidelines:

1. A *simple,* primary rule should be used to generate abbreviations for most items; a *simple* secondary rule should be used for those items where there is a conflict.

2. Abbreviations generated by the secondary rule should have a marker (for example, an asterisk) incorporated in them.

3. The number of words abbreviated by the secondary rule should be kept to a minimum.

4. Users should be familiar with the rules used to generate abbreviations.

5. Truncation should be used because it is an easy rule for users to comprehend and remember. When it produces a large number of identical abbreviations for different words, adjustments must be found.

6. Fixed-length abbreviations should be used in preference to variable-length ones.

7. Abbreviations should not be designed to incorporate endings (e.g., ING, ED, S).

8. Unless there is a critical space problem, abbreviations should not be used in messages generated by the computer and read by the user.

Abbreviations are an important part of system design and they are appreciated by experienced users. Users are more likely to use abbreviations if they are confident in their knowledge of the abbreviations and if the benefit is a savings of more than one to two characters (Benbasat and Wand, 1984). The dominance of GUIs has reduced the importance of abbreviations strategies, but when there are appropriate situations for command abbreviations, empirical tests with users should be applied.

8.6   Command Menus

To relieve the burden of memorization of commands, some designers offer users brief prompts of available commands, in a format called a *command menu*. For example, a text-only web browser called lynx displays this prompt:

```
H)elp O)ptions P)rint G)o M)ain screen Q)uit
        /=search [delete]=history list
```

Experienced users come to know the commands and do not need to read the prompt or the help screens. Intermittent users know the concepts and refer to the prompt to jog their memory and to get help in retaining the syntax for future uses. Novice users do not benefit as much from the prompt and must take a training course or consult the online help.

The prompting approach emphasizes syntax and serves frequent users. It is closer to but more compact than a numbered menu, and preserves screen space for task-related information. The early WORDSTAR editor offered the novice and intermittent user help menus containing commands with one- or two-word descriptions (Fig. 8.3). Frequent users could turn off the display of help menus, thereby gaining screen space for additional text.

```
          A:GETTYS  PAGE 1 LINE 9 COL 62                    INSERT ON
                      < < <      M A I N   M E N U     > > >
      --Cursor Movement--     : -Delete- :   -Miscellaneous-  :  -Other   Menus-
  ^S char left ^D char right :^G  char  :  ^I Tab   ^B Reform :  (from Main only)
  ^A word left ^F word right :DEL chr lf:  ^V INSERT ON/OFF   :^J Help   ^K Block
  ^E line  up  ^X line down  :^T word rt:^L Find/Replce again:^Q Quick ^P Print
         --Scrolling--       :^Y  line  :RETURN End paragraph:^O Onscreen
  ^Z line down ^W line up    :          :  ^N Insert a RETURN :
  ^C screen up ^R screen down:          :  ^U Stop a command  :
  L----!----!----!----!----!----!----!----!----!----!----!--------R
      Fourscore  and seven years ago our fathers brought forth on
  this continent a new nation conceived in liberty and dedicated to
  the  proposition  that  all men are created equal.   Now  we  are
  engaged in a great civil war testing whether that nation,  or any
  nation so conceived and so dedicated, can long endure.

      We are met on a great battlefield of that war.  We have come
  to dedicate a portion of that field as a final resting-place  for
  those  who here gave their lives that that nation might live.
```

Figure 8.3

The early WORDSTAR help menus, which offered the novice and intermittent users commands with one- or two-word descriptions.

In many Command menus, users can use the mouse or arrow keys to highlight their choices, or can type single-letter choices, but frequent users do not even look at the menus as they type sequences of two, three, four, or more single letters that come to be thought of as a command. Windows 95 shows the single-letter command by underscoring a letter in the menu, allowing users to perform all operations with keyboard commands (see Color Plate A1). With a fast display, command menus blur the boundaries between commands and menus.

8.7 Natural Language in Computing

Even before there were computers, people dreamed about creating machines that would accept *natural language*. It is a wonderful fantasy, and the success of word-manipulation devices such as word processors, tape recorders, and telephones may give encouragement to some people. Although there has been some progress in machine translation from one natural language to another (for example, Japanese to English), most effective systems require constrained or preprocessed input, or postprocessing of output. Undoubtedly, improvements will continue and constraints will be reduced, but high-quality reliable translations of complete documents without human intervention seem difficult to attain. Structured texts such as weather reports are translatable; technical papers are marginally translatable; novels or poems are not translatable. Language is subtle; there are many special cases, contexts are complex and emotional relationships have a powerful and pervasive effect in human–human communication.

Although full comprehension and generation of language seems inaccessible, there are still many ways that computers can be used in dealing with natural language, such as for interaction, queries, database searching, text generation, and adventure games (Allen, 1995). So much research has been invested in natural-language systems that undoubtedly some successes will emerge, but widespread use may not develop because the alternatives may be more appealing. More rapid progress can be made if carefully designed experimental tests are used to discover the users, tasks, and interface designs for which natural-language applications are most beneficial (Oviatt, 1994; King, 1996).

8.7.1   Natural-language interaction

Researchers hope to fulfill the Star Trek scenario in which computers will respond to commands users issue by speaking (or typing) in natural language. *Natural-language interaction* (NLI) might be defined as the operation of computers by people using a familiar natural language (such as English) to give instructions and receive responses. Users do not have to learn a command syntax or to select from menus. Early attempts at generalized "automatic programming" from natural-language statements have faded, but there are continuing efforts to provide domain-specific assistance.

The problems with NLI lie in not only implementation on the computer, but also desirability for large numbers of users for a wide variety of tasks. People are different from computers, and human–human interaction is not necessarily an appropriate model for human operation of computers. Since computers can display information 1000 times faster than people can enter commands, it seems advantageous to use the computer to display large amounts of information, and to allow novice and intermittent users simply to choose among the items. Selection helps to guide the user by making clear what functions are available. For knowledgeable and frequent users, who are thoroughly aware of the available functions, a precise, concise command language is usually preferred.

In fact, the metaphors of artificial intelligence (smart machines, intelligent agents, and expert systems) may prove to be mind-limiting distractions that inhibit designers from creating the powerful tools that become commercially successful. Spreadsheets, WYSIWYG word processors, and direct-manipulation graphics tools emerged from a recognition of what users were using effectively, rather than from the misleading notions of intelligent machines. Similarly, the next generation of groupware to support collaboration, visualization, simulation, tele-operated devices, and hypermedia stem from user-centered scenarios, rather than from the machine-centered artificial-intelligence scenarios.

The OAI model may help us to sort out the issues. Most designs for NLI do not provide information about task actions and objects; users are usually presented with a simple prompt that invites a natural-language statement. Users who are knowledgeable about the task—for example, stock-market objects and permissible actions—could make buy or sell orders by voice or typing in natural language, but compact command languages are reliable and have been preferred by these users. NLI designs also do not usually convey information about the interface—for example, tree-structuring of information, implications of a deletion, Boolean operations, or query strategies. NLI designs should relieve users from learning new syntactic rules, since they presumably will accept familiar English language requests. Therefore, NLI can be effective for users who are knowledgeable about specific tasks and interface concepts but who are intermittent users who cannot retain the syntactic details of the interface.

By this analysis, NLI might apply to checkbook maintenance (Shneiderman, 1980), where the users recognize that there is an ascending sequence of integer-numbered checks, and that each check has a single payee field, single amount, single date, and one or more signatures. Checks can be issued, voided, searched, and printed. Following this suggestion, Ford (1981) created and tested a textual NLI system for this purpose. Subjects were paid to maintain their checkbook registers by computer using an APL-based program that was refined incrementally to account for unanticipated entries. The final system successfully handled 91 percent of users' requests, such as these:

```
Pay to Safeway on 3/24/86 $29.75.
June 10 $33.00 to Madonna.
Show me all the checks paid to George Bush.
Which checks were written on October 29?
```

Users reported satisfaction with the system and were eager to use the system after completing the several months of experimentation. This study can be seen as a success for NLI, but direct-manipulation alternatives (for example, Quicken from Intuit) have proved more attractive in the marketplace. Showing a full screen of checkbook entries with a blank line for new entries might allow users to accomplish most tasks without any commands and with minimal typing. Users could search by entering partial information (for example, Bill Clinton in the payee field) and then pressing a query key.

There have been numerous informal tests of NLI systems, but only a few have been controlled experimental comparisons against some other design. Researchers seeking to demonstrate the advantage of NLI over command-language and menu approaches for creating business graphics were surprised to find no significant differences for task time, user errors, or user attitudes (Hauptmann and Green, 1983).

A more positive result was found with users of HAL, the restricted natural-language addition to Lotus 1–2–3 (Napier et al., 1989). HAL users could avoid the command-menu /WEY (for Worksheet Erase Yes), and could type requests such as \erase worksheet, \insert row, or \total all `columns`, starting with any of the 180 permissible verbs. In an empirical study, after 1.5 days of training, 19 HAL users and 22 Lotus 1–2–3 users worked on three substantial problem sets for another 1.5 days. Performance and preference strongly favored the restricted natural-language version, but the experimenters had difficulty identifying the features that made a difference: "It is not clear whether Lotus HAL was better because it is more like English or because it takes advantage of context, but we suspect the latter is more important." By context, the authors meant features such as the cursor position or meaningful variable names that indicate cell ranges. HAL is no longer marketed.

Some NLI work has turned to automatic speech recognition and speech generation to reduce the barriers to acceptance (Oviatt, 1994). There is some advantage to use of these technologies, but the results are still meager. A promising application is the selection of painting tools by discrete-word recognition (see Section 9.4.1), thus eliminating the frustration and delay of moving the cursor from the object to the tool menu on the border and back again (Pausch, 1991). Selections are voiced, but feedback is visual. Users of the mouse plus the voice commands performed their tasks 21-percent faster than did the users who had only the mouse. Alternatives to voice, such as keyboard or touchscreen, were not tested.

There is some portion of the user spectrum that can benefit from NLI, but it may not be as large as promoters believe. Computer users usually seek predictable responses and are discouraged if they must engage in clarification dialogs frequently. Since NLI has such varied forms, the users must constantly be aware of the computer's response, to verify that their actions were recognized. Finally, visually oriented interactions, embracing the notions of direct manipulation (see Chapter 6), make more effective use of the computer's capacity for rapid display. In short, pointing and selecting in context is often more attractive than is typing or even speaking an English sentence.

8.7.2 Natural-language queries

Since general interaction is difficult to support, some designers have pursued a more limited goal of *natural-language queries* (NLQ) against relational databases. The *relational schema* contains attribute names and the database contains attribute values, both of which are helpful in disambiguating queries. A simulated query system was used to compare a subset of the structured SQL database facility to a natural-language system (Small and Weldon, 1983). The SQL simulation resulted in faster performance on a benchmark set of tasks. Similarly, a field trial with a real system, users, and queries pointed to the advantages of SQL over the natural-language alternative (Jarke et al., 1985). Believers in NLQ may claim that more research and system development is needed before that approach can be excluded, but improvements in menus, command languages, and direct manipulation seem equally likely.

Supporters of NLQ can point with some pride at the modest success of the INTELLECT system, which had approximately 400 installations on large mainframe computers during the 1980s. The system's appeal has faded in recent years as users have turned to other approaches. Business executives, sales representatives, and other people use INTELLECT to search databases on a regular basis. Several innovative implementation ideas helped to make INTELLECT appealing. First, the parser used the contents of the database to parse queries; for example, the parser could determine that a query containing Cleveland referred to city locations, because Cleveland is an instance in the database. Second, the system administrator could conveniently include guidance for handling domain-specific requests, by indicating fields related to who, what, where, when, why, and how queries. Third, INTELLECT rephrased the user's query and displayed a response, such as PRINT THE CHECK NUMBERS WITH PAYEE = GEORGE BUSH. This structured response served as an educational aid, and users gravitated toward expressions that mimicked the style. Eventually, as users became more knowledgeable, they often used concise, commandlike expressions that they believed would be parsed successfully. Even the promoters of INTELLECT recognized that novice users who were unfamiliar with the task domain would have a difficult time, and that the ideal user might be a knowledgeable intermittent user.

A more successful product was Q&A from Symantec, which provided rapid, effective query interpretation and execution on IBM PCs (Fig. 8.4). The package made a positive impression, but few data have been collected about actual usage. The designers cited many instances of happy users of NLQ, and found practical applications in the users' daily work, but the popularity of the package seems to have been more closely tied to its word processor, database, and form-fillin facilities (Church and Rau, 1995). Q&A and most other NLQ packages are no longer sold. The dream of NLQ remains alive in some quarters, such as in Microsoft's Research Laboratories, where a talking parrot named Peedy is under development (Fig. 8.5).

8.7.3 Text-database searching

Text-database searching is a growing application for natural-language enthusiasts who have developed filters and parsers for queries expressed in natural language (Lewis and Jones, 1996). At one end of the spectrum is the full understanding of the meaning of a query and fulfillment of the users information needs. For example, in a legal application (Find cases of tenants who have sued landlords unsuccessfully for lack of heat), the system parses the text grammatically, provides synonyms from a thesaurus (renters for tenants), deals with singulars versus plurals, and handles other

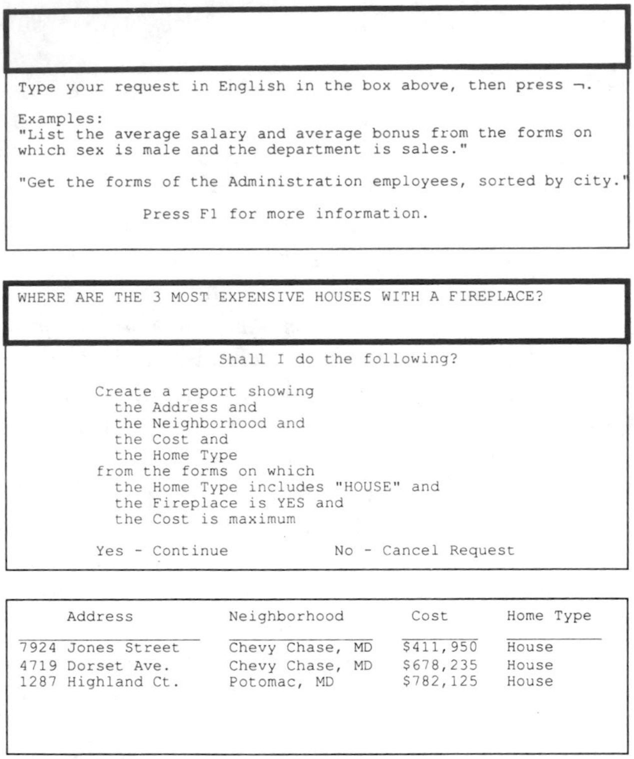

```
┌─────────────────────────────────────────────────────────────┐
│                                                             │
└─────────────────────────────────────────────────────────────┘
 Type your request in English in the box above, then press ¬.

 Examples:
 "List the average salary and average bonus from the forms on
 which sex is male and the department is sales."

 "Get the forms of the Administration employees, sorted by city."

             Press F1 for more information.
```

```
┌─────────────────────────────────────────────────────────────┐
│ WHERE ARE THE 3 MOST EXPENSIVE HOUSES WITH A FIREPLACE?      │
└─────────────────────────────────────────────────────────────┘
                     Shall I do the following?

         Create a report showing
            the Address and
            the Neighborhood and
            the Cost and
            the Home Type
         from the forms on which
            the Home Type includes "HOUSE" and
            the Fireplace is YES and
            the Cost is maximum

         Yes - Continue          No - Cancel Request
```

```
      Address          Neighborhood       Cost       Home Type
   ─────────────       ────────────     ────────     ─────────
 7924 Jones Street    Chevy Chase, MD   $411,950     House
 4719 Dorset Ave.     Chevy Chase, MD   $678,235     House
 1287 Highland Ct.    Potomac, MD       $782,125     House
```

Figure 8.4

Q&A supported a natural-language front end for its database. Users could type a question in English and get the result of a structured database search. In this example, the user has typed a query, the system has responded with a verification, and then the system has generated the result. (Q&A was a product of Symantic Corp., Cupertino, CA.)

problems such as misspellings or foreign terms. Then, the analyzer separates the query into standard components—such as plaintiff, defendant, and cause—and finds all meaningfully related legal citations.

More realistic and typical scenarios are for parsers to eliminate noise words (for example, *the*, *of*, or *in*) provide stemming (plurals or alternate endings), and produce a relevance ranked list of documents based on term frequencies. These systems do not deal with negation, broader or narrow terms, and relationships (such as plaintiff sues defendants), but they can be effective with skilled users. A comparative-evaluation contest among information-retrieval programs that use natural-language strategies to select documents from a large collection continues to be extremely successful in promoting rapid progress (Harman, 1995). Many of the popular search tools on the World Wide Web (e.g., Lycos, Infoseek, AltaVista) use modest natural-

[Peedy, a parrot, is asleep on his perch]

User: Good morning, Peedy.   [Peedy rouses]

Peedy: Good morning.

User: Let's do a demo.   [Peedy stands up, smiles]

Peedy: Your wish is my command, what would you like to hear?

User: What have you got by Bonnie Raitt?

[Peedy waves in a stream of notes and grabs one]

Peedy: I have "The Bonnie Raitt Collection" from 1990.

User: Pick something from that.

Peedy: How about "Angel from Montgomery"?

User: Sounds good.   [Peedy drops note on pile]

Peedy: OK.

User: Play some rock after that.

Figure 8.5

Sample dialog from Microsoft Research exemplifying the goals for that company's natural-language system. (Used with permission of Microsoft Corp., Redmond, WA.)

language techniques, such as stemming, relevance ranking by word-frequency analyses, latent semantic indexing, and filtering of common words.

Another application with textual databases is extraction, in which a natural-language parser analyzes the stored text and creates a more structured format, such as a relational database. The advantage is that the parsing can be done once in advance to structure the entire database and to speed searches when users pose relational queries. Legal (Supreme Court decisions or state laws), medical (scientific journal articles or patient histories), and journalistic (Associated Press news stories or Wall Street Journal reports) texts have been used. This application is promising because even a modest increase in suitable retrievals is appreciated by users, and incorrect retrievals are tolerated better than are errors in natural-language interaction. Extraction is somewhat easier than is the task of writing a natural-language summary of a long document. Summaries must capture the essence of the content, and must convey it accurately in a compact manner. A variant task is to make categories of documents based on contents. For example, it would be useful to have an automated analysis of business news stories to separate out mergers, bankruptcies, and initial public offerings for companies in the electronics, pharmaceutical, or oil industries. The categorization task is appealing because a modest rate of errors would be tolerable (Church and Rau, 1995).

8.7.4   Natural-language text generation

Although the artificial-intelligence community often frowns on *natural-language text generation* (NLTG), this modest application does seem to be a worthy one (Fedder, 1990). It handles certain simple tasks, such as the preparation of structured weather reports (80-percent chance of light rain in northern suburbs by late Sunday afternoon) from complex mathematical models (Church and Rau, 1995). These reports can be sent out automatically, or even can be used to generate spoken reports available over the telephone in multiple languages.

More elaborate applications of NLTG include preparation of reports of medical laboratory or psychological tests. The computer generates not only readable reports (White-blood-cell count is 12,000), but also warnings (This value exceeds the normal range of 3000 to 8000 by 50 percent) or recommendations (Further examination for systemic infection is recommended). Still more involved scenarios for NLTG involve the creation of legal contracts, wills, or business proposals.

On the artistic side, computer generation of poems and even novels is a regular discussion point in literary circles. Although computer-generated combinations of randomly selected phrases can be provocative, it is still the creative work of the person who chose the set of possible words and decided which of the outputs to publish. This position parallels the custom of crediting the human photographer, rather than the camera or the subject matter of the photograph.

8.7.5   Adventure and educational games

Natural-language interaction techniques have enjoyed a notable and widespread success in a variety of adventure games. Users may indicate directions of movement or type commands, such as TAKE ALL OF THE KEYS, OPEN THE GATE, or DROP THE CAGE AND PICK UP THE SWORD. Part of the attraction of using natural-language interaction in this situation is that the system is unpredictable, and some exploration is necessary to discover the proper incantation. However, such games have largely disappeared from the market.

8.8   Practitioner's Summary

Command languages can be attractive when frequent use of a system is anticipated, users are knowledgeable about the task and interface concepts, screen space is at a premium, response time and display rates are slow, and numerous functions can be combined in a compact expression. Users have to learn the semantics and syntax, but they can initiate, rather than respond, and can rapidly specify actions involving several objects and options. Finally, a complex sequence of commands can be easily specified and stored for future use as a macro.

Designers should begin with a careful task analysis to determine what functions should be provided. Hierarchical strategies and congruent structures facilitate learning, problem solving, and human retention over time. Laying out the full set of commands on a single sheet of paper helps to show the structure to the designer and to the learner. Meaningful specific names aid learning and retention. Compact abbreviations constructed according to consistent rules facilitate retention and rapid performance for frequent users.

Command menus can be effective if rapid response to screen actions can be provided. Natural-language interaction and queries can be implemented partially, but their advantages are limited. Natural-language support has clearer niches in text searching, text generation, extraction, and games.

8.9   Researcher's Agenda

The benefits of structuring command languages based on hierarchy, congruence, consistency, and mnemonicity have been demonstrated in specific cases, but replication in varied situations should lead to a comprehensive cognitive model of command-language learning and use (Box 8.1). Novel input devices and high-speed, high-resolution displays offer new opportunities—such as command and pop-up menus—for breaking free from the traditional syntax of command languages.

Natural-language interaction still holds promise in certain applications, and empirical tests offer us a good chance to identify the appropriate niches and design strategies.

Box 8.1

Command Language Guidelines

- Create explicit model of objects and actions
- Choose meaningful, specific, distinctive names
- Try to achieve hierarchical structure
- Provide consistent structure
  (hierarchy, argument order, action-object)
- Support consistent abbreviation rules
  (prefer truncation to one letter)
- Offer frequent users the ability to create macros
- Consider command menus on high-speed displays
- Limit number of commands and ways of accomplishing a task

World Wide Web Resources   WWW

Some information on command languages but lots of activity on natural language translation, interaction, queries, and extraction.

http://www.aw.com/DTUI

References

Allen, James, *Natural Language Understanding* (Second Edition), Addison-Wesley, Reading, MA (1995).

Barnard, P. J., Hammond, N. V., Morton, J., Long, J. B., and Clark, I. A., Consistency and compatibility in human–computer dialogue, *International Journal of Man–Machine Studies*, 15, (1981), 87–134.

Benbasat, Izak and Wand, Yair, Command abbreviation behavior in human–computer interaction, *Communications of the ACM*, 27, 4 (April 1984), 376–383.

Black, J., and Moran, T., Learning and remembering command names, *Proc. Conference on Human Factors in Computer Systems*, ACM, Washington, D.C. (1982), 8–11.

Carroll, John M., Learning, using and designing command paradigms, *Human Learning*, 1, 1 (1982), 31–62.

Church, Kenneth W. and Rau, Lisa F., Commercial applications of natural language processing *Communications of the ACM*, 38, 11 (November 1995), 71–79.

Ehrenreich, S. L., and Porcu, Theodora, Abbreviations for automated systems: Teaching operators and rules. In Badre, Al, and Shneiderman, Ben, (Editors), *Directions in Human–Computer Interaction*, Ablex, Norwood, NJ (1982), 111–136.

Fedder, Lee., Recent approaches to natural language generation. In Diaper, D., Gilmore, D., Cockton, G., and Shackel, B. (Editors), *Human–Computer Interaction: Interact '90*, North-Holland, Amsterdam, The Netherlands (1990), 801–805.

Ford, W. Randolph, *Natural Language Processing by Computer—A New Approach*, Ph. D. Dissertation, Department of Psychology, Johns Hopkins University, Baltimore, MD (1981).

Grudin, Jonathan and Barnard, Phil, When does an abbreviation become a word and related questions, *Proc. CHI '85 Conference on Human Factors in Computer Systems*, ACM, New York (1985), 121–126.

Hanson, Stephen J., Kraut, Robert E., and Farber, James M., Interface design and multivariate analysis of Unix command use, *ACM Transactions on Office Information Systems*, 2, 1 (1984), 42–57.

Harman, Donna (Editor), *Proc. Third Text Retrieval Conference (TREC)*, Morgan Kaufmann, San Mateo, CA (1995).

Hauptmann, Alexander G. and Green, Bert F., A comparison of command, menu-selection and natural language computer programs, *Behaviour and Information Technology*, 2, 2 (1983), 163–178.

Jarke, Matthias, Turner, Jon A., Stohr, Edward A., Vassiliou, Yannis, White, Norman H., and Michielsen, Ken, A field evaluation of natural language for data retrieval, *IEEE Transactions on Software Engineering*, SE–11, 1 (January 1985), 97–113.

King, Margaret, Evaluating natural language processing systems, *Communications of the ACM*, 39, 1 (January 1996), 73–79.

Landauer, T. K., Calotti, K. M., and Hartwell, S., Natural command names and initial learning, *Communications of the ACM*, 26, 7 (July 1983), 495–503.

Ledgard, H., Whiteside, J. A., Singer, A., and Seymour, W., The natural language of interactive systems, *Communications of the ACM*, 23, (1980), 556–563.

Lewis, David and Jones, Karen Sparck, Natural language processing for information retrieval, *Communications of the ACM*, 39, 1 (January 1996), 92–101.

Napier, H. Albert, Lane, David, Batsell, Richard R., and Guadango, Norman S., Impact of a restricted natural language interface on ease of learning and productivity, *Communications of the ACM*, 32, 10 (October 1989), 1190–1198.

Norman, Donald, The trouble with Unix, *Datamation*, 27, (November 1981), 139–150.

Oviatt, Sharon, Interface techniques for minimizing disfluent input to spoken language systems, *Proc. CHI '94 Conference on Human Factors in Computing Systems*, ACM, New York (1994), 205–210.

Pausch, Randy and Leatherby, James H., An empirical study: Adding voice input to a graphical editor, *Journal of the American Voice Input/Output Society*, 9, 2 (July 1991), 55–66.

Rosenberg, Jarrett, Evaluating the suggestiveness of command names, *Behaviour and Information Technology*, 1, (1982), 371–400.

Scapin, Dominique L., Computer commands labeled by users versus imposed commands and the effect of structuring rules on recall, *Proc. Conference on Human Factors in Computer Systems*, ACM, Washington, D.C. (1982), 17–19.

Schneider, M. L., Ergonomic considerations in the design of text editors. In Vassiliou, Y. (Editor), *Human Factors and Interactive Computer Systems*, Ablex, Norwood, NJ (1984), 141–161.

Schneider, M. L., Hirsh-Pasek, K., and Nudelman, S., An experimental evaluation of delimiters in a command language syntax, *International Journal of Man–Machine Studies*, 20, 6 (June 1984), 521–536.

Shneiderman, Ben, *Software Psychology: Human Factors in Computer and Information Systems*, Little, Brown, Boston (1980).

Small, Duane and Weldon, Linda, An experimental comparison of natural and structured query languages, *Human Factors*, 25, (1983), 253–263.

Mark Kostabi, *Industrial Interior,* 1996

Interaction Devices

The wheel is an extension of the foot,
the book is an extension of the eye,
clothing, an extension of the skin,
electric circuitry an extension of the central nervous system.

Marshall McLuhan and Quentin Fiore,
The Medium Is the Massage, **1967**

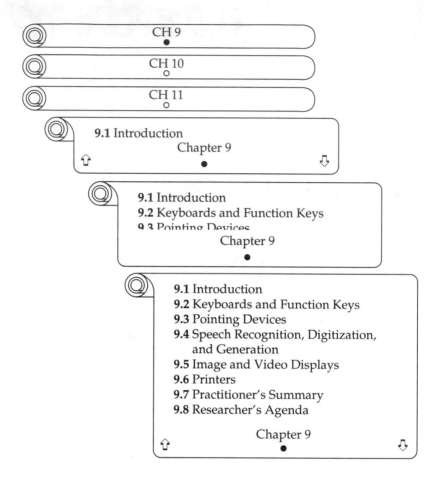

9.1 Introduction

The remarkable progress since 1960 in computer-processor speeds and storage capabilities is matched by improvements in many input-output devices. Ten-character-per-second Teletypes have been replaced by high-speed megapixel graphical displays for output, and the 100-year-old keyboard is giving way to rapid and high-precision pointing devices for carrying out user actions. Although the common Sholes keyboard layout is likely to remain the primary device for text input, pointing devices increasingly free users from keyboards for many tasks. The future of computing is likely to include gestural input, two-handed input, three-dimensional pointing, more voice input–output, wearable devices, and whole-body involvement for some input and output tasks.

The increased concern for human factors has led to hundreds of new devices and variants of the old devices. Novel keyboards with tilted and curved profiles to lessen repetitive-strain injuries and touchscreen or stylus replacements testify to the vital importance of textual input, even in the age of GUIs. Pointing devices such as the mouse, touchscreen, stylus, and trackball have gone through hundreds of refinements to accommodate varied users and to squeeze out another five percent improvement in performance. The still-improving speech recognizers are joined by more mundane but widely used speech store-and-forward technologies with increased emphasis on telephone-based applications. Proponents of eyetrackers, datagloves, and force-feedback devices are trying to expand from their niches.

Color displays for desktops and most laptops are standard, but monochrome displays (especially flat-plate liquid-crystal panels) continue to proliferate in small and large formats. Compact digital cameras with instant viewing on small LCDs are creating a steadily growing success story. Low-cost printers, even with color, are widely available. Innovative input devices, sensors, and effectors, and integration of computers into the physical environment, open the door to new applications (Sherr, 1988; Greenstein and Arnaut, 1988; Foley et al., 1990; Card et al., 1991; Jacob et al., 1993).

9.2 Keyboards and Function Keys

The primary mode of textual data entry is still the keyboard. This often-criticized device is impressive in its success. Hundreds of millions of people have managed to use keyboards with speeds of up to 15 keystrokes per second (approximately 150 words per minute), although rates for beginners are less than one keystroke per second, and rates for average office workers are five keystrokes per second (approximately 50 words per minute). Contemporary keyboards generally permit only one keypress at a time, although dual keypresses (SHIFT plus a letter) are used to produce capitals and special functions (CTRL or ALT plus a letter).

More rapid data entry can be accomplished by chord keyboards that allow several keys to be pressed simultaneously to represent several characters or a word. Courtroom recorders regularly use chord keyboards serenely to enter the full text of spoken arguments, reaching rates of up to 300 words per minute. This feat requires months of training and frequent use to retain the complex pattern of chordpresses. The piano keyboard is an impressive data-entry device that allows several fingerpresses at once and is responsive to different pressures and durations. It seems that there is potential for higher rates of data entry than is possible with the current computer keyboards.

Keyboard size and packaging also influence user satisfaction and usability. Large keyboards with many keys give an impression of professionalism and complexity, but may threaten novice users. Small keyboards seem lacking in power to some users, but their compact size is an attraction to others. A thin profile (20 to 40 millimeters thick) allows users to rest the keyboards on their laps easily and permits a comfortable hand position when the keyboard is on a desk. Adjustable keyboards that tilt forward or back, or that split in the middle to reduce stressful ulnar abduction and pronation, are currently popular.

9.2.1   Keyboard layouts

The Smithsonian Institution's National Museum of American History in Washington, D.C. has a remarkable exhibit on the development of the typewriter. During the middle of the nineteenth century, hundreds of attempts were made to build typewriters, with a stunning variety of positions for the paper, mechanisms for producing a character, and layouts for the keys. By the 1870s, Christopher Latham Sholes's design was becoming successful because of a good mechanical design and a clever placement of the letters that slowed down the users enough that key jamming was infrequent. This *QWERTY layout* put frequently used letter pairs far apart, thereby increasing finger travel distances.

Sholes's success led to such widespread standardization that, a century later, almost all English-language keyboards use the QWERTY layout (Fig. 9.1). The development of electronic keyboards eliminated the mechanical problems and led many twentieth-century inventors to propose alternative layouts to reduce finger travel distances (Montgomery, 1982; Kroemer, 1993).

Figure 9.1

QWERTY keyboard from the Macintosh, with function keys, numeric keypad, separate cursor-control keys, and special functions.

Figure 9.2

Dvorak layout on an IBM keyboard with function keys, separate cursor-control keys, and special functions. The keycaps also show the APL character set.

The *Dvorak layout* (Fig. 9.2), developed in the 1920s, supposedly reduces finger travel distances by at least one order of magnitude, thereby increasing the typing rate of expert typists from about 150 words per minute to more than 200 words per minute, while reducing errors (Potosnak, 1988).

Acceptance of the Dvorak design has been slow despite the dedicated work of devotees. Those people who have tried the keyboard report that it takes about 1 week of regular typing to make the switch, but most users have been unwilling to invest this much effort. We are confronted with an interesting example of how even documented improvements are hard to disseminate because the perceived benefit of change does not outweigh the effort.

A third keyboard layout of some interest is the *ABCDE style* that has the 26 letters of the alphabet laid out in alphabetical order. The rationale here is that nontypists will find it easier to locate the keys. A few data-entry terminals for numeric and alphabetic codes still use this style. The widespread availability of QWERTY keyboards has made typing a more common skill and has reduced the importance of the ABCDE style. Our study and those of other researchers have shown no advantage for the ABCDE style; users with little QWERTY experience are eager to acquire this expertise and often resent having to use an ABCDE style.

Beyond the letters, many debates rage about the placement of additional keys. The early IBM PC keyboard was widely criticized because of the placement of a few keys, such as a backslash key where most typists expected to find the SHIFT key, and the placement of several special characters near the ENTER

Figure 9.3

Early IBM PC keyboard with 10 function keys on the left, numeric keypad on the right, and cursor-control keys embedded in the numeric keypad.

key (Fig. 9.3). Later versions relocated the offending keys, to the acclaim of critics. Other improvements included a larger ENTER key and LEDs to signal the status of the CAPS LOCK, NUM LOCK, and SCROLL LOCK keys (Fig. 9.4). Even on laptop or notebook computers, keyboards are fullsize, but some pocket computers used a greatly reduced keyboard (Fig. 9.5).

Number pads are another source of controversy. Telephones have the 1–2–3 keys on the top row, but calculators place the 7–8–9 keys on the top row. Studies have shown a slight advantage for the telephone layout, but most computer keyboards use the calculator layout.

Some researchers have recognized that the wrist and hand placement required for standard keyboards is awkward. Redesigned keyboards that

Figure 9.4

Full-size keyboard. (Produced by Gateway 2000 Corp.)

Figure 9.5

Pocket computers have reduced-sized keyboards. Many users type with one finger on each hand.

separated the keys for the left and right hands by 9.5 centimeters, had an opening angle of 25 degrees with an inclination of 10 degrees, and offered large areas for forearm—wrist support led to lower reported tension, better posture, and higher preference scores (Nakaseko et al., 1985). However, separated keyboards have the disadvantage that visual scanning is disrupted, so various geometries have been tried with split and tilted keyboards (for example, the Microsoft Natural; Fig. 9.6), but empirical verification of benefits to typing speed, accuracy, or reduced repetitive strain injury is elusive.

9.2.2   Keys

Modern electronic keyboards use 1/2-inch-square keys (12 mm square) with about a 1/4-inch space (6 mm square) between keys. This design has been refined carefully and tested thoroughly in research laboratories and the marketplace. The keys have a slightly concave surface for good contact with fingertips, and a matte finish to reduce both reflective glare and the chance of finger slips. The keypresses require a 40- to 125-gram force and a displacement of 3 to 5 millimeters. The force and displacement have been shown to produce rapid typing with low error rates while providing suitable feedback to users. As user experience increases and the chance of a misplaced finger is reduced, the force and displacement can be lowered.

   An important element in key design is the profile of force displacement. When the key has been depressed far enough to send a signal, the key gives way and emits a click. The tactile and audible feedback is extremely important in touch typing. For these reasons, membrane keyboards that use a non-moving touch-sensitive surface are unacceptable for touch typing. However,

Figure 9.6

Microsoft's Natural keyboard. The curved layout and adjustable rests underneath help to reduce repetitive-strain injuries.

they are durable and therefore effective for public installations at museums or amusement parks.

Certain keys, such as the space bar, ENTER key, SHIFT key, or CTRL key, should be larger than others to allow easy, reliable access. Other keys, such as the CAPS LOCK or NUM LOCK should have a clear indication of their state, such as by physical locking in a lowered position or by an embedded light. Key labels should be large enough to read, meaningful, and permanent. Discrete color coding of keys helps to make a pleasing, informative layout. A further design principle is that some of the home keys—F and J in the QWERTY layout—may have a deeper concavity or a small raised dot to reassure users that their fingers are placed properly.

9.2.3   Function keys

Many keyboards contain a set of additional *function keys* for special functions or programmed functions. These keys are often labeled F1 ... F10 or PF1 ... PF24. Users must remember the functions, learn about them from the screen, or consult an attachable plastic template, but some keys have meaningful labels, such as CUT, COPY, or PASTE. This strategy attempts to reduce user keystrokes by replacing a command name with a single keystroke. Most function-key strategies do not require users to press the ENTER key to invoke the function.

Function keys can reduce keystroke numbers and errors, thereby speeding work for novice users who are poor typists and for expert users who readily recall the purpose of each function key. Unfortunately, some systems confuse users with inconsistent key use. For example, the HELP key may be F1, F9, or F12, depending on the system.

The placement of function keys is important if the task requires users to go from typing to using function keys. The greater the distance of the function keys from the home position on the keyboard, the more severe the problem. Some users would rather type six or eight characters than remove their fingers from the home position. Layout of function keys also influences ease of use. A 3 by 4 layout of 12 keys is helpful, because users quickly learn functions by the keys' placement on the upper-left or lower-right. A 1 by 12 layout only has two anchors and leads to slower and more error-prone selection of middle keys. A small gap between the sixth and seventh keys could aid users by grouping keys. A 2 by 5 layout is a reasonable intermediate style.

Function keys are sometimes built in to the display-screen bezel so that they are close to displayed labels—a popular technique with bank machines. This position supports novices who need labels, but it still requires hands to stray from the home position. Lights can be built into and next to function keys to indicate availability or ON-OFF status.

If all work can be done with labeled function keys, as on some CAD systems, this solution is appealing. WordPerfect became a worldwide success partly because all actions are initiated by function keys (plus CTRL, ALT, and SHIFT) and refined by onscreen menus. Some WordPerfect devotees refuse to move to pull-down menus, since their proficiency with the keys enables them to beat many mouse users. However, most word-processor users have now adopted more graphic interfaces, including many with toolbars with icons for frequent tasks. Frequent movements between the home position on the keyboard and the mouse or distant function keys can be disruptive. An alternative strategy is to use nearby CTRL or ALT keys plus a letter to invoke a function. This approach has some mnemonic value, keeps hands on the home keys, and reduces the need for extra keys.

9.2.4 Cursor movement keys

A special category of function keys is the *cursor-movement keys*. There are usually four keys—up, down, left, and right. Some keyboards have eight keys to simplify diagonal movements. The placement of the cursor-movement keys is important in facilitating rapid and error-free use. The best layouts place the keys in their natural positions (Fig. 9.7a–d), but designers have attempted several variations (Fig. 9.7e–g). The increasingly popular inverted-T arrangement (Fig. 9.7a) allows users to place their middle three fingers in a way that reduces hand and finger movement. The cross-arrangement (Fig. 9.7b) is a better choice for novice users than the linear arrangement (Fig. 9.7e) or the box arrangement (Fig. 9.7f).

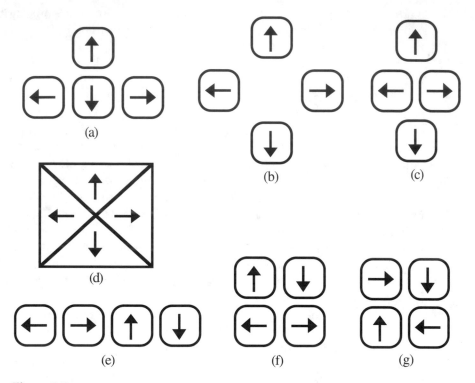

Figure 9.7

Seven styles of key layout for arrow keys. These layouts are only a subset of what is commercially available. (a–d) Key layouts that are compatible with the arrow directions. (e–g) Incompatible layouts that may result in slower performance and higher error rates.

Cursor-movement keys often have a *typamatic (auto-repeat) feature;* that is, repetition occurs automatically with continued depression. This feature is widely appreciated and may improve performance, especially if users can control the rate to accommodate their preferences (important for users who are very young, elderly, or handicapped).

Cursor-movement keys have become more important with the increased use of form-fillin and direct manipulation. Additional cursor movements might be performed by the TAB key for larger jumps, the HOME key to go to the top left, or the END key to go to the bottom right of the display. Other accelerators are popular, such as CTRL with up, down, left, or right keypresses, to jump a word or a paragraph. Cursor-movement keys can be used to select items in a menu or on a display, but more rapid pointing at displays than can be provided by cursor-movement keys is often desired.

9.3   Pointing Devices

With complex information displays—such as those used in air-traffic control, word processing, and CAD—it is often convenient to point at and select items. This direct-manipulation approach is attractive because the users can avoid learning commands, reduce the chance of typographic errors on a key-board, and keep their attention on the display. The results are often faster performance, fewer errors, easier learning, and higher satisfaction. The diversity of tasks and variety of devices plus strategies for using them create a rich design space (Buxton, 1985; Card et al., 1991). Physical device attrib-utes (rotation or linear movement), dimensionality of movement (1, 2, 3, ...), and positioning (relative or absolute) are useful ways of categorizing devices; here, we discuss the tasks and degree of directness.

9.3.1   Pointing tasks

Pointing devices are applicable in six types of interaction tasks (Foley et al., 1984):

1. *Select*   The user chooses from a set of items. This technique is used for traditional menu selection, identification of a file in a directory, or mark-ing of a part in an automobile design.
2. *Position*   The user chooses a point in a one-, two-, three-, or higher-dimensional space. Positioning may be used to create a drawing, to place a new window, or to drag a block of text in a figure.
3. *Orient*   The user chooses a direction in a two-, three-, or higher-dimen-sional space. The direction may simply rotate a symbol on the screen, indicate a direction of motion for a space ship, or control the operation of a robot arm.
4. *Path*   The user rapidly performs a series of position and orient opera-tions. The path may be realized as a curving line in a drawing program, the instructions for a cloth-cutting machine, or the route on a map.
5. *Quantify*   The user specifies a numeric value. The quantify task is usu-ally a one-dimensional selection of integer or real values to set parame-ters, such as the page number in a document, the velocity of a ship, or the amplitude of a sound.

6. *Text*   The user enters, moves, and edits text in a two-dimensional space. The pointing device indicates the location of an insertion, deletion, or change. Beyond the simple manipulation of the text are more elaborate tasks, such as centering, margin setting, font sizes, highlighting (bold-face or underscore), and page layout.

It is possible to perform all these tasks with a keyboard by typing: numbers or letters to select, integer coordinates to position, a number representing an angle to point, a number to quantify, and cursor-control commands to move about in text. In the past, the keyboard was used to perform all these tasks, but now users employ pointing devices to perform these tasks more rapidly and with fewer errors. Even in modern GUIs, however, some tasks are invoked so frequently that special keys may be appropriate, such as a HELP key or CTRL-C to copy a marked item.

Pointing devices can be grouped into those that offer (1) *direct control* on the screen surface, such as the lightpen, touchscreen, and stylus, and (2) *indirect control* away from the screen surface, such as mouse, trackball, joystick, graphics tablet, and touchpad. Within each category are many variations, and novel designs emerge frequently.

9.3.2   Direct-control pointing devices

The *lightpen* was an early device that enabled users to point to a spot on a screen and to perform a select, position, or other task (Fig. 9.8). In fact, the lightpen could be used to perform all six tasks. The lightpen was attractive

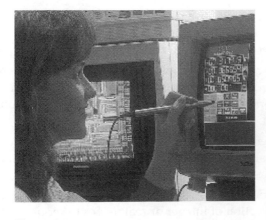

Figure 9.8

Lightpens. Users can point directly to a spot on the screen with these input devices.

because it allowed the user to gain direct control by pointing to a spot on the display, as opposed to having the indirect control provided by a graphics tablet, joystick, or mouse. Most lightpens incorporate a button for the user to press when the cursor is resting on the desired spot on the screen. Lightpens vary in thickness, length, weight, and shape (the lightgun, with a trigger, was one variation), and in position of buttons. Unfortunately, direct control on an upright screen can cause arm fatigue. The lightpen had three further disadvantages: users' hands obscured part of the screen, users had to remove their hands from the keyboard, and users had to pick up the lightpen.

Some of these disadvantages are overcome by the *touchscreen*, which does not require picking up some device, but instead allows the user to make direct-control touches on the screen with a finger (Fig. 9.9) (Shneiderman, 1991). Early touchscreen designs were rightly criticized for causing fatigue, hand obscuring the screen, hand off keyboard, imprecise pointing, and the eventual smudging of the display. Some touchscreen implementations had a further problem: The software accepted the touch immediately (*land-on strategy*), denying users the opportunity to verify the correctness of the selected spot, which they could do with lightpens. These early designs were based on physical pressure, impact, or interruption of a grid of infrared beams.

Figure 9.9

Touchscreen. The user needs only to point with a finger to make a selection. High-precision touchscreens increase the range of possible applications, especially if they are mounted in a position that is convenient for pointing and reading (30 to 45 degrees from the horizontal).

Newer designs have dramatically improved touchscreens to permit high precision (Sears and Shneiderman, 1991). The resistive, capacitive, or surface acoustic-wave hardware can provide 1024 × 1024 sensitivity, and the *lift-off strategy* enables users to point at a single pixel. The lift-off strategy has three steps. The users touch the surface, and then see a cursor that they can drag around on the display; when the users are satisfied with the position, they lift their fingers off the display to activate. The availability of high-precision touchscreens has opened the doors to many applications (Sears et al., 1992).

Refinements to touchscreens can be expected as they are integrated into applications directed at novice users, in which the keyboard can be eliminated and touch is the only interface mechanism. Touchscreens are valued by designers of public-access systems because there are no moving parts, durability in high-use environments is good (touchscreens are the only input devices that have survived at EPCOT), and the price is relatively low. Touchscreens have found a home in building-management, air-traffic–control, medical, and military systems. In these systems, space is at a premium, rugged design with no moving parts is appreciated, and users can be guided through a complex activity.

Touchscreens can produce varied displays to suit the task. Form fillin or menu selection works naturally by touchscreen, as does typing on a touchscreen keyboard. In our studies with keyboards that were 7 and 25 centimeters wide, users could, with some practice, type from 20 to 30 words per minute, respectively (Sears et al., 1993). Studies of touchscreen use for panning graphical displays show that users are more rapid and accurate when pushing the background, rather than shifting the viewpoint (Johnson, 1995).

As touchscreens are fabricated integrally with display surfaces, cost is likely to drop and parallax problems from an attached glass panel will decrease. A touchable surface on a flat-plate LCD enables construction of novel car-borne navigation displays and museum placards that contain extensive information. Every office-door nameplate, refrigerator, camera, TV, or appliance could have helpful explanations, information resources, or complete user manuals constantly available.

Palmtop computers make it natural to have pointing on the LCD surface, which is held in the hand, placed on a desk, or rested on the lap. Handwriting recognition, selection from a keyboard displayed on the surface, or selection from menus and forms permits simple and rapid data entry. The *stylus* is attractive to designers because it is familiar and comfortable for users, and because it permits high precision with good control to limit inadvertent selections. Users can guide the stylus tip to the desired location while keeping the critical sections of the display in view. These advantages over touchscreens are balanced against the need to pick up and put down a stylus.

Compact lightweight machines, such as the Apple Newton or MessagePad, Sharp Zaurus, US Robotics Pilot (see Fig. 1.6), and others are growing in popularity. The market should be large if the price can be brought down while screen resolution and readability are improved.

Alternatives to keyboard entry are gaining popularity with touchscreen or stylus entry on virtual keyboards, but these mechanisms have data-entry rates of only 20 to 30 words per minute (Sears et al., 1993). Novel data entry based on pie-menu gestures (Venolia and Neiberg, 1994) and handwriting recognition (Frankish et al., 1995) are competing with ever-faster pull-down–menu and direct-manipulation strategies.

Recognition of handwritten block or script characters has been supplemented by word-pattern recognition against a stored database of 10,000 or more words. Contextual clues and stroke speed plus direction can enhance recognition rates. The Apple Newton brought handwriting input and recognition to a wide market, but high error rates were troubling to many users. For some languages, such as Japanese or Chinese, handwriting input and recognition may dramatically increase the user population.

9.3.3 Indirect-control pointing devices

Indirect pointing devices eliminate the hand-fatigue and hand-obscuring-the-screen problems, but must overcome the problem of indirection. As they do with the lightpen, the off-keyboard hand position and pick-up problems remain. Also, indirect-control devices require more cognitive processing and hand–eye coordination to bring the onscreen cursor to the desired target.

The *mouse* is appealing because the hand rests in a comfortable position, buttons on the mouse are easily pressed, even long motions can be rapid, and positioning can be precise (Fig. 9.10). However, the user must grab the

Figure 9.10

Three versions of the mouse: three buttons (Sun Microsystems), two buttons (Microsoft), and one button (Apple Macintosh).

mouse to begin work, desk space is consumed, the mouse wire can be distracting, pickup and replace actions are necessary for long motions, and some practice (5 to 50 minutes) is required to develop skill. The variety of mouse technologies (physical, optical, or acoustic), number of buttons, placement of the sensor, weight, and size indicate that designers and users have yet to settle on one alternative. Personal preferences and the variety of tasks leave room for lively competition. Wireless mice that allow pointing from 5 to 30 feet away from the display without a mousepad are gaining acceptance for lecturing situations and for home entertainment in living-room environments. Infrared technologies refined from television remote controllers or more sophisticated gyroscopic designs are being promoted.

The *trackball* has sometimes been described as an upside-down mouse. It is usually implemented as a rotating ball 1 to 15 centimeters in diameter that moves a cursor on the screen as it is moved. The trackball is firmly mounted in a desk or a solid box to allow the user to hit the ball vigorously and to make it spin. The trackball has been the preferred device in the high-stress world of air-traffic control and in some video games. Small trackballs make a convenient pointing device when installed in portable laptop computers (Fig. 9.11).

The *joystick,* whose long history began in aircraft-control devices (Fig. 9.12), now has dozens of computer versions with varying stick lengths and thicknesses, displacement forces and distances, buttons or triggers, anchoring strategies for bases, and placement relative to the keyboard and screen.

Figure 9.11

Small trackball embedded in a laptop computer.

Figure 9.12

A joystick. This input device makes it easy for users to move a cursor around on the screen rapidly, but precise or drawing actions are difficult.

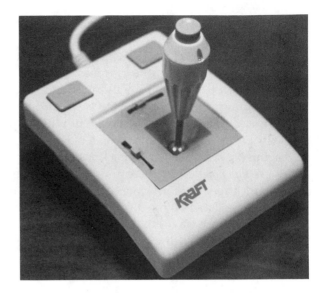

Joysticks are appealing for tracking purposes (i.e., to follow a moving object on a screen), partly because of the relatively small displacements needed to move a cursor and the ease of direction changes. The trackpoint is a small isometric joystick embedded in laptop keyboards that has a rubber tip to facilitate finger contact (Fig. 9.13). With modest practice, users can be quick and accurate while keeping their fingers on the keyboard home position.

Figure 9.13

The trackpoint. This device is a small isometric joystick mounted between the G and H keys.

The *graphics tablet* is a touch-sensitive surface separate from the screen, usually laid flat on the table (Fig. 9.14) or in the user's lap. This separation allows for a comfortable hand position and keeps the users' hands off the screen. Furthermore, the graphics tablet permits a surface even larger than the screen to be covered with printing to indicate available choices, thereby providing guidance to novice users and preserving valuable screen space. Limited data entry can be done with the graphics tablet. The graphics tablet can be operated by placement of a finger, pencil, puck, or stylus, using acoustic, electronic, or contact position sensing.

A *touchpad* (5- by 8-centimeters touchable surface) built in near the keyboard offers the convenience and precision of a touchscreen while keeping the user's hand off the display surface. Users can make quick movements for long-distance traversals, and can gently rock their fingers for precise positioning, before lifting off. The lack of moving parts and the thin profile make touchpads appealing for portable devices.

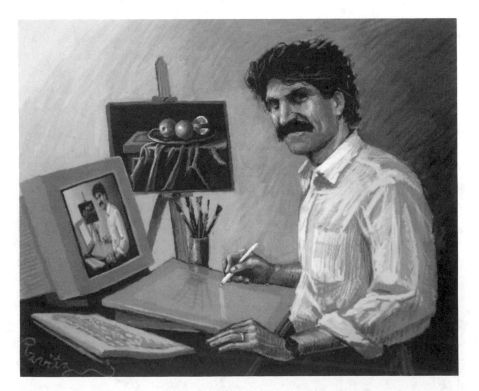

Figure 9.14

An all-electronic painting created by Larry Ravitz using Adobe PhotoShop and a Wacom tablet. The Wacom stylus and graphics tablet allow the precise pointing and accurate control that artists need. (Photograph courtesy of Larry Ravitz, Takoma Park, MD.)

Among these indirect pointing devices, the mouse has been the basis for the greatest success story. Given its rapid high-precision pointing and a comfortable hand position, the modest training period is only a small impediment to its use. Most desktop computer systems offer a mouse, but the battle for the laptop rages.

9.3.4   Comparisons of pointing devices

Each pointing concept has its enthusiasts and detractors, motivated by commercial interests, by personal preference, and increasingly by empirical evidence. Human-factors variables of interest are speed of motion for short and long distances, accuracy of positioning, error rates, learning time, and user satisfaction. Other variables are cost, durability, space requirements, weight, left- versus right-hand use, likelihood to cause repetitive-strain injury, and compatibility with other systems.

In early studies, direct pointing devices such as the lightpen or touchscreen were often the fastest but the least accurate devices (Stammers and Bird, 1980; Haller et al., 1984). The speed appears to accrue from the directness of pointing, and the inaccuracy from problems with feedback, physical design, and use strategies. New strategies such as lift-off and greater precision in the devices have made it feasible to build high-precision touchscreens, graphics tablets, and pens.

Indirect pointing devices have been the cause of much controversy. The graphics tablet is appealing when the user can remain with the device for long periods without switching to a keyboard. Pens accompanying graphics tablets allow a high degree of control that is appreciated by artists using drawing programs. The Wacom tablet with its wireless pen allows freedom and control (Fig. 9.14). The mouse was found to be faster than the isometric joystick (English et al., 1967; Card et al., 1978; Rutledge and Selker, 1990) due to tremors in finger motion during fine finger movements (Mithal and Douglas, 1996).

The usual belief is that pointing devices are faster than keyboard controls, such as cursor-movement keys, but this assertion depends on the task. When a few (two to 10) targets are on the screen and the cursor can be made to jump from one target to the next, then using the cursor jump keys can be faster than using pointing devices (Fig. 9.15) (Ewing et al., 1986). For tasks that mix typing and pointing, cursor keys have also been shown to be faster than and preferred to the mouse (Karat et al., 1984). Since muscular strain is low for cursor keys (Haider et al., 1982), they should be considered for this special case. This result is supported by Card et al. (1978), who reported that, for short distances, the cursor keys were faster than the mouse (Fig. 9.16). The positioning time increases rapidly with distance for cursor keys, but only slightly for the mouse or trackball.

Figure 9.15

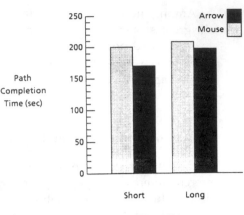

Path completion time for arrow-jump and mouse as a function of average target distance of the traversed path (Ewing et al., 1986). Long-distance targets were farther away from the start point than were short-distance targets. The arrow-jump strategy was faster, since a single keypress produced a jump to the target, whereas mouse users had to move the cursor across the screen.

In summary, much work remains to sort out the task and individual differences with respect to pointing devices. The touchscreen and trackball are durable in public-access, shop-floor, and laboratory applications. The mouse, trackball, trackpoint, graphics tablet, and touchpad are effective for pixel-level pointing. Cursor jump keys are attractive when there is a small number of targets. Joysticks are appealing to game or aircraft-cockpit designers, apparently because of the firm grip and easy movement, but they are slow and inaccurate in guiding a cursor to a fixed destination in office automation and personal computing. Indirect-control pointing devices require more learning than do direct-control devices.

Figure 9.16

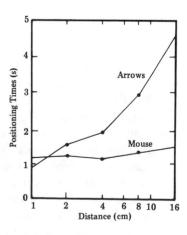

The effect of target distance on position time for arrow keys and mouse (Card et al., 1978). The positioning time for arrow keys increased dramatically with distance, because users had to make many keypresses to move the cursor to the target. The mouse time is independent of time over these distances. With very short distances and a few character positions, the arrow keys afforded a shorter mean time. (Adapted from S. K. Card, W. K. English, and B. J. Burr, Evaluation of mouse, rate-controlled isometric joystick, step keys, and task keys for text selection on a CRT, *Ergonomics*, 17, 6 [1965].)

9.3.5 Fitts' Law

The major pointing devices depend on hand movement to control a cursor on the display. An effective predictive model of time to move a given distance, D, to a target of width, W, was developed by Paul Fitts (1954). He discovered that the pointing time is a function of the distance and the width; farther away and smaller targets take longer to point to. The *index of difficulty* is defined as

$$Index\ of\ difficulty = \log_2(2D/W).$$

The index of difficulty is a unitless number, but it is traditionally measured in bits. The time to perform the point action is

$$Time\ to\ point = C_1 + C_2\ (Index\ of\ difficulty),$$

where C_1 and C_2 are constants that depend on the device. Once data have been collected for a given device, C_1 and C_2 can be computed, and then predictions can be made regarding the time for other tasks. For example, for a 1 cm-wide target at a distance of 8 cm, the *Index of difficulty* is $\log_2(2*8/1) = \log_2(16) = 4$ bits. If tests show that, for a given device, $C_1 = 0.2$, $C_2 = 0.1$, then the *Time to point* $= 0.2 + 0.1\ (4) = 0.6$ seconds.

MacKenzie (1992) lucidly describes what Fitts' law is, how it has been applied, and what the many refinements are for cases such as two-dimensional pointing. In our studies of high-precision touchscreens (Sears and Shneiderman, 1991), we found that, in addition to the gross arm movement predicted by Fitts, there was also a fine-tuning motion of the fingers to move in on small targets such as a single pixel. A three-component equation was thus more suited for the high-precision pointing task:

$$Time\ for\ precision\ pointing = C_1 + C_2\ (index\ of\ difficulty) + C_3 \log_2 (C_4\ /\ W).$$

The third term, time for fine tuning, increases as the target width, W, decreases. This extension to Fitts' law is quite understandable and simple; it suggests that the *Time for precision pointing* at an object consists of a time for initiation of action, C_1, a time for gross movement, and time for fine adjustment. Fitts's studies focused on moderate movements, but current studies deal with a greater range of arm motion as well as precise finger positioning, even in three-dimensional space (Zhai et al., 1996). An open problem is how to design devices that produce smaller constants for the predictive equation.

9.3.6   Novel pointing devices

The popularity of pointing devices and the quest for new ways to engage diverse users for diverse tasks has led to provocative innovations. Since a user's hands might be busy on the keyboard, several designers have explored other methods for selection and pointing. Foot controls are popular with rock-music performers, organists, dentists, medical-equipment users, car drivers, and pilots, so maybe computer users could benefit from them as well. A foot mouse was tested and was found to take about twice as much time to use as a hand-operated mouse, but benefits in special applications may exist (Pearson and Weiser, 1986).

Eye-tracking, gaze-detecting controllers have been developed by several researchers and companies who make devices to assist the handicapped (Jacob, 1991). Nonintrusive and noncontact equipment using video-camera image recognition of pupil position can give 1- to 2-degree accuracy, and fixations of 200 to 600 milliseconds are used to make selections. Unfortunately, the "Midas touch problem" intrudes, since every gaze has the potential to activate an unintended command. For the moment, eye tracking remains a research tool and an aid for the handicapped.

The VPL DataGlove appeared in 1987 and attracted serious researchers, game developers, cyberspace adventurers, and virtual-reality devotees (see Section 6.8). Descendants of the original DataGlove are still often made of sleek black spandex with attached fiber-optic sensors to measure finger position. The displayed feedback can show the placement of each finger; thus, commands such as a closed fist, open hand, index-finger pointing, and thumbs-up gesture can be recognized. With a *Polhemus tracker,* complete three-dimensional placement and orientation can be recorded. Control over three-dimensional objects seems a natural application, but comparisons with other strategies reveal low precision and slow response. Devotees claim that the naturalness of gestures will enable use by many keyboard-averse or mouse-phobic users, although users require substantial training to master more than a half-dozen gestures. Gestural input with the glove can have special applications such as input of American Sign Language or musical performance.

An alternative to the goggles-and-gloves approach is the Fakespace *Binocular Omni-Orientation Monitor (BOOM)* (see Fig. 6.21), which allows users to step up to a viewer with handles and look in the binocular-like device while holding the handles to shift vantage points within the range of the mechanical boom. The display updates to create the illusion that the user is moving in three dimensions, and users have an immersive experience without the heavy and confining head-mounted goggles.

Support for virtual reality (see Chapter 6) is one motivation, but many design, medical, and other tasks may require three-dimensional input or even six degrees of freedom to indicate a position and an orientation. Commercial devices include the Logitech 3D mouse, Ascension Bird, and Polhemus 3Ball. Glove-mounted devices or tethered balls are being refined (Zhai et al., 1996). The bat brush gives flexibility for artistic effects (Ware and Baxter, 1989), and other graspable user interfaces seem ripe for exploration (Fitzmaurice et al., 1995; Fitzmaurice, 1993). Matching of task with device and refining the input plus feedback strategies are common themes (Jacob et al., 1994).

Pointing devices with *haptic feedback* are an intriguing research direction. Several technologies have been employed to allow users to push a mouse or other device and to feel resistance (for example, as they cross a window boundary) or a hard wall (for example, as they navigate a maze). Three-dimensional versions, such as the Phantom, are still more intriguing, but compelling commercial applications have yet to emerge. Sound is a good substitute for haptic feedback in many cases, and the special-purpose applications of current haptic devices limit widespread use.

9.4   Speech Recognition, Digitization, and Generation

The dream of speaking to computers and having computers speak has lured many researchers and visionaries. Arthur C. Clarke's 1968 fantasy of the HAL 9000 computer in the book and movie *2001* has set the standard for future performance of computers in science fiction and for some advanced developers. The reality is more complex and sometimes more surprising than the dream. Hardware designers have made dramatic progress with speech and voice-manipulation devices, but current successes are sobering compared to the science-fiction fantasy (Yankelovich et al., 1995; Schmandt, 1994; Strathmeyer, 1990). Even science-fiction writers have shifted their scenarios, as shown by the reduced use of voice interaction in favor of larger visual displays in Star Trek's *Next Generation* and *Voyager*.

The vision of a computer that has a leisurely chat with the user seems more of a fantasy than a desired or believable reality. Instead, practical applications for specific tasks with specific devices are more effective in serving the user's need to work rapidly with low error rates. Designers are reluctantly recognizing that, even as technical problems are solved and the recognition algorithms improve, voice commanding is more demanding of users' working memory than is hand–eye coordination, which is processed elsewhere in the brain. Unfortunately, background noise and variations in user speech performance make the challenge still greater. By contrast, *speech store and forward* and *speech generation* are satisfyingly predictable and appealingly available because of the telephone's ubiquity, but they will always be slower and more difficult to traverse than are textual and graphical displays. Speech store and forward is a success because the emotional content and prosody in human speech is compelling in voice messaging, museum tours, and instructional contexts.

The benefits to people with certain physical handicaps are rewarding to see, but the general users of office or personal computing are not rushing toward speech input and output. However, speech store-and-forward systems and telephone-based information services are growing in popularity. Speech is the bicycle of user-interface design: It is great fun to use and has an important role, but it can carry only a light load. Sober advocates know that it will be tough to replace the automobile: graphic user interfaces.

Speech enthusiasts can claim huge successes in *telephony*, where digital circuitry has increased the capacity of networks and have improved voice quality. Cellular telephones have been a huge success in developed countries and often bring telephone service rapidly to less developed countries. Internet telephony is rising rapidly, giving many users low-cost long-distance service even though sound quality is lower. The immediacy and emotional impact of a telephone conversation is a compelling component of human–human communication.

For designers of human–computer interaction, speech technology has four variations: discrete-word recognition, continuous-speech recognition, speech store and forward, and speech generation. A related topic is the use of audio tones, audiolization, and music. These components can be combined in creative ways: from simple systems that merely play back or generate a message, to complex interactions that accept speech commands, generate speech feedback, provide audiolizations of scientific data, and allow annotation plus editing of stored speech (Blattner et al., 1989).

A deeper understanding of neurological processing of sounds would be helpful. Why does listening to Mozart symphonies encourage creative work, whereas listening to radio news reports suspends it? Is the linguistic processing needed to absorb a radio news report disruptive, whereas background Mozart is somehow invigorating? Of course, listening to Mozart with the serious intention of a musicologist would be completely absorbing of mental resources. Are there uses of sound or speech and ways of shifting attention, that might be less disruptive or even supportive of symbolic processing, analytic reasoning, or graphic designing? Could sound be a more useful component of drawing software than of word processors?

9.4.1 Discrete-word recognition

Discrete-word–recognition devices recognize individual words spoken by a specific person; they can work with 90- to 98-percent reliability for 20- to 200-

word vocabularies. *Speaker-dependent training,* in which the user repeats the full vocabulary once or twice, is a part of most systems. *Speaker-independent* systems are beginning to be reliable enough for certain commercial applications. Quiet environments, head-mounted microphones, and careful choice of vocabularies improve recognition rates.

Applications for the physically handicapped have been successful in enabling bedridden, paralyzed, or otherwise disabled people to broaden the horizons of their life. They can control wheelchairs, operate equipment, or use personal computers for a variety of tasks.

Other applications have been successful when at least one of these conditions exist:

- Speaker's hands are busy.
- Mobility is required.
- Speaker's eyes are occupied.
- Harsh (underwater or battlefield) or cramped (airplane-cockpit) conditions preclude use of a keyboard.

Example applications include those for aircraft-engine inspectors who wear a wireless microphone as they walk around the engine opening coverplates or adjusting components. They can issue orders, read serial numbers, or retrieve previous maintenance records by using a 35-word vocabulary. Baggage handlers for a major airline speak the destination city names as they place bags on a moving conveyor belt, thereby routing the bag to the proper airplane loading gate. For this application, the speaker-dependent training produced higher recognition rates when done in the noisy but more realistic environment of the conveyor belt rather than in the quiet conditions of a recording studio. Implementers should consider conducting speaker-dependent training in the task environment.

Consumer products include a wireless VCR controller with voice recognition for play, rewind, stop, and record (plus date and time commands); on this device, a sliding panel reveals the usual buttons if recognition fails because of a sore throat or a noisy room. Telephone companies are offering voice-dialing services to allow users simply to say "Call Mom" and be connected. Difficulties with training for multiple users in a household and reliable recognition are apparently slowing acceptance.

Many advanced development efforts have tested speech recognition in military aircraft, medical operating rooms, training laboratories, and offices. The results reveal problems with recognition rates even for speaker-dependent training systems, when background sounds change, when the user is ill or under stress, and when words in the vocabulary are similar (dime–time or Houston–Austin).

For common computing applications when a screen is used, speech input has not been beneficial. Studies of users controlling cursor movement by voice and keyboard (Murray et al., 1983) found that cursor-movement keys were twice as fast and were preferred by users. In a study with four one-hour sessions, 10 typists and 10 nontypists used typed and spoken commands to correct online documents using the UNIX ed editor (Morrison et al., 1984). For both typed and spoken commands, the user still had to type parameter strings. Typists preferred to use the keyboard. Nontypists began with a preference for spoken commands, but switched to favor using the keyboard by the end of the four sessions. No significant differences were found for task-completion time or error rates.

In a study of 24 knowledgeable programmers, a voice editor led to a lower task-completion rate than did a keyboard editor. However, the keyboard entry produced a higher error rate (Leggett and Williams, 1984) (see Table 9.1). The authors suggest that further experience with voice systems, beyond the 90 minutes of this study, might lead to better performance. A speed advantage for voice entry over a menu-selection strategy was found in a study of two beginners and three advanced users of a CAD system (Shutoh et al., 1984).

A study of eight MacDraw users drawing eight diagrams each showed that allowing users to select one of 19 commands by voice instead of selection from a palette improved performance times by an average of 21 percent (Pausch and Leatherby, 1991). The advantage seems to have been gained through avoidance of the time-consuming and distracting effort of moving the cursor repeatedly from the diagram to the tool palette and back. A replication confirmed this result with word-processing tasks using 18 spoken commands such as "boldface," "down," "italic," "paste," and

Table 9.1

Average percentage scores for input and editing tasks with subjects using keyboard and voice editors. (Data from Leggett, John, and Williams, Glen, An empirical investigation of voice as an input modality for computer programming, *International Journal of Man–Machine Studies*, 21, (1984), 493–520.)

	Key editor	Voice editor
Input task		
Input task completed	70.6	50.7
Erroneous input	11.0	3.8
Edit Task		
Edit task completed	70.3	55.3
Erroneous commands	2.4	1.5
Erroneous input	14.3	1.2

"undo" (Karl et al., 1993). Although overall voice recognition was 19 percent faster than mouse pointing, mainly due to mouse acquisition time, error rates were higher for voice users in tasks that required high short-term–memory load. This unexpected result was explained by psychologists, who pointed out that short-term memory is sometimes referred to as "acoustic memory." Speaking commands is more demanding of working memory than is performing the hand–eye coordination needed for mouse pointing, which apparently is handled in parallel by other parts of the brain.

This result may explain the slower acceptance of speech interfaces as compared with GUIs; speaking commands or listening disrupts problem solving more than does selecting actions from a menu with a mouse. This phenomenon was noted by product evaluators for an IBM dictation package. They wrote that "thought, for many people is very closely linked to language. In keyboarding, users can continue to hone their words while their fingers output an earlier version. In dictation, users may experience more interference between outputting their initial thought and elaborating on it." (Danis et al., 1994)

Current research projects are devoted to improving recognition rates in difficult conditions, eliminating the need for speaker-dependent training, and increasing the vocabularies handled to 10,000 and even 20,000 words. IBM's speech-dictation system is trained by users reading a passage from Mark Twain for about 90 minutes. Users report satisfactory recognition rates when speaking with brief pauses between words. A newer version called Voice Type 3.0 promises simpler training, higher recognition rates, and an improved interface. With specialized vocabularies such as in radiology, even greater success has been demonstrated.

Whether continuous speech will gain widespread acceptance is still an open question. Speech recognition for discrete words works well for special-purpose applications, but it does not serve as a general interaction medium. Keyboards, function keys, and pointing devices with direct manipulation are often more rapid, and the actions or commands can be made visible for easy editing. Error handling and appropriate feedback with voice input are difficult and slow. Combinations of voice and direct manipulation may be useful, as indicated by Pausch and Leatherby's study.

9.4.2   Continuous-speech recognition

HAL's ability to understand the astronauts' spoken words and even to read their lips was an appealing fantasy, but the reality is more sobering. Although many research projects have pursued *continuous-speech recognition*, commercially successful products are still restricted to specialty niches such as radiologists (Lai and Vergo, 1997). The difficulty lies in recognizing the boundaries between spoken words. Normal speech patterns blur the boundaries.

The hope is that, with a continuous-speech–recognition system, users could dictate letters, compose reports verbally for automatic transcription, and enable computers to scan long audio soundtracks, radio programs, or telephone calls for specific words or topics. Simply segmenting a movie by speakers would be a useful contribution. Using voice for identification purposes could be a benefit for security systems. Users would be asked to speak a novel phrase, and the system would ascertain which of the registered users was speaking.

Continuous-speech–recognition products are offered by manufacturers such as Verbex, which claims greater than 99.5-percent accuracy with speaker-dependent training with vocabularies of up to 10,000 words, and Speech Systems, which claims 95-percent accuracy for speaker-independent systems with 40,000 word vocabularies. IBM has tested a continuous-speech recognizer that uses subgrammars to increase recognition rates. Target tasks include operating-system control, police requests for information on car licenses, and stock-broker orders, but troubling error rates have delayed commercial distribution. Microsoft's Peedy, a graphically attractive conversational parrot, is cute at first, but I wonder whether users will become annoyed with it by their second and third encounter. A telephone message service called Wildfire is also appealing, but moving from a good demo to a working product may prove to be difficult.

Although progress has been made by the many companies and research groups, the following evaluation is still valid: "Comfortable and natural communication in a general setting (no constraints on what you can say and how you say it) is beyond us for now, posing a problem too difficult to solve" (Peacocke and Graf, 1990).

9.4.3   Speech store and forward

Less exciting but more immediately useful are the systems that enable storing and forwarding of spoken messages. Stored messages are commonly used for weather, airline, and financial information, but personal messaging through the telephone network is growing more popular. After registering with the service, users can touch commands on a 12-key telephone to store spoken messages and can have the messages sent to one or more people who are also registered with the service. Users can receive messages, replay messages, reply to the caller, forward messages to other users, delete messages, or archive messages. Automatic elimination of silences and speedup with frequency shifting can cut listening time in half.

Voice-mail technology works reliably, is fairly low cost, and is generally liked by users. Problems arise mainly because of the awkwardness of using the 12-key telephone pad for commands, the need to dial in to check whether messages have been left, and the potential for too many "junk" telephone messages because of the ease of broadcasting a message to many people.

Telephone-based information systems have also been a great success, although many users are frustrated by the lengthy and deep menu structures, or by long informational speeches in which it seems that the needed fact is always at the end or is omitted. Well-designed systems (Resnick and Virzi, 1995) can provide reasonable customer service and timely information at relatively low cost.

Personal tape recorders are moving toward digital approaches, with small handheld voice note takers carving out a successful consumer market. Credit-card–sized devices that cost about $40 can store and randomly access several minutes of voice-quality notes. More ambitious handheld devices enable users to manage audio databases and to retrieve selected music segments or recorded lecture segments (Schmandt, 1994).

Audio tours in museums have been successful because they allow user control of the pace, while conveying the curator's enthusiasm. Educational psychologists conjecture that, if several senses (sight, touch, hearing) are engaged, then learning can be facilitated. Adding a spoken voice to an instructional system or an online help system may improve the learning process. However, there is evidence that users of instructional systems prefer textual displays to voice presentations (Resnick and Lammers, 1985). Adding voice annotation to a document may make it easier for teachers to comment on student papers, or for business executives to leave detailed responses or instructions. Editing the voice annotation is possible, but is still difficult.

9.4.4 Speech generation

Speech generation is an example of a successful technology that is used, but whose applicability was overestimated by some developers. Inexpensive, compact, reliable speech-generation (also called synthesis) devices have been used in cameras ("too dark—use flash"), soft-drink vending machines ("insert correct change and make your selection," "thank you"), automobiles ("your door is ajar"), children's games, and utility-control rooms ("danger").

In some cases, the novelty wears off leading to removal of the speech generation. Talking supermarket checkout machines that read products and prices were found to violate shoppers' sense of privacy about purchases and to be too noisy. Automobile speech-generation devices are now less widely used; a few tones and red-light indicators were found to be more acceptable. Spoken warnings in cockpits or control rooms were sometimes missed, or were in competition with human–human communication.

Applications for the blind are an important success story (Songco et al., 1980). The Kurzweil Reader is used in hundreds of libraries. Patrons can place a book on a copierlike device that scans the text and does an acceptable job of reading the text one word at a time.

The quality of the sound can be good when the words and pronunciation for digitized human speech can be stored in a dictionary. When algorithms are used to generate the sound, the quality is sometimes degraded. Digitized human speech for phrases or sentences is often a useful strategy, since human intonation provides more authentic sound. For some applications, a computerlike sound may be preferred. Apparently, the robotlike sounds used in the Atlanta airport subway drew more attention than did a tape recording of a human giving directions.

Michaelis and Wiggins (1982) suggest that speech generation is frequently preferable when the

1. message is simple.

2. message is short.

3. message will not be referred to later.

4. message deals with events in time.

5. message requires an immediate response.

6. visual channels of communication are overloaded.

7. environment is too brightly lit, too poorly lit, subject to severe vibration, or otherwise unsuitable for transmission of visual information.

8. user must be free to move around.

9. user is subjected to high G forces or anoxia (lack of oxygen, typically occuring at high altitudes). The magnitude of G forces or anoxia at which eyesight begins to be impaired is well below that needed to affect hearing.

These criteria apply to digitized human speech and to simple playbacks of tape recordings.

Digitized speech segments can be concatenated to form more complex phrases and sentences. Telephone-based voice information systems for banking (Fidelity Automated Service Telephone (FAST)), credit-card information (Citibank Customer Service), airline schedules (American Airlines Dial-AA-Flight), and so on have touchtone keying of codes and voice output of information.

In summary, speech generation is technologically feasible. Now, clever designers must find the situations in which it is superior to competing technologies. Novel applications may be by way of the telephone as a supplement to the CRT or through embedding in small consumer products.

9.4.5 Audio tones, audiolization, and music

In addition to speech, auditory machine outputs include individual *audio tones;* more complex information presentation by combinations of sound or *audiolization;* and *music.* Early Teletypes did include a bell tone to alert users that a message was coming or that paper had run out. Later computer systems added a range of tones to indicate warnings or simply to acknowledge the completion of an action. Even keyboards were built with the intent to preserve sound feedback. As digital-signal-processing chips to perform digital-to-analog and analog-to-digital conversions have become more powerful and cheaper, innovations have begun to appear. Gaver's SonicFinder (1989) added sound to the Macintosh interface by offering a dragging sound when a file was being dragged, a click when a window boundary was passed, and a thunk when the file was dropped into the trashcan for deletion. The effect for most users is a satisfying confirmation of actions; for visually impaired users, the sounds are vital. On the other hand, after a few hours the sound can become a distraction rather than a contribution, especially in a room with several machines and users. An auditory-enhanced scroll bar that provided feedback about user actions produced a 20- to 25-percent speedup in search and navigation tasks when tested with 12 experienced users (Brewster et al., 1994).

Auditory browsers for blind users (see Section 1.5.5) or telephonic usage have been proposed. Each file might have a sound whose frequency is related to its size, and might be assigned an instrument (violin, flute, trumpet). Then, when the directory is opened, each file might play its sound simultaneously or sequentially (in alphabetical order?). Alternatively, files might have sounds associated with their file types so that users could hear whether there were only spreadsheet, graphic, or text files (Blattner et al., 1989).

More ambitious audiolizations have been proposed (Smith et al., 1990; Blattner et al., 1991) in which scientific data are presented as a series of stereophonic sounds rather than as images. Other explorations have included audio tones for mass-spectrograph output to allow operators to hear the differences between a standard and a test sample, and appealing musical output to debug the execution of a computer with 16 parallel processors.

Adding traditional music to user interfaces seems to be an appropriate idea to heighten drama, to relax users, to draw attention, or to set a mood (patriotic marches, romantic sonatas, or gentle waltzes). These approaches have been used in video games and educational packages; they might also be suitable for public access, home control, sales kiosks, bank machines, and other applications.

The potential for novel musical instruments seems especially attractive. With a touchscreen, it should be possible to offer appropriate feedback to give musicians an experience similar to a piano keyboard, a drum, a wood-wind, or a stringed instrument. There is a possibility of inventing new instruments whose frequency, amplitude, and effect are governed by the placement of the touch, as well as by its direction, speed, and even acceleration. Music composition using computers expanded as powerful musical-instrument digital-interface (MIDI) hardware and software has become widely available at reasonable prices, and user interfaces effectively combine piano and computer keyboards (Baggi, 1991).

9.5   Image and Video Displays

The *visual display unit (VDU)* has become the primary source of feedback to the user from the computer (Cakir et al., 1980; Grandjean, 1987; Helander, 1987). The VDU has many important features, including these:

- *Rapid operation*   Thousands of characters per second or a full image in a few milliseconds.
- *Reasonable size*   Early displays had 24 lines of 80 characters, but current devices show graphics and often more than 66 lines of 166 characters.
- *Reasonable resolution*   Typical resolution is 768×1024 pixels, but 1280×1024 is common.
- *Quiet operation*
- *No paper waste*
- *Relatively low cost*   Displays can cost as little as $100.
- *Reliability*
- *Highlighting*   Overwriting, windowing, and blinking are examples.
- *Graphics and animation*

Health concerns—such as visual fatigue, stress, and radiation exposure—are being addressed by manufacturers and government agencies, but remain active.

9.5.1   Display devices

For certain applications, *monochrome displays* are adequate and are attractive because of their lower cost. Color displays can make video games, educational simulations, CAD, and many other applications more attractive and effective for users. There are, however, real dangers in misusing color and difficulties in ensuring color constancy across devices.

Display technologies include:

- *Raster-scan cathode-ray tube (CRT)*   This popular device is similar to a television monitor, with an electron beam sweeping out lines of dots to form letters and graphics. The refresh rates (the reciprocal of the time required to produce a full screen image) vary from 30 to 70 per second. Higher rates are preferred, because they reduce *flicker*. Early CRT displays were often green because the P39 green phosphor has a long decay time, permitting relatively stable images. Another important property of a phosphor is the low *bloom level*, allowing sharp images because the small granules of the phosphor do not spread the glow to nearby points. The maximum resolution of a CRT is about 100 lines per inch but higher resolutions are being developed. CRT sizes (measured diagonally) range from less than 2 inches to more than 30 inches; popular models are in the range of 11 to 17 inches.

- *Liquid-crystal displays (LCDs)*   Voltage changes influence the polarization of tiny capsules of liquid crystals, turning some spots darker when viewed by reflected light. LCDs are flickerfree, but the size of the capsules limits the resolution. Portable computers usually have LCD displays because of the latter's thin form and light weight. Resolutions have moved up from 640 × 480 to 768 × 1024, with improved viewing from oblique angles, brighter images with better contrast, and more rapid adaptation to movement. Watches and calculators often use LCDs because of small size, light weight, and low power consumption.

- *Plasma panel*   Rows of horizontal wires are slightly separated from vertical wires by small glass-enclosed capsules of neon-based gases. When the horizontal and vertical wires on either side of the capsule receive a high voltage, the gas glows. Plasma displays are usually orange and are flickerfree, but the size of the capsules limits the resolution. Plasma computer displays have been built to display up to 62 lines of 166 characters, and bright multicolor plasma displays are being built.

- *Light-emitting diodes (LEDs)*   Certain diodes emit light when a voltage is applied. Arrays of these small diodes can be assembled to display characters. Here again, the resolution is limited by manufacturing techniques and costs are still high.

The technology employed affects these display attributes:

- Size
- Refresh rate
- Capacity to show animation

- Resolution
- Surface flatness
- Surface glare from reflected light
- Contrast between characters and background
- Brightness
- Line sharpness
- Character formation
- Tolerance for vibration

Each display technology has advantages and disadvantages with respect to these attributes. Users should expect these features:

- User control of contrast and brightness
- Software highlighting of characters by brightness
- Underscoring, reverse video, blinking (possibly at several rates)
- Extensive character set (alphabetic, numeric, special and international characters)
- Multiple type styles (for example, italic, bold) and fonts
- User control of cursor shape, blinking, and brightness
- Scrolling mechanism (smooth scrolling is preferred)
- User control of number of lines or characters per line displayed
- Support of negative and positive polarity (light on dark or dark on light)

Some frequent users place contrast-enhancement filters or masks in front of displays. Filters reduce reflected glare by using polarizers or a thin film of antireflective coating. Masks may be made of nylon mesh or simple matte surfaces. These devices are helpful to some users, but they can reduce resolution and are subject to smudging from fingerprints.

Dramatic progress in computer graphics has led to increasing use in motion pictures and television. Startling images have been created by George Lucas's Industrial Light and Magic and by Walt Disney Studios for movies, such as the *Star Wars* series, *Terminator 2*, *Jurassic Park*, and *Toy Story*. Many television commercials, station-identification segments, and news-related graphics have been constructed by computer animation. Finally, video games are another source of impressive computer-graphics images. The ACM's SIGGRAPH (Special Interest Group on Graphics) has an exciting annual conference with exhibitions of novel graphics devices and applications. The conference proceedings and videotape digest are rich sources of information.

9.5.2 Digital photography and scanners

Digital photography has become widespread in the news media and photographic agencies, where rapid electronic editing and dissemination is paramount. Many suppliers offer specialized cameras or add-ons for existing cameras (such as Kodak's attachment for Nikon cameras) that can take 100 images on a portable battery-driven hard-disk drive. Professional and amateur photographers are warming up to the digital cameras offered by Canon, Casio, Kodak, and SONY. Downloading to personal computers is simple, and display on the World Wide Web is a popular pursuit. The community of interested photographers has been enlarged with Kodak's PhotoCDs, which are produced from standard 35-millimeter negatives at the same time as prints are made. The PhotoCD's high resolution and good integration with personal computers are attractive to professional and amateur photographers who are seeking images for everything from professional documents to electronic family albums.

The increasing use of images has stimulated the need to scan photos, maps, documents, or handwritten notes. Page-sized scanners with 300-points-per-inch resolution are commonly available for a few hundred dollars, and larger scanners with higher resolution can be had for higher prices. Scanning packages often include character-recognition software that can convert text in printed documents into electronic forms with good reliability, but verification is necessary for demanding applications.

9.5.3 Digital video

The first generation of video applications was based on videodisk sources provided by producers who have access to interesting visual resources. Producers such as National Geographic (GEO), the Library of Congress (American Memory), ABC News (Election of 1988, Middle East history), Voyager (National Gallery of Art), and many others generated videodisks with tens of thousands of still images or hundreds of motion video segments. Each package had its own access software, and the thrill was to view the treasured images on command. Success often depended more on content than on design.

The 12-inch videodisks can store up to 54,000 still images, or 30 minutes of motion video, per side. Access time has been reduced steadily; on new players, it is under 1 second. Videodisk databases are a major application in museums (paintings, photos, and so on), travel (previews of hotels, tourist attractions, and so on), education (microbiology slides, environmental awareness, current events, and so on), industrial training (truck drivers, financial sales, power-plant control, and so on), and sales (shoes, sports equipment, real estate, and so on). User-interface issues revolve around access to indexes, searching methods, action sets (start, pause, replay, stop, fast forward or backward), branching capability to allow individual exploration, capacity to extract and export, annotation, and synchronization with other activities.

Abbe Don, a multimedia artist who created "We Make Memories," used a HyperCard stack and videodisk to display family history as told by herself, her sister, her mother, and her grandmother. In this electronic version of a family photo album, events take on universal themes, and the emotional engagement foretells future applications that deal more with the heart than the head.

Videodisks are still suited for full-length motion pictures, but cheap *CD-ROMs* can provide up to 600 megabytes of textual or numeric data, or approximately 6000 graphic images, 1 hour of music, or 6 to 72 minutes (depending on effectiveness of compression and the resolution of the images) of motion video. CD-ROMs are relatively cheap, are small, and have reading devices smaller than those of videodisks. CD-ROMs are restructuring libraries and offices as the latter acquire more electronic reference sources and the computers to search that material. The next generation of CD-ROMs, *digital video disks (DVDs)*, will have an order-of-magnitude greater storage space, to allow storage of 2 hours of medium-resolution video.

Second-generation digital video capabilities—which allow users to create and store their own images and videos and to send this material to other people—have already begun to spice the pot of computing applications. Applications include video electronic mail, video conferences, personal image databases, video tutorials, video online help, and remote control with video feedback. Medical image-processing applications include X-ray images, sonograms, nuclear magnetic-resonance images (MRI), and computed-axial-tomography (CAT) scans.

Since video storage can consume many megabytes, efficient and rapid compression and decompression techniques become vital. The *Motion Picture Experts Group (MPEG)* approach has made digital-video servers a workable reality, even for full-length motion pictures. MPEG algorithms can compress 1 second of full-motion video into approximately 150 kilobytes—approximately 5 kilobytes per frame. MPEG algorithms attempt to store only differences across frames, so that stable images are compressed more than active or panning sequences. The elimination of special videodisk players and the capacity for recording video with standard magnetic media are attractive.

User-interface issues for these video environments are just beginning to be explored. For retrieval-oriented applications, the key question is how to find the desired videos in a library or a segment within a two-hour video.

Computer-based video-conferencing systems allow users to send an image over normal telephone lines in compressed data formats in a fraction of a second for low-resolution images, and in from 5 to 30 seconds for higher-resolution images. Increasingly available higher-speed lines—such as ISDN, leased lines, cable TV, and direct broadcast satellites—are enabling good-quality images and video to be used in a wide range of applications.

9.5.4   Projectors, heads-up displays, helmet-mounted displays

The desire to show and see computer-generated images has inspired several novel products. *Projector* television systems have been adapted to show the higher-resolution images from computers. These devices can generate 2 by 3 meter displays with good saturation, and larger displays with some loss of fidelity. An important variation is to use an LCD plate in connection with a common overhead projector to show color computer displays for meetings of 10 to 1000 people. These devices are rapidly declining in price and increasing in quality.

Personal display technology involves small portable monitors, often made with LCD in monochrome or color. A *heads-up display* projects information on a partially silvered windscreen of an airplane or car, so that the pilots or drivers can keep their attention focused on the surroundings while receiving computer-generated information. An alternative, the *helmet-mounted display (HMD)*, consists of a small partially silvered glass mounted on a helmet or hat that lets users see information even while turning their heads. In fact, the information that they see may be varied as a function of the direction in which they are looking.

The Private Eye technology uses a line of 200 LEDs and a moving mirror to produce 720- by 200-pixel resolution images in a lightweight and small display that can be mounted on a pair of glasses. This early example of wearable computers has focused attention on small portable devices that people can use while moving or accomplishing other tasks, such as jet engine repair or inventory control.

Attempts to produce three-dimensional displays include vibrating surfaces, holograms, polarized glasses, red–blue glasses, and synchronized shutter glasses. The CrystalEyes glasses from Stereographics shift from left-to right-eye vision at 120 hertz, and with a synchronized display, give users a strong sense of three-dimensional vision.

Still more innovative approaches come from performance artists such as Vincent Vincent, whose Mandala system is a three-dimensional environment for theatrical exploration. Performers or amateur users touch images of harps, bells, drums, or cymbals, and the instruments respond. Myron Krueger's artificial realities contain friendly video-projected cartoonlike creatures who playfully crawl on your arm or approach your outstretched hand. In both of these environments, input is from video cameras or body sensors that do not require the user–performers to wear special equipment. Such environments invite participation, and the serious research aspects fade as joyful exploration takes over and you step inside the computer's world.

9.6 Printers

Even when they have good-quality and high-speed displays, people still have a great desire for hardcopy printouts. Paper documents can be easily copied, mailed, marked, and stored. The following are the important criteria for printers:

- Speed
- Print quality
- Cost
- Compactness
- Quietness of operation
- Type of paper (fanfolded or single sheet)
- Character set
- Variety of typefaces, fonts, and sizes
- Highlighting techniques (boldface, underscore, and so on)
- Support for special forms (printed forms, different lengths, and so on)
- Reliability

Early computer printers worked at 10 characters per second and did not support graphics. Personal-computer *dot-matrix printers* print more than 200 characters per second, have multiple fonts, can print boldface, use variable width and size, and have graphics capabilities. *Inkjet printers* offer quiet operation and high-quality output on plain paper. *Thermal printers* (often used in *fax machines*) offer quiet, compact, and inexpensive output on specially coated or plain paper.

Printing systems on mainframe computers with *impact line printers* that operate at 1200 lines per minute have all but vanished in favor of *laser printers* that operate at 30,000 lines per minute. The laser printers, now widely available for microcomputers, support graphics and produce high-quality images. Speeds vary from 4 to 40 pages per minute; resolution ranges from 200 to 1200 points per inch. Software to permit publication-quality typesetting has opened the door to *desktop-publishing* ventures.

Compact laser printers offer users the satisfaction of producing elegant business documents, scientific reports, novels, or personal correspondence. Users should consider output quality, speed, choice of faces and fonts, graphics capabilities, and special paper requirements.

Color printers allow users to produce hardcopy output of color graphics, usually by an inkjet approach with three colored inks and a black ink. The printed image is often of lower quality than the screen image and may not be faithful to the screen colors. Color laser printers or dye-transfer methods bring the satisfaction of bright and sharp color images, but at a higher price.

Plotters enable output of graphs, bar charts, line drawings, and maps on rolls of paper or sheets up to 100 by 150 cm. Plotters may have single pens, multiple pens, or inkjets for color output. Other design factors are the precision of small movements, the accuracy in placement of the pens, the speed of pen motion, the repeatability of drawings, and the software support.

Photographic printers allow the creation of 35-millimeter or larger slides (transparencies) and photographic prints. These printers are often designed as add-on devices in front of a display, but high-quality printing systems are independent devices. *Newspaper-* or *magazine-layout systems* allow electronic editing of images and text before generation of production-quality output for printing.

9.7 Practitioner's Summary

Choosing hardware always involves making a compromise between the ideal and the practical. The designer's vision of what an input or output device should be must be tempered by the realities of what is commercially available within the project budget. Devices should be tested in the application domain to verify the manufacturer's claims, and testimonials or suggestions from users should be obtained.

Designers should pay attention to current trends for specific devices, such as the mouse, touchscreen, stylus, or voice recognizer. Since new devices and refinements to old devices appear regularly, device-independent architecture and software will permit easy integration of novel devices. Avoid being locked into one device; the hardware is often the softest part of the system. Also, remember that a successful software idea can become even more successful if reimplementation on other devices is easy to achieve.

Keyboard entry is here to stay for a long time, but consider other forms of input when text entry is limited. Selecting rather than typing has many benefits for both novice and frequent users. Direct-pointing devices are faster and more convenient for novices than are indirect-pointing devices, and accurate pointing is now possible. Beware of the hand-off-the-keyboard problem for all pointing devices, and strive to reduce the number of shifts between the keyboard and the pointing device.

Speech input and output are commercially viable and should be applied where appropriate, but take care to ensure that performance is genuinely improved over other interaction strategies. Display technology is moving rapidly and user expectations are increasing. Higher-resolution, color, and larger displays will be sought by users. Even when they have sharp, rapid, and accurate color displays, users still need high-quality hardcopy output.

9.8   Researcher's Agenda

Novel text-entry keyboards to speed input and to reduce error rates will have to provide significant benefits to displace the well-entrenched QWERTY design. For numerous applications not requiring extensive text entry, opportunities exist to create special-purpose devices or to redesign the task to permit direct-manipulation selection instead. Increasingly, input can be accomplished via conversion or extraction of data from online sources. Another input source is optical character recognition of printed text or of bar codes printed in magazines, on bank statements, in books, or on record albums.

Pointing devices will certainly play an increasing role. A clearer understanding of pointing tasks and the refinement of pointing devices to suit each task seem inevitable. Improvements can be made not only to the devices, but also to the software with which the devices are used. The same mouse hardware can be used in many ways to speed up movement, to provide more accurate feedback to users, and to reduce errors.

Research on speech systems can also be directed at improving the device and at redesigning the application to make more effective use of the speech input and output technology. Complete and accurate continuous-speech recognition does not seem attainable, but if users will modify their speaking style in specific applications, then more progress is possible. Another worthy direction is to increase rates of continuous-speech recognition for such tasks as finding a given phrase in a large body of recorded speech.

Larger, higher-resolution displays seem attainable. Thin, lightweight, durable, and inexpensive displays will spawn many applications, not only in portable computers, but also for embedding in briefcases, appliances, telephones, and automobiles. A battery-powered book-sized computer could contain the information from thousands of books or support Internet access.

A low-cost *webtop* computer for reading only could do away with keyboards, hard-disk drives, and floppy-disk drives.

Among the most exciting developments will be the increased facility for manipulating video and images. Many possibilities will open with improved graphics editors; faster image-processing hardware and algorithms; and cheaper image input, storage, and output devices. How will people search for images, integrate images with text, or modify images? What level of increased visual literacy will schools expect? How can animation be used as a more common part of computer applications? Can the hardware or software evoke more emotional responses and broaden the spectrum of computer devotees?

World Wide Web Resources   WWW

Rich resources are available on commercial input devices, especially pointing devices and handwriting input. Promoters of speech recognition offer commercial packages, software tools, and demonstrations. MIDI tools and virtual reality devices enable serious hobbyists and researchers to create novel experiences for users.

http://www.aw.com/DTUI

References

Baggi, Dennis L., Computer-generated music, *IEEE Computer*, 24, 7 (July 1991), 6–9.

Blattner, Meera M., Greenberg, R. M., and Kamegai, M., Listening to turbulence: An example of scientific audiolization. In Blattner, M. and Dannenberg, R. B. (Editors), *Interactive Multimedia Computing*, ACM Press, New York (1991).

Blattner, Meera M., Sumikawa, Denise A., and Greenberg, R. M., Earcons and icons: Their structure and common design principles, *Human–Computer Interaction*, 4, (1989), 11–44.

Brewster, Stephen A., Wright, Peter C., and Edwards, Alistair D. N., The design and evaluation of an auditory-enhanced scrollbar, *Proc. CHI '94: Human Factors in Computing Systems*, ACM, New York (1994), 173–179.

Buxton, William, There's more to interaction than meets the eye: Some issues in manual input. In Norman, D. A., and Draper, S. W. (Editors), *User Centered System Design: New Perspectives on Human–Computer Interaction*, Lawrence Erlbaum Associates, Hillsdale, NJ (1985) 319–337.

Cakir, A., Hart, D. J., and Stewart, T. F. M., *The VDT Manual*, John Wiley and Sons, New York (1980).

Card, Stuart K., Mackinlay, Jock D., and Robertson, George G., A morphological analysis of the design space of input devices, *ACM Transactions on Information Systems, 9*, 2 (1991), 99–122.

Card, S. K., English, W. K., and Burr, B. J., Evaluation of mouse, rate-controlled isometric joystick, step keys, and task keys for text selection on a CRT, *Ergonomics, 21*, 8 (August 1978), 601–613.

Danis, Catalina, Comerford, Liam, Janke, Eric, Davies, Ken, DeVries, Jackie, and Bertran, Alex, StoryWriter: A speech oriented editor, *Proc. CHI '94: Human Factors in Computing Systems: Conference Companion*, ACM, New York (1994), 277–278.

Dunsmore, H. E., Data entry. In Kantowitz, Barry H., and Sorkin, Robert D., *Human Factors: Understanding People–Systems Relationships*, John Wiley and Sons, New York (1983), 335–366.

Emmons, W. H., A comparison of cursor-key arrangements (box versus cross) for VDUs. In Grandjean, Etienne (Editor), *Ergonomics and Health in Modern Offices*, Taylor and Francis, London and Philadelphia (1984), 214–219.

English, William K., Engelbart, Douglas C., and Berman, Melvyn L., Display-selection techniques for text manipulation, *IEEE Transactions on Human Factors in Electronics, HFE–8*, 1 (March 1967), 5–15.

Ewing, John, Mehrabanzad, Simin, Sheck, Scott, Ostroff, Dan, and Shneiderman, Ben, An experimental comparison of a mouse and arrow-jump keys for an interactive encyclopedia, *International Journal of Man–Machine Studies, 23*, 1 (January 1986), 29–45.

Fitts, Paul M., The information capacity of the human motor system in controlling amplitude of movement, *Journal of Experimental Psychology, 47*, (1954), 381–391.

Fitzmaurice, George W., Situated information spaces and spatially aware palmtop computers, *Communications of the ACM, 36*, 7 (1993), 38–49.

Fitzmaurice, George, W, Ishii, Hiroshi, and Buxton, William, Bricks: Laying the foundation for graspable user interfaces, *CHI '95: Human Factors in Computing Systems*, ACM, New York (1995), 442–449.

Foley, James D., Van Dam, Andries, Feiner, Steven K., and Hughes, John F., *Computer Graphics: Principles and Practice* (Second Edition), Addison-Wesley, Reading, MA (1990).

Foley, James D., Wallace, Victor L., and Chan, Peggy, The human factors of computer graphics interaction techniques, *IEEE Computer Graphics and Applications, 4*, 11 (November 1984), 13–48.

Frankish, Clive, Hull, Richard, and Morgan, Pam, Recognition accuracy and user acceptance of pen interfaces, *Proc. CHI '95 Conference: Human Factors in Computing Systems*, ACM, New York (1995), 503–510.

Gaver, William W., The SonicFinder: An interface that uses auditory icons, *Human–Computer Interaction, 4*, 1 (1989), 67–94.

Grandjean, E., Design of VDT workstations. In Salvendy, Gavriel (Editor), *Handbook of Human Factors*, John Wiley and Sons, New York (1987), 1359–1397.

Greenstein, Joel and Arnaut, Lynn, Input devices. In Helander, Martin, *Handbook of Human–Computer Interaction*, North-Holland, Amsterdam, The Netherlands (1988), 495–516.

Haider, E., Luczak, H., and Rohmert, W., Ergonomics investigations of workplaces in a police command-control centre equipped with TV displays, *Applied Ergonomics*, 13, 3 (1982), 163–170.

Haller, R., Mutschler, H., and Voss, M., Comparison of input devices for correction of typing errors in office systems, *INTERACT 84* (1984), 218–223.

Helander, Martin G., Design of visual displays. In Salvendy, Gavriel (Editor), *Handbook of Human Factors*, John Wiley and Sons, New York (1987), 507–548.

Jacob, Robert J. K., The use of eye movements in human–computer interaction techniques: What you look at is what you get, *ACM Trans. on Information Systems*, 9, 3 (1991), 152–169.

Jacob, Robert J. K., Leggett, John, Myers, Brad A., and Pausch, Randy, Interaction styles and input/output devices, *Behaviour & Information Technology*, 12, 2 (1993), 69–79.

Jacob, Robert J. K., Sibert, Linda E., McFarlane, Daniel C., and Mullen, Jr., M. Preston, Integrality and separability of input devices, *ACM Trans. on Computer–Human-Interaction*, 1, 1 (March 1994), 3–26.

Johnson, Jeff A., A comparison of user interfaces for panning on a touch-controlled display, *Proc. ACM CHI '95: Human Factors in Computing Systems*, ACM, New York (1995), 218–225.

Karat, John, McDonald, James, and Anderson, Matt, A comparison of selection techniques: Touch panel, mouse and keyboard, *INTERACT 84* (September 1984), 149–153.

Karl, Lewis, Pettey, Michael, and Shneiderman, Ben, Speech versus mouse commands for word processing applications: An empirical evaluation, *International Journal for Man–Machine Studies*, 39, 4 (1993), 667–687.

Kroemer, K. H. E., Operation of ternary chorded keys, *International Journal of Human–Computer Interaction*, 5, 3 (1993), 267–288.

Lai, Jennifer and Vergo, John, MedSpeak: Report creation with continuous speech recognition, Proc. *ACM CHI '97: Human Factors in Computing Systems*, ACM, New York (1997), 431–438.

Leggett, John, and Williams, Glen, An empirical investigation of voice as an input modality for computer programming, *International Journal of Man–Machine Studies*, 21, (1984), 493–520.

MacKenzie, I. Scott, Movement time prediction in human–computer interfaces, *Graphics Interface '92*, Morgan Kaufmann, San Francisco (1992), 140–150.

Michaelis, Paul Roller, and Wiggins, Richard H., A human factors engineer's introduction to speech synthesizers. In Badre, A. and Shneiderman, B. (Editors), *Directions in Human–Computer Interaction*, Ablex, Norwood, NJ (1982), 149–178.

Mithal, Anant Kartik and Douglas, Sarah A., Differences in movement microstructure of the mouse and the finger-controlled isometric joystick, *Proc. ACM CHI '96: Human Factors in Computing Systems*, ACM, New York (1996), 300–307.

Montgomery, Edward B., Bringing manual input into the twentieth century, *IEEE Computer*, 15, 3 (March 1982), 11–18.

Morrison, D. L., Green, T. R. G., Shaw, A. C., and Payne, S. J., Speech-controlled text-editing: effects of input modality and of command structure, *International Journal of Man–Machine Studies*, 21, 1 (1984), 49–63.

Murray, J. Thomas, Van Praag, John, and Gilfoil, David, Voice versus keyboard control of cursor motion, *Proc. Human Factors Society—Twenty-Seventh Annual Meeting*, Human Factors Society, Santa Monica, CA (1983), 103.

Nakaseko, M., Grandjean, E., Hunting, W., and Gierer, R., Studies of ergonomically designed alphanumeric keyboards, *Human Factors*, 27, 2 (1985), 175–187.

Pausch, Randy and Leatherby, James H., An empirical study: Adding voice input to a graphical editor, *Journal of the American Voice Input/Output Society*, 9, 2 (July 1991), 55–66.

Peacocke, Richard D. and Graf, Daryl H., An introduction to speech and speaker recognition, *IEEE Computer*, 23, 8 (August 1990), 26–33.

Pearson, Glenn and Weiser, Mark, Of moles and men: The design of foot controls for workstations, *Proc. ACM CHI '86: Human Factors in Computing Systems*, ACM, New York (1986), 333–339.

Potosnak, Kathleen M., Input devices. In Helander, Martin (Editor), *Handbook of Human–Computer Interaction*, North-Holland, Amsterdam, The Netherlands (1988), 475–494.

Resnick, Paul and Virzi, Robert A., Relief from the audio interface blues: Expanding the spectrum of menu, list, and form styles, *ACM Trans. on Computer-Human-Interaction*, 2, 2 (June 1995), 145–176.

Resnick, P. V. and Lammers, H. B., The influence of self esteem on cognitive responses to-machine-like versus human-like computer feedback, *Journal of Social Psychology*, 125, 6 (1985), 761–769.

Rutledge, J. D. and Selker, T., Force-to-motion functions for pointing in human–computer interaction, *Proc. INTERACT '90*, North-Holland, Amsterdam, The Netherlands (1990), 701–706.

Schmandt, Christopher, *Voice Communication with Computers*, Van Nostrand Reinhold, New York (1994).

Sears, Andrew, Plaisant, Catherine, and Shneiderman, Ben, A new era for touchscreen applications: High-precision, dragging, and direct manipulation metaphors. In Hartson, R. H. and Hix, D. (Editors), *Advances in Human–Computer Interaction*, Volume 3, Ablex, Norwood, NJ (1992), 1–33.

Sears, Andrew, Revis, Doreen, Swatski, Jean, Crittenden, Robert, and Shneiderman, Ben, Investigating touchscreen typing: The effect of keyboard size on typing speed, *Behaviour & Information Technology*, 12, 1 (Jan–Feb 1993), 17–22.

Sears, Andrew and Shneiderman, Ben, High precision touchscreens: Design strategies and comparison with a mouse, *International Journal of Man–Machine Studies*, 34, 4 (April 1991), 593–613.

Sherr, Sol (Editor), *Input Devices*, Academic Press, San Diego, CA (1988).

Shneiderman, B., Touch screens now offer compelling uses, *IEEE Software*, 8, 2 (March 1991), 93–94, 107.

Shutoh, Tomoki, Tsuruta, Shichiro, Kawai, Ryuichi, and Shutoh, Masamichi, Voice operation in CAD system. In Hendrick, H. W., and Brown, O., Jr., (Editors), *Human Factors in Organizational Design and Management*, Elsevier Science Publishers B.V. (North-Holland), Amsterdam, The Netherlands (1984), 205–209.

Smith, Stuart, Bergeron, R. Daniel, and Grinstein, Georges, G., Stereophonic and surface sound generation for exploratory data analysis, *Proc. CHI '90: Conference:
Human Factors in Computing Systems*, ACM, New York (1990), 125–132.

Songco, D. C., Allen, S. I., Plexico, P. S., and Morford, R. A., How computers talk to
the blind, *IEEE Spectrum*, [VOLUME, ISSUE] (May 1980), 34–38.

Stammers, R. B. and Bird, J. M., Controller evaluation of a touch input air traffic data
system: An indelicate experiment, *Human Factors*, 22, 5 (1980), 581–589.

Strathmeyer, Carl R., Voice in computing: An overview of available technologies,
IEEE Computer, 23, 8 (August 1990), 10–16.

Venolia, Dan and Neiberg, Forrest, T-Cube: A fast self-disclosing pen-based alphabet, *Proc. CHI '94 Conference: Human Factors in Computing Systems*, ACM, New
York (1994), 265–270.

Ware, Colin and Baxter, Curtis, Bat Brushes: On the uses of six position and orientation parameters in a paint program, *Proc. CHI '89 Conference: Human Factors in
Computing Systems*, ACM, New York (1989), 155–160.

Yankelovich, Nicole, Levow, Gina-Anne, and Marx, Matt, Designing SpeechActs:
Issues in speech user interfaces, *Proc. CHI '95 Conference: Human Factors in Computing Systems*, ACM, New York (1995), 369–376.

Zhai, Shuman, Milgram, Paul and Buxton, William, The influence of muscle groups on
performance of multiple degree-of-freedom input, *Proc. CHI '96 Conference: Human
Factors in Computing Systems*, ACM, New York (1996), 308–315.

Mark Kostabi, *The Listeners (Post Modern Rome)*, 1996

Response Time and Display Rate

Stimulation is the indispensable requisite for pleasure in an experience,
and the feeling of bare time is the least stimulating experience we can have.

William James, *Principles of Psychology,* **Volume I, 1890**

Nothing can be more useful to a man than a determination not to be hurried.

Henry David Thoreau, *Journal*

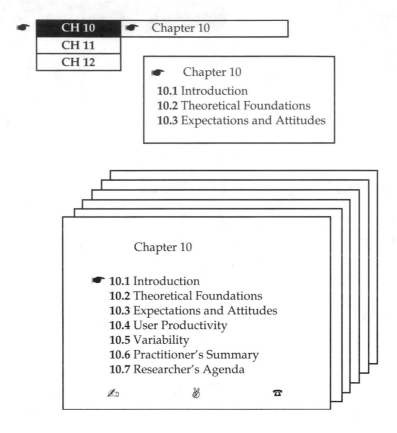

10.1 Introduction

Time is precious. When externally imposed delays impede progress on a task, many people become frustrated, annoyed, and eventually angry. Lengthy or unexpected system response times and slow display rates produce these reactions in computer users, leading to frequent errors and low satisfaction. Some users accept the situation with a shrug of their shoulders, but most users prefer to work more quickly than the computer allows.

There is a danger in working too quickly. As users pick up the pace of a rapid interaction sequence, they may learn less, read with lower comprehension, make more ill-considered decisions, and commit more data-entry errors. Stress can build in this situation if it is hard to recover from errors, or if the errors destroy data, damage equipment, or imperil human life (for example, in air-traffic control or medical systems) (Emurian, 1989; Kuhmann, 1989).

The computer system's *response time* is the number of seconds it takes from the moment users initiate an activity (usually by pressing an ENTER

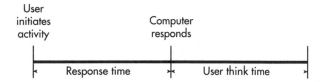

Figure 10.1

Simple model of system response time and user think time.

key or mouse button) until the computer begins to present results on the display or printer (Fig. 10.1). When the response is completely displayed, users begin formulating the next action. The *user think time* is the number of seconds during which users think before entering the next action. In this simple model, users initiate, wait for the computer to respond, watch while the results appear, think for a while, and initiate again.

In a more realistic model (Fig. 10.2), users plan while reading results, while typing, and while the computer is generating results or retrieving information across the network. Most people will use whatever time they have to plan ahead; thus, precise measurements of user think time are difficult to obtain. The computer's response is usually more precisely defined and measurable, but there are problems here as well. Some systems respond with distracting messages, informative feedback, or a simple prompt immediately after a command is initiated, but actual results may not appear for a few seconds.

Designers who specify response times and display rates in human–computer interactions have to consider the complex interaction of technical feasibility, costs, task complexity, user expectations, speed of task performance, error rates, and error-handling procedures. Decisions about these variables are further complicated by the influence of users' personality differences, fatigue, familiarity with computers, experience with the task, and motivation (Carbonell et al., 1968; Shneiderman, 1980).

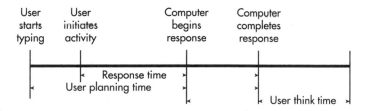

Figure 10.2

Model of system response time, user planning time, and user think time. This model is more realistic than the one in Fig. 10.1.

Although some people are content with a slower system for some tasks, the overwhelming majority prefer rapid interactions. Overall productivity depends not only on the speed of the system, but also on the rate of human error and the ease of recovery from those errors. Lengthy (longer than 15-second) response times are generally detrimental to productivity, increasing error rates and decreasing satisfaction. More rapid (less than 1-second) interactions are generally preferred and can increase productivity, but may increase error rates for complex tasks. The high cost of providing rapid response times or display rates and the loss from increased errors must be evaluated in the choice of an optimum pace.

For alphanumeric displays, the *display rate* is the speed, in *characters per second (cps)*, at which characters appear for the user to read. The rate may be limited by inexpensive modems to 30 to 120 cps or the display may fill instantaneously (typical for many personal computers and workstations). In World Wide Web applications, the display rate of a page may be limited by network transmission speed or server performance. Portions of images or fragments of a page may appear with interspersed delays of several seconds. Display rates for graphics are measured in bytes per second; a typical home user has a 28.8Kbps modem, which is capable of receiving approximately 3600 bytes per second but more commonly receives 500 to 2000 bytes per second. At that rate, a 100-Kbyte image takes more than one minute to load—a long delay. Faster communications lines by more advanced network connections (such as Asynchronous Transfer Mode (ATM)), satellites, or cable modems could reduce times to a few seconds.

Reading textual information from a screen is a challenging cognitive and perceptual task—it is more difficult than reading from a book. If the display rate can be made so fast that the screen appears to fill instantly (beyond the speed at which someone might feel compelled to keep up), subjects seem to relax, to pace themselves, and to work productively. Since users often scan a web page looking for highlights or links, rather than reading the full text, it is useful to display text first, leaving space for the graphical elements that are slower to display.

This chapter begins in Section 10.2 by discussing a model of short-term human memory and identifying the sources of human error. Section 10.3 focuses on the role of users' expectations and attitudes in shaping users' subjective reactions to the computer-system response time. Section 10.4 concentrates on productivity as a function of response time. Section 10.5 reviews the research on the influence of variable response times.

10.2   Theoretical Foundations

A cognitive model of human performance that accounts for the experimental results in response time and display rates would be useful in making predictions, designing systems, and formulating management policies. A complete, predictive model that accounts for all the variables may never be realized, but even fragments of such a model are useful to designers.

Robert B. Miller's review (1968) presented a lucid analysis of response-time issues and a list of 17 situations in which preferred response times might differ. Much has changed since his paper was written, but the principles of closure, short-term–memory limitations, and chunking still apply.

10.2.1   Limitations of short-term and working memory

Any cognitive model must emerge from an understanding of human problem-solving abilities and information-processing capabilities. A central issue is the limitation of *short-term memory* capacity.

George Miller's classic 1956 paper, "The magical number seven—plus or minus two," identified the limited capacities people have for absorbing information (Miller, 1956). People can rapidly recognize approximately seven (this value was contested by later researchers, but serves as a good estimate) *chunks* of information at a time and can hold those chunks in short-term memory for 15 to 30 seconds. The size of a chunk of information depends on the person's familiarity with the material.

For example, most people could look at seven binary digits for a few seconds and then recall the digits correctly from memory within 15 seconds. However, performing a distracting task during those 15 seconds, such as reciting a poem, would erase the binary digits. Of course, if people concentrate on remembering the binary digits and succeed in transferring them to long-term memory, then they can retain the binary digits for much longer periods. Most Americans could also probably remember seven decimal digits, seven alphabetic characters, seven English words, or even seven familiar advertising slogans. Although these items have increasing complexity, they are still treated as single chunks. However, Americans might not succeed in remembering seven Russian letters, Chinese pictograms, or Polish sayings. Knowledge and experience govern the size of a chunk for each individual.

People use short-term memory in conjunction with *working memory* for processing information and for problem solving. Short-term memory processes perceptual input, whereas working memory is used to generate and implement solutions. If many facts and decisions are necessary to solve a problem, then short-term and working memory may become overloaded. People learn to cope with complex problems by developing higher-level concepts that bring together several lower-level concepts into a single chunk. Novices at any task tend to work with smaller chunks until they can cluster concepts into larger chunks. Novices will break a complex task into a sequence of smaller tasks that they are confident about accomplishing.

This chunking phenomenon was demonstrated by Neal (1977), who required 15 experienced keypunch operators to type data records organized into numeric, alphanumeric, and English word fields. The median interkey-stroke time was 0.2 seconds, but it rose to more than 0.3 seconds at field boundaries and 0.9 seconds at record boundaries.

Short-term and working memory are highly volatile; disruptions cause loss of information, and delays can require that the memory be refreshed. Visual distractions or noisy environments also interfere with cognitive processing. Furthermore, anxiety apparently reduces the size of the available memory, since the person's attention is partially absorbed in concerns that are beyond the problem-solving task.

10.2.2   Sources of errors

If people are able to construct a solution to a problem in spite of interference, they must still record or implement the solution. If they can implement the solution immediately, they can proceed quickly through their work. On the other hand, if they must record the solution in long-term memory, on paper, or on a complex device, the chances for error increase and the pace of work slows.

Multiplying two four-digit numbers in your head is difficult because the intermediate results cannot be maintained in working memory and must be transferred to long-term memory. Controlling a nuclear reactor or air traffic is a challenge in part because these tasks often require integration of information (in short-term and working memory) from several sources, as well as maintenance of awareness of the complete situation. In attending to newly arriving information, operators may be distracted and may lose the contents of their short-term or working memory.

When using an interactive computer system, users may formulate plans and then have to wait while they execute each step in the plan. If a step produces an unexpected result or if the delays are long, then the user may forget part of the plan or be forced to review the plan continually.

Long (1976) studied delays of approximately 0.1 to 0.5 seconds in the time for a keystroke to produce a character on an impact printer. He found that unskilled and skilled typists worked more slowly and made more errors with longer response times. Even these brief delays were distracting in the rapid process of typing. If users try to work too quickly, they may not allow sufficient time to formulate a solution plan correctly, and error rates may increase. As familiarity with the task increases, users' capacity to work more quickly and with fewer errors should increase.

This model leads to the conjecture that, for a given user and task, there is a preferred response time. Long response times lead to wasted effort and more errors because a solution plan is reviewed repeatedly. Shorter response times may generate a faster pace in which solution plans are prepared hastily and incompletely. More data from a variety of situations and users would clarify these conjectures.

10.2.3 Conditions for optimum problem solving

As response times grow longer, users may become more anxious because the penalty for an error increases. As the difficulty in handling an error increases, their anxiety levels increase, further slowing performance and increasing errors. As response times grow shorter and display rates increase, users pick up the pace of the system and may fail to comprehend the presented material, may generate incorrect solution plans, and may make more execution errors. Wickelgren (1977) reviews speed–accuracy tradeoffs.

Car driving may offer a useful analogy. Although higher speed limits are attractive to many drivers and do produce faster completion of trips, they also lead to higher accident rates. Since automobile accidents have dreadful consequences, we accept speed limits. When incorrect use of computer systems can lead to damage to life, property, or data, should not speed limits be provided?

Another lesson from driving is the importance of progress indicators. Drivers want to know how far it is to their destination and what progress they are making by seeing the declining number of miles on road signs. Similarly, computer users want to know how long it will take for a web page to load or a database search to complete. Users given graphical dynamic progress indicators rather than a static ("Please wait"), blinking, or numeric (number of seconds left) message had higher satisfaction and shorter perceived elapsed times to completion (Meyer et al., 1995; 1996).

Users may achieve rapid task performance, low error rates, and high satisfaction if the following criteria are met:

- Users have adequate knowledge of the objects and actions necessary for the problem-solving task.
- The solution plan can be carried out without delays.
- Distractions are eliminated.
- User anxiety is low.
- There is feedback about progress toward solution.
- Errors can be avoided or, if they occur, can be handled easily.

These conditions for optimum problem solving, with acceptable cost and technical feasibility, are the basic constraints on design. However, other conjectures may play a role in choosing the optimum interaction speed:

- Novices may exhibit better performance with somewhat slower response time.
- Novices prefer to work at speeds slower than those chosen by knowledgeable frequent users.
- When there is little penalty for an error, users prefer to work more quickly.

- When the task is familiar and easily comprehended, users prefer more rapid action.
- If users have experienced rapid performance previously, they will expect and demand it in future situations.

These informal conjectures need to be qualified and verified. Then a more rigorous cognitive model needs to be developed to accommodate the great diversity in human work styles and in computer-use situations. Practitioners can conduct field tests to measure productivity, error rates, and satisfaction as a function of response times in their application areas.

The experiments described in the following sections are tiles in the mosaic of human performance with computers, but many more tiles are necessary before the fragments form a complete image. Some guidelines have emerged for designers and information-system managers, but local testing and continuous monitoring of performance and satisfaction are still necessary. The remarkable adaptability of computer users means that researchers and practitioners will have to be alert to novel conditions that require revisions of these guidelines.

10.3   Expectations and Attitudes

How long will users wait for the computer to respond before they become annoyed? This simple question has provoked much discussion and several experiments. There is no simple answer to the question; more important, it may be the wrong question to ask.

Related design issues may clarify the question of acceptable response time. For example, how long should users have to wait before they hear a dial tone on a telephone or see a picture on their television? If the cost is not excessive, the frequently mentioned 2-second limit (Miller, 1968) seems appropriate for many tasks. In some situations, however, users expect responses within 0.1 second, such as when turning the wheel of a car; pressing a key on a typewriter, piano, or telephone; or changing channels on a television. Two-second delays in these cases might be unsettling because users have adapted a working style and expectation based on responses within a fraction of a second. In other situations, users are accustomed to longer response times, such as waiting 30 seconds for a red traffic light to turn green, two days for a letter to arrive, or one month for flowers to grow.

The first factor influencing acceptable response time is that people have established expectations based on their past experiences of the time required to complete a given task. If a task is completed more quickly than expected, people will be pleased; but if the task is completed much more quickly than expected, they may become concerned that something is wrong. Similarly, if a task is completed much more slowly than expected, users become concerned or frustrated. Even though people can detect 8-percent changes in a 2- or 4-second response time (Miller, 1968), users apparently do not become concerned until the change is much greater.

Two installers of shared computer systems have reported a problem concerning user expectations with new systems. The first users are delighted because the response is short when the load is light. As the load builds, however, these first users become unhappy because the response time deteriorates. The users who come on later may be satisfied with what they perceive as normal response times. Both installers devised a *response-time choke* by which they could slow down the system when the load was light. This surprising policy makes the response time uniform over time and across users, thus reducing complaints.

Computer-center managers have similar problems with varying response times as new equipment is added or as large projects begin or complete their work. The variation in response time can be disruptive to users who have developed expectations and working styles based on a specific response time. There are also periods within each day when the response time is short, such as at lunch time, or when it is long, such as midmorning or late afternoon. Some users rush to complete a task when response times are short, and as a result they may make more errors. Some workers refuse to work when the response time is slow relative to their expectations.

A second factor influencing response-time expectations is the individual's tolerance for delays. Novice computer users may be willing to wait much longer than are experienced users. In short, there are large variations in what individuals consider acceptable waiting time. These variations are influenced by many factors, such as personality, costs, age, mood, cultural context, time of day, noise, and perceived pressure to complete work. The laid-back web surfer may enjoy chatting with friends while pages appear, but the anxious deadline-fighting journalist may start banging on desks or keys in a vain attempt to push the computer along.

Other factors influencing response-time expectations are the task complexity and the users' familiarity with the task. For simple repetitive tasks that require little problem solving, users want to perform rapidly and are annoyed by delays of more than a few tenths of a second. For complex problems, users can plan ahead during longer response times and will perform well even as response time grows. Users are highly adaptive and can change their working style to accommodate different response times. This factor was found in early studies of batch-programming environments and in recent studies of interactive-system usage. If delays are long, users will seek alternate strategies that reduce the number of interactions, whenever possible. They will fill in the long delays by performing other tasks, daydream-ing, or planning ahead in their work. These long delays may or may not increase error rates when they are in the range of 3 to 15 seconds, but they probably will increase error rates when they are above 15 seconds if people must remain at the keyboard waiting for a response. Even if diversions are available, dissatisfaction grows with longer response times.

An increasing number of tasks place high demands on rapid system per-formance; examples are user-controlled three-dimensional animations, flight simulations, graphic design, and dynamic queries for information visualiza-tion. In these applications, users are continuously adjusting the input con-trols, and they expect changes to appear with no perceived delay—that is, within less than 100 milliseconds.

In summary, three primary factors influence users' expectations and atti-tudes regarding response time:

1. Previous experiences
2. Individual personality differences
3. Task differences

Experimental results show interesting patterns of behavior for specific backgrounds, individuals, and tasks, but it is difficult to distill a simple set of conclusions. Several experiments attempted to identify acceptable waiting times by allowing subjects to press a key if they thought that the waiting time was too long. Subjects who could shorten the response time in future interac-tions took advantage of that feature as they became more experienced. They forced response times for frequent commands down to well below 1 second. It seems appealing to offer users a choice in the pace of the interaction. Video-game designers recognize the role of user-controlled pace setting and the increased challenge from fast pacing. Differing desires open opportuni-ties to charge premiums for faster service; for example, many World Wide Web users are willing to pay extra for faster network performance.

In summary, three conjectures emerge:

1. Individual differences are large and users are adaptive. They will work faster as they gain experience, and will change their working strategies as response times change. It may be useful to allow people to set their own pace of interaction.
2. For repetitive tasks, users prefer and will work more rapidly with short response times.
3. For complex tasks, users can adapt to working with slow response times with no loss of productivity, but their dissatisfaction increases as response times lengthen.

10.4   User Productivity

Shorter system response times usually lead to higher productivity, but in some situations users who receive long system response times can find clever shortcuts or ways to do concurrent processing to reduce the effort and time to accomplish a task. Working too quickly may lead to errors that reduce productivity.

In computing, just as in driving, there is no general rule about whether the high-speed highway or the slower, clever shortcut is better. The designer must survey each situation carefully to make the optimal choice. The choice is not critical for the occasional excursion, but becomes worthy of investigation when the frequency is great. When computers are used in high-volume situations, more effort can be expended in discovering the proper response time for a given task and set of users. It should not be surprising that a new study must be conducted when the tasks and users change, just as a new route evaluation must be done for each trip.

10.4.1   Repetitive tasks

The nature of the task has a strong influence on whether changes in response time alter user productivity. A repetitive control task involves monitoring a display and issuing commands in response to changes in the display. Although the operator may be trying to understand the underlying process, the basic activities are to respond to a change in the display, to issue commands, and then to see whether the commands produce the desired effect. When there is a choice among commands, the problem becomes more interesting and the operator tries to pick the optimal command in each situation. With shorter system response times, the operator picks up the pace of the system and works more quickly, but decisions on commands may be less than optimal. On the other hand, with short response times, the penalty for a poor choice may be small because it may be easy to try another command. In fact, operators may learn to use the system more quickly with short system response times because they can explore alternatives more easily.

Goodman and Spence (1981) studied a control task involving multiparameter optimization. The goal was to force "a displayed graph to lie wholly within a defined acceptance region." Operators could adjust five parameters by using lightpen touches, thus altering the shape of the graph. There were response times of 0.16, 0.72, or 1.49 seconds. Each of the 30 subjects worked at each of the three response times in this repeated-measures experiment.

The total times to solution (just over 500 seconds) and the total user think time (around 300 seconds) were the same for the 0.16- and 0.72-second treatments. The 1.49-second treatment led to a 50-percent increase in solution time and to a modest increase in user think time. In this case, reducing the response time to less than one second was beneficial in terms of human productivity. A pilot study of this task with six subjects provided further support for the productivity benefit of short response time: A response time of three seconds drove the solution time up to more than 1200 seconds.

In a data-entry task, users adopted one of three strategies, depending on the response time (Teal and Rudnicky, 1992). With response times under one second, users worked automatically without checking whether the system was ready for the next data value. This behavior resulted in numerous anticipation errors, in which the users typed data values before the system could accept those values. With response times above two seconds, users monitored the display carefully to make sure that the prompt appeared before they type. In the middle ground of one to two seconds, users paced themselves and waited an appropriate amount of time before attempting to enter data values.

10.4.2   Problem-solving tasks

When complex problem solving is required and many approaches to the solution are possible, users will adapt their work style to the response time. A demonstration of this effect emerged from early studies (Grossberg et al., 1976) using four experienced subjects doing complex matrix manipulations. The response time means were set at 1, 4, 16, and 64 seconds for commands that generated output or an error message. Nonoutput commands were simply accepted by the system. Each subject performed a total of 48 tasks of approximately 15 minutes duration each, distributed across the four response-time treatments.

The remarkable outcome of this study was that the time to solution was invariant with respect to response time! When working with 64-second delays, subjects used substantially fewer output commands and also fewer total commands. Apparently, with long response times, subjects thought carefully about the problem solution, since there were also longer intervals between commands. There were differences across subjects, but all subjects stayed within a limited range of solution times across the four system response times with which they worked.

Although the number of subjects was small, the results are strong in support of the notion that, if possible, users will change their work habits as the response time changes. As the cost in time of an error or an unnecessary output command rose, subjects made fewer errors and issued fewer commands. These results were closely tied to the study's complex, intellectually demanding task, for which there were several solutions.

Productivity with statistical problem-solving tasks was also found to be constant despite response-time changes over the range of 5.0 to 0.1 seconds (Martin and Corl, 1986). The same study with 24 regular users found linear productivity gains for simple data-entry tasks. The simpler and more habitual the task, the greater the productivity benefit of a short response time.

Barber and Lucas (1983) studied 100 professional circuit-layout clerks who assigned telephone equipment in response to service requests. Ten or more interactions were needed to complete each of these complex tasks. Data were collected about normal performance for 12 days with an average response time of 6 seconds. Then, 29 clerks were given response times averaging 14 seconds for 4 days. When the response time was as short as 4 seconds, there were 49 errors out of 287 transactions. As the response time increased to 12 seconds, the errors decreased to 16 of 222 transactions; and as the response time increased further to 24 seconds, the errors *increased* to 70 of 151 transactions (Fig. 10.3). The volume of transactions was recorded during sessions of 200 minutes. For this complex task, the data reveal that the lowest error rate occurred with a 12-second response time. With shorter response times, the workers made hasty decisions; with longer response times, the frustration of waiting burdened short-term memory. It is important to recognize that the number of productive transactions (total minus errors) increased almost linearly with reductions in response time. Apparently, reduced error rates were not sufficient to increase satisfaction, since subjective preference was consistently in favor of the shorter response time.

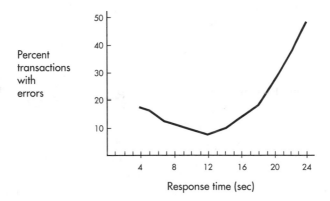

Figure 10.3

Error rates as a function of response time for complex telephone-circuit–layout task by Barber and Lucas (1983). Although error rates were lowest with long response times (12 seconds), productivity increased with shorter times because the system could detect errors and thus users could rapidly correct them.

10.4.3   Summary

It is clear that users pick up the pace of the system to work more quickly with shorter response times and that they consistently prefer a faster pace. The profile of error rates at shorter response times varies across tasks. Not surprisingly, each user-task situation appears to have an optimal pace—response times that are shorter or longer than this pace lead to increased errors. The ease of error recovery and the damage caused by an error must be evaluated carefully by managers who are choosing the optimal pace of interaction. If they desire higher throughput of work, then they must pay attention to minimizing the cost and delay of error recovery. In short, the optimal response time may be longer than the minimum possible response time.

10.5   Variability

People are willing to pay substantial amounts of money to reduce the variability in their life. The entire insurance industry is based on the reduction of present pleasures, through the payment of premiums, to reduce the severity of a future loss. Most people appreciate predictable behavior that lessens the anxiety of contemplating unpleasant surprises.

When they use computers, users cannot see into the machine to gain reassurance that the commands are being executed properly, but the response time can provide a clue. If users come to expect a response time of three seconds for a common operation, they may become apprehensive if this operation takes 0.5 or 15 seconds. Such extreme variation is unsettling and should be prevented or acknowledged by the system, with some indicator for unusually fast response, and a progress report for an unusually slow response.

The more difficult issue is the effect of modest variations in response time. As discussed earlier, Miller (1968) raised this issue and reported that 75 percent of subjects tested could perceive 8-percent variations in time for periods in the interval of two to four seconds. These results prompted some designers to suggest restrictive rules for variability of response time.

Since it may not be technically feasible to provide a fixed short response time (such as one second) for all commands, several researchers have suggested that the time be fixed for classes of commands. Many commands could have a fixed response time of less than one second, other commands could take four seconds, and still other commands could take 12 seconds. Experimental results suggest that modest variations in response time do not severely affect performance. Users are apparently capable of adapting to varying situations, although some of them may become frustrated when performing certain tasks.

Goodman and Spence (1981) attempted to measure performance changes in a problem-solving situation (a similar situation was used in their earlier experiment, described in Section 10.4.1). Subjects used lightpen touches to manipulate a displayed graph. The mean response time was set at 1.0 second with three levels of variation: quasinormal distributions with standard deviations of 0.2, 0.4, and 0.8 seconds. The minimum response time was 0.2 seconds, and the maximum response time was 1.8 seconds. Goodman and Spence found no significant performance changes as the variability was increased. The time to solution and the profile of command use were unchanged. As the variability increased, they did note that subjects took more advantage of fast responses by entering subsequent commands immediately, balancing the time lost in waiting for slower responses.

Similar results were found by researchers using a mean response time of 10 seconds and three variations: standard deviations of 0.0, 2.5, and 7.5 seconds (Bergman et al., 1981). The authors concluded that an increase in variability of response time "does not have any negative influence on the subject's performance on a rather complicated problem-solving task."

Two studies detected modest increases in user think time as variability increased. Butler (1983) studied six subjects who worked for two hours at each of 10 response-time conditions: the means were 2, 4, 8, 16, and 32 seconds, each with low and high variability. Subjects performed simple data-entry tasks but had to wait for the system response before they could proceed. Accuracy and rate of typing were unaffected by the duration or variability of response time. User think time increased with the duration and with variability of the computer's response time. Butler describes a second experiment with a more complex task whose results are similar.

The physiological effect of response-time variability was studied by Kuhmann and colleagues (1987), who found no dramatic effects between constant and variable treatments for detection and correction tasks with 68 subjects. Constant response times of two and eight seconds were compared with variable response times ranging over 0.5 to 5.75 seconds (mean two seconds) and 2.0 to 22.81 seconds (mean eight seconds). Statistically significantly higher error rates, higher systolic blood pressure, and more pronounced pain symptoms were found with shorter response times. However, no significant differences were found for response-time variability at either the short or long response times. Similarly, Emurian (1991) compared an 8-second constant response time to a variable response time ranging from one to 30 seconds (mean eight seconds). His 10 subjects solved 50 database queries with 45-second time limits. Although diastolic blood pressure and masseter (jaw-muscle) tension did increase when compared to resting baseline values, there were no significant differences in these physiological measures between constant and variable treatments.

In summary, modest variations in response time (plus or minus 50 percent of the mean) appear to be tolerable and to have little effect on performance.

As the variability grows, performance speed may decrease some. Frustration emerges only if delays are unusually long—at least twice the anticipated time. Similarly, anxiety about an erroneous command may emerge only if the response time is unusually short—say, less than one-quarter of the anticipated time. But even with extreme changes, users appear to be adaptable enough to complete their tasks.

It may be useful to slow down unexpected fast responses to avoid surprising the user. This proposal is controversial but would affect only a small fraction of user interactions. Certainly, designers should make a serious effort to avoid extremely slow responses, or, if responses must be slow, should give users information to indicate progress toward the goal. One graphics system displays a large clock ticking backward; the output appears only when the clock has ticked down to zero. Many print-spooling programs and document-formatting systems display the page numbers to indicate progress and to confirm that the computer is at work productively on the appropriate document.

10.6   Practitioner's Summary

Computer-system response time and display rate are important determinants of user productivity, error rates, working style, and satisfaction (Box 10.1). In most situations, shorter response times (less than one second) lead to higher productivity. For mouse actions, direct manipulation, typing feedback, and animation, even faster performance is necessary (less than 0.1 second). Satisfaction generally increases as the response time decreases, but there may be a danger from stress induced by a rapid pace. As users pick up the pace of the system, they may make more errors; if these errors are detected and corrected easily, then productivity will generally increase. If errors are hard to detect or are excessively costly, then a moderate pace may be most beneficial.

Designers can determine the optimal response time for a specific application and user community by measuring the change in productivity associated with, cost of errors resulting from, and cost of providing short response times. Managers must be alert to changes in work style as the pace quickens; productivity is measured by correctly completed tasks rather than by interactions per hour. Novices may prefer a slower pace of interaction. When technical feasibility or costs prevent response times of less than one second, each class of commands can be assigned to a response-time category—for example, two to four seconds, four to eight seconds, eight to 12 seconds, and more than 12 seconds. Modest variations around the mean response time are acceptable, but large variations (less than one-quarter of the mean or more than twice the mean) should be accompanied by an informative message. An alternative approach is to slow down overly rapid responses and thus to avoid the need for a message.

Box 10.1

Response-time guidelines.

- Users prefer shorter response times
- Longer response times (> 15 secs) are disruptive
- Users change usage profile with response time
- Shorter response time leads to shorter user think time
- A faster pace may increase productivity, but may increase error rates
- Error recovery ease and time influence optimal response time
- Response time should be appropriate to the task:
  - Typing, cursor motion, mouse selection: 50–150 milliseconds
  - Simple frequent tasks: 1 second
  - Common tasks: 2–4 seconds
  - Complex tasks: 8–12 seconds
- Users should be advised of long delays
- Modest variability in response time is acceptable
- Unexpected delays may be disruptive
- Empirical tests can help to set suitable response times

10.7 Researcher's Agenda

In spite of the experiments described here, many unanswered questions remain. The taxonomy of issues provides a framework for research, but a finer taxonomy of tasks, of relevant cognitive-style differences, and of work situations is needed if we are to specify adequate experimental controls. Next, a sound theory of problem-solving behavior with computers is necessary if we are to generate useful hypotheses.

Doherty and Kelisky (1979) suggest that longer response times lead to slower work, more emotional upset, and more errors. This statement appears to be true with long response times of more than 15 seconds, but there is little evidence to support the claim that fewer errors are made with short response times of less than one second. Barber and Lucas (1983) found a U-shaped error curve, with the lowest error rate at a 12-second response time. It would be productive to study error rates as a function of response time for a range of tasks and users.

It is understandable that error rates vary with response times, but how else are users' work styles affected? Do users issue more commands as response times shorten? Grossberg et al. (1976) found this result for a complex task with extremely long response times of up to 64 seconds, but there is little evidence with more common tasks and speeds. Does the profile of commands shift to a smaller set of more familiar commands as the response time shortens? Does the session length increase or decrease with response-time increases? Are workers more willing to pursue higher-quality results when they are given shorter response times that enable multiple quick changes?

Many other questions are worthy of investigation. When technical feasibility prevents short responses, can users be satisfied by diversionary tasks, or are progress reports sufficient? Do warnings of long responses relieve anxiety or simply further frustrate users?

Operating-system implementers can also contribute by providing better user control over response time. It should be possible for a user-interface designer to specify upper and lower limits for response time for each command. It is still difficult on large shared computers to specify a response time, even on an experimental basis.

World Wide Web Resources   WWW

Response time issues have a modest presence on the net, although the issue of long network delays gets discussed frequently.

http://www.aw.com/DTUI

References

Barber, Raymond E. and Lucas, H. C., System response time, operator productivity and job satisfaction, *Communications of the ACM*, 26, 11 (November 1983), 972–986.

Bergman, Hans, Brinkman, Albert, and Koelega, Harry S., System response time and problem solving behavior, *Proc. of the Human Factors Society—Twenty-fifth Annual Meeting*, Rochester, NY (October 12–16, 1981), 749–753.

Butler, T. W., Computer response time and user performance, ACM CHI '83 Proceedings: Human Factors in Computer Systems (December 1983), 56–62.

Carbonell, J. R., Elkind, J. I., and Nickerson, R. S., On the psychological importance of time in a timesharing system, *Human Factors*, 10, 2 (1968), 135–142.

Doherty, W. J. and Kelisky, R. P., Managing VM/CMS systems for user effectiveness, *IBM Systems Journal*, 18, 1, (1979) 143–163.

Emurian, Henry H., Physiological responses during data retrieval: Consideration of constant and variable system response times, *Computers and Human Behavior*, 7 (1991), 291–310.

Emurian, Henry H., Human–computer interactions: Are there adverse health consequences?, *Computers and Human Behavior*, 5, (1989), 265–275.

Goodman, T. J., and Spence, R., The effect of computer system response time variability on interactive graphical problem solving, *IEEE Transactions on Systems, Man, and Cybernetics*, 11, 3 (March 1981), 207–216.

Goodman, Tom and Spence, Robert, The effects of potentiometer dimensionality, system response time, and time of day on interactive graphical problem solving, *Human Factors*, 24, 4 (1982), 437–456.

Grossberg, Mitchell, Wiesen, Raymond A., and Yntema, Douwe B., An experiment on problem solving with delayed computer responses, *IEEE Transactions on Systems, Man, and Cybernetics*, 6, 3 (March 1976), 219–222.

Kuhmann, Werner, Experimental investigation of stress-inducing properties of system response times, *Ergonomics*, 32, 3 (1989), 271–280.

Kuhmann, Werner, Boucsein, Wolfram, Schaefer, Florian, and Alexander, Johanna, Experimental investigation of psychophysiological stress-reactions induced by different system response times in human–computer interaction, *Ergonomics*, 30, 6 (1987), 933–943.

Lambert, G. N., A comparative study of system response time on program developer productivity, *IBM System Journal*, 23, 1 (1984), 36–43.

Long, John, Effects of delayed irregular feedback on unskilled and skilled keying performance, *Ergonomics*, 19, 2 (1976), 183–202.

Martin, G. L. and Corl, K. G., System response time effects on user productivity, *Behaviour and Information Technology*, 5, 1 (1986), 3–13.

Meyer, Joachim, Bitan, Yuval, and Shinar, David, Displaying a boundary in graphic and symbolic "wait" displays: Duration estimates and users' preferences, *International Journal of Human–Computer Interaction*, 7, 3 (1995), 273–290.

Meyer, Joachim, Shinar, David, Bitan, Yuval, and Leiser, David, Duration estimates and users' preferences in human–computer interaction, *Ergonomics*, 39, (1996), 46–60.

Miller, G. A., The magical number seven, plus or minus two: Some limits on our capacity for processing information, *Psychological Science*, 63, (1956), 81–97.

Miller, Robert B., Response time in man–computer conversational transactions, *Proceedings Spring Joint Computer Conference 1968*, 33, AFIPS Press, Montvale, NJ (1968), 267–277.

Neal, Alan S., Time interval between keystrokes, records, and fields in data entry with skilled operators, *Human Factors*, 19, 2 (1977), 163–170.

Shneiderman, Ben, *Software Psychology: Human Factors in Computer and Information Systems*, Little, Brown, Boston (1980).

Teal, Steven L. and Rudnicky, Alexander I., A performance model of system delay and user strategy selection, *Proc. CHI '92 Human Factors in Computer Systems*, ACM, New York (1992), 295–305.

Wickelgren, Wayne A., Speed-accuracy tradeoff and information processing dynamics, *Acta Psychologica*, 41, (1977), 67–85.

Mark Kostabi, *Update*, 1996

Presentation Styles: Balancing Function and Fashion

Words are sometimes sensitive instruments of precision with which delicate operations may be performed and swift, elusive truths may be touched.

Helen Merrell Lynd, *On Shame and the Search for Identity*

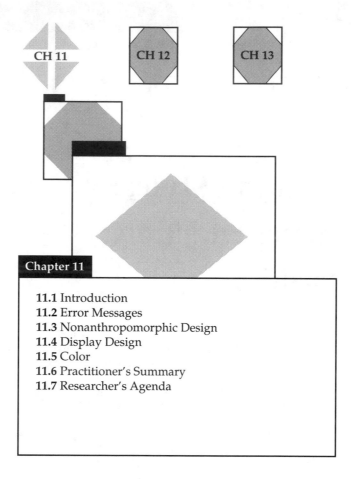

CH 11

CH 12

CH 13

Chapter 11

11.1 Introduction
11.2 Error Messages
11.3 Nonanthropomorphic Design
11.4 Display Design
11.5 Color
11.6 Practitioner's Summary
11.7 Researcher's Agenda

11.1 Introduction

Interface design has yet to match the high art of architecture or trendiness of clothing design. However, we can anticipate that, as the audience for computers expands, competition over design will heighten. Early automobiles were purely functional and Henry Ford could joke about customers getting any color as long as it was black, but modern car designers have learned to balance function and fashion. This chapter deals with four design matters that are functional issues with many human factors criteria, but that also leave room for varying styles to suit a variety of customers. They are error messages, nonanthropomorphic design, display design, and color.

User experiences with computer-system prompts, explanations, error diagnostics, and warnings play a critical role in influencing acceptance of software systems. The wording of messages is especially important in systems designed for novice users; experts also benefit from improved messages. Messages are sometimes meant to be conversational, as modeled by human–human communication, but this strategy has its limits because people are different from computers and computers are different from people. This fact may be obvious, but a section on nonanthropomorphic design seems necessary to steer designers toward comprehensible, predictable, and controllable interfaces.

Another opportunity for design improvements lies in the layout of information on a display. Cluttered displays may overwhelm even knowledgeable users; but with only modest effort, we can create well-organized information-abundant layouts that reduce search time and increase subjective satisfaction. Large, fast, high-resolution color displays offer many possibilities and challenges for designers. Some guidelines are useful, but there are too many variables and situations to ensure success without repeated trials even by experienced designers.

Recognition of the creative challenge of balancing function and fashion might be furthered by having designers put their names and photos on a title or credits page, just as authors do in a book. Such acknowledgment is common in games and in some educational software, and seems appropriate for all software. Credits provide recognition for good work, and identify the people responsible. Having their name in lights may also encourage designers to work a bit harder, since their identities will be public.

11.2   Error Messages

Normal prompts, advisory messages, and system responses to user actions may influence user perceptions, but the phrasing of error messages or diagnostic warnings is critical. Since errors occur because of lack of knowledge, incorrect understanding, or inadvertent slips, users are likely to be confused, to feel inadequate, and to be anxious. Error messages with an imperious tone that condemns users can heighten anxiety, making it more difficult to correct the error and increasing the chances of further errors. Messages that are too generic, such as WHAT? or SYNTAX ERROR, or that are too obscure, such as FAC RJCT 004004400400 or 0C7, offer little assistance to most users.

These concerns are especially important with respect to novices, whose lack of knowledge and confidence amplify the stress that can lead to a sequence of failures. The discouraging effects of a bad experience in using a computer are not easily overcome by a few good experiences. In some cases, systems are remembered more for what happens when things go wrong than for when things go right. Although these concerns apply most forcefully to novice computer users, experienced users also suffer. Experts in one system or part of a system are still novices in many situations.

Producing a set of guidelines for writing system messages is not an easy task because of differences of opinion and the impossibility of being complete (Dean, 1982). However, explicit guidelines generate discussions and help less experienced designers to produce better systems. Improving the error messages is one of the easiest and most effective ways to improve an existing system. If the software can capture the frequency of errors, then people can focus on fixing the most important messages.

Error-frequency distributions also enable system designers and maintainers to revise error-handling procedures, to improve documentation and training manuals, to alter online help, or even to change the permissible actions. The complete set of messages should be reviewed by peers and managers, tested empirically, and included in user manuals.

Specificity, constructive guidance, positive tone, user-centered style, and appropriate physical format are recommended as the bases for preparing system messages. These guidelines are especially important when the users are novices, but they can benefit experts as well. The phrasing and contents of system messages can significantly affect user performance and satisfaction.

11.2.1 Specificity

Messages that are too general make it difficult for the novice to know what has gone wrong. Simple and condemning messages are frustrating because they provide neither enough information about what has gone wrong nor the knowledge to set things right. The right amount of specificity therefore is important.

Poor	Better
SYNTAX ERROR	Unmatched left parenthesis
ILLEGAL ENTRY	Type first letter: Send, Read, or Drop
INVALID DATA	Days range from 1 to 31
BAD FILE NAME	File names must begin with a letter

Execution-time messages in programming languages should provide the user with specific information about where the problem arose, what objects were involved, and what values were improper. One system for hotel checkin required the desk clerk to enter a 40- to 45-character string containing the name, room number, credit-card information, and so on. If the clerk made a data-entry error, the only message was INVALID INPUT. YOU MUST RETYPE THE ENTIRE RECORD. This led to frustration for users and delays for irritated guests. Interactive systems should be designed to minimize input errors by proper form-fillin strategies (see Chapter 7); when an error occurs, the users should have to repair only the incorrect part.

Systems that offer an error-code number leading to a paragraph-long explanation in a manual are also annoying because the manual may not be available, or consulting it may be disruptive and time consuming. In most cases, system developers can no longer hide behind the claim that printing meaningful messages consumes too many system resources.

11.2.2   Constructive guidance and positive tone

Rather than condemning users for what they have done wrong, messages should, where possible, indicate what users need to do to set things right:

Poor: DISASTROUS STRING OVERFLOW. JOB ABANDONED. (From a well-known compiler-compiler.)

Better: String space consumed. Revise program to use shorter strings or expand string space

Poor: UNDEFINED LABELS (From a FORTRAN compiler.)

Better: Define statement labels before use

Poor: ILLEGAL STA. WRN. (From a FORTRAN compiler.)

Better: RETURN statement cannot be used in a FUNCTION subprogram.

Unnecessarily hostile messages using violent terminology can disturb nontechnical users. An interactive legal-citation–searching system uses this message: FATAL ERROR, RUN ABORTED. A popular operating-system threatens many users with CATASTROPHIC ERROR; LOGGED WITH OPERATOR. There is no excuse for these hostile messages; they can easily be rewritten to provide more information about what happened and what must be done to set things right. Such negative words as ILLEGAL, ERROR, INVALID, or BAD should be eliminated or used infrequently.

It may be difficult for the software writer to create a program that accurately determines what was the user's intention, so the advice to be constructive is often difficult to apply. Some designers argue for automatic error correction, but the disadvantage is that the user may fail to learn proper syntax and may become dependent on alterations that the system makes.

Another approach is to inform the user of the possible alternatives and to let the user decide. A preferred strategy is to prevent errors from occurring (see Section 2.6).

11.2.3   User-centered phrasing

The term *user-centered* suggests that the user controls the system—initiating more than responding. Designers partially accomplish this scenario by avoiding the negative and condemning tone in messages and by being courteous to the user. Prompting messages should avoid such imperative forms as ENTER DATA, and should focus on such user control as READY FOR COMMAND or simply READY.

Brevity is a virtue, but the user should be allowed to control the kind of information provided. Possibly, the standard system message should be less than one line; but, by keying a ?, the user should be able to obtain a few lines of explanation. ?? might yield a set of examples, and ??? might produce explanations of the examples and a complete description. Most application software offer a special HELP button to provide contest-sensitive explanations when the user needs assistance.

Some telephone companies, long used to dealing with nontechnical users, offer this tolerant message: "We're sorry, but we were unable to complete your call as dialed. Please hang up, check your number, or consult the operator for assistance." They take the blame and offer constructive guidance for what to do. A thoughtless programmer might have generated a harsher message: "Illegal telephone number. Call aborted. Error number 583-2R6.9. Consult your user manual for further information."

11.2.4   Appropriate physical format

Although professional programmers have learned to read uppercase-only text, most users prefer and find easier to read mixed uppercase and lowercase messages (Section 11.4). Uppercase-only messages should be reserved for brief, serious warnings. Messages that begin with a lengthy and mysterious code number serve only to remind the user that the designers were insensitive to the user's real needs. If code numbers are needed at all, they might be enclosed in parentheses at the end of a message.

There is disagreement about the optimal placement of messages in a display. One school of thought argues that the messages should be placed on the display near where the problem has arisen. A second opinion is that the messages clutter the display and should be placed in a consistent position on the bottom of the display. The third approach simply pops up a dialog box in the middle of the display, possibly obscuring the relevant part.

Some applications ring a bell or sound a tone when an error has occurred. This alarm can be useful if the operator could miss the error, but can be embarrassing if other people are in the room and is potentially annoying even if the operator is alone. The use of audio signals should be under user control.

The early high-level language Michigan Algorithmic Decoder (MAD) printed out a full-page picture of Alfred E. Neuman if syntactic errors were in the program. Novices enjoyed this playful approach, but after they had accumulated a drawer full of pictures, the portrait became an annoying embarrassment. Designers must walk a narrow path between calling attention to a problem and avoiding embarrassment to the user. Considering the wide range of experience and temperament in users, maybe the best solution is to offer the user control over the alternatives—this approaches coordinates well with the user-centered principle.

11.2.5   Development of effective messages

The designer's intuition can be supplemented by simple, fast, and inexpensive design studies with actual users and several alternative messages. If the project goal is to serve novice users, then ample effort must be dedicated to designing, testing, and implementing the user interface. This commitment must extend to the earliest design stages so that interfaces can be modified in a way that contributes to the production of specific error messages. Messages should be evaluated by several people and tested with suitable subjects (Isa et al., 1983). Messages should appear in user manuals and be given greater visibility. Records should be kept on the frequency of occurrence of each error. Frequent errors should lead to software modifications that provide better error handling, to improved training, and to revisions in user manuals.

Users may remember the one time when they had difficulties with a computer system rather than the 20 times when everything went well. Their strong reaction to problems in using computer systems comes in part from the anxiety and lack of knowledge that novice users have. This reaction may be exacerbated by a poorly designed, excessively complex system; by a poor manual or training experience; or by hostile, vague, or irritating system messages. Improving the messages will not turn a bad system into a good one, but it can play a significant role in improving the user's performance and attitude.

Five controlled experiments explored the influence of error messages on user performance (Shneiderman, 1982). In one study, COBOL syntax error messages were modified, and undergraduate novice users were asked to repair the COBOL statements. Messages with increased specificity generated 28-percent higher repair scores.

Subjects using a text editor with only a ? for an error message made an average of 10.7 errors, but made only 6.1 errors when they switched to an editor offering brief explanatory messages. In another experiment, students corrected 4.1 out of 10 erroneous text-editor commands using the standard system messages. Using improved messages, the experimental group corrected 7.5 out of the 10 commands.

In a study of the comprehensibility of job-control–language error messages from two popular contemporary systems, students scored 2.9 and 3.8 out of 6, whereas students receiving improved messages scored 4.8. Subjective preferences also favored the improved messages.

Mosteller (1981) studied error patterns in IBM's MVS Job Entry Control Language by capturing actual runs in a commercial environment. Analysis of the 2073 errors resulted in specific suggestions for revisions to the error messages, parser, and command language. Remarkably, 513 of the errors were exact retries of the previous runs, confirming concerns over the persistence of errors when messages are poor. As improvements were made to the messages, Mosteller found lower error rates.

These early experiments support the contentions that improving messages can upgrade performance and result in greater job satisfaction. They have led to the following recommendations for system developers (Box 11.1):

1. *Increase attention to message design*   The wording of messages should be considered carefully. Technical writers or copy editors can be consulted about the choice of words and phrasing to improve both clarity and consistency.

2. *Establish quality control* Messages   should be approved by an appropriate quality-control committee consisting of programmers, users, and human-factors specialists. Changes or additions should be monitored and recorded.

3. *Develop guidelines*   Error messages should meet these criteria:
   - *Have a positive tone*   Indicate what must be done, rather than condemning the user for the error. Reduce or eliminate the use of such terms as ILLEGAL, INVALID, ERROR, or WRONG PASSWORD. Try Your password did not match the stored password. Please try again.
   - *Be specific and address the problem in the user's terms*   Avoid the vague SYNTAX ERROR or obscure internal codes. Use variable names and concepts known to the user. Instead of INVALID DATA in an inventory application, try Dress sizes range from 5 to 16.
   - *Place the users in control of the situation*   Provide them with enough information to take action. Instead of INCORRECT COMMAND, try Permissible commands are: SAVE, LOAD, or EXPLAIN.
   - *Have a neat, consistent, and comprehensible format*   Avoid lengthy numeric codes, obscure mnemonics, and cluttered displays.

Writing good messages—like writing good poems, essays, or advertisements—requires experience, practice, and a sensitivity to how the reader

Box 11.1

Error-message guidelines for the end product and for the development process. These guidelines are derived from practical experience and empirical data.

- Product
    - Be as specific and precise as possible.
    - Be constructive: Indicate what the user needs to do.
    - Use a positive tone: Avoid condemnation.
    - Choose user-centered phrasing.
    - Consider multiple levels of messages.
    - Maintain consistent grammatical form, terminology, and abbreviations.
    - Maintain consistent visual format and placement.

- Process
    - Establish a message quality-control group.
    - Include messages in the design phase.
    - Place all messages in a file.
    - Review messages during development.
    - Design the product to eliminate the need for most messages.
    - Carry out acceptance tests.
    - Collect frequency data for each message.
    - Review and revise messages over time.

will react. It is a skill that can be acquired and refined by programmers and designers who are intent on serving the user. However, perfection is impossible and humility is the mark of the true professional.

4. *Carry out usability tests*   System messages should be subjected to a usability test with an appropriate user community to determine whether they are comprehensible. The test could range from a rigorous experiment with realistic situations (for life-critical or high-reliability systems) to an informal reading and review by interested users (for personal computing or low-threat applications). Complex interactive systems that involve thousands of users are never really complete until they are obsolete. Under these conditions, the most effective designs emerge from iterative testing and evolutionary refinement (Chapter 4).

5. *Collect user-performance data*   Frequency counts should be collected for each error condition on a regular basis. If possible, the user's actions

should be captured for a more detailed study. If you know where users run into difficulties, you can then revise the message, improve the training, modify the manual, or change the interface. The error rate per 1000 actions should be used as a metric of system quality and a gauge of how improvements affect performance. An error-counting option is useful for internal systems and can be a marketing feature for software products.

Improved messages will be of the greatest benefit to novice users, and regular users and experienced professionals will also benefit. As examples of excellence proliferate, complex, obscure, and harsh systems will seem increasingly out of place. The crude environments of the past will be replaced gradually by systems designed with the user in mind. Resistance to such a transition should not be allowed to impede progress toward the goal of serving the growing user community.

11.3   Nonanthropomorphic Design

There is a great temptation to have computers "talk" as though they were people. It is a primitive urge that designers often follow, and that children and many adults accept without hesitation (Nass et al., 1994, 1995). Children accept human-like references and qualities for almost any object, from Humpty Dumpty to Tootle the Train. Adults reserve the *anthropomorphic* references for objects of special attraction, such as cars, ships, or computers.

The words and graphics in user interfaces can make important differences in people's perceptions, emotional reactions, and motivations. Attributions of intelligence, autonomy, free will, or knowledge to computers can deceive, confuse, and mislead users. The suggestion that computers can think, know, or understand may give users an erroneous model of how computers work and what the machines' capacities are. Ultimately, the deception becomes apparent, and users may feel poorly treated. Martin (1995/96) carefully traces the media impact of the 1946 ENIAC announcements: "Readers were given hyperbole designed to raise their expectations about the use of the new electronic brains. . . . This engendered premature enthusiasm, which then led to disillusionment and distrust of computers on the part of the public when the new technology did not live up to these expectations."

A second reason for using nonanthropomorphic phrasing is to clarify the differences between people and computers. Relationships with people are different from relationships with computers. Users operate and control computers, but they respect the unique identity and autonomy of individuals. Furthermore, users and designers must accept responsibility for misuse of computers rather than blaming the machine for errors. It is worrisome that, in one study (Friedman, 1995), 24 of 29 computer-science students "attributed aspects of agency—either decision-making and/or intentions—to computers" and six "consistently held computers morally responsible for errors."

A third motivation is that, although an anthropomorphic interface may be attractive to some people, it can be anxiety producing for others. Some people express anxiety about using computers and believe that computers "make you feel dumb." Presenting the computer through the specific functions it offers may be a stronger stimulus to user acceptance than is promoting the fantasy that the computer is a friend, parent, or partner. As users become engaged, the computer becomes transparent, and they can concentrate on their writing, problem solving, or exploration. At the end, they have the experience of accomplishment and mastery, rather than the feeling that some magical machine has done their job for them.

Individual differences in the desire for internal locus of control will be important, but there may be an overall advantage to clearly distinguishing human abilities from computer powers for most tasks and users (Shneiderman, 1995). On the other hand, there are advocates of creating an anthropomorphic computer and of creating lifelike autonomous agents (Laurel, 1990; Maes, 1995). Apple Computer created a videotape in 1987, "The Knowledge Navigator," with a preppie bow-tied young male agent carrying out tasks for an environmental researcher. Some futurists celebrated this vision, but skeptics scorned the scenario as a deception; most viewers, meanwhile, seemed mildly amused. Advocates of anthropomorphic interfaces assume that human–human communication is an appropriate model for human operation of computers. It may be a useful starting point, but I find it hard to understand why some designers pursue the human imitation approach long after it becomes counterproductive. Mature technology has managed to overcome the *obstacle of animism*, which has been a trap for technologists for centuries (Mumford, 1934). A visit to the Museum of Automata in York, England, reveals the ancient sources and persistent fantasies of animated dolls and robotic toys.

Historical precedents of failed anthropomorphic bank tellers (Tillie the Teller, Harvey Wallbanker, BOB (Bank of Baltimore)) or abandoned talking automobiles and soda machines do not seem to register on some designers. The bigger-than-life-sized Postal Buddy was supposed to be cute and friendly while providing several useful automated services, but this pseudo-postal clerk was rejected by users after incurring costs of over $1 billion.

Empirical studies offer further evidence. In an experimental test with 26 college students, the anthropomorphic interface (HI THERE, JOHN! IT'S NICE TO MEET YOU, I SEE YOU ARE READY NOW) was seen as less honest than a mechanistic dialog (PRESS THE ENTER KEY TO BEGIN SESSION) (Quintanar et al., 1982). In this computer-assisted instruction task, subjects took longer with the anthropomorphic design, possibly contributing to the observed improved scores on a quiz, but the students felt less responsible for their performance.

In another study, a stern face and a neutral talking face were compared with a text-only display (Walker et al., 1994). The authors concluded that "incautiously adding human characteristics like face, voice, and facial expressions could make the experience for users worse rather than better." The designers generated the talking faces by texture mapping an image onto a geometric wire frame model to produce a 512×320 pixel face. The lip movements were synchronized with the voice-generation algorithm; the stern expression was produced by contraction of the corrugator muscles in the underlying physical model to pull the inner eyebrows in and down. The 42 experienced users rated the text-only version as statistically significantly more likable, friendly, comfortable, happy, less stiff, and less sad than the talking faces. Subjects also found the questions clearer and were more willing to continue with the text-only versions. Evidence in favor of the faces was that subjects in the face treatments produced fewer invalid answers and wrote lengthier commentaries, especially with the stern face. In a follow-up study to assess willingness to cooperate, subjects "kept their promises as much with a text-only computer as with a person, but less with a more human-like computer" (Kiesler et al., 1996).

A more elaborate computer-generated face (16 muscles and 10 parameters controlling 500 polygons) was compared with a three-dimensional arrow in guiding user attention to moves in a card game (Takeuchi and Naito, 1995). Although the face was appreciated as being "entertaining," the arrow was seen as "useful." The authors noted that "subjects tend to try to interpret facial displays and head behaviors. Such involvement prevents them from concentrating on the game" and led to fewer wins than subjects had in the arrow treatments.

Similar questions arise in the use of value judgments as reinforcement for correct answers in educational software. Our study with 24 third-grade students found that positive reinforcement with value-judgment phrases (EXCELLENT, THAT'S GOOD!, YOU'RE DOING GREAT, and so on) did not improve performance or satisfaction in an arithmetic drill-and-practice lesson. On the other hand, the presence of a simple numerical counter (6 CORRECT 2 INCORRECT) improved learning.

In a study with 36 junior–high-school students conducted by Lori Gay and Diane Lindwarm under my direction, the style of interaction was varied. Students received a computer-assisted instruction session in one of three forms:

1. *I:* HI! I am the computer. I am going to ask you some questions.
2. *You:* You will be answering some questions. You should. . . .
3. *Neutral:* This is a multiple-choice exercise.

Before and after the three sessions at the computer, subjects were asked to describe whether using a computer was "easy" or "hard." Most subjects initially thought that using a computer was "hard" and did not change their opinion. Of the seven who changed their minds, the five who moved toward "hard" were all using the *I* or *neutral* interface. The two subjects who moved toward "easy" were using the *you* interface. Performance measures on the tasks were not significantly different, but anecdotal evidence and the positive shift for the group that used *you* messages warrant further study.

A study of error-message wording found similar results with 49 business-school undergraduates (Resnik and Lammers, 1986). Subjects reported being less confused and nervous with constructive (Use letters only) than with human-like (I don't understand these numbers) or condemning (Numerics illegal) message tones.

These results suggest that anthropomorphic interfaces that use first-person pronouns may be counterproductive because they deceive, mislead, and confuse. It may seem cute on first encounter to be greeted by I am SOPHIE, the sophisticated teacher, and I will teach you to spell correctly. By the second session, however, this approach strikes people as uselessly repetitive; by the third session, it is an annoying distraction from the task.

The alternative for the software designer is to focus on the user and to use third-person singular pronouns or to avoid pronouns altogether; for example,

Poor: I will begin the lesson when you press RETURN.

Better: You can begin the lesson by pressing RETURN.

Better: To begin the lesson, press RETURN.

The *you* form seems preferable for introductory screens; however, once the session is underway, reducing the number of pronouns and words avoids distractions from the task. A travel-reservation task was carried out by 33 students with a simulated natural-language interface using the *I, you,* or *neutral* styles (called *anthropomorphic, fluent,* and *telegraphic* by the authors; Brennan and Ohaeri, 1994). Users' messages mimicked the style of messages they received, leading to lengthier user inputs and longer task completion times in the anthropomorphic treatment. Users did not attribute greater intelligence to the anthropomorphic computer.

Some designers of children's educational software believe that it is appropriate and acceptable to have a fantasy character, such as a teddy bear or busy beaver, serve as a guide through a lesson. A cartoon character can be drawn on the screen and possibly animated, adding visual appeal. Successful software packages such as Reader Rabbit provide support for this position. Unfortunately, cartoon characters were not successful in the heavily promoted, but short-lived, home-computing product from Microsoft called *BOB*. Users could choose from a variety of on-screen characters who spoke in cartoon bubbles with phrases such as: What a team we are, What shall we do next, Ben? and Good job so far, Ben. This style might be accept-able in children's games and educational software, but is probably not acceptable for adults performing meaningful tasks.

A more likely approach is to identify the human author of a lesson or soft-ware package, and to allow that person to speak to the reader, much as tele-vision news announcers speak to the viewer. Instead of making the computer into a person, designers can show identifiable and appropriate personalities. For example, President Clinton might welcome visitors to a web site about the White House, or Bill Gates might provide a greeting for new users of Windows.

Once past these introductions, several styles are possible. One is a contin-uation of the guided-tour metaphor, in which the respected personality introduces segments, but allows users to control the pace, to repeat seg-ments, and to decide when they are ready to move on. This approach works for museum tours, tutorials on software, and certain educational lectures. A second strategy is to support user control by showing an overview of the modules from which users can choose. Users decide how much time to spend visiting parts of museums, browsing a timeline with details of events, or jumping among articles in hyperlinked encyclopedia.

These overviews give users a sense of the magnitude of information avail-able and allow them to see their progress in covering the topics. Overviews also support users' needs for closure and the satisfaction of completely tour-ing the contents. Overviews also offer a comprehensible environment with predictable actions that foster a comforting sense of control. Furthermore, they support the need for replicability of actions (to revisit an appealing or confusing module, or to show it to a colleague) and reversibility to return to a known landmark. By contrast, game designers have long understood the challenge of confusion, hidden controls, and unpredictability, but games are certainly different from most applications. A summary of nonanthropomor-phic guidelines appears in Box 11.2.

11.4   Display Design

For most interactive systems, the displays are a key component to successful designs, and are the source of many lively arguments. Dense or cluttered dis-plays can provoke anger, and inconsistent formats can inhibit performance. The complexity of this issue is suggested by the 162 guidelines for data display offered by Smith and Mosier (1986). This diligent effort (see Box 11.3 for exam-ples) represents progress over the vague guidelines given in earlier reviews. Display design will always have elements of art and require invention, but per-

Box 11.2

Guidelines for avoiding anthropomorphism and building appealing interfaces.

Nonanthropomorphic Guidelines

- Avoid presenting computers as people.
- Choose appropriate humans for introductions or guides.
- Use caution in designing computer-generated human faces or cartoon characters.
- Use cartoon characters in games or children's software, but usually not elsewhere.
- Design comprehensible, predictable, and controllable interfaces.
- Provide user-centered overviews for orientation and closure.
- Do not use "I" when the computer responds to human actions.
- Use "you" to guide users, or just state facts.

ceptual principles are becoming clearer (Tullis, 1988a, 1988b; Tufte, 1990; Marcus, 1992; Galitz, 1994), and theoretical foundations are emerging (Mackinlay, 1986; Casner, 1991; Lohse, 1991), and are being applied in research prototypes (Roth et al., 1994). Innovative information visualizations with user interfaces to support dynamic control is a rapidly emerging theme (Chapter 15).

Designers should begin, as always, with a thorough knowledge of the users' tasks, free from the constraints of display size or available fonts. Effective display designs must provide all the necessary data in the proper sequence to carry out the task. Meaningful groupings of items (with labels suitable to the user's knowledge), consistent sequences of groups, and orderly formats all support task performance. Groups can be surrounded by blank spaces or boxes. Alternatively, related items can be indicated by highlighting, background shading, color, or special fonts. Within a group, orderly formats can be accomplished by left or right justification, alignment on decimal points for numbers, or markers to decompose lengthy fields.

Graphic designers have produced principles suited to print formats, and are now adapting these principles for display design. Mullet and Sano (1995) offer thoughtful advice with examples of good and bad design in commercial systems. They propose six categories of principles that reveal the complexity of the designer's task:

1. *Elegance and simplicity*   Unity, refinement, and fitness
2. *Scale, contrast, and proportion*   Clarity, harmony, activity, and restraint
3. *Organization and visual structure*   Grouping, hierarchy, relationship, and balance

Box 11.3

Samples of the 162 data-display guidelines from Smith and Mosier (1984).

- Ensure that any data that a user needs, at any step in a transaction sequence, are available for display.
- Display data to users in directly usable form; do not require that users convert displayed data.
- Maintain consistent format, for any particular type of data display, from one display to another.
- Use short, simple sentences.
- Use affirmative statements, rather than negative statements.
- Adopt a logical principle by which to order lists; where no other principle applies, order lists alphabetically.
- Ensure that labels are sufficiently close to their data fields to indicate association, yet are separated from their data fields by at least one space.
- Left-justify columns of alphabetic data to permit rapid scanning.
- Label each page in multipaged displays to show its relation to the others.
- Begin every display with a title or header, describing briefly the contents or purpose of the display; leave at least one blank line between the title and the body of the display.
- For size coding, make larger symbols be at least 1.5 times the height of the next-smaller symbol.
- Consider color coding for applications in which users must distinguish rapidly among several categories of data, particularly when the data items are dispersed on the display.
- When you use blink coding, make the blink rate 2 to 5 Hz, with a minimum duty cycle (ON interval) of 50 percent.
- For a large table that exceeds the capacity of one display frame, ensure that users can see column headings and row labels in all displayed sections of the table.
- Provide a means for users (or a system administrator) to make necessary changes to display functions, if data-display requirements may change (as is often the case).

4. *Module and program*   Focus, flexibility, and consistent application
5. *Image and representation*   Immediacy, generality, cohesiveness, and characterization
6. *Style*   Distinctiveness, integrity, comprehensiveness, and appropriateness

This section deals with a fraction of the issues, and offers empirical support for concepts where available.

11.4.1 Field layout

Exploration with a variety of layouts can be a helpful process. These design alternatives should be developed directly on a display screen. An employee record with information about a spouse and children could be displayed crudely as

Poor: TAYLOR, SUSAN034787331WILLIAM TAYLOR
      THOMAS102974ANN082177ALEXANDRA090872

This record may contain the necessary information for a task, but extracting the information will be slow and error-prone. As a first step at improving the format, blanks and separate lines can distinguish fields:

Better: TAYLOR, SUSAN 034787331   WILLIAM TAYLOR
      THOMAS 102974
      ANN 082177
      ALEXANDRA 090872

The children's names can be listed in chronological order, with alignment of the dates. Familiar separators for the dates and the employee's social-security number also aid recognition:

Better: TAYLOR, SUSAN 034-78-7331   WILLIAM TAYLOR
      ALEXANDRA 09-08-72
      THOMAS   10-29-74
      ANN   08-21-77

The reversed order of "last name, first name" for the employee may be desired to highlight the lexicographic ordering in a long file. However, the "first name, last name" order for the spouse is usually more readable. Consistency seems important, so a compromise might be made to produce

Better: SUSAN TAYLOR   034-78-7331   WILLIAM TAYLOR
      ALEXANDRA 09-08-72
      THOMAS   10-29-74
      ANN   08-21-77

For frequent users, this format may be acceptable, since labels have a cluttering effect; for most users, however, labels will be helpful:

Better: Employee: SUSAN TAYLOR Social Security
      Number: 034-78-7331
      Spouse: WILLIAM TAYLOR
      Children: Names   Birthdates
      ALEXANDRA 09-08-72
      THOMAS   10-29-74
      ANN   08-21-77

Lowercase letters have been used for labels, but the coding might be switched with bold face for the contents. The lengthy label for social-security number might be abbreviated if the users are knowledgeable. Indenting the information about children might help to convey the grouping of these repeating fields:

```
Better: EMPLOYEE: Susan Taylor    SSN: 034-78-7331
        SPOUSE: William Taylor
        CHILDREN:
          NAMES       BIRTHDATES
        Alexandra   09-08-72
        Thomas       10-29-74
        Ann          08-21-77
```

Finally, if boxes are available, then an orderly pattern is sometimes more appealing, although it may consume more screen space:

```
Better: ┌──────────────────────────────────────────────┐
        │ EMPLOYEE: Susan Taylor SSN: 034-78-7331      │
        │                                              │
        │ SPOUSE: William Taylor                       │
        ├──────────────────────────────────────────────┤
        │ CHILDREN                                     │
        │ NAMES              BIRTHDATES                │
        ├──────────────────────────────────────────────┤
        │ Alexandra          09-08-72                  │
        │ Thomas             10-29-74                  │
        │ Ann                08-21-77                  │
        └──────────────────────────────────────────────┘
```

Even in this simple example, the possibilities are numerous. In any situation, a variety of designs should be explored. Further improvements could be made with other coding strategies, such as background shading, color, and graphic icons. An experienced graphic designer can be a great benefit to the design team. Pilot testing with prospective users can yield subjective satisfaction scores and objective times to complete tasks plus error rates for a variety of proposed formats.

11.4.2 Empirical results

A few empirical tests of alternative display designs have been conducted. A narrative form (Fig. 11.1a), taken from a telephone-line–testing program, was replaced with a structured form (Fig. 11.1b) (Tullis, 1981). The structured form eliminated unnecessary information, grouped related information, and emphasized the information relevant to the required tasks. After practice in reading these displays, Bell System employees were required to carry out typical tasks. The narrative form required an average of 8.3 seconds per task, whereas the structured form took only 5.0 seconds, resulting in an estimated saving of 79 person-years over the life of the system.

A NASA study with space-shuttle displays demonstrated that improving the data labels, clustering related information, using appropriate indentation and underlining, aligning numeric values, and eliminating extraneous characters could improve performance (Burns et al., 1986). Task times were reduced by 31 percent and error rates by 28 percent for a population of 16 technical and clerical employees at NASA and Lockheed who were unfamiliar with either version. Sixteen experts with the existing system did not perform statistically significantly faster with the improved displays, but they did perform significantly more accurately. A follow-up study validated the benefit of redesign and showed that appropriate highlighting further reduced search times (Donner et al., 1991).

Expert users can deal with dense displays and may prefer these displays because they are familiar with the format and they must initiate fewer actions. Performance times are likely to be shorter with fewer, but denser displays than with more numerous but sparse displays. This improvement will be especially marked if tasks require comparison of information across displays. Systems for stock-market data, air-traffic control, and airline reservations are examples of successful applications that have dense packing, limited labels, and highly coded fields.

In a study of 12 telephone operators, Springer (1987) found that suppressing the presentation of redundant family names in a directory-assistance listing reduced target-location time by 0.8 seconds. She also found that, when the target was in the upper quarter of the display, users found it more quickly if the screen were only one-quarter full, as opposed to one-half full or completely full. This result suggests that screen contents should contain only task-relevant information, and that extraneous information does slow performance.

In another study, 110 nurses were shown laboratory reports of blood tests in the standard commercial format of three screens, in a compressed

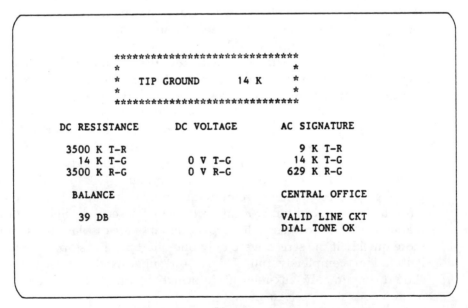

```
   TEST RESULTS     SUMMARY: GROUND

   GROUND, FAULT T-G
   3 TERMINAL DC RESISTANCE
      >  3500.00 K OHMS T-R
      =     14.21 K OHMS T-G
      >  3500.00 K OHMS R-G
   3 TERMINAL DC VOLTAGE
      =      0.00 VOLTS  T-G
      =      0.00 VOLTS  R-G
   VALID AC SIGNATURE
   3 TERMINAL AC RESISTANCE
      =      8.82 K OHMS T-R
      =     14.17 K OHMS T-G
      =    628.52 K OHMS R-G
   LONGITUDINAL BALANCE POOR
      =     39     DB
   COULD NOT COUNT RINGERS DUE TO
      LOW RESISTANCE
   VALID LINE CKT CONFIGURATION
   CAN DRAW AND BREAK DIAL TONE
```

(a)

```
     ********************************
     *                              *
     *    TIP GROUND       14 K      *
     *                              *
     ********************************

   DC RESISTANCE       DC VOLTAGE       AC SIGNATURE

   3500 K T-R                              9 K T-R
     14 K T-G          0 V T-G           14 K T-G
   3500 K R-G          0 V R-G          629 K R-G

     BALANCE                            CENTRAL OFFICE

     39 DB                              VALID LINE CKT
                                        DIAL TONE OK
```

(b)

Figure 11.1

Two versions of screens in a Bell Laboratories study (Tullis, 1981). (a) The narrative format. (b) The structured format.

two-screen version, and in a densely packed one-screen version (Staggers. 1993). Search times dropped in half (approximately) over the five trial blocks for novice and experienced nurses, demonstrating a strong learning effect. The dramatic performance result was that search times were longest on the three-screen version (9.4 seconds per task) compared to the densely packed one-screen version (5.3 seconds per task) (Fig. 11.2). The high cost of turning pages and of reorienting to the new material appears to be far more destructive of concentration than scanning dense displays. Accuracy and subjective satisfaction were not significantly different across the three versions.

Every guideline document implores designers to preserve consistent location, structure, and terminology across displays. Supportive evidence for consistent location comes from a study of 40 inexperienced computer users of a menu system (Teitelbaum and Granda, 1983). The position of the title, page number, topic heading, instruction line, and entry area were varied across displays for one-half of the subjects, whereas the other half saw constant positions. Mean response time to questions about these items for subjects in the varying condition was 2.54 seconds, but was only 1.47 seconds for those seeing constant positions. A student project with 60 experienced computer users showed similar benefits from consistent placement, size, and color of buttons in GUIs.

Sequences of displays should be similar throughout the system for similar tasks, but exceptions will certainly occur. Within a sequence, users should be offered some sense of how far they have come and how far they have to go to reach the end. It should be possible to go backward in a sequence to correct errors, to review decisions, or to try alternatives.

11.4.3   Display-complexity metrics

Although knowledge of the users' tasks and abilities is the key to designing effective screen displays, an objective, automatable metric of screen complexity is an attractive aid. After a thorough review of the literature, Tullis (1988a) developed four task-independent metrics for alphanumeric displays:

1. *Overall density*   Number of filled character spaces as a percentage of total spaces available

2. *Local density*   Average number of filled character spaces in a five-degree visual angle around each character, expressed as a percentage of available spaces in the circle and weighted by distance from the character

Low Density Screens

```
Patient Laboratory Inquiry    Large University Medical Center    Pg 1 of 3

Robinson, Christopher  #XXX-20-4627  Unit: 5E, 5133D  M/13  Ph:301-XXX-5885

       <CBC>      Result      Normal  Range      Units
       ---------------------------------------------------
11/20  Wbc        5.0         4.8  -  10.8       th/cumm
22:55  Rbc        4.78        4.7  -   6.1       m/cumm
       Hgb       12.8        14.0  -  18.0       g/dL
       Hct       37.9        42.0  -  52.0       %
       Plt      163.0       130.0  - 400.0       th/cumm
       Mcv       88.5        82.0  - 101.0       fL
       Mch       30.6        27.0  -  34.0       picogms
       Mchc      34.6        32.0  -  36.0       g/dL
       Rdw       14.5        11.5  -  14.5       %
       Mpv        9.3         7.4  -  10.4       fL
       ---------------------------------------------------
       Key:   * = abnormal
                                               PgDn for more


Patient Laboratory Inquiry    Large University Medical Center    Pg 2 of 3

Robinson, Christopher  #XXX-20-4627  Unit: 5E, 5133D  M/13  Ph:301-XXX-5885

       <DIFF>     Result      Norm Range      Unit
       ---------------------------------------------------
11/20  Segs        35        34  - 75          %
22:55  Bands        5         0  -  9          %
       Lymphs      33        10  - 49          %
       Monos       33         2  - 14          %
       Eosino       5         0  -  8          %

       Baso         2         0  -  2          %
       Atyplymph   20         0  -  0          %
       Meta         0         0  -  0          %
       Myleo        0         0  -  0          %
       Platelets(estimated)                  adeq
       ---------------------------------------------------
       Key:   * = Abnormal
                                               PgDn for more


Patient Laboratory Inquiry    Large University Medical Center    Pg 3 of 3

Robinson, Christopher  #XXX-20-4627  Unit: 5E, 5133D  M/13  Ph:301-XXX-5885

11/20  22:55

<MORPHOLOGY     Macrocytosis  1+   Basophilic Stippling 1+   Toxic Gran Occ
Hypochromia 1+  Polychromasia 1+   Target Cells         3+   Normocytic  No
Key: * = Abnormal Priority:  Routine        Acc#: 122045-015212
Ordered by: Holland, Daniel on 10/22/91, 10:00      Ord#: 900928-HH1131
   Personal Data  -  PRIVACY ACT OF 1974  (PL  93-579)
      End of report
```

Figure 11.2

In a study with 110 nurses, results showed an average task time of 9.4 seconds with the low-density version, versus 5.3 seconds with the high-density version (Staggers, 1993).

High Density Screen

```
Patient Laboratory Inquiry        Large University Medical Center      Pg 1 of 1

Robinson, Christopher    #XXX-20-4627   Unit: 5E, 5133D    M/13   Ph:301-XXX-5885

         <CBC>    Result   Normal Range    Units    <DIFF>    Result   Norm Range    Unit
         --------------------------------------------------------------------------------
10/23    Wbc       5.0      4.8 -  10.8   th/cumm   Segs       40      34 - 74        %
0600     Rbc       4.78     4.7 -   6.1   m/cumm    Bands       5       0 -  9        %
         Hgb      15.1     14.0 -  18.0   g/dL      Lymphs     33      10 - 49        %
         Hct      47.9     42.0 -  52.0     %       Monos      10       2 - 14        %
         Plt     163.0    130.0 - 400.0   th/cumm   Eosino      5       0 -  8        %
         Mcv      88.5     82.0 - 101.0    fL       Baso        2       2 -  2        %
         Mch      30.6     27.0 -  34.0   picogms   Atyplymph   0       0 -  0        %
         Mchc     34.6     32.0 -  36.0   g/dL      Meta        0       0 -  0        %
         Rdw      14.5     11.5 -  14.5     %       Myelo       0       0 -  0        %
         Mpv       8.3      7.4 -  10.4    fL                  Plt    (estm)        adeq
         --------------------------------------------------------------------------------
<MORPHOLOGY        Macrocytosis  1+    Basophilic Stippling  1+    Toxic Gran  Occ
Hypochromia 1+     Polychromasia 1+    Target Cells          3+    Normocytic  No

Key: * = Abnormal Priority:   Routine       Acc#: 122045-015212
Ordered by:   Holland, Daniel on 10/22/91, 10:00        Ord#: 900928-HH1131
   Personal Data   -   PRIVACY ACT OF 1974   (PL  93-579)
```

Figure 11.2 *(continued)*

3. *Grouping* (1)   Number of groups of "connected" characters, where a connection is any pair of characters separated by less than twice the mean of the distances between each character and its nearest neighbor; (2) average visual angle subtended by groups, and weighted by number of characters in the group

4. *Layout complexity*   Complexity, as defined in information theory, of the distribution of horizontal and vertical distances of each label and data item from a standard point on the display

The argument for local density emerges from studies of visual perception indicating that concentration is focused in a five-degree visual angle. At normal viewing distances from displays, this area translates into a circle approximately 15 characters wide and seven characters high. Lower local and overall densities should yield easier-to-read displays. The grouping metric was designed to yield an objective, automatable value that assesses the number of clusters of fields on a display. Typically, clusters are formed by characters that are separated by no more than one intervening space horizontally and that are on adjacent lines. Layout complexity measures the variety of shapes that confront the user on a display. Neat blocks of fields that start in the same column will have a lower layout complexity. These metrics do not account for coding techniques, uppercase versus lowercase characters, continuous text, graphics, or multidisplay issues.

Ten Bell Laboratories employees did motel- and airline-information retrieval tasks on 520 different displays in a variety of formats (Fig. 11.3). Performance times and subjective evaluations were collected to generate a predictive equation. The efficacy of the predictor equations for performance times and subjective ratings were validated in a second study, in which 14 Bell Laboratories employees did author- and book-information retrieval tasks on 150 displays using 15 different display formats (Fig. 11.4). Correlations between predicted and actual values were 0.80 for search times and 0.79 for subjective ratings.

This impressive result is encouraging; however, the metrics require a computer program to do the computations on the alphanumeric-only displays, and they do not include coding techniques, user-experience levels, or multidisplay considerations. Tullis is cautious in interpreting the results and emphasizes that displays that optimize search times do not necessarily optimize subjective ratings. Grouping of items led to fast performance, but high subjective ratings were linked to low local density and low layout complexity. A simple interpretation of these results is be that effective display designs contain a middle number of (six to 15) groups that are neatly laid out, surrounded by blanks, and similarly structured. This conclusion is a satisfying confirmation of a principle that, when stated, seems intuitively obvious, but has not emerged explicitly in the numerous guidelines documents. Further study of human visual search strategies would be helpful in preparing design guidelines (Treisman, 1982).

A more accurate prediction of performance is likely to come with metrics that integrate task frequencies and sequences. Sears' (1993) developed a task-dependent metric called *layout appropriateness* to assess whether the spatial layout is in harmony with the users' tasks (Fig. 11.5). If users can accomplish frequent tasks by moving through a display in a top-to-bottom pattern, then faster performance is likely, compared to that with a layout that requires numerous jumps around widely separated parts of the display. Layout appropriateness is a widget-level metric that deals with buttons, boxes, and lists. Designers specify the sequences of selections that users make and the frequencies for each sequence. Then, the given layout of widgets is evaluated by how well it matches the tasks. An optimal layout that minimizes visual scanning can be produced, but since it may violate user expectations about positions of fields, the designers must make the final layout decisions.

Layouts in which related information was clustered were found to benefit users when the cognitive load on working memory was large. Accuracy increased when related items were clustered, thus reducing the scanning needed to locate distant items (Vincow and Wickens, 1993).

```
To: Atlanta, GA

    Departs    Arrives    Flight

Asheville, NC          First: $92.57   Coach: $66.85
    7:20a     8:05a      PI 299
   10:10a    10:55a      PI 203
    4:20p     5:00p      PI 259

Austin, TX             First: $263.00  Coach: $221.00
    8:15a    11:15a      EA 530
    8:40a    11:39a      DL 212
    2:00p     5:00p      DL 348
    7:15p    11:26p      DL 1654

Baltimore, MD          First: $209.00  Coach: $167.00
    7:00a     8:35a      DL 1767
    7:50a     9:32a      EA 631
    8:45a    10:20a      DL 1610
   11:15a    12:35p      EA 147
    1:35p     3:10p      DL 1731
    2:35p     4:16p      EA 141
```

(a)

```
To: Knoxville, TN
Atlanta, GA  Dp: 9:28a  Ar: 10:10a  Flt: DL 1704  1st: 97.00  Coach: 86.00
Atlanta, GA  Dp: 12:28p Ar: 1:10p   Flt: DL 152   1st: 97.00  Coach: 86.00
Atlanta, GA  Dp: 4:58p  Ar: 5:40p   Flt: DL 418   1st: 97.00  Coach: 86.00
Atlanta, GA  Dp: 7:41p  Ar: 8:25p   Flt: DL 1126  1st: 97.00  Coach: 86.00
Chicago, Ill.  Dp: 1:45p  Ar: 5:39p  Flt: AL 58   1st: 190.00 Coach: 161.00
Chicago, Ill.  Dp: 6:30p  Ar: 9:35p  Flt: DL 675  1st: 190.00 Coach: 161.00
Chicago, Ill.  Dp: 6:50p  Ar: 9:55p  Flt: RC 398  1st: 190.00 Coach: 161.00
Cincinnati, OH  Dp: 12:05p Ar: 1:10p  Flt: FW 453  1st: 118.00 Coach: 66.85
Cincinnati, OH  Dp: 5:25p  Ar: 6:30p  Flt: FW 455  1st: 118.00 Coach: 66.85
Dallas, TX  Dp: 5:55p  Ar: 9:56p  Flt: AL 360  1st: 365.00 Coach: 215.00
Dayton, OH  Dp: 11:20a  Ar: 1:10p  Flt: FW 453  1st: 189.00 Coach: 108.00
Dayton, OH  Dp: 4:40  Ar: 6:30p  Flt: FW 455  1st: 189.00 Coach: 108.00
Detroit, Mich.  Dp: 9:10a  Ar: 1:10p  Flt: FW 453  1st: 183.00 Coach: 106.00
Detroit, Mich.  Dp: 2:35p  Ar: 6:30p  Flt: FW 455  1st: 183.00 Coach: 106.00
```

(b)

Figure 11.3

Two versions of screens from the first experiment by Tullis (1984). (a) A structured format that leads to superior performance and preference. (b) Unstructured format. The results of this experiment led to predictive equations.

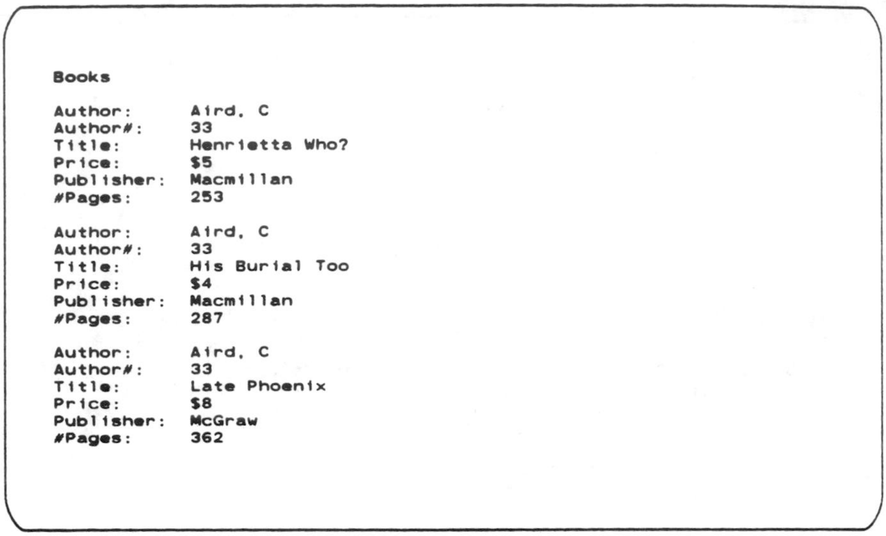

```
Books

Author:       Aird, C
Author#:      33
Title:        Henrietta Who?
Price:        $5
Publisher:    Macmillan
#Pages:       253

Author:       Aird, C
Author#:      33
Title:        His Burial Too
Price:        $4
Publisher:    Macmillan
#Pages:       287

Author:       Aird, C
Author#:      33
Title:        Late Phoenix
Price:        $8
Publisher:    McGraw
#Pages:       362
```

(a)

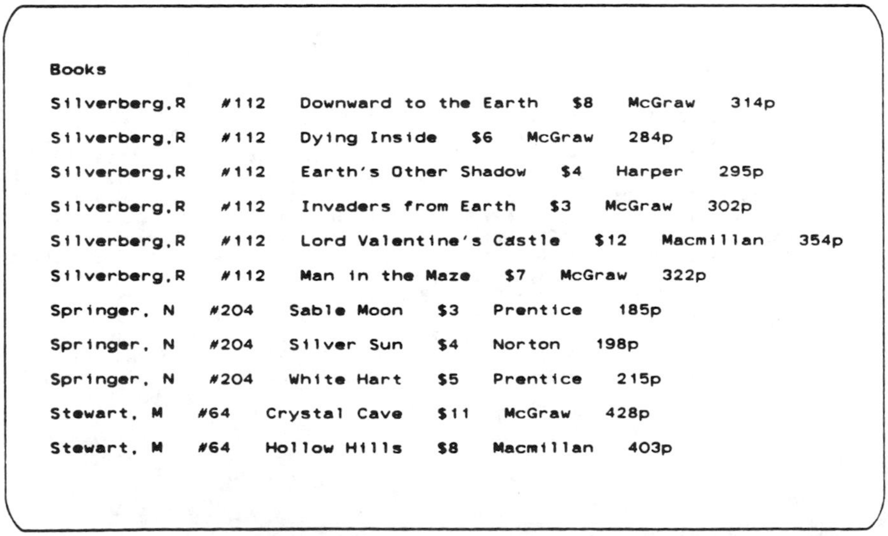

```
Books

Silverberg,R    #112    Downward to the Earth    $8    McGraw      314p

Silverberg,R    #112    Dying Inside    $6    McGraw      284p

Silverberg,R    #112    Earth's Other Shadow    $4    Harper      295p

Silverberg,R    #112    Invaders from Earth    $3    McGraw      302p

Silverberg,R    #112    Lord Valentine's Castle    $12    Macmillan      354p

Silverberg,R    #112    Man in the Maze    $7    McGraw      322p

Springer, N    #204    Sable Moon    $3    Prentice      185p

Springer, N    #204    Silver Sun    $4    Norton      198p

Springer, N    #204    White Hart    $5    Prentice      215p

Stewart, M    #64    Crystal Cave    $11    McGraw      428p

Stewart, M    #64    Hollow Hills    $8    Macmillan      403p
```

(b)

Figure 11.4

Two versions of screens in the second experiment by Tullis (1984). Equations based on objective metrics predicted performance and preference scores accurately, indicating the superiority of version (a) over version (b).

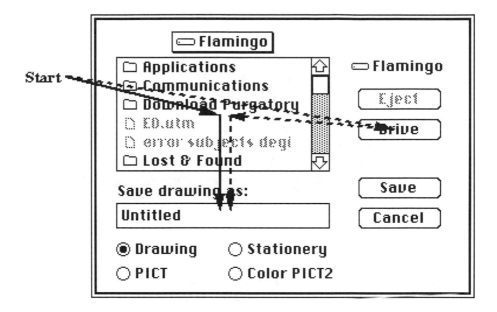

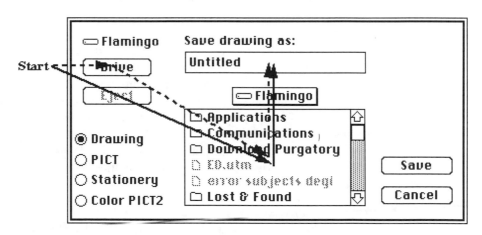

Figure 11.5

Layout appropriateness can help designers to analyze and redesign dialog boxes. (a) The existing dialog box. (b) The redesigned versions based on frequencies of action sequences. The solid line represents the most frequent sequence of actions; the dashed line represents the second most frequent sequence of actions. (Sears, 1993.)

11.5   Color

Color displays are attractive to users and can often improve task performance, but the danger of misuse is high. Color can

- Soothe or strike the eye
- Add accents to an uninteresting display
- Facilitate subtle discriminations in complex displays
- Emphasize the logical organization of information
- Draw attention to warnings
- Evoke strong emotional reactions of joy, excitement, fear, or anger

The principles developed by graphic artists for using color in books, magazines, highway signs, and television are being adapted for computer displays (Thorell and Smith, 1990; Travis, 1991; Marcus, 1992; Shubin et al., 1996). Programmers and interactive-systems designers are learning how to create effective computer displays and to avoid the pitfalls (Weitzman, 1985; Brown, 1988; Salomon, 1990; Galitz, 1994) (see Color Plates for examples).

There is no doubt that color makes video games more attractive to users, conveys more information on power-plant or process-control diagrams, and is necessary for realistic images of people, scenery, or three-dimensional objects (Foley et al., 1990; Gardiner, 1994). These applications require color. Greater controversy exists about the benefits of color for alphanumeric displays, spreadsheets, graphs, and user-interface components. High-resolution displays with multiple type fonts, sizes, and styles offer designers many options with black-on-white displays, which have been shown to be more readable than white-on-black (Snyder et al., 1990) however, color still has powerful attractions.

No simple set of rules governs use of color, but these guidelines are a starting point for designers:

- *Use color conservatively*   Many programmers and novice designers are eager to use color to brighten up their displays, but the results are often counterproductive. One home information system had the seven letters in its name in large letters, each with a different color. At a distance, the display appeared inviting and eye-catching; up close, however, it was difficult to read.

  Instead of showing meaningful relationships, inappropriately colored fields mislead users into searching for relationships that do not exist. In one poorly designed display, white lettering was used for input fields and for explanations of PF (Programmed Function) keys, leading users to think that they had to type the letters PF3 or PF9.

Using a different color for each of 12 items in a menu produces an overwhelming effect. Using four colors (such as red, blue, green, and yellow) for the 12 items will still mislead users into thinking that all the similarly colored items are related. An appropriate strategy would be to show all the menu items in one color, the title in a second color, the instructions in a third color, and error messages in a fourth color. Even this strategy can be overwhelming if the colors are too striking visually. A safe approach is always to use black letters on a white background, with italics or bold for emphasis, and to reserve color for special highlighting.

- *Limit the number of colors* Many design guides suggest limiting the number of colors in a single alphanumeric display to four, with a limit of seven colors in the entire sequence of displays. Experienced users may be able to benefit from a larger number of color codes.

- *Recognize the power of color as a coding technique* Color speeds recognition for many tasks, and is more effective than texture coding (Perlman and Swan, 1993). However, color coding can inhibit performance of tasks that go against the grain of the coding scheme. For example, in an accounting application, if data lines with accounts overdue more than 30 days are coded in red, they will be readily visible among the nonoverdue accounts coded in green. In air-traffic control, high-flying planes might be coded differently from low-flying planes to facilitate recognition. In programming workstations, newly added programming-language statements might be coded differently from the old statements, to show progress in writing or maintaining programs.

- *Ensure that color coding supports the task* If, in the accounting application with color coding by days overdue, the task is now to locate accounts with balances of more than $55, the coding by days overdue may inhibit performance on the second task. In the programming application, the coding of recent additions may make it more difficult to read the entire program. Designers should attempt to make a close linkage between the users' tasks and the color coding.

- *Have color coding appear with minimal user effort* In general, the color coding should not have to be assigned by the users each time that they perform a task, but rather should appear because they, for example, initiate the program to check for accounts overdue by more than 30 days. When the users perform the task of locating accounts with balances of more than $55, the new color coding should appear automatically.

- *Place color coding under user control* When appropriate, the users should be able to turn off the color coding. For example, if a spelling checker color codes possibly misspelled words in red, then the user should be able to accept or change the spelling and to turn off the coding. The presence of the highly visible red coding is a distraction from reading the text for comprehension.

- *Design for monochrome first*   The primary goal of a display designer should be to lay out the contents in a logical pattern. Related fields can be shown by contiguity or by similar structural patterns; for example, successive employee records may have the same indentation pattern. Related fields can also be grouped by a box drawn around the group. Unrelated fields can be kept separate by blank space—at least one blank line vertically or three blank characters horizontally. It may be advantageous to design for monochrome because color displays may not be universally available.

- *Consider the needs of color-deficient users*   Approximately 8 percent of North American and European users have some color deficiency in their vision. The most common deficiency is red–green blindness, in which both of these colors appear gray. Black on white or white on black will work for these and most other users.

- *Use color to help in formatting*   In densely packed displays where space is at a premium, similar colors can be used to group related items. For example, in a police dispatcher's tabular display of assignments, the police cars on emergency calls might be coded in red, and the police cars on routine calls might be coded in green. Then, when a new emergency arose, it would be relatively easy to identify the cars on routine calls and to assign one to the emergency. Dissimilar colors can be used to distinguish physically close but logically distinct fields. In a block-structured programming language, designers could show the nesting levels by coding the statements in a progression of colors—for example, dark green, light green, yellow, light orange, dark orange, red, and so on.

- *Be consistent in color coding*   Use the same color-coding rules throughout the system. If some error messages are displayed in red, then make sure that every error message appears in red; a change to yellow may be interpreted as a change in importance of the message. If colors are used differently by several designers of the same system, then users will hesitate as they attempt to assign meaning to the color changes. A set of color-coding standards should be written down for the benefit of every designer.

- *Be alert to common expectations about color codes*   The designer needs to speak to users to determine what color codes are applied in the task domain. From automobile-driving experience, red is commonly considered to indicate stop or danger, yellow is a warning, and green is go. In investment circles, red is a financial loss and black is a gain. For chemical engineers, red is hot and blue is cold. For map makers, blue means water, green means forests, and yellow means deserts. These multiple conventions can cause problems for designers. A designer might consider using red to signal that an engine is warmed up and ready, but a user might understand the red coding as an indication of danger. A red light is often used to indicate power ON for electrical equipment, but some users are made anxious by this decision since red has a strong association with danger or stopping. When appropriate, indicate the color-code interpretations on the display or in a help panel.

- *Be alert to problems with color pairings*   If saturated (pure) red and blue appear on a display at the same time, it may be difficult for users to absorb the information. Red and blue are on the opposite ends of the spectrum, and the muscles surrounding the human eye will be strained by attempts to produce a sharp focus for both colors simultaneously. The blue will appear to recede and the red will appear to come forward. Blue text on a red background would present an especially difficult challenge for users to read. Similarly, other combinations will appear to be garish and difficult to read—for example, yellow on purple, magenta on green. Too little contrast also is a problem: Imagine yellow letters on a white background or brown letters on a black background. On each color monitor, the color appears differently, and careful tests with various text and background colors are necessary. Pace (1984) tested 24 color combinations using 36 undergraduate subjects. He found that error rates ranged from approximately one to four errors per 1000 characters read. Black on blue and blue on white were two color schemes associated with low error rates in both tasks, and magenta on green and green on white were two color schemes associated with high error rates. Tests with other monitors and tasks are necessary to reach a general conclusion about the most effective color pairs.

- *Use color changes to indicate status changes*   If an automobile speedometer had a digital readout of the driving speed, it might be helpful to change from green numbers below the maximum speed limit to red above the maximum speed limit to act as a warning. Similarly, in an oil refinery, pressure indicators might change color as the value went above or below acceptable limits. In this way, color acts as an attention-getting method. This technique is potentially valuable when there are hundreds of values displayed continuously.

- *Use color in graphic displays for greater information density*   In graphs with multiple plots, color can be helpful in showing which line segments form the full graph. The usual strategies for differentiating lines in black-on-white graphs—such as dotted lines, thicker lines, and dashed lines—are not as effective as is using separate colors for each line. Architectural plans benefit from color coding of electrical, telephone, hot-water, cold-water, and natural-gas lines. Similarly, maps can have greater information density when color coding is used.

The complexity of using color was demonstrated in studies of decision-making tasks, rather than of simple location of information or recall, with management-information systems (Benbasat et al., 1986). Although color coding was found to be beneficial and preferred, there was an interaction with personality factors. Further intricate relationships were found in a comparison of monochrome versus color-coded pie charts, bar charts, line graphs, and data tables, in which color coding sped performance in all but the line graphs (Hoadley, 1990). Hoadley concludes that "uncritical addition of color may not be uniformly beneficial. Color is a subtle variable that can significantly enhance the decision maker's ability to extract information."

Box 11.4

Guidelines that highlight the complex potential benefits and dangers of using color coding.

Guidelines for using color
- Use color conservatively: Limit the number and amount of colors.
- Recognize the power of color to speed or slow tasks.
- Ensure that color coding should supports the task.
- Make color coding appear with minimal user effort.
- Keep color coding under user control.
- Design for monochrome first.
- Use color to help in formatting.
- Be consistent in color coding.
- Be alert to common expectations about color codes.
- Use color changes to indicate status changes.
- Use color in graphic displays for greater information density.

Benefits of using color
- Various colors are soothing or striking to the eye.
- Color can improve an uninteresting display.
- Color facilitates subtle discriminations in complex displays.
- A color code can emphasize the logical organization of information.
- Certain colors can draw attention to warnings.
- Color coding can evoke more emotional reactions of joy, excitement, fear, or anger.

Dangers of using color
- Color pairings may cause problems.
- Color fidelity may degrade on other hardware.
- Printing or conversion to other media may be a problem.

Color displays are becoming nearly universal, even in laptops, and designers usually make heavy use color in system designs. There are undoubtedly benefits of increased user satisfaction and often increased performance; however, there are real dangers in misusing color. Care should be taken to make appropriate designs and to conduct thorough evaluations (Box 11.4).

11.6 Practitioner's Summary

The wording of system messages may have an effect on performance and attitudes, especially for novices whose anxiety and lack of knowledge put them at a disadvantage. Designers might make improvements by merely using more specific diagnostic messages, offering constructive guidance rather than focusing on failures, employing user-centered phrasing, choosing a suitable physical format, and avoiding vague terminology or numeric codes.

When giving instructions, focus on the user and the user's tasks. Avoid anthropomorphic phrasing and use the *you* form to guide the novice user. Avoid judging the user. Simple statements of status are more succinct and usually are more effective.

Pay careful attention to display design, and develop a local set of guidelines for all designers. Use spacing, indentation, columnar formats, and field labels to organize the display for users. Denser displays, but fewer of them, may be advantageous. Color can improve some displays and can lead to more rapid task performance with higher satisfaction; but improper use of color can mislead and slow users.

Organizations can benefit from careful study of display-design guidelines documents and from the creation of their own set of guidelines tailored to local needs (see Section 3.2.1). This document should also include a list of local terminology and abbreviations. Consistency and thorough testing are critical.

11.7 Researcher's Agenda

Experimental testing could refine the proposed error-message guidelines proposed here, and could identify the sources of user anxiety or confusion. Message placement, highlighting techniques, and multiple-level message strategies are candidates for exploration. Improved analysis of sequences of user actions to provide more effective messages automatically would be useful.

There is a great need for testing to validate data-display and color-design guidelines. Basic understanding and cognitive models of visual perception of displays would be a dramatic contribution. Do users follow a scanning pattern from the top left? Do users whose natural language reads from right to left or users from different cultures scan displays differently? Does use of whitespace around or boxing of items facilitate comprehension and speed interpretation? When is a single dense display preferable to two sparse displays? How does color coding reorganize the pattern of scanning?

World Wide Web Resources   WWW

Usage guidelines for color are nicely done on the World Wide Web with some empirical results, but the most informative and enjoyable experience is simply browsing through the lively and colorful websites. Styles and fashions come and go quickly, so save the examples you like best.

http://www.aw.com/DTUI

References

Benbasat, I., Dexter, A. S., and Todd, P., The influence of color and graphical information presentation in a managerial decision simulation, *Human–Computer Interaction*, 2 (1986), 65–92.

Brennan, Susan E. and Ohaeri, Justina O., Effects of messages style on users' attributions towards agents, *Proc. ACM CHI '94 Human Factors in Computing Systems: Conference Companion*, ACM, New York (1994), 281–282.

Brown, C. Marlin, *Human–Computer Interface Design Guidelines*, Ablex, Norwood, NJ (1988).

Burns, Michael J., Warren, Dianne L., and Rudisill, Marianne, Formatting space-related displays to optimize expert and nonexpert user performance, *Proc. ACM SIGCHI '86 Human Factors in Computing Systems*, ACM, New York (1986), 274–280.

Casner, Stephen M., A task-analytic approach to the automated design of information graphic presentations, *ACM Transactions on Graphics*, 10, 2 (April 1991), 111–151.

Dean, M., How a computer should talk to people, *IBM Systems Journal*, 21, 4 (1982), 424–453.

Donner, Kimberly A., McKay, Tim, O'Brien, Kevin M., and Rudisill, Marianne, Display format and highlighting validity effects on search performance using complex visual displays, *Proc. Human Factors Society—Thirty-Fifth Annual Meeting*, Santa Monica, CA (1991), 374–378.

Foley, James D., van Dam, Andries, Feiner, Steven K., and Hughes, John F., *Computer Graphics: Principles and Practice* (Second Edition), Addison-Wesley, Reading, MA (1990).

Friedman, Batya, "It's the computer's fault"—Reasoning about computers as moral agents, *Proc. ACM CHI '95 Human Factors in Computing Systems: Conference Companion*, ACM, New York (1995), 226–227.

Galitz, Wilbert O., *It's Time to Clean Your Windows: Designing GUIs that Work*, John Wiley and Sons, New York (1994).

Gardiner, Jeremy, *Digital Photo Illustration*, Van Nostrand Reinhold, New York (1994).

Hoadley, Ellen D., Investigating the effects of color, *Communications of the ACM*, 33, 2 (February 1990), 120–139.

Isa, Barbara S., Boyle, James M., Neal, Alan S., and Simons, Roger M., A methodology for objectively evaluating error messages, *Proc. ACM CHI '83 Human Factors in Computing Systems*, ACM, New York (1983), 68–71.

Kiesler, Sara, Sproull, Lee, and Waters, Keith, A prisoner's dilemma experiment on cooperation with people and human-like computers, *Journal of Personality and Social Psychology*, 70, 1 (1996), 47–65.

Laurel, Brenda, Interface agents: Metaphors with character. In Laurel, Brenda (Editor), *The Art of Human–Computer Interface Design*, Addison-Wesley, Reading, MA (1990), 355–365.

Lohse, Jerry. A cognitive model for perception and understanding of graphs, *Proc. ACM CHI '91 Human Factors in Computing Systems*, ACM, New York (1991), 137–144.

Mackinlay, Jock, Automating the design of graphical presentations of relational information, *ACM Transactions on Graphics*, 5, 2 (1986), 110–141.

Maes, Pattie, Artificial life meets entertainment: Lifelike autonomous agents, *Communications of the ACM*, 38, 11 (November 1995), 108–114.

Marcus, Aaron, *Graphic Design for Electronic Documents and User Interfaces*, ACM Press, New York (1992).

Martin, Dianne, ENIAC: Press conference that shook the world, *IEEE Technology and Society Magazine*, 14, 4 (Winter 1995/96), 3–10.

Mosteller, W., Job entry control language errors, *Proceedings of SHARE 57*, SHARE, Chicago (1981), 149–155.

Mullet, Kevin and Sano, Darrell, *Designing Visual Interfaces: Communication Oriented Techniques*, Sunsoft Press, Englewood Cliffs, NJ (1995).

Mumford, Lewis, *Technics and Civilization*, Harcourt Brace and World, New York (1934), 31–36

Nass, Clifford, Steuer, Jonathan, and Tauber, Ellen R., Computers are social actors, *Proc. ACM CHI '94 Human Factors in Computing Systems*, ACM, New York (1994), 72–78

Nass, Clifford, Lombard, Matthew, Henriksen, Lisa, and Steuer, Jonathan, Anthropocentrism and computers, *Behaviour & Information Technology*, 14, 4 (1995), 229–238.

Pace, Bruce J., Color combinations and contrast reversals on visual display units, *Proceedings of the Human Factors Society Twenty-Eighth Annual Meeting*, Santa Monica, CA (1984), 326–330.

Perlman, Gary and Swan, II, J. Edward, Color versus texture coding to improve visual search performance, *Proc. Human Factors Society—Thirty-Seventh Annual Meeting*, Santa Monica, CA (1993), 343–347.

Quintanar, Leo R., Crowell, Charles R., and Pryor, John B., Human–computer interaction: A preliminary social psychological analysis, *Behavior Research Methods and Instrumentation*, 14, 2 (1982), 210–220.

Resnik, P. V. and Lammers, H. B., The influence of self-esteem on cognitive response to machine-like versus human-like computer feedback, *Journal of Social Psychology*, 125, (1986), 761–769.

Roth, Steven F., Kolojejchick, John, Mattis, Joe, and Goldstein, Jade, Interactive graphic design using automatic presentation knowledge, *Proc. ACM CHI '94 Human Factors in Computing Systems*, ACM, New York (1994), 112–117.

Salomon, Gitta, New Uses for Color, In Laurel, Brenda (Editor), *The Art of Human–Computer Interface Design*, Addison-Wesley, Reading, MA (1990), 269–278.

Sears, Andrew, Layout appropriateness: Guiding user interface design with simple task descriptions, *IEEE Transactions on Software Engineering*, 19, 7 (1993), 707–719.

Shneiderman, Ben, System message design: Guidelines and experimental results. In Badre, A., and Shneiderman, B. (Editors), *Directions in Human/Computer Interaction*, Ablex, Norwood, NJ (1982), 55–78.

Shneiderman, Ben, Looking for the bright side of agents, *ACM Interactions*, 2, 1 (January 1995), 13–15.

Shubin, Hal, Falck, Deborah, and Johansen, Ati Gropius, Exploring color in interface design, *ACM interactions III.4* (August 1996), 36–48.

Smith, Sid L. and Mosier, Jane N., *Guidelines for Designing User Interface Software*, Report ESD-TR-86-278, MITRE, Bedford, MA (August 1986).

Snyder, Harry L., Decker, Jennie J., Lloyd, Charles J. C., and Dye, Craig, Effect of image polarity on VDT task performance, *Proc. Human Factors Society—Thirty-Fourth Annual Meeting*, Santa Monica, CA (1990), 1447–1451.

Springer, Carla J., Retrieval of information from complex alphanumeric displays: Screen formatting variables' effect on target identification time. In Salvendy, Gavriel (Editor), *Cognitive Engineering in the Design of Human–Computer Interaction and Expert Systems*, Elsevier, Amsterdam, The Netherlands (1987), 375–382.

Staggers, Nancy, Impact of screen density on clinical nurses' computer task performance and subjective screen satisfaction, *International Journal of Man–Machine Studies*, 39, 5 (November 1993), 775–792.

Takeuchi, Akikazu and Naito, Taketo, Situated facial displays: Towards social interaction, *Proc. ACM CHI '95 Human Factors in Computing Systems*, ACM, New York (1995), 450–455.

Teitelbaum, Richard C., and Granda, Richard F., The effects of positional constancy on searching menus for information, *Proc. ACM CHI '83 Human Factors in Computing Systems*, ACM, New York (1983), 150–153.

Thorell, L. G., and Smith, W. J., *Using Computer Color Effectively*, Prentice-Hall, Englewood Cliffs, NJ (1990).

Travis, David S., *Effective Color Displays: Theory and Practice*, Academic Press, New York (1991).

Treisman, Anne, Perceptual grouping and attention in visual search for features and for objects, *Journal of Experimental Psychology: Human Perception and Performance*, 8, 2 (1982), 194–214.

Tufte, Edward, *Envisioning Information*, Graphics Press, Cheshire, CT (1990).

Tullis, T. S., An evaluation of alphanumeric, graphic and color information displays, *Human Factors*, 23, (1981), 541–550.

Tullis, T. S., Screen design. In Helander, Martin (Editor), *Handbook of Human–Computer Interaction*, Elsevier Science Publishers, Amsterdam, The Netherlands (1988a), 377–411.

Tullis, T. S., A system for evaluating screen formats: Research and application. In Hartson, H. Rex, and Hix, Hartson (Editors), *Advances in Human–Computer Interaction* (Volume 2), Ablex, Norwood, NJ (1988b), 214–286.

Vincow, Michelle A. and Wickens, Christopher, Spatial layout of displayed information: Three steps toward developing quantitative models, *Proc. Human Factors Society—Thirty-Seventh Annual Meeting*, Santa Monica, CA (1993), 348–352.

Walker, Janet H., Sproull, Lee, and Subramani, R., Using a human face in an interface, *Proc. ACM CHI '94 Human Factors in Computing Systems*, ACM, New York (1994), 85–91.

Weitzman, Donald O., Color coding re-viewed, *Proc. Human Factors Society—Twenty-ninth Annual Meeting*, Santa Monica, CA (1985), 1079–1083.

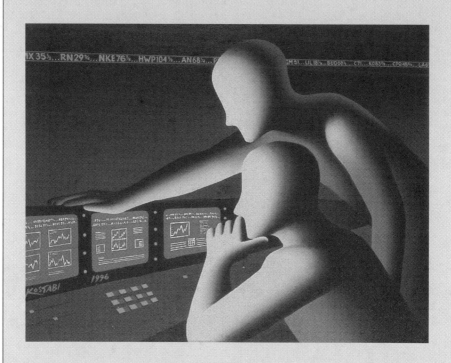

Mark Kostabi, *Computer Virus*, 1992

Printed Manuals, Online Help, and Tutorials

What is really important in education is . . . that the mind is matured, that energy is aroused.

Soren Kierkegaard, *Either/Or, Volume II*

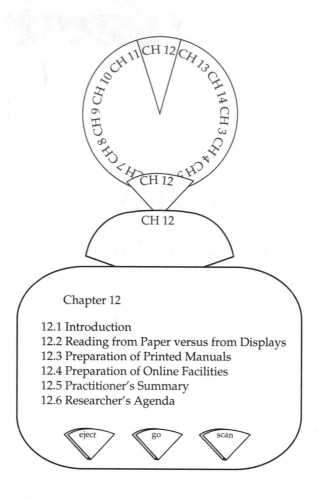

Chapter 12

12.1 Introduction
12.2 Reading from Paper versus from Displays
12.3 Preparation of Printed Manuals
12.4 Preparation of Online Facilities
12.5 Practitioner's Summary
12.6 Researcher's Agenda

12.1 Introduction

All users of interactive computer systems require training. Many users learn from another person who knows the system, but training materials are often necessary. Traditional printed manuals are sometimes poorly written, but this medium can be effective and convenient if prepared properly (Price, 1984; Brockmann, 1990). Online help, manuals, and tutorials that use the same interactive system to provide training, reference, and reminders about specific features and syntax have become expected components of most systems. In fact, as display devices appear in cars, cameras, VCRs, and elsewhere, ubiquitous help should be the norm.

Learning anything new is a challenge. Although challenge can be joyous and satisfying, when it comes to learning about computer systems, many people experience anxiety, frustration, and disappointment. Much of the difficulty flows directly from the poor design of the menus, displays, or instructions that lead to error conditions, or simply from the inability of users to know what to do next.

Even though increasing attention is being paid to improving user-interface design, the complexity of online systems grows. There will always be a need for supplemental materials that aid users, in both paper and online form. Some of the many forms of paper user manuals are:

- *Brief getting-started notes* to enable eager first-time users to try out features
- *Introductory tutorial* to explain common features
- *Thorough tutorial* that covers typical and advanced tasks
- *Quick reference card* with a concise presentation of the syntax
- *Conversion manual* that teaches the features of the current system to users who are knowledgeable about some other system
- *Detailed reference manual* with all features covered

There is also a variety of online materials:

- *Online user manual*   This simple conversion of the traditional user manual to electronic form may make the text more readily available, but more difficult to read and absorb
- *Online help facility*   The most common form of online help is a list of article titles (possibly searchable for keywords) and an index of terms that lead to articles.
- *Online tutorial*   This potentially appealing and innovative approach uses the electronic medium to teach the novice user by showing simulations of the working system, by displaying attractive animations, and by engaging the user in interactive sessions.
- *Online demonstration*   Potential users who want an overview of the software can benefit from an online demonstration that gives them a guided tour through the software.

Duffy and colleagues (1992) classify paper and online materials by user's goals:

User's Goal	Medium of Delivery	
	Paper	*Online*
I want to *buy* it	sales brochure fact sheet	demonstration program
I want to *learn* it	tutorial manual	guided tour
I want to *use* it	user's manual	online help online document

Other forms of instruction or information acquisition include classroom instruction, personal training and assistance, telephone consultation, videotapes, and audio tapes. These forms are not discussed here, but many of the same instructional design principles apply.

12.2   Reading from Paper versus from Displays

The technology of printing text on paper has been evolving for more than 500 years. The paper surface and color, the typeface, character width, letter sharpness, text contrast with the paper, width of the text column, size of margins, spacing between lines, and even room lighting all have been explored in efforts to produce the most appealing and readable format.

In the last 40 years, the cathode ray tube *(CRT)*, often called the *visual display unit (VDU) or tube (VDT),* has emerged as an alternate medium for presenting text, but researchers have only begun the long process of optimization (Cakir et al., 1980; Grandjean and Vigliani, 1982; Heines, 1984; Helander, 1987; Hansen and Haas, 1988; Oborne and Holton, 1988; Creed and Newstead, 1988; Horton, 1990) to meet user needs. Serious concerns about CRT radiation or other health hazards have lessened as manufacturers, labor unions, and government agencies have funded major research in this area. One advantage of the increasingly popular liquid crystal displays (LCDs) is the lessened concerns about radiation.

The widespread reports about visual fatigue and stress have been confirmed, but these conditions respond well to rest, frequent breaks, and task diversity. But even before users are aware of visual fatigue or stress, their capacity to work with displays may be below their capacity to work with printed materials.

Approximately 10 studies during the 1980s found 15- to 30-percent slower task times for comprehension or proofreading of text on computer displays, compared to on paper. The potential disadvantages of reading from displays include these:

- *Fonts* may be poor, especially on low resolution displays. The dots composing the letters may be so large that each is visible, making the user expend effort to recognize the character. Monospace (fixed width) fonts, lack of appropriate kerning (for example, adjustments to bring "V" and "A" closer together), inappropriate interletter and interline spacing, and inappropriate colors may all complicate recognition.

- *Low contrast* between the characters and the background, and *fuzzy character* boundaries also can cause trouble.

- *Emitted light* from displays may be more difficult to read by than reflected light from paper; glare may be greater, *flicker* can be a problem, and the *curved display surface* may be troubling.

- *Small displays* require frequent *page turning*; issuing the page-turning commands is disruptive, and the page turns are unsettling, especially if they are slow and visually distracting.
- *Reading distance* can be greater than for paper, displays are *fixed* in place, and display *placement* may be too high for comfortable reading (optometrists suggest reading be done with the eyes in a downward-looking direction); the "near quintad" are the five ways eyes adjust to seeing close items (Grant, 1990): *accommodation* (lens-shape change), *convergence* (looking toward the center), *meiosis* (pupillary contraction), *excyclotorsion* (rotation), and *depression of gaze* (looking down).
- *Layout and formatting* can be problems, such as improper margins, inappropriate line width (35 to 55 characters is recommended), or awkward justification (left justification and ragged right are recommended).
- *Reduced hand and body motion* with displays as compared to paper, and *reduce rigid posture* for displays, as both may be fatiguing.
- *Unfamiliarity of displays* and the *anxiety* that the image may disappear can increase *stress*.

The fascinating history of this issue goes back at least to Hansen and associates (1978) who found that seven students who were asked to take examinations on paper and on PLATO terminals took almost twice as long online. Much of the increased time could be attributed to system delays, poor software design, and slower output rates, but the authors could not thus account for 37 percent of the longer time on PLATO. They conjecture that this additional time could be attributed to uncertainty about how to control the medium, what the system would do, and what the system had done.

Wright and Lickorish (1983) studied proofreading of 134-line texts that contained 39 errors (typographical errors, spelling errors, missing words, and repeated words). Thirty-two subjects read from an Apple II using an 80-column display on a 12-inch black-and-white display screen or from hardcopy generated by a dot-matrix printer. There was a modest, but significant, increase in detected errors with the printed text. There was also a 30- to 40-percent advantage in speed with the printed text.

Gould and Grischkowsky (1984) studied proofreading for typographic errors on displays and on output from a computer-controlled photocomposer. Both the displays and the hardcopy texts had 23 lines per page, with about nine words per line. Twenty-four subjects spent 8 hours reading in each format. The reading rate was significantly faster on hardcopy (200 words per minute) than on the screens (155 words per minute). Accuracy was slightly, but reliably, higher on hardcopy. The subjective ratings of readability were similar for both forms. A later series of studies with improved displays led to much smaller differences and even to the elimination of differences (Gould et al., 1987a; 1987b).

More recent results demonstrate no difference between reading text on displays versus paper when researchers control for enough of the variables. Oborne and Holton (1988) believe that earlier studies may have been flawed by lack of control and comparing low-resolution displays to high-quality print. In their comprehension studies using a within-subjects design with approximately 380-word passages, there were no statistically significant differences between displays and photographs of displays. They controlled for position, distance to retina, line length, layout, and illumination. Jorna's study (1991) solidly demonstrates that, when the resolution of the display matches that of the hardcopy, there is no difference in reading speed or perceived image quality. Since computer displays do not yet have the resolution of paper, it is still easier to read from paper.

These empirical studies isolated the issues and led to a clear message for designers: High-resolution displays are recommended if users are to read lengthy texts online. Related studies clarify that short response times, fast display rates, black text on white background, and page-sized displays are important considerations if displayed text is meant to replace paper documents.

12.3   Preparation of Printed Manuals

Traditionally, training and reference materials for computer systems were printed manuals. Writing these manuals was often left to the most junior member of the development team as a 5-percent effort at the end of the project. As a result, the manuals were often poorly written, were not suited to the background of the users, were delayed or incomplete, and were tested inadequately.

There is a growing awareness that users are not like designers, that system developers might not be good writers, that it takes time and skill to write an effective manual, that testing and revisions must be done before widespread dissemination, and that system success is closely coupled to documentation quality.

In an early experiment, Foss, Rosson, and Smith (1982) modified a standard text-editor manual. The standard manual presented all the details about a command; the modified manual offered a progressive, or *spiral*, approach to the material by presenting subsets of the concepts. The standard manual used an abstract formal notation to describe the syntax of the commands; the modified manual showed numerous examples. Finally, the standard manual used terse technical prose; the modified manual included readable explanations with fewer technical terms.

During the experiment, subjects took 15 to 30 minutes to study the manuals, and were then asked to complete nine complex text-editing or creation tasks within a 3-hour period. On all five dependent measures, the subjects with the modified manual demonstrated superior performance (Table 12.1).

Table 12.1

Results of a study comparing standard manual with a modified manual (spiral approach, numerous examples, more readable explanations) (Foss et al., 1982).

	Standard Manual	Modified Manual
Tasks Completed	7.4	8.8
Average Minutes per Task	26.6	16.0
Average Edit Errors per Task	1.4	.3
Average Commands per Task	23.6	13.0
Average Requests for Verbal Help	5.5	2.6

The results make a strong case for the effect of the manual on the success of the user with the system.

The iterative process of refining a text-editor manual and evaluating its effectiveness is described by Sullivan and Chapanis (1983). They rewrote a manual for a widely used text editor, conducted a walk-through test with colleagues, and performed a more elaborate test with five temporary secretaries. Subjective and objective metrics showed substantial benefits from the rewriting. Allwood and Kalen (1997) realized similar improvements by keeping sentences short, by avoiding jargon, by using a new paragraph for each command, and by emphasizing tasks.

The benefits of well-designed manuals include shorter learning times, better user performance, increased user satisfaction and fewer calls for support (Spencer and Yates, 1995).

12.3.1 Use of the OAI Model to design manuals

The objects–actions interface (OAI) model offers insight to the learning process, and thus provides guidance to instructional-materials designers. If the user has only partial knowledge of the task objects and actions (Fig. 12.1), then training in the task is the first step. For a task such as letter writing, users must learn about address blocks, salutations, content, and signatures. Once users know the hierarchy of objects from the high-level down to the atomic and recognize the range of their high-level intentions down to their specific action steps (Fig. 12.2), they are equipped to learn about the interface representations. The instructional materials should start from familiar objects and actions in the letter-writing task, link these concepts to the high-level interface objects and actions (Fig. 12.3), and then show the syntax needed to accomplish each task. Knowledgeable users who understand the task and interface (see Fig. 2.2) can move on to expert levels of usage with shortcuts that speed performance.

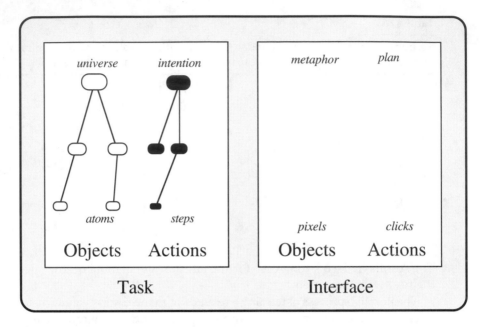

Figure 12.1

A representation of users who know some of task objects and actions, but know nothing about the interface. A deeper knowledge of task objects and actions will give them a framework for learning about the interface.

Some users are knowledgeable about letter writing and word processing, but must learn a new word processor. They need a presentation that shows the relationship between the metaphors and plans they know and the new ones. Increasingly, the metaphors and plans are shared among word processors, but the dialog boxes, clicks, and keystrokes may vary.

Some users have learned the task and interface objects and actions, but cannot recall details of how to convert their plans into detailed actions.

These three scenarios demonstrate three popular forms of printed materials: the *introductory tutorial*, the *conversion manual*, and the *quick reference* (cheat sheet).

The OAI model can also help researchers to map the current levels of knowledge in learning systems. For example, a user who is learning about database-management systems for Congressional voting patterns might have some knowledge about the database and its manipulation, the query-language concepts, and the syntax needed. This user would benefit from seeing typical queries that would demonstrate the syntax and serve as templates for other queries. In fact, complete *sample sessions* are extremely helpful in giving a portrait of the system features and interaction style (Fig. 12.4). Many users will work through these sessions to verify their under-

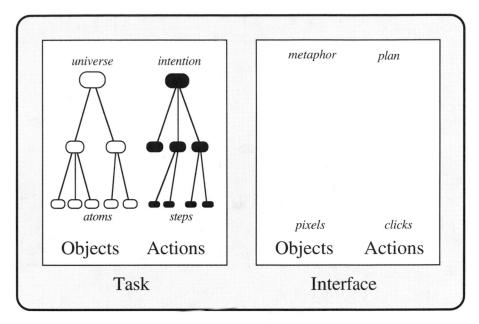

Figure 12.2

A representation of users who know the task adequately, but do not know the interface. Educational materials for this community should explain the interface objects and actions, starting with plans.

standing, to gain a sense of competence in using the system, and to see whether the system and the manual match.

Another helpful guide to using a system is an overall *flow diagram* of activity (Fig. 12.5). Such visual overviews provide a map that orients users to the transitions from one activity to another. Similarly, if the system uses a complex model of data objects, an overview diagram may help users to appreciate the details.

12.3.2   Organization and writing style

Designing instructional materials is a challenging endeavor. The author must be knowledgeable about the technical content; sensitive to the background, reading level, and intellectual ability of the reader; and skilled in writing lucid prose. Assuming that the author has acquired the technical content, the primary job in creating a manual is to understand the readers and the tasks that they must perform.

A precise statement of the *educational objectives* (Mager, 1962) is an invaluable guide to the author and the reader. The sequencing of the instructional

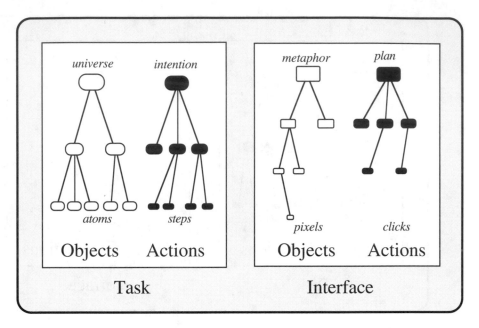

Figure 12.3

A representation of users who are knowledgeable about the task and high-level interface aspects, and need to learn only the specific visual representations and syntactic details. For example, someone who knows about writing scientific articles and is familiar with at least one word processor will find it relatively easy to acquire the low-level objects and actions in another word processor.

contents is governed by the reader's current knowledge and ultimate objectives. Precise rules are hard to identify, but the author should attempt to present concepts in a logical sequence with increasing order of difficulty, to ensure that each concept is used in subsequent sections, to avoid forward references, and to construct sections that contain approximately equal amounts of new material. In addition to these structural requirements, the manual should have sufficient examples and complete sample sessions.

Within a section that presents a concept, the author should begin with the reason for the concept, describe the concept in task-domain semantic terms, then show the computer-related semantic concepts, and, finally, offer the syntax.

The choice of words and their phrasing is as important as the overall structure. A poorly written sentence mars a well-designed manual, just as an incorrect note mars a beautifully composed sonata. The classic book on writing, *The Elements of Style* (Strunk and White, 1979) is a valuable resource. Style guides for organizations represent worthy attempts at ensuring consis-

SEARCH: I am looking for an image of Goleta Beach.

Steps:

1. MAP BROWSER: The user selects zoom 10X IN for the Zoom Factor, and clicks with the mouse on point near Goleta in Southern California.

2. MAP BROWSER: The Zoom Factor is changed to 5X IN. The Map Database is changed from World to USA, so that the next map redraw will display additional features; then, the user again clicks on a point near Goleta.

3. MAP BROWSER: The user now selects GAZETTEER to aid in the location of Goleta Beach through search by feature name.

4. GAZETTEER SEARCH FORM: Limit search to items CONTAINED within for the spatial search method and Current Map Region are preselected by system. The user inputs Goleta into the Sort Name field and selects Show Terms.

5. GAZETTEER SUGGESTIONS: A page is displayed to inform the user that the domain of this field is too large to display. The user is then given the option to use a fuzzy text search engine to help her to identify valid terms. Conquest search is selected, and the user is taken to a page to suggest values for that field (Sort Name).

6. GAZETTEER SUGGESTIONS: If a term was entered on the Gazetteer Search Form page, this term is seeded into the selection box and the user selects Suggest. Otherwise, the user provides a term to be used to suggest values for Sort Name.

7. GAZETTEER SUGGESTIONS: The terms GOLETA BEACH, GOLETA POINT, GOLETA PIER, GOLETA COVE, AND GOLETA are selected, and ADD is selected to add these items to the search selection list for the Gazetteer.

Figure 12.4

A sample walkthrough is often a convenient way to explain system usage. Many users try the sample and then make variations to suit their needs. This sample shows the first seven of 21 steps to retrieve a map image for the Alexandria Digital Library. (University of California at Santa Barbara, CA.)

tency and high quality. Of course, no set of guidelines can turn a mediocre writer into a great writer. Writing is a highly creative act; effective writers are national treasures.

Writing style should match the users' reading ability (Roemer and Chapanis, 1982). After a tutorial was written at the fifth-, tenth-, and fifteenth-grade levels, 54 subjects were divided into groups with low, middle, and high reading ability. Higher reading ability led to significant reductions in the completion time and number of errors, and to higher scores on a concepts test. Increased complexity of the writing style did not lead to significant differences on the performance variables, but subjective preferences significantly

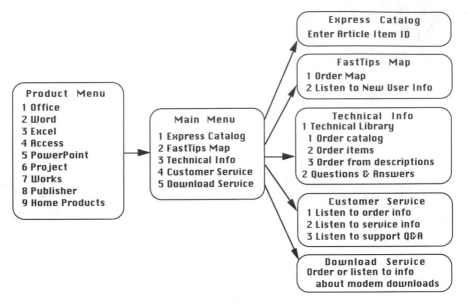

Figure 12.5

A transition diagram can be a helpful aid for users. This FastTips map, adapted from the Microsoft Support Network, gives telephone callers an overview and therefore capability to move rapidly within the support service. Users identify relevant articles, which are faxed to them. (Used with permission of Microsoft Corp., Redmond, WA.)

favored the fifth-grade version. Subjects could overcome the complex writing style, but the authors conclude that "the most sensible approach in designing computer dialogue is to use the simplest language."

Thinking-aloud studies (see Section 4.3) of subjects who were learning word processors revealed the enormous difficulties that most novices have and the strategies that they adopt to overcome those difficulties (Carroll and Mack, 1984). Learners are actively engaged in trying to make the system work, to read portions of the manual, to understand the screen displays, to explore the function of keys, and to overcome the many problems that they encounter. Learners apparently prefer trying out actions on the computer, rather than reading lengthy manuals. They want to perform meaningful, familiar tasks immediately, and to see the results for themselves. They apply real-world knowledge, experience with other computer systems, and frequent guesswork, unlike the fanciful image of the new user patiently reading through and absorbing the contents of a manual.

These observations led to the design of *minimal manuals* that drastically cut verbiage, encourage active involvement with hands-on experiences as soon as possible, and promote *guided exploration* of system features (Carroll, 1984; 1990). The key principles have been refined over time (van der Meij and Carroll, 1995):

- Choose an action-oriented approach
- Anchor the tool in the task domain
- Support error recognition and recovery
- Support reading to do, study, and locate

Results of field trials and of dozens of empirical studies demonstrate that with improved manuals, the learning time can be reduced substantially and user satisfaction increased (van der Meij and Lazonder, 1993).

Visual aspects are helpful to readers, especially with highly visual direct-manipulation and GUIs. Showing numerous well-chosen screen prints that demonstrate typical uses enables users to develop an understanding and a *predictive model* of the system. Often, users will mimic the examples in the manual during their first trials of the software. Figures containing complex data structures, transition diagrams, and menu maps (Parton et al., 1985) can improve performance dramatically by giving users access to fundamental structures created by designers.

Of course, every good manual should have a *table of contents* and an *index*. *Glossaries* can be helpful for clarifying technical terms. *Appendices* with error messages are recommended.

Whether to give *credit* to authors and designers is a lively and frequently debated issue. Advocates, including me, encourage giving credit in the manuals to honor good work, to encourage contributor responsibility for doing an excellent job, and to build the users' trust. Responsibility and trust are increased because the contributors were willing to have their names listed publicly. Having names in the manual makes software fit in with other creative human endeavors, such as books, films, and music, in which contributors are acknowledged, even if there are dozens of them. Opponents say that it is difficult to identify each contribution or that unwelcome telephone calls might be received by contributors.

12.3.3 Nonanthropomorphic descriptions

The metaphors used in describing computer systems can influence the user's reactions. Some writers are attracted to an anthropomorphic style that suggests that the computer is close to human in its powers. This suggestion can anger some users; more likely, it is seen as cute the first time, silly the second, and annoyingly distracting the third time (see Section 11.3).

Many designers prefer to focus attention on the users and on the tasks that the users must accomplish. In introductory sections of user manuals and online help, use of the second-person singular pronoun ("you") seems appropriate. Then, in later sections, simple descriptive sentences place the emphasis on the user's tasks.

In a transportation-network system, the user might have to establish the input conditions on the screen and then to invoke the program to perform an analysis:

> **Poor:** The expert system will discover the solution when the F1 key is pressed.
>
> **Better:** You can get the solution by pressing F1.
>
> **Better:** To solve, press F1.

The first description emphasizes the computer's role, the second focuses on the user and might be used in an introduction to the system. In later sections, the briefer third version is less distracting from the task.

In discussing computers, writers might be well advised to avoid such verbs as these:

> **Poor:** know, think, understand, have memory

In their place, use more mechanical terms, such as

> **Better:** process, print, compute, sort, store, search, retrieve

When describing what a user does with a computer, avoid such verbs as

> **Poor:** ask, tell, speak to, communicate with

In their place, use such terms as

> **Better:** use, direct, operate, program, control

Still better is to eliminate the reference to the computer, and to concentrate instead on what the user is doing, such as writing, solving a problem, finding an answer, learning a concept, or adding up a list of numbers:

> **Poor:** The computer can teach you Spanish words.
>
> **Better:** You can use the computer to learn Spanish words.

Make the user the subject of the sentence:

> **Poor:** The computer will give you a printed list of employees.
>
> **Poor:** Ask the computer to print a list of employees.
>
> **Better:** You can get the computer to print a list of employees.
>
> **Better:** You can print a list of employees.

The final sentence puts the emphasis on the user and eliminates the computer.

Poor: The computer needs to have the disk in the disk drive to boot the system.

Better: Put the disk labeled A2 in the disk drive before starting the computer.

Better: To begin writing, put the Word Processor disk in the drive.

The final form emphasizes the function or activity that the user is about to perform.

Poor: The computer knows how to do arithmetic.

Better: You can use the computer to do arithmetic.

Focus on the user's initiative, process, goals, and accomplishments.

12.3.4   Development process

Recognizing the difference between a good and a bad manual is necessary to producing a successful manual on time and within a reasonable budget. *Production of a manual*, like any project, must be managed properly, staffed with suitable personnel, and monitored with appropriate milestones (Box 12.1).

Getting started early is invaluable. If the manual-writing process begins before the implementation, then there is adequate time for review, testing, and refinement. Furthermore, the user's manual can act as a more complete and comprehensible alternative to the formal specification for the software. Implementers may miss or misunderstand some of the design requirements when reading a formal specification; a well-written user manual may clarify the design. The manual writer becomes an effective critic, reviewer, or question asker who can stimulate the implementation team. Early development of the manual enables pilot testing of the software's learnability even before the system is built. In the months before the software is completed, the manual may be the best way to convey the designers' intentions to potential customers and users, as well as to system implementers and project managers.

Ample lead time in the development of the manual allows for reviews and suggestions by designers, other technical writers, potential customers, intended users, copy editors, graphic artists, lawyers, marketing personnel, instructors, telephone consultants, and product testers (Brockmann, 1990).

Beyond informal reviews by people with different backgrounds, there are other strategies for evaluating the manual. Checklists of features have been developed by many organizations based on experience with previous manuals. Automated metrics of reading level or difficulty are available to help

Box 12.1

User-manual guidelines based on practice and empirical studies.

User Manual Guidelines
- Product
  - Let user's tasks guide organization (outside-in).
  - Let user's learning process shape sequencing.
  - Present task concepts before interface objects and actions.
  - Keep writing style clean and simple.
  - Show numerous examples.
  - Offer meaningful and complete sample sessions.
  - Draw transition or menu-tree diagrams.
  - Try advance organizers and summaries.
  - Provide table of contents, index, and glossary.
  - Include list of error messages.
  - Give credits to all project participants.
- Process
  - Seek professional writers and copy writers.
  - Prepare user manuals early (before implementation).
  - Review drafts thoroughly.
  - Field test early editions.
  - Provide a feedback mechanism for readers.
  - Revise to reflect changes regularly.

designers isolate complex sections of text. Computer-based style evaluations and spelling checkers are useful tools in refining any document.

Informal walkthroughs with users are usually an enlightening experience for software designers and manual writers. Potential users are asked to read through the manual and to describe aloud what they are seeing and learning. More controlled experiments with groups of users may help authors to make design decisions about the manual. In such studies, subjects are assigned tasks; their time to completion, error rates, and subjective satisfaction are the dependent variables.

Field trials with moderate numbers of users constitute a further process for identifying problems with the user manual and the software. Field trials can range from 1/2 hour with a half-dozen people to several months with thousands of users. One effective and simple strategy is for field-trial users to mark up the manual while they are using it. They can thus rapidly indicate typos, misleading information, and confusing sections.

Software and the accompanying manuals are rarely completed. Rather, they go into a continuous process of evolutionary refinement. Each version eliminates known errors, adds refinements, and extends the functionality. If the users can communicate with the manual writers, then there is a greater chance of rapid improvement. Most manuals offer a tear-out sheet for users to indicate comments for the manual writers. This device can be effective, but other routes should also be explored: electronic mail, interviews with users, debriefing of consultants and instructors, written surveys, group discussions, and further controlled experiments or field studies.

Brockmann (1990) offers a nine-step process for writing user documentation:

1. Develop the document specifications:
   - Use task orientation
   - Use minimalist design
   - Handle diverse audiences
   - State the purpose
   - Organize information and develop visualizations
   - Consider layout and color
2. Prototype
3. Draft
4. Edit
5. Review
6. Field test
7. Publish
8. Perform postproject review
9. Maintain

12.4   Preparation of Online Facilities

There is a great attraction to making technical manuals available on the computer. The positive reasons for doing so are these:

- Information is available whenever the computer is available. There is no need to locate the correct manual—which activity could cause a minor disruption if the proper manual is close by, or a major disruption if the manual must be retrieved from another building or person. The harsh reality is that many users lose their manuals or do not keep the manuals current with new versions of the software.

- Users do not need to allocate physical work space to opening up manuals. Paper manuals can be clumsy to use and can clutter a workspace.
- Information can be electronically updated rapidly and at low cost. Electronic dissemination of revisions ensures that out-of-date material cannot be retrieved inadvertently.
- Specific information necessary for a task can be located rapidly if the online manual offers electronic indexing or text searching. Searching for one page in hundreds can usually be done more quickly on a computer than with printed material.
- Authors can use graphics, sound, color, and animations that may be helpful in explaining complex actions and creating an engaging experience for users.

However, these positive attributes can be compromised by several potentially serious negative side effects:

- Displays may not be as readable as printed materials (see Section 12.2).
- Each display may contain substantially less information than a sheet of paper, and the rate of paging is slow compared to the rate of paging through a manual. The display resolution is lower than that for paper, which is especially important when pictures or graphics are used.
- The user interface of help systems may be novel and confusing to novices. By contrast, most people are thoroughly familiar with the "user interface" of paper manuals. The extra mental effort required for navigating through many screens may interfere with concentration and learning.
- Splitting the display between work and help or tutorial windows reduces the space for work displays. If users must switch to a separate application, then the burden on the user's short-term memory can be large. Users lose their context of work and have difficulty remembering what they read in the online manual. Multiple displays or windows provide a potential resolution for this problem.

Even recent studies (Hertzum and Forkjaer, 1996) have shown that paper manuals can yield faster learning. Still, the online environment opens the door to a variety of helpful facilities (Roesler and McLellan, 1995) that might not be practical in printed form. Relles and Price (1981) offer this list:

- Successively more detailed explanations of a displayed error message
- Successively more detailed explanations of a displayed question or prompt
- Successive examples of correct input or valid commands
- Explanation or definition of a specified term
- A description of the format of a specified command

- A list of allowable commands
- A display of specified sections of documentation
- A description of the current values of various system parameters
- Instruction on the use of the system
- News of interest to users of the system
- A list of available user aids

Houghton (1984) reviews online help facilities and points out the great difficulty in helping the novice user to get started, as well as helping the expert user who needs one specific piece of information. Kearsley (1988) offers examples, empirical data about online help systems, and these guidelines:

- Make the help system easy to access and easy to return from.
- Make helps as specific as possible.
- Collect data to determine what helps are needed.
- Give users as much control as possible over the help system.
- Supply different helps for different types of users.
- Make help messages accurate and complete.
- Do not use helps to compensate for poor interface design.

Results demonstrating the efficacy of online help facilities come from a study with 72 novice users of a text editor (Cohill and Williges, 1982). A control group receiving no online help facilities was compared with groups in eight experimental conditions formed from all combinations of initiation (user versus computer causes the help session to begin), presentation (printed manual versus online), and selection of topics (user versus computer selects which material is displayed). The control group with no online facilities performed significantly less well than did the experimental groups (Table 12.2). Of the eight experimental groups, the best performance was achieved by the user-initiated, user-selected, and printed-manual group.

Magers (1983) revised an online help facility to offer context-sensitive help instead of keyword-indexed help, wrote tutorial screens in addition to the reference material, reduced computer jargon, used examples instead of a mathematical notation, provided an online dictionary of command synonyms, and wrote task-oriented rather than computer-oriented help screens. Thirty computer novices were split into two groups; half received the original and half the modified help facility. The subjects with the revised help achieved a task score of 90.6, compared with 43.0 for the other subjects. Time was reduced from 75.6 to 52.0 minutes with the improved help facility. Subjective-satisfaction scores also strongly favored the revised help facility.

In spite of improvements, many users wish to avoid paper or online manuals, and prefer to learn system features by exploration (Rieman, 1996).

Table 12.2

Results from a study comparing nine styles of online help facilities (Cohill and Williges, 1982).

Help Configurations

Initiation	Presentation	Selection	Time in Subtask	Errors per Subtask	Commands per Subtask	Subtasks Completed
User	Manual	User	293.1	0.4	8.4	5.0
User	Manual	System	442.2	2.0	17.7	4.9
User	Online	User	350.9	1.1	13.5	5.0
User	Online	System	382.2	1.8	17.6	4.9
System	Manual	User	367.9	1.3	13.1	4.8
System	Manual	System	399.1	0.9	13.8	4.9
System	Online	User	425.9	2.8	15.1	5.0
System	Online	System	351.5	1.2	13.7	4.9
Control: No HELP Available			679.1	5.0	20.2	3.4

Nonetheless, for most contemporary software, failure to provide online manuals or help will be seen as a deficiency by most reviewers and users. The form and content of the online help facility make a profound difference. Good writing, task orientation, context sensitivity, and appropriate examples contribute to improved online manuals and help.

12.4.1   Online manuals

Developers of traditional paper manuals are often proud of their work, and may be tempted to load the text automatically to make it available online. This course is attractive, but the results are likely to be less than optimal. Page layouts for paper may not be convertible to a useful online or web formats, and dealing with the figures automatically is risky. The automatic conversion to online or web text is most attractive if the users have a display large enough to show a full page of text; then, precise images of the printed text can be scanned in with text, figures, photographs, page numbers, and so on. A close match between printed and online manuals can be useful, but if the quality of the displayed image is significantly lower than that of the printed version, users may prefer the paper.

Online manuals can be enhanced by availability of string search, multiple indices, tables of contents, tables of figures, electronic bookmarks, annotation, hypertext traversal, and automatic history keeping (Fig. 12.6). The designers will be most effective if they can redesign the manuals to fit the electronic

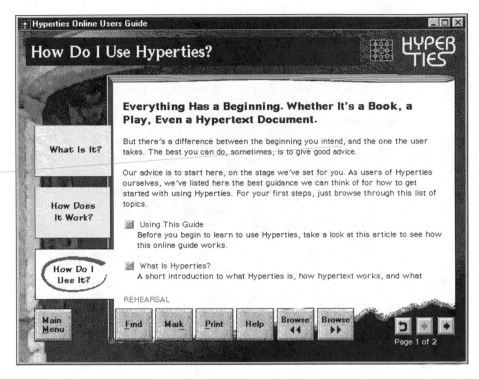

Figure 12.6

Online Manual for Hyperties hypertext electronic-publishing system, using three topic categories related to the user's goals described by Duffy and colleagues (1992). (Used with permission of Cognetics Corp., Princeton Junction, NJ.)

medium and to take advantage of multiple windows, text highlighting, color, sound, animation, and especially string search with relevance feedback.

Several workstation manufacturers have attempted to put their user manuals online. Symbolics was an early success, with 4000 pages online in such a convenient browser that many purchasers never removed the shrink-wrap plastic from their printed manuals (Walker, 1987). The growing availability plus low production and shipping costs of CD-ROMs has encouraged hardware suppliers to produce browsers for online manuals that are exact images of the printed manuals. Apple put its six-volume *Inside Macintosh* series for developers onto a single CD-ROM with scanned images and hypertext links. This HyperCard product took only 1 month of intense effort to develop (Bechtel, 1990). Another Apple (1993) innovation was to create a CD-ROM guide for interface designers with more than a hundred animations of poor, good, and better designs.

A vital feature for online manuals is a properly designed table of contents that can remain visible to the side of the page of text. Selection of a chapter or other entry in the table of contents should immediately produce the appropriate page on the display. Expanding or contracting tables of contents (Egan et al., 1989) or multiple panes to show several levels at once are beneficial (see Fig. 13.10) (Chimera and Shneiderman, 1994).

A more primitive approach to online manuals is the Unix man facility, which has textual descriptions and associated options for each command. Users must know the command names to find the material, but a clever and simple system called apropos helps substantially. The apropos file contains the name of each Unix command with a carefully written one-line description. Users can type apropos sort to get this listing, and then can display the manual pages:

sortm	**sort messages**
comm	select, reject lines common to two sorted files
look	find lines in a sorted file
qsort	quick sort
scandir, alphasort	scan a directory
sort	sort or merge files
sortbib	sort bibliographic database
tsort	topological sort

This approach can work some of the time, but seems to be more effective for experienced than for novice users.

Online help that offers concise descriptions of the interface syntax and semantics is probably most effective for intermittent knowledgeable users, but is likely to be difficult for novices who have more need for tutorial training. The traditional approach is to have the user type or select a help-menu item, and to display six or 60 or 600 alphabetically arranged command or menu names for which there is a paragraph or more of help that the user can retrieve by typing help followed by the command name. This method can also work, but it is often frustrating for those users who are not sure of the correct name for the task they wish to accomplish; for example, the name might be search, query, select, browse, find, reveal, display, info, or view. They may see several familiar terms but not know which one to select to accomplish their task. Worse still, there may not be a single command that accomplishes the task, and there is usually little information about how to assemble commands to perform tasks, such as converting graphics into a different format.

Designers can improve *keyword lists* by clustering keywords into meaningful categories, and indicating a starter set of commands for novices. Users may also be able to set the level of detail and the kind of information (for example, descriptions with or without options, examples, complete syntax) that they obtain about each command.

Two other useful lists might be of *keystrokes* or *menu items*. Each might have an accompanying feature description, such as the first few lines from the help list of the early keyboard-oriented WordPerfect:

Key	Feature	Key Name
Ctrl-F5	Add Password	Text In/out,2
Shft-F7	Additional Printers	Print,S
Shft-F8	Advance Up, Down or Line	Format,4
Ctrl-PgUp	Advanced Macros	Macro Commands
Ctrl-F10	Advanced Macros, Help on	Macro Definition
Shft-F8	Align/Decimal Character	Format,4

Many designers recognized that the keyword lists are overwhelming and that users probably want to have local information about the task that they are performing. They developed *context-sensitive help,* in which users get different messages from the help processor, depending on where they are in the software. Help requested from inside a dialog box produces a window with information about that dialog box, preferably in a nearby pop-up window.

Another approach to context-sensitive help in form-fillin or menu systems is to have the user position the cursor and then to press F1 or a help key to produce information about the item on which the cursor is resting. A subtle variation is to use a mouse to click on a help button or a ? to turn the cursor into a question mark. Then, the cursor is dropped on a field, icon, or menu item, and a pop-up window describes that item. In an accelerated version of this technique, the user simply drags the cursor over items, causing a small windows to pop up with explanations of those items. This strategy is the idea behind Apple's balloon help (Fig. 12.7).

A variant of balloon help is to turn on all the balloons at once, so that the user can see all the explanations simultaneously. A mode switch might change from the balloons to a set of marks that indicate which parts of the display are clickable, double-clickable, draggable, and so on.

Searching through the full text of online manuals is increasingly rapid, and the user-interface strategies are being refined steadily. An expanding and contracting table of contents was combined with string search and relevance feedback indicating number of "hits" on the table-of-contents listing (Egan et al., 1989). A series of three empirical studies showed the effects of several improvements and the advantage over print versions of the same document. The electronic version was advantageous, especially when the

Figure 12.7

Apple's balloon help pops up a single balloon with an explanation of the item on which the cursor is resting on. Users can turn off the balloon help. (Used with permission of Apple Computer, Cupertino, CA.)

search questions contained words that were in the document headings or text. Browsing strategies were found to be most effective in a study of 87 computer-science students, but search by keywords proved to be a useful complement (Hertzum and Frokjaer, 1996).

The Microsoft Windows 95 help facility offers users access to large numbers of hyperlinked articles. Users begin by selecting a topic word; then, they can scroll a list of relevant article titles to find the most appropriate one. The help articles are task oriented with step-by-step instructions, but the large number of articles and the complexity of information often makes it hard for novices to get what they need. Some level structuring of the help articles to limit the novices to seeing novice topics would be an improvement. Popular features are the Wizards and CueCards that guide users through sequences of actions to accomplish a task such as preparing a macro.

The online help in Microsoft Windows 95 offers four ways of finding relevant articles, called *topics*. Users can browse a meaningfully organized table of contents that lists the topics hierarchically. They can also browse an alphabetical list of terms and topics, or find a topic by typing the first few letters of a keyword (Fig. 12.8). This huge list is searched rapidly, and variant

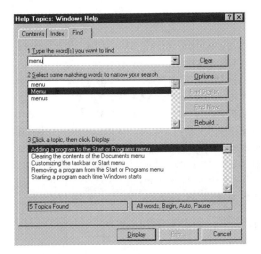 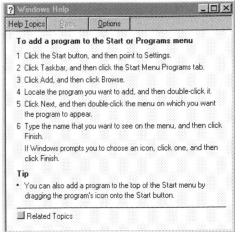

Figure 12.8

Microsoft Windows 95 offers elaborate online help, including an index, bookmarks, definition buttons, and other features to assist navigation. (Used with permission of Microsoft Corp., Redmond, WA.)

forms of capitalization are shown for the exact words as they appear in the topics. Finally, the Answer Wizard approach allows users to type a request using natural-language statements; the program then selects the relevant keywords and offers a list of topics organized into three categories. For example, typing "Tell me how to print addresses on envelopes" produces:

How Do I
>
> Print an address on an envelope
>
> Change the size of an envelope
>
> Print envelopes by merging an address list
>
> ...

Tell Me About
>
> Field codes: UserAddress field
>
> Form letters, envelopes, and mailing labels
>
> Making a list of names and addresses for a mail merge
>
> ...

Programming and Language Reference
>
> Mail Merge statements and functions
>
> Tool statements and functions

This example query produces an effective result as the first topic, but other topics are not appropriate. Results will vary depending on the situation.

12.4.2   Online tutorials, demonstrations, and animations

First-time users of a software package need an interactive tutorial environment in which the computer instructs the user to carry out commands right on the system. One introductory tutorial for the Lotus 1-2-3 package displays the exact keystrokes the user must type, and then carries out the commands. The user can type the exact keystrokes or just keep pressing the space bar to speed through the demonstration. Adobe's PhotoDeluxe includes an online tutorial that leads users through the multiple steps needed for graphical image manipulation (Fig. 12.9). Some users find this guided approach attractive; others are put off by the restrictive sequencing that prevents errors and exploration.

Online tutorials can be effective because the user (Al-Awar et al., 1981)

- Does not have to keep shifting attention between the terminal and the instructional material
- Practices the skills needed to use the system
- Can work alone at an individual pace and without the embarrassment of mistakes made before a human instructor or fellow students

The opportunity for carrying out practice tasks as part of an online tutorial is one of the latter's greatest strengths. Getting users to be active is one of the key tenets of the minimal-manual approach, and it applies especially well to

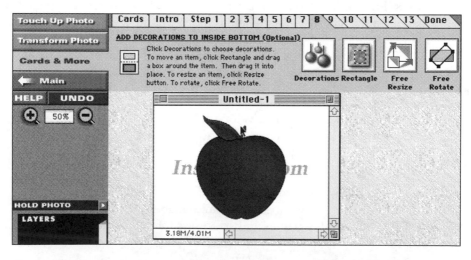

Figure 12.9

This online tutorial for Adobe PhotoDeluxe leads users through the multiple steps needed for graphical image manipulation. It shows three levels of menus simultaneously, giving users flexibility in moving rapidly among tasks. (Used with permission of Adobe Systems, Seattle, WA.)

online tutorials. Subjects who carried out online exercises learned better than did those who used only guided exploration (Wiedenbeck et al., 1995).

Creators of interactive tutorials must address the usual questions of instructional design and also the novelty of the computer environment. A library of common tasks for users to practice is a great help. Sample documents for word processors, slides for presentation software, and maps for geographic-information systems help users to experience the application. Repeated testing and refinement is highly recommended for tutorials.

Demonstration (demo) disks have become a modern high-tech art form. Someday soon, someone should start a museum of demo disks to preserve these innovative, flashy, and slick byproducts of the computer era. Demo disks are designed to attract potential users of software or hardware by showing off system features using the best animations, color graphics, sound, and information presentation that advertising agencies can produce. The technical requirement that the demo fit on a single diskette makes development challenging, but this requirement is giving way as demos are put on CD-ROMs or on the World Wide Web. Animated text (words zooming, flipping, or spinning), varied transitions (fades, wipes, mosaics, or dissolves), sound effects, bright graphics, and finally an address or telephone number to use for ordering the software are typically included. The user-interface requirements are to capture and maintain the users' interest, while conveying information and building a positive product image. Automatic pacing or manual control satisfies hands-off or hands-on users, respectively. Sessions should be alterable to suit the user who wants a three-minute introduction and the user who wants a one-hour in-depth treatment. Additional control to allow users to stop, replay, or skip parts adds to the acceptability.

Animations as part of online help are increasingly common as hardware improves and competition increases (Apple, 1993). A simple and ingenious approach is to animate the action icons in a display to give a quick demonstration of usage (Baecker et al., 1991). An artist created brief animations for the 18 icons in the HyperCard tool menu (paint brush, lasso, eraser, and so on) that ran within each icon's 20- by 22-pixel box. A usability test was conducted to refine the designs and to demonstrate their effectiveness: "In every case in which static icons were not understood, the dynamic icons were successful in conveying the purpose of the tool." Another approach to animated help showed sequences of menu or icon selections that performed a complex task, such as moving a block of text (Sukaviriya and Foley, 1990). This project produced a working system that generated the animations automatically from task descriptions. The benefits of animations for learners of user interfaces are still unclear, although users do enjoy this presentation style (Palmiter and Elkerton, 1991; Payne et al., 1992; Harrison, 1995).

12.4.3   Helpful guides

Sometimes, friendly guides, such as the marketing manager for the software, or a famous personality related to the content, or a cartoon character for children, can lead users through a body of knowledge. A pioneering effort was the GUIDES 3.0 project, in which a Native American chief, a settler wife, and a cavalry man appear as small photographs on the display to guide readers through the materials by offering their points of view on the settling of the American West (Oren et al., 1990). When selected, the guides tell their stories through video sequences from laser disk. In addition, a modern woman is available in TV format to help guide the readers through using the system. This approach does not anthropomorphize the computer, but rather makes the computer a medium of communication, much like a book enables the author to speak to readers by way of the printed page.

Introductions to online services such as CompuServe or America Online, web sites such as for the Library of Congress, and Bill Gates's CD-ROM book *The Road Ahead* (1995) welcome new users and offer guidance about which features to begin using. Audio tours of art galleries have become popular at many museums. An informed and engaging curator such as J. Carter Brown can lead visitors through the National Gallery of Art in Washington, D.C., but users can control the pace and replay sections. The well-designed CD-ROM *A Passion for Art* has several authoritative guides explaining the software, history, and impressionist art in the Barnes collection (Corbis, 1995). A still photo of the speaker is accompanied by spoken text to guide the users through the software and the collection.

Natural-language dialog was proposed for interactive learning about an operating-system command language, but this strategy has not proved to be effective (Shapiro and Kwasny, 1975; Wilensky et al., 1984). An optimistic discussion of advice-giving expert systems (Carroll and McKendree, 1987) laments the lack of behavioral research and focuses on questions such as these: In what ways do people voluntarily restrict their use of natural language when interacting with a recognition facility? Can user models that incorporate learning transitions and trajectories (as well as end states) be developed? A simulated "intelligent help" system was tested with eight users doing business tasks, such as printing a mailing list (Carroll and Aaronson, 1988). The researchers prepared messages for expected error conditions, but they found that "people are incredibly creative in generating errors and misconceptions, and incredibly fast." The results, even with a simulated system, were mixed; the authors concluded that "development of intelligent help systems faces serious usability challenges." In a Smalltalk programming environment, cartoonlike gurus appear onscreen and offer audio commentaries with animated demonstrations of the GUI (Alpert et al., 1995). The designers consider many of the problems of anthropomorphic help, such as user initiation, pacing, and user control of remediation; unfortunately, however, no empirical evidence of efficacy is offered.

The newer and apparently more effective approach is to have a help network, in which email is used to support question asking and responses (Eveland, 1994; Ackerman, 1994; Ackerman and Palen, 1996). Electronic-mail help questions can be sent to a designated help desk or staff person, or to a general list within an organization. Responses can be received in seconds or, more typically, minutes or hours, but users must publicly expose their lack of knowledge and risk getting incorrect advice. In one simple example a broadcast message produced the answer in 42 seconds:

```
Time: 18:57:10 Date: Fri Oct 29, 1993
From: <azir>
after i change a list to a group, how long before
I can use it?
```

```
Time: 18:57:52 Date: Fri Oct 29, 1993
From: starlight on a moonless night <clee>
you can use it immediately
```

Increasingly the communal broadcast approach is appealing because of low cost, and respondents have a sense of satisfaction from being able to help and demonstrate their abilities. The social nature of computing networks encourages question asking. Recording questions and answers into files of *frequently asked questions (FAQs)* enables newcomers to browse typical problems discussed in the past. For example, this question and brief answer come from the Netscape Mail Server FAQ:

```
Can the Mail Server deliver mail using UUCP?
```

```
No, the Mail Server doesn't support UUCP at present. We
recommend the use of more current standards, such as PPP
and SLIP.
```

12.5   Practitioner's Summary

Paper manuals and online help can determine the success or failure of a software product. Sufficient personnel, money, and time should be assigned to these support materials. User manuals and online help should be developed before the implementation to help the development team to define the interface and to allow adequate time for testing. Both manuals and online help segments should be tailored to specific user communities and to accomplishment of specific goals (offer task instruction or describe interface objects and actions). Instructional examples should be realistic, encourage prompt action, use consistent terminology, and support error recognition and recovery. Online manuals and help are increasingly attractive, as screen resolution, size, and speed increase, but designers should minimize extra commands, preserve the context of work, and avoid forcing memorization of information. Online guides or tutorials can lend a human touch, if they contain presentations by real humans. Help networks provide a powerful low-cost support mechanism.

12.6   Researcher's Agenda

The main advantage of online materials is the potential for rapid retrieval and traversal of large databases, but little is known about how to offer this advantage conveniently without overwhelming the user. Layered approaches, in which users can set their level of expertise, seem helpful but are untested. The cognitive model of turning pages in a book is too simple, but if elaborate hyperlinked networks are used, disorientation is a danger. Users' navigation among online help segments should be recorded and studied, so that we can gain a better understanding of what help segments are effective. Multiple windows help users by allowing the users to see the problem and the online help or tutorial at the same time, but better automatic layout strategies are needed. Cognitive models of how different classes of people learn to use computer systems need refinement.

World Wide Web Resources   WWW

The World Wide Web contains many online manuals and tutorials that can be studied. There are also guidelines for writing better manuals and some empirical studies.

http://www.aw.com/DTUI

References

Ackerman, Mark S., Augmenting the organizational memory: A field study of Answer Garden, *Proc. Conference on Computer Supported Cooperative Work '94*, ACM, New York (1994), 243–252.

Ackerman, Mark S. and Palen, Leysia, The Zephyr help instance: Promoting ongoing activity in a CSCW system, *Proc. CHI '96 Human Factors in Computer Systems*, ACM, New York (1996), 268–275.

Al-Awar, J., Chapanis, A., and Ford, W. R., Tutorials for the first-time computer user, *IEEE Transactions on Professional Communication*, PC-24, (1981), 30–37.

Allwood, C. M. and Kalen, T., Evaluating and improving the usability of a user manual, *Behaviour & Information Technology*, 16, 1 (January–February 1997), 43–57.

Alpert, Sherman R., Singley, Mark K., and Carroll, John M., Multiple multimodal mentors: Delivering computer-based instruction via specialized anthropomorphic advisors, *Behaviour & Information Technology*, 14, 2 (1995), 69–79.

Apple Computer, *Making it Macintosh*, Cupertino, CA (1993), CD-ROM animated guide.

Baecker, Ronald, Small, Ian, and Mander, Richard, Bringing icons to life, *Proc. CHI '91 Human Factors in Computer Systems*, ACM, New York (1991), 1–6.

Bechtel, Brian, Inside Macintosh as hypertext. In Rizk, A., Streitz, N., and Andre, J. (Editors), *Hypertext: Concepts, Systems and Applications*, Cambridge University Press, Cambridge, U.K. (1990), 312–323.

Brockmann, R. John, *Writing Better Computer User Documentation: From Paper to Hypertext: Version 2.0*, John Wiley and Sons, New York (1990).

Cakir, A., Hart, D. J., and Stewart, T. F. M., *Visual Display Terminals: A Manual Covering Ergonomics, Workplace Design, Health and Safety, Task Organization*, John Wiley and Sons, New York (1980).

Carroll, John M., Minimalist training, *Datamation*, 30, 18 (1984), 125–136.

Carroll, John M., *The Nurnberg Funnel: Designing Minimalist Instruction for Practical Computer Skill*, MIT Press, Cambridge, MA (1990).

Carroll, John M. and Aaronson, Amy P., Learning by doing with simulated intelligent help, *Communications of the ACM*, 31, 9 (September 1988), 1064–1079.

Carroll, John M. and Mack, R. L., Learning to use a word processor: By doing, by thinking, and by knowing. In Thomas, J. C., and Schneider, M. (Editors), *Human Factors in Computing Systems*, Ablex, Norwood, NJ (1984), 13–51.

Carroll, John M. and McKendree, Jean, Interface design issues for advice-giving expert systems, *Communications of the ACM*, 30, 1 (January 1987), 14–31.

Chimera, R. and Shneiderman, B., Evaluating three user interfaces for browsing tables of contents, *ACM Transactions on Information Systems*, 12, 4 (October 1994), 383–406.

Cohill, A. M. and Williges, Robert C., Computer-augmented retrieval of HELP information for novice users, *Proc. Human Factors Society—Twenty-Sixth Annual Meeting* (1982), 79–82.

Corbis Publishing, *A Passion for Art*, Bellevue, WA (1995).

Creed, A., Dennis, I., and Newstead, S., Effects of display format on proof-reading on VDUs, *Behaviour & Information Technology*, 7, 4 (1988), 467–478.

Duffy, Thomas, Palmer, James, and Mehlenbacher, Brad, *Online Help Systems: Theory and Practice*, Ablex, Norwood, NJ (1992).

Egan, Dennis E., Remde, Joel R., Gomez, Louis M., Landauer, Thomas K., Eberhardt, Jennifer, and Lochbum, Carol C., Formative design-evaluation of SuperBook, *ACM Transactions on Information Systems*, 7, 1 (January 1989), 30–57.

Eveland, J. D., Blanchard, Anita, Brown, William, and Mattocks, Jennifer, The role of "help networks" in facilitating use of CSCW tools, *Proc. Conference on Computer Supported Cooperative Work '94*, ACM, New York (1994), 265–274.

Foss, D., Rosson, M. B., and Smith, P., Reducing manual labor: An experimental analysis of learning aids for a text editor, *Proc. Human Factors in Computer Systems*, ACM, Washington, D.C. (March 1982).

Gates, Bill, *The Road Ahead*, Viking Penguin, New York (1995).

Gould, John, and Grischkowsky, Nancy, Doing the same work with hardcopy and with cathode ray tube (CRT) terminals, *Human Factors*, 26 (1984), 323–337.

Gould, J., Alfaro, L., Barnes, V., Finn, R., Grischkowsky, N., and Minuto, A., Reading is slower from CRT displays than from paper: Attempts to isolate a single-variable explanation, *Human Factors*, 29, 3 (1987a), 269–299.

Gould, J., Alfaro, L., Finn, R., Haupt, B., and Minuto, A., Reading from CRT displays can be as fast as reading from paper, *Human Factors*, 29, 5 (1987b), 497–517.

Grandjean, E. and Vigliani, E. (Editors), *Ergonomic Aspects of Visual Display Terminals*, Taylor and Francis, London (1982).

Grant, Allan, Homo quintadus, computers and ROOMS (repetitive ocular orthopedic motion stress), *Optometry and Vision Science*, 67, 4 (1990), 297–305.

Hansen, Wilfred J., Doring, Richard, and Whitlock, Lawrence R., Why an examination was slower on-line than on paper, *International Journal of Man–Machine Studies*, 10, (1978), 507–519.

Hansen, Wilfred J. and Haas, Christine, Reading and writing with computers: A framework for explaining differences in performance, *Communications of the ACM*, 31, 9 (1988), 1080–1089.

Harrison, Susan M., A comparison of still, animated, or nonillustrated on-line help with written or spoken instructions in a graphic user interface, *Proc. CHI '95 Conference: Human Factors in Computing Systems*, ACM, New York (1995), 82–89.

Heines, Jesse M., *Screen Design Strategies for Computer-Assisted Instruction*, Digital Press, Bedford, MA (1984).

Helander, Martin G., Design of visual displays. In Salvendy, Gavriel (Editor), *Handbook of Human Factors*, John Wiley and Sons, New York (1987), 507–548.

Hertzum, Morten and Frokjaer, Erik, Browsing and querying in online documentation: A study of user interfaces and the interaction process, *ACM Transactions on Computer–Human Interaction*, 3, 2 (June 1996), 136–161.

Horton, William K., *Designing and Writing Online Documentation: Help Files to Hypertext*, John Wiley and Sons, New York (1990).

Houghton, Raymond C., Online help systems: A conspectus, *Communications of the ACM*, 27, 2 (February 1984), 126–133.

Jorna, Gerard C., Image quality determines differences in reading performance and perceived image quality with CRT and hard-copy displays, *Proc. Human Factors Society—Thirty-Fifth Annual Meeting*, Human Factors Society, Santa Monica, CA (1991), 1432–1436.

Kearsley, Greg, *Online Help Systems: Design and Implementation*, Ablex, Norwood, NJ (1988).

Mager, Robert F., *Preparing Instructional Objectives*, Fearon, Palo Alto, CA (1962).

Magers, Celeste S., An experimental evaluation of on-line HELP for non-programmers, *Proc. CHI '83 Conference: Human Factors in Computing Systems*, ACM, New York (1983), 277–281.

Oborne, David J. and Holton, Doreen, Reading from screen versus paper: There is no difference, *International Journal of Man–Machine Studies*, 28, (1988), 1–9.

Oren, Tim, Salomon, Gitta, Kreitman, Kristee, and Don, Abbe, Guides: Characterizing the interface. In Laurel, Brenda (Editor), *The Art of Human–Computer Interface Design*, Addison Wesley, Reading, MA (1990), 367–381.

Palmiter, Susan and Elkerton, Jay, An evaluation of animated demonstrations for learning computer-based tasks, *Proc. CHI '91 Conference: Human Factors in Computing Systems*, ACM, New York (1991), 257–263.

Parton, Diana, Huffman, Keith, Pridgen, Patty, Norman, Kent, and Shneiderman, Ben, Learning a menu selection tree: Training methods compared, *Behaviour and Information Technology*, 4, 2 (1985), 81–91.

Payne, S. J., Chesworth, L., and Hill, E., Animated demonstrations for exploratory learners, *Interacting with Computers*, 4, (1992), 3–22.

Price, Jonathan, and staff, *How to Write a Computer Manual*, Benjamin/Cummings, Addison-Wesley, Reading, MA (1984).

Relles, Nathan and Price, Lynne A., A user interface for online assistance, *Proc. Fifth International Conference on Software Engineering*, IEEE, Silver Spring, MD (1981).

Rieman, John, A field study of exploratory learning strategies, *ACM Trans. on Computer–Human Interaction*, 3, 3 (September 1996), 189–218.

Roemer, Joan M. and Chapanis, Alphonse, Learning performance and attitudes as a function of the reading grade level of a computer-presented tutorial, *Proc. Human Factors in Computer Systems*, ACM, Washington, D.C. (1982), 239–244.

Roesler, A. W. and McLellan, S. G., What help do users need? Taxonomies for on-line information needs and access methods, *Proc. CHI '95 Conference: Human Factors in Computing Systems*, ACM, New York (1995), 437–441.

Shapiro, Stuart C. and Kwasny, Stanley C., Interactive consulting via natural language, *Communications of the ACM*, 18, 8 (August 1975), 459–462.

Spencer, C. J. and Yates, D. K., A good user's guide means fewer support calls and lower support costs. *Technical Communication*, 42, 1 (1995), 52.

Strunk, William, Jr. and White, E. B., *The Elements of Style* (Third Edition), Macmillan, New York (1979).

Sukaviriya, Piyawadee "Noi" and Foley, James D., Coupling a UI framework with automatic generation of context-sensitive animated help, *Proc. User Interface Software and Technology*, 3, ACM, New York (1990), 152–166.

Sullivan, Marc A. and Chapanis, Alphonse, Human factoring a text editor manual, *Behaviour and Information Technology*, 2, 2 (1983), 113–125.

van der Meij, Hans and Carroll, John M., Principles and heuristics in designing minimalist instruction, *Technical Communication* (Second Quarter 1995), 243–261.

van der Meij, Hans and Lazonder, Ard W., Assessment of the minimalist approach to computer user documentation, *Interacting with Computers*, 5, 4 (1993), 355–370.

Walker, Janet, Issues and strategies for online documentation, *IEEE Transactions on Professional Communication PC*, 30 (1987), 235–248.

Wiedenbeck, Susan, Zila, Patti L., and McConnell, Daniel S., End-user training: An empirical study comparing on-line practice methods, *Proc. CHI '95 Conference: Human Factors in Computing Systems*, ACM, New York (1995), 74–81.

Wilensky, R., Arens, Y., and Chin, D., Talking to UNIX in English: An overview of UC, *Communications of the ACM*, 27, 6 (June 1984), 574–593.

Wright, P. and Lickorish, A., Proof-reading texts on screen and paper, *Behaviour and Information Technology*, 2, 3 (1983), 227–235.

Mark Kostabi, *Market Research*, 1996

Multiple-Window Strategies

Through even the smallest window the eye can reach the most distant horizon.

A. Bergman, *Visual Realities,* **1992**

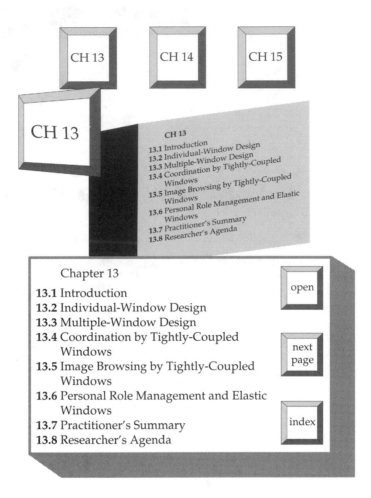

13.1   Introduction

The output of early computers was printed by Teletype on an ever-growing scroll of paper. As designers switched to displays, the need to go back was sometimes supported by electronic scrolling of the session. This technique is useful, but designers became aware of similar situations in which users have to jump around to related text or graphics. Programmers have to jump from procedural code to data declarations, or from procedure invocations to procedure definitions. Authors of scientific papers jump from writing the text to adding a bibliographic reference to reviewing empirical data to creating figures to reading previous papers. Airline reservationists jump from working on a client itinerary to reviewing schedules to choosing seat assignments.

The general problem for many computer users is the need to consult multiple sources rapidly, while minimally disrupting their concentration on their task. With large desk- or wall-sized displays, many related documents can be displayed simultaneously, but visibility and eye–head movement might be a problem. With small displays, windows are usually too small to provide adequate information or context. In the middle ground, with 20–70 cm displays (approximately 640 × 480 to 2048 × 2048 pixels), it becomes a design challenge to offer users sufficient information and flexibility to accomplish their tasks while reducing window housekeeping actions, distracting clutter, and eye–head movement. The animation characteristics, three-dimensional appearance, and graphic design play key roles in efficacy and acceptance (Gait, 1985; Kobara, 1991; Marcus, 1992).

If users' tasks are well understood and regular, then there is a good chance that an effective *multiple-window display* strategy can be developed. The airline reservationist might start a client-itinerary window, review flight segments from a schedule window, and drag selected flight segments to the itinerary window. Windows labeled Seat Selection or Food Preferences might appear as needed, and then the charge-card information window would appear to complete the transaction. When the sequence is varied and unpredictable, users will need to have more control of the layout and will need more training.

Window housekeeping is an activity related to the interface and not directly related to the user's task. If window-housekeeping actions can be reduced, then users can complete their tasks more rapidly. In an empirical test with eight experienced users, the windowed version of a system produced longer task-completion times than did the nonwindowed (full-screen) environment (Bury et al., 1985). Multiple smaller windows led to more time arranging information on the display and more scrolling activity to bring necessary information into view. However, after the time to arrange the display was eliminated, the task-solution times were shorter for the windowed environment. Fewer errors were made in the windowed environment. These results suggest that there are advantages to using windows, but these advantages may be compromised unless effective window arrangement is provided.

On small displays with poor resolution, opportunities for using multiple windows are limited because users are annoyed by frequent horizontal and vertical scrolling. With medium-resolution displays and careful design, multiple windows can be practical and esthetically pleasing. Window-border decorations can be made to be informative and useful. On larger, high-resolution displays, windows become still more attractive, but the manipulation of windows can remain as a distraction from the user's task. Opening windows, moving them around, changing their size, or closing them are the most common operations supported (Card et al., 1984; Myers, 1988).

The visual nature of window use has led many designers to apply a direct-manipulation strategy (see Chapter 6) to window actions. To stretch, move, and scroll a window, users can point at appropriate icons on the window border and simply click on the mouse button (Billingsley, 1988; Kobara, 1991; Marcus 1992). Since the dynamics of windows have a strong effect on user perceptions, the animations for transitions (zooming boxes, sequencing of repainting when a window is opened or closed, blinking outlines, or highlighting during dragging) must be designed carefully.

It is hard to trace the first explicit description of windows (Hopgood et al., 1985), although several sources credit Doug Engelbart with the invention of the mouse, windows, outlining, collaborative work, and hypertext as part of his pioneering NLS system during the mid-1960s (Engelbart, 1988). Movable, overlapping windows appeared in the Smalltalk graphical environment (Fig. 13.1) as it evolved in the 1970s at Xerox PARC, with contributions from Alan Kay, Larry Tesler (1981), Daniel Ingalls, and others. In 1981, the highly graphical Xerox Star (Fig. 13.2) (Smith et al., 1982; Johnson et al., 1990) allowed up to six nonoverlapping windows (with limited size control and movement, but with no dragging of windows or icons) to cover the desktop, plus multiple property sheets to overlay temporarily parts of the windows or desktop. Soon after, the Apple Lisa and, in 1984, the Apple Macintosh (see Fig. 1.1) made popular their style of GUI with overlapping windows (Apple, 1987).

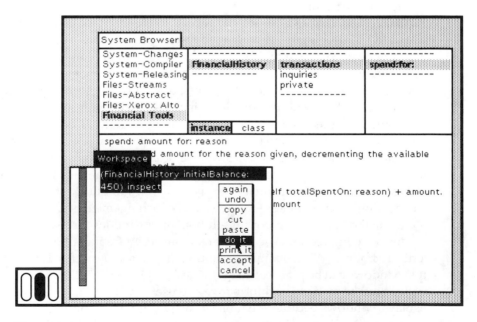

Figure 13.1

Many versions of Smalltalk were created in the 1970s, but the user interface is remembered for overlapping windows, a multipane hierarchical browser, window titles that stick out like tabs, pop-up menus for window actions, and an unorthodox scroll bar. (Courtesy of Parc Place Systems, Mountain View, CA.)

Figure 13.2

The Xerox 8010 Star. The Star played a leading role in popularizing high-resolution, WYSIWYG editing for document preparation in office environments. The Star system pioneered the use of the display screen as an electronic desktop, as well as commercially introducing the mouse, symbolic icons, multiple display windows, and a bitmapped display that showed graphics in detail. (Courtesy of Xerox Corp., Rochester, N.Y.)

Microsoft followed with the graphical MS Windows 1.0 (tiled windows) (Fig. 13.3), 2.03 (Fig. 13.4), 3.0 (Fig. 13.5), and Windows 95 (Color Plate A1) for IBM PCs, while IBM offered OS/2.

The notion of collections of windows assembled into *rooms* is an important step forward in matching window strategies to users' tasks (Henderson and Card, 1986; Card and Henderson, 1987). Users can open and leave in one room a set of windows for reading electronic mail; another room might have a set of windows for composing an article or a program. Rooms can be seen as a form of window macro that enables users to specify actions on several windows at a time. Hewlett-Packard's HP-VUE implements the rooms idea

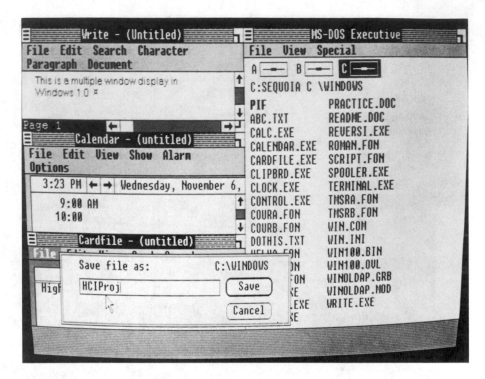

Figure 13.3

Microsoft Windows 1.0, which permitted variable size/place/number and space-filling tiling only. Dialog boxes could appear on top of the tiled windows. (Reprinted with permission from Microsoft Corporation, Redmond, WA.)

as a set of workspaces that users can visit. Sun Microsystems offers virtual workspaces with an overview window to support navigation among clusters of windows. An effective historic overview of windowing strategies is available in videotape form (Myers, 1990).

Much progress has been made, but there is still an opportunity to reduce dramatically the housekeeping chores with individual windows and to provide task-related multiple-window coordination. Innovative features, inventive borders or color combinations, individual tailoring, programmable actions, and cultural variations should be expected.

13.2   Individual-Window Design

The *MS Windows 3.0 User's Guide* (1990) identifies a window as "a rectangular area that contains a software application, or a document file. Windows can be opened and closed, resized and moved. You can open several of them

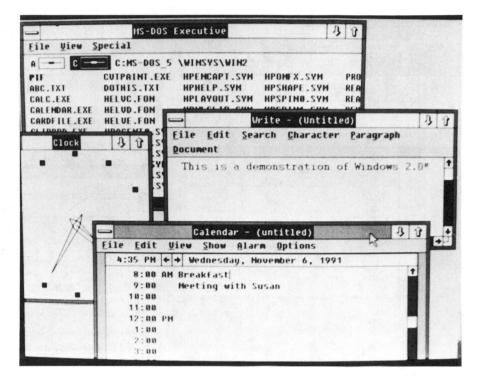

Figure 13.4

Microsoft Windows 2.0, which permitted arbitrary overlapping windows.
(Reprinted with permission from Microsoft Corporation, Redmond, WA.)

on the desktop at the same time and you can shrink windows to icons or enlarge them to fill the entire desktop." Although some people might disagree with aspects of this definition (for example, windows are not always rectangular, and other window actions are possible), it is useful. Window interface objects include:

- *Titles*   Most windows have an identifying title at the top center, top left, or bottom center, or on a tab that extends from the window (Fig. 13.6). Tabbed window titles can be helpful in locating a window on a cluttered desktop. To save window space, designers may create some windows with no titles. Title bars may change shading or color to show which window is currently active (the active window is the one that receives keystrokes from the keyboard). When a window is closed, it may be represented as an icon, and it may show a title to its right, below it and centered, or below it and left justified. Other approaches show the titles in a pop-up menu list or as a tab sticking out of a pile of windows.

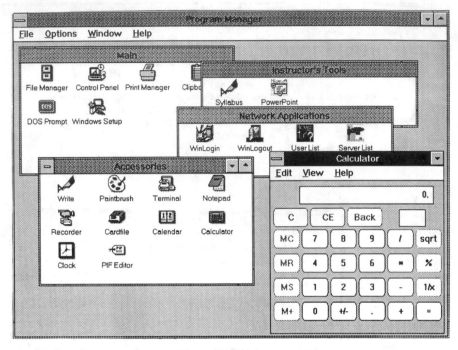

Figure 13.5

Microsoft Windows 3.0 and 3.1x, which had higher-resolution displays and overlapping windows, and became enormously popular. (Reprinted with permission from Microsoft Corporation, Redmond, WA.)

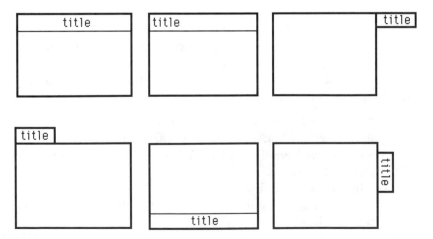

Figure 13.6

Titles may be inside the window in various locations, or protruding from it in various positions.

- *Borders or frames* The window border or frame may be one or more pixels thick to accommodate selection for resizing or to distinguish windows from the background. Several systems use three-dimensional lighting models and may show a shadow below each window. Three-dimensional buttons and icons on the borders have become popular. This three-dimensional effect is attractive to many users (although some users find it distracting), but it may also use precious pixels that could be devoted to window contents. Border thickness or color changes can be used to highlight the currently active window.

- *Scroll bars* Since a window may be small compared to its contents, some method for moving the window over the contents or moving the contents under the window is needed. The basic operation of a scroll bar is to move up or down and left or right, but many variations have been implemented. Small and large motions must be supported, incremental and destination actions are appreciated, and feedback is necessary to help users formulate their plans (Fig. 13.7a). Most scroll bars have some form of up and down arrows on which the user can click to produce a small motion, such as a single-line scroll. An important feature is to permit smooth scrolling when the up or down arrow is selected continuously (for example, when the user holds down the

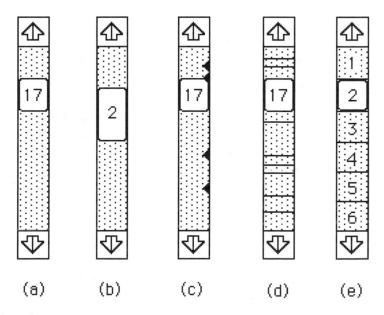

(a)   (b)   (c)   (d)   (e)

Figure 13.7

Scroll bars showing existing and proposed features. (a) Page number in scroll box. (b) Proportional scroll box. (c) Selectable position markers. (d) Value bar showing sections. (c) Page bar with discrete positions.

mouse button). This strategy is preferable to repeated mouse clicks, which distract the user from reading the contents. Scrolling by a full window or page turning is often supported by clicks above or below the scroll box. Users can get to a specific destination in a document, such as the end, by dragging the scroll box to the desired destination.

Feedback in scroll bars is important for ensuring confidence and correct operations. An important approach uses proportional scroll boxes that indicate what portion of the document is visible currently. Another appreciated feature displays a page number inside the scroll box, so that, as users drag the scroll box, they can see where they are in a document (Fig. 13.7b). If the scroll bar is used on a list, such as alphabetically organized document names, then the scroll box can show the first letter of the names.

There is room for improvement of scroll bars. For example, it might be nice to mark a particular position and to see a small triangle on the scroll bar (Fig. 13.7c). Then, merely clicking on the triangle would cause the scroll bar and the window's contents to jump to that location. Scroll bars can contain document-visualization tools (see Chapter 15) using techniques such as *value bars* to show document section boundaries (Fig. 13.7d) (Chimera, 1992) and *page bars* to facilitate discrete page turning (Fig. 13.7e).

Scroll-bar arrows usually indicate the direction for movement of the window, but they could also represent the direction of movement of the contents. An early study (Bury et al., 1982) showed that a majority of users thought that a down arrow meant that the window moved down to show later portions of a document, but many users are still confused and make errors. Recovery of errors is rapid, but creative designers might still pursue visual cues to give users a better indication of which motion will occur.

Window interface actions include:

- *Open action*   A window can be opened from its icon or text-menu list onto the display by a typed command, a menu selection, a voice command, or a double click. The icons can be of varying size (.5 to 3 cm square) and labels can be placed in varying locations.

Feedback during opening can vary from simply having the window appear after the full display repaints, to blanking or blackening of the window destination followed by appearance of the window border and then the contents. Visually appealing animations are possible, such as zoom boxes (animated series of growing boxes emanating from the icon growing into the window), zoom lines (streaks, dots, or other representations of light going to the corners of the window), window-shade opening (the window appears to pull down like a window shade), or three-dimensional flips or spins from the icon to the full window (Silicon Graphics Iris). Open actions may have accompanying sounds.

- *Open place and size*   A key determinant of the usability of window systems is the choice of where the window opens. Most window systems support the most-recently-used place and size approach, which has a better chance to satisfy user needs than a fixed position. Often, the most effective solution is to open the new window close to the current focus (icon, menu item, field, and so on) to limit eye motion, but far enough away to avoid obscuring the current focus. For example, if a control-panel icon is selected, then the control panel could appear just below the icon. Similarly, if a fillin field for a form is selected with a help action, the help window should appear to the side but should not obscure the field in question.

- *Close action*   Windows may have a small icon (typically in the upper-left or upper-right corner) to close them and show animation in a way that is symmetric with the open action. Feedback during closing varies from none (which can be a problem for users who do not know where the icon is located) to zoom boxes (animated series of shrinking boxes moving toward where the window rests on the desktop as an icon), or three-dimensional flips or spins of the window as it shrinks to an icon. Most systems close windows smoothly and rapidly; in slower systems, however, awkward sequences of display painting can be unsettling—for example, if the window is cleared in strips that break up the window frame or the contents.

- *Resize action*   There is great diversity in approaches to resizing a window. The Macintosh permits sizing only from a size box on the lower-right corner, whereas MS Windows, OSF/Motif, OS/2, and many other systems permit sizing by all four corners and by each of the four sides. Some systems will resize adjacent windows automatically. An interesting question is whether or not resizing the window causes reformatting of text (reflowing of documents or changing fontsize), graphics (size changes to ensure that the full object is seen no matter what the window size) or icon layouts (icons are moved to ensure that they remain visible in a smaller window). Another way in which window systems vary is on size limits. Some systems allow windows to be made extremely small (for example, 1×2 centimeters); other systems require windows to be larger than a certain minimum (for example, 4×6 centimeters, or big enough to show the contents). Most window systems have window-size upper bounds that are as large as the display.

- *Move action*   There is also great diversity in approaches to moving a window. The Xerox STAR and MS Windows 1.0 had a Move menu item; users selected it and then clicked on the destination, but the results were sometimes surprising because of the complex layout strategies. The Macintosh designers use the entire title bar as a handle and have the users drag an outline of the window until satisfied with the placement. A variety of visual feedback has been created. Display rates have become faster, and some systems now support displays of the full window as it is dragged. Some systems require that the full window be visible on the display, whereas others permit portions of a window to be off the display in three (typically left, right, and bottom), or in all four, directions. Some systems constrain a window (the child) to be contained within another window (the parent).

- *Bring forward or activation*   When overlapping windows are used, users need a mechanism to bring forward and make active a window that is totally or partially obscured by other windows. Approaches to bringing a window forward include clicking on a menu list of open windows to select one, selecting an action such as Top from a pop-up menu associated with each window, clicking in any part of a window (or a restricted part, such as the title bar), or simply moving the cursor into a window. Variations include the possibility that all windows are active with text flowing into the window that contains the cursor, and that a window is made active but is not brought to the top. Activation may be shown by changes to the border (color or thickness changes), title (color or stripes are added), or text background (brightness increases). An important part of activation is the smoothness and sequence of the painting process. Although some systems are so rapid that the entire window and its contents appear virtually instantaneously (in less than 100 milliseconds), many systems may clear the area first, then paint the border, and finally fill the window top to bottom. Awkward painting strategies—such as painting different-colored parts of a frame one at a time, or filling the window from the bottom to the top—can be unsettling.

These basic window-interface objects and actions are shared by many systems, but there are numerous variations and extensions. An interesting extension is to use spoken commands and speech-recognition technology (see Section 9.4) to control window actions. An initial version of an X Window implementation, called Xspeak, was tested by four users to explore useful features (Schmandt et al., 1990). The authors concluded that "navigation in a window can be handled with speech input," but, in the current implementation they "found the use of voice in navigation an incomplete substitute for the mouse."

13.3 Multiple-Window Design

The challenge of providing access to multiple sources of information has stimulated many solutions:

- *Multiple monitors* Stock-market traders or process-control operators sometimes use multiple physical monitors because that is the only way to see all the information needed with the hardware available. Experience suggests that a smaller number of higher-resolution monitors with multiple windows is superior in most cases, because the distraction of eye motion across the gaps between monitors slows work.

- *Rapid display flipping* Another alternative is rapid alternation or flipping among displays, automatically or by user control. This strategy can be helpful, but it too has been shown to place greater burdens on users to recognize where they are, to know the commands, to formulate a plan to reach the desired display, and to execute the plan. User-controlled rapid display flipping can be usefully applied with knowledgeable users to supplement windowing. Automatic page flipping can be useful in public-access information systems, but airport designers have recognized that, if budget and space permit, having a bank of six or eight displays for departures and another six or eight displays for arrivals is superior to using an automatic page-flipping strategy on one display.

- *Split displays* Many early word processors enabled users to split their display to show two (or more) parts of a document, or two (or more) documents. Split displays were available in early text-oriented systems such as emacs, WordPerfect (two windows), MS Word on IBM-PCs (eight windows), and many other word processors. Splits could be made horizontally (to create two full-width windows) or vertically (to allow side-by-side comparisons—but this arrangement was effective for only those files with narrow lists). A split display is a simplified approach to multiple windows, and offers fewer features than window systems.

- *Space-filling tiling with fixed number, size, and place* Simple display splits are often described as being *tiled*, since the display space is often covered completely with rectangular sections resembling the ceramic tiles on a floor. Tiling usually is meant to convey space filling and no overlapping, but there are many variations. Making a simple dichotomy between tiling and overlapping ignores many interesting variations. The simplest case is a fixed number of fixed-sized and fixed-placement tiles—for example, two, four, six, or eight rectangles filling the display—with the possible exception of some control or icon region.

- *Space-filling tiling with variable size, place, and number*   A common strategy is to start with a single large window and, when a second window is opened, to cut the first one in half horizontally or vertically to make space for the second. Microsoft Windows 1.0 used this tiling strategy with splits occurring when a document or application icon was dragged to the horizontal or vertical borders to cause a vertical or horizontal splits, respectively. Moving a window was possible, but the results were often surprising to users. Similarly, closing a window in a variable-number space-filling tiled layout could produce unexpected results, such as other windows growing to use the space, windows moving, or simply blank space appearing.

- *Non–space-filling tiling*   Variations emerged that did not require the entire display to be covered. The Xerox Star allowed blank space on the right half of the two-column display. In the original Xerox Star, the first window to open would be a full-page size on the left side of the display (see Fig. 13.2); then, the second window would cause the left side of the display to be shared by upper and lower halves. The third window would result in each window getting one-third of the left side of the display. The fourth through sixth (a maximum of six was allowed) windows would fill the right side of the display. This strategy avoided narrow windows that require annoying and frequent horizontal scrolling.

- *Piles of tiles*   Variations on the basic tiling strategy include the piles-of-tiles strategy, in which windows are stacked on top of one another, so that tiles can be popped to reveal previously used windows. Typically, piles of tiles are of fixed size and fixed position to simplify usage. Subsequent windows are placed on the least recently used pile, with tabs protruding to allow selection.

- *Window zooming*   Since users often need to expand a window temporarily, some systems offer a convenient feature to enlarge a window—even to full display size—and then to shrink the window back to the previous size. This technique, often used in slide-presentation programs that show thumbnails of the slide show, allows users to zoom in on a single slide (Fig. 13.8).

- *Arbitrary overlaps*   There is a great appeal to seeing multiple windows on a display with the appearance of partial and arbitrary overlaps. With this now popular strategy, windows can be moved to any point on the display, and portions of the window may be off the display, clipped by the display boundary. This approach has been called *two-and-one-half dimensional programming* to characterize the appearance of multiple windows overlapping as though they were floating one above the other. This strategy was used in Smalltalk, the Apple Lisa, the Apple Macintosh, MS Windows 2.03, and many later window systems. Arbitrary overlapping windows can be advantageous if independent tasks are

Figure 13.8

Microsoft PowerPoint display showing an overview of a slide show by thumbnail views that the user can select to produce full-sized images. (Reprinted with permission from Microsoft Corporation, Redmond, WA.)

being carried out. For example, in the middle of using a word processor, a user can decide to send a piece of electronic mail, to use a calculator, or to consult a personal schedule. The user can pop up a new window, take care of the task, and return to the main task without losing context or restarting the work. However, overlapping windows have the potential to obscure relevant material and to increase the housekeeping load.

- *Cascades* Designers have applied the familiar deck-of-cards metaphor by positioning a sequence of windows from the upper left down to the lower right (or from the lower left up to the upper right). Successive windows are offset below (or above) and to the right to allow each window title to remain visible. Some systems automatically lay out successively opened windows in the cascade. Other systems allow users to select a cascade action from a menu, which places the currently open windows in a cascade, but newly opened windows appear elsewhere on the display. Tombaugh et al. (1987) demonstrated that, with sufficient practice, users could answer questions more rapidly from a multiple-window cascade representing chapters of a book than they could from a paged single window.

There are certainly other approaches to designing multiple windows, and a comprehensive guiding theory is still needed. A theory might emerge from computational geometry or from a more task-related model, such as the working-set model (Card, 1989).

Empirical studies are needed to clarify the issues and to establish methods for measuring performance and ability in windowing environments. Enthusiasts of the greater flexibility of arbitrary overlaps may have been disappointed by an empirical comparison with a tiled approach of the early Xerox Star (Bly and Rosenberg, 1986). Tasks requiring little window manipulation were carried out more quickly with the tiled strategy, but other tasks were carried more quickly with the overlapping strategy by some users. Overlapping window manipulation appeared to require the users to have experience before they could use it effectively. Overall, the authors suggest that, for users with a higher level of expertise, tiled windows may be better.

We implemented program browsing with a multiwindow hypertext environment using a tiled approach using automatic window placement plus zooming (Seabrook and Shneiderman, 1989). Typical program-exploration tasks were performed more rapidly than with a standard single-window editor.

13.4   Coordination by Tightly-Coupled Windows

Designers may break through to the next generation of window managers by developing coordinated windows, in which windows appear, change contents, and close as a direct result of user actions in the task domain (Norman et al., 1986; Shneiderman et al., 1986). For example, in medical insurance-claims processing, when the agent retrieves information about a client, such fields as the address, telephone numbers, and membership numbers should appear on the display. Simultaneously, and with no additional commands, the medical history might appear in a second window, and the record of previous claims might appear in a third window. A fourth window might contain a form for the agent to complete to indicate payment or exceptions. Scrolling the medical-history window might produce a synchronized scroll of the previous claims window to show related information. When the claim is completed, all window contents are saved and the windows are closed. Such sequences of actions can be established by designers, or by users with end-user programming tools.

Coordination is a task concept that describes how information objects change based on user actions. *Tight coupling* among windows is the interface concept that supports coordination. A careful study of user tasks can lead to task-specific coordinations based on sequences of actions; there are also certain generic coordinations that might be supported by interface developers:

- *Synchronized scrolling*   A simple coordination is synchronized scrolling, in which the scroll bar of one window is tightly coupled to another scroll bar, and action on one scroll bar causes the other to scroll the associated window contents. This technique is useful for comparing two versions of a program or document. Synchronization might be on a line-for-line basis, on a proportional basis, or keyed to matching tokens in the two windows. Another way to do synchronization might be as an option on an open action that would specify two windows to open side by side with a single scroll bar between them.

- *Hierarchical browsing*   Tightly coupled windows can be used to support hierarchical browsing (Fig. 13.9). If one window contains the table of contents of a document, selection of a chapter title by a pointing device should lead to display, in an adjoining window, of the chapter contents (Fig. 13.10). Hierarchical browsing was nicely integrated into the Windows 95 Explorer to allow users to browse hierarchical directories, and is increasingly used in web-sites.

- *Direct selection*   Another tight-coupling idea is direct selection, in which pointing at an icon, a word in the text, or a variable name in a program pops up an adjoining window with the details of the icon, word definition, or the variable declaration (Fig. 13.11). Macintosh balloon help and Windows tool-tips are applications of direct selection, and users should be able to define such coordinations easily.

- *Two-dimensional browsing*   A two-dimensional cousin of hierarchical browsing shows an overview of a map, graphic, or photograph in one window, and the details in a second window. Users can move a field-

Figure 13.10

Multiple coordinated windows that create a convenient browsing environment. Clicking in the top window automatically fills the lower windows. (Chimera and Shneiderman, 1991.)

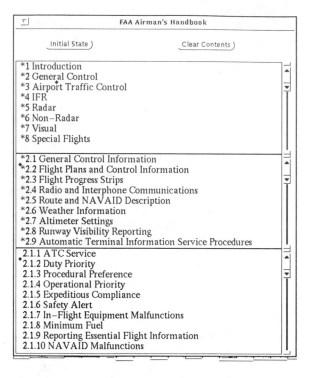

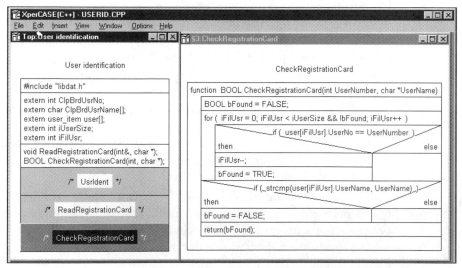

Figure 13.9

Hierarchical browsing in the XperCASE tool (now called EasyCASE with EasyCODE. The specification is on the left. As users click on components (CheckRegistrationCard), the detail view in a Nassi–Shneiderman Chart appears on the right. (Used with permission of Siemens AG Austria.)

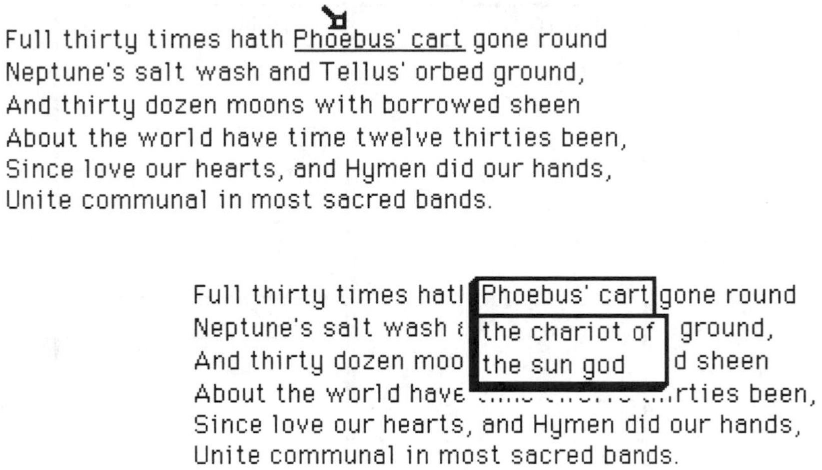

```
Full thirty times hath Phoebus' cart gone round
Neptune's salt wash and Tellus' orbed ground,
And thirty dozen moons with borrowed sheen
About the world have time twelve thirties been,
Since love our hearts, and Hymen did our hands,
Unite communal in most sacred bands.
```

```
Full thirty times hatl Phoebus' cart gone round
Neptune's salt wash ε the chariot of  ground,
And thirty dozen moo the sun god    d sheen
About the world have ..... ..... ....rties been,
Since love our hearts, and Hymen did our hands,
Unite communal in most sacred bands.
```

Figure 13.11

Direct selection of the phrase Phoebus' cart in this sample of Shakespearian text produces an immediate, in-place explanation. This technique is effective in showing data definitions for program variables.

of-view box in the overview to adjust the detail-view content (see Section 13.5).

- *Dependent-windows opening*   An option on opening a window might be to open dependent windows in a nearby and convenient location. For example, when users are browsing a program, when they open a main procedure, the dependent set of procedures could open up (Fig. 13.12).
- *Dependent-windows closing*   An option on closing a window would be to close all the dependent windows. This option might be applied to closing dialog, message, and help windows with a single action. For example, in filling in a form, users might have seen a dialog box with a choice of preferences. That dialog box might have led the user to activate a pop-up or error-message window, which in turn might have led to an invocation of the help window. After the user indicates the desired choice in the dialog box, it would be convenient for a double click on the dialog box close icon (or to select from a menu) to close all three or four windows (Fig. 13.13).
- *Save or open window state*   A natural extension of saving a document or a set of preferences is to save the current state of the display, with all the windows and their contents. This feature might be implemented by a simple addition of a Save screen as... menu item to the

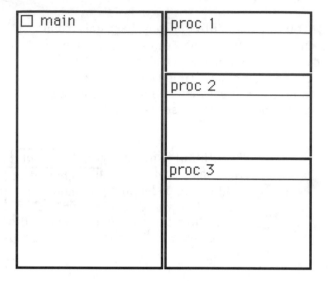

Figure 13.12

Dependent windows. When such windows open, several other windows may open automatically. In this example the main procedure of a program has been opened, and the dependent procedures 1, 2, and 3 have been opened and placed at a convenient location. Connecting lines, shading, or decoration on the frame might indicate the parent and child relationships.

File menu of actions. This action would create a new icon representing the current state; it could be opened to reproduce that state. This feature is a simple version of the rooms approach (Henderson and Card, 1986).

13.5   Image Browsing by Tightly-Coupled Windows

When the user is browsing large images from medical, geographic information, or graphic-design systems, a pair of scroll bars is adequate when the image size is less than three to five times the screen size. With larger images, many designers have found that a tight coupling between an overview and a detail view provides many advantages over a single zoom-

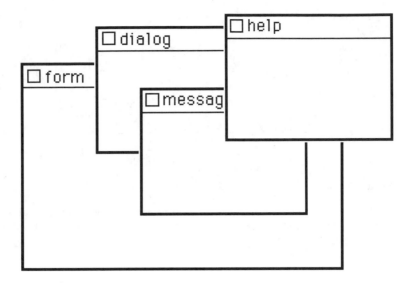

Figure 13.13

Dependent windows. When such windows close, other windows may close too.
Here, all four windows will be closed automatically when the parent window, form,
is closed. Lines, shading, or border decorations may indicate families of windows,
with special marks to indicate parents and children.

ing or several independent windows. A field-of-view box on the overview
can be moved to update the detail view. Similarly, if users pan in the detail
view, the field-of-view box should move in the overview. Well-designed
tightly coupled windows have matching aspect ratios in the field-of-view
box and the detail view, and changes to the shape of either produces a corresponding change in the other.

The magnification from the overview to the detail view is called the *zoom
factor*. When the zoom factors are between 5 and 30, the tightly coupled
overview and detail view pair are effective; for larger zoom factors, however,
an additional intermediate view is needed. For example, if an overview
shows a map of the France, then a detail view showing the Paris region is
effective. However, if the overview were of the entire world, then intermediate views of Europe and France would preserve orientation (Fig. 13.14).

Side-by-side placement of overview and detail views is the most common
layout, since it allows users to see the big picture and the details at the same
time. Some systems provide a single view, either smooth zooming to move in
on a selected point (Bederson and Hollan, 1994), or simply replacing the

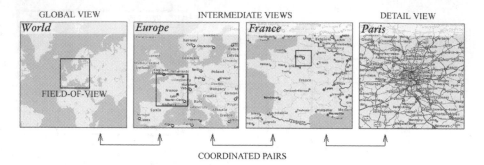

Figure 13.14

Global and intermediate views, which provide overviews for the detail view of Paris. Movements of the field-of-view boxes change the content in the detail view. (Plaisant et al., 1994.)

overview with the detail view. This zoom-and-replace approach is simple to implement and gives the maximal screen space for each view, but it denies the users the chance to see the overview and detail view at the same time. A variation is to have the detail view overlap the overview, even though it may obscure key items.

Attempts to provide detail views (focus) and overviews (context) without obscuring anything have motivated interest in *fisheye views* (Sarkar and Brown 1994; Bartram et al., 1995) (Fig. 13.15). The focus area (or areas) is magnified to show detail, while preserving the context, all in a single display. This approach is visually appealing, but the changing distortion may be disorienting, and the zoom factor in published examples never exceeds 5.

The design for image browsers should be governed by the users' tasks, which can be classified as follows (Plaisant et al., 1995):

- *Image generation*   Paint or construct a large image or diagram.
- *Open-ended exploration*   Browse to gain an understanding of the map or image.
- *Diagnostic*   Scan for flaws in an entire circuit diagram, medical image or newspaper layout.
- *Navigation*   Have knowledge of overview, but need to pursue details along a highway or vein.
- *Monitoring*   Watch the overview and, when problem occurs, zoom in on details.

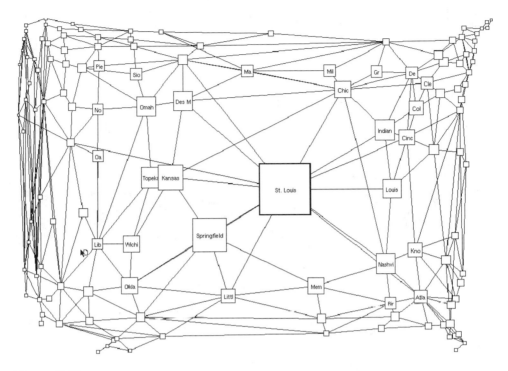

Figure 13.15

Fisheye view of U.S. cities, with the focus on St. Louis. The context is preserved, although the distortions can be disorienting. (Sarkar and Brown, 1994.) (Used with permission of Marc Brown, DEC Systems Research Center, Palo Alto, CA.)

Within these high-level tasks, users carry out many low-level actions, such as moving the focus (jumping from city to city on a map), comparing (viewing two harbors at the same time to compare their facilities, or viewing matching regions in X-ray images of left and right lungs), traversing (following a vein to look for blockages), or marking locations to return to them at a later time.

A taxonomy of browser-interface objects (Fig. 13.16) and actions (Fig. 13.17) reveals the rich possibilities that will be sorted out in the coming years as certain strategies gain commercial dominance. Tight couplings between windows and other interface widgets—especially sliders and data-entry fields—are proving to be helpful in many tasks (see Chapter 15).

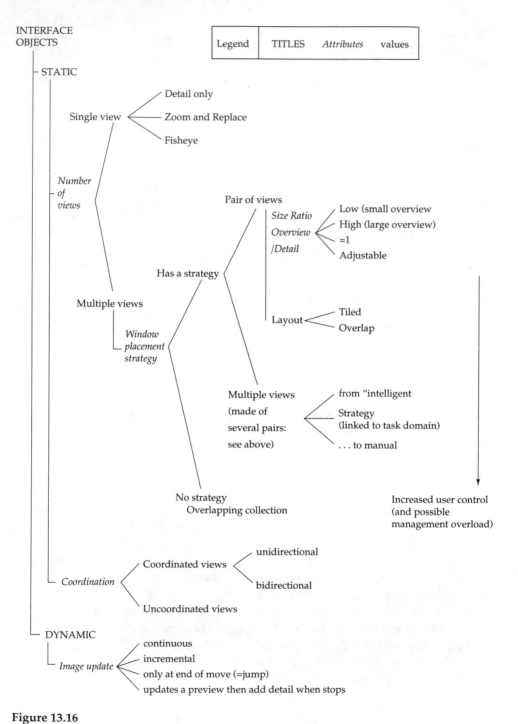

Figure 13.16

Taxonomy of browser strategies, focusing on interface objects. (Plaisant et al., 1994.)

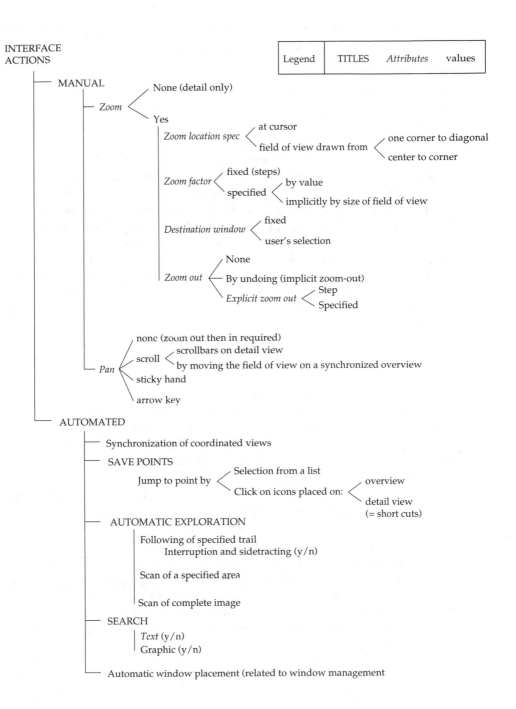

Figure 13.17

Taxonomy of browser strategies, focusing on interface actions. (Plaisant et al., 1994.)

13.6   Personal Role Management and Elastic Windows

Window coordination by tight coupling will facilitate handling of larger images and tasks that have been too complex to deal with in the past. However, there are even more potent opportunities to improve window management radically. The current GUIs offer a desktop with applications represented as icons and documents organized into folders.

Novel approaches emphasize a *docucentric* design (Microsoft's Object Linking and Embedding or Apple's OpenDoc Architecture), in which documents become more important and applications fade into the background. The enriched documents contain multiple object types, such as text, drawings, photos, spreadsheets, and sound, with links across documents to share common objects. Actions that earlier had required opening a new window for an application—such as spell checking, thesaurus referencing, or document faxing—are now integrated into the unified docucentric interface.

Although these are useful steps away from the underlying technology and more in harmony with the users' perceptions of their work, larger steps are needed to reach the next generation of user interfaces. A natural progression is toward a *role-centered* design, which emphasizes the users' tasks rather than the documents. This design concept is in harmony with the current movement toward computer-supported cooperative work and groupware (Chapter 14). These tools are aimed at coordination of several people performing a common task with a common schedule. By contrast, a role-centered design could substantially improve support for individuals in managing their multiple roles in an organization. Each role brings these individuals in contact with different people for carrying out a hierarchy of tasks following an independent schedule. A *personal role manager* (PRM), instead of a window manager, could improve performance and reduce distraction while the user is working in a given role, and could facilitate shifting of attention from one role to another (Shneiderman and Plaisant, 1994; Plaisant and Shneiderman, 1995).

In a personal role manager, each role has a vision statement (a document that describes responsibilities, quotas, and goals) that is established by the user or manager. The explicitness of the vision can simplify the training and integration of new personnel into the organization, and also can facilitate the temporary covering of responsibilities among employees (during vacations or parental leave, for example).

For example, a professor may have roles such as a teacher of courses, advisor to graduate students, member of the recruiting committee, principal investigator of grants, author of technical reports, and liaison to industry. In the teacher role, the professor's vision statement might include the intention to apply electronic mail to facilitate a large undergraduate course. Files might include homework assignments, bibliography, course outline, and so on. The task hierarchy might begin with tasks such as choosing a textbook and end with administering the final exam. The subtasks for administering the final exam might include preparing the exam, photocopying the exam, reserving a room, proctoring the exam, and grading the exam. The set of people includes the students, teaching assistants, bookstore manager, registrar, and colleagues teaching other sections of the course. The schedule would begin with deadlines for submitting the book order to the bookstore manager and end with turning in the final grades to the registrar.

The personal role manager was stimulated by experiences in managing multiple projects with many participants, plus observations and interviews with 15 experienced users to understand their needs. Although there are scheduling, time management, address book, document-management packages available, the coordination of these tools is often underemphasized. The personal role manager would simplify and accelerate the performance of common coordination tasks, in the same way that GUIs simplify file-management tasks.

The key to PRM is organizing information according to the roles that an individual has in an organization. When users are working in a role, they have most relevant information visually available. These visual cues remind them of their goals, related individuals, required tasks, and scheduled events. The initial layout of roles may be established by a manager for a new employee, but then the employee can adjust, combine, or split roles as the demands change.

Screen management is one of the key functions of the personal role manager. All roles should be visible, but the current focus of attention could occupy most of the screen. As users shift attention to a second role, the current one shrinks and the second one grows to fill the screen. Users could simultaneously enlarge two roles if there were interactions between them. The task objects in a personal role manager are these:

- *Vision statement* Each role has a vision statement that reminds users of their goals. As a professor, my teaching role might have a vision statement about my desire to "increase class participation by collaborative methods, improve teamwork on term projects by requiring regular management meetings, prepare careful notes to facilitate future teaching of the same course, and coordinate with my teaching assistants by weekly meetings and electronic-mail discussions."

- *Set of people* When acting in a given role, users interact with a set of people that is a subset of the people in an organization's telephone book. Making the role-relevant group of people continuously visible (for example, with names or small photos on the border of the large screen) has at least two benefits. First, the images will act as cues to remind the user of the need to inform, makes request of, or communicate with that individual (similar to seeing someone in the hallway, and thus triggering communication to coordinate work). Second, the images act as active menus to initiate telephone, fax, or electronic-mail communication. For example, a document can be dragged and dropped onto an image, triggering electronic mail plus a log of the action. Providing direct access to these people without the need of a directory search speeds performance and reduces cognitive load.

- *Task hierarchy* Tasks are hierarchically organized into subtasks via an outlining tool. The professor role may have a task for each of several courses, or the principal-investigator role may have tasks for multiple grants. Each course has multiple subtasks, such as writing the syllabus, ordering textbooks, giving exams, and preparing final grades. The task hierarchy acts as a to-do list, and is linked to the schedule calendar to remind users of upcoming deadlines.

- *Schedule* Each role has an associated schedule that is a component of a user's master schedule. When viewing a role, the user initially sees only the role-related schedule. For example, when the user is viewing the professor role, the semester schedule is visible; when the principal-investigator role is on view, the 2-year grant schedule is visible. Schedules can be combined to reveal a master schedule that allows users to allocate time and to ensure that travel, vacations, and required meetings are blocked off on every schedule.

The requirements for a personal role manager include these:

- Support a *unified framework* for information organization according to users' roles.
- Provide a *visual, spatial layout* that matches tasks.
- Support *multiwindow actions* for fast arrangement of information.
- Support *information access* with partial knowledge of an information item's nominal, spatial, temporal, and visual attributes, and relationships to other pieces of information.
- Allow *fast switching* and *resumption* among *roles*.
- Free users' *cognitive resources* to work on *task-domain actions,* rather than making users concentrate on interface-domain actions.
- Use *screen space* efficiently and productively for tasks.

The Rooms model for multiple-window workspaces provides improved support for these requirements, but does not provide sufficiently smooth transition among roles. *Elastic windows* organize windows in a space-filling, hierarchically nested, tiled layout that was designed to support the personal role manager's requirements (Kandogan and Shneiderman, 1997). Actions, such as an `open` or `close`, can be applied to a group of windows to open six related electronic-mail messages or 10 resumes of job applicants. In a study with 12 sophisticated users, multiwindow operations were shown to enable faster task switching and structuring of the work environment, by opening, closing, or changing the size of 10 to 20 windows at a time.

Figure 13.18 depicts an example mapping of different roles of a student onto a hierarchical window organization. This student takes two courses this semester: Software Engineering and Computer Networks. Project materials and partners; homework assignments; and correspondence with the professor, TAs, and classmates for each course are organized in a hierarchical fashion. This student has a number of other roles, in which he manages home duties, job responsibilities, and the planning of a birthday party. Partners,

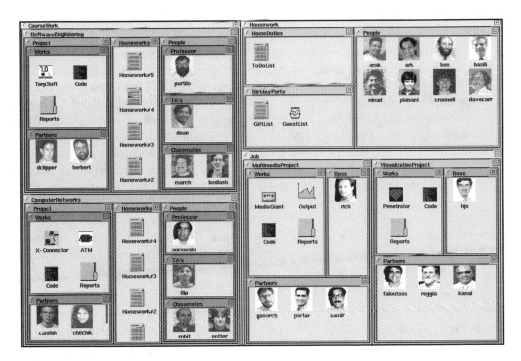

Figure 13.18

Role-manager prototype for a student doing coursework (in Software Engineering and Computer Networks), housework, and a job (with a Multimedia Project and a Visualization Project). Users can resize, open, close, or move groups of windows. (Kandogan and Shneiderman, 1997.)

schedules, tools, and documents pertaining to each of these roles are mapped hierarchically into different windows. The interface layout provides an overview of the roles, enables direct access on demand to details of any role, and can be custom-tailored for a specific task.

In elastic windows, users can change the layout according to tasks quickly, by applying operations on groups of windows (for example, *container* windows that surround their *member* windows). Elastic-window resizing, which the system does by enlarging a window or a group of windows while reducing the size of other windows in the group, enables users to focus easily on information in different windows. Also, a subhierarchy of windows can be collapsed into a single visual primitive (for example, icon or textual item). Then, for example, all windows containing the code for the software-engineering class project can be opened with a single action, thus enabling fast switching among roles.

13.7 Practitioner's Summary

Multiple windows are an accepted feature of contemporary computers. Window-frame designs are distinctive, and graphic-design style is important, as are features such as title bars, action menus, and scroll bars. Users expect to perform rapidly, conveniently, and comprehensibly typical actions, such as opening, closing, moving, and sizing. The popular style of overlapping windows has an appealing three-dimensional (or two-and-one-half–dimensional) look and serves some purpose, but it can produce clutter and be inefficient. Approaches that limit the overlap can be helpful in many situations. Coordination strategies based on user tasks can bring further benefits by automating multiple-window actions, bringing windows close to where they are needed, reducing the housekeeping burden, and avoiding unwanted overlaps. Scrolls bars are applied widely and are usually successful, but there is room for improvement. Browsing large images with tightly-coupled windows simplifies and speeds the users' task completion.

13.8 Researcher's Agenda

Windows provide visually appealing possibilities and intriguing opportunities for designers, but advantages and disadvantages of design features are still poorly understood. Eye-motion studies might provide data for effective design, and basic task analysis can still be productive in classifying the information needs and action sequences of users. A theory of window layouts, based on psychological principles and task analysis, would be a significant contribution. Even without a deeper theory, there seems to be much room for innovation in tight coupling of multiple-window layouts. As higher-resolution and larger displays appear, dense presentations and novel three-dimensional layouts may be possible, with dramatic animations and eye-catching designs. The addition of coordinated windows and window macros is possible, and may lead to a new generation of GUIs that support personal role management.

World Wide Web Resources   WWW

Window management is changing because of the World Wide Web, where new ideas such as frames can be tried, debated, and studied. Novel window management strategies are offered by some developers in demos and commercial products.

http://www.aw.com/DTUI

References

Apple Human Interface Guidelines: The Apple Desktop Interface, Addison-Wesley, Reading, MA (1987).

Bartram, Lyn, Ho, Albert, Dill, John, and Henigman, Frank, The continuous zoom: A constrained fisheye technique for viewing and navigating large information spaces, *Proc. User Interface Software and Technology '95*, ACM, New York (1995), 207–215.

Bederson, B., Hollan, J. D., Pad++: A zooming graphical interface for exploring alternate interface physics, *Proc. of the UIST '94, User Interface Software and Technology*, ACM, New York (1994), 17–26.

Billingsley, Patricia A., Taking panes: Issues in the design of windowing systems. In Helander, M. (Editor), *Handbook of Human–Computer Interaction*, Elsevier Science Publishers B.V., Amsterdam, The Netherlands (1988), 413–436.

Bly, Sara and Rosenberg, Jarrett, A comparison of tiled and overlapping windows, *Proc. CHI '86 Conference: Human Factors in Computing Systems*, ACM, New York (1986), 101–106.

Bury, K. F., Boyle, J. M., Evey, R. J., and Neal, A. S., Windowing versus scrolling on a visual display terminal, *Human Factors*, 24, 4 (1982), 385–394.

Bury, Kevin F., Davies, Susan E., and Darnell, Michael J., Window management: A review of issues and some results from user testing, IBM Human Factors Center Report HFC-53, San Jose, CA (June 1985).

Card, Stuart K., Theory-driven design research. In McMillan, Grant R., Beevis, David, Salas, Eduardo, Strub, Michael H., Sutton, Robert, and Van Breda, Leo (Editors), *Applications of Human Performance Models to System Design*, Plenum Press, New York (1989), 501–509.

Card, Stuart K., Pavel, M., and Farrell, J. E., Window-based computer dialogues, *INTERACT '84, First IFIP Conference on Human–Computer Interaction*, London (1984), 239–243.

Card, Stuart K. and Henderson, Austin, A multiple virtual-workspace interface to support task switching, *Proc. CHI '87 Conference: Human Factors in Computing Systems*, ACM, New York (1987), 53–59.

Chimera, Richard, Value bars: An information visualization and navigation tool for multiattribute listings, *Proc. CHI '92 Conference: Human Factors in Computing Systems*, ACM, New York (1992), 293–294.

Engelbart, Douglas C. and English, William K., A research center for augmenting human intellect. In Greif, I. (Editor), *Computer-Supported Cooperative Work: A Book of Readings*, Morgan Kaufmann, Palo Alto, CA (1988), 81–105.

Gait, Jason, An aspect of aesthetics in human–computer communications: Pretty windows, *IEEE Transactions on Software Engineering*, SE-11, 8 (August 1985), 714–717.

Henderson, Austin and Card, and Stuart K., Rooms: The use of multiple virtual workspaces to reduce space contention in a window-based graphical user interface, *ACM Transactions on Graphics*, 5, 3 (1986), 211–243.

Hopgood, F. R. A., Duce D. A., Fielding, E. V. C., Robinson, K., and Williams, A. S. (Editors), *Methodology of Window Management*, Springer-Verlag, Berlin (April 1985).

Johnson, Jeff, Roberts, Teresa L., Verplank, William, Smith, David C., Irby, Charles H., Beard, Marian, and Mackey, Kevin, The Xerox Star: A Retrospective, *IEEE Computer*, 22, 9 (September 1989), 11–29.

Kandogan, Eser and Shneiderman, Ben, Elastic windows: Evaluation of multi-window operations, *Proc. CHI '97 Conference: Human Factors in Computing Systems*, ACM, New York (1997), 250–257.

Kobara, Shiz, *Visual Design with OSF/Motif*, Addison-Wesley, Reading, MA (1991).

Marcus, Aaron, *Graphic Design for Electronic Documents and User Interfaces*, ACM Press, New York (1992).

Myers, Brad, Window interfaces: A taxonomy of window manager user interfaces, *IEEE Computer Graphics and Applications*, 8, 5 (September 1988), 65–84.

Myers, Brad, *All the Widgets, SIGGRAPH Video Review #57*, ACM, New York (1990).

Norman, Kent L., Weldon, Linda J., and Shneiderman, Ben, Cognitive layouts of windows and multiple screens for user interfaces, *International Journal of Man–Machine Studies*, 25, (1986), 229–248.

Plaisant, Catherine, Carr, David, and Shneiderman, Ben, Image browsers: Taxonomy and design guidelines, *IEEE Software*, 12, 2 (March 1995), 21–32.

Plaisant, Catherine and Shneiderman, Ben, Organization overviews and role management: Inspiration for future desktop environments, *Proc. IEEE Fourth Workshop on Enabling Technologies: Infrastructure for Collaborative Enterprises*, IEEE Press, Los Alamitos, CA (April 1995), 14–22.

Sarkar, Manojit and Brown, Marc H., Graphical fisheye views, *Communications of the ACM*, 37, 12 (July 1994), 73–84.

Schmandt, Chris, Ackerman, Mark S., and Hindus, Debby, Augmenting a window system with speech input, *IEEE Computer*, 23, 8 (August 1990), 50–56.

Seabrook, Richard and Shneiderman, Ben, The user interface in a hypertext, multi-window browser, *Interacting with Computers*, 1, 3 (1989), 299–337.

Shneiderman, Ben and Plaisant, Catherine, The future of graphic user interfaces: Personal role managers, *People and Computers IX*, Cambridge University Press, Cambridge, U.K. (1994), 3–8.

Shneiderman, Ben, Shafer, Phil, Simon, Roland, and Weldon, Linda, Display strategies for program browsing: Concepts and experiment, *IEEE Software*, 3, 3 (May 1986), 7–15.

Smith, D. C., Irby, C., Kimball, R., and Verplank, W. L., Designing the Star user interface, *Byte*, 7, 4 (April 1982), 242–282.

Tesler, Larry, The Smalltalk Environment, *Byte*, 6, (August 1981), 90–147.

Tombaugh, J., Lickorish, A., and Wright P., Multi-window displays for readers of lengthy texts, *International Journal of Man–Machine Studies*, 26, (1987), 597–615.

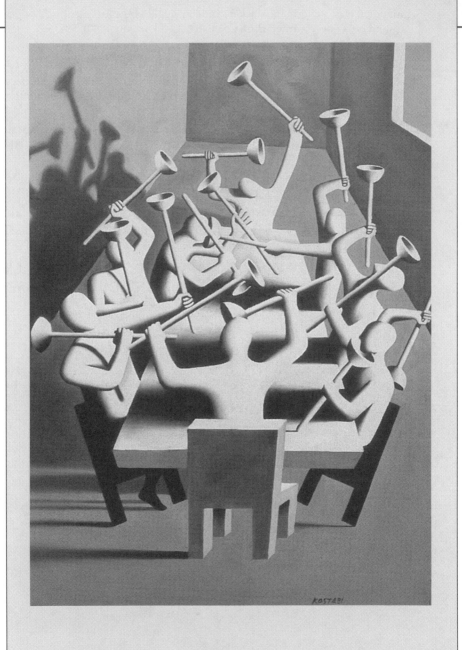

Mark Kostabi, *Upheaval*, 1982

Computer-Supported Cooperative Work

Three helping one another will do as much as six working singly.

Spanish proverb

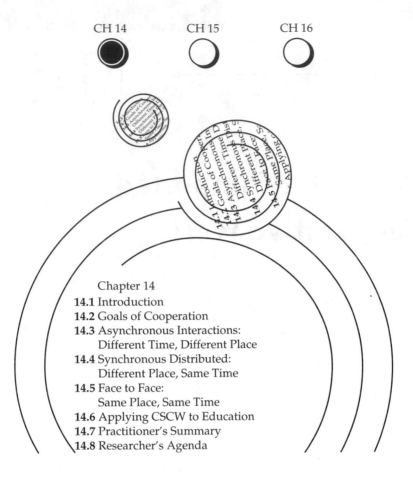

CH 14 CH 15 CH 16

Chapter 14
14.1 Introduction
14.2 Goals of Cooperation
14.3 Asynchronous Interactions:
Different Time, Different Place
14.4 Synchronous Distributed:
Different Place, Same Time
14.5 Face to Face:
Same Place, Same Time
14.6 Applying CSCW to Education
14.7 Practitioner's Summary
14.8 Researcher's Agenda

14.1   Introduction

The introversion and isolation of early computer users has given way to lively online communities of busily interacting dyads and bustling crowds of chatty users. The pursuit of human connections has prompted millions of users to join mailing lists, visit chat rooms, and fill newsgroups with useful information and helpful responses, peppered with outrageous humor. But, as in any human community, there is also controversy, slander, and pornography. The World Wide Web (Chapter 16) has dramatically expanded the communications richness, with colorful graphics and sometimes too-dazzling Java animations. The Web is sometimes derided as a playground, but serious work and creative endeavors are enormously facilitated by the easy flow of information.

Goal-directed people quickly recognized the benefits of electronic cooperation and the potential to live in the immediacy of the networked global village. The distance to colleagues is measured not in miles, but rather in intellectual compatibility and responsiveness; a close friend is someone who responds from 3000 miles away within three minutes at three A.M. with the reference that you need to finish a paper.

The good news is that computing, once seen as alienating and antihuman, is becoming a socially respectable and interpersonally positive force. Enthusiasts hail cooperative technologies, groupware, team processes, coordination science, and other communal utopias, but there may be a dark side to the force. Even optical fiber is not a channel through which you can send a handshake or a hug. How does intimacy survive when mediated by the remoteness in time and physical space? Can laughter and tears mean the same thing for electronic-dialog partners as for face-to-face partners? Will the speedup in work improve or reduce quality? Can cooperative systems be turned into oppressive tools or confrontive environments?

New terminology and metaphors are appearing daily. Although the conferences on *computer-supported cooperative work* have established CSCW as a new acronym, even the organizers debate whether that acronym covers *cooperative, collaborative,* and *competitive* work. The focus of CSCW researchers is on the design and evaluation of new technologies to support the social processes of work, often among distant partners. The implementers and marketeers quickly gravitated to *groupware* as a term to describe the team-oriented commercial products (Baecker, 1993). For researchers, new paradigms and fresh ideas are flowing from psychologists, sociologists, and anthropologists (Vaske and Grantham, 1990; Sproull and Kiesler, 1991). For educators, the movement toward social construction theories of learning is fostered by the World Wide Web and by classroom tools and techniques (Hiltz, 1994; Harasim et al., 1995; Shneiderman et al., 1995).

Networked communities have become talk-show topics, with social commentators celebrating or warning about the transformational power of CSCW. Howard Rheingold's (1993) popular book on *Virtual Communities* tells charming and touching stories of cooperation and support in the San Francisco–based WELL. At the same time, clinical psychologists analyze network addictions and deconstruct manufactured cyber-identities (Turkle, 1995).

14.2   Goals of Cooperation

People cooperate because doing so is satisfying or productive. Communication can have purely emotionally rewarding purposes or specific task-related goals. Communication can be sought individually or imposed managerially.

Relationships can be one-time encounters or enduring. The analysis of cooperative systems is governed by the goals and tasks of the participants:

- *Focused partnerships* are cooperations between two users who need each other to complete a task, such as joint authors of a technical report, two pathologists consulting about a cancer specimen, programmers debugging a program together, or astronaut and ground-controller repairing a faulty satellite. Often, there is an electronic document or image to "conference over." Partners can use electronic mail, voice mail, telephone, or video mail.

- *Lecture or demo* formats have one person sharing information with many users at remote sites. The start time and duration is the same for all; questions may be asked by the recipients. No history keeping is required, but a replay may be possible at a later time.

- *Conferences* allow groups to communicate at the same time or spread out over time, but with participants distributed in space. Many-to-many messaging may be used, with a record of previous conversations: a scientific-meeting program committee might discuss the plans for an upcoming event, or a group of students might discuss the most recent class examination. In more directed conferences, a leader or moderator supervises the online discussion to achieve goals within deadlines.

- *Structured work processes* let people with distinct roles cooperate on some task: a scientific-journal editor arranges online submission, reviewing, revisions, and publication; a health-insurance agency receives, reviews, and reimburses or rejects medical bills; or a university admissions committee registers, reviews, chooses, and informs high-school applicants.

- *Electronic commerce* includes short-term collaborations to inquire about and then order a standard product, and long-term negotiations to craft a major business deal or contract. Electronic negotiations can be distributed in time and space, while producing an accurate record and rapid dissemination of results.

- *Meeting and decision support* can be done in a face-to-face meeting, with each user working at a computer and making simultaneous contributions. Shared and private windows plus large-screen projectors, enable simultaneous shared comments that may be anonymous. Anonymity not only encourages shy participants to speak up, but also allows forceful leaders to accept novel suggestions without ego conflicts.

- *Teledemocracy* allows city, state, or national governments to conduct online town-hall meetings; to expose officials to comments from constituents; or to produce consensus through online conferences, debates, and votes.

There are undoubtedly other cooperative tasks; this list simply indicates the diversity. Within each task, there are numerous variations, and the potential market for innovative software products is large. However, designing for cooperation is a challenge because of the numerous and subtle questions of etiquette, dominance, ego, anxiety, and posturing. The tasks in our list are serious and professional, but there are also opportunities for entertaining multiperson games, challenging contests, or playful social encounters.

The traditional way (Ellis et al., 1991) to decompose cooperative systems is by a time–space matrix:

	Same Time	*Different Times*
Same place	face to face (classrooms, meeting rooms)	asynchronous interaction (project scheduling, coodination tools)
Different places	synchronous distributed (shared editors, video windows)	asynchronous distributed (email, listservs, conferences)

This decomposition focuses on two critical dimensions, and thus guides designers and evaluators.

Research in cooperative systems is more difficult than is that in single-user interfaces. The multiplicity of users makes it nearly impossible to conduct controlled experiments, and the flood of data from multiple users defies orderly analysis. Small-group psychology, industrial and organization behavior, sociology, and anthropology provide useful research paradigms, but many researchers must invent their own methodologies. Subjective reports, case studies, and users' eagerness to continue using the groupware tools are the strongest indicators of success (Kraut et al., 1994).

Cooperative systems are maturing, but the determinants of success are still not clear. Electronic mail is a widespread success story, and videoconferencing use grows slowly but steadily, while shared calendar programs are repeatedly spurned. Grudin (1994) outlines some of the causes of groupware failures: disparity between who does the work and who gets the benefit, threats to existing political power structures, insufficient critical mass of users who have convenient access, violation of social taboos, and rigidity that counters common practice or prevents exception handling.

Arguments over measures of success also complicate analysis. Whereas some people cite the high utilization of electronic mail, others question whether electronic mail aids or hinders job-related productivity. Videoconferencing may initially reduce travel expenses, but it can encourage cooperation with more distant partners, thus leading to increasing costs and possibly more travel.

In educational environments, outcomes can be measured by comparison of scores on final exams, but students are often learning new skills when they work collaboratively in networked environments. These skills are needed in the workplace, where teamwork and effective communication are essential.

Cooperation and discussion are a natural part of democratic processes, so online campaigning, organizing, and consensus building are likely to become required skills for politicians. Electronic mail to public officials and online town-hall meetings are already possible, but electronic parliaments with consensus building, committee caucusing, deal making, and voting are still to emerge. Utopian visionaries suggest increased and constructive participation in democratic processes, but other people warn about the dangers of uninformed citizens influencing legislation and of harmful speedup that reduces thoughtful deliberation.

Community networks are already successful and are spreading (Rheingold, 1993; Schuler, 1996). Some communities are geographically confined, such as the ones in Seattle, Washington, Taos, New Mexico, and Blacksburg, Virginia (Carroll and Rosson, 1996), whereas others have a global perspective but are topically focused, such as the ones for AIDS patients, archaeologists, and agronomists. The positive side is the facilitation of communication among like-minded people who have shared interests; the negative side is that electronic communities may have less commitment than do those that attend to face-to-face meetings of clubs, civic groups, and parent–teacher associations.

14.3   Asynchronous Interactions: Different Time, Different Place

Cooperation across time and space is one of the gifts of technology. Durable messages transmitted electronically enable cooperation and therefore, for many users, electronic mail is a popular starting point. Electronic mail is widely appreciated, but it can be too loosely structured (endless chatting with no process or leader to reach a goal or to make a decision), too overwhelming (hundreds of messages per day can be difficult to absorb effectively), and too transient (lack of storage organization may make it difficult to locate relevant messages, and late joiners in a discussion have no means to catch up on earlier comments). To remedy these problems, structured methods for electronic conferencing have been created (Hiltz and Turoff, 1978; Hiltz, 1984) and have been applied in widely used software such as COSY and FirstClass. Filtering and archiving tools in commercial electronic-mail packages—such as Eudora, Lotus cc:Mail, or Microsoft Mail—enable users to manage incoming and previously received electronic mail. Web browsers, such as Netscape Navigator and Microsoft Internet Explorer, and commercial services such as CompuServe and America Online, provide mail handling as well. Setting up private mailing lists, web sites, and discussion groups is also getting easier. Support for teams, whole organizations, or larger communities is beginning to emerge, along with more structured work processes that are supported by computing networks.

14.3.1   Electronic Mail

The atomic unit of cooperation is the electronic-mail message; the FROM party sends a message to the TO party. Electronic-mail systems (Fig. 14.1) share the notion that an individual can send a message to another individual or a list of individuals. Messages usually are delivered in seconds or minutes, and replying is easy and rapid.

Electronic-mail messages typically contain text only, but increasingly graphics, spreadsheets, sounds, animations, web pointers, or other structured objects can be included. The quests for more flexibility and for instantaneous distribution are persistent. Sending graphics or spreadsheets is becoming more common as standard formats and effective conversions emerge. Still rare is the availability of video electronic mail, but it should spread during the next decade. Those users who have been able to add video comments to their electronic mail say that they like this feature and use it regularly—it does seem to have the capacity to add a more personal touch. Problems of standardization

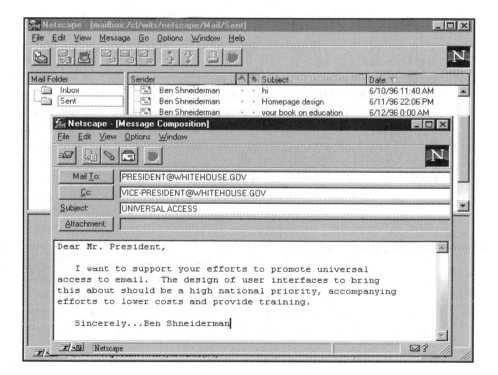

Figure 14.1

Electronic-mail system for Netscape Navigator, showing Inbox, Sent mail list, and a current note being composed. (© 1996 Netscape Communication Corporation. Used with permission.)

across video systems and the need for good user interfaces are apparent in the reports from early projects (Borenstein, 1991; Hoffert and Gretsch, 1991).

Voice mail is effectively sent by the normal telephone networks, but the inclusion of a voice annotation in an electronic-mail message is possible. Telephone service by way of the Internet is also possible, although speech quality is generally below the quality on the telephone network.

Most electronic-mail systems provide fields for TO (list of recipients), FROM (sender), CC (list of copy recipients), DATE, and SUBJECT. Malone and collegues (1987) showed the surprising benefit of semistructured messages in their pioneering system called the Information Lens. If messages were identified as being a lecture announcement, then they would have fields with the time, date, place, speaker, title, and host, in addition to the talk abstract. The semistructured portions of the message enable more automatic filtering of incoming messages or automatic routing and replies. Users can specify that they do not want to receive lecture announcements with times after 5 P.M. or on weekends. Alternatively, users can specify that copies of certain messages will be sent to colleagues, to the secretarial staff, or to their assistants. This feature provides a basis for dealing with the dangers of information overload as users begin to receive dozens or hundreds of messages per day.

A still more structured version of electronic mail was based on a *speech-acts theory* of requests and commitments that compelled users to be explicit about their expectations for responses when a message was sent. However, many users found this approach too rigid (Flores et al., 1988).

An interesting and successful product is Lotus Notes, which was sold only in 200-unit lots to large corporations, but was successful in reaching more than 75 sites with over 50,000 licenses after its first year on the market. Notes provides support to integrate electronic mail, newsgroups, telephone-call tracking, status reporting, text-database searching, document sharing, meeting scheduling, and other cooperation tools. Some large multinational corporations recognized Notes as providing a competitive advantage because widely distributed communities of employees could conveniently share information, make decisions, and carry out complex action plans. The emergence of the World Wide Web has challenged the success of Notes, but Notes still has advantages in better security control and a more structured environment.

Electronic mail has become widespread, but making it universal will require increased simplification, improved training, easier filtering, and lower-cost hardware plus network service (Anderson et al., 1995). The incompatibility of the dozens of systems is slowly being overcome, in part by the efforts of the Electronic Mail Association, by pressure from users, and by commercial realities that force cooperation. The possibility of including media richer than text is an attraction for some users who still prefer FAX machines to electronic mail, because even poor graphics are better than no graphics. Online directories, which are emerging on the web, might be facilitators, since it is still necessary to know a person's electronic mail address before sending a message. Such online directories would also include group lists and the capacity to create new group lists conveniently, so that whole communities could be reached easily. Finally, improved archiving and retrieval systems would enable users to find old electronic-mail messages conveniently and rapidly. The dangers of junk electronic mail remain, and even noble ideas of cooperation can be undermined by users who fail to be polite, nuisances who persistently disrupt, electronic snoopers who do not respect privacy, or calculating opportunists who abuse their privileges.

14.3.2   Newsgroups and network communities

Electronic mail is a great way to get started in electronic communication, but its basic features need extension to serve the needs of communities. When a group of people use electronic mail for focused discussions, tools to organize the discussion and to provide an accessible historical record are needed. One popular strategy is the *USENET newsgroups,* in which thousands of topics are listed. Newsgroups users initiate action by selecting the newsgroup they want and reading as many previous notes and related comments as they wish. Typically, the past few weeks of notes are maintained on the user's machine. Global search of all newsgroups has only lately become an option by way of the web search engines. A more orderly community structure is the *listserv,* to which individuals must subscribe to receive electronic-mail notices. Still more structured is the *online conference,* in which additional tools are available for voting and for using online directories of users and documents.

Listservs can be moderated by a leader or can simply act as a mail reflector, sending out copies of received electronic-mail notes to all people who have subscribed. Users can get flooded with listserv electronic-mail notes, so the decision to subscribe can be a serious commitment. The listserv server machine keeps an archive of notes that is searchable, and a subscriber list. Users can obtain listserv commands by sending a one-word `help` command to the listserv host.

```
LISTSERV Version 1.8b: Most commonly used commands
Info         <topic|listname>          Order documentation
Lists        <Detail|Short|Global>     Get a description of all lists
SUBscribe    listname <full name>      Subscribe to a list
SIGNOFF      listname                  Sign off from a list
SIGNOFF      * (NETWIDE                 - from all lists on all servers
REView       listname <options>        Review a list
Query        listname                  Query your subscription options
SET          listname options          Update your subscription options
INDex        <filelist_name>           Order a list of LISTSERV files
GET          filename filetype         Order a file from LISTSERV
REGister     full_name|OFF             Tell LISTSERV about your name
```

Thousands of newsgroups, listservs, and conferences have emerged around the world, administered by devoted individuals who keep the discussion moving, filter malicious or unsavory messages, and act as the

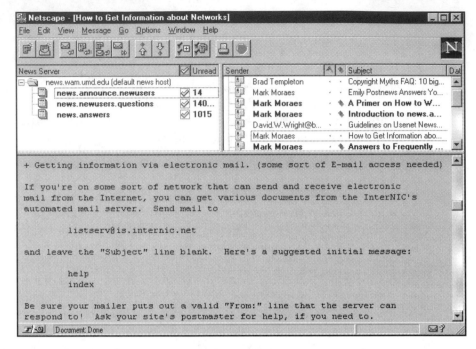

Figure 14.2

News reader system for Netscape Navigator, showing News Server list, a list of announcements for new users, and part of one announcement. (© 1996 Netscape Communication Corporation. Used with permission.)

Gertude Steins of the modern electronic salons. Notes may contain a question, an offer to buy or sell, interesting news, a joke, or a "flame" (abusive criticism) (Fischer and Stevens, 1991). Each item has a short one-line heading and an arbitrarily long body (Fig. 14.2).

The user interfaces tend to be simple to accommodate even low-speed dial-in access. Choices are few; the intrigue lies in the complexity of the conversations, especially in spirited replies and debates. As usage increases, the systems operator (often known as the SYSOP) must decide whether to split topics into more focused subtopics to avoid the overwhelming participants with thousands of new messages. Ensuring that the communities remain interesting is a challenge; if a group of advanced programmers discussing esoteric details is invaded by novices asking beginner-level questions, the experts will want to split off to re-form their own discussion group. Communities can be found for most computer-related issues, but other topics—such as movies, kayaking, rap music, folk dancing, and restaurants—are popular.

Practical information exchange is common for diverse groups such as cancer researchers, NASA scientists, handicapped users, and human-factors researchers. Within corporations, universities, or government agencies, specialized groups may be established for topics such as corporate policy, medical-insurance information, or product updates.

Newsgroups or listservs are usually open to all, whereas conferences are designed to provide access to a known community (Hiltz, 1984; Hiltz and Turoff, 1985). A conference is usually moderated, meaning that a conference leader invites participants, poses an issue or theme, and keeps the discussion going if a question is unanswered or if some participants fail to read new notes in a timely manner. Conferences are more likely to have voting features to allow consensus formation or decision making. Votes may be required within 48 hours, with results posted by the moderator. Thoughtful discussions within a conference are encouraged because participants can consider their position judiciously, consult other materials, and phrase their contributions carefully, without the pressure for an immediate comment that is inherent in a telephone call or face-to-face meeting.

Online magazines and newsletters are proliferating, with audiences growing rapidly. *HotWired, Electric Minds,* and *C|Net* focus on the web world; *Slate* is a general news and opinion magazine; and specialized newsletters are emerging in every discipline. Often, they are paid for by advertising, but some charge subscription fees. Hundreds of online newspapers complement the printed editions, and it seems likely that traditional newspaper features, such as financial tables and classified ads, will shift to online-only modes. Similarly, small scientific journals with fewer than 1000 subscribers seem likely to become available in electronic-only form.

Network communities have become controversial. In one case U.S. federal-government agents confiscated computer equipment alleging that illegal information was being posted, and the hacker community joined forces to protect the accused. The First Amendment principle of freedom of speech should be extended to electronic speech, but there are dangers of illegal activities. Some network communities have been criticized for spreading racist material, so the challenge is to preserve valued freedoms and rights without allowing harm. Congressional advocates of controlling online obscenity succeeded in quickly passing the Communications Decency Act of 1996, but it was just as quickly struck down as unconstitutional by federal judges.

Instead of seeking a conversation, many computer-network users are eager to scour remote databases for useful materials to download (load onto their personal computers). Creators of programs, images, databases, and so on often seek to publish their materials electronically, or to *upload* them, for people who can put these products to use. Some services provide informative listings of available materials, but more could be done to provide effective library resources.

Enthusiasts delight in the free exchange of *shareware, freeware, and public-access software*. A slight variation is the honor system in which downloaded software includes a request for a modest fee ($10 to $100) to become a registered user; such users might receive notices of changes or a printed user manual.

14.4   Synchronous Distributed: Different Place, Same Time

The dream of being in two places at one time became realizable with modern technologies such as telephone and television; now, being in 10 places at once is possible through *synchronous distributed applications* such as *group editing*. For example, in the groundbreaking GROVE (for GRoup Outline Viewing Editor system), multiple users can edit the same document simultaneously (Ellis et al, 1991). Coordination is accomplished by voice communication. The default mode in GROVE is to allow every user to type simultaneously—there is no locking. Although the authors report that collisions are surprisingly infrequent, since users tend to work on different parts of a document, locking by sentence or paragraph would seem to be a necessary option for some situations. Both GROVE and a follow-on system, rIBIS (Rein et al., 1991) included small images of current users.

Important features in the development of ShrEdit (for shared editor) at the University of Michigan were the mixture of private and public workspaces, identity of participants, location of actions, and care with updating (Olson et al., 1990). These same issues of ownership and control were highly visible in groups of inner-city sixth graders who used a group editor to write a magazine on prejudice (Mitchell et al., 1995). Shared workspaces for drawing (Greenberg et al., 1995), creating hypermedia documents (Mark et al., 1996), performing flexible teamwork (Roseman & Greenberg, 1996), and doing collaborative design (Ishii et al., 1994) expand the possibilities (Figs. 14.3 and 14.4).

Shared-editor sessions or shared spreadsheets seem to be simple yet potentially popular applications. IBM's early CVIEW demonstrated the benefits of shared screens for customer assistance. Users with problems could call the customer engineer, and both could see the same screens as the engineer walked through the solution. People have given demonstrations of new software at multiple sites by showing screens to dozens of people while talking on a conference call. Another potential application is to allow sharing of

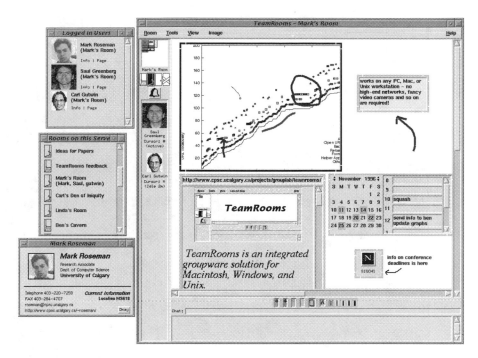

Figure 14.3

TeamRooms, a program that simulates real-life team meeting rooms that provide a shared space for a workgroup. When people enter, they are automatically connected with everyone in the room. In this example of Mark's room, Saul and Carl are commenting on and marking scientific data. Multiple graphical groupware applications can be active. (Used with permission of the University of Calgary, Alberta, Canada.)

information for applications such as airlines reservations. When the agent has located a selection of possible flights, it would be convenient to be able to *show* the customer rather than to read the list. The customer could then make the selection and would have an electronic copy to save, print, or include in other documents. An innovative commercial direction is the development of interactive games that permit two or more people to participate simultaneously in poker, chess, or complex fantasies.

Even simple exchanges of text messages in systems such as CHAT, Internet Relay Chat (IRC), or TALK produce lively social clubhouses on many distributed online information services. Participants may be genuinely caring and helpful, or maybe wisecracking *flamers* more intent on a putdown with a

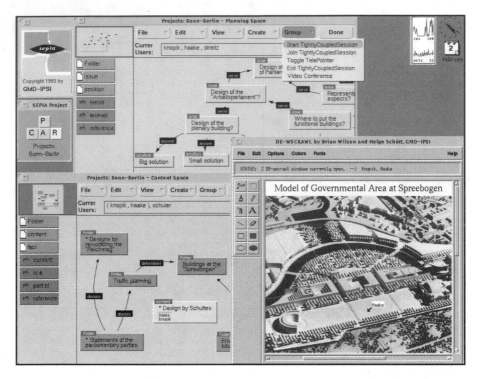

Figure 14.4

SEPIA (Structured Elicitation and Processing of Ideas for Authoring), a program that supports hypermedia-document production by group discussions with multiple remote users (Streitz et al., 1996). In this example, the users Knopik, Haake, Streitz, and Schuler are working in different Activity Spaces in loosely (top) and in tightly coupled (bottom) collaboration modes. They can share views at the network level of typed hypermedia nodes and links, as well as sharing the content of nodes (lower right) and using telepointers at all levels. SEPIA laid the basis for the DOLPHIN system (Mark et al., 1996), which supports electronic meeting collaboration. (Used with permission of Norbert Streitz, GMD-IPSI, Darmstadt, Germany.)

tendency to violent or obscene language. Sometimes, users take on new personalities with engaging names such as Gypsy, Larry Lightning, or Really Rosie. The social chatter can be light, provocative, or intimidating.

Elaborate MUD (for Multi-User Dungeons or Dimensions systems) offer fantasy environments (although most are still text-oriented), where users can take on novel identities, personas, or avatars while on heroic quests (Turkle, 1995). According to a web MUD page: "You can walk around, chat with other characters, explore dangerous monster-infested areas, solve puzzles, and even create your very own rooms, descriptions and items."

The hardware, network, and software architectures to support synchronous applications with multimedia capabilities are being developed at many sites (Crowley et al., 1990; Patterson et al., 1990; Greenberg and Marwood, 1994); each project is dealing with the problems of delays, locking, sharing, and synchronization.

Innovative attempts to use video to bridge distance have been made. A simple approach is to have two video cameras and displays so that you can have an informal chat:

> Imagine sitting in your workplace lounge having coffee with colleagues. Now imagine that you and your colleagues are still in the same room, but are separated by a large sheet of glass that does not interfere with your ability to carry on a clear, two-way conversation. Finally, imagine that you have split the room into two parts and moved one part 50 miles down the road, without impairing the quality of your interaction with your friends.

That scenario illustrates the goal of the VideoWindow project (Fish et al., 1990): to extend a shared space over considerable distance without impairing the quality of the interactions among users or requiring any special actions to establish a conversation.

Approaches to videoconferencing range from special rooms to users working at their own desks using their normal computer systems while seeing one or more other participants in the video conference (Watabe, 1990; Mantei et al., 1991; Bly et al., 1993; Isaacs et al., 1995, 1996). The convenience of *desktop videoconferencing (DTVC)* is great, since this strategy permits users to have access to their papers and computer systems during the conference. Specialized videoconferencing rooms that are reserved by appointment give the event greater significance, and the equipment quality is usually higher because the equipment can be a shared resource.

In the University of Toronto's early DTVC system, called CAVECAT (for Computer Audio Video Enhanced Collaboration and Telepresence), up to four sites could be viewed on a single monitor. Problems included slow response time for entering or leaving a session, distracting background audio that exacerbated the difficulty of determining who was speaking, inappropriate lighting, difficulty in making eye contact (participants would look at their monitors rather than into the cameras), changed social status, small image size, and potential invasion of privacy.

The move from research prototypes to widely used DTVC systems is happening as costs drop, adequate bandwidth becomes available, and interfaces improve. Cornell University's CU-SeeMe system offers free software that runs on most personal computers with no special hardware and ordinary video cameras (Dorcey, 1995 and http://cu-seeme.cornell.edu). The low resolution (320 × 240) grayscale images are transmitted via the Internet at whatever frame rates are possible (Fig. 14.5). The images are often jerky, but CU-SeeMe is used for many personal conferences, professional work, and distance learning. More sophisticated commercial systems include Intel's

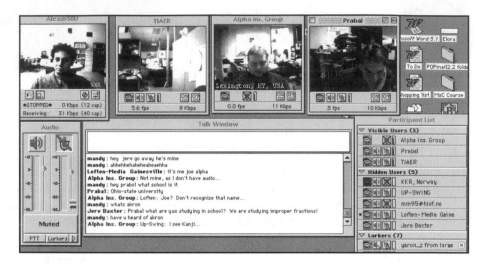

Figure 14.5

CUSee-Me used as a videoconferencing system. Four users are displayed in video windows as they share a common talk window. (Prepared by Alessandro Barabesi.)

ProShare II, which provides good images on Integrated Services Digital Network (ISDN) lines and supports shared workspaces for document processing, spreadsheets, and so on.

The PictureTel line of videoconferencing platforms provides increasingly higher-quality services on telephone lines, the Internet, local-area networks, and leased lines (Fig. 14.6) (http://www.picturetel.com). Once users have had the pleasure of seeing one another on video, done the required hand waving, and adjusted their lighting, cameras, hair, and clothes, it is time to get down to business. Some meetings are simple discussions that replace face-to-face visits, and the improvement over the telephone is the capacity to assess facial-expression and body-language cues for enthusiasm, disinterest, or anger. Many meetings include conferencing over some object of interest, such as a document, map, or photo. Developers emphasize the need for convenient turn taking and document sharing by using terms such as *smooth, lightweight,* or *seamless integration.*

Controlled experimentation on performance with different media is guiding designers in shaping effective systems. Chapanis's classic studies (1975) and recent work confirm that a voice channel is an important component for discussion of what participants see on a shared display. In one comparison, a shared workspace on a computer display was used without audio or video, with audio alone, and with audio and video (Gale, 1990). One group of four performed three tasks five times in each media format. Significant differences were found for the meeting-scheduling task, which took almost twice as long with the

Figure 14.6

The PictureTel Venue 2000 Model 50, a system that supports high-quality videocon-ferencing, such as this discussion between architects and construction engineers. (Used with permission of PictureTel Corp.)

workspace-alone treatment as it did with the two other treatments. This result reinforces the importance of having a clear voice channel for coordination while users are looking at the objects of interest. The capacity for remote groups to produce work of a quality similar to that of face-to-face groups was demon-strated in studies of audio- and video-supported groups (Olson et al., 1995). Video support improved quality of work over audio only, and users preferred having the video support. The importance of audio and the marginal benefits of video for turn taking or interruption were highlighted in a comparison of three systems, but users expressed desire for video (Sellen, 1994).

Ethnographic observations and field studies reveal actual usage patterns and support competing theories. Kraut and associates (1994) found evidence that "critical mass—the numbers of people one can reach on a system—and social influence—the norms that grow up around a medium" are the key determinants of video-system success. Those people whose jobs involved substantial personnel management used video more than did those with more structured and document-oriented jobs.

The promise of video windows, tunnels, spaces, and so on is that they enable an enriched form of communication compared to a telephone confer-ence or electronic mail, with less disruption than a trip. They enable partici-pants to access the resources of their office environments while affording a chance for successful communication and emotional contact. Successful entrepreneurs will be those who best understand these new media and find the situations for which the media are best suited.

14.5   Face to Face: Same Place, Same Time

Teams of people often work together and use complex shared technology. Pilot and copilot cooperation in airplanes has been designed carefully with shared instruments and displays. Coordination among air-traffic controllers has a long history that has been studied thoroughly (Wiener and Nagel, 1988). Stock-market trading rooms and commodity markets are other existing applications of face-to-face teamwork or negotiations that are computer mediated.

Newer applications in office and classroom environments are attracting more attention because of the large numbers of potential users and the potential for innovative approaches to work and to learning. These applications include:

- *Shared display from lecturer workstation*   In this simple form of group computing, a professor or lecturer may use the computer with a large-screen projector to demonstrate a computing application, to show a set of slides with business graphics, to retrieve images, or to run an animation. Fred Hofstetter (1995) of the University of Delaware developed a multimedia lectureware package, PODIUM, that allows instructors to compose illustrated lectures using slides, computer graphics, animations, videos, and audio sequences. Many speakers are happy to use standard commercial packages such as Microsoft PowerPoint, Lotus Freelance, or Adobe Persuasion. User-interface issues include simplicity in moving to the next slide, capacity to jump out of sequence, and ease of making spontaneous changes.

- *Audience response units*   Simple keypads have been used effectively in training courses. Students can answer multiple-choice questions at their desks, and results can be shown to the full class on a large display. Similar units have been used by advertising researchers who ask test audiences to respond to commercials shown on a large screen. Votes in parliamentary forums can be rapid and accurate. Promoters claim that this simple technology is easy to learn, is acceptable to most people, is nonthreatening, and heightens attention because of the participatory experience. The National Geographic interactive exhibit gallery in Washington, D.C., has five-button response units that allow visitors to try their hand at answering multiple-choice questions such as "What percentage of the earth is covered by water?" The set of answers is shown on the shared display, but the presentation sequence is unaffected by the audience's selections.

- *Text-submission workstations*   By giving each participant a keyboard and simple software, it is possible to create an inviting environment for conversation or brainstorming. Batson (Bruce et al., 1992) at Gallaudet University constructed a highly successful networking program that allows each participant to type a line of text that is shown immediately, with the author's name, on every participant's display. With 10 people typing, new comments appear a few times per second and lively conversations ensue. Batson's goal was to overcome his frustrated efforts at teaching college-level English writing, and his English Natural Form Instruction (ENFI) network software was spectacularly successful:

> It seems slightly ironic that the computer, which for twenty-five years has been perceived as anti-human, a tool of control and suppression of human instinct and intuition, has really humanized my job. For the first time in a long time, I have real hope that we might make some progress. . . . Freed of having to be the cardboard figure at the front of the classroom, I became a person again, with foibles, feelings and fantasies. As a group, we were more democratic and open with each other than any other writing class I'd had. (Bruce et al., 1992).

The clatter of the keyboards adds to the laughter, groans, cheers, and grimaces to create a good atmosphere.

- *Brainstorming, voting, and ranking* Beyond talking, structured social processes can produce dramatic educational discussions and highly productive business meetings. The University of Arizona was a pioneer in developing the social process, the physical environment, and the software tools (Valacich et al., 1991) to "reduce or eliminate the dysfunctions of the group interaction so that a group reaches or exceeds its task potential" (Fig. 14.7). By allowing anonymous submission of suggestions and ranking of proposals, the authors introduced a wider range of possibilities; also, ideas were valued on their merits, independently of the originator (Fig. 14.8a–c). Because ego investments and conflicts were reduced, groups seemed to be more open to novel suggestions. IBM has built 19 Decision Center rooms based on the Arizona model for its internal use, and another

Figure 14.7

Semicircular classroom with 24 personal computers built into the desks at the University of Arizona. (Group Systems is a registered trademark of Ventana Corporation.)

Figure 14.8

Sample screens from
GroupSystems Electronic
Meeting software. Online
restaurant survey (top).
Results of a vote in part of
the restaurant survey (bot-
tom). (Used with permis-
sion from Ventana Corp.,
Tucson, AZ.) (Group
Systems is a registered
trademark of Ventana
Corporation.)

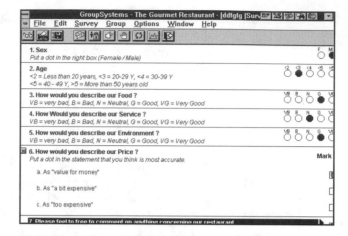

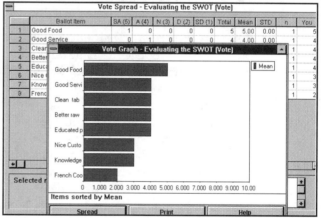

20 for rental to users under the TeamFocus name. Well-trained facilitators with backgrounds in social dynamics consult with the team
leader to plan the decision session and to write the problem statement. In a typical task, 45 minutes of brainstorming by 15 to 20 people can produce hundreds of lines of suggestions for questions such
as, "How can we increase sales?" Or, "What are the key issues in
technological support for group work?" Then, items can be filtered,
clustered into similar groups, and presented to participants for
refinement and ranking. Afterward, a printout and electronic-file
version of the entire session is immediately available. Numerous
studies of electronic meeting systems with thousands of users have
demonstrated and explored the benefits (Nunamaker et al., 1991):

- Parallel communication promotes broader input into the meeting process and reduces the chance that a few people dominate
  the meeting.

- Anonymity mitigates evaluation apprehension and conformance pressure, so issues are discussed more candidly.
- The group memory constructed by participants enables them to pause and reflect on information and on opinions of others during the meeting, and serves as a permanent record of what occurred.
- Process structure helps to focus the group on key issues, and discourages digressions and unproductive behaviors.
- Task support and structure provide information and approaches to analyze that information.

The University of Arizona system is marketed under the name Group-Systems (Ventana Corp.).

- *File sharing*   A simple but powerful use of networked computers in a workplace, classroom, or meeting room is to share files. Participants may arrive with sales reports that can be shared with other people in the room rapidly. Alternatively, the group leaders may have agenda or budgets that they wish to broadcast to all participants, who may then annotate or embed these documents in others. Shared files may contain text, programs, spreadsheets, databases, graphics, animations, sound, X-ray images, or video. Presumably, distribution can go beyond the meeting room to allow participants to access the files from their offices and homes.

- *Shared workspace*   The complement to each person receiving a personal copy of a file is to have a shared view of a workspace that every user can access. The pioneering Capture Lab at Electronic Data Systems contained an oval desk with eight Macintosh computers built into the desk to preserve the business-meeting atmosphere (Mantei, 1988). The large display in front of the desk is visible to all attendees, who can each take control of the large screen by pressing a button on a machine. At Xerox PARC, the research system Colab has generated the commercial large-screen (167-cm-diagonal) display, LiveBoard (Fig. 14.9), on which users can see the current list of topics or proposals, and can point to, edit, move, or add to under the policy sometimes called WYSIWIS (what you see is what I see) (Stefik et al., 1987). The advantage of a shared workspace is that everyone sees the same display and can work communally to produce a joint and recorded result (Weiser, 1991).

- *Group activities*   With the proper networking software among workstations, users can be assigned a problem, and those needing assistance can "raise their hands" to show their display on a large shared display or on the group leader's display. Then, the group leader or other participants can issue commands to resolve the problem. Similarly, if participants have a particularly noteworthy result, graphic, or comment, they can share it with the group either on the large shared display or on individual workstations.

Figure 14.9

The LiveBoard Interactive Meeting System from LiveWorks, Inc., a Xerox company. Team discussions with groups at multiple locations can be facilitated with a 167-cm LiveBoard display. (Used with permission of LiveWorks, Inc.)

14.6   Applying CSCW to Education

The potential for a groupware-mediated paradigm shift in education evokes passion from devotees, but there is ample reason for skepticism and resistance. No single technology will dominate, but successful combinations will have to be suited to the goals of the institution, pedagogic style of the instructor, and availability of equipment for students. The long-promised but slow education revolution is speeding up as use of electronic mail and the web become widespread (Gilbert, 1996). Same-time, same-place electronic classrooms and a rich variety of distance-education strategies are promoted as ways to improve quality or to lower costs, but a change in teaching and learning styles and the inclusion of new students are often the main result (Harasim et al., 1995).

Coordination of students in a *virtual classroom* is a complex process but it can enable a stimulating educational experience for people who cannot travel to a regular classroom (Hiltz, 1992). Multiple trials with sociology, computer-science, and philosophy courses demonstrated the efficacy of a conference format for college courses, complete with homework assignments, projects, tests, and final examinations. Instructors found the constant flow of messages to be a rewarding challenge, and students were generally satisfied with the experience:

> The essence of the Virtual Classroom is an environment to facilitate collaborative learning. For distance education students, the increased ability to be in constant communication with other learners is obvious. But even for campus-based courses the technology provides a means for a rich, collaborative learning environment which exceeds the traditional classroom in its ability to 'connect' students and course materials on a round-the-clock basis. (Hiltz, 1992)

Distance education with broadcast-quality video lectures is common, but interactivity with students is often by telephone, electronic mail, or web exchanges. DTVC has the potential to create livelier two-way interactions for discussion, mentoring, and remediation. The greatest beneficiaries are professionals who can attend courses electronically from their offices or special learning centers, and home-oriented students who cannot commit the time for travel to a traditional campus. Current desktop videoconferencing facilitates communication, but improvements are needed to give instructors better awareness of reactions at multiple sites and ways to manage smoother turn taking (Ramsay et al., 1996). Improved resolution will help to convey gesture, gaze direction, and body language, but seeing detail and context simultaneously at multiple sites is a challenge (Fussel and Benimoff, 1995).

The electronic classrooms at the University of Maryland balance the pursuit of new technologies with the exploration of new teaching and learning styles (Shneiderman et al., 1995). Three classrooms were built with 40 seats and 20 high-resolution monitors partially recessed into the desks to preserve sightlines (Fig. 14.10). The computers were placed in a side room to increase security and room space and to reduce noise and heat. A workstation and two large rear-projected displays enable instructors to show everyone their screen or any student screen. Keys to success included provision of the necessary infrastructure for faculty training and support, and collection of ample evaluation data to guide the process.

Over the first six years, 68 faculty (30 tenured, 16 nontenured, 22 other staff) from 21 departments offered 233 courses with over 6782 students. Courses filled most slots from 8 A.M. to 10 P.M., and were as diverse as "The Role of Media in the American Political Process," "Chinese Poetry into English," "Marketing Research Methods," "Database Design," and "Saving the Bay."

Faculty members who used the electronic classrooms explored novel teaching and learning styles that can create more engaging experiences for students. While traditional lectures with or without discussion remain common, electronic-classroom technologies can enliven lectures (Hofstetter,

Figure 14.10

AT&T Teaching/Learning Theater at the University of Maryland has 20 high-resolution displays built into custom desks with seats for 40 students.

1995) while enabling active individual learning, small-group collaborative learning, and entire-class collaborative learning. Most faculty acknowledge spending more preparation time to use the electronic classroom especially in their first semester, but one wrote that it is "well worthwhile in terms of greater learning efficiency."

The assumption that improved lectures were the main goal changed as faculty tried collaborative teaching methods and talked about these methods with one another. Faculty who had used paper-based collaborations appreciated the smoothness of showing electronic student submissions to the whole class. Faculty who had not used collaborative methods appreciated the ease and liveliness of an anonymous electronic brainstorming session.

More active individual learning experiences include using software during class time

- To write essays in English or poems in a foreign language
- To find antecedents of Impressionism in an art-history library of 9000 images
- To run business simulations to increase product quality
- To perform statistical analyses of psychology studies

- To do landscaping with computer-assisted design and graphics packages
- To compose computer programs
- To search the Internet

A common teacher strategy (Norman, 1994) is to assign time-limited (3 to 10 minutes) tasks, and then to use the video switcher to review the students' work, to give individual help when necessary, and to show the students' work to the entire class. The transformational breakthrough lies in opening the learning process by rapidly showing many students' work to the entire class. Doing so at first generates student and faculty anxiety, but quickly becomes normal. Seeing and critiquing exemplary and ordinary work by fellow students provides feedback that inspires better work on subsequent tasks.

Small-group collaborative-learning experiences include having pairs of students work together at a machine on a time-limited task. Pairs often learn better than individuals, because people can discuss their problems, learn from each other, and split their roles into problem solver and computer operator. With paired teams, the variance of completion time for tasks is reduced compared to individual use, and fewer students get stuck in completing a task. Verbalization of problems has often been demonstrated to be advantageous during learning and is an important job skill to acquire for modern team-oriented organizations.

Innovative approaches with larger teams include simulated hostage negotiations with terrorist airplane hijackers in a course on conflict resolution, and business trade negotiations in a United Nations format for a course on commercial Spanish. Teams work to analyze situations, to develop position statements online, and to communicate their positions to their adversaries over the network. In an introductory programming course, 10 teams wrote components and sent them through the network to the lead team, who combined the pieces into a 173-line program, all in 25 minutes. The class performed a walkthrough of the code using the large-screen display, and quickly identified bugs.

Some faculty find that adapting to the electronic-classroom environment changes their styles so much that they teach differently even in traditional classrooms. Other faculty vow that they will never teach in a traditional classroom again. Most faculty users want to continue teaching in these electronic classrooms and discover that more than their teaching styles change— their attitudes about the goals of teaching and about the content of the courses often shift as well. Many faculty develop higher expectations for student projects. Some become evangelists within their disciplines for the importance of teamwork and its accompanying communications skills.

On the negative side, a math professor who used the computers only to do occasional demonstrations returned to teaching in a traditional classroom, where he had much more blackboard space. Some reluctant instructors express resistance to changing their teaching styles and anticipate having to make a large effort to use the electronic classrooms.

Evaluations included standard course evaluations, use of anonymous electronic ratings, and specially prepared questionnaires. A controlled study with 127 students (Alavi, 1994) indicated that electronic-classroom students had higher perceived skill development, self-reported learning, and evaluation of classroom experience than did students in a collaborative-learning traditional classroom. Electronic-classroom students also had statistically significantly higher final-exam grades. Popular features were the electronic note taking, interactivity, idea sharing, and brainstorming.

Evaluations revealed problems with network access from outside the classrooms and with file-sharing methods within the classroom. Students generally were positive, and often were enthusiastic: "Everyone should have a chance to be in here at least once. . . . Great tech. Great education technique. . . . Easy to use, but tends to crash and die at times. . . . the best thing that I could think of to improve the ability to teach interactively. Even though there were a few humps to get over at the beginning—it was well worth the effort (and money)."

Intense interest in educational technology and in new teaching strategies is widespread. Resource-rich universities are investing in teaching–learning theaters; others are making innovative use of electronic mail, listservs, and the web (Gilbert, 1996). Distance learning using CSCW technologies seems likely to expand.

14.7   Practitioner's Summary

Computing has become a social process. The networks and telephone lines have opened up possibilities for cooperation. Electronic mail has made it easy to reach out and touch someone, or thousands of someones. Newsgroups, electronic conferences, and the web have enabled users to be in closer communication. Coordination within projects or between organizations is facilitated by text, graphic, voice, and even video exchanges. Even face-to-face meetings are getting a facelift with new tools for electronic meetings and with teaching–learning theaters. The introspective and isolated style of past computer use is giving way to a lively social environment where training has to include *netiquette* (network etiquette). These collaboration tools are beginning to have a visible effect; it seems that their success will continue spreading. However, as there are in all new technologies, there will be failures and surprising discoveries, because our intuitions about the design of groupware are based on shallow experience (Box 14.1). Thorough testing of new applications is necessary before widespread dissemination.

Box 14.1

Questions for consideration. The novelty and diversity of computer-supported cooperative work means that clear guidelines have not emerged, but these sobering questions might help designers and managers.

Computer-Supported Cooperative Work Questions

- How would facilitating communication improve or harm teamwork?
- Where does the community of users stand on centralization versus decentralization?
- What pressures exist for conformity versus individuality?
- How is privacy compromised or protected?
- What are the sources of friction among participants?
- Is there protection from hostile, aggressive, or malicious behavior?
- Will there be sufficient equipment to support convenient access for all participants?
- What network delays are expected and tolerable?
- What is the user's level of technological sophistication or resistance?
- Who is most likely to be threatened by computer-supported cooperative work?
- How will high-level management participate?
- Which jobs may have to be redefined?
- Whose status will rise or fall?
- What are the additional costs or projected savings?
- Is there an adequate phase-in plan with sufficient training?
- Will there be consultants and adequate assistance in the early phases?
- Is there enough flexibility to handle exceptional cases and special needs (disabilities)?
- What international, national, organizational standards must be considered?
- How will success be evaluated?

14.8   Researcher's Agenda

The opportunities for new products and for refinements of existing products seem great. Even basic products such as electronic mail could be improved dramatically by inclusion of advanced features, such as online directories, filtering, and archiving tools, as well as by universal-access features, such as improved tutorials, better explanations, and convenient assistance. Conferencing methods and cooperative document production will change as bandwidth increases and video is added. The most dramatic projects thus far are the ambitious electronic-meeting systems and teaching–learning theaters. They are costly, but are so attractive that many organizations are likely to spend heavily on these new technologies during the next decade. Although user-interface design of applications will be a necessary component, the larger and more difficult research problems lie in studying the social processes. How will home life and work be changed? How might interfaces differ for games, cooperative work, and conflict-laden online negotiations? Some of the excitement for researchers in computer-supported cooperative work stems from the vast uncharted territory: theories are sparse, controlled studies are difficult to arrange, data analysis is overwhelming, and predictive models are nonexistent (Olson et al., 1993).

World Wide Web Resources   WWW

Computer Supported Cooperative Work is naturally a part of the World Wide Web and novel tools are springing up on many websites. You can try various chat services, download special purpose software, or shop for conferencing tools (video, audio, or text-based). Evaluations are also available online.

http://www.aw.com/DTUI

References

Alavi, Maryam, Computer mediated collaborative learning: An empirical evaluation, *MIS Quarterly*, 18, 2 (June 1994), 159–173.

Anderson, Robert H., Bikson, Tora K., Law, Sally Ann, and Mitchell, Bridger M., *Universal Access to Email: Feasibility and Societal Implications*, RAND, Santa Monica, CA (1995), also at http://www.rand.org.

Baecker, Ron, *Readings in Groupware and Computer-Supported Cooperative Work: Assisting Human–Human Collaboration*, Morgan Kaufmann, San Francisco, CA (1993).

Bly, Sara A., Harrison, Steve R., and Irwin, Susan, MediaSpaces: Bringing people together in a video, audio, and computing environment, *Communications of the ACM*, 36, 1 (January 1993), 28–47.

Bruce, Bertram, Peyton, Joy, and Batson, Trent, *Network-Based Classrooms*, Cambridge University Press, Cambridge, U.K. (1992).

Borenstein, Nathaniel S., Multimedia electronic mail: Will the dream become a reality? *Communications of the ACM*, 34, 4 (April 1991), 117–119.

Carroll, John M. and Rosson, Mary Beth, Developing the Blacksburg Electronic Village. *Communications of the ACM*, 39, 12 (December 1996), 69–74.

Chapanis, Alphonse, Interactive human communication, *Scientific American*, 232, 3 (March 1975), 36–42.

Crowley, Terrence, Milazzo, Paul, Baker, Ellie, Forsdick, Harry, and Tomlinson, Raymond, MMConf: An infrastructure for building shared multimedia applications, *Proc. Third Conference on Computer-Supported Cooperative Work*, ACM, New York (1990), 329–355.

Dorcey, Tim, CU-SeeMe desktop videoconferencing software, *Connexions*, 9, 3 (March 1995). Also at http://cu-seeme.cornell.edu/DorceyConnexions.html.

Ellis, C. A., Gibbs, S. J., and Rein, G. L., Groupware: Some issues and experiences, *Communications of the ACM*, 34, 1 (January 1991), 680–689.

Fischer, Gerhard and Stevens, Curt, Information access in complex, poorly structured information spaces, *Proc. ACM CHI '91 Human Factors in Computing Systems*, ACM, New York (1991), 63–70.

Fish, Robert S., Kraut, Robert E., and Chalfonte, Barbara, The VideoWindow System in informal communications, *Proc. Third Conference on Computer-Supported Cooperative Work*, ACM, New York (1990), 1–11.

Flores, F., Graves, M., Hartfield, B., and Winograd, T. Computer systems and the design of organizational interaction, *ACM Transactions on Office Information Systems*, 6, 2 (April 1988), 153–172.

Fussel, S. R. and Benimoff, I., Social and cognitive processes in interpersonal communications: Implications for advanced telecommunications technologies, *Human Factors*, 27, 2 (1995), 228–250.

Gale, Stephen, Human aspects of interactive multimedia communication, *Interacting with Computers*, 2, 2 (1990), 175–189.

Gilbert, Steven, Making the most of a slow revolution, *Change: The Magazine of Higher Learning*, 28, 2 (March/April 1996), 10–23.

Greenberg, Saul, Hayne, Stephen, and Rada, Roy (Editors), *Groupware for Real Time Drawing: A Designer's Guide*, McGraw-Hill, New York (1995).

Greenberg, Saul and Marwood, David, Real time groupware as a distributed system: Concurrency control and its effect on the interface, *Proc. Conference on Computer Supported Cooperative Work '94*, ACM, New York (1994), 207–217.

Grudin, Jonathan, Groupware and social dynamics: Eight challenges for developers, *Communications of the ACM*, 37, 1 (January 1994), 93–105.

Harasim, Linda, Hiltz, Starr Roxanne, Teles, Lucio, and Turoff, Murray, *Learning Networks: A Field Guide to Teaching and Learning Online*, MIT Press, Cambridge, MA (1995).

Hiltz, S. R., *Online Communities: A Case Study of the Office of the Future*, Ablex, Norwood, NJ (1984).

Hiltz, S. R., *The Virtual Classroom*, Ablex, Norwood, NJ (1992).

Hiltz, S. R. and Turoff, M., *The Network Nation: Human Communication via Computer*. Addison-Wesley, Reading, MA (1978).

Hiltz, S. R., and Turoff, M., Structuring computer-mediated communication systems to avoid information overload, *Communications of the ACM*, 28, 7 (July 1985), 680–689.

Hoffert, Eric M. and Gretsch, Greg, The digital news system at EDUCOM: A convergence of interactive computing, newspapers, television and high-speed networks, *Communications of the ACM*, 34, 4 (April 1991), 113–116.

Hofstetter, Fred T., *Multimedia Literacy*, McGraw-Hill, New York (1995).

Isaacs, Ellen, Morris, Trevor, Rodriguez, Thomas K., and Tang, John C., A comparison of face-to-face and distributed presentations, *Proc. CHI '95 Conference: Human Factors in Computing Systems*, ACM, New York (1995), 354–361.

Isaacs, Ellen, Tang, John C., and Morris, Trevor, *Proc. Conference on Computer Supported Cooperative Work '96*, ACM, New York (1996), 325–333.

Ishii, H., Kobayashi, M., and Arita, K., Iterative design of seamless collaboration media: From TeamWorkStation to ClearBoard, *Communications of the ACM*, 37, 8 (1994), 83–97.

Kraut, Robert E., Cool, Colleen, Rice, Ronald E., and Fish, Robert S., Life and death of new technology: Task, utility and social influences on the use of a communications medium, *Proc. Conference on Computer Supported Cooperative Work '94*, ACM, New York (1994), 13–21.

Malone, T., and Crowston, K. What is coordination theory and how can it help design cooperative work systems? In *Proc. Third Conference on Computer-Supported Cooperative Work*, ACM, New York (1990), 357–370.

Malone, T. W., Grant, K. R., Turbak, F. A., Brobst, S. A., and Cohen, M. D., Intelligent information-sharing systems, *Communications of the ACM*, 30 (1987), 390–402.

Mantei, M., Capturing the capture lab concepts: A case study in the design of computer supported meeting environments, *Proc. Second Conference on Computer-Supported Cooperative Work*, ACM, New York (1988), 257–270.

Mantei, Marilyn M., Baecker, Ronald S., Sellen, Abigail J., Buxton, William A. S., and Milligan, Thomas, Experiences in the use of a media space, *Proc. Conference: CHI '91 Human Factors in Computing Systems*, ACM, New York (1991), 203–208.

Mark, Gloria Haake, Jorg M., and Streitz, Norbert A., Hypermedia Structures and the Division of Labor in Meeting Room Collaboration, *Proc. Conference on Computer Supported Cooperative Work '96*, ACM, New York (1996), 170–179.

Mitchell, Alex, Posner, Ilona, and Baecker, Ronald, Learning to write together using groupware, *Proc. CHI '95 Conference: Human Factors in Computing Systems*, ACM, New York (1995), 288–295.

Norman, Kent, Navigating the educational space with HyperCourseware, *Hypermedia*, 6, 1 (January 1994), 35–60.

Nunamaker, J. F., Dennis, Alan R., Valacich, Joseph S., Vogel, Douglas R., and George, Joey F., Electronic meeting systems to support group work, *Communications of the ACM*, 34, 7 (July 1991), 40–61.

Olson, Judith S., Card, Stuart K., Landauer, Thomas K., Olson, Gary M., Malone, Thomas, and Leggett, John, Computer supported co-operative work: Research issues for the 90s, *Behaviour & Information Technology*, 12, 2 (1993), 115–129.

Olson, Judith S., Olson, Gary M., Mack, Lisbeth A., and Wellner, Pierre, Concurrent editing: The group's interface. In Diaper, D., Gilmore, D., Cockton, G., and Shackel, B. (Editors), *Human–Computer Interaction—INTERACT '90*, Elsevier Science Publishers, Amsterdam, The Netherlands (1990), 835–840.

Olson, Judith S., Olson, Gary M., and Meader, David K., What mix of video and audio is useful for small groups doing remote real-time design work?, *Proc. CHI '95 Conference: Human Factors in Computing Systems*, ACM, New York (1995), 362–368.

Patterson, John F., Hill, Ralph D., and Rohall, Steven L., Rendezvous: An architecture for synchronous multi-user applications, *Proc. Third Conference on Computer-Supported Cooperative Work*, ACM, New York (1990), 317–328.

Ramsay, J., Barabesi, A. and Preece, J. (1996) Informal communication is about sharing objects in media, Interacting with Computers, 8, 3, 227–283.

Rein, Gail L. and Ellis, Clarence A., rIBIS: a real-time group hypertext system, *International Journal of Man–Machine Studies*, 34, 3 (1991), 349–367.

Rheingold, Howard, *The Virtual Community: Homesteading on the Electronic Frontier*, Addison-Wesley, Reading, MA (1993).

Roseman, Mark and Greenberg, Saul, TeamRooms: Network places for collaboration, *Proc. Conference on Computer Supported Cooperative Work '96*, ACM, New York (1996), 325–333.

Schuler, Doug, *New Community Networks: Wired for Change*, Addison-Wesley, Reading, MA (1996).

Sellen, Abigail J., Remote conversations: The effects of mediating talk with technology, *Human–Computer Interaction*, 10, 4 (1994), 401–444.

Shneiderman, Ben, Alavi, Maryam, Norman, Kent, and Borkowski, Ellen Y., Windows of opportunity in electronic classrooms, *Communications of the ACM*, 38, 11 (November 1995), 19–24.

Sproull, Lee and Kiesler, Sara, *Connections: New Ways of Working in the Networked Organization*, MIT Press, Cambridge, MA (1991).

Stefik, M., Bobrow, D. G., Foster, G., Lanning, S., and Tartar, D., WYSIWIS revised: Early experiences with multiuser interfaces, *ACM Transactions on Office Information Systems*, 5, 2 (April 1987), 147–186.

Streitz, N., Haake, J., Hannemann, J., Lemke, A., Schuler, W., Schuett, H., and Thuering, M., SEPIA: A cooperative hypermedia authoring environment, In Rada, Roy (Editor), *Groupware and Authoring*, Academic Press, London, U.K. (1996), 241–264.

Turkle, Sherry, *Life on the Screen: Identity in the Age of the Internet*, Simon and Schuster, New York (1995).

Valacich, J. S., Dennis, A. R., and Nunamaker, Jr., J. F., Electronic meeting support: The GroupSystems concept, *International Journal of Man–Machine Studies*, 34, 2 (1991), 261–282.

Vaske, Jerry and Grantham, Charles, *Socializing the Human–Computer Environment*, Ablex, Norwood, NJ (1990).

Watabe, Kazuo, Sakata, Shiro, Maeno, Kazutoshi, Fukuoka, Hideyuki, and Ohmori, Toyoko, Distributed multiparty desktop conferencing system: MERMAID, *Proc. Third Conference on Computer-Supported Cooperative Work*, ACM, New York (1990), 27–28.

Weiser, Mark, The computer for the twenty-first century, *Scientific American*, 265, 3 (September 1991), 94–104.

Wiener, Earl L. and Nagel, David C. (Editors), *Human Factors in Aviation*, Academic Press, New York (1988).

Mark Kostabi, *The Industrial Revolution (Luminary)*, 1994

Information Search
and Visualization

Everything points to the conclusion that the phrase "the language of art" is more than a loose metaphor, that even to describe the visible world in images we need a developed system of schemata.

E. H. Gombrich, *Art and Illusion*, 1959 (p. 76)

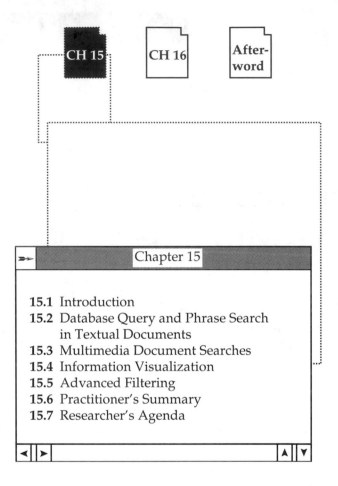

CH 15 CH 16 After-word

Chapter 15

15.1 Introduction
15.2 Database Query and Phrase Search in Textual Documents
15.3 Multimedia Document Searches
15.4 Information Visualization
15.5 Advanced Filtering
15.6 Practitioner's Summary
15.7 Researcher's Agenda

15.1 Introduction

Information exploration should be a joyous experience, but many commentators talk of information overload and anxiety (Wurman, 1989). However, there is promising evidence that the next generation of digital libraries will enable convenient exploration of growing information spaces by a wider range of users. User-interface designers are inventing more powerful search and visualization methods, while offering smoother integration of technology with task.

The terminology swirl in this domain is especially colorful. The older terms of *information retrieval* (often applied to bibliographic and textual document systems) and *database management* (often applied to more structured relational database systems with orderly attributes and sort keys), are being pushed aside by newer notions of *information gathering, seeking, filtering,* or *visualization*. Business-oriented developers focus on the huge volumes of data when they talk of *data mining* and *warehousing,* while expert-system visionaries talk about *knowledge networks*. The distinctions are subtle; the common goals range from finding a narrow set of items in a large collection that satisfy a well-understood information need (known-item search) to browsing to discover unexpected patterns within the collection (Marchionini, 1995).

Exploring information collections becomes increasingly difficult as the volume and diversity grows. A page of information is easy to explore, but when the information representation becomes the size of a book, or library, or even larger, it may be difficult to locate known items or to browse to gain an overview. The strategies to focus and narrow are well understood by librarians and information-search specialists, and now these strategies are being implemented for widespread use. The computer is a powerful tool for searching, but traditional user interfaces have been a hurdle for novice users (complex commands, Boolean operators, unwieldy concepts) and an inadequate tool for experts (difficulty in repeating searches across multiple databases, weak methods for discovering where to narrow broad searches, poor integration with other tools) (Borgman, 1986). This chapter suggests novel possibilities for first-time or intermittent versus frequent computer users, and also for task novices versus experts. Improvements on traditional text and multimedia searching seem possible as a new generation of visualization strategies for query formulation and information presentation emerges.

Designers are just discovering how to use rapid and high-resolution color displays to present large amounts of information in orderly and user-controlled ways. Perceptual psychologists, statisticians, and graphic designers (Bertin, 1983; Cleveland, 1993; Tufte, 1983, 1990) offer valuable guidance about presenting static information, but the opportunity for dynamic displays takes user-interface designers well beyond current wisdom.

The objects–actions interface (OAI) model (see Fig. 2.2) helps by separating task concepts (do you think of your organization as a hierarchy or a matrix?) from interface concepts (is your hierarchy can best represented as an outline, node–link diagram, or a treemap?). The OAI model also separates high-level interface issues (are overview diagrams necessary for navigation?) from low-level interface issues (will color or size coding be used to represent salary levels?).

First-time users of an information-exploration system (whether they have little or much task knowledge) are struggling to understand what they see on the display while keeping in mind their information needs. They would be distracted if they had to learn complex query languages or elaborate shape-coding rules. They need the low cognitive burdens of menu and direct-manipulation designs and simple visual-coding rules. As users gain experience with the interface, they can request additional features by adjusting control panels. Knowledgeable and frequent users want a wide range of search tools with many options that allow them to compose, save, replay, and revise increasingly elaborate query plans.

To facilitate discussion, we need to define a few terms. *Task objects,* such as Leonardo's notebooks or sports-video segments from the Olympics, are represented by *interface objects* in structured relational databases, textual document libraries, or multimedia document libraries. A *structured relational database* consists of *relations* and a *schema* to describe the relations. Relations have *items* (usually called *tuples* or *records*), and each item has multiple *attributes* (often called *fields*), which each have *attribute values.* In the relational model, items form an unordered set (although one attribute can contain sequencing information or be a unique key to identify or sort the other items) and attributes are *atomic.*

A *textual document library* consists of a set of *collections* (typically up to a few hundred collections per library) plus some *descriptive attributes* about the library (for example, name, location, owner). Each collection has a *name* plus some descriptive attributes about the collection (for example, location, media type, curator, donor, dates, geographic coverage), and a set of items (typically 10 to 100,000 items per collection). Items in a collection may vary greatly, but usually a moderate-sized superset of attributes exists that covers all the items. Attributes may be blank, have single values, have multiple values, or be lengthy texts. A collection is owned by a single library, and an item belongs to a single collection, although exceptions are possible. A *multimedia document library* consists of collections of documents that can contain images, sound, video, animations, and so on.

Task actions such as *fact finding* are decomposed into *browsing* or *searching,* and are represented by *interface actions* such as scrolling, zooming, joining, or linking. Users begin by formulating their information needs in the task domain. Tasks can range from specific fact finding, where there is a single readily identifiable outcome, to more extended fact finding, with uncertain but replicable outcomes. Relatively unstructured tasks include open-ended browsing of known collections and exploration of the availability of information on a topic:

Specific fact finding (known-item search)

Find the Library of Congress call number of "Future Shock."
Find the telephone number of Bill Clinton.
Find the highest-resolution LANDSAT image of College Park at noon on Dec. 13, 1997.

Extended fact finding

What other books are by the author of Jurassic Park?
What genres of music is Sony publishing?
Which satellites took images of the Persian Gulf War?

Open-ended browsing

> Does the Mathew Brady Civil War photo collection show the role of women in that war?
>
> Is there new work on voice recognition being reported from Japan?
>
> Is there a relationship between carbon-monoxide levels and desertification?

Exploration of availability

> What genealogy information is available at the National Archives?
>
> What information is available on the Grateful Dead band members?
>
> Do NASA datasets demonstrate acid-rain damage to soy crops?

Once users have clarified their information needs, the first step in satisfying those needs is to decide where to search (Marchionini, 1995). The conversion of information needs, stated in task-domain terminology, to interface actions is a large cognitive step, but it must be accomplished before expression of these actions in a query language or via a series of mouse selections can begin.

Supplemental *finding aids* can help users to clarify and pursue their information needs. Examples include tables of contents or indexes in books, descriptive introductions, concordances, key-word-in-context (KWIC) lists, and subject classifications. Careful understanding of previous and potential search requests, and of the task analysis, can improve search results by allowing the system to offer hot-topic lists and useful classification schemes. For example, the U.S. Congressional Research Service has a list of approximately 80 hot topics covering current bills before Congress, and has 5000 terms in its Legislative Indexing Vocabulary. The National Library of Medicine maintains the Medical Subject Headings (MeSH), with 14,000 items in a seven-level hierarchy.

This chapter covers database query and textual-document searches briefly, then suggests innovative directions for multimedia-document searches and introduces a four-phase framework. The main contribution is a taxonomy of information-visualization strategies based on data types and user tasks. The final section explores advanced filtering methods.

15.2   Database Query and Phrase Search in Textual Documents

Searching in structured relational database systems is a well-established task for which the SQL language has become a widespread standard (Reisner, 1988). Users write queries that specify matches on attribute values, such as author, date of publication, language, or publisher. Each document has values for the attributes, and database-management methods enable rapid retrieval even with millions of documents. For example, an SQL-like command might be

```
SELECT DOCUMENT#
FROM JOURNAL-DB
WHERE    (DATE >= 1994 AND DATE <= 1997)
    AND  (LANGUAGE = ENGLISH OR FRENCH)
    AND  (PUBLISHER = ASIS OR HFES OR ACM).
```

SQL has powerful features, but using it requires training (2 to 20 hours), and even then users make frequent errors for many classes of queries (Welty, 1985). Alternatives such as *query-by-example* can help users to formulate simpler queries, such as requesting all English-language ACM articles published during or after 1994:

```
JOURNAL | DOCUMENT# | DATE    | AUTHOR | LANGUAGE | PUBLISHER
-----------------------------------------------------------------
        | P._X      | >=1994  |        | ENGLISH  | ACM
        |           |         |        |          |
```

The full set of Boolean expressions, however, is difficult to express except inside a special *condition box*.

Form-fillin queries can substantially simplify many queries, and, if the user interface permits, some Boolean combinations (usually a conjunction of disjuncts (ORs) within attributes with ANDs between attributes) can be easy to express:

```
JOURNAL DATABASE
    DOCUMENT#:
          DATE: 1994..1997
        AUTHOR:
      LANGUAGE: ENGLISH, FRENCH
     PUBLISHER: ASIS, HFES, ACM
```

Although SQL is a standard, many form-fillin variants for expressing relational database queries have been proposed to aid novice searchers. The diversity is itself an impediment to easy use, but designers assume that users are willing to invest minutes or hours to learn each interface. This assumption is not valid for walk-up kiosks or for web pages offering textual-document library searches, in which users are often invited to type keywords or *natural-language queries* in a box, and to click on a run button. This presentation is meant to be appealing, but the computer's capacity for responding to the natural-language query is often limited to eliminating frequent terms or commands ("please list the documents that deal with") and searching for remaining words. A ranked list of documents is usually presented, and users must do their best in choosing relevant items from the list.

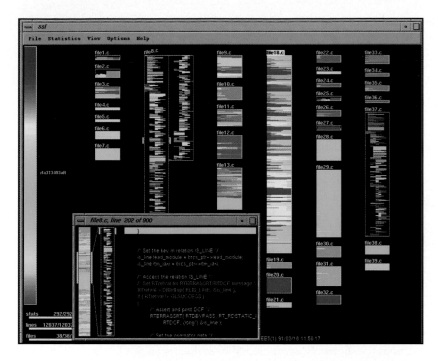

Plate B1: A computer program with 4000 lines of code. The newest lines are in red; the oldest are in blue. The smaller browser window shows a code overview and detail view. (Used with permission of ATT Bell Labs, Naperville, IL.)

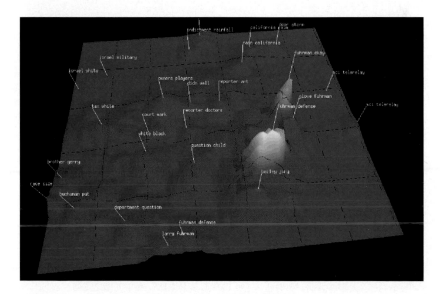

Plate B2: Information-retrieval themescape, showing a multidimensional information space pressed down into a two-dimensional topological map. Some clustering of points can be interesting, but they carry the danger of misinterpretations of the meaning of adjacency. (Wise et al., 1995.) (Used with permission of Battelle Pacific Northwest National Laboratory, Richland, WA.)

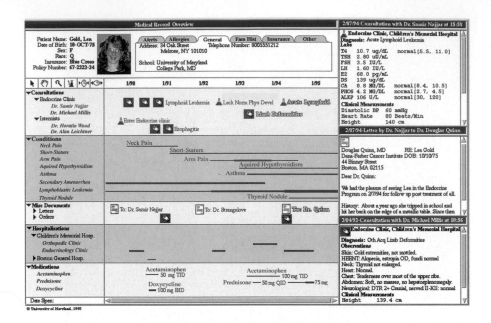

Plate B3: Medical version of LifeLines. Physician visits, conditions, hospitalizations, and medications are shown. Every item in the record is seen as a line or icon in the overview, with color coding by doctor. Line thickness indicates severity and dosage. Windows on the right side show the details. (Plaisant et al., 1997.)

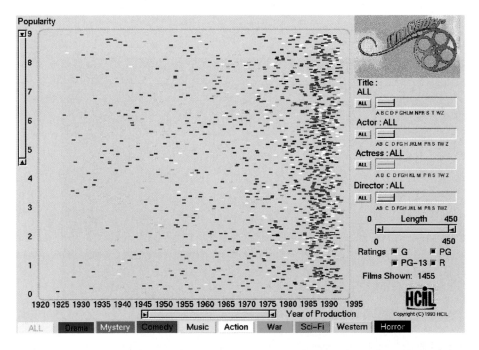

Plate B4 (a): FilmFinder showing 1500 films in a starfield display, where the location of each point is determined by the year of the film (x axis) and by the film's popularity in video store rentals (y axis). The color encodes the film type.

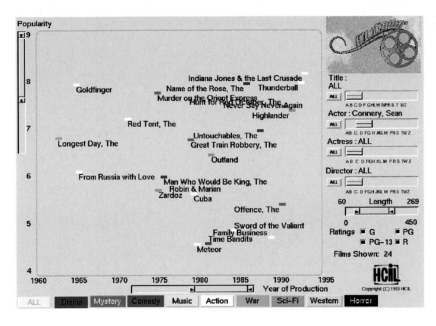

Plate B4 (b): FilmFinder after zooming in on recent popular films. When less than 25 films remain, the titles appear automatically.

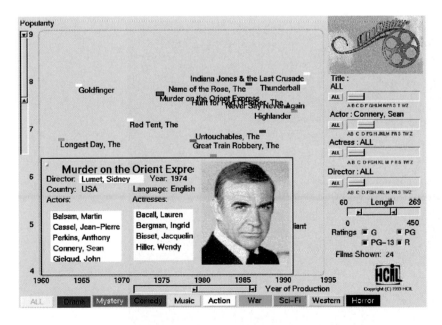

Plate B4 (c): FilmFinder after selection of a single film. The info card pops up with details on demand. (Ahlberg and Shneiderman, 1997.)

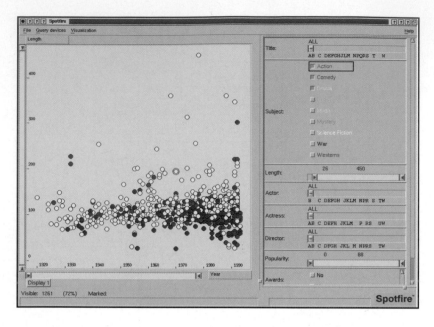

Plate B5: Spotfire version of FilmFinder, which provides increased user controls. Users can set axes (set to length in minutes and year) and glyph attributes (color is set to subject, and larger size indicates award-winning film). (Used with permission of IVEE Development, Goteborg, Sweden.) (http://www.ivee.com)

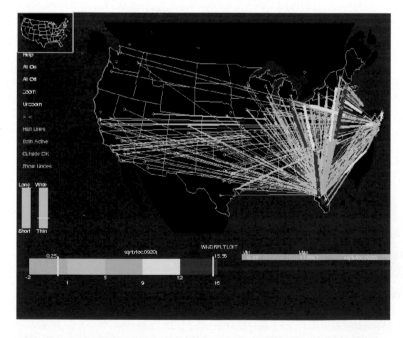

Plate B6: Telephone network traffic represented by thickness and color of the half-line segments between cities. (Used with permission of ATT Bell Labs, Naperville, IL.)

Although an easy-to-use interface is a good idea, if users cannot express their intentions or are uncertain about the meaning of the results, then the interface may need improvement. Finding a way to provide powerful search without overwhelming novice users is a current challenge. Existing interfaces often hide important aspects of the search (by poor design or to protect proprietary relevance-ranking schemes), or make query specification so difficult and confusing that they discourage use. Evidence from empirical studies shows that users perform better and have higher subjective satisfaction when they can view and control the search (Koenemann and Belkin, 1996).

An analogy to the evolution of automobile user interfaces might clarify the goals. Early competitors offered a profusion of controls, and each manufacturer had a distinct design. Some designs—such as having a brake pedal that was far from the gas pedal—were dangerous. Furthermore, if you were accustomed to driving a car with the brake to the left of the gas pedal, and your neighbor's car had the reverse design, it might be risky to trade cars. It took a half-century to achieve good design and appropriate consistency in automobiles; let's hope that we can make the transition faster for text-search user interfaces.

Improved designs and consistency across multiple systems can bring faster performance, reduce mistaken assumptions, and increase success in finding relevant items. For example, with the variety of web search systems, such as Lycos, Infoseek, and AltaVista, users might expect that the search string `direct manipulation` would produce one of the following:

- Search on the exact string `direct manipulation`
- Probabilistic search for `direct` and `manipulation`
- Probabilistic search for `direct` and `manipulation`, with some weighting if the terms are in close proximity
- Boolean search on `direct` AND `manipulation`
- Boolean search on `direct` OR `manipulation`
- Error message indicating missing AND/OR operator or other delimiters

In many systems, there is little or no indication regarding which interpretation has been chosen and whether stemming, case matching, stop words, or other transformations are being applied. Often, the results are displayed in a relevance-ranked manner that is a mystery to many users (and sometimes is a proprietary secret).

To coordinate design practice, we might use a *four-phase framework* to satisfy the needs of first-time, intermittent, and frequent users who are accessing a variety of textual and multimedia libraries (Shneiderman et al., 1997). Finding common ground will be difficult; not finding it will be tragic. Although early adopters of technology are willing to overcome difficulties, the middle and late adopters are not so tolerant. The future of search services on the World Wide Web and elsewhere may depend on the degree to which user frustration and confusion are reduced, while the ability to find reliably sought items in the surging sea of information is increased.

The four-phase framework (Box 15.1) gives great freedom to designers to offer features in an orderly and consistent manner. The phases are

1. *Formulation:* expressing the search
2. *Initiation of action:* launching the search
3. *Review of results:* reading messages and outcomes
4. *Refinement:* formulating the next step

Formulation includes the *source* of the information, the *fields* for limiting the source, the *phrases*, and the *variants*. Even if technically and economically feasible, searching all libraries or collections in a library is not always the preferred approach. Users often prefer to limit the sources to a specific library, collection in a library, or subcollection range of items (users may choose date ranges, languages, media types, publishers, and so on). Users may wish to limit their search to specific *fields* (for example, the title, abstract, or full text of a scientific article) of items within a collection. Typically, users searching on common phrases would prefer to retrieve only those documents whose title contains those phrases. Sources may also be restricted by structured fields (year of publication, volume number, and so on).

In textual databases, users often seek items that contain meaningful *phrases* (Civil War, Environmental Protection Agency, George Washington, air pollution, carbon monoxide), and multiple entry windows should be provided to allow for multiple phrases. Searches on phrases have proved to be more accurate than are searches on words. Since some relevant items may be missed by a phrase approach, users should have the option to expand a search by breaking the phrases into separate words. Phrases also facilitate searching on names (for example, search on George Washington should not turn up George Bush or Washington, D.C.). If Boolean operations, proximity restrictions, or other combining strategies are specifiable, then the users should be able to express them. Users or service providers should have control over stop lists (common words, single letters, obscenities).

When users are unsure of the exact value of the field (subject term, or spelling or capitalization of a city name), they may want to relax the search constraints by allowing *variants* to be accepted. In structured databases, the variants may include a wider range on a numeric attribute. In a textual-document search, interfaces should allow user control over variant capitalization (case sensitivity), stemmed versions (the keyword teach retrieves variant suffixes such as teacher, teaching, or teaches), partial matches (the keyword biology retrieves sociobiology and astrobiology), phonetic variants from soundex methods (the keyword Johnson retrieves Jonson, Jansen, Johnsson), synonyms (the keyword cancer retrieves oncology), abbrevia-

Box 15.1

Four-phase framework to clarify user interfaces for textual search.

---

1. *Formulation*
   - Search the appropriate sources in libraries and collections
   - Use *fields* for limiting the source: structured fields such as year, media, or language, and text fields such as titles or abstracts of documents
   - Recognize *phrases* to allow entry of names such as `George Washington` or `Environmental Protection Agency`, and concepts such as `abortion rights reform` or `gallium arsenide`.
   - Permit *variants* to allow relaxation of search constraints, such as case sensitivity, stemming, partial matches, phonetic variations, abbreviations, or synonyms from a thesaurus.

2. *Action*
   - Include *explicit actions* initiated by buttons with consistent labels (such as "Search"), location, size, and color.
   - Include *implicit actions* initiated by changes to a parameter of the formulation phase that immediately produce a new set of search results.

3. *Results*
   - Read explanatory messages.
   - View textual lists.
   - Manipulate visualizations.
   - Control what the size of the result set is and which fields are displayed.
   - Change sequencing (alphabetical, chronological, relevance ranked, etc.).
   - Explore clustering (by attribute value, topics, etc.).

4. *Refinement*
   - Use meaningful messages to guide users in progressive refinement; for example, if the two words in a phrase are not found near each other, then offer easy selection of individual words or variants.
   - Make changing of search parameters convenient.
   - Allow search results and the setting of each parameter to be saved, sent by email, or used as input to other programs, such as visualization or statistical tools.

---

tions (the keyword `IBM` retrieves International Business Machines, and vice versa), and broader or narrower terms from a thesaurus (the keyphrase `New England` retrieves Vermont, Maine, Rhode Island, New Hampshire, Massachusetts, and Connecticut).

The second phase is the initiation of *action*, which may be explicit or implicit. Most current systems have a search button for explicit initiation, or for delayed or regularly scheduled initiation. The button label, size, and color should be consistent across versions. An appealing alternative is *implicit initiation*, in which each change to a component of the formulation phase immediately produces a new set of search results. *Dynamic queries*—in which users adjust query widgets to produce continuous updates—have proved to be effective and satisfying. They require adequate screen space and rapid processing, but their advantages are great.

The third phase is the review of *results*, in which the users read messages, view textual lists, or manipulate visualizations. Users may be given control over what the size of the result set is, which fields are displayed, how results are sequenced (alphabetical, chronological, relevance ranked), and how results are clustered (by attribute value, by topics) (Pirolli et al., 1996).

The fourth phase is the *refinement*. Search interfaces should provide meaningful messages to explain search outcomes and to support progressive refinement. For example, if a stop word, obscenity, or misspelling is eliminated from a search input window, or if stemmed terms, partial matches, or variant capitalizations are included, users should be able to see these changes to their query. If two words in a keyphrase are not found proximally, then feedback should be given about the occurrence of the words individually. If multiple phrases are input, then items containing all phrases should be shown first and identified, followed by items containing subsets; but if no documents are found with all phrases, that failure should be indicated. There is a fairly elaborate decision tree (maybe 60 to 100 branches) of search outcomes and messages that needs to be specified. Another aspect of feedback is that, as searches are made, the system should keep track of them in a *history buffer* to allow review of earlier searches. Progressive refinement, in which the results of a search are refined by changing of the search parameters, should be convenient. Search results and the settings of all parameters should be objects that can be saved, sent by electronic mail, or used as input to other programs—for example, for visualization or statistical tools.

The four-phase framework can be applied by designers to make the search process more visible, comprehensible, and controllable by users. This approach is in harmony with movement toward direct manipulation, in which the state of the system is made visible and is placed under user control. Novices may not want to see all the components of the four phases initially, but, if they are unhappy with the search results, they should be able to view the settings and change their queries easily. A revised interface for the Library of Congress' THOMAS system (Fig. 15.1) shows how the framework might be applied to full-text searching of proposed legislation.

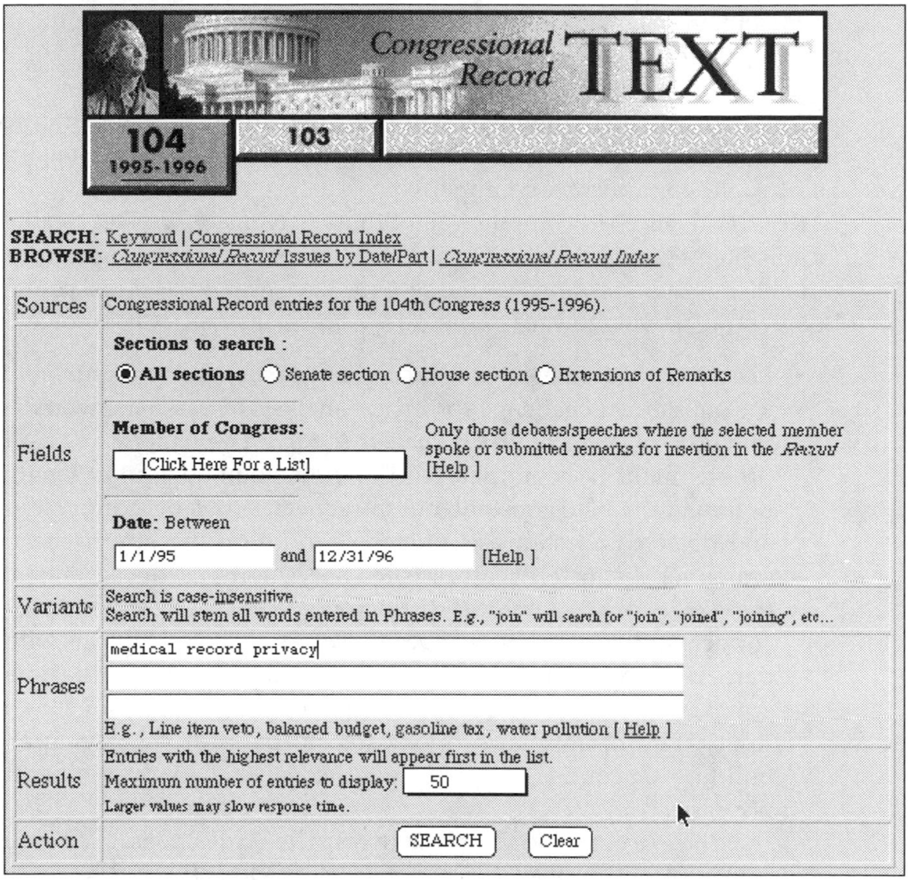

Figure 15.1

A revised interface for the Library of Congress' THOMAS system. The display shows how the four-phase framework might be applied to text searching on Congressional Record articles. Implemented by Bryan Slavin at the University of Maryland Human–Computer Interaction Laboratory. (Shneiderman et al., 1997.)

15.3   Multimedia Document Searches

Interfaces to search structured databases and textual-document libraries are good and getting better, but searching in multimedia document libraries is still in a primitive stage. Current approaches to locating images, videos, sound, or animation depend on a parallel database or document search to locate the items. For example, searches in photo libraries can be done by date, photographer, medium, location, or text in captions, but finding photos showing a ribbon-cutting ceremony or videos of a sunset is difficult. In the near term, those people who must search multimedia documents should push for ambitious captioning and attribute recording. Classification according to useful search categories (agriculture, music, sports, personalities) is helpful, although costly and imperfect.

Recent advances in computer algorithms may enable greater flexibility in locating items in multimedia libraries. User-interface designs to specify the permissible matches are varied. Some systems have elaborate textual commands, but most are moving toward graphical specification of query components:

- *Photo search*   Finding photos with images such as the Statue of Liberty is a substantial challenge for image-analysis researchers, who describe this task as *query by image content (QBIC)*. Lady Liberty's distinctive profile might be identifiable if the orientation, lens focal length, and lighting were held constant, but the general problem is difficult in large and diverse collections of photos. Two promising approaches are to search for distinctive features such as the torch or the seven spikes in the crown, or to search for distinctive colors, such as the faded green copper verdigris. Users can specify features or color patterns with standard drawing tools, and even can indicate where in the image to search. For example, users could specify red, white, and blue in the upper third of an image to look for an American flag flying above a building. Of course, separating out the British, French, or other flags is not easy.

  More success is attainable with restricted collections, such as of glass vases, for which users could draw a desired profile and retrieve vases with long narrow necks. Other candidate collections include photos of constellations, subatomic particle tracks, or red blood cells. Users could specify their requests by selecting from a set of templates and adjusting the templates to describe their query. For critical applications, such as fingerprint matching, current successes depend on human identification of as many as 20 distinct features, but automatic recognition is improving. Even if completely automatic recognition is not possible, it will still be useful to have computers perform filtering, such as finding all the portraits with neutral backgrounds in a photo library.

- *Map search*   Computer-generated maps are increasingly available online. Locating a map by latitude and longitude is the structured-database solution, but search by features is becoming possible because the tools used to build maps preserve the structural aspects and the multiple layers in maps. For example, users might specify a search for all port cities with a population greater than 1 million and an airport within 10 miles. Search on simpler maps such as airline routes might find flights to a given destination with no more than two connections on the same airline. Another candidate is weather maps, in which structured data—such as temperature, winds, or barometric pressure—make the search specification convenient.

- *Design or diagram search* Some computer-assisted design packages offer users limited search capabilities within a single design or across design collections. Finding red circles inside blue squares may help in some cases, but more elaborate strategies for finding engine designs with pistons smaller than 6 centimeters could prove more beneficial. Diagramming tools for making flowcharts or organization charts can add search capabilities to locate organizations that have more than five levels of management or situations where vice presidents are managing more than seven projects. Newspaper-layout packages could allow search for all occasions of headlines using fonts larger than 48 points, or headlines that span the front page.

- *Sound search* Imagine a music database system that would respond when users hum a few notes by producing a list of symphonies that contain that string of notes. Then, with a single touch, users could listen to the full symphony. Implementing this idea in the unstructured world of analog-encoded or even digitally encoded music is difficult, but imagine that the score sheets of symphonies were stored with the music and that string search over the score sheets was possible. Then, the application becomes easier to conceive. Identification of the users' hummed input might not be reliable, but if visual feedback were provided or if users entered the notes on a staff, then the fantasy would become feasible. Finding a spoken word or phrase in databases of telephone conversations is still difficult, but is becoming possible, even on a speaker-independent basis.

- *Video search* Searching a video or film involves more than simply searching through each of the frames. Users may wish to have a video segmented into scenes or cuts, and to identify zooming in or out and panning left or right. Gaining an overview of a 2-hour video by a time line of scenes would enable better understanding, editing, or selection. Combinations of structured databases and textual documents with video libraries lead to powerful services. Television news or sports libraries maintain structured databases and textual documents to support search for presidential appearances, disasters, or football highlights, carefully indexed for rapid future retrieval.

- *Animation search* Animation-authoring tools are still in early stages of development, but it might be possible to specify searches for certain kinds of animation—for example, spinning globes, moving banners, bouncing balls, or morphing faces. Although it might be less useful, it should be relatively easy to search for slides in a presentation that have moving text that comes in from the left, or in which the transition from one slide to another is by a barndoor animation.

15.4   Information Visualization

Grasping the whole is a gigantic theme. Arguably, intellectual history's most important. Ant-vision is humanity's usual fate; but seeing the whole is every thinking person's aspiration.

David Gelernter, *Mirror Worlds*, 1992

Visualization is a method of computing. It transforms the symbolic into the geometric, enabling researchers to observe their simulations and computations. Visualization offers a method for seeing the unseen. It enriches the process of scientific discovery and fosters profound and unexpected insights. In many fields it is already revolutionizing the way scientists do science.

McCormick et al., 1987

The success of direct-manipulation interfaces is indicative of the power of using computers in a more visual or graphic manner. A picture is often said to be worth a thousand words and, for some tasks, a visual presentation—such as a map or photograph—is dramatically easier to use or comprehend than is a textual description or a spoken report. As computer speeds and display resolution increase, information visualization and graphical interfaces are likely to have an expanding role. If a map of the United States is displayed, then it should be possible to point rapidly at one of 1000 cities to get tourist information. Of course, a foreigner who knows a city's name (for example, New Orleans), but does not know its location, may do better with a scrolling alphabetical list. Visual displays become even more attractive to provide orientation or context, to enable selection of regions, and to provide dynamic feedback for identifying changes (for example, on a weather map). Scientific visualization has the power to make visible and comprehensible atomic, cosmic, and common three-dimensional phenomena (such as heat conduction in engines, airflow over wings, or ozone holes). Abstract-information visualization has the power to reveal patterns, clusters, gaps, or outliers in statistical data, stock-market trades, computer directories, or document collections.

Overall, the bandwidth of information presentation is potentially higher in the visual domain than it is for media reaching any of the other senses. Humans have remarkable perceptual abilities that are greatly underutilized in current designs. Users can scan, recognize, and recall images rapidly, and can detect subtle changes in size, color, shape, movement, or texture. They can point to a single pixel, even in a megapixel display, and can drag one object to another to perform an action. User interfaces thus far have been largely text oriented, so as visual approaches are explored, appealing new opportunities are emerging.

There are many visual design guidelines. The central principle might be summarized as this *visual-information-seeking mantra:*

Overview first, zoom and filter, then details on demand
Overview first, zoom and filter, then details on demand
Overview first, zoom and filter, then details on demand
Overview first, zoom and filter, then details on demand
Overview first, zoom and filter, then details on demand
Overview first, zoom and filter, then details on demand
Overview first, zoom and filter, then details on demand
Overview first, zoom and filter, then details on demand
Overview first, zoom and filter, then details on demand
Overview first, zoom and filter, then details on demand
Overview first, zoom and filter, then details on demand
Overview first, zoom and filter, then details on demand

Each line represents one project in which I found myself rediscovering this principle and therefore wrote it down as a reminder. The mantra proved to be a good starting point when I was trying to characterize the multiple information-visualization innovations occurring at university, government, and industry research laboratories. To sort out the numerous prototypes and to guide researchers to new opportunities, Box 15.2 gives a *data type by task taxonomy (TTT)* of information visualizations.

As in the case of search, users are assumed to be viewing collections of items, where items have multiple attributes. In all seven data types (one-, two-, three-dimensional data; temporal and multi-dimensional data; and tree and network data) the items have one or more attributes. A basic search task is to select all items that match target attributes—for example, find all divisions in an company that have a budget greater than $500,000.

The data types of the TTT characterize the task-domain information objects and are organized by the problems that users are trying to solve. For example, in two-dimensional information such as maps, users are trying to grasp adjacency or to navigate paths, whereas in tree-structured information, users are trying to understand parent–child–sibling relationships. The tasks in the TTT are task-domain information actions that users wish to perform.

The seven tasks are at a high level of abstraction. Refinements and additions to these tasks would be natural next steps in expanding this taxonomy. The seven tasks are overview, zoom, filter, details-on-demand, relate, history, extract. Further discussion of the seven tasks follows the descriptions of the seven data types.

Box 15.2

Data Type by Task Taxonomy (TTT) to identify visualization data types and the tasks that need to be supported.

Data Type by Task Taxonomy (TTT)

Data Types

1-D Linear	Document Lens, SeeSoft
	Information Mural
2-D Map	GIS, Arcinfo, ThemeMap
	LyberWorld, InfoCrystal
3-D World	Desktops, WebBook, VRML
	CAD, Medical, Molecules
Temporal	Perspective Wall, ESDA
	MSProjects, LifeLines
Multi-Dimensional	Parallel Coordinates, Starfield, Visage
	Influence Explorer, TableLens
Tree	Outliners, Superbook, FileManager
	Cone/Cam/Hyperbolic, TreeBrowser, Treemaps
Network	Netmap, SemNet, SeeNet, Butterfly

Tasks

Overview	Gain an overview of the entire collection.
Zoom	Zoom in on items of interest.
Filter	Filter out uninteresting items.
Details-on-demand	Select an item or group and get details when needed.
Relate	View relationships among items.
History	Keep a history of actions to support undo, replay, and progressive refinement.
Extract	Allow extraction of subcollections and of the query parameters.

1-D Linear Data

Linear data types include textual documents, program source code, and alphabetical lists of names, all of which are all organized in a sequential manner. Each item in the collection is a line of text containing a string of characters. Additional attributes might be the date of most recent update or author name. Interface-design issues include what fonts, color, size to use, and what overview, scrolling, or selection methods can be used. User tasks might be to find the number of items, to see items having certain attributes (show only lines of a document that are section titles, lines of a program that were changed from the previous version, or people in a list who are older than 21 years), or to see an item with all its attributes.

An early approach to dealing with large one-dimensional data sets was the *bifocal display*, which provided detailed information in the focus area and less information in the surrounding context area (Spence and Apperley, 1982). A selected issue of a scientific journal had details about each article; the older and newer issues of the journal were to the left and right on the bookshelf with decreasing space. Another effort to visualize one-dimensional data showed the attribute values of thousands of items in a fixed-sized space using a scrollbar-like display called *value bars* (Fig. 15.2) (Chimera, 1992). Even greater compressions were accomplished in compact displays of tens of thousands of lines of program source code in See Soft (Color Plate B1) (Eick et al., 1992) or lines in Hamlet (Fig. 15.3). Other examples of one-dimensional data include large textual documents in Document Lens (Fig. 15.4) (Robertson and Mackinlay, 1993) and historical

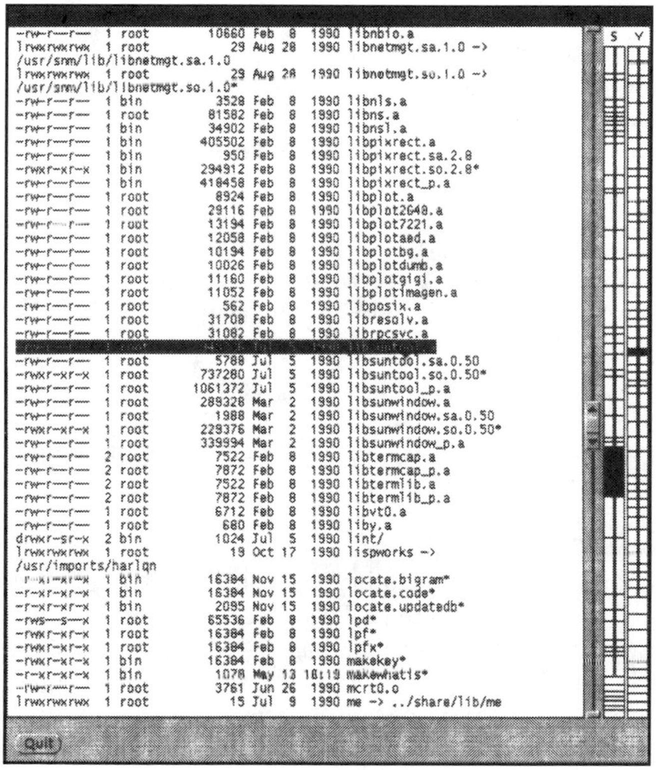

Figure 15.2

Each value bar shows one attribute of the linear list of items. In this Unix directory example, the two value bars on the right represent the file size (S) and file modification recency, or youth (Y). The currently selected file is one of the biggest in size and is moderately youthful. (Chimera, 1992.)

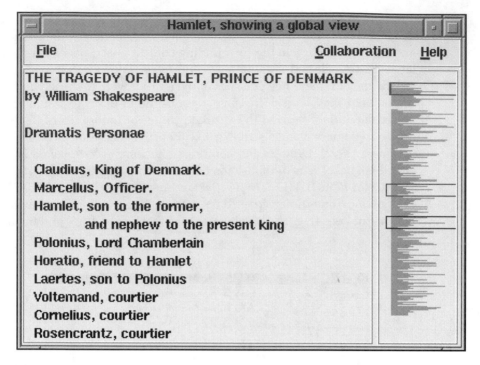

Figure 15.3

Shakespeare's Hamlet, viewed with a one-dimensional overview on the right side showing where three users are reading the document. Each person's field-of-view box shows their location. This user is at the start. (Used with permission of the University of Calgary, Alberta, Canada.)

data about sunspots using the information-mural algorithms (Fig. 15.5) (Jerding and Stasko, 1995).

2-D Map data

Planar or map data include geographic maps, floorplans, and newspaper layouts. Each item in the collection covers some part of the total area and may or may not be rectangular. Each item has task-domain attributes, such as name, owner, and value, and interface-domain features, such as size, color, and opacity. Many systems adopt a multiple-layer approach to dealing with map data, but each layer is two-dimensional. User tasks are to find adjacent items, containing items and paths between items, and to perform the seven basic tasks.

Examples include geographic-information systems, which are a large research and commercial domain (Laurini and Thompson, 1992; Egenhofer and Richards, 1993) with numerous systems available (see Fig. 6.5). Information-visualization researchers have used spatial dis-

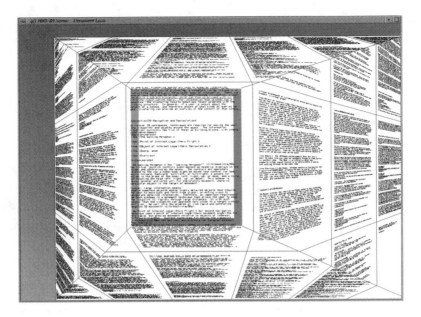

Figure 15.4

Document Lens showing many pages of a document in miniature form. Users can zoom in on any page easily and quickly. (Used with permission from Xerox PARC, Palo Alto, CA.)

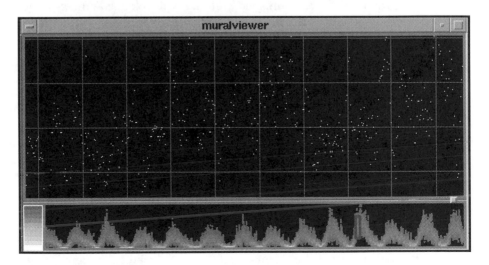

Figure 15.5

The information-mural overview at the bottom uses an antialiasing algorithm to show 52,000 readings of sun spots from 1850 to 1993. The field-of-view box at the bottom shows the context for the detail view on top. (Jerding & Stasko, 1995.) (Used with permission of Georgia Tech University, Atlanta, GA.)

plays of document collections (Color Plate B2) (Korfhage, 1991; Hemmje et al., 1993; Wise et al., 1995) organized proximally by term co-occurrences.

3-D World

Real-world objects such as molecules, the human body, and buildings have items with volume and with potentially complex relationships with other items. Computer-assisted design systems for architects, solid modelers, and mechanical engineers are built to handle complex three-dimensional relationships. Users' tasks deal with adjacency plus above–below and inside–outside relationships, as well as the seven basic tasks. In three-dimensional applications, users must cope with their position and orientation when viewing the objects, plus must handle the serious problems of *occlusion*. Solutions are proposed in many prototypes with techniques such as overviews, landmarks, perspective, stereo display, transparency, and color coding.

Examples of three-dimensional computer graphics and computer-assisted design are numerous, but information-visualization work in three dimensions is still novel. Some virtual-environment researchers have sought to present information in three-dimensional structures (see Section 6.8). Navigating high-resolution images of the human body is the challenge in the National Library of Medicine's Visible Human project (Fig. 15.6) (North et al., 1996). Architectural walkthroughs or flythroughs can give users an idea of what a finished building will look like. A three-dimensional desktop is thought to be appealing to users, but disorientation, navigation, and hidden data problems remain (Fig. 15.7) (Card et al., 1996).

Temporal data

Time lines are widely used and are sufficiently vital for medical records, project management, or historical presentations that researchers have created a data type that is separate from one-dimensional data. The distinctions of *temporal data* are that items have a start and finish time, and that items may overlap. Frequent tasks include finding all events before, after, or during some time period or moment, plus the seven basic tasks.

Many project-management tools exist; novel visualizations of time include the perspective wall (Fig. 15.8) (Robertson et al., 1993) and Life-Lines (see Fig. 1.5 and Color Plate B3) (Plaisant et al., 1996). LifeLines shows a youth's history keyed to the needs of the Maryland Department of Juvenile Justice, but is intended to present medical patient histories as a compact overview with selectable items that allow users to get details-on-demand. Temporal-data visualizations appear in systems for editing video data, composing music, or preparing animations, such as Macromedia Director.

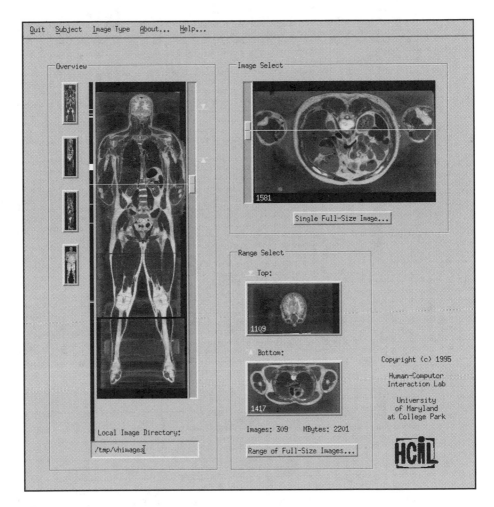

Figure 15.6

Visible Human Explorer user interface, showing a reconstructed coronal section overview (on the left) and an axial preview image of the upper abdominal region (on the upper right). Dragging the sliders animates the cross-sections through the body. (North et al., 1996.) (Available at http://www.nlm.nih.gov)

Multidimensional data

Most relational- and statistical-database contents are conveniently manipulated as multidimensional data, in which items with n attributes become points in a *n-dimensional space*. The interface representation can be dynamic two-dimensional scattergrams, with each additional dimension controlled by a slider (Ahlberg and Shneiderman, 1994). Buttons can used

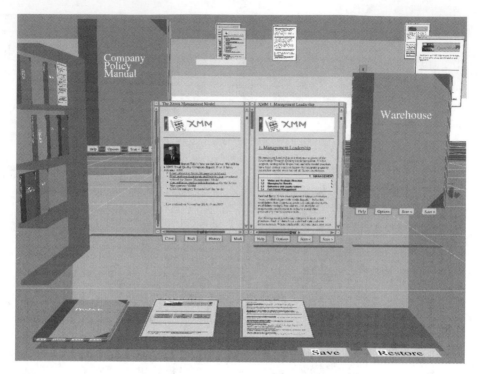

Figure 15.7

WebBook and WebForager. These three-dimensional worlds are used for browsing and recording web pages. (Used with permission from Xerox PARC, Palo Alto, CA.)

for attribute values when the cardinality is small—say, less than 10. Tasks include finding patterns, clusters, correlations among pairs of variables, gaps, and outliers. Multidimensional data can be represented by a three-dimensional scattergram, but disorientation (especially if the user's point of view is from inside the cluster of points) and occlusion (especially if close points are represented as being larger) can be problems. The technique of using parallel coordinates (Fig. 15.9) is a clever innovation that makes certain tasks easier, but takes practice for users to comprehend (Inselberg, 1985).

The early HomeFinder (Fig. 15.10) developed dynamic queries and sliders for user-controlled visualization of multidimensional data (Williamson and Shneiderman, 1992). The successor FilmFinder (Color Plate B4a–c) refined the techniques (Ahlberg and Shneiderman, 1994) for starfield displays (zoomable, color-coded, user-controlled scattergrams), and laid the basis for the commercial product Spotfire (Color Plate B5) (Ahlberg and Wistrand, 1995). Extrapolations include the Aggregate Manipulator (Goldstein and Roth, 1994), movable filters (Fishkin and

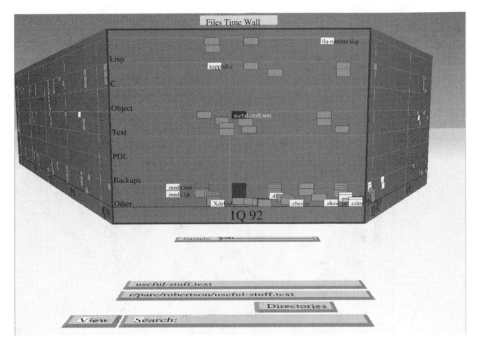

Files Time Wall

ilu-runtime.lisp

Lisp

xapp.edit

C

Object

useful-stuff.text

Text

PDL

Backups

.med ginit
.med lgt

Other

Xdefan

All

ches.tc

sho

em

eshr

IQ 92

useful-stuff.text

r/parc/robertson/useful-stuff.text

Directories

View   Search:

Figure 15.8

A perspective wall, showing time moving from left to right, with the focus in the center. Different categories of programs are shown on each level of the wall. Color or size coding can be used. (Used with permission from Xerox PARC, Palo Alto, CA.)

Stone, 1995), and Selective Dynamic Manipulation (Chuah et al., 1995). Related works include VisDB for multidimensional database visualization (Keim and Kreigal, 1994), the spreadsheet-like Table Lens (Fig. 15.11) (Rao and Card, 1994), and the multiple linked histograms in the Influence Explorer (Tweedie et al., 1996).

Tree data

Hierarchies or tree structures are collections of items, in which each item (except the root) has a link to one parent item. Items and the links between parent and child can have multiple attributes. The basic tasks can be applied to items and links, and tasks related to structural properties become interesting—for example, how many levels are in the tree, or how many children does an item have? While it is possible to have similar items at leaves and internal nodes, it is also common to find different items at each level in a tree. Fixed-level trees, with all leaves equidistant from the root, and fixed-fanout trees, with the same number of children for every parent, are easier to handle. High-fanout (broad) and small-fanout (deep) trees are important special cases. Inter-

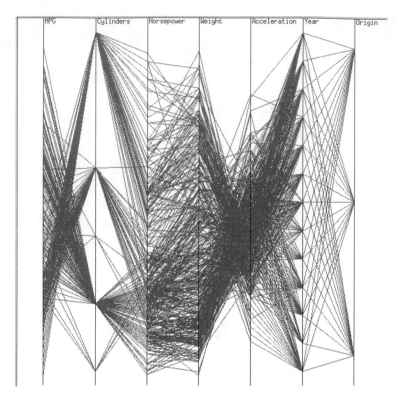

Figure 15.9

Parallel coordinate plot of seven dimensions of automobile data (CARS dataset obtained from StatLib at Carnegie Mellon University). There is a range of MPG (miles per gallon) values, but clear clusters of two-, four-, and six-cylinder cars are visible. More cylinders generally produce higher horsepower. Also notable is the generally inverse relationship of weight to acceleration. (Used with permission of Matt Ward, Worcester Polytechnic Institute, Worcester, MA.)

face representations of trees can use the outline style of indented labels used in tables of contents (Chimera and Shneiderman, 1993); a node-and-link diagram; or a *treemap,* in which child items are rectangles nested inside parent rectangles.

Tree-structured data has long been displayed with indented outlines (Egan et al., 1989), or with connecting lines, as in many computer-directory file managers. Attempts to show large tree structures as node-and-link diagrams in compact forms include the three-dimensional cone (Fig. 15.12) and cam trees (Robertson et al., 1993; Carriere and Kazman, 1995), dynamic pruning in the TreeBrowser (Fig. 15.13) (Kumar et al., 1997), and the appealingly animated hyperbolic trees (Fig. 15.14) (Lamping et al.,

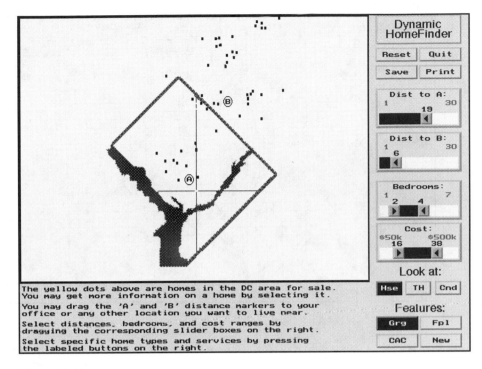

The yellow dots above are homes in the DC area for sale.
You may get more information on a home by selecting it.

You may drag the 'A' and 'B' distance markers to your
office or any other location you want to live near.

Select distances, bedrooms, and cost ranges by
dragging the corresponding slider boxes on the right.

Select specific home types and services by pressing
the labeled buttons on the right.

Figure 15.10

Dynamic HomeFinder, an early application of dynamic queries. Homes for sale in the Washington, D.C., area were shown as 1100 points of light. As users moved the sliders on the right, the screen was updated immediately to show the points matching the current query. By clicking on any point, users could get a detailed description. (Williamson and Shneiderman, 1992.)

1995). The space-filling mosaic approach, treemaps, shows an arbitrary-sized tree in a fixed rectangular space (Shneiderman, 1992; Johnson and Shneiderman, 1991). The treemap approach was applied successfully to libraries (Fig. 15.15), computer directories (Fig. 15.16), sales data, business decision making (Asahi et al., 1995), and web browsing (Mitchell et al., 1995; Mukherjea et al., 1995), but first-time users take 10 to 20 minutes to accommodate to treemaps.

Network data

Sometimes, relationships among items cannot be captured conveniently with a tree structure, and it is useful to have items linked to an arbitrary number of other items. Although many special cases of networks exist (acyclic, lattices, rooted versus unrooted, directed versus undirected), it is

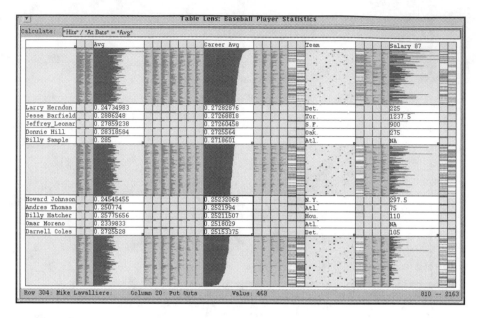

Figure 15.11

Table Lens, a program that provided a spreadsheetlike world that also supported information-visualization methods to find rankings and correlations among baseball players. (Used with permission from Xerox PARC, Palo Alto, CA.)

convenient to consider them all as one data type. In addition to performing the basic tasks applied to items and links, network users often want to know about shortest or least costly paths connecting two items or traversing the entire network. Interface representations include a node-and-link diagram, and a square matrix of the items with the value of a link attribute in the row and column representing a link.

Network visualization is an old but still imperfect art because of the complexity of relationships and user tasks. Commercial packages can handle small networks or simple strategies, such as Netmap's layout of nodes on a circle with links criss-crossing the central area. Specialized visualizations can be designed to be more effective for a given task, such as a network diagram showing heavy telephone traffic on holidays (Color Plate B6). An ambitious three-dimensional approach allowed users to fly into a network and control the visualization (Fairchild et al., 1988). New interest in this topic has been spawned by attempts to visualize the World Wide Web (Andrews, 1995; Hendley et al., 1995).

The seven data types that we have discussed reflect an abstraction of the reality. There are many variations on these themes (two-and-one-half

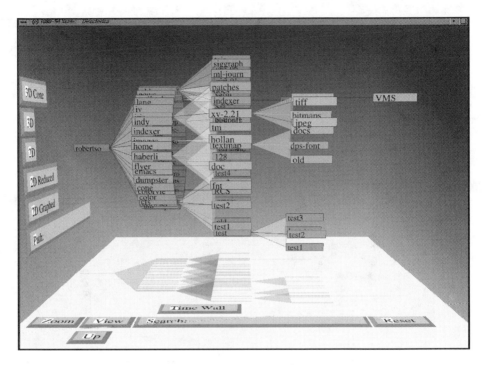

Figure 15.12

Cam-tree design, showing a hierarchical directory from left to right side. Users can rotate the trees smoothly in this three-dimensional viewer. When the root of the tree is shown at the top, this representation is called a cone-tree. (Used with permission from Xerox PARC, Palo Alto, CA.)

or four-dimensional data, multitrees) and many prototypes use combinations of these data types. This taxonomy is useful only if it facilitates discussion and leads to useful discoveries. We can get an idea of missed opportunities by looking at the tasks and data types in depth.

Overview task

We can gain an overview of the entire collection. Overview strategies (Section 13.5) include zoomed-out views of each data type that allow the user to see the entire collection plus an adjoining detail view. The overview contains a movable field-of-view box with which the user controls the contents of the detail view, allowing zoom factors of 3 to 30. Replication of this strategy with intermediate views enables users to reach larger zoom factors. Another popular approach is the fisheye strategy (Furnas, 1986), which has been applied most commonly for network browsing (Fig.

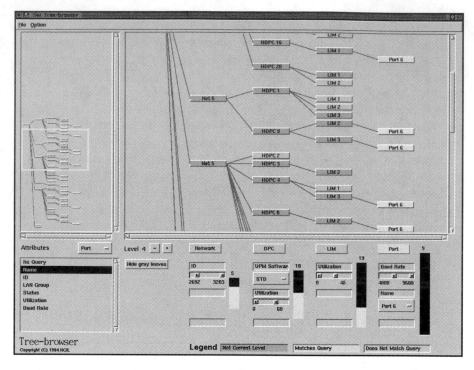

Figure 15.13

PDQ TreeBrowser, which supports pruning of nodes at every level of a tree. A user has pruned an 1100-node tree of a satellite network, using dynamic query sliders at four levels; only nine possible ports (leaf nodes) remain in the result set. (Kumar et al., 1997)

15.17) (Sarkar and Brown, 1994; Bartram et al., 1995; Schaffer et al., 1996). The fisheye distortion magnifies one or more areas of the display, but zoom factors in prototypes are limited to about 5. Although query-language facilities made it difficult to gain an overview of a collection, information-visualization interfaces support some overview strategy—or should do so. Adequate overview strategies are a useful criterion to judge such interfaces. In addition, look for navigation tools to pan or scroll through the collection.

Zoom task

We can zoom in on items of interest. Users typically have an interest in some portion of a collection, and they need tools to enable them to control the zoom focus and the zoom factor. Smooth zooming helps users to pre-

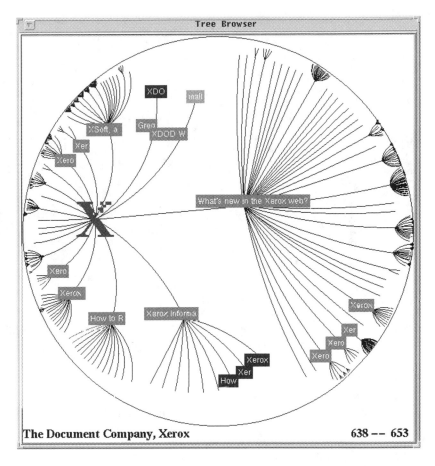

Figure 15.14

A hyperbolic tree browser that allows 10 to 30 nodes near the center to be seen clearly; branches are reduced gradually as they get closer to the periphery. This display technique guarantees that large trees can be accommodated in a fixed screen size. As the focus is shifted among nodes, the display updates smoothly, producing a satisfying animation. Landmarks or other features can be introduced to reduce the disorienting effect of movement (Lamping, Rao et al., 1995). (Used with permission of InXight Software, Palo Alto, CA.)

serve their sense of position and context (Schaffer et al., 1996). A user can zoom on one dimension at a time by moving the zoombar controls or by adjusting the size of the field-of-view box. A satisfying way to zoom in is to point to a location and to issue a zooming command, usually by holding down a mouse button (Bederson and Hollan, 1993). Zooming in one dimension has proved useful in starfield displays (Jog and Shneiderman, 1995).

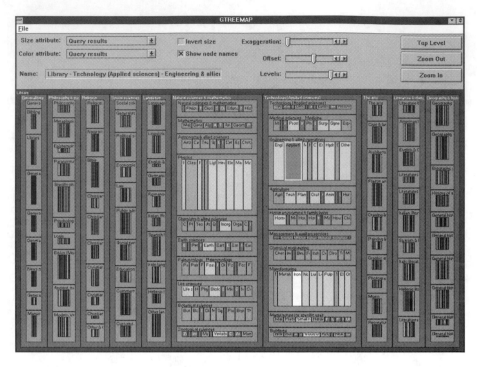

Figure 15.15

The first three levels of the Dewey Decimal System shown as a treemap in which
size indicates the number of books held in each of the 1000 categories. Color indicates frequency of utilization, with darker indicating high utilization (hot) and
lighter indicating low utilization. Implemented by Marko Teittinen at the University
of Maryland Human–Computer Interaction Laboratory.

Filter task

We can filter out uninteresting items. Dynamic queries applied to the
items in the collection constitute one of the key ideas in information visualization (Ahlberg et al., 1992; Williamson and Shneiderman, 1992; Kumar
et al., 1997). When users control the contents of the display, they can
quickly focus on their interests by eliminating unwanted items. Sliders,
buttons, or other control widgets coupled to rapid (less than 100 milliseconds) display update is the goal, even when there are tens of thousands of
displayed items.

Details-on-demand task

We can select an item or group to get details. Once a collection has been
trimmed to a few dozen items, it should be easy to browse the details
about the group or individual items. The usual approach is to simply click
on an item to get a pop-up window with values of each of the attributes.

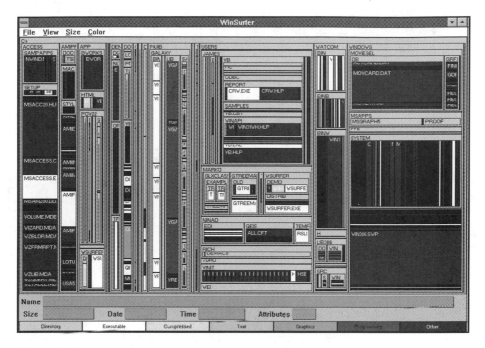

Figure 15.16

Winsurfer treemap that shows the 4900 files at several levels on a hard disk. Area is set to be proportional to file size and color to file type. Moving the cursor over an area produces an immediate display of attribute values on the bottom. Developed by Marko Teittinen at the University of Maryland Human–Computer Interaction Laboratory.

In Spotfire (Color Plate B5), the details-on-demand window can contain HTML text with links to further information.

Relate task

We can view relationships among items. In the FilmFinder details-on-demand window (Ahlberg and Shneiderman, 1994), users could select an attribute, such as the film's director, and cause the director alphaslider to be reset to the director's name, thereby displaying only films by that director. Similarly, in SDM (Chuah et al., 1995), users can select an item and then highlight items with similar attributes. In LifeLines (Color Plate B3) (Plaisant et al., 1996), users can click on a medication and see the related visit report, prescriptions, and laboratory test results. Designing user-interface actions to specify which relationship is to be manifested is still a challenge. The Influence Explorer (Tweedie et al., 1996) emphasizes exploration of relationships among attributes. The Table Lens (Fig. 15.11) emphasizes finding correlations among pairs of numerical attributes (Rao and Card, 1994).

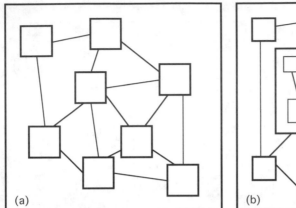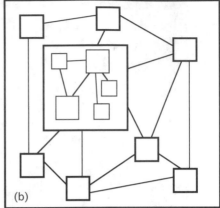

Figure 15.17

A fisheye view or variable zooming on a hierarchical network diagram. These techniques can help to focus attention on details while preserving context. (a) A central node has been selected for zooming. (b) The node is expanded by a zoom factor of 3, exposing five nodes at the next level. (Schaffer et al., 1996.)

History task

We can keep a history of actions to support undo, replay, and progressive refinement. It is rare that a single user action produces the desired outcome. Information exploration is inherently a process with many steps, so keeping the history of actions and allowing users to retrace their steps is important. However, most prototypes fail to deal with this requirement. Maybe they are reflecting the current state of GUIs, but designers would do better to model information-retrieval systems, which typically preserve the sequence of searches so that these searches can be combined or refined.

Extract task

We can allow extraction of subcollections and of the query parameters. Once users have obtained the item or set of items that they desire, it would be useful for them to be able to extract that set and to save it to a file in a format that would facilitate other uses, such as sending by electronic mail, printing, graphing, or insertion into a statistical or presentation package. As an alternative to saving the set, they might want to save, send, or print the settings for the control widgets. Few prototypes support such actions, although Roth's recent work on Visage provides an elegant capability to extract sets of items and simply drag-and-drop them into the next application window (Roth et al., 1996).

The attraction of visual displays, when compared to textual displays, is that they make use of the remarkable human perceptual ability for visual information. Within visual displays, there are opportunities for showing relationships by proximity, by containment, by connected lines, or by color coding. Highlighting techniques (for example, boldface text or brightening, inverse video, blinking, underscoring, or boxing) can be used to draw attention to certain items in a field of thousands of items. Pointing to a visual display can allow rapid selection, and feedback is apparent. The eye, the hand, and the mind seem to work smoothly and rapidly as users perform actions on visual displays.

15.5 Advanced Filtering

Users have highly varied needs for filtering features. The dynamic-queries approach of adjusting numeric range sliders, alphasliders for names or categories, or buttons for small sets of categories is appealing to many users for many tasks (Shneiderman, 1994). Dynamic queries might be called *direct-manipulation queries,* since they share the same concepts of visual display of actions (the sliders or buttons) and objects (the query results in the task-domain display); the use of rapid, incremental, and reversible actions; and the immediate display of feedback (less than 100 milliseconds). Additional benefits are the prevention of syntax errors and an encouragement of exploration.

Dynamic queries can reveal global properties, as well as assist users in answering specific questions. As the database grows, it is more difficult to update the display fast enough, and specialized data structures or parallel computation is required. Dynamic queries have attracted attention, although many user-interface problems remain; for example, we need to discover how to perform these tasks:

- Select a set of sliders from a large set of attributes.
- Specify greater than, less than, or greater than and less than.
- Deal with Boolean combinations of slider settings.
- Choose among highlighting by color, by points or light, by regions, by blinking, and so on.
- Cope with tens of thousands of points.
- Permit weighting of criteria.

The dynamic-query approach to the chemical table of elements was tested in an empirical comparison with a form-fillin query interface (Ahlberg et al., 1991). The counterbalanced-ordering within-subjects design with 18 chemistry students showed strong advantages for the dynamic queries, in terms of faster performance and lower error rates (Ahlberg et al., 1991).

Commercial information-retrieval systems, such as DIALOG or First-Search, permit complex Boolean expressions with parentheses, but their widespread adoption has been inhibited by their difficulty of use. Numerous proposals have been put forward to reduce the burden of specifying complex Boolean expressions (Reisner, 1988). Part of the confusion stems from informal English usage, in which a query such as "List all employees who live in New York and Boston" usually would result in an empty list because the "and" would be interpreted as an intersection; only employees who live in both cities would qualify! In English, "and" usually expands the options; in Boolean expressions, AND is used to narrow a set to the intersection of two others. Similarly, in the English "I'd like Russian or Italian salad dressing," the "or" is exclusive, indicating that you want one or the other but not both; in Boolean expressions, an OR is inclusive, and is used to expand a set.

The desire for *full Boolean expressions*, including nested parentheses and NOT operators, has led to novel metaphors for query specification. *Venn diagrams* (Michard, 1982) and *decision tables* (Greene et al., 1990) have been used, but these representations become clumsy as query complexity increases. To support arbitrarily complex Boolean expressions with a graphical specification, we applied the metaphor of water flowing from left to right through a series of filters, where each filter lets through only the appropriate documents, and the flow paths indicate AND or OR (Young and Shneiderman, 1993).

In this filter–flow model, ANDs are shown as a linear sequence of filters, suggesting the successive application of required criteria. As the flow passes through each filter, it is reduced, and the visual feedback shows a narrower stream of water. In Fig. 15.18(a) a journal database containing 6741 articles passes through the Date filter, about one-half of the articles satisfy the Date requirements of 94 to 97 (years 1994 to 1997). Only about one quarter of those articles pass through the Language filter, which selects English OR French. Users can also specify ORs across attributes, by putting filters in parallel flow paths (Fig. 15.18b). When the parallel flow paths converge, the width reflects the size of the union of the document sets.

Negation is handled by a NOT operator that, when selected, inverts all currently selected items in a filter (Fig. 15.18b). In the example, NOT 91 allows about 80 percent of the articles to pass the Date filter. Clusters of filters and flow paths (with one ingoing and one outgoing flow) can be made into a single labeled filter. Creation of clusters ensures that the full query can be shown on the display at once, and allows named clusters to be saved in a library for later reuse.

The filter-flow approach has been shown to help novices and intermittent users to specify complex Boolean expressions and to learn Boolean concepts. A usability study was conducted with 20 subjects who had had little experience using Boolean algebra. The prototype filter-flow interface was preferred over textual interface by all 20 subjects, and statistically significant advantages emerged on comprehension and composition tasks.

Another form of filtering is to apply a user-constructed set of keywords to dynamically generated information, such as incoming electronic-mail mes-

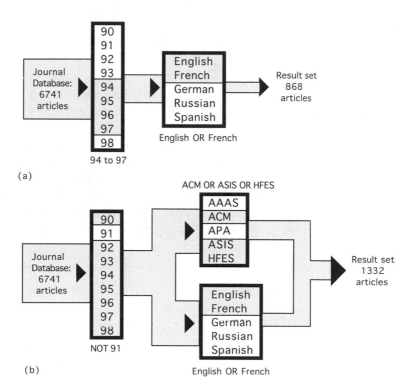

Figure 15.18

(a) Filter-flow model for the query (Date between 94 to 97) AND (Language is English OR French).

(b) Filter-flow model for query (Date NOT 91) AND (Publisher is ACM OR ASIS OR HFES) OR (Language is English OR French)).

sages, newspaper stories, or scientific journal articles (Belkin and Croft, 1992). The users create and store their profiles, which are evaluated each time that a new document appears. Users can be notified by electronic mail that a relevant document has appeared, or the results can be simply collected into a file until the users seek them out. These approaches are a modern version of traditional information-retrieval strategy called *selective dissemination of information (SDI)*, which was used in the earliest days of magnetic-tape distribution of document collections. Elaborate strategies for using the user-supplied set of keywords include latent semantic indexing, use of thesauri for find narrower or broader terms, and natural-language parsing techniques (Foltz and Dumais, 1992). Use of these strategies and term-frequency data can produce relevance rankings of retrieved documents that are appealing to many users and are successful in increasing the recall and precision of searches. A series of text-retrieval conferences (TREC) organized by Donna Harman at the National Institute for Standards and

Technology (http://potomac.ncsl.nist.gov/TREC) has allowed developers of research and commercial products to compare their strategies against a large test collection of textual documents.

A social form of filtering is *collaborative filtering*, in which groups of users combine their evaluations to help one another find interesting items in a large document collection (Resnick et al., 1994). Each user rates documents in terms of their interest. Then, the system can suggest unread articles that are close to the user's interests, as determined by matches with other people's interests. This method can also be applied to movies, music, restaurants, and so on. For example, if you rate six restaurants high, the algorithms will provide you with other restaurants that were rated high by people who liked your six restaurants. This strategy has an inherent appeal, and dozens of systems have been built for organizational databases, news files, music groups, and World Wide Web pages.

15.6   Practitioner's Summary

Improved user interfaces to traditional database-query and text- or multimedia-document search will spawn appealing new products. Flexible queries against complex text, sound, graphics, image, and video databases are emerging. Novel graphical and direct-manipulation approaches to query formulation and information visualization are now possible. Whereas research prototypes have typically dealt with only one data type (one-, two-, and three-dimensional data; temporal and multidimensional data; and tree and network data), successful commercial products will have to accommodate several. These products will need to provide smooth integration with existing software and to support the full task list: overview, zoom, filter, details-on-demand, relate, history, and extract. These methods are attractive because they present information rapidly and allow user-controlled exploration. If they are all to be fully effective, we will require advanced data structures, high-resolution color displays, fast data retrieval, and novel forms of user training. Many user interfaces for specifying advanced filtering are being built and are worthy of evaluation for commercial projects.

15.7   Researcher's Agenda

Although the computer contributes to the information explosion, it is potentially the magic lens for finding, sorting, filtering, and presenting the relevant items. Search in complex structured documents, graphics, images, sound, or video presents grand opportunities for the design of advanced user interfaces and powerful search engines to find the needles in the haystacks and the forests beyond the trees. The novel information-exploration tools—such as dynamic queries, treemaps, fisheye views, parallel coordinates, starfields, and perspective walls—are but a few of the inventions that will have to be tamed and validated by user-interface researchers. A better integration with perceptual psychology (understanding preattentive processes and the impact of varied coding or highlighting techniques) and with business decision making (identifying tasks and procedures that occur in realistic situations) is needed, as are theoretical foundations and practical benchmarks for choosing among the diverse emerging visualization techniques. Empirical studies would help to sort out the specific situations in which visualization was most helpful. Finally, software toolkits for building innovative visualizations would facilitate the exploration process.

World Wide Web Resources   WWW

The search services such as Alta Vista, Excite, Infoseek, and Lycos provide remarkable but flawed access to the World Wide Web. Other information retrieval topics such as collaborative filtering, document summarization, and indexing methods are covered. Information visualization tools are growing more effective for a wider range of tasks.

http://www.aw.com/DTUI

References

Ahlberg, Christopher and Shneiderman, Ben, Visual information seeking: Tight coupling of dynamic query filters with starfield displays, *Proc. CHI '94 Conference: Human Factors in Computing Systems*, ACM, New York (1994), 313–321 and color plates.

Ahlberg, Christopher and Shneiderman, Ben, AlphaSlider: A compact and rapid selector, *Proc. of ACM CHI '94 Conference Human Factors in Computing Systems*, ACM, New York (1994), 365–371.

Ahlberg, Christopher, Williamson, Christopher, and Shneiderman, Ben, Dynamic queries for information exploration: An implementation and evaluation, *Proc. ACM CHI '92: Human Factors in Computing Systems*, ACM, New York (1992), 619–626.

Ahlberg, Christopher and Wistrand, Erik, IVEE: An information visualization and exploration environment, *Proc. IEEE Information Visualization '95*, IEEE Computer Press, Los Alamitos, CA (1995), 66–73.

Andrews, Keith, Visualising cyberspace: Information visualisation in the Harmony internet browser, *Proc. IEEE Information Visualization '95*, IEEE Computer Press, Los Alamitos, CA (1995), 97–104.

Asahi, T., Turo, D., and Shneiderman, B., Using treemaps to visualize the analytic hierarchy process, *Information Systems Research*, 6, 4 (December 1995), 357–375.

Bartram, Lyn, Ho, Albert, Dill, John, and Henigman, Frank, The continuous zoom: A constrained fisheye technique for viewing and navigating large information spaces, *Proc. User Interface Software and Technology '95*, ACM, New York (1995), 207–215.

Becker, Richard A., Eick, Stephen G., and Wilks, Allan R. Visualizing network data, *IEEE Transactions on Visualization and Computer Graphics*, 1, 1 (March 1995), 16–28.

Bederson, Ben B. and Hollan, James D., PAD++: A zooming graphical user interface for exploring alternate interface physics, *Proc. User Interfaces Software and Technology '94* (1994), 17–27.

Belkin, Nick J. and Croft, Bruce W. Information filtering and information retrieval: Two sides of the same coin?, *Communications of the ACM*, 35, 12 (1992), 29–38.

Bertin, Jacques, *Semiology of Graphics*, University of Wisconsin Press, Madison, WI (1983).

Borgman, Christine, L., Why are online catalogs hard to use? Lessons learned from information-retrieval studies, *Journal of the American Society for Information Science*, 37, 6 (1986), 387–400.

Card, Stuart K., Robertson, George G., and York, William, The WebBook and the WebForager: An information workspace for the World-Wide Web, *Proc. CHI' 96 Conference: Human Factors in Computing Systems*, ACM, New York (1996), 111–117.

Carriere, Jeremy and Kazman, Rick, Interacting with huge hierarchies: Beyond cone trees, *Proc. IEEE Information Visualization '95*, IEEE Computer Press, Los Alamitos, CA (1995), 74–81.

Chimera, Richard, Value bars: An information visualization and navigation tool for multiattribute listings, *Proc. CHI '92 Conference: Human Factors in Computing Systems*, ACM, New York (1992), 293–294.

Chimera, Richard and Shneiderman, Ben, Evaluating three user interfaces for browsing tables of contents, *ACM Transactions on Information Systems*, 12, 4 (October 1994), 383–406.

Chuah, Mei C., Roth, Steven F., Mattis, Joe, and Kolojejchcik, John, SDM: Malleable Information Graphics, *Proc. IEEE Information Visualization '95*, IEEE Computer Press, Los Alamitos, CA (1995), 66–73.

Cleveland, William, *Visualizing Data*, Hobart Press, Summit, NJ (1993).

Egan, Dennis E., Remde, Joel R., Gomez, Louis M., Landauer, Thomas K., Eberhardt, Jennifer, and Lochbum, Carol C., Formative design-evaluation of SuperBook, *ACM Transactions on Information Systems*, 7, 1 (January 1989), 30–57.

Egenhofer, Max and Richards, J., Exploratory access to geographic data based on the map-overlay metaphor, *Journal of Visual Languages and Computing*, 4, 2 (1993), 105–125.

Eick, Stephen G., Steffen, Joseph L., and Sumner, Jr., Eric E., SeeSoft: A tool for visualizing line-oriented software statistics, *IEEE Transactions on Software Engineering*, 18, 11 (1992) 957–968.

Eick, Stephen G. and Wills, Graham J., Navigating large networks with hierarchies, *Proc. IEEE Visualization '93 Conference* (1993), 204–210.

Fairchild, Kim M., Poltrock, Steven E., and Furnas, George W., SemNet: Three-dimensional representations of large knowledge bases. In Guindon, Raymonde (Editor), *Cognitive Science and its Applications for Human–Computer Interaction,* Lawrence Erlbaum, Hillsdale, NJ (1988), 201–233.

Fishkin, Ken and Stone, Maureen C., Enhanced dynamic queries via movable filters, *Proc. CHI' 95 Conference: Human Factors in Computing Systems,* ACM, New York (1995), 415–420.

Foltz, Peter W. and Dumais, Susan T., Personalized information delivery: An analysis of information filtering methods. *Communications of the ACM,* 35, 12 (1992), 51–60.

Furnas, George W., Generalized fisheye views, *Proc. CHI' 86 Conference: Human Factors in Computing Systems,* ACM, New York (1986), 16–23.

Goldstein, Jade and Roth, Steven F., Using aggregation and dynamic queries for exploring large data sets, *Proc. CHI' 95 Conference: Human Factors in Computing Systems,* ACM, New York (1995), 23–29.

Greene, S. L., Devlin, S. J., Cannata, P. E., and Gomez, L. M., No IFs, ANDs, or ORs: A study of database querying, *International Journal of Man–Machine Studies,* 32, (March 1990), 303–326.

Hendley, R. J., Drew, N. S., Wood, A. S., Narcissus: Visualizing information, *Proc. IEEE Information Visualization '95,* IEEE Computer Press, Los Alamitos, CA (1995), 90–96.

Humphrey, Susanne M. and Melloni, Biagio John, *Databases: A Primer for Retrieving Information by Computer,* Prentice-Hall, Englewood Cliffs, NJ (1986).

Inselberg, Alfred, The plane with parallel coordinates, *The Visual Computer,* 1, (1985), 69–91.

Jarke, M., and Vassiliou, Y., A framework for choosing a database query language, *ACM Computing Surveys,* 11, 3 (1986), 313–340.

Jerding, Dean F. and Stasko, John T., The information mural: A technique for displaying and navigating large information spaces, *Proc. IEEE Information Visualization '95,* IEEE Computer Press, Los Alamitos, CA (1995), 43–50.

Jog, Ninad and Shneiderman, Ben, Information visualization with smooth zooming on a starfield display *Proc. Visual Databases 3* (March 1995), 1–10.

Johnson, Brian, and Shneiderman, Ben, Tree-maps: A space-filling approach to the visualization of hierarchical information structures, *Proc. IEEE Visualization '91,* IEEE, Piscataway, NJ (1991), 284–291.

Keim, D. A. and Kriegal, H., VisDB: Database exploration using multidimensional visualization, *IEEE Computer Graphics and Applications* (September 1994), 40–49.

Kim, H. J., Korth, H. F., and Silberschatz, A., PICASSO: A graphical query language, *Software: Practice and Experience,* 18, 3 (1988), 169–203.

Koenemann, Juergen and Belkin, Nicholas, A case for interaction: A study of interactive information retrieval behavior and effectiveness, *Proc. CHI '96 Human Factors in Computing Systems,* ACM Press, New York (1996), 205–212.

Korfhage, Robert, To see or not to see: Is that the query?, *Communications of the ACM,* 34 (1991), 134–141.

Kumar, Harsha, Plaisant, Catherine, and Shneiderman, Ben, Browsing hierarchical data with multi-level dynamic queries and pruning, *International Journal of Human–Computer Studies,* 46, 1 (January 1997), 103–124.

Lamping, John, Rao, Ramana, and Pirolli, Peter, A focus + context technique based on hyperbolic geometry for visualizing large hierarchies, *Proc. of CHI '95*

Conference: Human Factors in Computing Systems, ACM, New York (1995), 401–408.

Laurini, R. and Thompson, D., *Fundamentals of Spatial Information Systems,* Academic Press, New York (1992).

Marchionini, Gary, *Information Seeking in Electronic Environments,* Cambridge University Press, UK (1995).

Marchionini, Gary and Shneiderman, Ben, Finding facts and browsing knowledge in hypertext systems, *IEEE Computer,* 21, 1 (January 1988), 70–80.

Mark, Leo, A graphical query language for the binary relationship model, *Information Systems,* 14, 3 (1989), 231–246.

McCormick, B., DeFanti, T, and Brown, R. (Editors), Visualization in scientific computing and computer graphics, *ACM SIGGRAPH,* 21, 6 (November 1987).

Michard, A., A new database query language for non-professional users: Design principles and ergonomic evaluation, *Behavioral and Information Technology,* 1, 3 (July–September 1982), 279–288.

Mitchell, Richard, Day, David, and Hirschman, Lynette, Fishing for information on the internet, *Proc. IEEE Information Visualization '95,* IEEE Computer Press, Los Alamitos, CA (1995), 105–111.

Mukherjea, Sougata, Foley, James D., and Hudson, Scott, Visualizing complex hypermedia networks through multiple hierarchical views, *Proc. of ACM CHI '95 Conference: Human Factors in Computing Systems,* ACM, New York (1995), 331–337 plus color plate.

North, Chris, Shneiderman, Ben, and Plaisant, Catherine, User controlled overviews of an image library: A case study of the Visible Human, *Proc. 1st ACM International Conference on Digital Libraries* (1996), 74–82.

Pirolli, Peter, Schank, Patricia, Hearst, Marti, and Diehl, Christine, Scatter/gather browsing communicates the topic structure of a very large text collection, *Proc. of ACM CHI' 96 Conference,* ACM, New York (1996), 213–220.

Plaisant, Catherine, Rose, Anne, Milash, Brett, Widoff, Seth, and Shneiderman, Ben, LifeLines: Visualizing personal histories, *Proc. of CHI' 96 Conference: Human Factors in Computing Systems,* ACM, New York (1996), 221–227, 518.

Reisner, Phyllis, Query languages. In Helander, Martin (Editor), *Handbook of Human–Computer Interaction,* North-Holland, Amsterdam, The Netherlands (1988), 257–280.

Rao, Ramana and Card, Stuart K., The Table Lens; Merging graphical and symbolic representations in an interactive focus + context visualization for tabular information, *Proc. CHI '94 Conference: Human Factors in Computing Systems,* ACM, New York (1994), 318–322.

Resnick, Paul, Iacovou, Neophytos, Suchak, Mitesh, Bergstrom, Peter and Riedl, John, GroupLens: An open architecture for collaborative filtering of netnews, *Proc. Conference on Computer Supported Cooperative Work '94,* ACM, New York (1994), 175–186.

Robertson, George G., Card, Stuart K., and Mackinlay, Jock D., Information visualization using 3-D interactive animation, *Communications of the ACM,* 36, 4 (April 1993), 56–71.

Robertson George G. and Mackinlay, Jock D., The document lens, *Proc. 1993 ACM User Interface Software and Technology,* ACM New York (1993), 101–108.

Roth, Steven F., Lucas, Peter, Senn, Jeffrey A., Gomberg, Cristina C., Burks, Michael B., Stroffolino, Philip J., Kolojejchick, John A. and Dunmire, Carolyn, Visage: A user interface environment for exploring information, *Proc. IEEE Information Visualization '96*, IEEE Computer Press, Los Alamitos, CA (1996), 3–12.

Salton, G., Automatic Text Processing: *The Transformation, Analysis, and Retrieval of Information by Computer*, Addison-Wesley, Reading, MA (1989).

Sarkar, Manojit and Brown, Marc H., Graphical fisheye views, *Communications of the ACM*, 37, 12 (July 1994), 73–84.

Schaffer, Doug, Zuo, Zhengping, Greenberg, Saul, Bartram, Lyn, Dill, John, Dubs, Shelli and Roseman, Mark, Navigating hierarchically clustered networks through fisheye and full-zoom methods, *ACM Transactions on Computer–Human Interaction*, 3, 2 (June 1996), 162–188.

Shneiderman, Ben, Tree visualization with tree-maps: A 2-D space-filling approach, *ACM Transactions on Graphics*, 11, 1 (January 1992), 92–99.

Shneiderman, Ben, Dynamic queries for visual information seeking, *IEEE Software*, 11, 6 (1994), 70–77.

Shneiderman, Ben, Brethauer, Dorothy, Plaisant, Catherine and Potter, Richard, Three evaluations of museum installations of a hypertext system, *Journal of the American Society for Information Science*, 40, 3 (May 1989), 172–182.

Shneiderman, Ben, Byrd, Donald, and Croft, Bruce, Clarifying search: A user-interface framework for text searches, *D-LIB Magazine of Digital Library Research* (January 1997), http://www.dlib.org/.

Spence, Robert and Apperley, Mark, Data base navigation: An office environment for the professional, *Behaviour & Information Technology*, 1, 1 (1982), 43–54.

Spoerri, Anslem, InfoCrystal: A visual tool for information retrieval and management, *Proc. ACM Conf. on Information and Knowledge Management* (1993), 150–157.

Tufte, Edward, *The Visual Display of Quantitative Information*, Graphics Press, Cheshire, CT (1983).

Tufte, Edward, *Envisioning Information*, Graphics Press, Cheshire, CT (1990).

Tweedie, Lisa, Spence, Robert, Dawkes, Huw, and Su, Hua, Externalising abstract mathematical models, *Proc. of CHI' 96 Conference: Human Factors in Computing Systems*, ACM, New York (1996), 406–412.

Weiland, William J. and Shneiderman, Ben, A graphical query interface based on aggregation/generalization hierarchies,, *Information Systems*, 18, 4 (1993), 215–232.

Welty, C., Correcting user errors in SQL, *International Journal of Man–Machine Studies*, 22 (1985), 463–477.

Williamson, Christopher, and Shneiderman, Ben, The Dynamic HomeFinder: Evaluating dynamic queries in a real-estate information exploration system, *Proc. ACM SIGIR '92 Conference*, ACM, New York (1992), 338–346. Reprinted in Shneiderman, B. (Editor), *Sparks of Innovation in Human–Computer Interaction*, Ablex Publishers, Norwood, NJ (1993), 295–307.

Wise, James A., Thomas, James, J., Pennock, Kelly, Lantrip, David, Pottier, Marc, Schur, Anne, and Crow, Vern, Visualizing the non-visual: Spatial analysis and interaction with information from text documents, *Proc. IEEE Information Visualization '95*, IEEE Computer Press, Los Alamitos, CA (1995), 51–58.

Wurman, Richard Saul, *Information Anxiety*, Doubleday, New York (1989).

Young, Degi and Shneiderman, Ben, A graphical filter/flow model for Boolean queries: An implementation and experiment, *Journal of the American Society for Information Science*, 44, 6 (July 1993), 327–339.

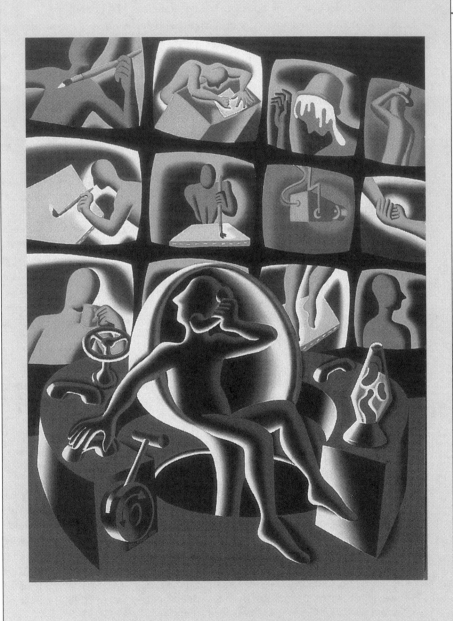

Mark Kostabi, *Quality Control*, 1990

Hypermedia and the World Wide Web

Gradually I began to feel that we were growing something almost organic in a new kind of reality, in cyberspace, growing it out of information . . . a pulsing tree of data that I loved to climb around in, scanning for new growth.

Mickey Hart, *Drumming at the Edge of Magic:*
A Journey into the Spirit of Percussion, **1990**

Look at every path closely and deliberately.
Try it as many times as you think necessary.
Then ask yourself, and yourself alone, one question . . .
Does this path have a heart?
If it does, the path is good; if it doesn't, it is of no use.

Carlos Castaneda, *The Teachings of Don Juan*

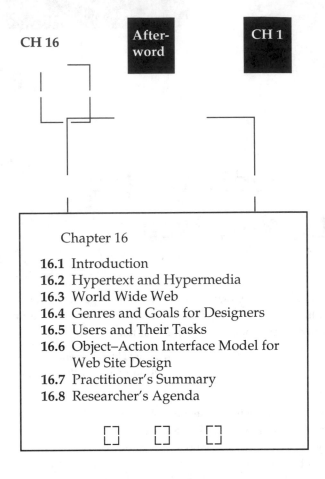

Chapter 16

16.1 Introduction
16.2 Hypertext and Hypermedia
16.3 World Wide Web
16.4 Genres and Goals for Designers
16.5 Users and Their Tasks
16.6 Object–Action Interface Model for Web Site Design
16.7 Practitioner's Summary
16.8 Researcher's Agenda

16.1 Introduction

In July 1945, Vannevar Bush, President Franklin Roosevelt's Science Adviser, wrote a provocative article (Bush, 1945) offering his vision of science projects that might become feasible in the post-World War II period. He wisely identified the information-overload problem and sought to make cross-references within and across documents easy to create and traverse. His desktop information-exploration tool, *memex*, was based on microfilm and eye-tracking technology. Memex would enable readers to follow cross-references by merely staring at them:

> Wholly new forms of encyclopedias will appear, ready-made with a mesh of associative trails running through them, ready to be dropped into the memex

and there amplified. The lawyer has at his touch the associated opinions and decisions of his whole experience, and of the experience of friends and authorities. . . . There is a new profession of trail blazers, those who find delight in establishing useful trails through the enormous mass of the common record. The inheritance from the master becomes, not only his addition to the world's record, but for his disciples the entire scaffolding by which they were erected. (Bush, 1945)

It has taken 50 years to create effective—although somewhat revised—models of Bush's vision. Now the technology is beginning to make possible a useful reading, browsing, linking, and annotating environment to support communal nonlinear writing and reading. The name *hypertext*, or *hypermedia*, has been applied to networks of nodes (also called articles, documents, files, cards, pages, frames, screens) containing information (in text, graphics, video, sound, and so on) that are connected by links (also called pointers, cross-references, citations). *Hypertext* is more commonly applied to text-only applications, whereas *hypermedia* is used to convey the inclusion of other media, especially sound and video. The World Wide Web extends the hypermedia to a vast network of computers in which millions of users can create and retrieve multimedia materials from around the world in seconds.

Ted Nelson coined the term *hypertext* in the 1960s as he was writing about his universal library and *docuverse*, with *stretch text* that expands when selected. Nelson's enthusiasm and imagination infected many people who shared his *computopian* hopes. Using less flamboyant terms, Douglas Engelbart created his Human Augmentation system at SRI during the 1960s, with hypertext point-and-click features, expanding outline processors, multiple windows, remote collaboration, and the mouse (Engelbart, 1984). In parallel, Andries van Dam developed early electronic books at Brown University using colorful dynamic graphics and three-dimensional animation (Yankelovich et al., 1985; van Dam, 1988).

By the mid-1980s, many research and commercial packages offered hypertext features to enable convenient jumps among articles (Conklin, 1987; Halasz, 1988; Shneiderman and Kearsley, 1989; Nielsen, 1995). Pioneering hypertext systems include NoteCards, developed at Xerox PARC; KMS, from Knowledge Systems, Inc.; Guide from OWL International; and Hyperties, originated at the University of Maryland (Shneiderman, 1989) and commercially developed by Cognetics Corporation of Princeton, New Jersey (Fig 7.5, Fig. 12.6, and Color Plate C1).

Hyperties was conceived as a publication tool, with which authors produce hypermedia for thousands of readers. It has separate tools for browsing and authoring documents. Hyperties was based on the metaphor of an electronic encyclopedia. Each document was called an article, and cross-references were implemented as highlighted text links and image maps. Using the metaphor of an encyclopedia comprising a collection of titled articles made acceptance easy and facilitated navigation. Built into Hyperties were author-generated and alphabetical tables of contents, including every article plus history lists supporting reversible actions. The Hyperties browser was one of the first software packages that needed no error messages, because the design prevented the user from making syntactic errors.

In the late 1980s, commercial hypertext applications began to appear. In 1987, Apple provided Bill Atkinson's HyperCard system free with every Macintosh. Although the brochures referred to Vannevar Bush's vision, Apple refrained from using the term *hypertext* in describing HyperCard (Fig. 16.1a–b). Building on the metaphor of cards arranged in stacks, Apple claimed in the online help that "you can use HyperCard to create your own applications for gathering, organizing, presenting, searching and customizing information."

The July 1988 *Communications of the ACM* contained eight papers from the first hypertext conference. Three electronic versions of this issue, built with KMS, HyperCard, and Hyperties (Shneiderman, 1988), were marketed by ACM to thousands of professionals. We used Hyperties the following year to create the first commercial electronic book, *Hypertext Hands-On!* (Shneiderman and Kearsley, 1989). Hewlett-Packard used Hyperties to distribute electronic documentation for its LaserJet 4 printers in 15 languages. That may have been the first world-wide distribution of hypertext prior to implementation of the World Wide Web.

Today, the World Wide Web uses hypertext to link tens of millions of documents together. The basic highlighted text link can be traced back to an innovation, developed in 1983, as part of *The Interactive Encyclopedia System (TIES)*, the research predecessor to Hyperties. The original concept was to eliminate menus by embedding highlighted link phrases directly in the text (Koved and Shneiderman, 1986). Earlier designs required typing codes, selecting from menu lists, or clicking on visually distracting markers in the text. The embedded-text-link idea was adopted by developers such as Tim Berners-Lee, who described "hot spots" in his 1989 proposal for the World Wide Web (Berners-Lee, 1994).

Other Hyperties features anticipated the World Wide Web. Charles Kreitzberg, Whitney Quesenbery, and programmers at Cognetics implemented image maps, animations, and a markup language called Hyperties Markup Language (HTML). It is quite similar to the HTML markup language used with web browsers; both drew on concepts in SGML, which continues to be an important markup language within the publishing community. Hyperties also had a Java-like scripting language that allowed processes to be attached to pages or to links.

Hypertext has become a mainstream interface paradigm with the emergence of the World Wide Web. In the web, the basic vision of Vannevar Bush, Ted Nelson and the researchers who picked up their challenge has become a reality. Some people might argue that the web does not capture the vision of the early hypertext pioneers, but the distinctions are modest, and innovations are added weekly.

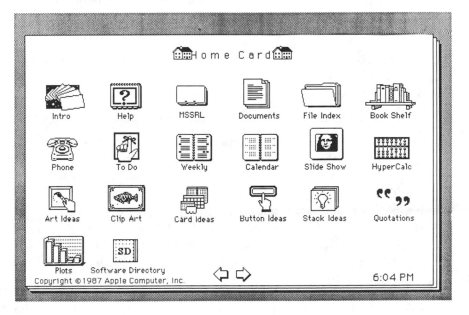

Figure 16.1

HyperCard displays from the original 1987 version. An iconic index of stacks is included. (Courtesy of Apple Computer, Cupertino, CA.)

With a simple mouse click, users can jump to related web pages, which may be delivered from millions of server computers located around the world. With graphics, maps, photos, sound, and the increasing degree of animation supplied by Java applets or VRML, the web is limited only by the bandwidth of the network and the imagination of designers.

16.2   Hypertext and Hypermedia

The intrigue of hypertext is that it extends traditional linear text with the opportunity for jumping to multiple related articles. Convenient backtracking, clickable indexes and tables of contents, string searching, bookmarks, and other navigation tools profoundly alter the reader's experience. For some purposes, hypertext can be a welcome improvement over linear paper documents, but there is a danger that jumping can also lead to hyperchaos. To reduce confusion, hypertext authors need to choose appropriate projects, to organize their articles suitably, and to adjust their writing style to make the best use of this new medium. The first step in creating effective hypertexts is to choose projects that adhere to the *Golden Rules of Hypertext* (Shneiderman, 1989):

1.   There is a large body of information organized into numerous fragments.

2.   The fragments relate to one another.

3.   The user needs only a small fraction of the fragments at any time.

The dual dangers are that hypertext may be inappropriate for some projects and that the design of the hypertext may be poor (for example, too many links or a confusing structure). A traditional novel is written linearly, and the reader is expected to read the entire text from beginning to middle to end. Most poems, fairy tales, newspaper articles, and even the chapters of this book are written in a linear form. Of course, hypernovels, hyperpoems, hyper—fairy tales, hypernewspapers, and hyperbooks are possible, but they require creative rethinking of the traditional forms to satisfy the Golden Rules of Hypertext.

Poor design of hypertext is common: too many links, long chains of links to reach relevant material, or too many long dull articles (Rivlin et al., 1994). Inadequate tables of contents or overviews make it difficult for users to determine what is contained in the hypertext. Breaking a text into linked fragments does not ensure that the result will be effective or attractive. Just as turning a theater production into a movie requires learning new techniques of zooming, panning, closeups, and so on, creating successful hypertext requires learning to use the features of the new medium (Jones and Shneiderman, 1990).

Enthusiasts of hypertext systems often dwell on nonlinear reading, yet there is also a great sense of novelty and adventure in *writing* nonlinear hypertexts. Authoring tools should support at least the features in this tableau of actions and objects:

Actions	Objects
import	an article or node
edit	a link
export	collections of articles or nodes
print	webs of links
search	entire hypertext

In constructing the first commercial hyperbook, *Hypertext Hands-On!* (Shneiderman and Kearsley, 1989), we faced two key authoring issues: managing the articles and specifying the links. Hypertext systems should provide an index of all the articles that have been referenced or created, and should allow rapid specification of links. Marking a phrase or a region can usually be accomplished easily, but then it should also be easy to indicate the link destination. Furthermore, if the same phrase appears many times, it should be possible to resolve the link more easily the second time. Other features to consider in an authoring tool for stand-alone or the World Wide Web (for example, Claris HomePage or Microsoft Front Page) are these:

- *Range of editing functions* available (for example, copying, moving, insertion, deletion, global change within and across articles)
- *Availability of lists of links* (in and out), index terms, synonyms, and so on
- *Link verification* to check correctness of links
- *Range of display-formatting commands*, fonts, sizes, highlighting
- *Availability of search-and-replace functions* for making global changes across multiple articles
- *Control of color* (text, background); color can make the text look attractive, but it can also be distracting; since users have different preferences and tasks, it should be possible to reset color-usage parameters
- *Capability to switch easily* between author and browser modes to test ideas
- *Availability of graphics and video* facilities; embedded graphics editors and mechanisms for exploring video segments

- *Possibility of collaboration;* more than one person should be able to edit the hypertext at one time; different people should be able to author components, which are then merged
- *Data compression;* compression algorithms can reduce the size and facilitate distribution
- *Security control;* password control can restrict access to the hypertext or parts of it
- *Encryption;* encryption of sensitive nodes enhances security
- *Reliability;* bug-free performance with no loss of data
- *Possibility of integration* with other software or hardware
- *Import and export of standard interchange formats,* such as SGML

For at least the past 3000 years, authors and editors have explored ways to structure knowledge to suit the linear medium of the written word. When appropriate, authors have developed strategies for linking related fragments of text and graphics even in the linear format. Now, hypertext encourages nonlinear interconnecting links among articles.

The first challenge is to structure the knowledge such that an overview can be presented to the reader in an introductory article. The overall structure of articles must make sense to readers so that they can form a mental image of the topics covered. This image facilitates traversal, reduces disorientation, and lets users know what is and what is *not* in the hypertext.

Hypertext is conducive to the inclusion of appendices, glossaries, examples, background information, original sources, and bibliographic references. Interested readers can pursue the details; casual readers can ignore them.

Creating documents for a hypertext database introduces considerations beyond the usual concerns of good writing. No list can be complete, but this list, derived from our experience, may be useful:

- *Know the users and their tasks*   Consult with users throughout the development process, and test your designs. You are not a good judge of your own design.
- *Ensure that meaningful structure comes first*   Build the project around the structuring and presentation of information, rather than around the technology. Develop a *high concept* for the body of information that you are organizing.
- *Apply diverse skills*   Make certain that the project team includes information specialists (trainers, psychologists, graphic artists), content specialists (users, marketers), and technologists (systems analysts, programmers).

- *Respect chunking* Organize information into chunks that deal with one topic, theme, or idea. Chunks may be 100 words or 1000 words—but when a chunk reaches 10,000 words, consider restructuring into multiple smaller chunks. Screens are still usually small and hard to read, so lengthy linear texts are not pleasant for users.
- *Show interrelationships* Write each article to contain links to other articles. Too few links bore readers; too many links overwhelm and distract. Author preferences range from putting in a maximum of one or two links per screen, to the more common range of two to 20 links per screen, to the extreme of dozens of links per screen. Although pages meant to be read thoroughly should have few links, index pages can contain hundreds of links.
- *Ensure simplicity in traversal* Design the link structure so that navigation is simple and consistent throughout the system.
- *Design each screen carefully* Design screens such they can be grasped easily. The focus of attention should be clear, headings should guide the reader, links should be useful guides that do not overwhelm the reader. Visual layout should be compact vertically, so as to minimize scrolling. Whitespace can be helpful, but blank space is wasteful.
- *Require low cognitive load* Minimize the burden on the user's short-term memory. Do not require the user to memorize terms or codes. The goal is to enable users to concentrate on the contents while the computer vanishes.

Key design questions are how to organize the hypertext, and how to convey that order to the reader. Authoring strategies for creating the introductory article include these:

- *Executive overview* Make the home page or introductory article an overview that summarizes the contents and contains links to all major concepts.
- *Top-down* Adopt a hierarchical approach in which the links in the home page are to major categories only.
- *Menu* Organize the home page as a detailed table of contents.
- *Search strategy* Make string search easily available as a possible first step.

A major concern of hypertext authors is the optimal length for articles. Research suggests that many short articles are preferable to a smaller number of long articles. An experiment at the University of Maryland using the Hyperties system compared two versions: 46 short articles (four to 83 lines) and five long articles (104 to 150 lines). Participants in the study were given

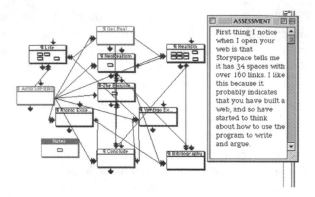

Figure 16.2

Eastgate Systems Storyscape, showing hypertext link structure and an assessment window with a comment. (Used with permission of Eastgate Systems, Watertown, MA.)

30 minutes to locate the answers to a series of questions by using the database. The 16 participants who worked with the short articles answered more questions correctly and took less time to answer the questions. The optimal article length will be affected by screen size, response time, nature of task, and experience of the users. With the longer time for retrieving articles on the web, the preferred length of home pages would be larger. Higher numbers of pointers per page can reduce the number of steps to reach a desired article.

Hypertext authoring has continued as a cottage industry among literary types, encouraged by Eastgate Systems, who also market the Storyscape system (Fig. 16.2). Broader application of hypertext has appeared in Microsoft's and other companies' online help systems, as well as in numerous CD-ROM reference works and encyclopedias, such as Encarta or Compton's (Color Plate C2). These are excellent systems, but the volume of material is dwarfed by the enormous and continuously expanding contents of the World Wide Web.

16.3   World Wide Web

The deluge of web pages has generated dystopian commentaries on the tragedy of the flood of information. It has also produced utopian visions of harnessing the same flood for constructive purposes. Within this ocean of information there are also lifeboat web pages offering design principles, but often the style parallels the early user-interface writings of the 1970s. The well-intentioned Noahs, who write from personal experience as web-site designers, often draw their wisdom from specific projects, so their advice is incomplete or lacks generalizability. Their experience is valuable, but the paucity of empirical data to validate or sharpen insight means that some guidelines are misleading. As scientific evidence accumulates, foundational cognitive and perceptual theories will structure the discussion and guide designers in novel situations.

It may take a decade until sufficient experience, experimentation, and hypothesis testing clarify design issues, so we should be grateful for the early and daring attempts to offer guidance. One of the better guides (Lynch, 1995) offers this advice:

> Proper World Wide Web site design is largely a matter of balancing the structure and relationship of menu or "home" pages and individual content pages or other linked graphics and documents. The goal is to build a hierarchy of menus and pages that feels natural and well-structured to the user, and doesn't interfere with their [sic] use of the Web site or mislead them.

This advice is helpful, but it does not tell designers what to do or how to evaluate the efficacy of what they have done. Lynch goes on to give constructive advice about not being too broad or too deep, finding the proper length of pages, using gridded layouts, and the challenge of "balancing the power of hypermedia Internet linkages against the new ability to imbed graphics and motion media within networked WWW pages." He sorts out the issues better than most, but still leaves designers with uncertainties.

Jakob Nielsen (1995) goes a step further by reporting on his case study of designing a web site for Sun Microsystems to showcase that company's products. His usability-testing approach revealed specific problems, and the web site discusses nine different versions of the home page. The subjective data reveal problems and highlight key principles—for example "Users consistently praised screens that provided overviews of large information spaces." Empirical testing should reveal what kinds of overviews are most effective and whether performance times, error rates, or retention are enhanced by certain overviews.

Refinement of the web is more than a technical challenge or commercial goal. As governments offer information plus services online and educational institutions increase their dependence on the web, effective designs will be essential. Universal access is an important economic and policy issue; it is also a fundamental design issue.

Until the empirical data and experience from practical cases arrive, we can use knowledge from other user-interface design domains, such as menu systems and hypertext (Isakowitz et al., 1995; Shneiderman and Kearsley, 1989).

Designers can apply the theoretical framework of the OAI model and experience from information-retrieval research (Marchionini, 1995). Improved guidelines appear regularly (IBM, 1997), so check the booksite for fresh pointers.

16.4   Genres and Goals for Designers

As they do in any medium, criteria for web-design quality vary with the genre and authors' goals. A dizzying diversity of web sites is emerging from the creative efforts of bold designers who merge old forms to create new information resources, communication media, business services, and entertainment experiences. Web sites can range from a one-page personal biography (Color Plate C3) to millions of pages in the Library of Congress's (Color Plate A5) American Memory project organized by the National Digital Library program (Color Plate C4). Common high-level goals include visual appeal, comprehensibility, utility, efficacy, and navigability, but finer discriminations come into play if we examine the categories of web sites.

A primary way of categorizing web sites is by the originator's identity: individual, group, university, corporation, nonprofit organization, or government agency. The originator's identity gives a quick indication of what the likely goals are and what contents to expect: corporations have products to sell, museums have archives to promote, and government agencies have services to offer.

A second way of categorizing web sites is by goals of the originators, as interpreted by the designers (Table 16.1). Such goals may be simple informa-

Table 16.1

Web-site goals tied to typical organizations

Goal	Organizations
Sell products	publishers, airlines, department stores
Advertise products	auto dealers, real estate agents, movie studios
Inform and announce	universities, museums, cities
Provide access	libraries, newspapers, scientific organizations
Offer services	governments, public utilities
Create discussions	public-interest groups, magazines
Nurture communities	political groups, professional associations

Figure 16.3

Life history of the photographer David Seymour ("Chim"), with a timeline showing eight segments of his work. Presented by the International Center of Photography in New York, NY (http://ww.icp.org/chim/chim2.html).

tion presentation in a self-publishing style, where quality is uncontrolled and structure may be chaotic. Information may be an index to other web sites, or it may be original material. Carefully polished individual life histories (Fig. 16.3) and impressive organizational annual reports are becoming common as expectations and designer experience increase. As commercial usage increases, elegant product catalogs, eye-catching advertisements, and lively newsletters will become the norm. Commercial and scientific publishers will join newspapers (Fig. 16.4) and magazines in providing access to

Figure 16.4

The New York Times compact vertical page layout fits the typical home computer screen (http://www.nytimes.com). (Reprinted by permission © 1997 The New York Times Electronic Media Company.)

information while exploring the opportunities for feedback to editors, discussions with authors, and reader interest groups. Digital libraries of many varieties are appearing (Color Plate C6), but full recognition of their distinct benefits and design features is emerging only slowly. Entertainment web sites are growing as fast as the audience gets online.

A third way of categorizing web sites is by the number of web pages or amount of information that is accessible (Table 16.2): one-page bios and project summaries are small, organization overviews for internal and external use are medium, and airline schedules and the telephone directories are large. Taxonomies of web sites from many perspectives are likely. The Yahoo home page, with its thematic categories, provides a starting point, and it changes as the web grows (Color Plate C5).

A fourth way of categorizing web sites is by measures of success. For individuals, the measure of success for an online resume may be getting a job or making a friend. For many corporate web sites, the publicity is measured in number of visits, which may be millions per day, independent of whether users benefit. For others, the value lies directly in promoting sales of other products, such as movies, books, events, or automobiles. Finally, for access providers who earn fees from hourly usage charges, success is measured by the thousands of hours of usage per week. Other measures include diversity of access as defined by what the number of users is; what their countries of origin are; or whether the users came from university, military, or commercial domains.

Table 16.2

Web-site genres, with approximate sizes and examples

Number of Web pages	Example genres	
1–10	Personal bio Project summary	Restaurant review Course outline
5–50	Scientific paper Conference program	Photo portfolio or exhibit Organization overview
50–500	Book or manual Corporate annual report	City guide or tour Product catalog or advertisement
500–5,000	Photo library Technical reports	Museum tour Music or film database
5,000–50,000	University guide	Newspaper or magazine
50,000–500,000	Telephone directory	Airline schedule
500,000–5,000,000	Congressional digest	Journal abstracts
>5,000,000	Library of Congress	NASA archives

16.5   Users and Their Tasks

As in any user-interface design process, we begin by asking: Who are the users and what are the tasks? Even when broad communities are anticipated, there are usually implicit assumptions about users being able to see and read English. Richer assumptions about the users' age group or educational background should be made explicit to guide designers. Just as automobile advertisements are directed to college-age males, young couples, or mature female professionals, web sites are more effective when directed to specific audience niches. Gender, age, economic status, ethnic origin, educational background, and language are primary audience attributes. Physical disabilities such as poor vision, hearing, or muscle control call for special designs.

Users' specific knowledge of science, history, medicine, or other disciplines will influence design. A web site for physicians treating lung cancer will differ in content, terminology, writing style, and depth from a web site on the same topic for patients. Communities of users might be museum visitors, students, teachers, researchers, or journalists. Their motives may range from fact finding to browsing, professional to casual, or serious to playful.

Knowledge of computers or web sites can also influence design, but more important is the distinction between first-time, intermittent, and frequent users of a web site. First-time users need an overview to understand what the range of services is, what is not available, and what buttons select which actions. Intermittent users need an orderly structure, familiar landmarks, reversibility, and safety during exploration. Frequent users demand short-cuts or macros to speed repeated tasks and extensive services to satisfy their varied needs (Kellogg and Richards, 1995).

Since many applications focus on educational services, appropriate designs should accommodate teachers and students from elementary through university levels. Adult learners and elderly explorers may also get special services or treatments.

Evidence from a survey of 15,000 web users conducted at the Georgia Institute of Technology (Pitkow and Kehoe, 1996) showed that the average age of respondents is 35, the mean household income is above $60,000, and 69 percent are male. A remarkable 82 percent are daily users, and are likely to have a professional connection to computing or education. These profiles have shifted from previous surveys and will probably continue moving toward a closer match with the population at large. Of course, survey response was voluntary, from the web community, so the sample is biased, but the results are still thought provoking. More carefully con-trolled marketing and user studies are beginning to emerge (Hoffman et al., 1996).

Identifying the users' tasks also guides designers in shaping a web site. Tasks can range from specific fact finding to more unstructured open-ended browsing of known databases, to exploration of the availability of informa-tion on a topic (Section 15.1).

The great gift of the web is its support for all these possibilities. Specific fact finding is the more traditional application of computer-based databases with query languages such as SQL, but the web has dramatically increased the capability for users to browse and explore. Equal challenges are to sup-port users seeking specific facts and to help users with poorly formed infor-mation needs who are just browsing.

A *planning document* for a web site might indicate that the primary audi-ence is North American high-school environmental-science teachers and their students, with secondary audiences consisting of other teachers and students, journalists, environmental activists, corporate lobbyists, policy analysts, and amateur scientists. The tasks might be identified as providing access to selected LANDSAT images of North America clustered by and annotated with agricultural, ecological, geological, and meteorological fea-tures. Primary access might be by a hierarchical thesaurus of keywords about the features (for example, `floods`, `hurricanes`, `volcanoes`) from the four topics. Secondary access might be geographical with indexes by state, county, and city, plus selection by pointing at a map. Tertiary access might be by specification of latitude and longitude.

16.6   Object–Action Interface Model for Web Site Design

The OAI model (Section 2.3) employs a hierarchical decomposition of objects and actions in the task and interface domains (see Fig. 2.2). It can be a helpful guide to web-site designers in decomposing a complex information problem and fashioning a comprehensible and effective web site.

The task of information seeking is complex, but it can be described by hierarchies of task objects and actions related to the information. Then, the designer can represent the task objects and actions with hierarchies of interface objects and actions. For example, a music library might be presented as a set of objects such as collections, which have shelves, and then songs. Users may perform actions such as entering a collection, searching the index to a shelf, and reading the score for a song. The interface for the music library could have hierarchies of menus or metaphorical graphic objects accompanied by graphic representations of the actions, such as a magnifying glass for a search. Briefly, the OAI model encourages designers of web sites to focus on four components in two areas:

1. *Task*
   - *Structured information objects* (for example, hierarchies, networks)
   - *Information actions* (for example, searching, linking)
2. *Interface*
   - *Metaphors for information objects* (for example, bookshelf, encyclopedia)
   - *Handles* (affordances) *for actions* (for example, querying, zooming)

The boundaries are not always clear, but this decomposition into components may be helpful in organizing and evaluating web sites. It was useful in comparing alternatives and analyzing the complex possibilities for the Library of Congress. We shall explore the OAI model and give examples of decompositions of object and actions.

16.6.1   Design of task objects and actions

Information seekers pursue objects relevant to their tasks and apply task-action steps to achieve their intention. Although many people would describe a book as a sequence of chapters and a library as a hierarchy organized by the Dewey Decimal System, books also have book jackets, tables of contents, indexes, and so on, and libraries have magazines, videotapes, special collections, manuscripts, and so on. It would be still harder to characterize the structure of university catalogs, corporate annual reports, photo archives, or newspapers, because they have still less standardized structures and more diverse access paths.

When you are planning a web site to present complex information structures, it helps to have a clear definition of the atomic task objects, and the aggregates that can be combined to build the universe. Atoms can be a birthdate, name, job title, biography, resumé, or technical report. With image data, an atomic object might be a color swatch, icon, corporate logo, portrait photo, or music video.

Information atoms can be combined in many ways to form aggregates, such as a page in a newspaper, a city guidebook, or an annotated musical score. Clear definitions help to coordinate among designers and inform users about the intended levels of abstraction within each project. Information aggregates are further combined into collections and libraries that form the universe of concern relevant to a given set of tasks.

Strategies for aggregating information are numerous. Here is a starting list of possibilities:

- *Short unstructured lists*   City-guide highlights, organizational divisions, current projects (and this list)
- *Linear structures*   Calendar of events, alphabetic list, human-body slice images from head to toe, orbital swath
- *Arrays or tables*   Departure city/arrival city/date, latitude/longitude/time
- *Hierarchies, trees*   Continent–country–city (for example, Africa, Nigeria, Lagos), or concepts (for example, sciences, physics, semiconductors, gallium arsenide)
- *Multitrees, faceted retrieval*   Photos indexed by date, photographer, location, topic, film type
- *Networks*   Journal citations, genealogies, World Wide Web

These aggregates can be used to describe structured information objects. An encyclopedia is usually seen as a linear alphabetical list of articles, with a linear index of terms pointing to pages. Articles may have a hierarchical structure of sections and subsections, and cross references among articles create a network.

Some information objects, such as a book table of contents, have a dual role, since people may read them to understand the topic itself or may browse them to gain access to a chapter. In the latter role, they represent the actions for navigation in a book.

The information actions enable users to follow paths through the information. Most information resources can be scanned linearly from start to finish, but their size often dictates the need for shortcuts to relevant information. Atomic information actions include these:

- Looking for Hemingway's name in an alphabetical list
- Scanning a list of scientific article titles
- Reading a paragraph
- Following a reference link

Aggregate information actions are composed of atomic actions:

- Browsing an almanac table of contents, jumping to a chapter on sports, and scanning for skiing topics
- Locating a scientific term in an alphabetic index and reading articles containing that term
- Using a keyword search in a catalog to obtain a list of candidate book titles
- Following cross reference from one legal precedent to another, repeatedly, until no new relevant precedents appear
- Scanning a music catalog to locate classical symphonies by eighteenth century French composers

These examples and the list in Section 15.1 create a diverse space of actions. Some are learned from youthful experiences with books or libraries, others are trained skills such as searching for legal precedents or scientific articles. These skills are independent of computer implementation; they are acquired through meaningful learning, are demonstrated with examples, and are durable in memory.

16.6.2   Design of interface objects and actions

Since many users and designers have experience with information objects and actions on paper and other traditional media, designing for computer implementation can be a challenge. Physical attributes such as the length of a book or size of a map, which vanish when the information is concealed behind a screen, need to be made apparent for successful use. So web-site designers have the burden of representing the desired attributes of traditional media, but also the opportunity of applying the dynamic power of the computer to support the desired information actions. Successful designers can offer users compelling features that go well beyond traditional media, such as multiple indexes, fast string search, bookmarks, history keeping, comparison, and extraction.

Metaphors for interface objects The metaphoric representation of traditional physical media is a natural starting point: electronic books may have covers, jackets, page turning, bookmarks, position indicators, and so on, and electronic libraries may show varied size and color of books on shelves (Pejtersen, 1989). These may be useful starting points, but greater benefits will emerge as web-site designers find new metaphors and handles for showing larger information spaces and powerful actions.

Information hierarchies are the most frequently represented metaphor, with at least these examples:

- File cabinet with folders and documents
- Book with chapters
- Encyclopedia with articles
- Television with channels
- Shopping mall with stores
- Museum with exhibits

Richer environments include a library with doors, help desk, rooms, collections, and shelves, and the City of Knowledge with gates, streets, buildings, and landmarks. Of course, the information superhighway is often presented as a metaphor, but rarely is it developed as a visual search environment. The metaphor needs to be useful in presenting high-level concepts, appropriate for expressing middle-level objects, and effective in suggesting pixel-level details.

Design of computer-based metaphors extends to support tools for the information seeker. Some systems provide maps of information spaces as an overview to allow users to grasp the relative size of components and to discover what is not in the database. History stacks, bookmarks, help desks, and guides offering tours are common support tools in information environments. Communications tools can be included to allow users to send extracts, to ask for assistance from experts, or to report findings to colleagues.

Handles for interface actions The web-site representation of actions is often conveyed by action handles: the labels, icons, buttons, or image regions that indicate where users should click to invoke an action. Navigation action handles can be a turned page corner to indicate next-page operation, a highlighted term for a link, and a magnifying glass to zoom in or open an outline. Other action handles might be a pencil to indicate annotation, a funnel to show sorting, a coal car to indicate data mining, or filters to show progressive query refinement. Sometimes, the action handle is merely a pulldown–menu item or a dialog box offering rich possibilities. The ensemble of handles should allow users to decompose their action plan conveniently into a series of clicks and keystrokes.

16.6.3   Case study with the Library of Congress

The OAI model is still in need of refinement plus validation, but it may already be a useful guide for website designers and evaluators. It offers a way to decompose the many concerns that arise and provides a framework for structured design processes and eventually software tools. It is not a predictive model, but a guide to designers about how to break a large problem into many smaller ones and an aid in recognizing appropriate features to include in a website. In my experience, designers are most likely to focus on the task or interface objects, and the OAI model has been helpful in bringing out the issues of permissible task actions and visible representations of interface actions.

In the early 1990s, the U.S. Library of Congress staff developed a touch-screen catalog interface to replace the difficult-to-learn command-line interface. In this project, the design was relatively simple; the task objects were the set of catalog items that contained fields about each item. The task actions were to search the catalog (by author, title, subject, and catalog number), browse the result list, and view detailed catalog items. The interface objects were a search form (with instructions and a single data entry field), result lists, brief catalog items, and detailed catalog items. The interface actions were represented by buttons to select the type of search, to scroll the result lists, and to expand a brief catalog entry into a detailed catalog entry. Additional actions, also represented by buttons, were to start a new search, get help, print, and exit. Even in this simple case, explicit attention to these four domains helped to simplify the design.

In the more ambitious case of the Library of Congress website, many potential task objects and actions were identified; more than 150 items were proposed for inclusion on the homepage. The policy and many design decisions were made by a participative process involving the Librarian of Congress, an 18-person Policy Committee, four graphic designers, and staff from many divisions. The resulting design (Color Plate A5) for the hierarchy of task objects is rich, including the catalog, exhibits, copyright information, Global Legal Information, the THOMAS database of bills before Congress, and the vast American Memory resources, but it does not include the books. The exclusion of books is a surprise to many users, but copyright is usually held by the publishers and there is no plan to make the full text of the books available. Conveying the absence of expected objects or actions is also a design challenge.

For brevity we focus on the American Memory component. It will contain 200 collections whose items may be searchable documents, scanned page images, and digitized photographs, videos, sound, or other media. A collection also has a record that contains its title, dates of coverage, ownership, keywords, etc. Each item may have a name, number, keywords, description, etc. The task actions are rich and controversial. They begin with the actions to browse a list of the collection titles, search within a collection, and retrieve an item for viewing. However, searching across all collections is difficult to support and is not currently available. Early analysis revealed that collection records might not have dates or geographic references, thereby limiting the ways that the collection list could be ordered and presented. Similarly, at the next level down, the item records may not contain the information to allow searching by date or photographer name, and restricting search to specific fields is not always feasible.

Continuing within the American Memory component, the interface objects and actions were presented explicitly on the homepage (Color Plate C4). Since many users seek specific types of objects, the primary ones were listed explicitly and made selectable: Prints & Photos, Documents, Motion Pictures, and Sound Recordings. The interface actions were stated simply and are selectable: Search, Browse, and Learn (about using the collections for educational purposes). Within each of these objects and actions, there were further decompositions based on what was possible and what a detailed needs analysis had revealed as important.

At the lowest level of interface objects were the images and descriptive text fields. At the lowest level of interface actions were the navigation, home page, and feedback buttons.

The modest nature of the OAI model means that it can lead to varying outcomes, but it would be unreasonable to assume that there is one best organization or decomposition of a website. In dealing with complex resources and services, it offers designers a way to think about solving their problems.

16.6.4 Detailed design issues

Many web-site design issues are not yet resolved properly. The four-phase framework (see Section 15.2) can provide guidance to web search-engine designers to improve the currently confusing situation. Other issues include query previews to reduce the zero-hit problem while facilitating browsing of large information spaces, and session management to support multiple step plans while providing user assistance.

Query Previews For large collections, especially when they are searched across the network, search actions can be split into two phases: a rapid rough search that previews only the number of items in the result set, followed by a query-refinement phase that allows users to narrow their search and to retrieve the result set (Doan et al., 1996).

For example, in a search for a restaurant (Color Plate C7), the query-preview screen gives users limited choices, with buttons to indicate the type of food (for example, Chinese, French, Indian), double-boxed range sliders to specify average price and time, and maybe a map to specify regions. As users make selections among these attributes, the query-preview bar at the bottom of the screen is updated immediately to indicate the number of items in the result set. Users can quickly discover that there are no cheap French restaurants in downtown New York, or that there are several Caribbean restaurants open after midnight. When the result set is too large, users can restrict their criteria; when the result set is too small, they can alter their plans.

Query previews require database maintainers to provide an updated table of contents that users can download from the server. Then, users can perform rapid searches on their client machines. The table of contents contains the number of items satisfying combinations of attributes, but the size of the table is only the product of the cardinality of the attributes, which is likely to be much smaller than the number of items in the database. With 12 kinds of restaurants, eight regions, and three kinds of charge cards, a simple table of contents would contain only 288 entries. Storing the table of contents burdens users who may have to keep tables of contents (1000 to 100,000 bytes) for each database that they search. Of course, the size of the table of contents can be cut down dramatically if there are simply fewer attributes or fewer values per attribute. The burden of storing tables of contents seems moderate when weighed against the benefits, especially if users search a database repeatedly. The table of contents is only as big as a typical image in a web site, and it can be downloaded for use automatically when Java applets are used.

Query previews are implemented for a complex search on NASA environmental databases. Users of the old system must understand the numerous and complex attributes of the database, which is distributed across eight archival centers. Many searches result in zero hits because users are uncertain about what data are available, and broad searches take many minutes yet yield huge and unwieldy result displays. The query preview uses only three parameters: locations (clustered into 15 geographic regions), 171 scientific parameters (soil type, ocean temperature, ozone, and so on), and dates (clustered into 10 1-year groups) (Fig. 16.5). There is thus a total of $15 \times 171 \times 10 = 25650$ data values in the table of contents. In the prototype, users could quickly discover that the archive held no ozone measurements in Antarctica before 1985. Once a reasonable-sized result set is identified, users can download the details about these data sets for the query-refinement phase.

Session Management Each search or jump is one action to accomplish a task within a session. When sessions cover many complex tasks, it is helpful

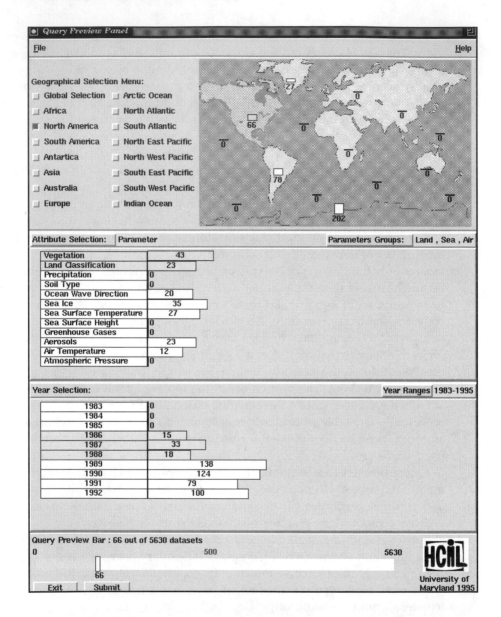

Figure 16.5

NASA query preview. The system applies this technique to a complex search for professional scientists. The set of more than 20 parameters is distilled to three, thus helping to speed the search and to reduce wasted effort. Users select values for the parameters and immediately see the size of the result bar on the bottom, thus avoiding zero-hit and mega-hit queries. (Doan et al., 1996) to have a history of the session, so that users can review their progress, return to key actions, learn from their failures, and save or edit or reapply previous actions (possibly on related databases). Other useful services allow users to annotate the objects that they have retrieved, and to extract text or images for use in their own projects. Communication with the owners or designers or maintainers of a web site and with other users should also be supported. Web-site users should be encouraged to comment about errors or suggest improvements.

No matter how well designed a web site is, there will always be a need for online and human assistance. The designer's goal should be to reduce the need for assistance, but with ever-greater numbers of users with ever-greater expectations, careful planning and trained personnel are needed. Online tutorials, descriptions of interface objects and actions, files with frequently asked questions (FAQs), electronic-mail help desks, and telephone service (possibly for a fee) should be made available.

16.6.5   Web-Page design

According to the OAI model, web-page designers should begin by identifying tasks in terms of information objects and actions. Then, designers can present interface metaphors for information objects accompanied by handles for actions. Success also requires wise choices during detailed page design to show objects (for example, menus, search results, fonts, colors) and to invoke actions (for example, button press, selection from a list). These visible design elements are often the most discussed aspects of design, and are the ones most directly implemented by HTML or Java coding. Initial subjective satisfaction is strongly determined by these surface features; therefore, they deserve intense attention (Horton et al., 1996).

Compactness and branching factors The most discussed issues are page length and number of links (branching factor). An extremely long page with no links is appealing only if users are expected to read the entire text sequentially. They rarely are, so some form of home or index page to point to fragments is necessary. Meaningful structures that guide users to the fragments that they want is the goal, but excessive fragmentation disrupts people who wish to read or print the full text. As the document and web site grow, the number of layers of index pages can grow as well, and that poses a severe danger. A higher branching factor is almost always preferred for index pages, especially if it can save an extra layer that users must traverse. The extra layers are more disorienting than are longer index pages. In a redesign for the Library of Congress home page (http://www.loc.gov) (Color Plate A5), the seven links to general themes were replaced with a compact display with 31 links to specific services. The Yahoo home page has almost 100 links in a compact two-column presentation.

Within a page, compact vertical design to reduce scrolling is recommended. Although some white space can help to organize a display, often web pages contain harmful dead space that lengthens the page without benefit to users. A typical mistake is to have a single left-justified column of links that leaves the right side of the display blank, thus forcing extra scrolling and preventing users from gaining an overview. A second common mistake is to use excessive horizontal rules or blank lines to separate items.

Sequencing, clustering, and emphasis Within a page—especially the highly visible home page of an organization—designers must consider carefully the sequencing, clustering, and emphasis for objects. Users expect the first item in a page to be an important one and are likely to select it. Clustering related items shows meaningful relationships. More important items can be emphasized with large fonts, color highlights, and surrounding boxes. The Library of Congress home page emphasizes the American Memory collections by placing them first and giving them a large fraction of the space. Public services such as the catalog and THOMAS (for searching legislation) are clustered in the center, and library services are clustered on the right side.

Support for universal access Designers must accommodate small and large displays, monochrome and color, slow and fast transmission, and various browsers that may not support desired features. The pressure for lowest-common-denominator design is often outweighed by the desires to assume larger displays, to use more detailed and more numerous graphics, to support Java applets, and to employ newer browser features. Fortunately, balanced approaches that enable users to indicate their environment and preferences are possible. Since many key design decisions involve task issues, several versions of the interface can be developed for relatively small incremental costs.

Providing text-only versions for users with small displays and low-bandwidth access is likely to be strongly recommended for many years to come. Users using low-cost devices, users in developing countries with poor communication infrastructure, users wanting low-bandwidth wireless access, users with small personal display devices, and handicapped users constitute a large proportion of the potential users.

The great disparity in transmission speeds (low-speed modems at 1200 baud to direct-connection lines at 4 megabits per second) has compelled many designers to build two versions of a web site: text only and graphical. Another solution is to display the textual components first, and to fill in the graphics as time permits. The use of image thumbnails that can be optionally expanded is another appropriate accommodation. Opinions are split over the use of low-resolution graphics that become enhanced as time permits.

Accommodating diverse users should be a strong concern for most designers, since it enlarges the market for commercial applications and provides democratic access to government services. Web sites should be tested an gray-scale displays, low-bandwidth transmission lines, and small displays. In addition, access by way of telephone or voice input–output devices will serve handicapped users and enlarge access. Access to web sites might also come from wristwatch projection displays, wallet-sized pocket PCs, or personal video devices mounted on eyeglasses.

Pointing devices could be the traditional mouse, trackball, trackpoint, touchpad, touchscreen, or eyegaze-detection devices. Cursor-control arrow keys could be used to support jumping among highlighted items.

Good graphical design Many personal web sites are developed by individuals who learn a modest amount of HTML or use a graphical interface to generate HTML. Simple web sites can be created successfully with these tools, but doing innovative and effective page layout for a large web site requires as much care and skill as does laying out a newspaper, magazine, or book. Page layout is a well-developed topic for graphic designers, whose expertise is vital for innovative and effective designs (Cotton and Oliver, 1993; McAdams, 1996; Weinman, 1996). Grid layouts and consistent structure help to guide the reader. Distinctive headings and graphics signal boundaries and provide familiar landmarks during navigation on the first visit and return visits. Indexes and shortcuts give frequent users paths for rapid traversal.

An hour spent browsing web sites will reveal diverse graphic-design philosophies. The poster designers use centered titles, large graphics, ample white space, and a small number of visually striking buttons, sometimes from the *Wired* magazine school of garish colors and extreme imagery. Book designers use left-justified titles, a few small graphics, dense text that goes on for many pages, and numerous text links. Newspaper designers start several stories on the home page, each with its own heading, font, column, inset photos, and continuations. GIF-heads are eager to show their scanned photos, art, scientific images, or logo, and place these graphics on the page with little care for captions, layout, or the burden on users who have low-bandwidth access. Hypertext fanatics chop up documents into paragraph-sized chunks or smaller, and put as many links as possible per sentence. Traditionalists simply put a lengthy text in a single file and expect users to scroll happily and linearly.

Each design philosophy is meant to appeal to certain users and to support certain tasks. Abuses that hinder task completion are likely to fade over time. Page layouts are likely to favor convenient online browsing, but special layouts may be needed to produce effective printed versions.

Traditional graphic-design rules often apply in the web environment. Large fonts or boldface type typically indicate major headings, and medium fonts can signal sub headings. Text is best left as black on white or gray, enabling links to be highlighted by color or underlining. A graphic logo is typical for an organization home page, and, as users move down in a hierarchy, moderate- or small-sized logos can indicate location in the hierarchy. Four sizes of logos are probably as many as most users can grasp quickly. For different branches of a large hierarchy, variant logos, and color coding of banners or backgrounds can be effective, with a limit of six to eight variations. These recommendations emerge from graphic-design books for paper documents; new opportunities will appear for electronic documents.

Navigation support In a paper book, the reader's progress is easily seen. Since this is not available online, innovative substitutes are appearing. The simple approach of indicating page 171 of 283 can be effective, but various analog progress indicators, such as scroll bars and page bars, are emerging. More elaborate indicators, such as a tree or network diagram, sometimes called a *site map*, help to orient users in larger sites (see Fig. 7.7). Dynamic indicators that respond to mouse cursor placement by opening up a hierarchy or popping up detailed information in a small window are still novel. Animated indicators that reveal underlying structures or offer more details are likely to emerge, along with auditory feedback, three-dimensional displays, and rich information visualizations.

Although scroll bars are the primary navigation tool because they provide a simple and standard mechanism, a paging strategy using page bars (a scroll bar with discrete jumps) is cognitively less demanding because users have a clearer sense of position in a document. Designers can make use of tops and bottoms of pages to provide navigational cues (headers, footers, page numbers). Users become familiar with a document by remembering a photo or figure at the top of a certain page. Unfortunately, this strategy is undermined by the wide variation in screen sizes, so designers have to commit to a specific size, such as 640×480 pixels, and then users of larger or smaller screens have to accommodate to the standard. When designers can assume a larger screen and resolution-indepen-

Plate C1: An electronic magazine Get Smart, built with Hyperties, that allows integration of images, video, and sound with embedded links to related topics. (Used with permission of Cognetics Corp., Princeton Junction, NJ.)

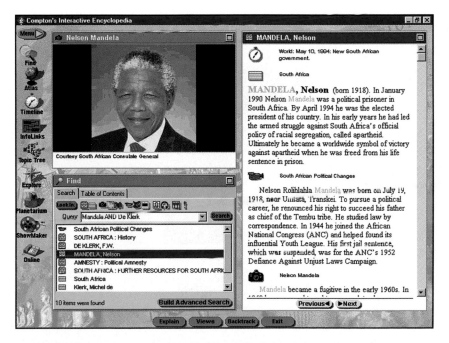

Plate C2: Compton's Encyclopedia uses multimedia and multiple windows to enrich the presentation and support browsing.

Ara Kotchian _and_ My Trip to Venus

Current Position: I am currently a programmer at Language Analysis Systems Inc. in Reston VA.
Academic Degree: I graduated with a B.S. in Computer Science on December 20, 1996

A little bit of information about me: I was born in the once beautiful city of Beirut, Lebanon.
Through some very strange events and mysterious occurrences over the years, I ended up here at the
University of Maryland. For three years I have worked at the Human-Computer Interaction Lab but as
of the end of September 1996 I have been working at my new job at L.A.S.. Aside from Computer
Science, I have a great interest in ancient and medieval world history and mythology. I am an amateur
armorer, I enjoy camping, reading and occasionally laying siege to castles.

Plate C3: One-page personal biography of Ara Kotchian, a student
at the University of Maryland. (Used with permission.)
(http://www.cs.umd.edu/projects/hcil/People/ara/index.html).

Plate C4: American Memory home page from the Library of Congress, which will offer more than 5 million images, texts, videos,
and so on by the year 2000. (http://lcweb2.loc.gov/ammem).

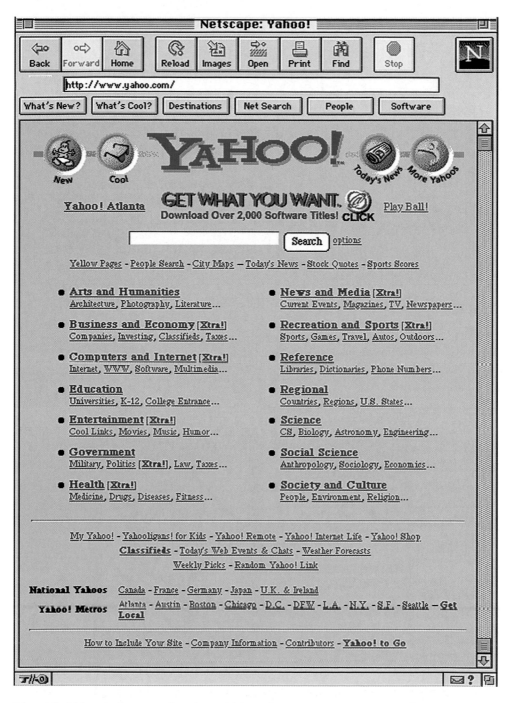

Plate C5: Yahoo index page showing a 14-item thematic categorization with 51 second-level links, and more than 30 other links. (http://www.yahoo.com) (Used with permission of Reuters, Inc.)

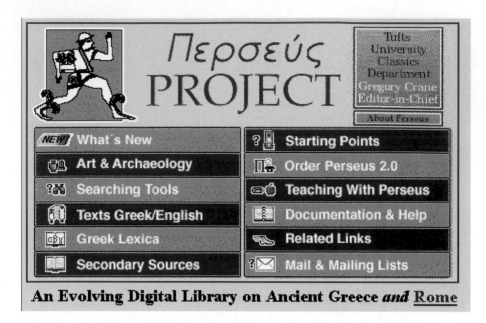

Plate C6: Perseus digital library, which contains ancient Greek texts in original and English forms with maps, photos, architectural plans, vases, coins, and so on for students and researchers. (http://www.perseus.tufts.edu).

Plate C7: Restaurant finder, a system that demonstrates query preview. Users can quickly adjust the parameters and see the effect on the size of the preview bar at the bottom. Zero-hit or mega-hit results are visible immediately, so users can always be sure that their search will produce an appropriate number of results. (Graphic design by Teresa Cronnell.) (Doan et al., 1997.)

dent layouts as standard, then the shift toward page orientation will be more common.

16.6.6   Testing and maintenance of web sites

Usability testing is recommended for all user-interface projects; in addition, there are special needs for web-site testing. As always, the questions of who the users are and what the tasks are guide designers. The testing should be done with representatives of each of the primary user communities and of as many of the secondary communities as time and money allow (Nielsen, 1995). Users of various ages, genders, and ethnic backgrounds, as well as international users, may be included. The task-frequency list developed during needs assessment provides guidance for construction of test tasks.

Users should be tested in realistic settings that resemble the office or home environments. The number of users and length of testing will depend on the project's importance. Various screen sizes and transmission speeds should be tested. Voice access should be tested for handicapped and other users. Since browsers have such varied features, testing should be done with several of them.

After early in-house testing with limited numbers of users, a more extensive in-house test might be conducted. Then, intensive field testing can begin, before a public announcement. A phased roll-out process will protect against disaster, improve quality, and ensure the highest satisfaction by the largest number of users.

The web-site developer's work is never done. The more successful a site is, the more opportunities there are for revision and improvement. Software logs should capture the frequency of use for each page, or at least for each component of a database. Such statistics can reveal patterns that provide guidance for improving a web site. If some components are never accessed, then they can be removed, or the references to these components can be improved to draw attention. Logging software can also reveal patterns of use over a month, week, or day, and can indicate the paths users take to arrive at and to traverse a web site.

In addition to using automated logging, web-site maintainers can solicit feedback from users by electronic mail or survey questionnaires embedded in the web site. Knowledge of user demographics and motivations may be helpful in refining a web site. To get in-depth understanding, web-site maintainers may interview users individually by telephone or personally, or conduct focus-group discussions among users.

User expectations and organizational policy guide the rate of change of the web-site contents and interface. Some web sites are stable, and users depend on the permanent availability of the contents; libraries, government archives, and online journals are examples. Other sites are volatile and are expected to change hourly, daily, weekly, or seasonally; weather information, newspapers, magazines, and train schedules are examples.

16.7   Practitioner's Summary

Linked information in text, graphics, image, sound, animation, and video formats can be used in commercial projects that satisfy the Golden Rules of Hypertext. Effective hypermedia products follow basic principles of user-interface design, but place a greater emphasis on content organization and presentation.

Careful web-site design makes the difference between a must-see, top-10 site and a worst–web page award. Specifying the users and setting the goals come first, followed by design of information objects and actions. Next, designers can create the interface metaphors (bookshelf, encyclopedia, shopping mall) and the handles for actions (scrolling, linking, zooming). Finally, the web-page design can be created in multiple visual formats and international versions, with access provided for handicapped or otherwise special readers. Every design project, including web-site development, should be subjected to usability testing and to other validation methods. Monitoring of use should guide revision.

16.8   Researcher's Agenda

Hypertext, hypermedia, multimedia, and the World Wide Web are still in the Ford Model T stage of development. Strategies for blending text, sound, images, and video are in need of refinement, and effective rhetorics for hypermedia are only now being created. Who will be the first to write the Great American Hypernovel or Hypermystery? Many results from other user-interface topics—such as menu selection, direct manipulation, and screen design—can be applied to web-site design. On the other hand, the novel communities of users, innovative databases, ambitious services, emphasis on linking and navigation, and intensive use of graphics present fresh challenges and rich opportunities to researchers to validate hypotheses in this environment. Theories of information structuring are emerging, as are standards for representing traversal actions. The creative frenzy on the web is likely to present new opportunities for design research for many years to come.

Controlled experimental studies are effective for narrow issues, whereas field studies, data logging, and online surveys are attractive alternative research methods in the wide-open web. Focus groups, critical-incident studies, and interviews may be effective for hypothesis formation. Other opportunities include sociological studies about impact of web use on home or office life, and political studies of web-use influence on democratic processes. Broader concerns—such as copyright violation, invasion of privacy, pornography, or criminal activity—merit attention as the impact of the World Wide Web increases. We can influence the direction and societal impact of technology only if we have the scientific foundation to understand the issues.

World Wide Web Resources   `WWW`

It should not be a surprise that World Wide Web contains numerous documents about the World Wide Web, including style guides for authors, numerous navigation tools, research and survey reports, and ample discussion.

http://www.aw.com/DTUI

References

Berners-Lee, Tim, Cailliau, Robert, Luotonen, Ari, and Nielsen, Henrik F., and Secret, Arthur, The World Wide Web, *Communications of the ACM*, 37, 8 (1994), 76–82.

Bush, Vannevar, As we may think, *Atlantic Monthly*, 76, 1 (July 1945), 101–108.

Chimera, R. and Shneiderman, B., Evaluating three user interfaces for browsing tables of contents, *ACM Transactions on Information Systems*, 12, 4 (October 1994), 383–406.

Conklin, Jeff, Hypertext: A survey and introduction, *IEEE Computer*, 20, 9 (September 1987), 17–41.

Cotton, Bob and Oliver, Richard, *Understanding Hypermedia: From Multimedia to Virtual Reality*, Phaidon Press, London, U.K. (1993).

Doan, Khoa, Plaisant, Catherine, and Shneiderman, Ben, Query previews for networked information services, *Proc. Advances in Digital Libraries Conference*, IEEE Computer Society, Los Alamitos, CA (May 1996), 120–129.

Engelbart, Douglas, Authorship provisions in AUGMENT, *Proc. IEEE CompCon Conference* (1984), 465–472.

Flynn, Laurie, Making searches easier in the web's sea of data, *The New York Times* (October 2, 1995).

Halasz, Frank, Reflections on NoteCards: Seven issues for the next generation of hypermedia systems, *Communications of the ACM*, 31, 7 (July 1988), 836–852.

Hoffman, Donna L., Kalsbeek, William D., and Novak, Thomas P., Internet and web usage in the U.S., *Communications of the ACM*, 39, 12 (December 1996), 36–46.

Horton, William, Taylor, Lee, Ignacio, Arthur, and Hoft, Nancy L., *The Web Page Design Cookbook*, John Wiley and Sons, New York (1996).

IBM, World Wide Web Design Guidelines, http://www.ibm.com/ibm/hci/guidelines/web/web_design.html (April 1997).

Isakowitz, Tomas, Stohr, Edward A., and Balasubramanian, P., RMM: A methodology for hypermedia design, *Communications of the ACM*, 38, 8 (August 1995), 34–44.

Jones, Trish and Shneiderman, Ben, Evaluating usability for a training-oriented hypertext: Can hyper-activity be good?, *Electronic Publishing 3*, 4 (November 1990), 207–225.

Kellogg, Wendy A. and Richards, John T., The human factors of information on the internet, In Nielsen, Jakob (Editor), *Advances in Human–Computer Interaction*, Volume 5, Ablex, Norwood, NJ (1995), 1–36.

Koved, Larry and Shneiderman, Ben, Embedded menus: Selecting items in context, *Communications of the ACM*, 29, 4 (April 1986), 312–318.

Lemay, Laura, *Teach Yourself Web Publishing with HTML in a Week*, Sams Publishing, Indianapolis, IN (1995).

Lynch, Patrick J., Yale, *University C/AIM WWW Style Guide*, http://info.med.yale.edu/caim/StyleManual_Top.HTML (September 5, 1995).

Marchionini, Gary, *Information Seeking in Electronic Environments*, Cambridge University Press, U.K. (1995).

Marchionini, Gary and Shneiderman, Ben, Finding facts and browsing knowledge in hypertext systems, *IEEE Computer*, 21, 1 (January 1988), 70–80.

McAdams, Melinda, Information design and the new media, *ACM interactions*, II.4, (October 1995), 38–46.

Nielsen, Jakob, *Multimedia and Hypermedia*, Academic Press, San Diego, CA (1995).

Nielsen, Jakob, A home-page overhaul using other web sites, *IEEE Software*, 12, 3 (May 1995), 75–78.

Nielsen, Jakob, Using paper prototypes in home-page design, *IEEE Software*, 12, 4 (July 1995), 88–97.

Nielsen, Jakob, Sun studies of WWW design, http://www.sun.com/sun-on-net/www.sun.com/uidesign.

Pejtersen, A. M., A library system for information retrieval based on a cognitive task analysis and supported by an icon-based interface, *Proc. ACM SIGIR Conference* (1989), 40–47.

Pitkow, Jim and Kehoe, Colleen, GVU's Fourth WWW User Survey, www-survey@cc.gatech.edu (1996).

Plaisant, Catherine, Guide to Opportunities in Volunteer Archaeology: Case study of the use of a hypertext system in a museum exhibit. In Berk, Emily and Devlin,

Joseph, (Editors), *Hypertext/Hypermedia Handbook,* McGraw-Hill, New York (1991), 498–505.

Rivlin, Ehud, Rotafogo, Rodrigo, and Shneiderman, Ben, Navigating in hyperspace: Designs for a structure-based toolbox, *Communications of the ACM,* 37, 2 (February 1994), 87–96.

Shneiderman, Ben (Editor), Hypertext on Hypertext, Hyperties disk with 1Mbyte data and graphics incorporating July 1988 *CACM,* ACM Press, New York, NY (July 1988).

Shneiderman, Ben, Reflections on authoring, editing, and managing hypertext. In Barrett, E. (Editor), *The Society of Text,* MIT Press, Cambridge, MA (1989), 115–131.

Shneiderman, Ben, Brethauer, Dorothy, Plaisant, Catherine and Potter, Richard, Three evaluations of museum installations of a hypertext system, *Journal of the American Society for Information Science,* 40, 3 (May 1989), 172–182.

Shneiderman, Ben and Kearsley, Greg, *Hypertext Hands-On! An Introduction to a New Way of Organizing and Accessing Information,* Addison-Wesley, Reading, MA (1989).

van Dam, Andries, Hypertext 87: Keynote Address, *Communications of the ACM,* 31, 7 (July 1988), 887–895.

Weinman, Lynda, *Designing Web Graphics,* New Riders Publishing, Indianapolis, IN (1996).

Yankelovich, Nicole, Meyrowitz, Norm, and van Dam, Andries, Reading and writing the electronic book, *IEEE Computer,* 18, 10 (October 1985), 15–30.

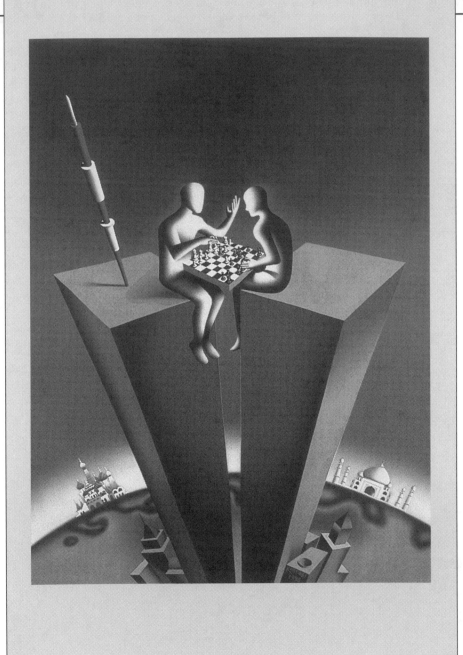

Mark Kostabi, *Grandmasters*, 1995

Societal and Individual Impact of User Interfaces

The machine itself makes no demands and holds out no promises: it is the human spirit that makes demands and keeps promises. In order to reconquer the machine and subdue it to human purposes, one must first understand it and assimilate it. So far we have embraced the machine without fully understanding it.

Lewis Mumford, *Technics and Civilization,* **1934**

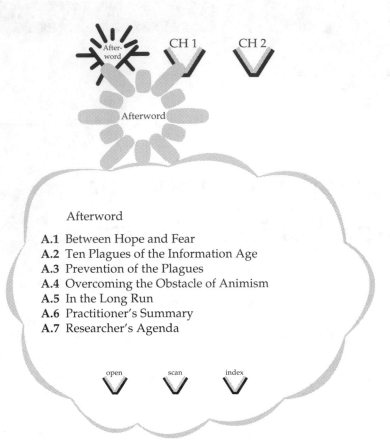

A.1   Between Hope and Fear

Hope is a vital human emotion, stimulated by the desire to make life better and infused with the belief that change is possible. Hope has a strong rational component that shapes plans and reasons about possible outcomes, but hope depends on passion for forward movement.

Deeply held hopes can invigorate other people to join in purposeful action. Martin Luther King's "I Have a Dream" speech is inspirational because of its image of racial harmony. Similarly, John F. Kennedy's vision of a human setting foot on the moon helped to bring about that event. His passion provided the propelling force for the rational scientific work that followed.

Often, hope must overcome resistance—the *fear* that action will fail or leave us worse off. Fear can be a terrifying barrier to change, but also can create energy for action. Confronting fears and summoning the courage to press forward requires self-confidence and a determination to succeed. Because of these challenges, people and civilizations are often remembered for their deep hopes, or, in the words of Ezra Pound, "One measure of a civilization, either of an age or of a single individual, is what that age or person really wishes to do."

Computing professionals can reflect proudly on 50 years of accomplishments, and it is appropriate for us to consider our deep hopes for the next 50 years. Computing has grown into a worldwide infrastructure that touches every country and soon may touch every individual on the planet. But what are our deep hopes for the next 50 years? If our hopes inspire action, our profession will be appreciated for contributing to a better society (Brooks, 1996; Shneiderman, 1995, 1990).

Through the half-century of our profession, visionaries have inspired constructive development. In the 1940s, Vannevar Bush envisioned memex, a desk with microfilm libraries to extend memory by accessing vast resources of patents, scientific papers, or legal citations (Bush, 1945). J.C.R. Licklider carried the digital-library idea into the world of electronic computers and recognized the potential for teleconferencing to bring people closer together (Licklider, 1965). Douglas Engelbart envisioned computers as symbol manipulators that could augment human intellect (Engelbart, 1968). He created an ambitious workstation with a mouse, a chorded keyboard, an outliner, and links across documents that he demonstrated at the Fall Joint Computer Conference of 1968. Later visionaries brought us personal computers, networks, electronic mail, GUIs, and more. These innovations helped to launch the modern computer industry; finding the next breakthrough is our next challenge.

An obvious vision of hope is by *technology extrapolation,* which posits that advances in technology are in themselves beneficial to society. This approach leads to dreams of gigahertz processors producing rapid user-controlled three-dimensional animations on gigapixel displays. Technology extrapolation also suggests terabyte hard disks and web spaces with petabytes of information at our fingertips. Progress is relatively easy to recognize if we follow technology extrapolation, but a more challenging path is to consider what technologies we want to change ourselves and our civilization.

A more elaborate form of technology extrapolation is to dream of intelligent agents, speech interaction, or information at our fingertips (Gates, 1995; Negroponte, 1995). These goals are technology-oriented, but they are not directly linked to clear societal benefits, such as world peace, improved health care, or civil rights. Linking grand goals to realistic scenarios for accomplishing them takes impassioned imagination combined with scientific rigor.

Let's start with imagination. The fisherman who rubbed Aladdin's lamp evoked a genie who offered three wishes. If rubbing your keyboard could produce a modern digital genie, what wishes would you choose to shape the

> **Web inspiration:** In trying to fathom the link between the emotional
> quality of hope and the rational world of technology, I ventured onto
> the World Wide Web. A quick search revealed an encouraging pattern:
> more than one million entries for hope, and only ⅓ million for fear.
> Some probing yielded a web site from a recent international conference
> in Japan on "The Future of Hope" (http://iij.asahi.com/paper/hope/
> english/index.html). Along with many speakers, Elie Wiesel called for
> recognition of past and current suffering. The closing *Hiroshima Decla-
> ration* stressed continued reduction in nuclear weapons and support
> for human and civil rights. It mentioned the potential for "revolution-
> ary technologies" that "offer ever more opportunities to bring people
> and leaders together in dialogue and thus resolve their conflicts."

future? After much reflection, my choices are for universal access to computing technology, universal medical records, and universal educational support.

A.1.1   Universal access to computing technology

My first hope is for universal access, in which progress is defined by the percentage of the population with convenient low-cost access to specific World
Wide Web services, such as electronic mail, distance education, or community networks (Anderson et al., 1995). Providing electricity, hardware, and
communications is just the beginning. Applications and services will have to
be reengineered to meet the differing needs of the many still forgotten users.
We must think about how electronic mail can be reshaped to accommodate
unskilled writers and readers, while helping to improve their skills. How can
job training and hunting be organized to serve those people with currently
poor employment skills and transient lifestyles? How can services such as
voting registration, motor-vehicle registration, or crime reporting be
improved if universal network access is assumed?

Perhaps we can begin by redesigning interfaces to simplify common
tasks. We can provide novel training and help methods so that using a computer is a satisfying opportunity, rather than a frustrating challenge. Evolutionary learning with level-structured interfaces would allow first-time users
to succeed with common tasks and would provide a growth path to reveal
more complex features. With millions of new users, improved strategies for
filtering electronic mail, searching directories, finding information, and getting online assistance will be needed. Low-cost manufacturing is a central
requirement to achieve universal access for low-income Americans or the
many still lower-income citizens in less technologically developed nations.

Facile tailoring of interfaces for diverse populations could be accomplished with control panels that allow users to specify their national language, units of measurement, skill level, and more. Portability to nonstandard hardware, accommodation of varying screen sizes or modem speeds, and design for handicapped or elderly users should be common practices.

Support for increased plasticity of information and services is technologically possible, but attention to this area has been limited. Convenient semantic tagging of items would enable software designers to reformat presentations, to remove unnecessary information selectively, or to integrate related materials dynamically to adjust to users' needs. Comprehensible software tools to support platform-independent authoring will enable many more people to contribute to the growing worldwide information infrastructure, as well as to their local resources.

Universal access is a policy issue: Common practices and a guiding vision are helpful to making it happen. Regulatory policies for telephones, television, and highways have been successful in creating near-universal access to these technologies, but computing economics, designs, and services apparently need revision to reach a broader audience. Fears of inappropriate intervention in free markets are legitimate, but commercial producers are likely to be major beneficiaries of universal-access policies. How might decision makers encourage industry to support universal access so as to create an expanding market that also benefits producers of commercial products and services?

In communities where adequate housing, sanitation, and food are still problems, telephones or computing are not primary needs, but the technology can still be helpful as part of an overall development plan. Community-networking technologies are being tried in well-off locales such as Taos, New Mexico, Seattle, Washington, and Blacksburg, Virginia, but adapting these designs to mountainous Nepal, urban Rio de Janeiro, or rural Botswana will take creative engineering, in addition to financial resources.

A.1.2   Universal medical records

My second hope is for improved medical record keeping. Resistance to changing the current paper-based approaches limits the availability of medical information for clinical decision making, quality control, and research. It is a paradox that airline reservations are available around the world, crossing hostile political boundaries and spanning networks of competing companies, but your medical records are inaccessible even when they might help to save your life.

A physician at any emergency room in the world should be able to review your history and see your most recent electrocardiogram or chest X-ray image within 15 seconds of your arrival, either via network or on a personal datacard. The display should appear in the local language, using familiar units of measurement, with easy access to details and convenient links for electronic consultation with physicians who know you personally.

Progress on standardizing clinical records, speeding data entry for patient histories, and designing effective overviews for viewing patient records (Color Plate B3) (Plaisant et al., 1996) could be dramatically accelerated. With a one-screen overview of patient histories, physicians could quickly spot previous surgeries or chronic diseases that might affect current decisions. Privacy protection, patient rights, and cost containment are serious concerns, but the potential for improved health care and reduced costs is compelling.

Further benefits of online medical records include assistance in formulating treatment plans and clinical research. Imagine if your physician were able to review the past year's outcomes for potential treatment plans in a sample of 10,000 patients who had your diagnosis? Imagine if scientists were able to study case histories retrospectively to support research on treatment plans and associated clinical outcomes?

With careful attention to personal privacy and costs, online medical records can become the basis for improved accountability of individual physicians and health-management organizations, as well as of improved medical understanding. Physicians may resist such visibility of their decisions, but objective comparisons with peer performance seem preferable to the current complexity and cost of malpractice litigation.

A.1.3   Universal educational support

Education is the hope of civilization. Computing is already dramatically altering education, but it is not enough to teach children about surfing the net—we must also teach them about making waves (Shneiderman, 1993). Finding information is useful only if students have a meaningful goal and a chance to influence their world.

My approach combines education with social benefit and authentic experiences to teach students how to participate in workgroups, political systems, and communities. Powerful information technologies enable students to collaborate effectively in constructing meaningful results that benefit someone outside the classroom. These action-oriented and authentic service projects done in teams produce a high level of motivation among students and give them the satisfaction of helping other people while learning.

A favorite student project involved a team that was interested in computing for the elderly. They read the literature, made a plan, brought computers to a nearby nursing home, and trained the elderly residents for several weeks. Then, their final report was written to the director of the home, with a well-reasoned plan for what might be done and pointers to helpful organi-

zations. Another project set up a database system for a charitable organization that continues to manage volunteer and donor lists with more than
20,000 names.

Student projects could be educationally oriented, such as writing an
online textbook for their course or developing an *Encyclopedia of X*, where *X*
is a variable in their discipline. Creating services for other groups is compelling to students and is in harmony with the efforts in many states, such as
Maryland, which requires 60 hours of community service for high-school
graduation.

This *relate–create–donate* approach enlivens the educational process,
pushes students to learn the relevant fundamentals, and encourages them to
strive for practical goals (Denning, 1992). I'm encouraged by reports from
other educators who have replicated and adapted this strategy from elementary schools (fifth graders creating a multimedia course on the animals of
Africa for third graders) to graduate business schools (M.B.A. candidates set
up web pages for two dozen campus and community groups).

Current technologies provide support for relate–create–donate styles of
education, but four phases of creative work could be improved with
advanced technology:

1. Reliable retrieval of existing knowledge relevant to team projects
2. Creative activities with brainstorming tools, simulation modeling,
    design exploration, and authoring tools
3. Consultation with peers and experts using convenient group-support
    tools
4. Dissemination of results through community-information tools

Imagine online science festivals in which student projects could build on
one another over the years. New student teams could view previous projects, conduct research, and develop creative contributions, while consulting
with other teams who are working on related problems or with professional
scientists. The results could be reviewed by award panels, disseminated to
interested people, and posted for future students.

Resistance to team projects is natural from faculty who have never had the
experience themselves, but many are learning to guide computer-mediated
team projects. The shift from "sage on the stage" to "guide on the side" is a
challenge, and finding appropriate team projects plus management strategies takes experience. Those educators who succeed are enthusiastic about
the power of collaboration and the thrill of intense experiences.

Taking responsibility for the future is a substantial challenge. It is my sin-
cere belief that we, as computing professionals, should accept the challenge

to look beyond the technology and to create a vision that inspires action. If we do so, we may be well remembered by history.

There are so many important problems to solve that there is room for everyone to contribute: jobs can be more rewarding, communities can be safer, and lives can be happier. Each one of us can make a difference.

Universal access to computing technology, universal medical records, and universal educational support are my ambitious hopes. There are surely other hopes and visions that can steer computing toward higher societal benefits, while providing unlimited challenges for researchers, entrepreneurs, and practitioners. For those people who feel inspired and wish to contribute, the time to begin is *now* and the leader to look to is *you*.

A.2   Ten Plagues of the Information Age

The real question before us lies here: do these instruments further life and enhance its values, or not?

Mumford, *Technics and Civilization,* **1934**

It would be naive to assume that widespread use of computers brings only benefits. There are legitimate reasons to worry that increased dissemination of computers might lead to a variety of oppressions—personal, organizational, political, or social. People who fear computers have good reason for their concerns. Computer-system designers have an opportunity and a responsibility to be alert to the dangers and to make thoughtful decisions about reducing the dangers they apprehend (Huff and Finholt, 1994). Here, then, is a personal list of potential and real dangers from use of computer systems:

1. *Anxiety*

   Many people avoid the computer or use it with great anxiety; they suffer from *computer shock, terminal terror,* or *network neurosis.* Their anxieties include fear of breaking the machine, worry over losing control to the computer, trepidation about appearing foolish or incompetent ("computers make you feel so dumb"), or more general concern about facing something new. These anxieties are real, should be acknowledged rather than dismissed, and can often be overcome with positive experiences. Can we build improved user interfaces and systems that will reduce or eliminate the current high level of anxiety experienced by many users?

2. *Alienation*

   As people spend more time using computers, they may become less connected to other people (Sheridan, 1980). Computer users as a group are
   more introverted than are other people, and increased time with the
   computer may increase their isolation. One psychologist (Brod, 1984)
   fears that computer users come to expect rapid performance, yes–no or
   true–false responses, and a high degree of control not only from their
   machines but also from their friends, spouses, and children. The dedicated video-game player who rarely communicates with another person
   is an extreme case, but what happens to the emotional relationships of a
   person who spends two hours per day dealing with electronic mail,
   rather than chatting with colleagues or family members (Kraut et al.,
   1996)? Can we build user interfaces that encourage more constructive
   human social interaction?

3. *Information-poor minority*

   Although some utopian visionaries believe that computers will eliminate the distinctions between rich and poor or will right social injustices,
   often computers are just another way in which the disadvantaged are
   disadvantaged (Friedman and Nissenbaum, 1996). Those people who
   are without computer skills may have a new reason for not succeeding
   in school or not getting a job. Already, great disparity exists in the distribution of educational computers. The high-income school districts are
   considerably more likely to have computer facilities than are the poorer
   school districts. Access to information resources is also disproportion-
   ately in the hands of the wealthy and established social communities.
   Can we build systems that empower low-skilled workers to perform at
   the level of experts? Can we arrange training and education for every
   able member of society?

4. *Impotence of the individual*

   Large organizations can become impersonal because the cost of handling special cases is great. Individuals who are frustrated in trying to
   receive personal treatment and attention may vent their anger at the
   organization, the personnel they encounter, or the technology that limits rather than enables. People who have tried to find out the current
   status of their social-security accounts or tried to have banks explain
   accounting discrepancies are aware of the problems, especially if they
   have language or hearing deficits, or other physical or cognitive handicaps. Interactive computer systems can be used to increase the influence of individuals or to provide special treatment, but this application

requires alert committed designers and sympathetic managers. How can we design so that individuals will feel more empowered and self-actualized?

5. *Bewildering complexity and speed*

The tax, welfare, and insurance regulations developed by computer-based bureaucracies are so complex and fast changing that it is extremely difficult for individuals to keep up and to make informed choices. Even knowledgeable computer users are often overwhelmed by the torrent of new software packages, each with hundreds of features and options. The presence of computers and other technologies can mislead managers into believing that they can deal with the complexities that they are creating. Rapid computer systems become valued, speed dominates, and more features are seen as preferable. This situation is apparent in nuclear-reactor control rooms, where hundreds of brightly lit annunciators overwhelm operators when indicating failures. Simplicity is a simple—but too often ignored—principle. Stern adherence to basic principles of design may be the only path to a safer, saner, simpler, and slower world where human concerns predominate.

6. *Organizational fragility*

As organizations come to depend on more complex technology, they can become fragile. When breakdowns occur, they can propagate rapidly and can halt the work of many people. With computer-based airline ticketing, telephone switching, or department-store sales, computer failures can mean immediate shutdowns of service. A more subtle example is that computer-based inventory control may eliminate or dramatically reduce stock on hand, after which disruptions spread rapidly. For example, a strike in a ball-bearing plant can force the closure of a distant automobile assembly line within a few days. Computers can cause concentration of expertise, and then a small number of people can disrupt a large organization. Can developers anticipate the dangers and produce robust designs?

7. *Invasion of privacy*

The widely reported threat of invasion of privacy is worrisome because the concentration of information and the existence of powerful retrieval systems make it possible to violate the privacy of many people easily and rapidly. Of course, well-designed computer systems have the potential of becoming more secure than paper systems if managers are dedicated to privacy protection. Airline, telephone, bank, medical, legal, and employment records can reveal much about an individual if confidentiality is compromised. Can managers seek policies and systems that increase rather than reduce the protection of privacy in a computer-based organization?

8. *Unemployment and displacement*

   As automation spreads, productivity and overall employment may increase, but some jobs may become less valued or eliminated. Retraining can help some employees, but others will have difficulty changing lifetime patterns of work. Displacement may happen to low-paid clerks or highly paid typesetters whose work is automated, as well as to the bank vice-president whose mortgage-loan decisions are now made by an expert system. Can employers develop labor policies that ensure retraining and guarantee jobs?

9. *Lack of professional responsibility*

   Faceless organizations may respond impersonally to, and deny responsibility for, problems. The complexity of technology and organizations provides ample opportunities for employees to pass the blame on to others or to the computer: "Sorry, the computer won't let us loan you the library book without your machine-readable card." Will users of medical diagnostic or defense-related systems be able to escape responsibility for decisions? Will computer printouts become more trusted than a person's word or a professional's judgment? Complex and confusing systems enable users and designers to blame the machine, but with improved designs, responsibility and credit will be given, and will be accepted by the users and designers.

10. *Deteriorating image of people*

    With the presence of *intelligent terminals, smart machines,* and *expert systems,* it seems that the machines have indeed *taken over* human abilities. These misleading phrases not only generate anxiety about computers, but also may undermine the image that we have of people and their abilities. Some behavioral psychologists suggest that we are little more than machines; some artificial-intelligence workers believe that the automation of many human abilities is within reach. The rich diversity of human skills, the generative or creative nature of daily life, the emotional or passionate side of human endeavor, and the idiosyncratic imagination of each child seem lost or undervalued (Rosenbrock, 1982). Rather than be impressed by smart machines, accept the misguided pursuit of the Turing test, or focus on computational skills in people, I believe that we should recognize that designs that empower users will increase users' appreciation of the richness and diversity of unique human abilities.

Undoubtedly, more plagues and problems exist. Each situation is a small warning for the designer. Each design is an opportunity to apply computers in positive, constructive ways that avoid these dangers.

A.3   Prevention of the Plagues

People who are so fascinated by the computer's lifelike feats—it plays chess! it writes poetry!—that they would turn it into the voice of omniscience, betray how little understanding they have of either themselves, their mechanical-electrical agents or the potentialities of life.

Lewis Mumford, *The Myth of the Machine,* **1970**

There is no sure vaccine for preventing the 10 plagues that we discussed. Even well-intentioned designers can inadvertently spread them, but alert, dedicated designers whose consciousness is raised can reduce the dangers. The strategies for preventing the plagues and reducing their effects include the following:

- *Human-centered design*   Concentrate attention on the users and on the tasks that they must accomplish. Make users the center of attention and build feelings of competence, mastery, clarity, and predictability. Construct well-organized menu trees, provide meaningful structure in command languages, present specific and constructive instructions and messages, develop uncluttered displays, offer informative feedback, enable easy error handling, ensure appropriate display rates and response time, and produce comprehensible learning materials.

- *Organizational support*   Beyond the software design, the organization must also support the user. Explore strategies for participatory design and elicit frequent evaluation and feedback from users. Techniques include personal interviews, focus groups, online surveys, paper questionnaires, and online consultants or suggestion boxes.

- *Job design*   European labor unions have been active in setting rules for computer users to prevent the exhaustion, stress, or burnout caused by an *electronic sweatshop*. Rules might be set to limit hours of use, to guarantee rest periods, to facilitate job rotation, and to support education. Similarly, negotiated measures of productivity or error rates can help to reward exemplary workers and to guide training. Monitoring or metering of work must be done cautiously, but both managers and employees can be beneficiaries of a thoughtful plan.

- *Education*   The complexity of modern life and computer systems makes education critical. Schools and colleges, as well as employers, all play a role in training. Special attention should be paid to continuing education, on-the-job training, and teacher education.

- *Feedback and rewards*   User groups can be more than passive observers. They can ensure that system failures are reported, that design improvements are conveyed to managers and designers, and that manuals and online aids are reviewed. Similarly, excellence should be acknowledged by awards within organizations and through public presentations. Professional societies in computing might promote awards, similar to the awards of the American Institute of Architects, the Pulitzer Prize Committee, or the Academy of Motion Picture Producers.

- *Public consciousness raising*   Informed consumers of personal computers and users of commercial systems can benefit the entire community. Professional societies, such as the ACM and the IEEE, and user groups can play a key role through public relations, consumer education, and professional standards of ethics.

- *Legislation*   Much progress has been made with legislation concerning privacy, right of access to information, and computer crime, but more work remains. Cautious steps toward regulation, work rules, and standardization can be highly beneficial. Dangers of restrictive legislation do exist, but thoughtful legal protection will stimulate development and prevent abuses.

- *Advanced research*   Individuals, organizations, and governments can support research to develop novel ideas, to minimize the dangers, and to spread the advantages of interactive systems. Theories of user cognitive behavior, individual differences, acquisition of skills, visual perception, and organizational change would be helpful in guiding designers and implementers.

A.4   Overcoming the Obstacle of Animism

Unlike machines, human minds can create ideas. We need ideas to guide us to progress, as well as tools to implement them. . . . Computers don't contain "brains" any more than stereos contain musical instruments. . . . Machines only manipulate numbers; people connect them to meaning.

Penzias, 1989

The emergence of computers is one of the fundamental historical changes. Such upheavals are neither all good nor all bad, but rather are an amalgam of many individual decisions about how a technology is applied. Each designer plays a role in shaping the direction. The computer revolution has passed its infancy, but there is still tremendous opportunity for change.

The metaphors, images, and names chosen for systems play a key role in the designers' and the users' perceptions. It is not surprising that many computer-system designers still mimic human or animal forms. The first attempts at flight imitated birds, and the first designs for microphones followed the shape of the human ear. Such primitive visions may be useful starting points, but success comes most rapidly to people who move beyond these fantasies and apply scientific analyses. Except for amusement, the goal is never to mimic the human form, but rather is to provide effective service to the users in accomplishing their tasks.

Lewis Mumford, in his classic book, *Technics and Civilization* (1934), characterized the problem of "dissociation of the animate and the mechanical" as the "obstacle of animism." He described Leonardo da Vinci's attempt to reproduce the motion of birds' wings, then Ader's batlike airplane (as late as 1897), and Branca's steam engine in the form of a human head and torso. Mumford wrote: "The most ineffective kind of machine is the realistic mechanical imitation of a man or another animal . . . for thousands of years animism has stood in the way of . . . development."

Choosing human or animal forms as the inspiration for some projects is understandable, but significant advances will come more quickly if we recognize the goals that serve human needs and the inherent attributes of the technology that is employed. Hand-held calculators do not follow human forms, but serve effectively for doing arithmetic. Designers of championship chess-playing programs no longer imitate human strategies. Vision-systems researchers realized the advantages of radar or sonar range finders and retreated from using humanlike stereo depth-perception cues.

Robots provide an informative case study. Beyond stone idols and voodoo dolls, we can trace modern robots back to the devices built by Pierre Jacquet-Droz, a Swiss watchmaker, from 1768 to 1774. The first child-sized mechanical robot, called the Scribe, could be programmed to write any message up to 40 characters long. It had commands to change lines, to skip a space, or to dip the quill in the inkwell. The second, called the Draughtsman, had a repertoire of four pencil sketches: a boy, a dog, Louis XV of France, and a pair of portraits. The third robot, the Musician, performed five songs on a working pipe organ and could operate for 1.5 hours on one winding. These robots made their creators famous and wealthy, since they were in great demand at the courts of the kings and in public showings. Eventually, however, printing presses became more effective than the Scribe and the Draughtsman, and tape players and phonographs were superior to the Musician.

Robots of the 1950s included electronic components and a metallic skin, but their designs were also strongly influenced by the human form. Robot arms were of the same dimension as human arms and the hands had five fingers. Designers of modern robots have finally overcome the obstacle of animism and now construct arms whose dimensions are appropriate for the steel and plastic technology and for the tasks. Two fingers are more common than five on robot hands, and the hands can often rotate more than 270 degrees. Where appropriate, fingers have been replaced by rubber suction cups with vacuum pumps to pick up parts.

In spite of these improvements, the metaphor and terminology of human form can still mislead the designers and users of robots. Programmers of one industrial robot were so disturbed by the labels "upper arm" and "lower arm" on the control panel that they scratched out the words. They thought that the anthropomorphic terms misled their intuitions about how to program the robot (McDaniel and Gong, 1982). The terms *programmable manipulators* and the broader *flexible manufacturing systems* are less exciting, but describe more accurately the newer generation of robotic systems.

The banking machine offers a simple example of the evolution from anthropomorphic imagery to a service orientation. Early systems had such names as Tillie the Teller or Harvey Wallbanker and were programmed with such phrases as "How can I help you?" These deceptive images rapidly gave way to a focus on the computer technology, with such names as the Electronic Teller, CompuCash, Cashmatic, or CompuBank. Over time, the emphasis has moved toward the service provided to the user: CashFlow, Money Exchange, 24-Hour Money Machine, All-Night Banker, and Money Mover.

The computer revolution will be judged not by the complexity or power of technology, but rather by the service to human needs. By focusing on users, researchers and designers will generate powerful yet simple systems that permit users to accomplish their tasks. These tools will enable short learning times, rapid performance, and low error rates. Putting users' needs first will lead to more appropriate choices of system features, giving users a greater sense of mastery and control, and the satisfaction of achievement. At the same time, users will feel increased responsibility for their actions and may be more motivated to learn about the tasks and the interactive system.

Sharpening the boundaries between people and computers will lead to a clearer recognition of computer powers and human reasoning (Weizenbaum, 1976; Winograd and Flores, 1986). Rapid progress will occur when designers accept that human–human communication is a poor model for human–computer interaction. People are different from computers, and human operation of computers is vastly different from human relationships. Vital factors that distinguish human behavior include the diversity of skills and background across individuals; the creativity, imagination, and inventiveness incorporated in daily actions; the emotional involvement in every act; the desire for social contact; and the power of intention.

Ignoring these primitive but enduring aspects of humanity leads to inappropriate technology and to hollow experiences. Embracing these aspects can bring about powerful tools, joy in learning, the capacity to realize goals, a sense of accomplishment, and increased social interaction.

Although designers may be attracted to the goal of making impressive and autonomous machines that perform tasks as well as humans do, realizing this goal will not provide what most users want. I believe that users want to have sense of their own accomplishment, rather than to admire a smart robot, intelligent agent, or expert system. Users want to be empowered by technology to apply their knowledge and experience to make judgments that lead to improved job performance and greater personal satisfaction. Sometimes, predefined objective criteria can be applied to a task, but often human values must be applied and flexibility in decision making is a necessity.

Some examples may help us to clarify this issue. Doctors do not want a machine that does medical diagnosis; rather, they want a machine that enables them to make a more accurate, reliable diagnosis; to obtain relevant references to scientific papers or clinical trials; to gather consultative support rapidly; and to record that support accurately. Similarly, air-traffic or manufacturing controllers do not want a machine that automatically does their job; rather they want one that increases their productivity, reduces their error rates, and enables them to handle special cases or emergencies effectively. I believe that an increase in personal responsibility will result in improved service.

A.5   In the Long Run

How do we use the power of technology
without adapting to it so completely
that we ourselves behave like machines, lost in the levers and cogs,
lonesome for the love of life,
hungry for the thrill of directly
experiencing the vivid intensity of the
ever-changing moment?

Al Gore, *Earth in the Balance,* **1992**

Successful interactive systems will bring ample rewards to the designers, but widespread use of effective tools is only the means to reach higher goals. A computer system is more than a technological artifact: Interactive systems, especially when linked by computer networks, create human social systems.

As Marshall McLuhan pointed out, "the medium is the message," and therefore each interactive system is a message from the designer to the user. That message has often been a harsh one, with the underlying implication that the designer does not care about the user. Nasty error messages are obvious manifestations; complex menus, cluttered screens, and confusing dialog boxes are also sentences in the harsh message.

Most designers want to send a more kind and caring message. Designers, implementers, and researchers are learning to send warmer greetings to the users with effective and well-tested systems. The message of quality is compelling to the recipients and can instill good feelings, appreciation for the designer, and the desire to excel in one's own work. The capacity for excellent systems to instill compassion and connection was noted by Sterling (1974) at the end of his guidelines for information systems: "In the long run what may be important is the *texture* of a system. By texture we mean the *quality* the system has to evoke in users and participants a feeling that the system increases the kinship among people."

At first, it may seem remarkable that computer systems can instill a kinship among people, but every technology has the potential to engage people in cooperative efforts. Each designer can play a role—not only that of fighting for the users, but also that of nurturing, serving, and caring for them.

A.6   Practitioner's Summary

High-level goals might include world peace, excellent health care, adequate nutrition, accessible education, communication, freedom of expression, support for creative exploration, safety, and socially constructive entertainment. Computer technology can help us to attain these high-level goals if we clearly state measurable objectives, obtain participation of professionals, and design effective human–computer interfaces. Design considerations include adequate attention to individual differences among users; support of social and organizational structures; design for reliability and safety; provision of access by the elderly, handicapped, or illiterate; and appropriate user-controlled adaptation.

A.7   Researcher's Agenda

The goals of universal access, advanced applications for life services, and tools to support innovation contain enough ambitious research projects for a generation. Medical information, education, and community networks are the most appealing candidates for early research, because the impact of changes could be so large. If we are to provide novel services to diverse users, we need effective theories and rigorous empirical research to achieve ease of learning, rapid performance, low error rates, and good retention over time, while preserving high subjective satisfaction.

World Wide Web Resources   WWW

Organizations dealing with ethics, social impact, and public policy are doing their best to make computing and information services as helpful as possible. Ways for you to become an activist are also included.

http://www.aw.com/DTUI

References

Anderson, Robert H., Bikson, Tora K., Law, Sally Ann, and Mitchell, Bridger M., *Universal Access to Email: Feasibility and Societal Implications*, RAND, Santa Monica, CA (1995). Also at http://www.rand.org.

Brod, Craig, *Technostress: The Human Cost of the Computer Revolution*, Addison-Wesley, Reading, MA (1984).

Brooks, Frederick, Jr., The computer scientist as toolsmith II, *Communications of the ACM*, 39, 3 (March 1996), 61–68.

Bush, Vannevar, As we may think, *Atlantic Monthly* (July 1945). Also at http://www2.theAtlantic.com/atlantic/atlweb/flashbks/computer/tech.htm.

Denning, Peter J., Educating a new engineer, *Communications of the ACM*, 35, 12 (December 1992), 83–97.

Engelbart, Douglas C. and English, William K., A research center for augmenting human intellect, *AFIPS Proc. Fall Joint Computer Conference*, 33 (1968), 395–410.

Friedman, Batya and Nissenbaum, Helen, Bias in Computer Systems, *ACM Transactions on Information Systems*, 14, 3 (July 1966), 330–347.

Gates, Bill, *The Road Ahead*, Viking Penguin, New York (1995).

Huff, Chuck W. and Finholt, Thomas (Editors) *Social Issues in Computing: Putting Computing in Its Place*, McGraw-Hill. New York (1994).

Kraut, Robert, Scherlis, William, Mukhopadhyay, Tridas, Manning, Jane, and Kiesler, Sara, The HomeNet field trial of residential internet services, *Communications of the ACM*, 39, 12 (December 1996), 55–63.

Licklider, J. C. R., *Libraries of the Future*, MIT Press, Cambridge, MA (1965).

McDaniel, Ellen, and Gong, Gwendolyn, The language of robotics: Use and abuse of personification, *IEEE Transactions on Professional Communications*, PC-25, 4 (December 1982), 178–181.

Mumford, Lewis, *Technics and Civilization*, Harcourt Brace and World, New York (1934).

Negroponte, Nicholas, *Being Digital*, Hodder and Stoughton, London, UK (1995).

Norman, Don, *The Psychology of Everyday Things*, Basic Books, New York (1988).

Penzias, Arno, *Ideas and Information*, Simon and Schuster, New York (1989).

Plaisant, Catherine, Rose, Anne, Milash, Brett, Widoff, Seth, and Shneiderman, Ben, LifeLines: Visualizing personal histories, *Proc. of ACM CHI '96 Conference: Human Factors in Computing Systems*, ACM, New York (1996), 221–227, 518.

Rosenbrock, H. H., Robots and people, *Measurement and Control,* 15, (March 1982), 105–112.

Sheridan, Thomas B., Computer control and human alienation, *Technology Review,* 83, 1 (October 1980), 51–73.

Shneiderman, B., Durango Declaration, *Communications of the ACM,* 38, 10 (1995), 13.

Shneiderman, B., Engagement and construction: Educational strategies for the post-TV era, *Journal of Computers in Higher Education,* 2, 4 (Spring 1993), 106–116.

Shneiderman, B., Human values and the future of technology: A declaration of empowerment, Keynote address, ACM SIGCAS Conference on Computers and the Quality of Life CQL '90, *SIGCAS Computers and Society,* 20, 3 (October 1990), 1–6.

Sterling, T. D., Guidelines for humanizing computerized information systems: A report from Stanley House, *Communications of the ACM,* 17, 11 (November 1974), 609–613.

Weizenbaum, Joseph, *Computer Power and Human Reason*, W. H. Freeman, San Francisco, CA (1976).

Winograd, Terry and Flores, Fernando, *Understanding Computers and Cognition: A New Foundation for Design*, Ablex, Norwood, NJ (1986).

Name Index

Subject Index

BEN SHNEIDERMAN

Ben Shneiderman is Professor in the Department of Computer Science, Head of the Human–Computer Interaction Laboratory, and Member of the Institutes for Advanced Computer Studies and for Systems Research, all at the University of Maryland at College Park. He taught previously at the State University of New York and at Indiana University. He regularly gives conference keynote speeches, tutorials, and short courses on user-interface design, information visualization, and educational technology. He also organizes an annual satellite–television presentation—*User Interface Strategies*—that has been seen by thousands of professionals since 1987. He has consulted and lectured for many organizations, including Apple, AT&T, Citicorp, GE, Honeywell, IBM, Intel, Library of Congress, NASA, and university research groups.

Recognized worldwide as a leader in human-computer interaction, Ben authored the first edition of *Designing the User Interface* in 1987, the second edition in 1992, and now this thoroughly updated third edition. His early works include another influential book, *Software Psychology: Human Factors in Computer and Information Systems* (1980), and a seminal paper (1981) in which he coined the term *direct manipulation* to describe graphical user interface design principles. Later, with Greg Kearsley, Ben coauthored the first commercial electronic book, *Hypertext Hands-On!* (Addison-Wesley, 1989). This book, comprising both a print version and a full hypertext version on diskettes, pioneered the highlighted embedded link. He developed this concept in the Hyperties hypermedia system.

A prolific writer and editor, Ben has coauthored two other textbooks, edited three technical books, and published nearly 200 technical papers and book chapters. His edited book, *Sparks of Innovation in Human-Computer Interaction* (Ablex, 1993), collects 25 papers from 10 years of research at the University of Maryland. He has been on the Editorial Advisory Boards of nine journals, including two important ACM publications, *Transactions on Computer–Human Interaction* and *Interactions*.

Ben received his B.S. from City College of New York in 1968, and his Ph.D. from State University of New York at Stony Brook in 1973. He received an Honorary Doctorate of Science from the University of Guelph, Ontario, Canada, in 1996, and was elected as a Fellow of the Association for Computing (ACM) in 1997.

You can learn more about Ben, the work at his lab, and resources for this book from the following World Wide Web sites:

http://www.cs.umd.edu/~ben
http://www.cs.umd.edu/projects/hcil
http://www.aw.com/DTUI